D0426814

FUNDAMENTALS OF
COMPUTER ALGORITHMS

Zeghong Peng

July 17, 1987

MD. U.S.A.

COMPUTER SOFTWARE ENGINEERING SERIES

ELLIS HOROWITZ, Editor

University of Southern California

CALINGAERT

Assemblers, Compilers and Program Translation

EVEN

Graph Algorithms

FINDLAY and WATT

PASCAL: An Introduction to Methodical Programming

HOROWITZ and SAHNI

Fundamentals of Computer Algorithms

HOROWITZ and SAHNI

Fundamentals of Data Structures

FUNDAMENTALS OF COMPUTER ALGORITHMS

ELLIS HOROWITZ
University of Southern California

SARTAJ SAHNI
University of Minnesota

ISBN 0-914894-22-6

發 行 人：楊　　鏡　　秋
發 行 所：儒 林 圖 書 有 限 公 司
地　　址：台北市重慶南路一段一一一號
電　　話：三 一 一 八 九 七 一 ～ 三 號
　　　　　三 一 四 四 〇 〇 〇 號
郵 政 劃 撥：〇 一 〇 六 七 九 二 一 號
印 刷 所：吉 豐 印 製 有 限 公 司
板橋市三民路二段正隆巷 46 弄 7 號
電　　話：九 六 一 四 三 四 八 號
中 華 民 國 七 十 四 年　　月
行政院新聞局局版台業字第一四九二號

dedicated to our wives
Neeta Sahni
Maryanne Horowitz

PREFACE

If we try to identify those contributions of computer science which will be long lasting, surely one of these will be the refinement of the concept called *algorithm*. Ever since man invented the idea of a machine which could perform basic mathematical operations, the study of what can be computed and how it can be done well was launched. This study, inspired by the computer, has led to the discovery of many important and clever algorithms. The discipline called computer science has embraced the study of algorithms as its own. It is the purpose of this book to organize what is known about them in a coherent fashion so that students and practitioners can learn to devise and analyze new algorithms for themselves.

But a book which contains every algorithm ever invented would be exceedingly large, and traditionally algorithms books have proceeded by examining only a small number of problem areas in depth. For each specific problem the most efficient algorithm for its solution is usually presented and analyzed. Having taught courses in this way for several years we were well aware that this approach has one major flaw. Though the student sees many fast algorithms and may master the tools of analysis, he remains unconfident about how to devise good algorithms in the first place.

The missing ingredient is a lack of emphasis on *design* techniques. A knowledge of design will certainly help one to create good algorithms, yet without the tools of analysis there is no way to determine the quality of the result. This observation that design should be taught on a par with analysis led us to a more promising line of approach: namely to organize our courses, and subsequently this book, around some fundamental strategies of algorithm design. The number of basic design strategies is reasonably small. Moreover all of the algorithms one would typically wish to study can easily be fit into these categories; for example, mergesort and quicksort are perfect examples of the divide-and-conquer strategy while Kruskal's minimum spanning tree algorithm and Dijkstra's single source shortest path algorithm are straightforward examples of the greedy strategy. An understanding of these strategies is an essential first step towards acquiring the skills of design.

Though we both strongly feel that the emphasis on design as well as analysis is the appropriate way to organize the study of algorithms, a cautionary remark is in order. First, we have not included every known design principle. One example is linear programming which is one of the most successful techniques, but is often discussed in a course of its own. Secondly, the student should be inhibited from taking a cookbook approach to algorithm design by assuming that each algorithm must derive from only a single technique. This is not so.

A major portion of this book, chapters 3 through 9, deal with the different design strategies. First each strategy is described in general terms. Typically a "program abstraction" is given which outlines the form that the computation will take if this strategy can be applied. Following this there are a succession of examples which reveal the intricacies and varieties of the general strategy. The examples are somewhat loosely ordered in terms of increasing complexity. The type of complexity may arise in several ways. Usually we begin with a problem which is very simple to understand and requires no data structures other than a one-dimensional array. For this problem it is usually obvious that the given design strategy yields a correct solution. Later examples may require a proof that an algorithm based on this design technique does work. Or, the later algorithms may require more sophisticated data structures (e.g. trees or graphs) and their analyses may be more complex. The major goal of this organization is to emphasize the arts of synthesis and analysis of algorithms. Auxiliary goals are to expose the student to good program structure and to proofs of algorithm correctness.

One of the most energetic areas of computer science research today is called *computational complexity*. That name denotes the study of what makes functions intrinsically difficult to compute. Two products of computational complexity have been the development of algorithms with the lowest asymptotic computing time and facts concerning the minimum number of operations required to compute a given function. Many of these results can be found here. However our decision in writing this book was to emphasize algorithms which were not only of theoretical interest but which are practical to use. Unfortunately many of the "best" algorithms, from an asymptotic point of view, are quite hard to program and require such a great amount of overhead that their practical value is limited. We have avoided lengthy presentations of such algorithms and contented ourselves with pointing to the available literature.

The algorithms presented here are written in SPARKS, the name we have given to our ALGOL/PASCAL-like language which we first introduced in *Fundamentals of Data Structures*. The syntax of some statements has been improved, but the changes are such that the meanings of all statements is still immediately discernible. Chapter one presents the precise semantics of each statement via flowcharts and gives some drill in the art of program structuring. We hope that by studying well-written programs the student will apply these same principles to his or her own program composition. Another important aspect of this book is *program testing*. Though computer science still lacks an adequate formal treatment of this subject, for some algorithms we show how to devise a range of data sets which can be used for debugging and performance measurement. Also we have felt obliged to provide programs which are essentially complete in all details. Though this may complicate the presentation of the algorithms, it has as its virtue the fact that each algorithm can be quickly programmed and executed. Of course, subroutines are used to improve clarity.

The material in this book does not correspond to any existing course within ACM's recommended Curriculum '68. However it does seem likely that the IEEE Computer Society will include an algorithms course within its new recommendations. As the course structure of many computer science programs is now firmly established, it has become harder to introduce new courses. Nevertheless we are confident that these subjects are of sufficient merit that many computer science educators will attempt to cover this material. Thus we offer the arguments we used to get our own departments to adopt a course on *The Design and Analysis of Algorithms*. First and foremost, we argued that "algorithm" is a fundamental concept of computer science and hence there should be a course devoted to its study. Secondly the skills of algorithm synthesis and analysis will improve both the students basic knowledge and his or her ability to comprehend more sophisticated algorithms in later courses. Finally there now exists some important theoretical results (e.g. NP-Completeness which is discussed in Chapter 11) which deserve to be covered.

We view the material presented here as ideal for a one semester or two quarter course given to juniors, seniors or graduate students. It does require prior experience with programming in a higher level language but everything else is self-contained. Practically speaking, it seems that a course on data structures is helpful, if only for the fact that the students have greater programming maturity. For a school on the quarter system, the first quarter might cover the basic design techniques as given in chapters 3 through 8: divide-and-conquer, the greedy method, dynamic programming, search and traversal, backtracking, and branch-and-bound. The second quarter would cover the more theoretical subjects of chapters 10 through 12: lower bound theory, NP-Completeness and approximation methods. For a semester schedule where the student has already encountered data structures and O-notation, chapters 3 through 11 is about the right amount of material. This includes the major design strategies as mentioned above plus the fast Fourier transform, lower bound theory, and the chapter on NP-Complete problems. A slower pace more typical of undergraduates would cover chapters 1 through 7 and 11, allowing more time for an introduction to the idea of algorithm analysis coupled with a review of the important data structuring techniques.

One question we are often asked is what do you do in class. Typically we devote each period to a discussion of one, or at most two problems. For each problem we try to emphasize how the solution can be arrived at by considering a design principle and showing that it applies. Perhaps alternative strategies are investigated and discarded. A clean separation is made between how the computation will proceed and decisions about data representation when that is possible. The best case and the worst case data of the resultant algorithm is made clear. Then an analysis of the time and space requirements is done. This scenario is a bit idealized, but on the whole it is accurate.

For homework there are numerous exercises at the end of each chapter. The most popular and instructive homework assignment we have found is one which requires the student to execute and time two programs using the same data sets. Since most of the algorithms in this book provide all of the implementation details they can easily be programmed in a variety of languages. The problem then reduces to devising suitable data sets and writing a main program which outputs the timing results. The timing results should agree with the asymptotic analysis that was done for the algorithm. This is a nontrivial task which can be both educational and fun. Most importantly it emphasizes an aspect of this field that is often neglected, that there is an experimental side to the practice of computer science.

Acknowledgments

We gratefully acknowledge the help of Arnold Rosenthal who carefully read the entire manuscript. In addition, Gary Bloom and our many algorithms students had many useful suggestions. Administrative credit goes to Martha Eul and typing assistance to Donald Aoki, Terrie Christian, Kathy Boyer and Sybil Wright. Also we thank the USC Information Sciences Institute for their computer resources and the inspiration of their program verification group including Ralph London, David Musser and Susan Gerhart.

CONTENTS

12.   APPROXIMATION ALGORITHMS FOR NP-HARD PROBLEMS

Chapter 1

INTRODUCTION

1.1 WHAT IS AN ALGORITHM?

The word algorithm comes from the name of a Persian author, Abu Ja'far
Mohammed ibn Musa al Khowarizmi (c. 825 A.D.) who wrote a textbook
on mathematics. An examination of the latest edition of Webster's dictionary defines its meaning as "any special method of solving a certain
kind of problem." But this word has taken on a special significance in
computer science, where *algorithm* has come to refer to a precise method
useable by a computer for the solution of a problem. This is what makes
the notion of an algorithm different from words such as process, technique
or method.

An algorithm is composed of a finite set of steps, each of which may require one or more operations. The possibility of a computer carrying out these
operations necessitates that certain constraints be placed on the type of
operations an algorithm can include. For example, each operation must
be *definite*, meaning that it must be perfectly clear what should be done.
Directions such as "compute 5/0" or "add 6 or 7 to x" are not permitted because it is not clear what the result is or which of the two possibilities should be done. Another important property each operation should
have is that it be *effective*; each step must be such that it can, at least in
principle, be done by a person using pencil and paper in a finite amount of
time. Performing arithmetic on integers is an example of an effective operation, but arithmetic with real numbers is not, since some values may be
expressible only by an infinitely long decimal expansion. Adding two such
numbers would violate the effectiveness property. An algorithm produces
one or more *outputs* and may have zero or more *inputs* which are externally
supplied.

Another important criterion we will assume about algorithms in this
book is that they *terminate* after a finite number of operations. There is
another word for an algorithm which obeys all of the above properties ex-

1

cept termination, and that is *computational procedure*. One important example of a computational procedure is the operating system of a digital computer. This procedure is designed to control the execution of jobs, such that when no jobs are available, it does not terminate, but continues in a waiting state until a new job is entered. Though computational procedures include important examples such as this one, we will restrict our study to those computational procedures which always terminate.

A related consideration is that the time for termination should be reasonably short. For example, an algorithm could be devised which, for any given position in the game of chess, decides if that is a winning position. The algorithm works by examining all possible moves and countermoves that could be made from the starting position. The difficulty with this algorithm is that even using the most modern computers it may take billions of years to make the decision. Therefore, we will be very concerned with analyzing the efficiency of each of our algorithms.

In order to help us achieve the criterion of definiteness, algorithms will be written in a programming language. Such languages are designed so that each legitimate sentence has a unique meaning. A *program* is the expression of an algorithm in a programming language. Sometimes words such as procedure or subroutine are used synonymously for program. Most readers of this book will have already programmed and run some algorithms on a computer. This is desirable because before one studies a concept in general it helps if one has had some practical experience with it. Perhaps you have had some difficulty getting started in formulating an initial solution to a problem, or perhaps you were unable to decide which of two algorithms was better. The goal of this book is to teach you how to make these decisions.

The study of algorithms includes many important and active areas of research. There are perhaps five distinct areas of study one can identify:

(*i*)   *How to devise algorithms*—The act of creating an algorithm is an art which may never be fully automated. A major goal of this book is to study various design techniques which have proven to be useful in that they have often yielded good algorithms. By mastering these design strategies, it will become easier for you to devise new and useful algorithms. Many of the chapters of this book are organized around what we believe are the major methods of algorithm design. The reader may now wish to glance back at the table of contents to see what these methods are called. Some of these techniques may already be familiar, and some have been found to be so useful that books have been written about them. Dynamic programming is one such technique. Some of the techniques are especially useful in fields other than computer science such as operations research and electrical engineering. In·this book we can only hope to give an introduction to these many approaches to algorithm formulation. All of the approaches we consider have applications in a variety of areas including computer science. But some important design techniques such as linear, nonlinear and integer programming are not covered here as they are traditionally covered in other courses.

(*ii*) *How to express algorithms*—The structured programming "movement" has as its central concern the clear and concise expression of algorithms in a programming language. We don't intend to give a tutorial on these subjects here and much good reading can be found in the books *Structured Programming* by Dahl, Dijkstra and Hoare (Academic Press), and *The Elements of Programming Style* by Kernighan and Plauger (McGraw-Hill). Nevertheless, section 1.3 covers a few structuring topics which will be important for us, e.g. recursion. In addition we shall express all of our algorithms using the best principles of structuring we can muster. The process of reading well composed programs should serve as a positive form of stimulation to the reader to improve his or her own skills.

(*iii*) *How to validate algorithms*—Once an algorithm is devised it is necessary to show that it computes the correct answer for all possible legal inputs. We refer to this process as *algorithm validation*. The algorithm need not as yet be expressed as a program. It is sufficient to state it in any precise way. The purpose of the validation is to assure us that this algorithm will work correctly independent of the issues concerning the programming language it will eventually be written in. Once the validity of the method has been shown, a program can be written and a second phase begins. This phase is referred to as *program proving* or sometimes as *program verification*. This area is now the object of intensive study and is still very much in its infancy. A proof of correctness requires that the solution be stated in two forms. One form is usually as a program which is annotated by a set of assertions about the input and output variables of the program. These assertions are often expressed in the predicate calculus. The second form is called a specification and this may also be expressed in the predicate calculus. A proof consists in showing that these two forms are equivalent in that for every given legal input they describe the same output. A complete proof of program correctness requires that each statement of the programming language be precisely defined and that all basic operations be proved correct. All these details may cause a proof to be very much longer than the program.

(*iv*) *How to analyze algorithms*—This field of study is called analysis of algorithms. As an algorithm is executed, it makes use of the computer's central processing unit (cpu) to perform operations and it uses the memory (both immediate and auxiliary) to hold the program and its data. *Analysis of algorithms* refers to the process of determining how much computing time and storage an algorithm will require. This area is a challenging one which sometimes requires great mathematical skill. One important result of this study is that it allows one to make quantitative judgments about the value of one algorithm over another. Another result is that it allows us to predict if our software will meet any efficiency constraints which may exist. Questions such as how well does an algorithm perform in the best case, in the worst case, or on the average are typical. For each algorithm which is presented here, an analysis will also be given. The exact nature of this process is more fully described in section 1.4.

(v) How to test a program—Testing a program really consists of two phases: debugging and profiling. *Debugging* is the process of executing programs on sample data sets to determine if faulty results occur and, if so, to correct them. However, as E. Dijkstra has pointed out, "debugging can only point to the presence of errors, but not to their absence." A proof of correctness is much more valuable than a thousand tests, (if that proof is correct), since it guarantees that the program will work correctly for *all* possible inputs. *Profiling* is the process of executing a correct program on data sets and measuring the time and space it takes to compute the results. These timing figures are useful in that they may confirm a previously done analysis and point out logical places to perform useful optimization. For some of the algorithms presented here we will show how to devise a range of data sets which will be useful for debugging and profiling.

These five categories just serve to outline the questions we will be asking about algorithms throughout this book. As we can't hope to cover all of these subjects completely, we will content ourselves with concentrating on design and analysis, spending less time on program construction and correctness. One can see that the subject of algorithms is a very diverse and challenging one.

1.2 WRITING ALGORITHMS IN SPARKS

Our choice of an algorithm description language was a difficult decision. We began by considering the use of some existing languages. Some names which came immediately to mind were ALGOL, ALGOL-W, APL, FORTRAN, LISP, PASCAL, and PL/I. Though some of these seemed more preferable than others, the choice of a specific language left us with many difficulties. First of all, we wished to be able to write our algorithms without dwelling on the idiosyncracies of a given language. Secondly, each language has its followers and its detractors. We would rather not have any individual rule us out simply because he did not know or, more particularly, disliked to use some specific language.

Futhermore, it is not really necessary to write algorithms in a language for which a compiler exists. As long as the language is close enough to many of the languages mentioned before, a hand translation will be relatively easy to accomplish. This encouraged us to develop a simple language which is tailored to describing the algorithms we wish to discuss. In this way we do not have to define many aspects of a programming language that we will never use here. We call our language SPARKS. It is close in form to ALGOL60 and PASCAL. Figure 1.1 shows how a SPARKS program could be executed on any machine. For information about obtaining a SPARKS translator see Appendix A.

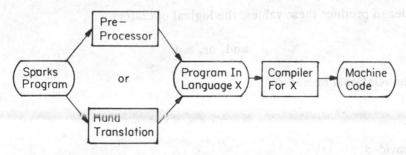

Figure 1.1   Translation of SPARKS

Some of you may already be familiar with SPARKS having read *Fundamentals of Data Structures* (Computer Science Press). Thus you may be surprised when you discover that the syntax of SPARKS has been changed, though modestly. The virtue of not being committed to a compiled language with actual users is that one can improve the syntax as better ideas are realized, without concern about creating incompatibilities with previous versions.

The primitive data types of SPARKS are integer, real, boolean and character. Variables may only hold values of a single type and this type can be declared by a statement of the form

$$\textbf{integer } x,y; \quad \textbf{boolean } a,b; \quad \textbf{char } c,d.$$

Identifiers having special significance in SPARKS are considered as reserved and they are printed in boldface. The rule for naming variables is to begin with a letter, use no special characters, don't be too long, and do not duplicate any reserved words of statements. Several statements may be included on a single line if they are separated by a semi-colon.

The method to accomplish assignment of values to variables is the assignment statement

$$< variable > \leftarrow < expression >$$

Contrary to FORTRAN and PL/I, the left arrow ($\leftarrow$) denotes the act of assigning the value of its right-hand side to the variable on its left.

There are two boolean values,

$$\text{ture and false}$$

In order to produce these values, the logical operators

$$\text{and, or, not}$$

and the relational operators

$$<, \leq, =, \neq, \geq, >$$

are provided.

Multidimensional arrays are available with arbitrary integer lower and upper bounds. An n-dimensional array of integers with lower and upper bounds $l_i, u_i, 1 \leq i \leq n$ may be declared by using the syntax **integer** A $(l_1:u_1, \ldots, l_n:u_n)$. The l_is are optional and if an l_i is not specified then the lower bound for that dimension is assumed to be 1. We have avoided introducing a record or structure feature. This feature can be useful in many programming situations. However our need for it here is minimal and we prefer to keep the syntax of SPARKS simple. Thus, all data objects will be constructed using the array as the basic building block.

A conditional statement has the form

if *cond* **then** S_1		**if** *cond* **then** S_1 **endif**	
	or		
else S_2			
endif			

where *cond* is a boolean expression and S_1, S_2 are arbitrary groups of SPARKS statements. The meaning of this statement is given by the flow charts of figure 12:

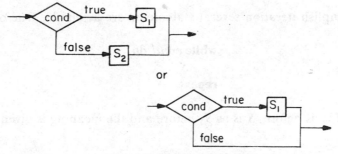

Figure 1.2 **If** statement

We will assume that conditional expressions are evaluated in "short circuit" mode: given the boolean expression (cond1 **or** cond2), if cond1 is true then cond2 is not evaluated; or given (cond1 **and** cond2), if cond1 is false then cond2 is not evaluated. Not all languages evaluate Boolean expressions in this way.

Another statement within SPARKS is the **case**, which allows one to easily distinguish between several alternatives without using multiple **if-then-else** statements. It has the form

case

: cond 1 : S_1

: cond 2 : S_2

·

·

·

: cond n : S_n

: **else** : S_{n+1}

endcase

where the S_i, $1 \le i \le n + 1$ are groups of SPARKS statements and the **else** clause is optional. The semantics of this statement is described by the following flowchart:

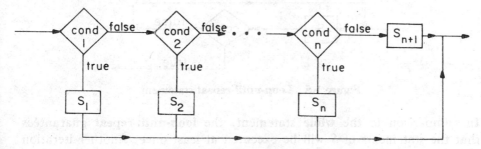

Figure 1.3 **Case** statement

To accomplish iteration several statements are available. One of them is

while *cond* **do**
S
repeat

where *cond* is as before, *S* is as S_1 before and the meaning is given by

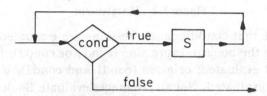

Figure 1.4   While statement

It is well known that all "proper" programs can be written using only the assignment, conditional and while statements. This result was obtained by Bohm and Jacopini (see *CACM* 1966). Though this is very interesting from a theoretical viewpoint, we should not take it to mean that this is the way to program. On the contrary, the more expressive our languages are, the more we can accomplish easily. So we will provide other statements such as a second iteration statement, the **loop-until-repeat**,

loop
S
until *cond* **repeat**

which has the meaning

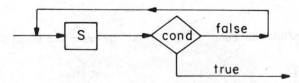

Figure 1.5   Loop-until-repeat statement

In comparison to the **while** statement, the **loop-until-repeat** guarantees that the statements of *S* will be executed at least once. Another iteration statement is called the **for**-loop, which has the form

for *vble* ← *start* **to** *finish* **by** *increment* **do**
   S
repeat

vble is a variable, while *start*, *finish* and *increment* are arithmetic expressions. A variable of type integer or real or a numerical constant is a simple form of an arithmetic expression. The clause "**by** increment" is optional and taken as +1 if it does not occur. We can write the meaning of this statement in SPARKS as

   vble ← *start*
   fin ← *finish*
   incr ← *increment*
  while (*vble* − *fin*) ∗ *incr* ≤ 0 **do**
    S
    vble ← *vble* + *incr*
  repeat

Notice how the expressions are evaluated only once and stored as the value of the variables *vble*, *fin*, and *incr* (two of which are new). These three variables will be the same type as the expressions on the right hand side of the arrow. *S* represents a sequence of SPARKS statements that do not alter the value of the variable *vble*.

A simpler form of the **loop-until-repeat** statement is given by

   loop
    S
   repeat

which has the meaning

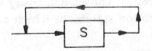

Figure 1.6 Loop-repeat statement

As it stands, this describes an infinite loop! However, we assume that this statement is used in conjunction with some test within *S* which will cause an exit. One way of exiting such a loop is by using a

   go to label

statement which transfers control to "label." A label may be attached to any statement by preceding that statement with an identifier and a colon. Though we will not normally need the **go to** statement, it will be useful when we translate recursive programs into iterative form. A more restricted form of the **go to** is the command

exit

which will cause a transfer of control to the first statement after the inner-most looping statement which contains it. This looping statement may be a **while-repeat, loop-repeat, loop-until-repeat** or a **for-repeat. exit** can be used either conditionally or unconditionally, for instance

loop
S_1
if *cond* **then exit endif**
S_2
repeat

will execute as

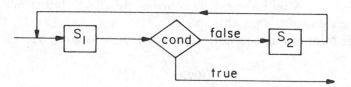

Figure 1.7   Loop-repeat with **exit**

Another statement which is a restricted form of the **go to** is the **cycle** statement. When encountered, it causes a transfer of control to the closing phrase of the innermost iteration statement which contains it. Thus

loop
S_1
if *cond1* **then cycle endif**
S_2
until *cond2* **repeat**

will execute as

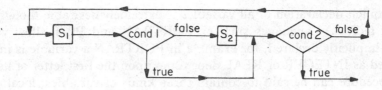

Figure 1.8 Cycle statement

The **cycle** statement works similarly when contained within the other looping constructs.

A complete SPARKS program is a collection of one or more procedures, the first one taken as the main program. Execution begins with the main program. If any SPARKS procedure, say A, reaches an **end** or a **return** statement, then control passes back to the SPARKS procedure which called procedure A. If procedure A is the main one, then control passes back to the operating system. A single SPARKS procedure has the form

procedure *NAME(parameter list)*
   declarations
   S
end *NAME*

A SPARKS procedure can be either a subroutine or a function. In either case the procedure is named and a set of formal parameters follow as a list within parentheses. The association of actual to formal parameters will be handled using the call-by-reference rule. This means that at run time the address of each parameter is passed to the called procedure. Parameters which are constants or values of expressions are assumed to be stored into internally generated words whose addresses are then passed to the procedure.

When a function is being written, the value to be returned is shown by enclosing it in parentheses immediately following the **return** statement; e.g.

return(*expr*)

where the value of *expr* is delivered as the value of the function. For procedures, the execution of an **end** implies a **return** with no value associated with it. To halt execution there is the command **stop**.

So far we have not said much about the declaration of variables other than to indicate how it might be done, for example **integer** *i,j*. Because SPARKS was devised as a language primarily for exposition we feel that the explicit declaration of all variables is extremely desirable though necessarily tedious. Languages such as FORTRAN and PL/I allow variables to be implicitly declared, for example in FORTRAN a variable is implicitly defined as INTEGER or REAL depending upon the first letter of its name. A procedure can be said to contain three kinds of variables: local, global, and formal parameters. A *local variable* is one which is declared in the current procedure. A *global variable* is one which has already been declared as local to a procedure which contains the current procedure. A *formal parameter* is not really a variable since it never actually contains a value. It is an identifier which is contained in the parameter list following the name of the procedure. At execution time formal parameters are replaced by the *actual parameters* (as described before) which are listed in the invoking statement.

As an example of how variables will be declared, consider the SPARKS procedure max which finds the maximum of n numbers, $n > 0$.

procedure *MAX(A, n, j)*
　//Set j so that A(j) is the maximum in A(1:n), n > 0.//
　$xmax \leftarrow A(1); j \leftarrow 1$
　for $i \leftarrow 2$ **to** n **do**
　　if $A(i) > xmax$ **then** $xmax \leftarrow A(i); j \leftarrow i$; **endif**
　repeat
end *MAX*

Algorithm 1.1　Finding the maximum of n items

It is easy to see that after execution of MAX, the actual parameter replacing j will have as its value the position in the array of the maximum element. It is unclear from the above whether $xmax$ is a local or global variable. Assuming it is a global variable makes sense because then its value at the end is the value of the largest element of A. The complete declaration for this procedure would appear as follows:

procedure *MAX(A, n, j)*
　global real *xmax;*
　parameters integer *j, n;* **real** *A(1:n)*
　local integer *i;*

We shall often prefer not to give a complete declaration when the context of variables is obvious. Since global variables are used infrequently, SPARKS will assume that all variables are either local or parameters unless declared otherwise. Another advantage of being less strict about enforcing declarations is that it allows a type of generalization called *polymorphism*. For example the way in which procedure MAX works applies equally well to $A(1:n)$ whether A contains integers, reals, or character strings. Most programming languages insist that we must specify the type of data that A contains and thus three separate procedures would have to be written. This makes no sense for us and as we are mostly interested in the algorithm's mode of processing we will often not declare the type of data in the array. This lack of specification, from our point of view, is more desirable.

Therefore the actual declarations which would appear in procedure MAX are simply **global** $xmax$; **integer** i, j, n. The type of $A(1:n)$ and $xmax$ remain undeclared and the fact that A, n, j are parameters and i is a local variable may be easily discerned by scanning the program and eliminating global variables.

Procedures may contain calls to other procedures which perform some task and then return to the next statement in the calling procedure. When a procedure includes a call to itself we refer to this as *direct recursion*. When a procedure calls another procedure which then causes the original procedure to be reinvoked, we call this *indirect recursion*. Both forms of recursion are permitted in SPARKS. Though recursion may carry with it some penalty at execution time, it remains an elegant way to describe many computing processes. This penalty will not deter us from using recursion. Many such programs are easily translatable so that the recursion is removed and efficiency achieved. This is discussed further in the next section.

For input and output we assume two functions

read(argument list);   **print**(argument list)

and we shall refrain from giving any details about formatting. A comment may be placed anywhere in a program by surrounding it with double slashes, e.g.

// this is a comment //

The language SPARKS as defined so far is not precise enough to presume to be complete. For example we have avoided rules about mixed mode arithmetic, about the formatting of I/O, scope rules, even the complete character set has not been stated. But none of these issues will concern us here so we needn't bother with them. Finally, there will be instances when it seems desirable to describe an operation by an English sentence, or by using familiar mathematical notation and we shall do so. Thus some of the algorithms in this book are actually written in what should be called pseudo-SPARKS.

1.3 WRITING STRUCTURED PROGRAMS

Since most of the SPARKS programs will be read many more times than they will be executed, we have tried to make our code readable. This is a goal which should be aimed at by everyone who writes programs. The SPARKS language is rich enough so that one can create a good looking program by applying some simple rules of style. Some of the commonly accepted rules of style are:

(i)   Every procedure should carefully specify its input and output variables.
(ii) The meaning of all local variables should be defined.
(iii) The flow of the program should generally be forward except for normal looping or unavoidable instances.
(iv) Indentation rules should be established and followed so that computational units of program text can more easily be identified.
(v)   Documentation should be short, but meaningful. Avoid comments like "i is increased by one."
(vi) Use subroutines where appropriate.

See the book *The Elements of Programming Style* by Kernighan and Plauger (McGraw-Hill) for more examples of good rules of programming.

Which iteration statement to use

Since SPARKS contains four different ways for getting a set of statements to be repeatedly executed, it is natural to ask under what circumstances we prefer to use one way rather than another. The four iteration statements are the (i) **loop-repeat**, (ii) **while-repeat**, (iii) **loop-until-repeat**, and (iv) **for-repeat**. Suppose we want to read a set of values until their sum exceeds a predefined limit, say n. This would naturally be expressed using the **while** loop as:

$y \leftarrow 0$
while $y \leq n$ **do**
  read(x)
  $y \leftarrow y + x$
repeat

On the other hand suppose we want to read in n values and process each one in some way. Using the **while** loop we might write:

```
i ← 1
while i ≤ n do
  read(x)
  call PROCESS(x)
  i ← i + 1
repeat
```

But in this case it is preferable to employ a **for** loop, as for example

```
for i ← 1 to n do
  read(x)
  call PROCESS(x)
repeat
```

The reason for favoring the **for** loop in this context is not so much because we save two statements ($i \leftarrow 1$ and $i \leftarrow i + 1$) but because the number of iterations was fixed by n and independent of the data being read. When we know exactly how many times we want to iterate a group of statements then the **for** statement should be used. When we want to iterate some statements until a certain condition becomes true or false then the **while** loop is favored.

Now suppose we want to read a set of values and process them until we read an end-of-file marker. Using the **while** loop we can express this as:

```
read(x)
while x ≠ eof do
  call PROCESS(x)
  read(x)
repeat
```

However a better way would be using the **loop-repeat**:

```
loop
  read(x)
  if x = eof then exit endif
  call PROCESS(x)
repeat
```

Now we have only one occurrence of the read statement which may prove useful if we have to modify this program segment. In fact suppose we now want to modify this program to test the result of **call** PROCESS(x), say PROCESS(x,y) and terminate processing if $y = 0$. Then the **loop-until-repeat** can be fruitfully used:

```
loop
    read(x)
    if x = eof then exit endif
    call PROCESS(x,y)
until y = 0 repeat
if x ≠ eof then ...
```

The Case for CASE

There are two statements in SPARKS for discriminating between alternatives: the **if-then-else** and the **case**. We could have gotten by with either one of these statements since we can simulate the **case**, as defined in Figure 1.3, using the nested sequence of **if-then-else**'s

```
if cond1 then S1
else if cond2 then S2
else if cond3 then S3
    :
else if condn then Sn
else Sn + 1
endif endif ... endif
```

The virtue of the case is that it eliminates the nesting of alternatives and brings the conditions out to the same level. The amount of syntax is reduced if many conditions are involved and the resulting program segment is easier to read.

Functions versus Subroutines

Most programming languages including SPARKS permit the definition of both functions and subroutines. But very few language primers discuss when one is preferable to the other. Before we can get close to answering this question, let us first reconsider the way variables get used in a procedure. In section 1.2 we noted that variables could be classified as either **local, global,** or **parameter**. There is another three category classification that pertains only to parameters and global variables. In one instance a variable may carry a value *in* to a procedure, but it remains unchanged throughout execution. A second possibility is that a variable is undefined upon entry but it is assigned a value which is carried *out* when the procedure ends. The third possibility is a variable which both brings a value *in* and (*a possibly changed value*) *out*. A language designer might even go so far as to insist that a programmer declare his variables in this way, as to whether they are **in, out,** or **inout** as this adds another measure of reliability. However we will refrain from adding this declaration feature to SPARKS, at least for now.

The reason for introducing these categories is to help us understand the notion of side effect. The words *subroutine* or *pure procedure* are used to denote a procedure which returns no function value but may alter either its parameters or global variables or both. A procedure which does alter one of its parameters or global variables is said to have a *side effect*. This is equivalent to a procedure which has at least an **out** or **inout** type of variable. Pure procedures work solely through side effects. A procedure which is a function may also have side effects. But in the interests of reliability SPARKS insists that one uses either functions without side effects or pure procedures.

In general we write a function when the value it returns will be used once in an expression. For example if we needed a procedure to determine whether two trees are equal we should create a function, say EQUAL(S, T), which returns either true or false (a Boolean function). Then in a program we could say

$$\text{if } EQUAL(S, T) \text{ then} \ldots$$

Or we might create a function for computing the greatest common divisor and use it in the assignment

$$z \leftarrow x * y / gcd(x, y)$$

However if we need the $gcd(x, y)$ more than once we can either assign its value to a variable ($t \leftarrow gcd(x, y)$) or we can make it a subroutine with a side effect (**call** $gcd(x, y, t)$).

Recursion

Recursion is a powerful programming technique which unfortunately is not employed to the extent it should. There are at least two reasons for this. One is the fact that FORTRAN does not permit recursion. Thousands of people who have learned the art of programming using FORTRAN have thus been unable to experience its benefits. Two is the fact that there is often a heavy penalty in terms of execution time when one uses recursion on some compilers. We shall be running some experiments later to see if we can quantify this penalty.

Let's take a look at some examples, both good and bad, which make use of recursion.

Example 1.1   The Fibonacci sequence 1,1,2,3,5,8,13,21,34, ... is defined as

$$F_0 = F_1 = 1, \quad F_i = F_{i-1} + F_{i-2}, \quad i > 1$$

This mathematical definition might naturally lead to the recursive SPARKS procedure:

procedure $F(n)$
    //*returns the nth Fibonacci number*//
    integer n
    if $n \leq 1$ **then return**(1)
            else return($F(n - 1) + F(n - 2)$)
    endif
end F

Algorithm 1.2   Fibonacci numbers

The virtue of this program is that it is almost syntactically identical to the mathematical definition. However it is atrociously inefficient from the standpoint of computing time. But the major source of the inefficiency does not arise because recursion is used. Rather it is because of the way the computation proceeds. Many values are recomputed many times; for example $F(n - 2)$ is computed twice, $F(n - 3)$ is computed three times, and $F(n - 4)$ is computed five times. Other recursive versions can be constructed which are far more efficient (see the exercises).

Example 1.2   Perhaps the oldest recorded nontrivial algorithm is due to Euclid. This algorithm is for computing the greatest common divisor of two nonnegative integers. The essential step which guarantees the validity of his method consists of showing that the greatest common divisor of a and b ($a > b \geq 0$) is equal to a if b is zero and is equal to the greatest common divisor of b and the remainder of a divided by b if b is nonzero. For ex ample:

$gcd(22,8) = gcd(8,6) = gcd(6,2) = gcd(2,0) = 2$

and

$gcd(21,13) = gcd(13,8) = gcd(8,5) = gcd(5,3) = gcd(3,2) = gcd(2,1) = gcd(1,0) = 1$

Expressing this process as a recursive procedure one gets

procedure *GCD(a,b)*
   //assume $a > b \geq 0$//
  if $b = 0$ **then return**(a)
         else return($GCD(b, a \bmod b)$)
  endif
end *GCD*

Algorithm 1.3   Greatest common divisor

Example 1.3 One often gets the mistaken impression that recursion is only appropriate for computing "mathematical" functions. Here is a procedure which searches for x in $A(1:n)$.

procedure *SEARCH(i)*
  //if there exists an index k such that $A(k) = x$ in $A(i:n)$//
  //then the first such k is returned else zero is returned.//
  global $n, x, A(1:n)$
  case
    : $i > n$: **return**(0)
    : $A(i) - x$: **return**(i)
    : **else** : **return**($SEARCH(i + 1)$)
    endcase
end *SEARCH*

Algorithm 1.4   Searching for x in $A(1:n)$

Normally we might have written this procedure using iteration. By using recursion the need for a looping statement has been removed. To determine if x is contained within $A(1:n)$ this function is initially invoked as ans ← $SEARCH(1)$. (See the exercises for an improvement to SEARCH).

Removing Recursion

We are in a mild dilemma. Some design techniques are inherently recursive and so recursion is a natural way to describe algorithms obtained from these techniques. Also, it is often easier to prove a recursive algorithm correct than it is to prove the corresponding iterative algorithm correct. Yet, many programming languages do not permit the use of recursion. Also, in some languages that do permit recursion, its cost is high. This is often due to the overhead of repeated procedure calls. But these difficulties should not prevent us from using recursion in the early stages of algorithm design. Once a recursive algorithm has been validated and we are satisfied that we have a good algorithm, the recursion may be removed by translating the algorithm into an equivalent one which uses only iteration. This translation may be accomplished using a simple set of rules. Then it is often possible to improve the efficiency of the resulting iterative procedure by making some simple transformations.

First let us see how to translate a recursive procedure into an equivalent procedure which uses only iteration. This translation involves replacing all recursive procedure calls and **return** statements by equivalent nonrecursive code. We describe the translation process for the case of direct recursion. Only a slight modification is needed to handle indirect recursion. To translate a directly recursive procedure one performs the following:

(i)   At the beginning of the procedure, code is inserted which declares a stack and initializes it to be empty. In the most general case, the stack will be used to hold the values of parameters, local variables, function value, and return address for each recursive call.

(ii) The label $L1$ is attached to the first executable statement.

Now, each recursive call is replaced by a set of instructions which do the following:

(iii) Store the values of all parameters and local variables in the stack. The pointer to the top of the stack can be treated as global.

(iv) Create the ith new label, Li, and store i in the stack. The value i of this label will be used to compute the return address. This label is placed in the program as described in rule (vii).

(v)   Evaluate the arguments of this call (they may be expressions) and assign these values to the appropriate formal parameters.

(vi) Insert an unconditional branch to the beginning of the procedure.

(vii)   If this procedure is a function, attach the label created in (iv) to a statement which retrieves the function value from the top of the stack. Add code to use this value in the way described in the recursive procedure. If this procedure is not a function then affix the label created in (iv) to the statement immediately following the branch of (vi).

These steps are sufficient to remove all recursive calls in a procedure. We must now alter all **return** statements in the following way. In place of each **return** do the following:

(viii) If the stack is empty then execute a normal return.
  (ix)   Otherwise take the current values of all output parameters (explicitly or implicitly understood to be of type **out** or **inout**) and assign these values to the corresponding variables which are in the top of the stack.
   (x)   Now insert code which removes the index of the return address from the stack if one has been placed there. Assign this address to some unused variable.
  (xi)   Remove from the stack the values of all local variables and parameters and assign them to their corresponding variables.
 (xii)   If this is a function, insert instructions to evaluate the expression immediately following **return** and store the result in the top of the stack.
(xiii) Use the index of the label of the return address to execute a branch to that label.

By following these rules carefully one can take any recursive program and produce a program which works in exactly the same way, yet which uses only iteration to control the flow of the program. On many compilers this resultant program will be much more efficient than its recursive version. On other compilers the times may be fairly close. Once the transformation to iterative form has been accomplished, one can often simplify the program even further thereby producing even more gains in efficiency.

Example 1.4.   Here we consider a problem which is most often thought of as best solved using iteration. The recursive program is not really any more intelligible. But we will use this example to illustrate the translation from recurisve to iterative form. The problem is one we've seen before, to write a procedure which finds the maximum element in an array $A(1:n)$.

procedure *MAX1*(*i*)
　　//this is a function which returns the largest integer k//
　　//such that A(k) is the maximum element in A(i:n)//
　　global integer *n*,*A* (1:*n*),*j*, *k* ;
　　integer *i*
　　if *i* < *n* **then** *j* ← *MAX1*(*i* + 1)
　　　　　if *A*(*i*) > *A*(*j*) **then** *k* ← *i*
　　　　　　　　　else *k* ← *j*
　　　　　endif
　　　else k ← n
　　endif
　　return(*k*)
end *MAX1*

　　　　　　　Algorithm 1.5   Recursively finding the maximum

This recursive version should be easy to follow, but you might try it on some
data before you proceed. The overhead at run time which accompanies the
procedure calls and the manipulation of the implicit stack naturally causes
us to consider removing the recursion before compilation.

procedure *MAX2*(*i*)
　　local integer *j*,*k;* **global integer** *n*, *A*(1:*n*);
　　integer *i*
　　integer *STACK* (1:2 * *n*);　　　　　　　//rule (i)//
　　top ← 0　　　　　　　　　　　　　　　//rule (i)//
*L*1: **if** *i* < *n*　　　　　　　　　　　　　　//rule (ii)//
　　　then *top* ← *top* + 1; *STACK(top)* ← *i*　　//rule (iii)//
　　　　　top ← *top* + 1; *STACK(top)* ← 2;　　//rule (iv)//
　　　　　i ← *i* + 1　　　　　　　　　　　//rule (v)//
　　　　　go to *L*1　　　　　　　　　　　//rule (vi)//
　　　　　*L*2: *j* ← *STACK(top)*; *top* ← *top* − 1　//rule (vii)//
　　　　　　　if *A*(*i*) > *A*(*j*) **then** *k* ← *i*
　　　　　　　　　　　else *k* ← *j*
　　　　　　　endif
　　　else *k* ← *n*
　　　endif
　　if *top* = 0 **then return** (*k*)　　　　　　//rule (viii)//
　　　　　else *addr* ← *STACK(top)*; *top* ← *top* − 1　//rule (x)//
　　　　　　　i ← *STACK(top)*; *top* ← *top* − 1　//rule (xi)//
　　　　　　　top ← *top* + 1; *STACK(top)* ← *k*　//rule (xii)//
　　　　　　　if *addr* = 2 **then go to** *L*2 **endif**　//rule (xiii)//
　　endif
end *MAX2*
　　　　　Algorithm 1.6   Iterative equivalent of Algorithm 1.5

As is often the case when we automatically remove recursion, the resulting program can look like a dish of spaghetti. But by religiously following the rules, we can have faith that the resulting version is semantically equivalent to the recursive version. Now we can begin to simplify the program by examining the way it operates. For example we needn't stack the return address since there is only one place to which the procedure returns. This leaves only the function value in the stack. However, at any point in time there is only one value of the function, that is, the index of the current maximum. Thus we can store this value in a single variable and eliminate the stack entirely. Another simplification is to remove the loop created by the statement **go to** $L1$. Equivalently we set i to n and use k to hold the index of the current maximum. The resulting simplified program follows.

```
procedure MAX3(A,n)
    integer i,k,n;
    i ← k ← n
    while i > 1 do
        i ← i - 1
        if A(i) > A(k) then k ← i endif
    repeat
    return(k)
end MAX3
```

Algorithm 1.7   A refined version of Algorithm 1.6

This example may be somewhat long but you shouldn't get discouraged. After you have tried a few examples on your own, you will be both more familiar with the way recursive procedures operate and quick to take advantage of many shortcuts as you translate out the recursion.

The rules just given are for the general case. Often there are occasions when simpler rules apply. For example if the last statement of a procedure is a recursive call, then remove it by simply evaluating the new values of the parameters and branching to the beginning. A stack is not needed. The gcd procedure is an example of this. Removing its recursion yields the following program:

```
procedure GCD1(a,b)
    L1: if b = 0 then return(a)
                 else t ← b; b ← a mod b; a ← t; go to L1
        endif
end GCD1
```

Algorithm 1.8   Iterative equivalent of Algorithm 1.3

With a little cleaning up we get

procedure $GCD2(a, b)$
  while $b \neq 0$ **do**
    $t \leftarrow b; b \leftarrow a \bmod b; a \leftarrow t$
  repeat
  return(a)
end $GCD2$

Algorithm 1.9   A refined version of Algorithm 1.8

The objective of removing recursion is to produce a more efficient but computationally equivalent iterative program. The fourteen rules stated previously need not always be followed if it is clear that one or more steps are unnecessary. Further, if your compiler translates recursive procedures into efficient code, then you may not need these rules at all. We shall return to recursive procedures and their translation as we meet the need in later chapters.

1.4 ANALYZING ALGORITHMS

Why do we bother to analyze an algorithm? For some of us analyzing algorithms is an intellectual activity that is fun. Another reason is the challenge of being able to predict the future and even though we are narrowing our predictions to algorithms, it is gratifying when we succeed. A third reason is because computer science attracts many people who enjoy being efficiency experts. Analyzing algorithms gives these people a chance to exhibit their skills by devising new ways of doing the same task even faster. This tendency has a large payoff in computing where time means money and efficiency saves dollars.

Before we can talk about how to analyze an algorithm we need to make explicit our assumptions about the kind of computer we expect the algorithm to be executed on. The assumptions we make can have important consequences with respect to how fast a problem can be solved. Though formal models of machines do exist (e.g. Turing machines or Random Access Machines), for most of this book it will be sufficient to consider our computer as a "conventional" one. By this we mean that the instructions of a program are assumed to be carried out one at a time and the major cost of an algorithm depends upon the number of operations it requires. We assume that a random access memory is available which permits one to either access or store any element in a fixed amount of time.

We admit that there are reasons to believe that these assumptions may become outmoded with future generations of machines. Already computers such as ILLIAC IV or the CDC STAR exist and offer a high degree of parallelism in the manner in which a sequence of operations can be executed. This invalidates to some extent the measurement of an algorithm's cost by the summing of its logical operations. A second though somewhat more remote factor is the dramatic decrease in the cost of logic circuits (microprocessors) to the point where configurations of these processors cause the movement of data to be more expensive than the arithmetic and logical operations. If these trends continue, a new theory of computation will be required. But until such machines becomes more pervasive the model of counting and summing logical operations on a sequential processor remains the most accurate predictor of performance and the one we will use.

Given an algorithm to be analyzed, the first task is to determine which operations are employed and what their relative costs are. These operations may include the four basic arithmetic operations on integers: addition, subtraction, multiplication and division. Other basic operations might include arithmetic on floating point numbers, comparisons, assigning values to variables and executing procedure calls. These operations typically take no more than a fixed amount of time and so we say that their time is bounded by a constant. This is not true of all operations of a computer. Some may be composed of an arbitrarily long sequence of more basic operations. For example, a comparison of two character strings may use a character compare instruction which may, in turn, use a shift and bit-compare instruction. The total time for the comparison of two strings will depend upon their lengths, while the time for each character compare is bounded by a constant.

The second task is to determine a sufficient number of data sets which cause the algorithm to exhibit all possible patterns of behavior. This is one of the important and creative tasks of algorithm analysis. It requires us to understand the workings of the algorithm well enough to concoct the data configurations which produce the best or worst or typical behavior. We will say more about this when we discuss particular algorithms.

In producing a complete analysis of the computing time of an algorithm, we distinguish between two phases: *a priori analysis* and *a posteriori testing*. In a priori analysis we obtain a function (of some relevant parameters) which bounds the algorithm's computing time. In a posteriori testing we collect actual statistics about the algorithm's consumption of time and space, while it is executing. Suppose there is the statement $x \leftarrow x + y$ somewhere in the middle of a program. We wish to determine the total time that statement will spend executing, given some initial state of input data.

This requires essentially two items of information, the statement's *frequency count* (i.e. the number of times the statement will be executed) and the time for one execution. The product of these two numbers is the total time. Since the time per execution depends on both the machine being used and the programming language together with its compiler, an a priori analysis limits itself to determining the frequency count of each statement. This number can be determined directly from the algorithm, independent of the machine it will be executed on and the programming language the algorithm is written in.

For example consider the three program segments a,b,c:

(a)	(b)	(c)
	for $i \leftarrow 1$ to n do	for $i \leftarrow 1$ to n do
		for $j \leftarrow 1$ to n do
$x \leftarrow x + y$	$x \leftarrow x + y$	$x \leftarrow x + y$
	repeat	repeat
		repeat

For each segment we assume the statement $x \leftarrow x + y$ is contained within no other loop than what is already visible. Thus for segment (a) the frequency count of this statement is 1. For segment (b) the count is n and for segment (c) it is n^2. These frequencies 1, n, n^2 are said to be different, increasing *orders of magnitude*. An order of magnitude is a common notion with which we are all familiar; for example walking, bicycling, riding in a car and flying in an airplane represent increasing orders of magnitude with respect to the distance we can travel per hour. In connection with algorithm analysis, the order of magnitude of a statement refers to its frequency of execution, while the order of magnitude of an algorithm refers to the sum of the frequencies of all of its statements. Given three algorithms for solving the same problem whose orders of magnitude are n, n^2, and n^3, naturally we will prefer the first since the second and third are progressively slower. For example, if $n = 10$ then these algorithms will require 10, 100, and 1000 units of time to execute respectively (assuming all basic operations are of equal duration). Determining the order of magnitude of an algorithm is very important and producing an algorithm which is faster by an order of magnitude is a significant accomplishment. The a priori analysis of algorithms is concerned chiefly with order of magnitude determination. Fortunately there is a convenient mathematical notation for dealing with this concept.

Asymptotic Notation

An a priori analysis of computing time ignores all of the factors which are machine or programming language dependent and concentrates on determining the order of magnitude of the frequency of execution of statements. There are several kinds of mathematical notation which are very useful for this kind of analysis. One of these is the O-notation.

Definition: $f(n) = O(g(n))$ (read as "f of n equals big oh of g of n") iff there exist two positive constants c and n_0 such that $|f(n)| \leq c |g(n)|$ for all $n \geq n_0$.

Suppose we are determining the computing time, $f(n)$, of some algorithm. The variable n might be the number of inputs or outputs, their sum or the magnitude of one of them. Since $f(n)$ is machine dependent, an a priori analysis will not suffice to determine it. However, an a priori analysis can be used to determine a $g(n)$ such that $f(n) = O(g(n))$. When we say that *an algorithm has computing time* $O(g(n))$ we mean that if the algorithm is run on some computer on the same type of data but for increasing values of n, the resulting times will always be less than some constant times $|g(n)|$. When determining the order of magnitude of $f(n)$ we shall always try to obtain the smallest $g(n)$ such that $f(n) = O(g(n))$.

Theorem 1.1: If $A(n) = a_m n^m + \cdots + a_1 n + a_0$ is a polynomial of degree m then $A(n) = O(n^m)$.

Proof: Using the definition of $A(n)$ and a simple inequality

$$|A(n)| \leq |a_m|n^m + \cdots + |a_1|n + |a_0|$$

$$\leq (|a_m| + |a_{m-1}|/n + \cdots + |a_0| /n^m)n^m$$

$$\leq (|a_m| + \cdots + |a_0|)n^m, \ n \geq 1.$$

Choosing $c = |a_m| + \cdots + |a_0|$ and $n_0 = 1$ the theorem immediately follows. $\square$

Theorem 1.1 says that if we can describe the frequency of execution of a statement in an algorithm by a polynomial such as $A(n)$, then that statement's computing time is $O(n^m)$. However the constant in the above theorem is not the best possible. Actually we can show that any constant greater than $|a_m|$ can be used (for sufficiently large n).

If an algorithm has k statements whose orders of magnitude are $c_1 n^{m_1}$, $c_2 n^{m_2}, \ldots, c_k n^{m_k}$ then the order of magnitude of the entire algorithm is given by $c_1 n^{m_1} + \ldots + c_k n^{m_k}$ which by Theorem 1.1 is equal to $O(n^m)$ where $m = \max\{m_i\}$, $1 \le i \le k$.

If we have two algorithms which perform the same task on n inputs, and the first has a computing time which is $O(n)$ and the second $O(n^2)$, which is superior? It is easy to see that for sufficiently large values of n, the time for the second algorithm will be larger than the time for the first. For example, if the actual computing times for these algorithms are $2n$ and n^2 respectively, then algorithm one is faster (i.e. has a smaller value) than algorithm two for all $n > 2$. On the other hand if the actual computing times are $10^4 n$ and n^2 then algorithm two is faster for all $n < 10^4$. For $n > 10^4$ algorithm one is faster. So, we cannot decide which of the two algorithms is better unless we know something about the constants associated with the orders of magnitude. If the constants are comparable then the lower order algorithm is better than the higher order algorithm. But this is not the whole story. The point at which one algorithm requires fewer operations than another also depends upon the low order terms. In practice these terms and their coefficients depend on many factors, such as the language and the machine one is using. Alas, it is far more difficult to derive the entire formula for the computing time than the leading term. Thus for a priori analysis, we content ourselves with determining the order of magnitude, and the establishment of its constant will be postponed until after the program has been written and executed. We will not usually derive any terms other than the order of magnitude, unless those terms significantly influence the comparison of two algorithms.

As an example of the usefulness of improving an algorithm by an order of magnitude, suppose we have two algorithms for solving the same task which require n^2 and $n \log n$ operations on n inputs. For $n = 1024$ they require 1,048,576 versus 10,240 operations. If it takes one microsecond to perform each operation then algorithm one requires about 1.05 seconds while algorithm two requires .01 seconds on the same input. If we double n to 2048, then the operation counts become 4,194,304 versus 22,528 or roughly 4.2 seconds versus .02 seconds. When the n is doubled an $O(n^2)$ algorithm takes four times as long to complete while an $O(n \log n)$ algorithm takes only a little more than twice as long to complete. Since an n of several thousand is not especially large, we see how important an order of magnitude improvement such as this can be.

The most common computing times for algorithms we will see here are

$$O(1) < O(\log n) < O(n) < O(n \log n) < O(n^2) < O(n^3) \text{ and } O(2^n)$$

$O(1)$ means that the number of executions of basic operations is fixed and hence the total time is bounded by a constant. The first six orders of magnitude have an important property in common, they are bounded by a polynomial. $O(n)$, $O(n^2)$, and $O(n^3)$ are themselves polynomials referred to by their degrees: linear, quadratic, and cubic. However, there is no integer m such that n^m bounds 2^n, or

$$2^n \neq O(n^m)$$

for any integer m. The order of this formula is $O(2^n)$.

An algorithm whose computing time is bounded by $O(2^n)$ is said to require *exponential time*. As n gets large, there becomes a tremendous difference between exponential and polynomial time algorithms. If one finds an algorithm which reduces the time to solve a problem from exponential to polynomial, that is a great accomplishment. See Chapter 11 for a further discussion of polynomial versus exponential time algorithms.

Figure 1.9 and Table 1.1 show how the computing times for six of the typical functions grow with a constant equal to one. Notice how the times $O(n)$ and $O(n \log n)$ grow much more slowly than the others. For large data sets, algorithms with a complexity greater than $O(n \log n)$ are often impractical. An algorithm which is exponential will be practical only for *very* small values of n and even if we decrease the leading constant, say by a factor of 2 or 3, we will not improve the amount of data we can handle by very much. To see more precisely why a change in the constant, rather than to the order, of an algorithm produces very little improvement in running time we look at an example.

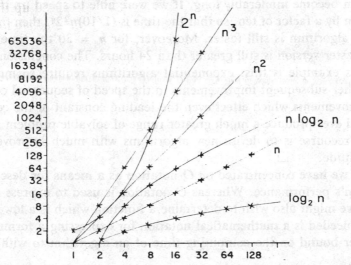

Figure 1.9   Rate of growth of common computing time functions

log n	n	n log n	n^2	n^3	2^n
0	1	0	1	1	2
1	2	2	4	8	4
2	4	8	16	64	16
3	8	24	64	512	256
4	16	64	256	4096	65536
5	32	160	1024	32768	4294967296

Table 1.1 Values for computing functions

Example 1.5 Suppose the orders of magnitude of two algorithms are $n^2 * 2^n$ and $n * 2^n$. Both algorithms are exponential, but in one case there is an extra factor of n. The leading constants are assumed to be one. The respective frequency counts are:

n	$n * 2^n$	$n^2 * 2^n$
5	160	800
10	10240	102400
15	491520	7372800
20	20971520	419430400
30	3.2×10^{10}	9.6×10^{11}

Using the same assumption as before of one operation per microsecond, we observe that for $n = 30$ the times are roughly 8.9 hours versus 11 days. Though the extra linear factor does make a considerable difference, the exponential character of these times dominates and implies that they will both soon become intolerably long. If we were able to speed up the second algorithm by a factor of ten, so that the time is $(1/10)n^2 2^n$, then for $n > 10$ the first algorithm is still faster. Moreover, for $n = 30$ the time required by this faster version is still greater than 24 hours. The conclusion we draw from this example is this: exponential algorithms require so much time, that neither subsequent improvements in the speed of sequential computers nor improvements which effect even the leading constant of the computing time, will ever produce a much greater range of solvable problem size. One possible recourse is to devise new algorithms with much improved orders of magnitude.   □

So far we have concentrated on O-notation as a means for describing an algorithm's performance. Whereas O-notation is used to express an upper bound, we might also wish to determine a function which is a lower bound. What is needed is a mathematical notation for expressing a formula which is a lower bound on the computing time of an algorithm to within a constant.

Definition: $f(n) = \Omega(g(n))$, (read as "f of n equals Ω of $g(n)$") iff there exist positive constants c and n_0 such that for all $n > n_0$, $|f(n)| \geq c|g(n)|$.

In some cases the time for an algorithm, $f(n)$, will be such that $f(n) = \Omega(g(n))$ and $f(n) = O(g(n))$. For this circumstance we will use the following notation.

Definition: $f(n) = \Theta(g(n))$ iff there exist positive constants c_1, c_2, and n_0 such that for all $n > n_0$, $c_1 |g(n)| \leq |f(n)| \leq c_2 |g(n)|$.

If $f(n) = \Theta(g(n))$ then $g(n)$ is both an upper and lower bound on $f(n)$. This means that the worst and best cases require the same amount of time to within a constant factor. As an example consider the algorithm which finds the maximum of n elements, Algorithm 1.1. The computing time for this algorithm is both $O(n)$ and $\Omega(n)$ since the **for** loop always makes $n - 1$ iterations. Thus, we say that its time is $\Theta(n)$. The procedure of algorithm 1.4 searches an array of n elements for a single value. It has a computing time which is $O(n)$ but $\Omega(1)$. In the best case it might find the value on the first comparison, but in the worst case it will look at all elements once.

An even stronger mathematical notation is given by the following.

Definition: $f(n) \sim o(g(n))$ (read as "f of n is asymptotic to $g(n)$") iff there exists a positive constant n_0 such that

$$limit \quad f(n)/g(n) \to 1 \text{ as } n \to \infty \text{ for } n > n_0$$

Since the ratio in the limit is one, the functions $f(n)$ and $g(n)$ must agree even closer than by a constant factor. If there is an algorithm whose exact computing time is $f(n)$ and we can determine a $g(n)$ such that f is asymptotic to g, then we will have a more precise description of the computing time than if we had used the big O-notation. In practice it implies we will know both the order of the leading term and its constant. For example if $f(n) = a_k n^k + \ldots + a_0$ then

$$f(n) = O(n^k)$$

and

$$f(n) \sim o(a_k n^k)$$

Sums of Integers

As we work to determine the frequency of execution of statements we shall often encounter expressions of the form

$$\sum_{g(n) \le i \le h(n)} f(i) \tag{1.1}$$

where $f(i)$ is a polynomial in i with rational number coefficients. The most common forms of this formula are

$$\sum_{1 \le i \le n} 1, \qquad \sum_{1 \le i \le n} i, \qquad \sum_{1 \le i \le n} i^2 \tag{1.2}$$

which are the first three Bernoulli polynomials. Since these sums are finite there exist formulas, polynomials in n, which are equal to these sums. The value of the first sum is easily seen to be n. But how do we determine the values of the others? One method is by using interpolation. For example we can think of the second summation as describing the set of points in two dimensional space, $(n, P(n))$, which are:

$$(1,1), (2,3), (3,6) (4,10), \ldots$$

$P(n)$ is the polynomial to be found. According to Lagrange's formula (see Chapter 9 for more details) we find that

$$\sum_{1 \le i \le n} i = n(n + 1)/2 = \theta(n^2) \tag{1.3}$$

$$\sum_{1 \le i \le n} i^2 = n(n + 1)(2n + 1)/6 = \theta(n^3) \tag{1.4}$$

In general we will find that

$$\sum_{1 \le i \le n} i^k = \frac{n^{k+1}}{k + 1} + \frac{n^k}{2} + \text{lower order terms} \tag{1.5}$$

Thus we can conclude that

$$\sum_{1 \le i \le n} i^k = \theta(n^{k+1}) \tag{1.6}$$

or more precisely

$$\sum_{1 \le i \le n} i^k \sim o\left(\frac{n^{k+1}}{k + 1}\right) \tag{1.7}$$

PROFILING

Suppose we assume at this stage that a program solving some problem has been devised, coded, proved correct, and debugged on a computer. How do we go about producing a *performance profile*, that is determining the precise amounts of time and storage this program will consume? In order to determine exact times, our computer must be equipped with a clock whose time can be read. Using this timing capability there are many factors of the program's performance we can check. The most important test of a program is the one which confirms the earlier analysis of the order of magnitude. A program whose time has been determined to be $\Theta(n)$ or $\Theta(n \log n)$, etc. will have a performance profile which looks like the curves in Figure 1.9. Using actual timing data we should be able to determine the exact shape of this curve given the programming language and the machine we are using.

Let the program be called SOLUTION(X, Y) where X denotes the input and Y the output. When the initial analysis was first done, a consideration of possible data sets was made. This was necessary to determine at least the worst and best possbile cases of the algorithm. Let these data sets be created to be used as input to this procedure. Then a program to produce a timing profile has the following general form:

procedure *PROFILE*
    // this program outlines the form that a main program//
    //will take when testing the program SOLUTION(X, Y)//

    //initialize any variables that may be needed for SOLUTION//
    print('Test of algorithm SOLUTION. Times in milliseconds')
    loop
       read(*DATA*)
       If *DATA* − *end-of-file* **then exit endif**
       print('*A new data set* =', *DATA*)
       call STIME(t)
       //Procedure STIME initializes t to the current//
       //value of the clock. Determining the time on a//
       //computer is machine dependent and varies greatly.//
       //See a consultant at your computing center for further details.//
       call SOLUTION(DATA,OUTPUT)
       call STIME(s)
       print('*Time* =', $s - t$)
    repeat
end *PROFILE*
    Algorithm 1.10   Schema for producing a program's performance profile

The above procedure will print out the times that SOLUTION takes to process each data set. Notice that we don't bother to print the result Y, since we are assuming that SOLUTION is known to work properly. Also, we assume that neither SOLUTION nor any of its subroutines perform any input or output. To produce an order of magnitude curve the data sets are chosen so that they grow in size. The resulting timing data will show the performance profile of SOLUTION. For a program whose computing time is described not by $\Theta(f(n))$ but by $O(f(n))$, separate runs should be made using the worst, best and average data over a range of sizes.

A second way to use the timing capability of your computer is to take two programs for performing the same task whose orders of magnitude are identical and run them as they process data. The resulting times will show which, if any, program is faster. Changes to one program which do not alter the order of magnitude but which purport to speed up the program can also be tested in this way.

The procedure STIME is used to read the computer's clock. Reading a clock varies widely from computer to computer and determining the precise times that an algorithm takes is not entirely trivial. Much of the difficulty comes from the idiosyncracies associated with computer clocks. Often they are not very accurate or it may be difficult to access them. A survey of some popular computers revealed that their clocks measured time in the given in units; see Table 1.2.

IBM 370/158	3.3	milliseconds
UNIVAC 1108	.2	milliseconds
PDP 11/45	16.7	milliseconds
CDC Cyber 74	1	milliseconds
HP 3000	1	milliseconds
B 3700	1	milliseconds
B 6700	2.64	microseconds

Table 1.2 Clocks and their accuracies

Another difficulty in getting reliable clock times comes about if your computer's operating system is in multiprogramming or time sharing mode. For instance, on the PDP-10 under the TENEX operating system, the clock times always includes a certain fraction of the time needed to swap out the user's program on disk. This time will vary depending upon the number of users who are currently logged into the system, and there is no way of discerning how much time that takes.

If we run an algorithm on an IBM 370 and the complete execution takes less than 1 millisecond, then the resulting timing figures will be just "noise", i.e., totally unreliable. There are two ways to solve this problem. One way is to increase the size of the input until the total time required is large enough to give a reliable measurement. A second possibility is to repeatedly execute the algorithm r times for r sufficiently large and then divide the total time by r.

In the remainder of this section we will take a specific problem, give several algorithms for its solution and compare their resulting running times. The problem we shall solve is a simple one. We are given n integers residing in the array $A(1:n)$. These integers are already in sorted order. The *mode* of A is an element which occurs most often. We wish to write an algorithm which determines both the mode of A and the number of times (frequency) the mode occurs in A. Procedure MODE presents what might be termed a straightforward solution.

procedure *MODE*$(A,n,mode,freq)$
  // In array $A(1:n)$, $n \geq 1$ which is already sorted,//
  //the mode and its frequency are found. In case//
  //of a tie the first mode encountered is chosen.//
  integer $i,n,freq,temp$;
  $mode \leftarrow A(1); freq \leftarrow 1; temp \leftarrow 1$
  for $i \leftarrow 2$ **to** n **do**
    if $A(i) \neq A(i) - 1)$ **then** $temp \leftarrow 1$ //a new element is encountered//
      else $temp \leftarrow temp + 1$ //increase the frequency of the current element//
        if $temp > freq$
          then $freq \leftarrow temp; mode \leftarrow A(i)$ //new frequency; possibly a new mode//
        endif
    endif
  repeat
end *MODE*

Algorithm 1.11 Finding a mode and its frequency

Now let us try to conceive of a recursive algorithm which finds the mode. Suppose we imagine that we already have a procedure RMODE(n,m,f) which finds the mode m and frequency f of the already sorted elements in $A(1:n)$. Suppose we apply the procedure to the first $n - 1$ elements, using **call** RMODE$(n - 1, m,f)$ and consider under what circumstances a new mode may occur by including $A(n)$. Thinking in this way leads to a recursive program and possibly to another mode finding program. Clearly, if $A(n) \neq$

$A(n - 1)$, m and f needn't be changed. If $A(n) = A(n - 1)$, how can we distinguish between the cases: (i) a new mode is found, (ii) the mode is unchanged, but its frequency is increased, (iii) no change need be made to m or f? The answer comes by considering if $A(n) = A(n - f)$, for then there are $n - (n - f) + 1 = f + 1$ occurences of $A(n)$ which makes it either a new mode or the same mode with a new frequency. Otherwise the mode needn't be changed. This leads to the elegant recursive procedure first given by M. Griffiths:

```
procedure RMODE(i,m,f)
   // the mode m and its frequency f in A(1:i) are found; i ≥ 1//
   global A(1:n); integer i,n,f;
   if i = 1 then m ← A(1); f ← 1
        else call RMODE(i - 1,m,f)
        if A(i) = A(i - f)
           then m ← A(i); f ← f + 1
        endif
   endif
end RMODE
```

Algorithm 1.12   Recursively finding a mode and its frequency

This program is very slick and needs to be studied. Initially RMODE is invoked by the statement **call** $RMODE$ $(n$, mode, freq) which sets i to n and begins execution. If i is one, it is obvious that it works! Otherwise, assuming RMODE will work correctly for $i - 1$ elements ($i \leq n$), we ask it to find the mode and frequency of the first $n - 1$ elements of A. It does this, returning the mode and frequency in m and f. If the frequency of the mode of the entire set $A(1:n)$ is g then the frequency of the mode of the first $n - 1$ elements, f, is $f = g$ or $f = g - 1$. The latter case occurs only if the last element, $A(n)$, is the mode. Then $A(n - f) = A(n - f + 1) = \ldots = A(n)$. The innermost **if** therefore correctly updates the mode.

If we examine the way RMODE actually works we see that it continually calls itself until $i = 1$. It then computes the final result by examining, in turn, the second, third, fourth, ..., nth element and updating the mode appropriately. This realization makes it natural to consider a translation of RMODE which would work iteratively. Since there is only one recursive call, no return address need be stacked. After performing a translation according to the rules in section 1.3 and then simplifying, procedure RMODE1 is obtained.

procedure $RMODE1(A,n,m,f)$
   // a non-recursive version of RMODE//
   integer i,n,f;
   $m \leftarrow A(1); f \leftarrow 1$
   for $i \leftarrow 2$ **to** n **do**
      if $A(i) = A(i - f)$
         then $m \leftarrow A(i); f \leftarrow f + 1$
     endif
   repeat
end $RMODE1$

Algorithm 1.13   A refined version of Algorithm 1.12

We now have three algorithms for finding the mode and its frequency in a sorted array. Which one is the best? RMODE is the shortest, but not by much. We might not have thought of RMODE1 if we hadn't searched for a recursive solution first. Since RMODE1 was derived from RMODE by removing the recursion, it will probably be faster. But how much faster? All three programs have computing times which are $\Theta(n)$ and an asymptotic analysis is unable to provide any more clues as to their relative efficiencies.

The solution is to devise some data sets and determine a performance profile for these three programs. Which data set will cause these programs to work the hardest? Clearly, sets containing only one distinct element will give the worst case. The frequency will continually be updated and each of the algorithms will do the maximum amount of work that is possible on each iteration. A best case data set would be the one with all distinct elements. Determining a data set which exhibits some average behavior is more complex. Elements should be repeated with varying frequencies. If there are k distinct elements out of n, where the ith occurs with frequency n_i, then $n_1 + \ldots + n_k = n$. This sum is called a k-partition of n. For random data sets we need to generate random k partitions of n for all values of k.

Table 1.3 gives the computing times in milleseconds, determined when RMODE, RMODE1, and MODE were run on the same data set, all numbers distinct. RMODE is consistently slower, by a factor between three and four over its iterative equivalent RMODE1. MODE, the originial solution, is also slower than RMODE1, but never by more than a factor of two. Notice that there is a severe penalty running a recursive program in PL/C (a diagnostic compiler for PL/1) versus its simplified iterative equivalent. We can use these times to estimate the constant of the leading term of the computing time. Let c_1n, c_2n, and c_3n be the best case times for RMODE,

RMODE1, and MODE respectively where the c_i are constants we wish to determine. From the table the approximate values for these constants are $11/10$, $3/10$, and $1/2$ respectively.

n	100	200	300	400	500	600	700	800	900	1000
RMODE	110	220	340	400	640	680	720	820	940	1050
RMODE1	40	60	80	120	150	170	200	240	260	280
MODE	60	100	150	180	250	300	350	410	440	500

(Run on an IBM 370/158 in PL/C)

Table 1.3   RMODE vs. RMODE1 vs. MODE, distinct numbers or best case

Another characteristic which we can test for is the difference in times obtained by writing an algorithm in different programming languages. To test this factor we wrote RMODE1 in FORTRAN and PLI/X and ran it using data with one distinct element. PLI/X is an optimizing compiler for PL/I. The table below summarizes the results.

n:	500	1000	1500	2000	2500	3000	3500	4000	4500	5000
FORTRAN G:	3	13	16	26	33	39	41	46	56	66
PLI/X:	9	19	33	43	56	69	76	86	99	113

(run on an IBM 370/158)

Table 1.4   Times in milliseconds for RMODE1, 1 element or worst case

Notice that despite the use of an optimizing compiler for PL/I the FORTRAN version is uniformly faster by slightly less than a factor of two.

There are many more experiments one could devise using these programs. The timing of programs and the collecting of performance profiles is an integral part of the analysis of algorithms. We will see more computational experiments as we study the algorithms in this book.

CONCLUSIONS

The first chapter has given us a glimpse of all of the phases we will go through as we study an algorithm and its variations. Informally speaking we perform in order: design, validation, analysis, coding, verification, debugging, and timing. Often we have to go back and repeat a phase. Though the creation of algorithms may never be fully automated, in Figure 1.10 we have even gone so far as to give a procedure for composing an algorithm. Look at it carefully. Maybe someday someone will write a system which automatically generates correct and efficient algorithms. In that case the need for this book will be removed. But in the meantime the development of algorithms remains both an art and a science.

In the following chapters you will find some of the most clever, most useful, and the most beautiful of algorithms that are known. The study of these algorithms is a fascinating adventure in itself. But the skills we hope you will learn here are useful for more than just recreation. They will have a payoff which you can apply to your own work and to the work of others.

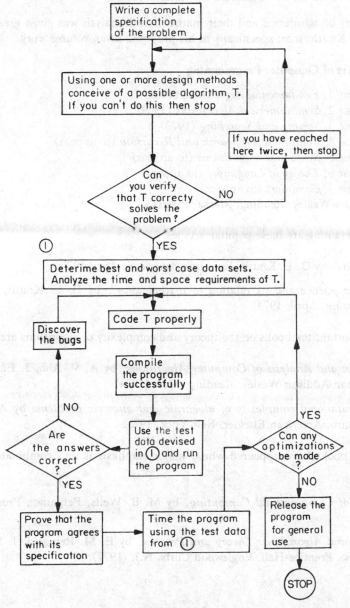

Figure 1.10

The ability to effectively analyze, criticize, and improve the programs that your colleagues develop will be a sign that your computer science training has paid off.

REFERENCES AND SELECTED READINGS

The study of algorithms and their mathematical analysis was given great impetus by Donald Knuth, most specifically in his projected seven volume work

The Art of Computer Programming

Volume 1, *Fundamental Algorithms* (1968)
Volume 2, *Seminumerical Algorithms* (1969)
Volume 3, *Sorting and Searching* (1973)
Volume 4, *Combinatorial Search and Recursion* (to appear)
Volume 5, *Syntactical Algorithms* (to appear)
Volume 6, *Theory of Languages* (to appear)
Volume 7, *Compilers* (to appear)
Addison-Wesley, Reading, Massachusetts

More entertaining are these popular articles

"Algorithms" by D. E. Knuth, *Scientific American*, April 1977.

"Computer science and its relation to mathematics", by D. E. Knuth, *American Math Monthly*, April, 1974.

Other important textbooks on the theory and complexity of algorithms are

The Design and Analysis of Computer Algorithms, by A. V. Aho, J. E. Hopcroft, J. D. Ullman Addison-Wesley, Reading, Mass (1974)

The computational complexity of algebraic and numeric problems by A. Borodin and I. Munro, American Elsevier, New York, 1975.

Several books have appeared whose major emphasis is on "combinatorial computing."

Elements of Combinatorial Computing, by M. B. Wells, Pergamon Press, Oxford (1971).

Combinatorial Algorithms: Theory and Practice, by E. M. Reingold, J. Nievergelt, and N. Deo, Prentice-Hall, Englewood Cliffs, N.J. (1977).

Combinatorial algorithms by A. Nijenhuis and H. S. Wilf, Academic Press, New York (1975).

Algorithmic combinatorics, by S. Even, Macmillan Company, New York, 1973.

Combinatorial optimization, by E. Lawler, Holt, Rinehart, Winston, New York, 1976.

More information on asymptotic analysis can be found in

Asymptotic Methods in Analysis, by N. G. de Bruijn, North Holland Publishers, Amsterdam (1961).

"Big Omicron and Big Omega and Big Theta," by D. E. Knuth, *SIGACT News*, ACM (April 1976).

The idea of translating recursive programs into iterative form is discussed in

"Structured Programming with Go-tos," by D. E. Knuth, *Computing Surveys*, vol. 6, no. 4, (January 1975)

"A system which automatically improves programs", by J. Darlington and R. M. Burstall, *Proceedings of the Third International Conference on Artificial Intell*, Stanford, (1973), 479–485. See also *JACM*, vol. 24, no. 1, January 1977, pp. 44–67.

"Toward automatic program systhesis" by Z. Manna and R. Waldinger, *CACM*, vol. 14, no. 3, (March 1971)

For an eloquent plea about the future directions of computer science theory see

"Microelectronics and computer science", by Ivan E. Sutherland and Carver A. Mead, *Scientific American*, September, 1977, 210–228.

For a nice introduction to the fields of program data flow analysis and program verification plus many references see

ACM Computing Surveys, vol. 8, no. 3, September 1976.

EXERCISES

1. Look up the words "algorism" and "algorithm" in your dictionary.

2. The shortened name al-Khowarizmi (algorithm) literally means "from the town of Khowarazm". This city is now known as Khiva, and is located in the province of Uzbekistan, USSR. See if you can find this city in an atlas.

3.   Rewrite the following program segments in a clearer way:

```
i ← n                if a > b
while i > 1 do       then if c > d
    y ← F(x)             then if e > f then x ← 1
    i ← i - 2                           else x ← 2
repeat                       endif
                         else x ← 3
                     endif
                 else x ← 4
                 endif
```

4.   Write FORTRAN equivalents of the **while, loop-until-repeat,** and **for** statements. Remember that according to the ANSI language standard, FORTRAN DO-loops always execute once and cannot count down.

5.   In an attempt to economize on the number of statements in SPARKS discuss the merits and demerits of removing the following statements: (i) **while** (ii) **while** and **loop-until-repeat** (iii) **go to** (iv) all iteration statements.

6.   Write a Boolean function which takes an array $A(1:n)$, $n \geq 1$, of zeros and ones and determines if the size of every sequence of consecutive ones is even. What is the computing time of your algorithm?

7.   Write a recursive algorithm for problem 6 if you have not already done so.

8.   If $t(n)$ is the time for **procedure** Fibonacci (n) as given in section 1.3 show that $t(n) = O(2^{n-2})$.

9.   Another recursive procedure which computes the nth Fibonacci number is the one below.

```
procedure F1(n)
    //a function which returns the nth Fibonacci number.//
    if n < 2 then return(1)
        else return (F2(2,n,1,1))
    endif
end F1

procedure F2(i,n,x,y)
    if i ≤ n
        then call F2(i + 1, n,y,x + y)
    endif
    return(y)
end F2
```

Trace out the algorithm as it computes F1(1), F1(2), F1(3), F1(4) and then compare its computing time to the time for procedure F(n), Algorithm 1.2.

10. Simulate **procedure** MAX1, Algorithm 1.5 on the data set $n = 5$ and $A(1:5) = 10,20,12,18,16$.

11. Which one of the following procedures correctly finds the maximum of the n distinct elements in $A(1:n)$?

procedure $MAX4(i,j)$
   global n, $A(1:n)$
   if $i \leq n$ **then if** $A(i) > A(j)$ **then** $j \leftarrow i$ **endif**
                              call $MAX4(i + 1, j)$
   endif
end $MAX4$

procedure $MAX5(i,j)$
   global n, $A(1:n)$
   if $i < n$ **then call** $MAX5(i + 1, j)$
               if $A(i) > A(j)$ **then** $j \leftarrow i$ **endif**
       else $j \leftarrow n$
   endif
end $MAX5$

How is each procedure initially invoked? Does the correct procedure work in the same way as Algorithm 1.5 if the elements of A are not distinct?

12. Take the five algorithms given in this chapter for finding the maximum and compare their computing times as you execute them on the data set whose values are in increasing order.

13. Procedure SEARCH(i) in the text will work faster if we do the following:

$$A(n + 1) \leftarrow x$$
$$k \leftarrow SEARCH(1)$$

Show how to rewrite SEARCH so it takes advantage of the fact that x occurs at least once at the end of the array.

14. Translate procedure SEARCH, Algorithm 1.4, into iterative form using the rules of section 1.3. First rewrite the recursive version so that there is only one **return** and then translate the result.

15. Write a procedure which finds the mode and frequency of an *unsorted* array. Analyze its computing time. Is your method better than sorting?

16. Program procedure RMODE1 in two different languages and run them on the same computer. Use a data set having all numbers distinct. Compare your results with Table 1.3.

17. Observe that for MODE or RMODE to work properly we needn't assume the set is sorted, but simply clustered. Define this notion precisely and devise an algorithm for clustering. If possible your algorithm should not necessarily sort the elements.

18. Devise an iterative version of mode finding which works faster than MODE (Algorithm 1.11). Your version will make fewer comparisons each time through the loop.

19. For the following pairs of functions determine the smallest value of n for which the second function becomes smaller than the first function.

   (i) n^2, $10n$
   (ii) 2^n, $2n^3$
   (iii) $n^2/\log n$, $n(\log n)^2$
   (iv) $n^3/2$, $n^{2.81}$

20. Write a recursive program which computes the binomial coefficient BINOM (n,m) using the recursive definition BINOM(n,m) = BINOM$(n - 1,m)$ + BINOM$(n - 1,m - 1)$ and BINOM$(n,0)$ = BINOM(n,n) = 1.

21. Compare the merits of computing binomial coefficients using the recursive program above with an iterative program based on factorials, BINOM(n,m) = $n!/(m!(n - m)!)$.

22. Prove that $1 + 2 + 3 + \cdots + n = n(n + 1)/2$. (Big hint: show that by grouping the terms as $(1 + n) + (2 + n - 1) + (3 + n - 2) + \cdots$ the formula holds.)

23. Using your calculator (or by hand) augment Table 1.1 by adding the values for the following columns: $\log \log n$, $n^2 \log n$, $n^3 \log n$, and n^n.

24. Using your calculator (or by hand) extend Table 1.1 by adding rows for the following values of n: 64, 128, 256, 512 and 1024. Use approximation where-ever it is necessary.

25. In procedure MAX3(A,n), Algorithm 1.7, the frequency of execution of every statement is fixed by n except "$k \leftarrow i$". Determine the average number of times this statement is executed using the following set of hints.

(i) Assume the values in A(1:n) are distinct and each of the n! permutations are equally likely to occur. Let p(n,k) be the number of permutations of n which create an execution frequency of k divided by n!.

(i) Determine the number of times that the frequency of execution of k ← i is either zero, one, or two when n = 3, namely find p(3,0), p(3,1), p(3,2).

(ii) The average frequency is defined as the sum of kp(n,k) as k varies from zero to n − 1. Explain why

$$p(n,k) = (1/n)p(n - 1, k - 1) + ((n - 1)/n)p(n - 1,k)$$

where initially $p(1,k) = \delta(0,1)$, and $p(n,k) = 0$ if $k < 0$.

(iii) Let $G(n,z) = p(n,0) + p(n,1)z + \cdots + p(n,n - 1)z^{n-1}$ and $G(1,z) = 1$. Using this definition and the previous formula show that

$$G(n,z) = (z/n)G(n - 1,z) + ((n - 1)/n)G(n - 1,z)$$
$$= ((z + n - 1)/n)G(n - 1,z)$$

(iv) Unwind the above formula to obtain

$$G(n,z) = (1/(z + n))\text{BINOM}\begin{pmatrix} z + n \\ n \end{pmatrix}$$

(v) Now show that

$$G'(n,z) = (1/n)G(n - 1,z) + ((z + n - 1)/n)G'(n - 1,z)$$

and

$$G'(n,1) = 1/n + G'(n - 1,1)$$
$$= \ldots = H_n - 1$$

where H_n is the nth Harmonic number, $H_n = 1 + 1/2 + 1/3 + 1/4 + \cdots + 1/n$

(vi) If you have gotten this far, you have no doubt observed that the average we are looking for is given by $G'(n,1)$ so you are already done.

These hints follow the derivation given by D. Knuth in *Fundamental Algorithms*.

26. In many cases it is advisable to compute the average time over a set of m trials when the input size is fixed. The test program to do this would look like

```
initialize the timer
for i ← 1 to m do
    call SOLUTION(x, y)
repeat
average ← TIME/m
```

It would also be nice to know how close the average is to the actual readings. This is given by the standard deviation. Look up the definition of the standard deviation and show how to compute it within the above program.

27. Another program for computing the mode and its frequency of a sorted set is

```
procedure MODE2(A,n,m,f)
    //n > 0//
    f ← 0; count ← 1; i ← 2
    A(n + 1) ← A(n) + 1          //We need to extend the array by one position//
    loop
        if A(i) = A(i − 1)
            then count ← count + 1
            else if count > f
                    then f ← count; m ← A(i − 1); count ← 1
                endif
        endif
        i ← i + 1
    until i > n + 1 repeat
end MODE2
```

Devise and execute some experiments which compare the computing times of MODE2 with the other versions of mode finding in this chapter.

28. Procedure $F(n)$ of section 1.3 computes the nth Fibonacci number. How many times is $F(i)$ computed for $i = 1,2,3,\cdots,n$?

29. Why does procedure PROFILE (Algorithm 1.10) assume that the call to SOLUTION contains no input or output statements?

30. Develop an algorithm which converts a Roman numeral into an Arabic integer. Note that $I = 1, V = 5, X = 10, L = 50, C = 100, M = 1000$.

31. Develop an algorithm which converts a positive Arabic integer into its corresponding Roman numeral.

32. Design and test an algorithm which determines how long it takes your computer to execute 2^n, n^n, and $n!$ additions for various values of n. Do the same for multiplications.

33. Modify the "algorithm" of Figure 1.10 so that it handles the case when two competing algorithms are developed to solve the same problem.

Chapter 2

ELEMENTARY DATA STRUCTURES

Now that we have presented the fundamental methods we need to express and analyze algorithms you might feel all set to begin. But alas we need to make one last diversion to which we devote this chapter, and that is a discussion of data structures. One of the basic techniques for improving algorithms is to structure the data in such a way that the resulting operations can be efficiently carried out. Though we can't possibly survey here all of the techniques that are known, in this chapter we have selected several which we feel occur most frequently. Maybe you have already seen these techniques in a course on data structures (hopefully having used *Fundamentals of data structures*). If so, you may either skip this chapter or scan it briefly. If you haven't been exposed to the ideas of stack, queues, sets, trees, graphs, heaps, or hashing then lets begin our study of algorithms right now with some interesting problems from the field of data structures.

2.1 STACKS AND QUEUES

One of the most common forms of data organization in computer programs is the ordered or linear list, which is often written as $A = (a_1, a_2, \ldots a_n)$. The $a_i s$ are referred to as *atoms* and they are chosen from some set. The null or empty list has $n = 0$ elements. A *stack* is an ordered list in which all insertions and deletions are made at one end, called the *top*. A *queue* is an ordered list in which all insertions take place at one end, the *rear*, while all deletions take place at the other end, the *front*.

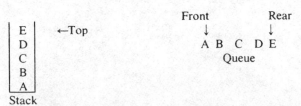

Figure 2.1   Example of a stack and a queue

48

The operations of a stack imply that if the elements A,B,C,D,E are inserted into a stack, in that order, then the first element to be removed/deleted must be E. Equivalently we say that the last element to be inserted into the stack will be the first to be removed. For this reason stacks are sometimes referred to as **Last In First Out** (LIFO) lists. The operations of a queue require that the first element which is inserted into the queue will be the first one to be removed. Thus queues are known as **First In First Out** (FIFO) lists. See Figure 2.1 for an example of a stack and a queue each containing the same five elements inserted in the same order. Note that the data object queue as defined here need not necessarily correspond to the concept of queue which is studied in queuing theory.

The simplest way to represent a stack is by using a one-dimensional array, say STACK(1:n), where n in the maximum number of allowable entries. The first or bottom element in the stack will be stored at STACK(1), the second at STACK(2) and the ith at STACK(i). Associated with the array will be a variable, typically called *top*, which points to the top element in the stack. To test if the stack is empty we ask "**if** *top* = 0". If not, the topmost element is at STACK(*top*). Two more substantial operations are inserting and deleting elements. The corresponding procedures are given as algorithms 2.1(a) and (b).

procedure *ADD(item, STACK, n, top)*
  //insert *item* into the STACK of maximum size n; *top* is the//
  //number of elements currently in STACK//
    if *top* ≥ n **then call** *STACKFULL* **endif**
    top ← *top* + 1
    STACK(top) ← *item*
end *ADD*

(a) Insertion of an element

procedure *DELETE(item, STACK, top)*
  //remove the top element of STACK and store it//
  //in *item* unless STACK is empty//
    if *top* ≤ 0 **then call** *STACKEMPTY* **endif**
    item ← *STACK(top)*
    top ← *top* − 1
end *DELETE*

(b) Deletion of an element

Algorithm 2.1   Stacking operations

Each execution of ADD or DELETE takes a constant amount of time and is independent of the number of elements in the stack. STACKFULL and STACKEMPTY are procedures which we leave unspecified since they will depend upon the particular application. Often a stack full condition will signal that more storage needs to be allocated and the program rerun. Stack empty is often a meaningful condition.

Another way to represent a stack is by using links (or pointers). A *node* is a collection of data and link information. A stack can be represented by using nodes with two fields, possibly called DATA and LINK. The data field of each node contains an item in the stack and the corresponding link field points to the node containing the next item in the stack. The link field of the last node is zero for we assume that all nodes have an address greater than zero. For example a stack with the items A,B,C,D,E inserted in that order, would look as in Figure 2.2.

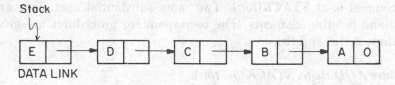

Figure 2.2   Example of a 5 element, linked stack

The variable STACK points to the topmost node (the last item inserted) in the list. The empty stack is represented by setting STACK = 0. Because of the way the links are pointing, insertion and deletion are easy to accomplish. For example to insert an item into the stack one should write the following:

call *GETNODE(T)*
DATA(T) ← *item*
LINK(T) ← *STACK*
STACK ← *T*

Procedure GETNODE assigns to the variable T the address of an available node. If no more exist it will terminate the program. The next two assignments store appropriate values into the two fields of the node. Then the variable STACK is updated to point to the new top element of the list.

Deletion would work as follows:

if $\underset{\sim}{STACK}$ = 0 **then call** $STACKEMPTY$ **endif**
$item \leftarrow DATA(STACK)$
$T \leftarrow STACK$
$STACK \leftarrow LINK(STACK)$
call $RETNODE(T)$

If the stack is empty, then trying to delete an item will prodcue a call of the procedure STACKEMPTY. Otherwise the top element is stored as the value of the variable *item*, a pointer to the first node is saved, and STACK is moved to point to the next node. Procedure RETNODE is designed to take a single node and place it into a list of available nodes for later use by GETNODE.

The use of links to represent a stack requires more storage than the sequential array STACK(1:n). However, there is greater flexibility when using links, for many structures can simultaneously use the same pool of available space. Most importantly the times for insertion and deletion using either representation are a constant which is independent of the size of the stack.

An efficient queue representation is obtained by taking an array, declared as $Q(0:n - 1)$, and treating it as if it was circular. Elements are inserted by increasing the variable *rear* to the next free position. When *rear* = $n - 1$, the next element is entered at $Q(0)$ in case that spot is free. *front* will always point one position counterclockwise from the first element in the queue. *front* = *rear* is and only if the queue is empty and initially we have *front* = *rear* = 0. Figure 2.3 illustrates two of the possible configurations for a circular queue containing the four elements J1–J4 with $n > 4$.

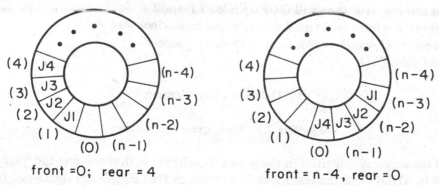

front =0; rear = 4   front = n−4, rear = 0

Figure 2.3 Circular queue of capacity *n* containing four elements J1,J2,J3,J4

In order to insert an element, it will be necessary to move *rear* one position clockwise. This can be done using the code:

if *rear* = $n - 1$ **then** *rear* $\leftarrow$ 0
               else *rear* $\leftarrow$ *rear* + 1
endif.

A more elegant way to do this is to use the built-in modulo operator which computes remainders. Before doing an insert we would increase the rear pointer by saying *rear* $\leftarrow$ (*rear* + 1) **mod** n. Similarly, it will be necessary to move *front* one position clockwise each time a deletion is made. An examination of the algorithms (algorithm 2.2 (a) and (b)) indicates that by treating the array circularly, addition and deletion for queues can be carried out in a fixed amount of time or $O(1)$.

procedure ADDQ(*item*, Q, *n*, *front*, *rear*)
   //insert *item* in the circular queue stored in $Q(0{:}n - 1)$;//
   //*rear* points to the last item and *front* is one position//
   //counterclockwise from the first item in Q//
   rear $\leftarrow$ (*rear* + 1) **mod** n '//advance rear clockwise//
   if *front* = *rear* **then call** *QUEUEFULL* **endif**
   Q(*rear*) $\leftarrow$ *item*   //insert new item//
end *ADDQ*

(a) Addition of an element

procedure DELETEQ(*item*, Q, *n*, *front*, *rear*)
   //removes the front element of the queue $Q(0{:}n - 1)$//
   //and stores it in *item*.//
   if *front* = *rear* **then call** *QUEUEEMPTY* **endif**
   front $\leftarrow$ (*front* + 1) **mod** n //advance front clockwise//
   item $\leftarrow$ Q(*front*)   //set item to front of queue//
end *DELETEQ*

(b) Deletion of an element

Algorithm 2.2   Basic queue operations

One surprising feature in these two algorithms is that the test for queue full in ADDQ and the test for queue empty in DELETEQ are the same. In the case of ADDQ, however, when *front* = *rear* there is actually one space free, $Q(rear)$, since the first element in the queue is not at $Q(front)$ but is one position clockwise from this point. However, if we insert an item there, then we will not be able to distinguish between the cases full and empty, since this insertion would leave $front = rear$. To avoid this, we signal queue full, thus permitting a maximum of $n - 1$ rather than n elements to be in the queue at any time. One way to use all n positions would be to use another variable, tag, to distinguish between the two situations, i.e. $tag = 0$ if and only if the queue is empty. This would however slow down the two algorithms. Since the ADDQ and DELETEQ algorithms will be used many times in any problem involving queues, the loss of one queue position will be more than made up for by the reduction in computing time.

The procedures QUEUEFULL and QUEUEEMPTY have been used without explanation, but they are similar to STACKFULL and STACK-EMPTY. Their function will depend on the particular application.

Another way to represent a queue would be by using links. Figure 2.4 shows a queue with the four elements A,B,C,D, entered in that order.

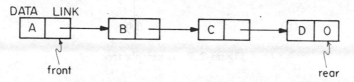

Figure 2.4 A linked queue with 4 elements

As with the linked stack example each node of the queue is composed of the two fields DATA and LINK. A queue is pointed at by two variables, *front* and *rear*. Deletions are made at the front and insertions at the rear. When *front* = 0 that signals an empty queue. Again, when using linked allocation one assumes the existence of procedures GETNODE and RET-NODE which operate as they did for stacks. The procedures for insertion and deletion of linked queues are left as exercises.

2.2 TREES

Definition A *tree* is a finite set of one or more nodes such that (i) there is a specially designated node called the root; (ii) the remaining nodes are partitioned into $n \geq 0$ disjoint sets $T1, \ldots, Tn$ where each of these sets is a tree. $T1, \ldots, Tn$ are called the *subtrees* of the root.

There are many terms which are often used when referring to trees. Consider the tree in Figure 2.5. This tree has 13 nodes, each data item of a node being a single letter for convenience. The root contains A, (though

we will usually say node A), and we will normally draw trees with their root
at the top. The number of subtrees of a node is called its *degree*. The degree
of A is 3, of C is 1, and of F is 0. Nodes that have degree zero are called
leaf or *terminal* nodes. The set $\{K, L, F, G, M, I, J\}$ is the set of leaf nodes
of Figure 2.5. The other nodes are referred to as *nonterminals*. The roots
of the subtrees of a node, X, are the *children* of X. X is the *parent* of its
children. Thus the children of D are H, I, J; the parent of D is A.

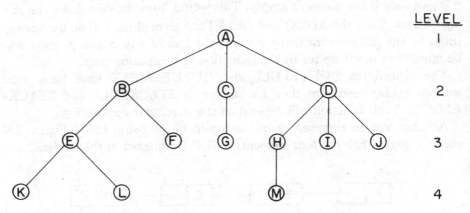

Figure 2.5   A sample tree

Children of the same parent are said to be *siblings*. For example H, I, and
J are siblings. We can extend this terminology if we need to so that we can
ask for the grandparent of M which is D, etc. The *degree* of a tree is the
maximum degree of the nodes in the tree. The tree in Figure 2.5 has degree
3. The *ancestors* of a node are all the nodes along the path from the root to
that node. The ancestors of M are A, D and H.

The *level* of a node is defined by initially letting the root be at level one.
If a node is at level p, then its children are at level $p + 1$. Figure 2.5 shows
the levels of all nodes in that tree. The *height* or *depth* of a tree is defined
to be the maximum level of any node in the tree.

A *forest* is a set of $n \geq 0$ disjoint trees. The notion of a forest is very
close to that of a tree because if we remove the root of a tree we get a forest.
For example, in Figure 2.5 if we remove A we get a forest with three trees.

Now how do we represent a tree in a computer's memory? If we wish to
use linked lists where one node in the list corresponds to one node in the
tree, then a node must have a varying number of fields depending upon
the number of branches. However it is often simpler to write algorithms for
a data representation where the node size is fixed. We can represent a
tree using a fixed node size list structure. Such a list representation for
the tree of Figure 2.5 is given in Figure 2.6. In this figure nodes have three

fields: TAG, DATA, and LINK. DATA and LINK are used as before with the exception that now TAG = 1, DATA contains a pointer to a list rather than a data item. A tree is represented by storing the root in the first node followed by nodes which point to publin, and contain each subtree of the root.

Binary Trees

A binary tree is an important type of tree structure which occurs very often. It is characterized by the fact that any node can have at most two children and there is no node with degree greater than two. For binary trees we distinguish between the children as left and on the right. element for tree the order of the subtrees is irrelevant. Furthermore a binary tree is allowed to have zero nodes while a tree must have at least one node. Thus a binary tree is NOT a special case of a tree.

Definition: A binary tree is a finite set of nodes which is either empty, or consists of a root and two disjoint binary trees called the left and right subtrees.

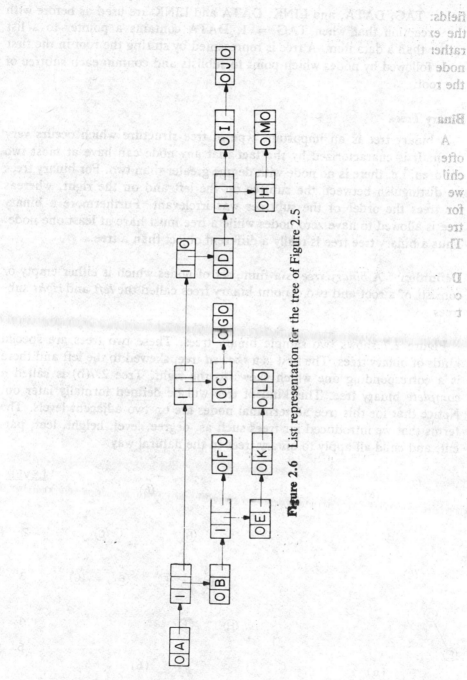

Figure 2.6 List representation for the tree of Figure 2.5

fields: TAG, DATA, and LINK. DATA and LINK are used as before with the exception that when TAG = 1, DATA contains a pointer to a list rather than a data item. A tree is represented by storing the root in the first node followed by nodes which point to sublists and contain each subtree of the root.

Binary Trees

A binary tree is an important type of tree structure which occurs very often. It is characterized by the fact that any node can have at most two children, i.e. there is no node with degree greater than two. For binary trees we distinguish between the subtree on the left and on the right, whereas for trees the order of the subtrees was irrelevant. Furthermore a binary tree is allowed to have zero nodes while a tree must have at least one node. Thus a binary tree tree is really a different object than a tree.

Definition: A *binary tree* is a finite set of nodes which is either empty or consists of a root and two disjoint binary trees called the *left* and *right* subtrees.

Figure 2.7 shows two sample binary trees. These two trees are special kinds of binary trees. The first is a *skewed* tree, skewed to the left and there is a corresponding one which skews to the right. Tree 2.7(b) is called a *complete* binary tree. This kind of tree will be defined formally later on. Notice that for this tree all terminal nodes are on two adjacent levels. The terms that we introduced for trees such as: degree, level, height, leaf, parent, and child all apply to binary trees in the natural way.

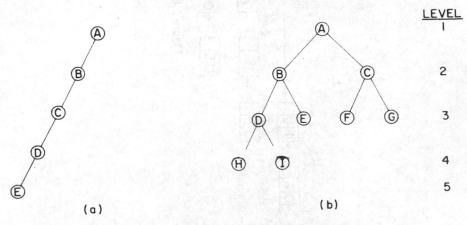

Figure 2.7   Two sample binary trees

Lemma 2.1 The maximum number of nodes on level i of a binary tree is 2^{i-1}. Also the maximum number of nodes in a binary tree of depth k is $2^k - 1, k > 0$. □

The binary tree of depth k which has exactly $2^k - 1$ nodes is called a *full* binary tree of depth k. Figure 2.8 shows a full binary tree of depth 4. A very elegant sequential representation for full binary trees results from sequentially numbering the nodes, starting with the node on level one, then going to those on level two and so on. Nodes on any level are numbered from left to right (see Figure 2.8). A binary tree with n nodes and of depth k is *complete* iff its nodes correspond to the nodes which are numbered one to n in the full binary tree of depth k. A consequence of this definition is that in a complete tree, leaf nodes occur on at most two adjacent levels. The nodes of a complete tree may be compactly stored in a one dimensional array, TREE, with the node numbered i being stored in TREE(i). The next lemma shows us how to easily determine the locations of the parent, left child and right child of any node i in the binary tree without explicitly storing any link information.

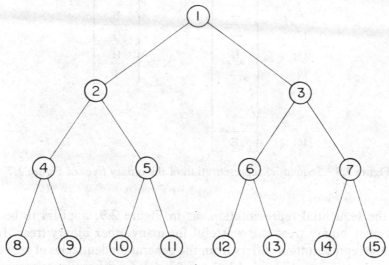

Figure 2.8 Full binary tree of depth 4

Lemma 2.2 If a complete binary tree with n nodes is represented sequentially as described before then for any node with index i, $1 \le i \le n$ we have:

(i) PARENT(i) is at $\lfloor i/2 \rfloor$ if $i \ne 1$. When $i = 1$, i is the root and has no parent.

(ii) LCHILD(i) is at $2i$ if $2i \leq n$. If $2i > n$ then i has no left child.
(iii) RCHILD(i) is at $2i + 1$ if $2i + 1 \leq n$. If $2i + 1 > n$ then i has no right child.

This representation can clearly be used for all binary trees though in most cases there will be a lot of unutilized space. For complete binary trees the representation is ideal as no space is wasted. For the skewed tree of Figure 2.7, however, less than a third of the array is utilized. In the worst case a right skewed tree of depth k will require $2^k - 1$ locations. Of these only k will be occupied.

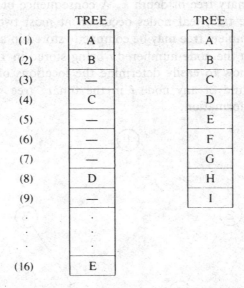

	TREE		TREE
(1)	A		A
(2)	B		B
(3)	—		C
(4)	C		D
(5)	—		E
(6)	—		F
(7)	—		G
(8)	D		H
(9)	—		I
·	·		
·	·		
·	·		
(16)	E		

Figure 2.9 Sequential representation of the binary trees of Figure 2.7

While the sequential representation, as in Figure 2.9, appears to be good for complete binary trees it is wasteful for many other binary trees. In addition, the representation suffers from the general inadequacies of sequential representations. Insertion or deletion of nodes requires the movement of potentially many nodes to reflect the change in level number of the remaining nodes. These problems can be easily overcome through the use of a linked representation. Each node will have three fields LCHILD, DATA, and RCHILD. While this node structure will make it difficult to determine the parent of a node, we shall see that for most applications it is adequate. In case it is often necessary to be able to determine the parent of a node, then a fourth field, PARENT, may be included with the obvious interpre-

tation. The representation of the binary trees of Figure 2.7 using a three
field structure is given in Figure 2.10.

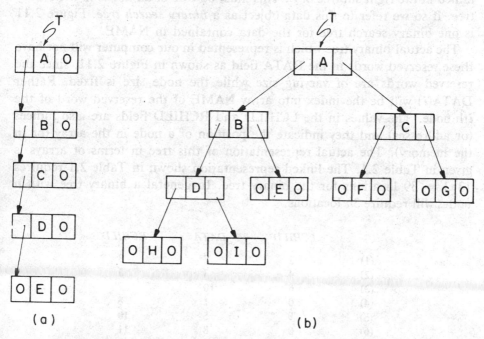

(a) (b)

Figure 2.10 Linked representation for the binary trees of Figure 2.7

As an example of the use of binary trees suppose we wish to maintain a
table which contains a subset of the reserved words of SPARKS. This would
be called a symbol table, and it could be used by a compiler which translates
SPARKS programs into some other, more primitive language (see Appendix
A for more details). We will select 13 SPARKS reserved words and store
them into the character array NAME(1:13):

NAME:	(1)	(2)	(3)	(4)	(5)	(6)	(7)
	case	do	else	end	endcase	endif	if

NAME:	(8)	(9)	(10)	(11)	(12)	(13)
	loop	procedure	repeat	return	then	while

A binary tree will be used to help us search if a particular character string,
X, is actually one of these reserved words. We insist that the binary tree be
constructed in such a way that the data associated with any node P is both

(*i*) alphabetically greater than the data in the nodes contained in the left subtree of *P*, and (*ii*) alphabetically less than the data in the nodes contained in the right subtree of *P*. This must be true of all nodes in the binary tree. If so we refer to this data object as a *binary search tree*. Figure 2.11 is one binary search tree for the data contained in NAME.

The actual binary tree which is represented in our computer will not have these reserved words in the DATA field as shown in Figure 2.11, since the reserved words are of varying size while the node size is fixed. Rather DATA(*i*) will be the index into array NAME of the reserved word of the *i*th node. The values in the LCHILD and RCHILD fields are also indices (or addresses) and they indicate the position of a node in the array (or in the memory). The actual representation of this tree in terms of arrays is given in Table 2.1. The linked representation shown in Table 2.1 requires 13*3 = 39 locations for the binary tree. In general a binary tree with *n* nodes will require 3*n* locations.

	LCHILD	DATA	RCHILD
(1)	2	7	3
(2)	4	3	5
(3)	6	10	7
(4)	0	1	8
(5)	9	5	10
(6)	0	8	11
(7)	12	12	13
(8)	0	2	0
(9)	0	4	0
(10)	0	6	0
(11)	0	9	0
(12)	0	11	0
(13)	0	13	0

Table 2.1   Array representation of Figure 2.12

It is easy to imagine how an algorithm would use a binary search tree to help it find out if *X* is present or not. This is asked for in the exercises. Sections 3.2 and 5.4 present more facts on this data structure.

There is a natural generalization of binary trees to the concept of *k*-ary trees, *k* ≥ 2. A node in a *k*-ary tree may have at most *k* children and these children are ordered. The sequential representation for binary trees can be extended to *k*-ary trees or a linked scheme using fixed size nodes can be used.

Let us return to the data structure tree where the subtrees are unordered and vary in number. We have a tree *T* with root T_1 and subtrees T_{11}, T_{12},

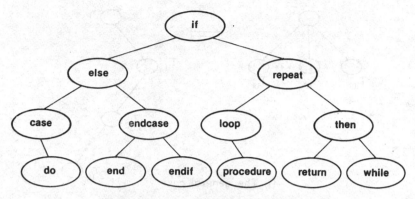

Figure 2.11 A binary search tree

..., T_{1k}. One way to represent this structure is to transform it into a binary tree. This is done by making T_1 the root of a binary tree, T_{11} the left child and then T_{1i} becomes the right child of $T_{1,i-1}$ for $2 \leq i \leq k$. Pictorially this looks like Figure 2.12. The virtue of this idea is that binary tree representations are simpler to process than using linked allocation with variable size nodes. Therefore this transformation may often result in less space and simpler algorithms.

We expect that most of our readers have already encountered the material in sections 2.1 and 2.2 and therefore they may have skimmed these sections. The next sections may offer new material for you and if so you are cautioned to now slow down and read more closely.

2.3 HEAPS AND HEAPSORT

In this section we study a way of structuring data which permits one to *insert* elements into a set and also to *find the largest element* efficiently. A data structure which provides for these two operations is called a *priority queue*. Many algorithms need to make use of priority queues and so an efficient way to implement these operations will be very useful.

We might first consider using a queue since inserting new elements would be very efficient. But finding the largest element would necessitate a scan of the entire queue. A second suggestion would be to use a sorted list which is stored sequentially. But an insertion could require moving all of the items in the list. What we want is a data structure which allows *both* operations to be done efficiently.

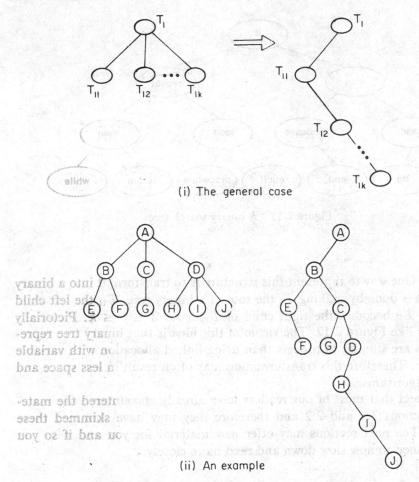

(i) The general case

(ii) An example

Figure 2.12   Transforming a tree into a binary tree

Definition: A *heap* is a complete binary tree with the property that the value at each node is at least as large as the values at its children (if they exist).

This definition implies that a largest element is at the root of the heap. If the elements are distinct, then the root contains the largest item. The relation greater than or equal to may be reversed so that the parent node contains a value as small as or smaller than its children. In this case the root contains the smallest element. But clinging to historical tradition we will assume that the larger values are closer to the root.

It is possible to take any binary tree containing values for which an ordering exists and move these values around so that the shape of the tree is preserved and the heap property is satisfied, see Figure 2.13. However, it is more often the case that we are given n items, say n integers and we are free to choose whatever shape binary tree seems most desirable. In this case the complete binary tree is chosen and represented sequentially, see Figure 2.14. This is why in the definition of heap we insist that a complete binary tree is used.

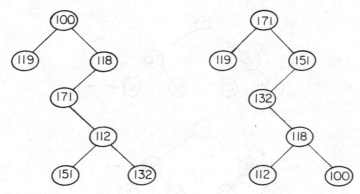

Figure 2.13 A binary tree and a heap that preserves the tree's shape

Now let us consider how to form a heap given n integers stored in $A(1:n)$. One strategy is to determine how to insert one element at a time into an already existing heap. If we can do this then we can apply the algorithm n times, first inserting one element into an empty heap and continuing in that way until all n elements have been inserted. The solution is simple, one adds a new item "at the bottom" of the heap and then compares it with its parent, grandparent, greatgrandparent, etc. until it is less than or equal to one of these values. Procedure INSERT, Algorithm 2.3 describes this process in full detail.

```
procedure INSERT(A,n)
  //inserts the value in A(n) into the heap which is stored//
  //at A(1) to A(n - 1)//
    integer i,j,n, ;
    j ← n; i ← ⌊n/2⌋ ; item ← A(n)
    while i > 0 and A(i) < item do
      A(j) ← A(i)            //move the parent down//
      j ← i; i ← ⌊i/2⌋      //the parent of A(i) is at A(⌊i/2⌋)//
    repeat
    A(j) ← item             //a place for A(n) is found//
end INSERT
```

Algorithm 2.3 Heap creation by inserting one item at a time

Figure 2.14 shows one example of how INSERT would insert a new value into an existing heap of six elements. It is clear from the program and the figure that the time for INSERT can vary. In the best case the new element is correctly positioned initially and no values need be rearranged. In the worst case the number of executions of the **while** loop is proportional to the number of levels in the heap.

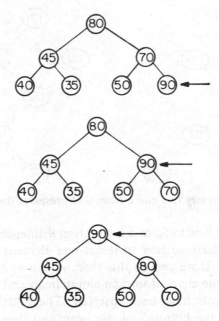

Figure 2.14   Action of INSERT inserting 90 as the seventh item into an existing heap

n items in $A(1:n)$ may be set up as a heap (which is also a complete binary tree) by the program segment

for $i \leftarrow 2$ **to** n **do**
    call *INSERT(A,i)*
repeat

Figure 2.15 shows how the data (40, 80, 35, 90, 45, 50, 70) is moved around until a heap is created. Trees in the left column represent the state of the array $A(1:i)$ before each call of INSERT. Trees in the right column show how the array was altered by INSERT to produce a heap. The array is drawn as a complete binary tree for clarity.

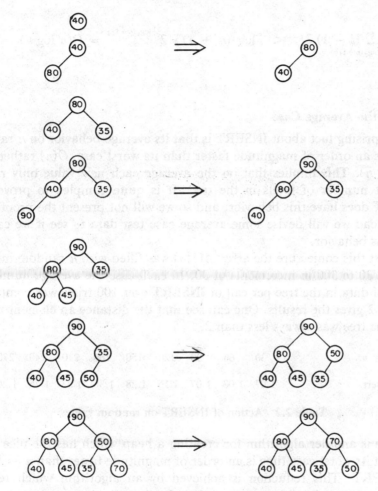

Figure 2.15 Forming a heap from the set (40,80,35,90,45,50,70)

Worst Case Analysis

The data set which causes the heap creation method using INSERT to behave in the worst way is when the elements are inserted in ascending order. Each new element will rise to become the new root.

There are at most 2^{i-1} nodes on level i of a complete binary tree, $1 \leq i \leq \lceil \log_2(n + 1) \rceil$. For a node on level i the distance to the root is $i - 1$. Thus the worst case time for heap creation using INSERT is

$$\sum_{1 \leq i \leq \lceil \log_2(n+1) \rceil} (i - 1) \, 2^{i-1} < \lceil \log_2(n + 1) \rceil \, 2^{\lceil \log_2(n+1) \rceil} = O(n \log n) \qquad (2.1)$$

Testing the Average Case

A surprising fact about INSERT is that its average behavior on n random inputs is an order of magnitude faster than its worst case, $O(n)$ rather than $O(n \log n)$. This implies that on the average each new value only rises a constant number of levels in the tree. It is quite complex to prove that INSERT does have this behavior, and so we will not present the proof here. But instead we will devise some average case test data to see if we can exhibit this behavior.

To test this conjecture the array $A(1:n)$ was filled with n random integers for $n = 30$ to 300 in increments of 30. In each case the average number of moves of data in the tree per call of **INSERT** over 100 trials was computed. Table 2.2 gives the results. Onc can see that the distance an element moved up in the tree was always less than 2.

n:	30	60	90	120	150	180	210	240	270	300
moves/insert:	1.07	1.08	1.07	1.16	1.28	1.36	1.33	1.76	1.28	1.52

Table 2.2   Action of INSERT on random values

There is another algorithm for creating a heap which has the nice property that its worst case time is an order of magnitude faster than $n - 1$ calls of INSERT. This reduction is achieved by an algorithm which regards $A(1:n)$ as a complete binary tree and works from the leaves up to the root, level by level. At each level, it will be the case that the left and right subtrees of any node are heaps. Only the value in the root node may violate the heap property. Hence it is sufficient to devise a method which converts a binary tree in which only the root may violate the heap property into a heap. Procedure ADJUST (Algorithm 2.4) does this for any binary tree whose root is at location i. The algorithm assumes that this binary tree is a subtree of a binary tree represented sequentially as discussed earlier.

procedure $ADJUST(A, i, n)$
>//The complete binary trees with roots $A(2*i)$ and $A(2*i + 1)$ are//
>//combined with $A(i)$ to form a single heap, $1 \leq i \leq n$.//
>//No node has an address greater than n or less than 1//
>>**integer** i, j, n;
>>$j \leftarrow 2 * i$; $item \leftarrow A(i)$
>>**while** $j \leq n$ **do**
>>>**if** $j < n$ **and** $A(j) < A(j + 1)$ //compare left and right child//
>>>**then** $j \leftarrow j + 1$ //j points to the larger child//
>>>**endif**
>>>**if** $item \geq A(j)$
>>>>**then exit**   //a position for item is found//
>>>>**else** $A(\lfloor j/2 \rfloor) \leftarrow A(j)$ //move the larger child up a level//
>>>>$j \leftarrow 2 * j$
>>>**endif**
>>>**repeat**
>>$A(\lfloor j/2 \rfloor) \leftarrow item$
>**end** $ADJUST$

Algorithm 2.4   Combining two heaps into a single heap

Given n elements in $A(1:n)$ we can create a heap by applying ADJUST. It is easy to see that leaf nodes are already heaps. So we may begin by calling ADJUST for the parents of leaf nodes and then work our way up, level by level, until the root is reached. In Figure 2.16 we observe the action of HEAPIFY as it creates a heap out of the given seven elements. The initial tree is drawn in Figure 2.16(*i*). Since $n = 7$ the first call to ADJUST has $i = 3$. In Figure 2.16(*ii*) the three elements 118, 151, 132 are rearranged to form a heap. Subsequently ADJUST is called with $i = 2$ and $i = 1$ yielding the trees in Figure 2.16(*iii*) and (*iv*).

procedure $HEAPIFY(A,n)$
>//Readjust the elements in $A(1:n)$ to form a heap//
>**integer** n,i
>**for** $i \leftarrow \lfloor n/2 \rfloor$ **to** 1 **by** -1 **do**
>>**call** $ADJUST(A, i, n)$
>**repeat**
end $HEAPIFY$

Algorithm 2.5   Creating a heap out of n arbitrary elements

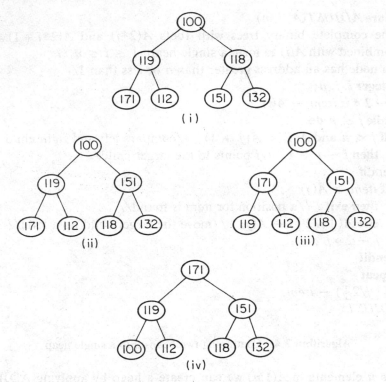

Figure 2.16 Action of HEAPIFY(A, 7) on the data of (100, 119, 118, 171, 112, 151, 132)

For the worst case analysis of HEAPIFY let $2^{k-1} \le n < 2^k$ where $k = \lceil \log(n + 1) \rceil$ and recall that the levels of the n node complete binary tree are numbered 1 to k. The worst case number of iterations for ADJUST is $k - i$ for a node on level i. Therefore the total time for HEAPIFY is proportional to

$$\sum_{1 \le i \le k} 2^{i-1}(k - i) = \sum_{1 \le i \le k-1} i\, 2^{k-i-1} \le n \sum i/2^i < n = O(n) \qquad (2.2)$$

Comparing HEAPIFY with repeated use of INSERT we see that the former is faster in the worst case, requiring $O(n)$ versus $O(n \log n)$ operations. However, HEAPIFY requires that all of the elements be available before heap creation begins. Using INSERT we can add a new element into the heap at any time.

In order to use a heap as a priority queue it is necessary to be able to insert or delete the largest element at any time. A simple way to accomplish this deletion is to remove the element at the root, $A(1)$, (this is the largest element), and then move the element $A(n)$ to $A(1)$. Now we have a binary tree in which only the root may violate the heap property so ADJUST may be used to recreate a heap. To insert elements we use procedure INSERT. Using the results of the analysis of ADJUST and INSERT we observe that both insertion into and deletion from a priority queue take $O(\log n)$ time.

We have discussed a heap as a data structure with the property that the value in every node is at least as large as the values in the children nodes. It should be easy to see that a parallel discussion could have been carried out with a definition requiring the value in every node to be at least as small as the values in the children nodes. In this case it is possible to delete the smallest element in $O(\log n)$ time and also to insert an element in $O(\log n)$ time. Later when we use heaps, we will refer to these two cases as max and min heaps respectively.

Heapsort

The most well known example of the use of a heap arises in its application to sorting. A conceptually simple sorting strategy is one which continually removes the maximum value from the remaining unsorted elements. A straightforward implementation of this idea leads to an algorithm whose worst case time is $O(n^2)$. A heap allows the maximum element to be found and deleted in $O(\log n)$ time thus yielding a sorting method whose worst case time is $O(n \log n)$.

```
procedure HEAPSORT(A,n)
//A(1:n) contains n elements to be sorted.//
//HEAPSORT rearranges them in-place into nondecreasing order.//

//first transform the elements into a heap//
call HEAPIFY(A,n)

//interchange the new maximum with the element at the//
//end of the tree//
for i ← n to 2 by −1 do
    t ← A(i); A(i) ← A(1); A(1) ← t
    call ADJUST(A, 1, i − 1)
repeat
end HEAPSORT
```

Algorithm 2.6   Heapsort

Though the call of HEAPIFY requires only $O(n)$ operations, ADJUST possibly requires $O(\log n)$ operations for each invocation. Thus the worst case time is $O(n \log n)$. Notice that the storage requirements, besides $A(1:n)$ are only for a few simple variables.

Final Comments on Priority Queues

There are many other applications of priority queues besides sorting. For example, simulation programming languages are usually organized around an "event list" which is a summary of actions which must be performed at different instants of simulated time. This event list is treated as a priority queue since new events with arbitrary times are inserted into this list and the next event to be deleted is the one with the earliest time. Another application of priority queues is for job scheduling according to a priority system. Jobs with priorities attached enter the system, which is continually looking for jobs to execute. The next job chosen is one with the largest priority.

There are many other ways to represent priority queues besides heaps. But their complete presentation is beyond our scope. Historically a sorted linear linked list was the structure which was originally used to implement event lists. For this representation deletion reduces to removing the front element, while insertion is done by scanning the list until the proper position is found. An additional property which is easily achieved by this representation is the ability to treat events with equal times on a first-in-first-out basis.

Insertion into sorted lists can be speeded up by using the balanced tree idea of Adel'son-Velskii and Landis (AVL trees). Both insertion and deletion can now be done in $O(\log n)$ steps, given n items in the tree. Unfortunately the algorithms are quite complex. Other structures which can be used for priority queues are leftist trees, 2-3 trees, p-trees and binomial queues. More details about all of these structures can be found in the references.

2.4   SETS AND DISJOINT SET UNION

Suppose we have some finite universe of n elements, U, out of which sets will be constructed. These sets may be empty or contain any subset of the elements of U. A common way to represent such sets is to allocate a bit vector of length n, SET$(1:n)$, such that SET$(i) = 1$ if the ith element of U

is in this set and zero otherwise. This array is called the *characteristic vector* for the set.

The advantage of this representation is that one can quickly determine whether or not any particular element i is present. Operations such as computing the union and intersection of two sets can be carried out using the "logical-and" and "logical-or" operations of your computer. This is especially efficient when n is "small", as each operation can be done by a single machine instruction. The disadvantage of this representation is that it is inefficient when n is large (say larger than the number of bits in one word) and the size of each set is small relative to n. The time to perform a union or an intersection is proportional to n rather than to the number of elements in the two sets.

An alternative representation for sets is to represent each set by a list of its elements. If there exists an ordering relation for these elements, then operations such as union and intersection can be done in time proportional to the sum of the lengths of the two sets.

In this section we study the use of trees for the representation of sets. We shall assume that the elements of the sets are the numbers 1, 2, 3, ..., n. These numbers might, in practice, be indices into a symbol table where the actual names of the elements are stored. We shall assume that the sets being represented are pairwise disjoint; i.e. if S_i and S_j, $i \neq j$, are two sets then there is no element which is in both S_i and S_j. For example, if we have 10 elements numbered 1 through 10, they may be partitioned into three disjoint sets $S_1 = \{1, 7, 8, 9\}$; $S_2 = \{2, 5, 10\}$ and $S_3 = \{3, 4, 6\}$.

The operations we wish to perform on these sets are:

(a) Disjoint set union ... if S_i and S_j are two disjoint sets, then their union $S_i \cup S_j = \{$all elements x such that x is in S_i or $S_j\}$. Thus, $S_1 \cup S_2 = \{1, 7, 8, 9, 2, 5, 10\}$. Since we have assumed that all sets are disjoint, following the union of S_i and S_j we can assume that the sets S_i and S_j no longer exist independently, i.e. they are replaced by $S_i \cup S_j$ in the collection of sets.

(b) Find (i) ... find the set containing element i. Thus, 4 is in set S_3 and 9 is in set S_1.

The challenge is to devise a data representation for disjoint sets such that these two operations can be carried out efficiently. The best we could hope for is to develop two algorithms whose times are both a constant, and so independent of the number of items in the sets. But we shall see that we will be unable to do that well. The sets will be represented by trees. One possible representation for the sets S_1, S_2 and S_3 is given in Figure 2.17:

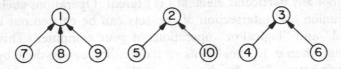

Figure 2.17   Representing disjoint sets by trees

Note that the nodes are linked on the parent relationship, i.e. each node other than the root is linked to its parent. The advantage of this will become apparent when we present the UNION and FIND algorithms. First, to take the union of S_1 and S_2 we simply make one of the trees a subtree of the other. $S_1 \cup S_2$ could then have one of the representations in Figure 2.18:

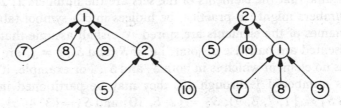

Figure 2.18   The two tree representations of $S1 \cup S2$

In order to find the union of two sets, all that has to be done is to set the parent field of one of the roots to the other root. In presenting the UNION and FIND algorithms we shall identify sets by the index of the roots of the trees. This will simplify the discussion. The transition to set names is easy and as we shall see, in many applications the set name is just the index of the root. The operation of FIND(i) now becomes: determine the root of the tree containing element i. UNION(i, j) requires two trees with roots i and j to be joined. We shall assume that the nodes in the trees are numbered 1 through n so that the node index corresponds to the element index. Thus, element 6 is represented by the node with index 6. Consequently, each node needs only one field, the PARENT field to link to its parent. Root nodes have a PARENT field of zero. Based on the above discussion, our first attempt at arriving at UNION, FIND algorithms would result in the procedures U and F in Algorithm 2.7.

procedure $U(i, j)$
    //replace the disjoint sets with roots i and j, $i \neq j$, by their union//
    integer i, j
    $PARENT(i) \leftarrow j$
end U

procedure $F(i)$
    //find the root of the tree containing element i//
    integer i, j
    $j \leftarrow i$
    while $PARENT(j) > 0$ **do**   //$PARENT(j) = 0$ if this node is a root//
        $j \leftarrow PARENT(j)$
    repeat
    return(j)
end F

Algorithm 2.7   Simple union and find algorithms

While these two algorithms are very easy to state, their performance characteristics are not very good. For instance, if we start off with n elements each in a set of its own, i.e. $S_i = \{i\}$, $1 \leq i \leq n$, then the initial configuration consists of a forest with n nodes and $PARENT(i) = 0$, $1 \leq i \leq n$. Now imagine that we process the following sequences of UNION-FIND operations:

$$U(1, 2), F(1), U(2, 3), F(1), U(3, 4)$$

$$F(1), U(4, 5), \ldots, F(1), U(n - 1, n)$$

This sequence results in the degenerate tree of Figure 2.19:

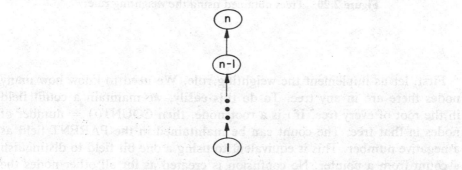

Figure 2.19   A worst case tree

Since the time taken for a union is constant, all the $n - 1$ unions can be processed in time $O(n)$. However, each FIND requires following a chain of PARENT links from node 1 to the root. The time required to process a FIND for an element at level i of a tree is $O(i)$. Hence, the total time needed to process the $n - 2$ finds is $O(n^2)$. It is easy to see that this example represents the worst case behavior of the UNION-FIND algorithms. We can do much better if care is taken to avoid the creation of degenerate trees. In order to accomplish this we shall make use of a *Weighting Rule* for UNION (i, j). *If the number of nodes in tree i is less than the number in tree j, then make j the parent of i, otherwise make i the parent of j.* Using this rule on the sequence of set unions given before we obtain the trees in Figure 2.20. Remember that the arguments of UNION must both be roots. Now the time required to process all the n finds is only $O(n)$ since in this case the maximum level of any node is 2. This however, is not the worst case. In lemma 2.3 we show that using the weighting rule, the maximum level for any node after any sequence of n union and find operations is $\lfloor \log n \rfloor + 1$.

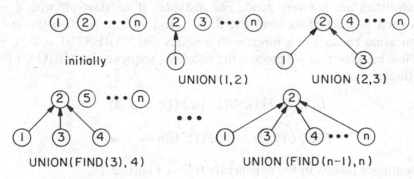

Figure 2.20   Trees obtained using the weighting rule

First, let us implement the weighting rule. We need to know how many nodes there are in any tree. To do this easily, we maintain a count field in the root of every tree. If i is a root node, then $COUNT(i)$ = number of nodes in that tree. The count can be maintained in the PARENT field as a negative number. This is equivalent to using a one bit field to distinguish a count from a pointer. No confusion is created as for all other nodes the PARENT is positive.

procedure *UNION(i,j)*
//union sets with roots *i* and *j*, *i* ≠ *j*, using the weighting rule.//
//PARENT(*i*) = − COUNT(*i*) and PARENT(*j*) = − COUNT(*j*).//
integer *i,j,x*
x ← PARENT(*i*) + PARENT(*j*)
if *PARENT(i) > PARENT(j)*
  then *PARENT(i)* ← *j* //*i* has fewer nodes//
    PARENT(j) ← *x*
  else *PARENT(j)* ← *i* //*j* has fewer nodes//
    PARENT(i) ← *x*
endif
end *UNION*

Algorithm 2.8 A more sophisticated union algorithm

The time required to perform a union has increased somewhat but is still bounded by a constant. The FIND algorithm remains unchanged. The maximum time to perform a find is now determined by lemma 2.3.

Lemma 2.3 Let T be a tree with n nodes created as a result of algorithm UNION. No node in T has level greater $\lfloor \log n \rfloor + 1$.
Proof: The lemma is clearly true for $n = 1$. Assume it is true for all trees with i nodes, $i \leq n - 1$. We shall show that it is also true for $i = n$. Let T be a tree with n nodes created by the UNION algorithm. Consider the last union operation performed, UNION(k,j). Let m be the number of nodes in tree j and $n - m$ the number in k. Without loss of generality we may assume $1 \leq m \leq n/2$. Then the maximum level of any node in T is either the same as that in k or is one more than that in j. If the former is the case, then the maximum level in T is $\leq \lfloor \log(n - m) \rfloor + 1 \leq \lfloor \log n \rfloor + 1$. If the latter is the case then the maximum level in T is $\leq \lfloor \log m \rfloor + 2 \leq \lfloor \log(n/2) \rfloor + 2 \leq \lfloor \log n \rfloor + 1$. $\square$

Example 2.1 shows that the bound of lemma 2.3 is achievable for some sequence of unions.

Example 2.1: Consider the behavior of algorithm UNION on the following sequence of unions starting from the initial configuration PARENT(*i*) = − COUNT(*i*) = −1, $1 \leq i \leq n = 2^3$

UNION(1, 2), UNION(3, 4), UNION(5, 6), UNION(7, 8)

UNION(1, 3), UNION(5, 7), UNION(1, 5)

The trees of Figure 2.21 are obtained. This example is easily generalized to obtain m node trees with $\lfloor \log m \rfloor + 1$ nodes.   □

As a result of lemma 2.3, the maximum time to process a find is at most $O(\log n)$ if there are n elements in a tree. If an intermixed sequence of n UNION and m FIND operations is to be processed, then the worst case time becomes $O(m \log n)$. Surprisingly, further improvement is possible. This time the modification will be made in the FIND algorithm using the *Collapsing Rule*: *If j is a node on the path from i to its root then set PARENT(j) ← root (i).* The new algorithm is procedure FIND(Algorithm 2.9):

```
procedure FIND(i)
    //Find the root of the tree containing element i. Use the//
    //collapsing rule to collapse all nodes from i to the root j//
    j ← i
    while PARENT(j) > 0 do   //find root//
        j ← PARENT(j)
    repeat
    k ← i
    while k ≠ j do   //collapse nodes from i to root j//
        t ← PARENT(k)
        PARENT(k) ← j
        k ← t
    repeat
    return(j)
end FIND
```

Algorithm 2.9   FIND using the collapsing rule

This modification roughly doubles the time for an individual find. Therefore one has to be very careful about claiming it is an improvement. For some applications, (e.g. when a lot of finds and few unions occur) this change to FIND may slow down the overall processing time. But in the worst case one can show that this change is a considerable improvement over just using the weighting rule.

Example 2.2: Consider the tree created by algorithm UNION on the sequence of unions of example 2.1. Now process the following 8 finds:

FIND(8), FIND(8), FIND(8), FIND(8)

FIND(8), FIND(8), FIND(8), FIND(8)

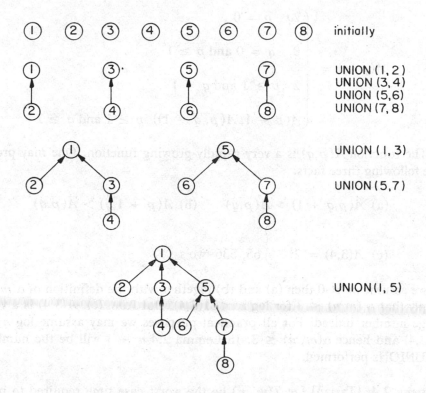

Figure 2.21 A worst case tree using the weighting rule

Using the old version of find, namely procedure F(8), requires going up 3 parent link fields for a total of 24 moves to process all 8 finds. In algorithm FIND, the first FIND(8) requires going up 3 links and then resetting 3 links. Each of remaining 7 finds requires going up only 1 link field. The total cost is now only 13 moves. □

The worst case behavior of the UNION-FIND algorithms while processing a sequence of unions and finds is stated in Lemma 2.4. Before stating this lemma, let us introduce a very slowly growing function $\alpha(m, n)$ which is related to a functional inverse of Ackermann's function $A(p, q)$ with which you may already be familiar. We have the following definition for $\alpha(m, n)$:

$$\alpha(m, n) = \min \{z \geq 1 | A(z, 4 \lceil m/n \rceil) > \log_2 n\}$$

The definition of Ackermann's function used here is:

$$A(p, q) = \begin{cases} 2q & p = 0 \\ 0, & q = 0 \text{ and } p \geq 1 \\ 2 & p \geq 1 \text{ and } q = 1 \\ A(p - 1, A(p, q - 1)) & p \geq 1 \text{ and } q \geq 2 \end{cases}$$

The function $A(p,q)$ is a very rapidly growing function. One may prove the following three facts:

(a) $A(p,q + 1) > A(p,q)$ (b) $A(p + 1,q) > A(p,q)$

(c) $A(3,4) = 2^{2^{.^{.^{2}}}} \Big\}$ 65, 536 two's

If we assume $m \neq 0$ then (a) and (b) together with the definition of $\alpha(m,n)$ imply that α $(m,n) \leq 3$ for $\log n < A(3,4)$. But from (c), $A(3,4)$ is a very large number indeed! For all practical purposes we may assume $\log n < A(3,4)$ and hence $\alpha(m, n) \leq 3$. In Lemma 2.4 $n - 1$ will be the number of UNIONs performed.

Lemma 2.4: [Tarjan] Let $T(m, n)$ be the worst case time required to process an intermixed sequence of $m \geq n$ FINDs and $n - 1$ UNIONs. Then $k_1 m\alpha(m,n) \leq T(m,n) \leq k_2 m\alpha(m,n)$ for some positive constants k_1 and k_2.   ☐

For a proof of this theorem see the paper by Tarjan, "Efficiency of a good but not linear set union algorithm,"*JACM*, (April 1975).

Even though the function $\alpha(m, n)$ is a very slowly growing function, the complexity of UNION-FIND is not linear in m, the number of FINDs. As far as the space requirements are concerned, the space needed is one node for each element.

Let us look briefly at an application of algorithms UNION and FIND; processing equivalence statements. The input is a set of pairs of the form $i \equiv j$ (i is equivalent to j). The goal is to be able to respond quickly to either new pairs or to questions which ask which equivalence class an element is currently in. This problem is an abstraction of what would have to be done to handle EQUIVALENCE statements in FORTRAN. The equivalence classes to be generated may be regarded as sets. These sets are disjoint as no variable can be in more than one equivalence class. To begin with all n variables are in equivalence classes of their own; thus PARENT(i) = $-1 \le i \le n$. If an equivalence pair, $i \equiv j$, is to be processed, we must first determine the sets containing i and j. If these are different, then the two sets are to be replaced by their union. If the two sets are the same, then nothing is to be done as the relation $i \equiv j$ is redundant; i and j are already in the same equivalence class. To process each equivalence pair we need to perform at most two finds and one union. Thus, if we have n variables and $m \ge n$ equivalence pairs, the total processing time is at most $O(m\alpha (m, n))$. The major advantage of this algorithm is that it works "on-line." This means that at any time it can answer questions about the equivalence class of an element rather than require all pairs to be presented to it first. In the following chapters we will see other fruitful uses of these two set manipulation algorithms.

2.5 GRAPHS

Now we consider the data object graph, an important structure which was first introduced by the mathematician L. Euler in 1736. A *graph* G consists of two sets called the *vertices* V and the *edges* E. V is a finite non-empty set of vertices (sometimes called nodes) usually numbered 1, 2, . . . , n and E is a finite set of pairs of vertices. Each pair in E is an edge of G.

If the pairs are ordered (i.e. the pair $<i, j>$ is different than the pair $<j, i>$) then we call the graph *directed*. Otherwise we call it *undirected*. We will use angle brackets to denote directed edges and parentheses to denote undirected edges. Thus, $<i, j>$ represents a directed edge while (i, j) represents an undirected edge. Note that edges of the type $\langle i,i \rangle$ or (i,i) are not permitted. For many applications there is often a positive real number, called a cost, which is attached to each edge. Such a graph is called a *network*.

In an undirected graph we say that the vertex i is *adjacent* to vertex j if the edge (i, j) exists. The degree of a vertex is the number of its adjacent vertices. For directed graphs we distinguish between the *in-degree* of a vertex i which is the number of edges with i as its second component, and the *out-degree* of i, the number of edges with i as the first component. If the directed edge $\langle i,j \rangle$ is present, then i is *adjacent-to* j and j is *adjacent-from* i.

A *path* from vertex v_p to v_q is a sequence of vertices v_p, v_{i1}, v_{i2}, . . . , v_{in}, v_q such that (v_p, v_{i1}), (v_{i1}, v_{i2}), . . . , (v_{in}, v_q) are edges in E(G). The *length* of a path is the number of edges on it. A *simple path* is a path in which all vertices except possibly the first and last are distinct. A *cycle* is a simple path in which the first and last vertices are the same.

In Figure 2.22 we have an example of a directed and an undirected graph both containing 5 vertices and 5 edges. In the directed graph vertex 1 has zero as its in-degree and three as its out-degree. The degree of vertex 1 in the undirected graph is three. In the undirected graph there is a path between every pair of vertices, whereas in the directed graph there is no way to go from vertex 3 (or vertex 5) to any other vertex. In Figure 2.22 (ii) the edges (1,2) (2,3) form a simple path and the path (1,2) (2,3) (3,1) is a cycle.

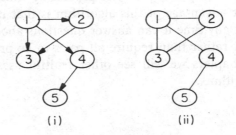

(i)   (ii)

Figure 2.22   Two sample graphs

The last notion we will define before discussing representations of graphs is connectedness. An undirected graph is called *connected* if for every pair of vertices there exists a path between them. If a graph is not connected then we refer to its connected subgraphs separately. A subgraph of a graph is a subset of the vertices in V say VB, and a subset of the edges of E which connect vertices in VB. A subgraph G' = (V', E') is a connected component of the undirected graph G = (V, E) iff G' is connected and there exists no other subgraph G" = (V", E") of G which is also connected and either V' ⊂ V" or E' ⊂ E". I.e., a connected component is a maximal connected subgraph. For directed graphs the connectedness idea is strengthened. If for every pair of vertices, i, j there exists a path from i to j and a path from j to i then we say that directed graph is *strongly connected*.

There are two common ways to represent graphs. These may be thought of as the sequential and linked representations. The sequential form uses a square table with n rows and columns where n is the number of vertices. This table is called the *adjacency matrix*. For an undirected graph, the adjacency matrix, GRAPH(1:n, 1:n), is defined such that GRAPH(i, j) = 1 if the edge (i, j) is present and 0 otherwise. If the graph is a network then GRAPH(i, j) = the cost of edge (i, j). If (i, j) is not present the value of GRAPH(i, j) is + ∞. For a directed graph, GRAPH(i, j) = 1 iff ⟨i,j⟩ is an edge. Graph (i, j) is similarly defined in case of a directed network.

Table 2.3 shows the adjacency matrices for the directed and undirected graphs of Figure 2.22. Both matrices are 5×5 and have entries which are zero or one. Note how in both cases the diagonal elements are zero indicating no "self-edges." The second matrix has a special structure which all undirected graphs will have, and that is that $GRAPH(i, j) = GRAPH(j, i)$. Such a matrix is said to be *symmetric*. Though the adjacency matrix normally requires n^2 locations, for undirected graphs it would suffice to keep only an upper triangular matrix, or $n(n - 1)/2$ elements. Note that the main diagonal need not be stored as $GRAPH(i, i) = 0$.

	1	2	3	4	5
1)	0	1	1	1	0
2)	0	0	1	0	0
3)	0	0	0	0	0
4)	0	0	0	0	1
5)	0	0	0	0	0

	1	2	3	4	5
	0	1	1	1	0
	1	0	1	0	0
	1	1	0	0	0
	1	0	0	0	1
	0	0	0	1	0

Table 2.3 Adjacency matrices for Figure 2.22

Before beginning any computation on a graph we will normally have to initialize an adjacency matrix so that it contains the graph we are going to operate on. This step will typically require at least $O(n^2)$ operations. Thus, the computing time of most any algorithm using this form of representation will be *at least* $O(n^2)$. This will be true even if the graph has only $O(n)$ edges! This fact leads us to consider an alternative representation.

Given a graph, its *adjacency list* representation consists of n lists, one for each vertex i. The list for vertex i contains just those vertices adjacent from i. Because we often need to access the adjacent vertices of a random vertex we insist that the heads of the lists are stored sequentially. But the list of a vertex's neighbors may be linked together. Figure 2.23 shows the adjacency lists for the two graphs of Figure 2.22.

For both graphs there are five sequential locations (head nodes) whose values are either zero (if no neighbors exist) or a pointer to a list of vertices. Each node on the list has two fields, a vertex and a pointer to the next element on the list. The directed graph has 5 nodes and the undirected graph has 10. In general, a directed graph with n vertices and e edges will require n locations plus e nodes while an undirected graph will require n locations plus $2e$ nodes. This can be quite a bit better than the requirements of the adjacency matrix representation.

In case no insertion or deletion of edges or vertices are to be performed on the graph, the adjacency lists may themselves be represented sequentially

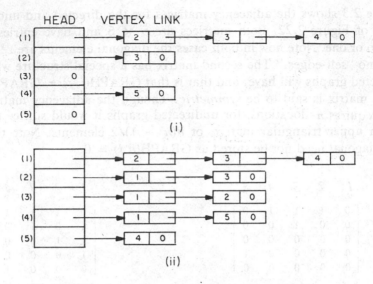

Figure 2.23   Adjacency lists for Figure 2.22

in a one dimensional array VERTEX(1:p) where $p = e$ if the graph is directed and $p = 2e$ if the graph is undirected. HEAD(i), $1 \leq i \leq n$ gives the starting point for the adjacency list for vertex i. If we define HEAD $(n + 1) = p + 1$ then the vertices on the adjacency list for vertex i are stored in VERTEX(j), where HEAD(i) $\leq j <$ HEAD($i + 1$). If the list for vertex i is empty, then HEAD(i) = HEAD($i + 1$). Figure 2.24 gives the sequential adjacency list representations corresponding to the linked representations of Figure 2.23.

This concludes section 2.5. In the following chapters we will encounter many algorithms on graphs, so make sure that you are familiar with these representation schemes.

2.6   HASHING

A *symbol table* is a data structure which allows one to easily determine the presence or absence of an arbitrary element. It also permits easy insertion and deletion of elements. In this section we present what is undoubtedly the most practical technique for maintaining a symbol table, hashing. Though many of the tree organizations of symbol tables (e.g. binary search trees) are useful when special information about the identifiers is known, in the absence of a priori statistical information, hashing is both conceptually simple and, as we shall see, very efficient.

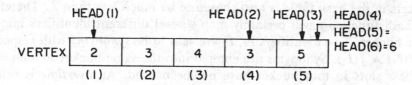

(i) Representation for the graph of Figure 2.22 (i)

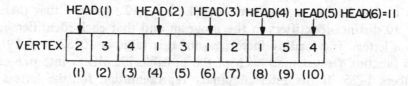

(ii) Representation for the graph of Figure 2.22(ii)

Figure 2.24 Sequential adjacency lists

In tree tables, the search for an identifier key is carried out via a sequence of comparisons. Hashing differs from this approach in that the address or location of an identifier, X, is obtained by computing some arithmetic function, f, of X. $f(X)$ gives the address where X should be placed in the table. This address will be referred to as the *hash address* of X. The memory available to maintain the symbol table is assumed to be sequential. This memory is referred to as the *hash table*, abbreviated HT. The hash table is partitioned into b buckets, HT(0), ..., HT($b - 1$). Each bucket is capable of holding s identifiers. Thus, a bucket is said to consist of s slots, each slot being large enough to hold 1 identifier. Usually $s = 1$ and each bucket can hold exactly one identifier. A hashing function, $f(X)$, is used to perform an identifier transformation on X. $f(X)$ maps the set of possible identifiers onto the integers 0 through $b - 1$. Let T be the size of the space from which the identifiers are drawn. This space is called the *identifier space*. For example if the identifiers are drawn from the set of all legal FORTRAN variable names then there are more than 1.6×10^9 distinct possible values. Any reasonable program, however, would use far less than all of these identifiers. For a table containing n identifiers, the ratio n/T is the *identifier density*, while $\alpha = n/(sb)$ is the *loading density* or *loading factor*.

Since the number of identifiers in use is usually several orders of magnitude less than the total number of possible identifiers, T, the number of buckets in the hash table is also chosen to be much less than T. Therefore, the hash function f will certainly map several different identifiers into the same bucket. Two identifiers I_1, I_2 are said to be *synonyms* with respect to f if $f(I_1) = f(I_2)$. Synonyms are entered into the same bucket so long as all of the s slots in that bucket have not been used. An *overflow* is said to occur when a new identifier I is mapped or hashed by f into a full bucket. A *collision* occurs when two nonidentical identifiers are hashed into the same bucket. When the bucket size s is 1, collisions and overflows occur simultaneously.

As an example, let us consider the hash table HT with $b = 26$ buckets, each bucket having exactly two slots, i.e., $s = 2$. Assume that there are $n = 10$ distinct identifiers in the program and that each identifier begins with a letter. The loading factor, α, for this table is $10/52 = 0.19$. The hash function f must map each of the possible identifiers into one of the numbers 1–26. If the internal binary representation for the letters A-Z corresponds to the numbers 1–26 respectively, then the function f defined by: $f(X) = $ the first character of X, will hash all identifiers X into the hash table. The identifiers GA, D, A, G, L, A2, A1, A3, A4 and E will be hashed into buckets 7, 4, 1, 7, 12, 1, 1, 1, 1 and 5 respectively by this function. The identifiers A, A1, A2, A3 and A4 are synonyms. So also are G and GA. Figure 2.25 shows the identifiers GA, D, A, G, and A2 entered into the hash table. Note that GA and G are in the same bucket and each bucket has two slots. Similarly, the synonyms A and A2 are in the same bucket gets hashed into HT(12). The next identifier, A1, hashes into the bucket HT(1). This bucket is full and a search of the bucket indicates that A1 is not in the bucket. An overflow has now occurred. Where in the table should

1	A	A2
2	0	0
3	0	0
4	D	0
5	0	0
6	0	0
7	GA	G
$\vdots$	$\vdots$	$\vdots$
26	0	0

Figure 2.25   Hash table

A1 now be entered so that it may be retrieved when needed? We will look into overflow handling strategies a little later. But before we do that we wish to say more about choosing a hashing function.

The hash function in the previous example is not very well suited for the use we have in mind because of the very large number of collisions and resulting overflows that may occur. This is so because it is not unusual to find that a collection of symbols such as identifiers in a computer program contain many which begin with the same letter. Ideally, we would like to choose a function f which is both easy to compute and results in very few collisions. But since the ratio b/T is usually very small, it is impossible to avoid collisions altogether.

In summary, hashing schemes perform an identifier transformation through the use of a hash function f. It is desirable to choose a function f which is easily computed and also minimizes the number of collisions. Since the size of the identifier space is usually several orders of magnitude larger than the number of buckets and s is small, overflows necessarily occur. Hence a mechanism to handle overflows is also needed.

Hash Function

A hashing functions, f, transforms an identifier X into a bucket address in the hash table. As mentioned earlier the desired properties of such a function are that it is easily computable and that it minimize the number of collisions. We would like the function to depend upon all the characters in the identifier rather than upon one character. In addition, we would like the hash function to be such that it does not result in a biased use of the hash table for random inputs. If X is an identifier chosen at random from the identifier space, then we want the probability that $f(X) = i$ to be $1/b$ for all buckets i. Then a random X has an equal chance of hashing into any of the b buckets. A hash function satisfying this property will be termed a *uniform hash function*. Many kinds of hash functions are in use. We shall discuss only two. A more detailed discussion may be found in any of the relevant references at the end of this chapter.

One simple and effective choice for a hash function is obtained by using the modulo (**mod**) operator. The identifier X is interpreted as an integer and it is divided by some number M and the remainder is used as the hash address for X.

$$f_D(X) = X \bmod M$$

This gives bucket addresses in the range 0 to $M - 1$ and so the hash table is at least of size $b = M$. The choice of M is critical. If M is a power of 2, then $f_D(X)$ depends only on the least significant bits of X. For instance, if each character is represented by six bits and identifiers are stored right justified in a 60-bit word with leading bits filled with zeros (Figure 2.26) then with $M = 2^i$, $i \le 6$ the identifiers A1, B1, C1, X41, DNTXY1 all have the same bucket address. With $M = 2^i$, $i \le 12$ the identifiers AXY, BXY, WTXY, have the same bucket address. Since programmers have a tendency to use many variables with the same suffix, the choice of M as a power of two would result in many collisions.

Figure 2.26   Identifier A1 right and left justified and zero filled

(6 bits per character)

Choosing M a power of 2 would have even more disastrous results if the identifier X is stored left justified zero filled. Then, all 1 character identifiers would map to the zeroth bucket for $M = 2^i$, $i \le 54$; all 2 character identifiers would map to the zeroth bucket for $M = 2^i$, $i \le 48$, etc. As a result of this observation, we see that when the division operation f_D is used as a hash function, the table size should not be a power of 2. Another problem about the choice of M is that if M is divisible by 2 then odd keys are mapped to odd buckets (as the remainder is odd) and even keys are mapped to even buckets. The use of the hash table is thus biased again.

Further analysis indicates that when M contains factors, a biased use of the table results if many of the identifiers are permutations of each other. These difficulties can be avoided by choosing M to be a prime number. Then, the only factors of M are M and 1. Knuth has shown that when M divides $r^k + a$ or $r^k - a$ where k and a are small numbers and r is the radix of the character set, then X **mod** M tends to be a simple superposition of the characters in X. Thus, a good choice for M would be: *M a prime number such that M does not divide* $r^k + a$ *or* $r^k - a$ *for small k and a*. In practice it has been observed that it is sufficient to choose M such that it has no prime divisors less than 20.

Another commonly used hash function is the "middle of the square" function. This function, f_m, is computed by squaring the identifier and then using an appropriate number of bits from the middle of the squared number to obtain the bucket address; the identifier is assumed to fit into one computer word. Since the middle bits of the square will usually depend upon all of the characters in the identifier, it is expected that different identifiers would result in different hash addresses with high probability even when some of the characters are the same. The number of bits to be used to obtain the bucket address depends on the table size. If r bits are used, the range of values is 2^r, so the size of hash tables is chosen to be a power of 2 when this kind of scheme is used.

Overflow Handling

In order to be able to detect collisions and overflows, it is necessary to initialize the hash table to represent the situation when all slots are empty. Assuming that no identifier has a value of zero, then all slots may be initialized to zero. When a new identifier gets hashed into a bucket already occupied, it is necessary to find another bucket for this identifier. The simplest solution would probably be to find the closest unfilled bucket. Let us illustrate this on a 26-bucket table with one slot per bucket. Assume the identifiers are GA, D, A, G, L, A2, A1, A3, A4, Z, ZA, E. For simplicity we choose the hash function $f(X)$ = first character of X. Initially, all the entries in the table are zero. $f(GA) = 7$, this bucket is empty, so GA (and any other information about this identifier) are entered into HT(7). D and A get entered into the buckets HT(4) and HT(1) respectively. The next identifier G has $f(G) = 7$. This slot is already used by GA. The next vacant slot is HT(8) and so G is entered there. L enters at HT(12). A2 collides with A at HT(1), the bucket overflows and A2 is entered at the next vacant slot HT(2). A1, A3 and A4 are entered at HT(3), HT(5) and HT(6) respectively. Z is entered at HT(26), ZA at HT(9), (the hash table is used circularly), and E collides with A3 at HT(5) and is eventually entered at HT(10). Figure 2.27 shows the resulting table. This method of resolving overflows is known as *linear probing* or *linear open addressing*.

In order to search the table for an identifier, X, it is necessary to first compute $f(X)$ and then examine keys at positions HT($f(X)$), HT($f(X) + 1$), ..., HT($f(X) + j$) such that HT($f(X) + j$) either equals X (X is in the table) or 0 (X is not in the table) or we eventually return to HT($f(X)$) (the table is full). The implementation of linear search is given in Algorithm 2.10.

```
procedure LINSRCH(X,HT,b,j)
//search the hash table HT(0:b − 1) (each bucket has exactly 1//
//slot) using linear probing. If HT(j) = 0 then the j-th bucket//
//is empty and X can be entered into the table. Otherwise//
//HT(j) = X and X is already in the table. f is the hash function//
    i ← f(X); j ← i
    while HT(j) ≠ X and HT(j) ≠ 0 do
        j ← (j + 1) mod b        //treat the table as circular//
        if j = i then call TABLE-FULL endif   //no empty slots//
    repeat
end LINSRCH
```

Algorithm 2.10   Linear hashing

1	A
2	A2
3	A1
4	D
5	A3
6	A4
7	GA
8	G
9	ZA
10	E
11	0
12	L
13	0
	0
	≈ ⋮ ≈
	0
26	Z

Figure 2.27 Hash table with linear probing. 26 buckets, 1 slot per bucket

Our earlier example shows that when linear probing is used to resolve overflows, identifiers tend to cluster together, and moreover, adjacent clusters tend to coalesce, thus increasing the search time. To locate the identifier, ZA, in the table of Figure 2.27, it was necessary to examine HT(26), HT(1), ..., HT(9), a total of ten comparisons. This is far worse than the worst case-behavior for tree tables. If each of the identifiers in the table of Figure 2.27 was retrieved exactly once, then the number of buckets examined would be 1 for A, 2 for A2, 3 for A1, 1 for D, 5 for A3, 6 for A4, 1 for GA, 2 for G, 10 for ZA, 6 for E, 1 for L and 1 for Z for a total of 39 buckets examined. The average number examined is 3.25 buckets per identifier. An analysis of this method in general shows that the expected average number of identifier comparisons, P, to look up an identifier is approximately $(2 - \alpha)/(2 - 2\alpha)$ where α is the loading density. This is the average over all possible sets of identifiers yielding the given loading density and using a uniform hashing function f. In the above example $\alpha = 12/26 = 0.46$ and $P = 1.42$. Even though the average number of probes is small, the worst case can be quite large.

One of the reasons linear probing and its variations perform poorly is that searching for an identifier involves comparison of identifiers with different hash values. In the hash table of Figure 2.25, for instance, searching for the identifier ZA involved comparisons with the buckets HT(1) to HT(8), even though none of the identifiers in these buckets had a collision with HT(26) and so could not possibly be ZA. Many of these comparisons could be avoided if we maintained lists of identifiers, one list per bucket, where each list contains only the synonyms for that bucket. If this were done, a search would then involve computing the hash address $f(X)$ and examining only those identifiers in the list for $f(X)$. Since the sizes of these lists is not known in advance, the best way to maintain them is as linked chains. Each chain will have a head node which will usually be much smaller than the other nodes since it has to retain only a link. Since the lists are to be accessed at random, the head nodes should be sequential. We assume they are numbered 1 to M if the hash function f has range 1 to M.

Using chaining to resolve collisions and the hash function used to obtain Figure 2.27, the hash chains of Figure 2.28 are obtained. When a new identifier, X, is being inserted into a chain, the insertion can be made at either end. This is so because the address of the last node in the chain is known as a result of the search that determined X was not in the list for $f(X)$. In the example of Figure 2.28 new identifiers were inserted at the front of the chains. The number of probes needed to search for any of the identifiers is now 1 for each of A4, D, E, G, L, and ZA; 2 for each of A3, GA and Z; 3 for A1; 4 for A2 and 5 for A for a total of 24. The average is now 2.0 which is considerably less than for linear probing. Additional storage, however, is needed for links.

```
procedure CHNSRCH(X,HT,b,j)
  //search the hash table HT(0:b − 1) for X. Either HT(i) = 0//
  //or it is a pointer to the list of identifiers X such that f(X) = i.//
  //List nodes have fields IDENT and LINK. Either j points//
  //to the node already containing X or j = 0//
  j ← HT(f(X))   //compute head node address//
  //search the chain starting at j//
  while j ≠ 0 and IDENT(j) ≠ X do
    j ← LINK(j)
  repeat
end CHNSRCH
```

Algorithm 2.11 Hashing with chaining

The expected number of identifier comparisons can be shown to be approximately equal to $1 + (\alpha/2)$ where α is the loading density n/b

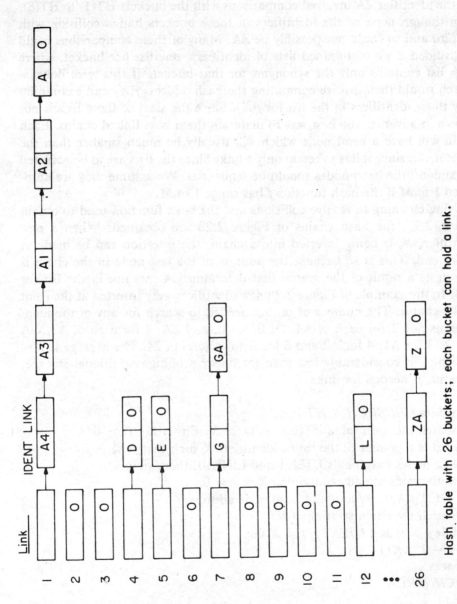

Hash table with 26 buckets; each bucket can hold a link.

Figure 2.28 Hash chains corresponding to Figure 2.27

(b = number of head nodes). For $\alpha = 0.5$ this figure is 1.25 and for $\alpha = 1$ it is 1.5. This scheme has the additional advantage that only the b head nodes must be sequential and reserved at the beginning. Each head node, however, will be at most 1/2 to 1 word long. The other nodes will be much bigger and need to be allocated only as needed. This could represent an overall reduction in space required for certain loading densities despite the links. If each record in the table is five words long, $n = 100$ and $\alpha = 0.5$, then the hash table will be of size $200 \times 5 = 1000$ words. Only 500 of these are used as $\alpha = 0.5$. On the other hand, if chaining is used with one full word per link, then 200 words are needed for the head nodes ($b = 200$). Each head node is one word long. One hundred nodes of six words each are needed for the records. The total space needed is thus 800 words, or 20% less than when no chaining was being used. Of course, when α is close to 1, chaining uses more space than linear probing. However, when α is close to 1, the average number of probes using linear probing or its variations becomes quite large and the additional space used for chaining can be justified by the reduction in the expected number of probes needed for retrieval. If one wishes to delete an entry from the table, then this can be done by just removing that node from its chain. The problem of deleting entries while using open addressing to resolve collisions is tackled in the exercises.

The results of this section tend to imply that the performance of a hash table depends only on the method used to handle overflows and is independent of the hash function so long as a uniform hash function is being used. While this is true when the identifiers are selected at random from the identifier space, it is not true in practice. In practice, there is a tendency to make a biased use of identifiers. Many identifiers in use have a common suffix or prefix or are simple permutations of other identifiers. Hence, in practice we would expect different hash functions to result in different hash table performance. The table of Figure 2.29 presents the results of an empirical study conducted by Lum, Yuen and Dodd. The values in each column give the average number of bucket accesses made in searching eight different tables with 33,575; 24,050; 4909; 3072; 2241; 930; 762 and 500 identifiers each. The table also gives the theoretical expected number of bucket accesses based on random keys. As expected, chaining outperforms linear open addressing as a method for overflow handling. In looking over the figures for the division and middle of square functions, we see that division is generally superior to middle of the square. Lum, Yuen, and Dodd have comparative figures for many other hash functions. Their conclusion is that division is generally the best hash function. For general applications, it is therefore recommended that the division method be used. The divisor should be a prime number, though it is sufficient to choose a divisor that has no prime factors less than 20.

$\alpha = n/b$

hash	.5		.75		.9		.95	
function	C	O	C	O	C	O	C	O
MIDSQ	1.26	1.73	1.40	9.75	1.45	27.14	1.47	37.53
DIV	1.19	4.52	1.31	7.20	1.38	22.42	1.41	25.79
THEO	1.25	1.50	1.37	2.50	1.45	5.50	1.48	10.5

C = chaining, O = open linear addressing, α = loading density, MIDSQ = middle of square, DIV = division, THEO = expectation

Figure 2.29   Average number of bucket accesses per identifier retrieved (condensed from Lum, Yuen and Dodd), "Key-to-Address Transform Techniques: A Fundamental Performance Study on Large Existing Formatted Files," CACM, April 1971, Vol. 14, No. 4, pp. 228–239.

The experimental evaluation of hashing techniques indicates a very good performance over conventional techniques such as balanced trees. The worst case performance for hashing can, however, be very bad. In the worst case an insertion or a search in a hash table with n identifiers may take $O(n)$ time. We now present a probabilistic analysis for the expected performance of the chaining method and state without proof the result of a similar analysis for linear open addressing. First, we formalize what we mean by expected performance.

Let HT(0:b − 1) be a hash table with b buckets, each bucket having one slot. Let f be a uniform hash function with range [0,b − 1]. If n identifiers $X_1, X_2, \ldots, X_n$ are entered into the hash table then there are b^n distinct hash sequences $f(X_1), f(X_2), \ldots, f(X_n)$. Assume that each of these is equally likely to occur. Let S_n denote the expected number of identifier comparisons needed to locate a randomly chosen X_i, $1 \le i \le n$. Then, S_n is the average number of comparisons needed to find the jth key, X_j; averaged over $1 \le j \le n$ with each j equally likely and averaged over all b^n hash sequences assuming each of these is also equally likely. Let U_n be the expected number of identifier comparisons when a search is made for an identifier not in the hash table. This hash table contains n identifiers. The quantity U_n may be defined in a manner analogous to that used for S_n.

Theorem 2.1   Let $\alpha = n/b$ be the loading density of a hash table using a uniform hashing function f. Then:

(i)   for linear open addressing

$$U_n \sim \frac{1}{2}\left(1 + \frac{1}{(1 - \alpha)^2}\right)$$

$$S_n \sim \frac{1}{2}\left(1 + \frac{1}{1 - \alpha}\right)$$

(ii)   for chaining

$$U_n \sim \alpha$$

$$S_n \sim 1 + \alpha/2$$

Exact derivations of U_n and S_n are fairly involved and can be found in Knuth's book: *The Art of Computer Programming: Sorting and Searching.* Here, we present a derivation of the approximate formulas for chaining. First, we must make clear our count for U_n and S_n. In case the identifier X being searched for has $f(X) = i$ and chain i has k nodes on it (not including the head node) then k comparisons are needed if X is not on the chain. If X is j nodes away from the head node, $1 \leq j \leq k$ then j comparisons are needed.

When the n identifiers distribute uniformly over the b possible chains, the expected number in each chain is $n/b = \alpha$. Since, U_n = expected number of identifiers on the chain, we get $U_n = \alpha$.

When the ith identifier, X_i, is being entered into the table, the expected number of identifiers on any chain is $(i - 1)/b$. Hence, the expected number of comparisons needed to search for X_i after all n identifiers have been entered is $1 + (i - 1)/b$ (this assumes that new entries will be made at the end of the chain). We therefore get:

$$S_n = \frac{1}{n} \sum_{1 \leq i \leq n} (1 + (i - 1)/b) \tag{2.3}$$

$$= 1 + (n - 1)/(2b) \sim 1 + \alpha/2 \quad \square$$

REFERENCES AND SELECTED READINGS

A wide ranging examination of data structures and their efficient implementation can be found in

Fundamentals of data structures. By Ellis Horowitz and Sartaj Sahni, Computer Science Press, Potomac, Maryland, 1976.

A complete analysis of many data structures including the topics discussed here can be found in the Knuth series, volumes I and III as cited in Chapter 1. Knuth's volume III and the data structures book by Horowitz and Sahni contain a more thorough discussion of hashing.

The following paper contains an analysis showing that the average time for insert is O(1):

"Analysis of heap insertion", by Istvan and Porter, Computer Science Department, Stanford University, 1977.

For more on priority queues see

"The analysis of a practical and nearly optimal priority queue", by Mark R. Brown, Computer Science Dept. STAN-CS-77-600, Stanford University, March 1977

"Priority queues with update and finding minimum spanning trees", by Donald B. Johnson *Information Processing Letters*, December 1975, 53–57.

"Analysis of an algorithm for priority queue administration", by Arne Jonassen and Ole-Johan Dahl, *BIT*, 1975, 409–422.

"A data structure for manipulating priority queues" by Jean Vuillemin, *C.ACM*, to appear.

For more on the disjoint set union problem see

"On the efficiency of a good but not linear set merging algorithm" by R. Tarjan, *J.ACM*, (22,2), April, 1975, 215–225.

"On the average behavior of set merging algorithms" by Andrew C. Yao, Proc. *8th symposium on the theory of computing*, ACM, May 1976, 192–195.

"The expected linearity of a simple equivalence algorithm" by Donald E. Knuth and Arnold Schonhage, STAN-CS-77-599, Computer Science, Stanford University, March 1977.

"Linear expected time of a simple UNION-FIND algorithm" by Jon Doyle and Ronald L. Rivest, *Information Processing Letters*, (1976) 146–148.

EXERCISES

1. Write algorithms for ADDQ and DELETEQ when the queue is represented as a linked list.

2. A linear list is being maintained circularly in an array C(0:n − 1) with F and and R set up as for circular queues.

(a) Obtain a formula in terms of F, R and n for the number of elements in the list.

(b) Write an algorithm to delete the kth element in the list.

(c) Write an algorithm to insert an element Y immediately after kth element.

What is the time complexity of your algorithms for (b) and (c)?

3. Let $X = (x_1, \ldots, x_n)$ and $Y = (y_1, \ldots, y_m)$ be two linked lists. Write an algorithm to merge the two lists together to obtain the linked list $Z = (x_1, y_1, x_2, y_2, \ldots, x_m, y_m, x_{m+1}, \ldots, x_n)$ if $m \leq n$ and $Z = (x_1, y_1, x_2, y_2, \ldots, x_m, y_n, y_{n+1}, \ldots, y_m)$ if $m > n$.

4. A double ended queue (deque) is a linear list where insertions and deletions can occur at either end. Show how to represent a deque in a one dimensional array and write algorithms which insert and delete at either end.

5. Consider the hypothetical data object $X2$. $X2$ is a linear list with the restriction that while additions to the list may be made at either end, deletions can be made from one end only. Design a linked list representation for $X2$. Write addition and deletion algorithms for $X2$. Specify initial and boundary conditions for your representation.

6. Write an algorithm to search a binary search tree T for an identifier X. Assume that each node in T has three fields: LCHILD, DATA and RCHILD. What is the computing time of your algorithm?

7. Write algorithms corresponding to ADJUST, HEAPIFY, INSERT and DELETE for the case of a min-heap represented as a complete binary tree.

8. Devise a suitable representation for graphs so they can be stored on punched cards. Write an algorithm which reads in such a graph and creates its adjacency matrix.

9. Write an algorithm which uses the external representation of exercise 8 to read in a graph and set up its adjacency lists.

10. Is the directed graph below strongly connected? List all of its simple paths.

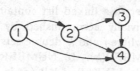

Figure 2.30 A directed graph

11. Show how the graph above would look if represented by its adjacency matrix or adjacency lists.

12. For an undirected graph G with n vertices and e edges show that the sum of the degrees of each vertex equals $2e$.

13. (a) Let G be a connected undirected graph on n vertices. Show that G must have at least $n - 1$ edges and that all connected undirected graphs with $n - 1$ edges are trees.
    (b) What is the minimum number of edges in a strongly connected digraph on n vertices? What shape do such digraphs have? Prove your answer.

14. For an undirected graph G with n vertices prove that the following are equivalent:

    (a) G is a tree;
    (b) G is connected, but if any edge is removed the resulting graph is not connected;
    (c) For every pair of distinct vertices $u \in V(G)$ and $v \in V(G)$ there is exactly one simple path from u to v;
    (d) G contains no cycles and has $n - 1$ edges;
    (e) G is connected and has $n - 1$ edges.

15. Program and run algorithm 2.6, HEAPSORT and compare its time against your favorite sorting method. If HEAPSORT is your favorite sorting method, rewrite it as a purely recursive program and compare both versions on selected data.

16. Verify for yourself that Algorithm 2.3, INSERT only uses a constant number of comparisons to insert a random element into a heap by repeating the experiment described in Table 2.7.

17. Equation 2.2 makes use of the fact that the sum $\Sigma(i/2^i)$ converges and is less than 2. Prove this fact.

18. Write an algorithm which prints all of the identifiers in a hash table in alphabetical order. How efficient is your algorithm?

19. Another way of solving the disjoint set union problem is as follows: let NAME (i) be the name of the set containing i, NUMBER(j) be the number of items in set j, LIST(j) a pointer to a linked list containing the items of set j. The FIND(i) operation is trivially accomplished by examining NAME(i). The UNION(j,k) operation, where j and k denote sets, is done by first comparing NUMBER(j) with NUMBER(k). If NUMBER$(j) \leq$ NUMBER(k) then NAME$(i) \leftarrow k$ for all i in LINK(j), LINK(j) is appended to LINK(k), and

NUMBER(k) is increased by NUMBER(j). The new set is j. Prove that for a total of n items the time for all UNION operations is at most $O(n \log n)$.

20. Knuth and Schonhage have shown that the average time to perform all unions by the method in the previous exercise is $O(n)$. For given values of n, generate random pairs of integers i and j and compare the times necessary to union i and j using the algorithms in the text (2.8 and 2.9) versus the procedure outlined above.

21. Write an algorithm to delete an identifier, X, from a hash table HT(0:$b - 1$) in which overflows are handled using linear probing.

22. [T. Gonzalez] Design a symbol table representation which allows one to search, insert and delete an identifier X in $O(1)$ time. Assume that $X \in [1, m]$ is integer valued that $m + n$ units of space are available where n is the number of insertions to be made. (Hint: use two arrays $A(1:n)$ and $B(1:m)$ where $A(i)$ will be the ith identifier inserted into the table. If X is the ith identifier inserted then $B(X) = i$). Write algorithms to search, insert and delete identifiers. Note that you cannot initialize either A or B to zero as this would take $O(m + n)$.

23. [T. Gonzalez] Let $S = (x_1, \ldots, x_n)$ and $T = (y_1, \ldots, y_r)$ be two sets. Assume $1 \leq x_i \leq m$, $1 \leq i \leq n$ and $1 \leq y_i \leq m$, $1 \leq i \leq r$. All x_is and y_is are integers. Using the idea of exercise 22 write an algorithm to determine if S is contained in T. Your algorithm should work in $O(n + r)$ time. Since S is equal to T iff S is contained in T and T is contained in S, this implies that one can determine in linear time if two sets are equal. How much space is needed by your algorithm?

Chapter 3

DIVIDE-AND-CONQUER

3.1 THE GENERAL METHOD

Given a function to compute on n inputs the *divide-and-conquer* strategy suggests splitting the inputs into k distinct subsets, $1 < k \leq n$ yielding k subproblems. These subproblems must be solved and then a method must be found to combine subsolutions into a solution of the whole. If the subproblems are still relatively large, then the divide-and-conquer strategy may possibly be reapplied. Often the subproblems resulting from a divide-and-conquer design are of the *same* type as the original problem. For those cases the reapplication of the divide-and-conquer principle is naturally expressed by a recursive procedure. Now smaller and smaller subproblems of the same kind are generated, eventually producing subproblems that are small enough to be solved without splitting.

To be more precise suppose we consider the divide-and-conquer strategy when it splits the input into two subproblems of the same kind as the original problem. This splitting is typical of many of the problems we will see here. We can write a control abstraction which mirrors the way an actual program based upon divide-and-conquer will look. By a *control abstraction* we informally mean a procedure whose flow of control is clear, but whose primary operations are specified by other procedures whose precise meaning is left undefined. Let the n inputs be stored (or pointed at) by the array $A(1:n)$ and we will assume this array is global to Algorithm 3.1. Procedure DANDC is a function which is initially invoked as DANDC($1, n$). DANDC (p, q) solves a problem instance defined by the inputs $A(p:q)$.

procedure *DANDC*(*p*, *q*)
  global *n*, *A*(1:*n*); **integer** *m*,*p*,*q*;   //1 ≤ *p* ≤ *q* ≤ *n*//
  if *SMALL*(*p*,*q*)
    then return (*G*(*p*, *q*))
    else m ← *DIVIDE*(*p*,*q*)   //*p* ≤ *m* < *q*//
      return(*COMBINE*(*DANDC*(*p*,*m*), *DANDC*(*m* + 1,*q*)))
  endif
end *DANDC*

Algorithm 3.1   Control abstraction for divide-and-conquer

SMALL(*p*,*q*) is a Boolean valued function which determines if the input size *q* − *p* + 1 is small enough so that the answer can be computed without splitting. If this is so the function *G* is invoked. Otherwise the function DIVIDE(*p*,*q*) is called. This function returns an integer which specifies where the input is to be split. Let *m* = DIVIDE(*p*,*q*). The input is split so that *A*(*p*:*m*) and *A*(*m* + 1, *q*) define instances of two subproblems. The solutions *x* and *y* respectively of these two subproblems are obtained by recursive application of DANDC. COMBINE(*x*, *y*) is a function which determines the solution to *A*(*p*:*q*) using the solutions *x* and *y* to the two subproblems *A*(*p*:*m*) and *A*(*m* + 1, *q*). If the sizes of the two subproblems are approximately equal then the computing time of DANDC is naturally described by the recurrence relation

$$T(n) = \begin{cases} g(n), & n \text{ small} \\ 2T(n/2) + f(n), & \text{otherwise} \end{cases}$$

where $T(n)$ is the time for DANDC on n inputs, $g(n)$ is the time to compute the answer directly for small inputs and $f(n)$ is the time for COMBINE. Recurrence relations will often arise for divide-and-conquer based algorithms and we will see how to work with them as they arise.

For divide-and-conquer based algorithms which produce subproblems of the same type as the original problem it is very natural to first describe such an algorithm using recursion. But to gain efficiency it may be desirable to translate the resulting program into iterative form. Algorithm 3.2 shows the result of applying the translation rules of section 1.3 to Algorithm 3.1.

procedure *DANDC*1 (*p,q*)
  //iterative version of DANDC//
  //declare a stack of appropriate size//
  local *s*, *t*
  top ← 0   //set the stack to empty//
  *L*1: **while not** *SMALL*(*p*, *q*) **do**
     m ← DIVIDE(*p,q*) //determine how to split the input//
     STACK gets p, q, m, 0, 2   //process the first recursive call;//
                                     //increment top//

     q ← *m*
  repeat
  t ← *G*(*p*, *q*)
  while *top* ≠ 0 **do**
    p, *q*, *m*, *s*, *ret removed from STACK* //decrement top appropri-//
                                                //ately//
    if *ret* = 2
      then *STACK gets p, q, m, t,* 3 //process the second recursive call//
         p ← *m* + 1
         go to *L*1
      else *t* ← COMBINE(*s*, *t*) //combine two solutions into one//
    endif
  repeat
  return(*t*)
end *DANDC*1

Algorithm 3.2 Iterative form of divide-and-conquer control abstraction

3.2 BINARY SEARCH

Let a_i, $1 \le i \le n$ be a list of elements which are sorted in nondecreasing order. Consider the problem of determining whether a given element x is present in the list. In case x is present, we are to determine a value j such that $a_j = x$. If x is not in the list then j is to be set to zero. Divide-and-conquer suggests breaking up any instance $I = (n, a_1, \ldots, a_n, x)$ of this search problem into subinstances. One possibility is to pick an index k and obtain three instances: $I1 = (k - 1, a_1, \ldots, a_{k-1}, x)$, $I2 = (1, a_k, x)$, and $I3 = (n - k, a_{k+1}, \ldots, a_n, x)$. The search problem for two of these three instances is easily solved by comparing x with a_k. If $x = a_k$ then $j = k$ and $I1$ and $I2$ need not be solved. If $x < a_k$ then for $I2$ and $I3$, $j = 0$ and only $I1$ remains to be solved. If $x > a_k$ then for $I1$ and $I2$, $j = 0$ and only *I3* remains to be solved. After a comparison with a_k, the instance remaining to be solved (if any) can be solved by using this divide-and-conquer scheme again. If k is always chosen such that a_k is the middle element (i.e. $k = \lfloor (n + 1)/2 \rfloor$ then the resulting search algorithm is known as binary search.

Algorithm 3.3 describes this binary search method using the language SPARKS. Procedure BINSRCH has three inputs, A, n and x, and one output, j. The **while** loop continues processing as long as there are more elements left to check. The **case** statement permits the selection of the three alternatives. The first two conditions are checked for, and if they do not occur, the "**else** clause" is automatically executed. At the conclusion of the procedure either $j = 0$ if x is not present, or $A(j) = x$.

procedure *BINSRCH(A,n,x,j)*
  //given an array $A(1:n)$ of elements in nondecreasing order,//
  //$n \geq 0$, determine if x is present, and if so, set j such that $x = A(j)$//
  //else $j = 0$.//
  integer *low, high, mid, j, n*;
  low ← 1; *high* ← *n*
  while *low* ≤ *high* **do**
     mid ← $\lfloor (low + high)/2 \rfloor$
   case
     : $x < A(mid)$: *high* ← *mid* − 1
     : $x > A(mid)$: *low* ← *mid* + 1
     : **else** : *j* ← *mid*; **return**
   endcase
  repeat
  j ← 0
end *BINSRCH*

Algorithm 3.3 Binary Search

Is BINSRCH an algorithm? We must be sure that all of the operations such as comparisons between x and $A(mid)$ are well defined. If the elements of A are integers, reals, or character strings then the relational operators will correctly carry out the comparisons. This will be true for those languages which offer these data types. Does BINSRCH terminate? We observe that *low* and *high* are integer variables such that each time through the loop either x is found or *low* is increased by at least one or *high* is decreased by at least one. Thus we have two sequences of integers approaching each other and eventually *low* will become greater than *high* causing termination in a finite number of steps if x is not present.

Let us select the nine entries,

$$-15, \ -6, 0, 7, 9, 23, 54, 82, 101$$

place them in $A(1:9)$, and simulate the steps that BINSRCH goes through as it searches for different values of x. Only the variables *low*, *high* and *mid* need to be traced as we simulate the algorithm. We shall try the following values for x: 101, -14, and 82 for two successful searches and one unsuccessful search.

$x = 101$	*low*	*high*	*mid*
	1	9	5
	6	9	7
	8	9	8
	9	9	9
			found

$x = -14$	*low*	*high*	*mid*
	1	9	5
	1	4	2
	1	1	1
	2	1	not found

$x = 82$	*low*	*high*	*mid*
	1	9	5
	6	9	7
	8	9	8
			found

Table 3.1   Three examples of binary search on nine elements

These examples may give us a little more confidence about Algorithm 3.3, but they by no means prove that it is correct. Proofs of programs are very useful because they establish the correctness of the program for *all* possible inputs, while testing gives much less in the way of guarantees. Unfortunately, program proving is a very difficult process and the complete proof of a program can be many times longer than the program itself. We shall content ourselves with an "informal proof" of BINSRCH.

Theorem 3.1   Procedure BINSRCH(A, n, x, j) works correctly.
Proof: We assume that all statements work as expected and that comparisons such as $x > A(mid)$ are appropriately carried out. Initially *low* = 1, *high* = $n, n \geq 0$ and $A(1) \leq \ldots \leq A(n)$. If $n = 0$ the **while** loop is not entered and j is set to zero. Otherwise we observe that each time through the loop the possible elements to be checked for equality with x are $A(low)$,

$A(low + 1), \ldots, A(mid), \ldots, A(high)$. If $x = A(mid)$ then the algorithm terminates successfully. Otherwise the range is narrowed by either increasing *low* to $mid + 1$ or decreasing *high* to $mid - 1$. Clearly this narrowing of the range does not affect the outcome of the search. If *low* becomes greater than *high* then x is not present and hence the loop is exited. $\square$

Notice that in order to fully test binary search we need not concern ourselves with the actual values of $A(1:n)$. By varying x sufficiently, we can observe all possible computation sequences of BINSRCH without devising different values for A. To test all successful searches x must take on the n values in A. To test all unsuccessful searches x need only take on $n + 1$ different values. Thus we might say that the complexity of testing BINSRCH is $2n + 1$ for each n.

Now lets analyze the execution profile of BINSRCH. The two relevant characteristics of this profile are the frequency counts and space required for the algorithm. For BINSRCH, storage is required for the n elements of the array plus storage for the variables *low*, *high*, *mid*, x and j or $n + 5$ locations. As for the time, there are three possibilities to consider: the best, average and worst case.

Suppose we begin by determining the time for BINSRCH on the previous data set. We observe that the only operations in the algorithm are comparisons and data movement. We will concentrate on comparisons between x. and the elements in A recognizing that the frequency count of all other operations will be of the same order as that for these comparisons. Comparisons between x and elements of A will be referred to as *element comparisons*. We assume that only one comparison is needed to determine which of the three possibilities of the **case** statement hold. The number of element comparisons needed to find each of the nine elements is:

A:	(1)	(2)	(3)	(4)	(5)	(6)	(7)	(8)	(9)
elements:	−15	−6	0	7	9	23	54	82	101
comparisons:	3	2	3	4	1	3	2	3	4

No element requires more than 4 comparisons to be found. The average is obtained by summing the comparisons needed to find all nine items and dividing by 9, yielding 25/9, or approximately 2.77 comparisons per successful search on the average. There are ten possible ways that an unsuccessful search may terminate depending upon the value of x. If $x < A(1)$, $A(1) < x < A(2)$, $A(2) < x < A(3)$, $A(5) < x < A(6)$, $A(6) < x < A(7)$, or $A(7) < x < A(8)$ the algorithm requires 3 element comparisons to determine that x is not present. For all of the remaining possibilities BINSRCH requires 4 element comparisons. Thus the average number of element comparisons for an unsuccessful search is $(3 + 3 + 3 + 4 + 4 + 3 + 3 + 3 + 4 + 4)/10 = 34/10 = 3.4$.

The analysis just done applies to any sorted sequence containing nine elements. But the type of result we would prefer is a formula for n elements. A good way to derive such a formula plus a better way to understand the algorithm is to consider the sequence of values for mid that are produced by BINSRCH for all possible values of x. These values are nicely described using a binary decision tree in which the value in each node is the value of *mid*. For example, if $n = 14$ then Figure 3.1 contains a binary decision tree which traces the way in which these values will be produced by procedure BINSRCH.

The first comparison is x with $A(7)$. If $x < A(7)$ then the next comparison is with $A(3)$; similarly, if $x < A(7)$ then the next comparison is with $A(11)$. Each path through the tree represents a sequence of comparisons in the binary search method. If x is present, then the algorithm will end at one of the circular nodes which lists the index into the array where x was found. If x is not present, the algorithm will terminate at one of the square nodes. Circular nodes are called *internal nodes* while square nodes are referred to as *external nodes*.

Theorem 3.2: If n is in the range $[2^{k-1}, 2^k)$ then BINSRCH makes at most k element comparisons for a successful search and either $k - 1$ or k comparisons for an unsuccessful search. (In other words the time for a successful search is $O(\log n)$ and for an unsuccessful search it is $\Theta(\log n)$).

Proof: Consider the binary decision tree describing the action of BINSRCH on n elements. All successful searches end at a circular node while all unsuccessful searches end at a square node. If $2^{k-1} \leq n < 2^k$ then all circular nodes are at levels 1, 2, ..., k while all square nodes are at levels k and $k + 1$ (note that the root is at level 1). The number of element comparisons needed to terminate at a circular node on level i is i while the number of element comparisons needed to terminate at a square node at level i is only $i - 1$. The theorem follows. $\square$

The previous theorem states the worst case time for binary search. To determine the average behavior we need to look more closely at the binary decision tree, equating its size to the number of element comparisons in the algorithm. The *distance* of a node from the root is one less than its level. The *internal path length*, I, is the sum of the distances of all internal nodes from the root. The *external path length*, E, is defined analogously as the sum of the distance of all external nodes from the root. It is easy to show by induction that for any binary tree with n internal nodes E and I are related by the formula

$$E = I + 2n$$

It turns out that there is a simple relationship between E, I and the average number of comparisons in binary search. Let $S(n)$ be the average number of comparisons in a successful search and $U(n)$ the average number of comparisons in an unsuccessful search. The number of comparisons needed to find an element represented by an internal node is one more than the distance of this node from the root. Hence,

$$S(n) = 1 + I/n$$

The number of comparisons on any path from the root to an external node is equal to the distance between the root and the external node. Since every binary tree with n internal nodes has $n + 1$ external nodes, it follows that

$$U(n) = E/(n + 1)$$

Using these formulas for E, $S(n)$, and $U(n)$ we find that

$$S(n) = (1 + 1/n)U(n) - 1$$

From this formula we see that $S(n)$ and $U(n)$ are directly related. The minimum value of $S(n)$ (and hence $U(n)$) is achieved by an algorithm whose binary decision tree has minimum external and internal path length. This minimum is achieved by the binary tree all of whose external nodes are on adjacent levels, and this is precisely the tree which is produced by binary search. From Theorem 3.2 it follows that E is proportional to $n \log n$. Using this in the preceeding formulas, we conclude that $S(n)$ and $U(n)$ are both proportional to $\log n$. Thus we conclude that the average and worst case number of comparisons for binary search is the same to within a constant factor. The best case analysis is easy. For a successful search only one element comparison is needed. For an unsuccessful search, Theorem 3.2 states that $\lfloor \log n \rfloor$ element comparisons are needed in the best case.

In conclusion we are now able to completely describe the computing time of binary search by giving formulas which describe the best, average and worst cases:

successful searches	unsuccessful searches
$\Theta(1)$, $\Theta(\log n)$, $\Theta(\log n)$	$\Theta(\log n)$
best average worst	best average and worst

Can we expect another searching algorithm to be significantly better than binary search in the worst case? This question will be pursued rigorously in chapter 10. But we can anticipate the answer here which is no. The method for proving such an assertion is to view the binary decision tree as a general model for any searching algorithm which depends upon comparisons of entire elements. Viewed in this way, we observe that the *longest* path to discover any element is minimized by binary search, and so any alternative algorithm will be no better from this point of view.

Before we end this section there is an interesting variation of binary search which is useful for programming languages which require two comparisons to implement the **case** statement of procedure BINSRCH. This variation appears as Algorithm 3.4. The correctness proof of this algorithm is left as an exercise.

```
procedure BINSRCH1(A,n,x,j)
  //Same specifications as BINSRCH except n > 0.//
  integer low, high, mid, j, n;
  low ← 1; high ← n + 1   //high is always one more than is possible//
  while low < high − 1 do
    mid ← ⌊(low + high)/2⌋
    if x < A(mid)      //only one comparison in the loop//
      then high ← mid
      else low ← mid   //x ≥ A(mid)//
    endif
  repeat
  if x = A(low) then j ← low     //x is present//
                else j ← 0       //x is not present//
  endif
end BINSRCH1
```

Algorithm 3.4 Binary search using one comparison per cycle

The virtue of this procedure is that it uses only one comparison between x and $A(mid)$ within the **while** loop. The **case** statement of BINSRCH can be implemented using the arithmetic-if statement in FORTRAN. In a language such as PL/I or Pascal, it may be implemented by the code equivalent to:

```
if x < A(mid) then high ← mid − 1
              else if x > A(mid) then low ← mid + 1
                                 else j ← mid; return
                   endif
endif
```

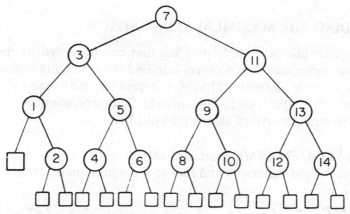

Figure 3.1 Binary decision tree for binary search, $n = 14$

In this case BINSRCH will sometimes make twice as many element comparisons as BINSRCH1 (for example when $x > A(n)$). However, for successful searches BINSRCH1 may in cases make $(\log n)/2$ more element comparisons than BINSRCH (for example when $x = A(mid)$). The analysis of BINSRCH1 is left as an exercise. It should be easy to see that the best, average and worst case times for BINSRCH1 are $\Theta(\log n)$ for both successful and unsuccessful searches.

These two algorithms were coded in FORTRAN and run on an IBM370/158. Also a version of BINSRCH called CBINSRCH, which uses the arithmetic IF statement was also coded and tested. The size of the arrays were 5000, 10000, 15000, 20000, 25000, 30000. The first three rows represent the average time for a successful search over all n times. The second set of three rows are the average times for all possible unsuccessful searches. For successful searches BINSRCH1 did marginally better than the other two methods. For unsuccessful comparisons BINSRCH was the winner. Based on this limited data sample and the usual inaccuracies of timing, the algorithms are judged to be indistinguishable in terms of performance.

Array sizes;	5000	10000	15000	20000	25000	30000
CBINSRCH	.356	.402	.421	.445	.456	.448
BINSRCH	.330	.410	.442	.462	.478	.447
BINSRCH1	.385	.398	.462	.475	.453	.433
		(successful searches)				
CBINSRCH	.373	.412	.450	.432	.430	.422
BINSRCH	.350	.377	.438	.382	.369	.386
BINSRCH1	.362	.422	.410	.412	.402	.430
		(unsuccessful searches)				

(times in seconds)

Table 3.2 Computing times for three binary search algorithms

3.3 FINDING THE MAXIMUM AND MINIMUM

Let us consider another simple problem that can be solved by the divide-and-conquer technique. The problem is to find the maximum and minimum items in a set of n elements. Though this problem may look so simple as to be contrived, it allows us to demonstrate divide-and-conquer in a simple setting. One straightforward algorithm looks like

procedure *STRAITMAXMIN(A, n, max, min)*
　　//Set *max* to the maximum and *min* to the minimum of $A(1{:}n)$//
　　integer *i, n*;
　　max ← *min* ← $A(1)$
　　for *i* ← 2 **to** *n* **do**
　　　　if $A(i) > max$
　　　　　　then *max* ← $A(i)$ **endif**
　　　　if $A(i) < min$
　　　　　　then *min* ← $A(i)$ **endif**
　　repeat
end *STRAITMAXMIN*

Algorithm 3.5　Straightforward maximum and minimum

In analyzing the time complexity of this algorithm, we shall once again concentrate on the number of element comparisons. The justification for this is that the frequency count for other operations in the above algorithm is of the same order as that for element comparisons. More importantly, when the elements in $A(1{:}n)$ are polynomials, vectors, very large numbers, or strings of characters the cost of an element comparison is much higher than the cost of the other operations. Hence the time is determined mainly by the total cost of the element comparisons.

It is easy to see that procedure STRAITMAXMIN requires $2(n - 1)$ element comparisons in the best, average and worst cases. An immediate improvement is possible by realizing that the comparison $A(i) < min$ is necessary only when $A(i) > max$ is false. Hence we may replace the contents of the **for** loop by:

if $A(i) > max$ **then** *max* ← $A(i)$
　　　　　　　　else if $A(i) < min$ **then** *min* ← $A(i)$ **endif**
endif

Now the best case occurs when the elements are in increasing order. The number of element comparisons is $n - 1$. The worst case occurs when the elements are in decreasing order. In this case the number of element comparisons is $2(n - 1)$. On the average, $A(i)$ will be greater than max half the time and so the average number of comparisons is $3n/2 - 1$.

A divide-and-conquer algorithm for this problem would proceed by dividing any instance $I = (n, A(1), \ldots, A(n))$ into smaller instances. For example we might divide I into the two instanced $I1 = (\lfloor n/2 \rfloor, A(1), \ldots, A \lfloor n/2 \rfloor)$ and $I2 = (n - \lfloor n/2 \rfloor, A(n/2 + 1, \ldots, A(n))$. If $MAX(I)$ and $MIN(I)$ are the maximum and minimum of the elements in I then $MAX(I) =$ the larger of $MAX(I1)$ and $MAX(I2)$, and $MIN(I) =$ the smaller of $MIN(I1)$ and $MIN(I2)$. If I contains only one element then the answer can be computed without any splitting.

Algorithm 3.6 shows the procedure which results by applying the strategy just described. MAXMIN is a recursive procedure which finds the maximum and minimum of the set of elements $\{A(i), A(i + 1), \ldots, A(j)\}$. The situation of set sizes one ($i = j$) and two ($i = j - 1$) are handled separately. For sets containing more than two elements, the midpoint is determined (just as in binary search) and two new subproblems are generated. When the maximum and minimum of these subproblems is determined, the two maxima are compared and the two minima are compared to achieve the solution for the entire set. **max** and **min** are considered to be built-in functions which require one comparison each to compute their result.

```
procedure MAXMIN(i, j, fmax, fmin)
    //A is a global array containing n numbers in A(1), ..., A(n).//
    //Parameters i, j are integers: 1 ≤ i ≤ j ≤ n. The effect is to//
    //assign to fmax and fmin the largest and smallest values in//
    //A(i:j) respectively.//
    integer i, j; global n, A(1:n)
    case
        : i = j : fmax ← fmin ← A(i)
        : i = j - 1 : if A(i) < A(j) then fmax ← A(j); fmin ← A(i)
                                     else fmax ← A(i); fmin ← A(j)
                      endif
        : else : mid ← ⌊(i + j)/2⌋
                 call MAXMIN(i, mid, gmax, gmin)
                 call MAXMIN(mid + 1, j, hmax, hmin)
                 fmax ← max(gmax, hmax)
                 fmin ← min(gmin, hmin)
    endcase
end MAXMIN
```

Algorithm 3.6 Recursively finding the maximum and minimum

The procedure is initially invoked by the statement

$$\text{call } MAXMIN(1, n, x, y).$$

max and **min** are functions that find the larger and smaller of two elements respectively. Note that each of these functions uses only one comparison per call. Suppose we simulate procedure MAXMIN on the following nine elements

A: *(1)* *(2)* *(3)* *(4)* *(5)* *(6)* *(7)* *(8)* *(9)*

22   13   −5   −8   15   60   17   31   47

A good way of keeping track of recursive calls is to build a tree so that a node is added each time a new call is made. For this program each node will have four items of information: $i, j, fmax, fmin$. On the array A above, the tree of Figure 3.2 is produced.

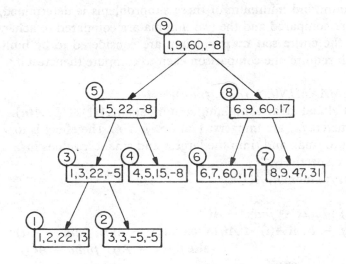

Figure 3.2   Trees of recursive calls of MAXMIN

Examining Figure 3.2 we see that the root node contains 1 and 9 as the values of i and j corresponding to the initial call to MAXMIN. This execution will produce two new calls to MAXMIN where i and j have the values 1, 5 and 6, 9 respectively thus splitting the set into two subsets of approximately the same size. From the tree we can immediately see that the maximum depth of recursion is four (including the first call). The circled numbers in the upper left hand corner of each node represent the order in which *fmax* and *fmin* are assigned a value.

Now what is the number of element comparisons needed for MAXMIN? If $T(n)$ represents this number, then the resulting recurrence relation is

$$T(n) = \begin{cases} T(\lfloor n/2 \rfloor) + T(\lceil n/2 \rceil) + 2, & n > 2 \\ 1, & n = 2 \\ 0, & n = 1 \end{cases}$$

When n is a power of two, $n = 2^k$ for some positive integer k, then

$$T(n) = 2T(n/2) + 2$$

$$= 2(2T(n/4) + 2) + 2$$
$$= 4\,T(n/4) + 4 + 2$$

$$\vdots \qquad\qquad\qquad\qquad\qquad (3.1)$$

$$= 2^{k-1}T(2) + \sum_{1 \le i \le k-1} 2^i$$

$$= 2^{k-1} + 2^k - 2 = 3n/2 - 2$$

Note that $3n/2 - 2$ is the best, average and worst case number of comparisons when n is a power of 2.

Compared with the $2n - 2$ comparisons for the straightforward method this is a savings of 25% in comparisons. It can be shown that no algorithm based upon comparisons uses less than $3n/2 - 2$ comparisons. So in this sense procedure MAXMIN is optimal (see chapter 10 for more details). But does this imply that MAXMIN is truly better in practice? Not necessarily. In terms of storage MAXMIN is worse than the straightforward algorithm because it requires stack space for $i, j, fmax$ and *fmin*. Given n elements there will be $\lfloor \log_2 n \rfloor + 1$ levels of recursion and we need to save five values for each recursive call (don't forget the return address is also needed). Of course we could remove the recursion using the translation rules of chapter 1. But even if we simplify the resulting iterative version, a stack whose depth is on the order log n is still needed. Another source of overhead is the comparisons needed to check if $i = j$ or $i = j - 1$. Perhaps it would be fairer not to distinguish between comparison of $A(i)$ and $A(j)$, and comparisons of i and j. This is especially true when the $A(i)$s are themselves small numbers.

Let us see what the count is when element comparisons have the same cost as comparisons between i and j. Let $C(n)$ be this number. First, we observe that the effect of the first two cases of the **case** statement can be achieved by deleting the case $i = j$ and replacing $i = j - 1$ by $i \geq j - 1$. Hence, a single comparison between i and $j - 1$ is adequate to implement the modified **case** statement. Assuming $n = 2^k$ for some positive integer k, we get

$$C(n) = \begin{cases} 2C(n/2) + 3, & n > 2 \\ 2 & , & n = 2 \end{cases}$$

Solving this equation we obtain

$$\begin{aligned} C(n) &= 2C(n/2) + 3 \\ &= 4C(n/4) + 6 + 3 \\ &\quad\cdot \\ &\quad\cdot \\ &= 2^{k-1}C(2) + \qquad\qquad 3 \ \ \Sigma_0^{k-2} 2^i \\ &= 2^k + 3*2^{k-1} - 3 \\ &= 5n/2 - 3 \end{aligned} \qquad (3.2)$$

The comparative figure for STRAITMAXMIN is $3(n - 1)$ (including the comparison needed to implement the **for** loop). This is larger than $5n/2 - 3$. Despite this, MAXMIN will be slower than STRAITMAXMIN because of the overhead of stacking $i, j, fmax$, and $fmin$ for the recursion.

Algorithm 3.6 makes several points. If comparisons among the elements of A are much more costly than comparisons of integer variables, then the divide-and-conquer technique has yielded a more efficient (actually an optimal) algorithm. On the other hand, if this assumption is not true, the technique yields a less efficient program. Thus the divide-and-conquer strategy is seen to be only a guide to better algorithm design which may not always succeed. Also we see that it is sometimes necessary to work out the constants associated with the computing time bound for an algorithm. Both MAXMIN and STRAITMAXMIN are $\Theta(n)$ so the use of asymptotic notation is not enough of a discriminator in this situation. The recursion of MAXMIN will make it run far slower than STRAITMAXMIN on most systems. Therefore for a fair comparison we might translate MAXMIN into an equivalent iterative program and test that against STRAITMAXMIN when the time for element comparisons is very long. Finally, see the exercises for another way to find the maximum and minimum using only $3n/2 - 2$ comparisons which uses iteration but requires no stack.

3.4 MERGESORT

As another example of divide-and-conquer, we investigate a sorting algorithm which has the nice property that in the worst case its complexity is $O(n \log_2 n)$. This algorithm is called mergesort. We shall assume throughout that the elements are to be sorted in nondecreasing order. Given a sequence of n elements (also called keys) $A(1), \ldots, A(n)$ the general idea is to imagine them split into two sets $A(1), \ldots, A(\lfloor n/2 \rfloor)$ and $A(\lfloor n/2 \rfloor + 1), \ldots, A(n)$. Each set is individually sorted and the resulting sequences are merged to produce a single sorted sequence of n elements. Thus we have another ideal example of the divide-and-conquer strategy where the splitting is into two equal size sets and the combining operation is the merging of two sorted sets into one.

Procedure MERGESORT describes this process very succinctly using recursion and a subprocedure MERGE which merges together two sorted sets.

procedure MERGESORT(*low, high*)
    //$A(low : high)$ is a global array containing $high - low + 1 \geq 0$//
    //values which represent the elements to be sorted.//
    integer *low, high*;
    if *low* < *high*;
        then *mid* ← $\lfloor (low + high)/2 \rfloor$ //find where to split the set//
             call *MERGESORT(low, mid)*   //sort one subset//
             call *MERGESORT(mid + 1, high)* //sort the other subset//
             call *MERGE(low, mid, high)* //combine the results//
    endif
end *MERGESORT*

Algorithm 3.7 Mergesort

procedure *MERGE(low, mid, high)*
//*A(low:high)* is a global array containing two sorted subsets   //
//in *A(low:mid)* and in *A(mid* + 1*:high)*.   //
//The objective is to merge these sorted sets into   //
//a single sorted set residing in *A(low:high)*. An auxiliary array *B* is used//
integer *h, i, j, k, low, mid, high*;   //*low* ≤ *mid* < *high*//
global *A(low:high)*; **local** *B(low:high)*
h ← *low*; *i* ← *low*; *j* ← *mid* + 1;
while *h* ≤ *mid* **and** *j* ≤ *high* **do**   //while both sets are not exhausted//
    if *A(h)* ≤ *A(j)* **then** *B(i)* ← *A(h)*; *h* ← *h* + 1
                else *B(i)* ← *A(j)*; *j* ← *j* + 1
    endif
    i ← *i* + 1
repeat
if *h* > *mid* **then for** *k* ← *j* **to** *high* **do**   //handle any remaining elements//
                    B(i) ← *A(k)*;   *i* ← *i* + 1
                repeat
            else for *k* ← *h* **to** *mid* **do**
                    B(i) ← *A(k)*;   *i* ← *i* + 1
                repeat
endif
for *k* ← *low* **to** *high* **do**   //copy the merged sets back into *A*//
    A(k) ← *B(k)*
repeat
end *MERGE*

Algorithm 3.8   Merging two sorted sets using auxiliary storage

Before executing procedure MERGESORT, the *n* elements should be placed in *A(1:n)* and the auxiliary array *B(1:n)* should also be declared. Then **call** MERGESORT(1, *n*) will cause the keys to be rearranged into nondecreasing order in *A*.

Consider the array of ten elements *A* = (310, 285, 179, 652, 351, 423, 861, 254, 450, 520). Procedure MERGESORT begins by splitting *A* into two subfiles of size five. The elements in *A(1:5)* are then split into two subfiles of size three and two. Then the items in *A(1:3)* are split into subfiles of size two and one. The two values in *A(1:2)* are split a final time into one element subfiles and now the merging begins. Note that no actual movement of data has yet taken place. A record of the subfiles is implicitly maintained by the recursive mechanism. Pictorially the file can now be viewed as

$$(310\,|\,285\,|\,179\,|\,652,\ 351\,|\,423,\ 861,\ 254,\ 450,\ 520)$$

with the vertical bars indicating the boundaries of subfiles. $A(1)$ and $A(2)$ are merged to yield

$$(285,\ 310\,|\,179\,|\,652,\ 351\,|\,423,\ 861,\ 254,\ 450,\ 520)$$

Then $A(3)$ is merged with $A(1:2)$ producing

$$(179,\ 285,\ 310\,|\,652,\ 351\,|\,423,\ 861,\ 254,\ 450,\ 520)$$

Next, elements $A(4)$ and $A(5)$ are merged

$$(179,\ 285,\ 310\,|\,351,\ 652\,|\,423,\ 861,\ 254,\ 450,\ 520)$$

followed by the merging of $A(1:3)$ and $A(4:5)$ to give

$$(179,\ 285,\ 310,\ 351,\ 652\,|\,423,\ 861,\ 254,\ 450,\ 520)$$

At this point the algorithm has returned to the first invocation of MERGE-SORT and it is about to process the second recursive call. Repeated recursive calls are invoked producing the following subfiles:

$$(179,\ 285,\ 310,\ 351,\ 652\,|\,423\,|\,861\,|\,254\,|\,450,\ 520)$$

$A(6)$ and $A(7)$ are merged and then $A(8)$ is merged with $A(6:7)$ giving

$$(179,\ 285,\ 310,\ 351,\ 652\,|\,254,\ 423,\ 861\,|\,450,\ 520)$$

Next $A(9)$ and $A(10)$ are merged followed by $A(6:8)$ and $A(9:10)$

$$(179,\ 285,\ 310,\ 351,\ 652\,|\,254,\ 423,\ 450,\ 520,\ 861)$$

At this point there are two sorted subfiles and the final merge produces the fully sorted result

$$(179,\ 254,\ 285,\ 310,\ 351,\ 423,\ 450,\ 520,\ 652,\ 861)$$

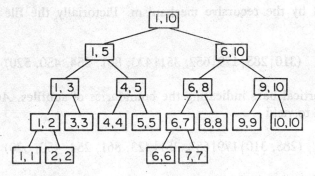

Figure 3.3 Tree of calls of MERGESORT(1, 10)

Figure 3.3 is a tree which represents the sequence of recursive calls that are produced by MERGESORT when it is applied to 10 elements. The pair of values in each node are the values of the parameters *low* and *high*. Notice how the splitting continues until sets containing a single element are produced. Figure 3.4 is a tree representing the calls to procedure MERGE by MERGESORT. For example the node containing 1, 2, 3 represents the merging of the elements in $A(1:2)$ with $A(3)$.

If the time for the merging operation is proportional to n then the computing time for mergesort is described by the recurrence relation

$$T(n) = \begin{cases} 0, & n = 1, \quad a \text{ a constant} \\ 2T(n/2) + cn, & n > 1, \quad c \text{ a constant} \end{cases}$$

When n is a power of 2, $n = 2^k$, we can solve this equation by successive substitutions, namely

$$T(n) = 2(2T(n/4) + cn/2) + cn$$

$$= 4T(n/4) + 2cn$$

$$= 4(2T(n/8) + cn/4) + 2cn$$

$$= \cdots = 2^k T(1) + kcn$$

$$= an + cn \log n$$

It is easy to see that if $2^k < n \le 2^{k+1}$ then $T(n) \le T(2^{k+1})$. Therefore

$$T(n) = O(n \log_2 n).$$

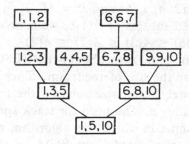

Figure 3.4 Tree of calls of MERGE

Further Refinements

Though Algorithm 3.7 nicely captures the divide-and-conquer nature of mergesort, there remain several inefficiencies which can and should be eliminated. In this subsection we present these refinements in an attempt to produce a version of mergesort which is good enough to execute. Despite these improvements the algorithm's complexity will remain $O(n \log n)$ in the worst case. We shall see in Chapter 10 that no sorting algorithm based upon comparisons of entire keys can do better.

One complaint we might raise concerning mergesort is its use of $2n$ locations. The additional n locations were needed because one couldn't reasonably merge two sorted sets in place. But despite the use of this space the algorithm must still work hard, copying the result placed into $B(low : high)$ back into $A(low:high)$ on each call of MERGE. An alternative to this copying is to associate a new field of information with each key. (The elements in A are called keys). This field will be used to link the keys and any associated information together in a sorted list (keys and related information are called records). Then the merging of the sorted lists proceeds by changing the link values and no records need be moved at all. A field which contains only a link will generally be smaller than an entire record so less space will also be used.

Along with the original array A we define an auxiliary array LINK$(1:n)$ which will contain integers in the range 1, 2, ..., n. These integers will be interpreted as pointers to elements of A. A list will be a sequence of pointers ending with a zero. Below is one set of values for LINK which contains two lists: Q and R. $Q = 2$ and $R = 5$ denotes the start of each list.

LINK:	(1)	(2)	(3)	(4)	(5)	(6)	(7)	(8)
	6	4	7	1	3	0	8	0

The two lists are $Q = (2, 4, 1, 6)$ and $R = (5, 3, 7, 8)$. Interpreting these lists as describing sorted subsets of $A(1:8)$ we conclude that $A(2) \leq A(4) \leq A(1) \leq A(6)$ and $A(5) \leq A(3) \leq A(7) \leq A(8)$.

Another complaint one could raise about MERGESORT is the stack space which is necessitated by the use of recursion. Since mergesort splits each set into two approximately equal size subsets, the maximum depth of the stack is proportional to $\log n$. The need for stack space seems necessitated by the "top-down" manner in which this algorithm was devised. The need for stack space can be eliminated if we build an algorithm which works "bottom-up", see the exercises for details.

As can be seen from procedure MERGESORT and the previous example, even sets of size two will cause two recursive calls to be made. For small set sizes most of the time will be spent processing the recursion instead of actually sorting. This situation can be improved by not allowing the recursion to go to the lowest level. In terms of the divide-and-conquer control abstraction we are suggesting that when SMALL is true for mergesort more work should be done then simply returning with no action. The work which would be helpful is to use a second sorting algorithm which works well on small size sets.

Insertion sort works exceedingly fast on arrays of less than, say 16 elements, though for large n its computing time is $O(n^2)$. Its basic idea for sorting the items in $A(1:n)$ is as follows:

for $j \leftarrow 2$ **to** n **do**
　place $A(j)$ in its correct position in the sorted set $A(1:j-1)$
repeat

Though all of the elements in $A(1:j-1)$ may have to be moved to accommodate $A(j)$, for small values of n the algorithm will work well. A completely stated procedure is given in Algorithm 3.9.

procedure *INSERTIONSORT*(A, n)
　//sort the values in $A(1:n)$ into nondecreasing order, $n \geq 1$//
　$A(0) \leftarrow -\infty$　　//create a dummy value at the beginning//
　for $j \leftarrow 2$ **to** n **do**　//$A(1:j-1)$ is sorted//
　　item $\leftarrow A(j); i \leftarrow j - 1$
　　while *item* $< A(i)$ **do**　//$0 \leq i < j$//
　　　$A(i+1) \leftarrow A(i); i \leftarrow i - 1$
　　repeat
　　$A(i+1) \leftarrow$ *item*
　repeat
end *INSERTIONSORT*

Algorithm 3.9　Insertionsort

The statements within the **while** loop may be executed zero up to a maximum of j times. Since j goes from 2 to n the worst case time of this procedure is bounded by

$$\sum_{2 \leq j \leq n} j = (n(n + 1)/2) - 1 = \Theta(n^2)$$

Its best case computing time is $\Omega(n)$ under the assumption that the body of the **while** loop is never entered. This will be true when the data is already in sorted order.

We are now ready to present the revised version of mergesort with the inclusion of insertionsort and the links.

procedure $MERGESORT1(low, high, p)$
  //The global array $A(low:high)$ is sorted into nondecreasing//
  //order using the auxiliary array LINK$(low, high)$. The values in//
  //LINK will represent a list of the indices low through $high$//
  //giving A in sorted order. p is set to point to the   //
  //beginning of the list.   //
  global $A(low:high), LINK(low:high)$
  if $high - low + 1 < 16$
    then call $INSERTIONSORT(A, LINK, low, high, p)$
    else mid $\leftarrow \lfloor (low + high)/2 \rfloor$
        call $MERGESORT1(low, mid, q)$ //return list q//
        call $MERGESORT1(mid + 1, high, r)$ //return list r//
        call $MERGE1(q, r, p)$ //merge lists q and r to p//
  endif
end $MERGESORT1$

Algorithm 3.10   Mergesort using links

Procedure MERGESORT1 is initially invoked by placing the keys of the records to be sorted in $A(1:n)$ and setting LINK$(1:n)$ to zero. Then one says **call** MERGESORT1$(1, n, p)$ and p is returned as a pointer to a list of indices which give the elements of A in sorted order. INSERTIONSORT is used whenever the number of items to be sorted is less than 16. The version of INSERTIONSORT as given by Algorithm 3.9 needs to be altered so that it sorts $A(low:high)$ into a linked list beginning at p.

Now we present the revised merging procedure.

procedure $MERGE1(q, r, p)$
//q and r are pointers to lists contained in the global array//
//LINK(1:n). These lists can be used to obtain sorted subsets//
//of elements in the global array $A(1:n)$. After execution, a new//
//list has been formed, pointed at by p, which can be used to obtain//
//a sorted list of the elements in A in nondecreasing order.//
//The lists pointed at by q and r are destroyed.//
//Assume that LINK(0) is defined and that zero terminates a list.//
global n, $A(1:n)$, LINK(0:n)
local integer i, j, k
$i \leftarrow q; j \leftarrow r; k \leftarrow 0$ //the new list starts at LINK(0)//
while $i \neq 0$ **and** $j \neq 0$ **do**   //while both lists are nonempty do//
  if $A(i) \leq A(j)$ //find the smaller key//
    then $LINK(k) \leftarrow i; k \leftarrow i; i \leftarrow LINK(i)$ //add a new key to the list//
    else $LINK(k) \leftarrow j; k \leftarrow j; j \leftarrow LINK(j)$
  endif
repeat
if $i = 0$ **then** $LINK(k) \leftarrow j$
          else $LINK(k) \leftarrow i$
endif
$p \leftarrow LINK(0)$
end $MERGE1$

Algorithm 3.11   Merging linked lists of sorted elements

As an aid to understanding this new version of mergesort, suppose we simulate the algorithm as it sorts the eight element sequence $(-50, 10, 25, 30, 15, 70, 35, 55)$. We will ignore the fact that less than 16 elements would normally be sorted using INSERTIONSORT. The LINK array is initialized to zero. Table 3.3 shows how the LINK array changes after each call of MERGESORT1 completes. On each row the value of p points to the list in LINK which was created by the last completion of MERGE1. To the right are the subsets of sorted elements which are represented by these lists. For example in the last row $p = 2$ which begins the list of links 2, 5, 3, 4, 7, 1, 8, 6 which implies $A(2) \leq A(5) \leq A(3) \leq A(4) \leq A(7) \leq A(1) \leq A(8) \leq A(6)$.

	(0)	(1)	(2)	(3)	(4)	(5)	(6)	(7)	(8)
A:	–	50,	10,	25,	30,	15,	70,	35,	55,
LINK	0,	0,	0,	0,	0,	0,	0,	0,	0,

q r p	(0)	(1)	(2)	(3)	(4)	(5)	(6)	(7)	(8)	
1 2 2 2	0	1	0	0	0	0	0	0	(10, 50)
3 4 3 3	0	1	4	0	0	0	0	0	(10, 50), (25, 30)
2 3 2 2	0	3	4	1	0	0	0	0	(10, 25, 30, 50)
5 6 5 5	0	3	4	1	6	0	0	0	(10, 25, 30, 50), (15, 70)
7 8 7 7	0	3	4	1	6	0	8	0	(10, 25, 30, 50), (15, 70), (35, 55)
5 7 5 5	0	3	4	1	7	0	8	6	(10, 25, 30, 50) (15, 70)
2 5 2 2	8	5	4	7	3	0	1	6	(10, 15, 25, 30, 35, 50, 55, 70)

Table 3.3   Example of how the LINK array changes when MERGESORT1 is applied to $A(1:8) = (50, 10, 25, 30, 15, 70, 35, 55)$.

3.5 QUICKSORT

The divide-and-conquer approach may be used to arrive at an efficient sorting method different from mergesort. In mergesort, the file $A(1:n)$ was divided at its midpoint into subfiles which were independently sorted and later merged. In quicksort, the division into two subfiles is made such that the sorted subfiles do not need to be later merged. This is accomplished by rearranging the elements in $A(1:n)$ such that $A(i) \leq A(j)$ for all i between 1 and m and all j between $m + 1$ and n for some m, $1 \leq m \leq n$. Thus, the elements in $A(1:m)$ and $A(m + 1:n)$ may be independently sorted. No merge is needed. The rearrangement of the elements is accomplished by picking some element of A, say $t = A(s)$, and then reordering the other elements so that all elements appearing before t in $A(1:n)$ are less than or equal to t and all elements appearing after t are greater than or equal to t. This rearranging is referred to as partitioning.

Procedure PARTITION of Algorithm 3.12 (due to C. A. R. Hoare) accomplishes an in-place partitioning of the elements of $A(m:p - 1)$. It is assumed that $A(p) \geq A(m)$ and that $A(m)$ is the partitioning element. If $m = 1$ and $p - 1 = n$ then $A(n + 1)$ must be defined and must be greater than or equal to those elements in $A(1:n)$. The assumption that $A(m)$ is the partition element is merely for convenience and we shall see that other choices for the partitioning element than the first item in the set will be better in practice. The procedure INTERCHANGE(x, y) performs the assignments: temp $\leftarrow x$; $x \leftarrow y$; $y \leftarrow$ temp.

procedure *PARTITION(m, p)*
//Within $A(m)$, $A(m + 1)$, ..., $A(p - 1)$ the elements are//
//rearranged in such a way that if initially $t = A(m)$,//
//then after completion $A(q) = t$, for some q between m and $p - 1$,//
//$A(k) \le t$ for $m \le k < q$ and $A(k) \ge t$ for $q < k < p$.//
//*The final value of p is changed to q*//
integer m, p, i; **global** $A(m - 1, p)$
$v \leftarrow A(m)$; $i \leftarrow m$ //$A(m)$ is the partition element//
loop
  loop $i \leftarrow i + 1$ **until** $A(i) \ge v$ **repeat**   //i moves left to right//
  loop $p \leftarrow p - 1$ **until** $A(p) \le v$ **repeat**   //p moves right to left//
  if $i < p$
    then call *INTERCHANGE(A(i), A(p))*   //exchange $A(i)$ and $A(p)$//
    else exit
  endif
repeat
$A(m) \leftarrow A(p)$; $A(p) \leftarrow v$ //the partition element belongs at position p//
end *PARTITION*

Algorithm 3.12   Partition the set $A(m:p - 1)$ about $A(m)$

As an example of how PARTITION works consider the following array of 9 elements. The procedure is initially invoked as **call** PARTITION(1, 10). The vertical bars connected by a horizontal line indicate those elements which were interchanged to produce the next row. $A(1) = 65$ is the partitioning element and it is eventually (in the sixth row) determined to be the 5th smallest element of the set. Notice that the remaining elements are unsorted but they are partitioned about $A(5) = 65$.

(1)	*(2)*	*(3)*	*(4)*	*(5)*	*(6)*	*(7)*	*(8)*	*(9)*	*(10)*	i	p
65	70	75	80	85	60	55	50	45	$+\infty$	2	9
65	45	75	80	85	60	55	50	70	$+\infty$	3	8
65	45	50	80	85	60	55	75	70	$+\infty$	4	7
65	45	50	55	85	60	80	75	70	$+\infty$	5	6
65	45	50	55	60	85	80	75	70	$+\infty$	6	5
60	45	50	55	65	85	80	75	70	$+\infty$		

Using Hoare's clever method of partitioning a set of elements about a chosen element we can directly devise a divide-and-conquer method for completely sorting n elements. Following a call to procedure PARTITION two sets S_1 and S_2 are produced. All elements in S_1 are less than or equal to the elements in S_2. Hence S_1 and S_2 may be sorted independently. Each set will be sorted by reusing procedure PARTITION. Algorithm 3.13 describes the complete process as a program.

procedure $QUICKSORT(p, q)$
   //sorts the elements $A(p), \ldots, A(q)$ which reside//
   //in the global array $A(1:n)$ into ascending order;//
   //$A(n + 1)$ is considered to be defined//
   //and must be $\geq$ all elements in $A(p:q)$; $A(n + 1) = +\infty$//
   integer p, q; **global** $n, A(1:n)$
   if $p < q$
     then $j \leftarrow q + 1$
       call $PARTITION(p, j)$
       call $QUICKSORT(p, j - 1)$ //j is the position of the partitioning//
                                      //element//
       call $QUICKSORT(j + 1, q)$
  endif
end $QUICKSORT$

Algorithm 3.13   Sorting by partitioning

Analysis of Quicksort

In analyzing QUICKSORT, we shall count only the number of element comparisons $C(n)$. It is easy to see that the frequency count of other operations is of the same order as $C(n)$. We make the following assumptions:

(i)   the n elements to be sorted are distinct;
(ii)   the partitioning element v in PARTITION is chosen using a random selection process.

If $RANDOM(i, j)$ is a function that generates a random integer in the interval $[i, j]$, then the selection element is chosen by replacing the statements $v \leftarrow A(m)$; $i \leftarrow m$ in PARTITION by $i \leftarrow RANDOM(m, p - 1)$; $v \leftarrow A(i)$; $A(i) \leftarrow A(m)$; $i \leftarrow m$.

First, let us obtain the worst case value $C_w(n)$ of $C(n)$. The number of element comparisons in each call of PARTITION is at most $p - m + 1$.

(Note that if the elements are not distinct then at most $p - m + 2$ comparisons may be made.) Let r be the total number of elements in all of the calls to PARTITION at any level of recursion. At level one only one call, PARTITION$(1, n + 1)$ is made and $r = n$; at level two at most two calls are made and $r = n - 1$; etc. At each level of recursion, $O(r)$ element comparisons are made by PARTITION. At each level r is at least one less than the r at the previous level as the partitioning elements of the previous level are eliminated. Hence $C_w(n)$ is the sum on r as r varies from 2 to n or $O(n^2)$. An exercise examines input data on which QUICKSORT uses $O(n^2)$ comparisons.

The average value $C_A(n)$ of $C(n)$ is much less than $C_w(n)$. Under the assumptions made earlier, the partitioning element v in the call to PARTITION(m, p) has an equal probability of being the ith smallest element $1 \le i \le p - m$, in $A(m : p - 1)$. Hence the two subfiles remaining to be sorted will be $A(m : j)$ and $A(j + 1 : p - 1)$ with probability $1/(p - m)$, $m \le j < p$. From this we obtain the recurrence

$$C_A(n) = n + 1 + \frac{1}{n} \sum_{1 \le k \le n} (C_A(k - 1) + C_A(n - k)) \qquad (3.4)$$

$n + 1$ is the number of element comparisons required by PARTITION on its first call. Note that $C_A(0) = C_A(1) = 0$. Multiplying both sides of (3.4) by n we obtain

$$nC_A(n) = n(n + 1) + 2(C_A(0) + C_A(1) + \cdots + C_A(n - 1)) \qquad (3.5)$$

Replacing n by $n - 1$ in (3.5) gives

$$(n - 1)C_A(n - 1) = n(n - 1) + 2(C_A(0) + \cdots + C_A(n - 2))$$

Subtracting this from (3.5) we get

$$nC_A(n) - (n - 1)C_A(n - 1) = 2n + 2C_A(n - 1)$$

or

$$C_A(n)/(n + 1) = C_A(n - 1)/n + 2/(n + 1)$$

Repeatedly using this equation to substitute for $C_A(n - 1)$, $C_A(n - 2)$, ... we get

$$C_A(n)/(n + 1) = C_A(n - 2)/(n - 1) + \frac{2}{n} + \frac{2}{n + 1}$$

$$= C_A(n - 3)/(n - 2) + \frac{2}{n - 1} + \frac{2}{n} + \frac{2}{n + 1}$$

$$\vdots$$

$$= C_A(1)/2 + 2 \sum_{3 \leq k \leq n+1} 1/k$$

$$= 2 \sum_{3 \leq k \leq n+1} 1/k \tag{3.6}$$

Since

$$\sum_{3 \leq k \leq n+1} 1/k \leq \int_3^{n + 2} 1/x \, dx < \log_e(n + 2)$$

(3.6) yields

$$C_A(n) < 2(n + 1) \log_e(n + 2) = O(n \log n)$$

Even though the worst case time is $O(n^2)$ the average is only $O(n \log n)$. Let us now look at the stack space needed by the recursion. In the worst case the maximum depth of recursion may be $n - 1$. This happens for example when the partition element on each call to PARTITION is the smallest value in $A(m: p - 1)$. The amount of stack space needed may be reduced to $O(\log n)$ by using an iterative version of quicksort in which the smaller of the two subfiles $A(p: j - 1)$ and $A(j + 1: q)$ is always sorted first. Also, the second recursive call may be replaced by some assignment statements and a jump to the beginning of the algorithm. Incorporating these changes QUICKSORT takes the form of Algorithm 3.14.

procedure $QUICKSORT2(p, q)$
  integer $STACK(1: max)$, top //max $= 2 \lfloor \log_2 n \rfloor$ //
  global $A(1:n)$; **local integer** j
  $top \leftarrow 0$
  loop
    while $p < q$ **do**
      $j \leftarrow q + 1$
      call $PARTITION(p, j)$
      if $j - p < q - j$ **then** $STACK(top + 1) \leftarrow j + 1$
                        $STACK(top + 2) \leftarrow q$
                        $q \leftarrow j - 1$
                    else $STACK(top + 1) \leftarrow p$
                        $STACK(top + 2) \leftarrow j - 1$
                        $p \leftarrow j + 1$
      endif
      $top \leftarrow top + 2$
    repeat   //sort the smaller subfile//
    if $top = 0$ **then return endif**
    $p \leftarrow STACK(top)$; $q \leftarrow STACK(top - 1)$
    $top \leftarrow top - 2$
  repeat
end $QUICKSORT2$

Algorithm 3.14   Iterative version of QUICKSORT

We may now verify that the maximum stack space needed is $O(\log n)$. Let $S(n)$ be the maximum stack space needed. Then it follows that

$$S(n) \leq \begin{cases} 2 + S(\lfloor (n - 1)/2 \rfloor), & n > 1 \\ 0 & n \leq 1 \end{cases}$$

which is less than $2 \log n$.

As remarked in Section 3.4 INSERTIONSORT is exceedingly fast for n less than about 16. Hence QUICKSORT2 may be speeded up by using INSERTIONSORT whenever $q - p < 16$. The exercises explore various possibilities for selection of the partition element.

Testing

The QUICKSORT and MERGESORT procedures were tested on an IBM 370/158. In both bases the recursive versions were used and programmed in PL/I. For QUICKSORT the PARTITION procedure was altered to carry out the median of three rule (i.e. the partitioning element was the median of $A(m)$, $A((m + p - 1)/2)$ and $A(p - 1)$). The data set consisted of random integers in the range (0,1000). Table 3.4 records the actual average computing times in milliseconds.

n	1000	1500	2000	2500	3000	3500	4000	4500
MERGESORT	500	750	1050	1400	1650	2000	2250	2650
QUICKSORT	400	600	850	1050	1300	1550	1800	2050

n	5000	5500	6000	6500	7000	7500	8000	8500
MERGESORT	2900	3450	3500	3850	4250	4550	4950	5200
QUICKSORT	2300	2650	2800	3000	3350	3700	3900	4100

Table 3.4   Average computing times for sorting algorithms

Scanning the table we immediately see that QUICKSORT is faster than MERGESORT for all values. Also we observe that with each increment of 500, the time for QUICKSORT roughly increases by 250 milliseconds. The behavior of MERGESORT is somewhat more erratic, increasing by roughly 350 milliseconds, on the average, for each increase of 500. Of course this is only an approximation since both algorithms require $O(n \log n)$ time on the average. The exercises discuss other tests which would make useful comparisons.

3.6   SELECTION

The PARTITION algorithm of the previous section may also be used to obtain an efficient solution to the selection problem. In this problem, we are given n elements $A(1:n)$ and are required to determine the kth smallest element. If the partitioning element v is positioned at $A(j)$, then $j - 1$ elements are less than or equal to $A(j)$ and $n - j$ elements are greater than or equal to $A(j)$. Hence if $k < j$ then the kth smallest element is in $A(1:j - 1)$; if $k = j$ then $A(j)$ is the kth smallest element; if $k > j$ then the kth smallest element is the $(k - j)$th smallest element in $A(j + 1:n)$. The resulting algorithm is procedure SELECT (Algorithm 3.15). This procedure places the kth smallest element into position $A(k)$ and partitions the remaining elements such that $A(i) \leq A(k)$, $1 \leq i < k$ and $A(i) \geq A(k)$, $k < i \leq n$.

procedure *SELECT*(A, n, k)

//Within the array $A(1), \ldots, A(n)$ the kth smallest//

//element s is found and placed at position k.//

//It is assumed that $1 \leq k \leq n$.//

//The remaining elements are rearranged in such a//

//manner that $A(k) = t, A(m) \leq t$ for $1 \leq m < k$, and//

//$A(m) \geq t$ for $k < m \leq n. A(n + 1) = +\infty$.//

integer n, k, m, r, j;

$m \leftarrow 1; r \leftarrow n + 1; A(n + 1) \leftarrow + \infty$;

loop //each time the loop is entered, $1 \leq m \leq k \leq r \leq n + 1$//

   $j \leftarrow r$ //set j to the high index + 1 of the remaining items//

   call *PARTITION*(m, j) //j returns such that $A(j)$ is the jth smallest//

                    //value//

   case

     :$k = j$: **return**

     :$k < j$: $r \leftarrow j$ //j is the new upper limit//

     :**else**: $m \leftarrow j + 1$ //$j + 1$ is the new lower limit//

   endcase

repeat

end *SELECT*

Algorithm 3.15   Finding the kth smallest element

Let us simulate SELECT as it operates on the same array used to test PARTITION in section 3.5. If $k = 5$ then the first, call of PARTITION will be sufficient since 65 is placed into $A(5)$. Instead lets assume that we are looking for the seventh smallest element of A, i.e. $k = 7$. The next invocation of PARTITION is **call** PARTITION(6,10).

A:	(5)	(6)	(7)	(8)	(9)	(10)	i	p
	65	85	80	75	70	$+\infty$	10	9
	65	70	80	75	85	$+\infty$		

This last call of PARTITION has uncovered the 9th smallest element of A. The next invocation is **call** PARTITION(6,9).

A:	(5)	(6)	(7)	(8)	(9)	(10)	i	p
	65	70	80	75	85	$+\infty$	7	6
	65	70	80	75	85	$+\infty$		

This time, the sixth element has been found. Since $k \neq j$ is still true in SELECT, another call to PARTITION is made, **call** PARTITION(7,9).

A:	(5)	(6)	(7)	(8)	(9)	(10)	i	p
	65	70	80	75	85	$+\infty$	9	8
			|-------|				
	65	70	75	80	85	$+\infty$		

Now 80 is the partition value and that is correctly placed at $A(8)$. However, SELECT has still not found the 7th smallest element. It needs one more call to PARTITION, which is **call** PARTITION(7, 8). This performs only an interchange between $A(7)$ and $A(7)$ and then returns having found the correct value.

ANALYSIS OF SELECT

In analyzing SELECT we shall make the same assumptions that were made for QUICKSORT viz.:

i)   the n elements are distinct and

ii)   the partitioning element is chosen at random so that each element in $A(m:p)$ has an equal probability of being the partitioning element.

PARTITION requires $O(p - m)$ time. On each successive call to PARTITION, either m increases by at least one or j decreases by at least one. Initially $m = 1$ and $j = n + 1$. Hence, at most n calls to PARTITION may be made. Thus, the worst case complexity of SELECT is at most $O(n^2)$. $O(n^2)$ behavior occurs, for example, when the input $A(1:n)$ is such that the partitioning element on the ith call to PARTITION is the ith smallest element and $k = n$. In this case, m increases by one following each call to PARTITION and j remains unchanged. Hence, n calls are made for a total cost of $O(\sum_1^n i) = O(n^2)$. The average computing time of SELECT is however only $O(n)$. Before proving this fact, we shall specify more precisely what we mean by the average time.

Let $T_A^k(n)$ be the average time to find the kth smallest element in $A(1:n)$. This average is taken over all $n!$ different permutations of n distinct elements. Now, define $T_A(n)$ and $R(n)$ as follows:

$$T_A(n) = \frac{1}{n} \sum_{1 \le k \le n} T_A^k(n)$$

and

$$R(n) = \max_k \{ T_A{}^k(n) \}$$

$T_A(n)$ is the average computing time of SELECT. It is easy to see that $T_A(n) \le R(n)$. We are now ready to show that $T_A(n) = O(n)$.

Theorem 3.3:   The average computing time, $T_A(n)$, of SELECT is $O(n)$.
Proof: On the first call to PARTITION, the partitioning element v is the ith smallest element with probability $1/n$, $1 \le i \le n$ (this follows from the random selection of v). The time required by PARTITION and the **case** statement in SELECT is $O(n)$. Hence, there is a constant c, $c > 0$ such that:

$$T_A{}^k(n) \le cn + \frac{1}{n}\left(\sum_{1 \le i < k} T_A{}^{k-i}(n - i) + \sum_{k < i \le n} T_A{}^k(i - 1) \right), n \ge 2$$

So,

$$R(n) \le cn + \frac{1}{n}\max_k\left\{ \sum_{1 \le i < k} R(n - i) + \sum_{k < i \le n} R(i - 1) \right\}$$

$$= cn + \frac{1}{n} \max_k\left\{ \sum_{n-k+1}^{n-1} R(i) + \sum_{k}^{n-1} R(i) \right\}, \quad n \ge 2 \quad (3.7)$$

We shall assume that c is chosen such that $R(1) \le c$ and show, by induction on n, that $R(n) \le 4cn$.
Induction Base: For $n = 2$, (3.7) gives:

$$R(n) \le 2c + \frac{1}{2} \max \{ R(1), R(1) \}$$

$$\le 2.5c < 4cn.$$

Induction Hypothesis: Assume $R(n) \le 4cn$ for all n, $2 \le n < m$.
Induction Step: For $n = m$, (3.7) gives:

$$R(m) \le cm + \frac{1}{m}\max_k\left\{ \sum_{m-k+1}^{m-1} R(i) + \sum_{k}^{m-1} R(i) \right\}$$

Since we know that $R(n)$ is a nondecreasing function of n, it follows that

$$\sum_{m-k+1}^{m-1} R(i) + \sum_{k}^{m-1} R(i)$$

is maximized if $k = m/2$ when m is even and $k = (m + 1)/2$ when m is odd. Thus, if m is even we obtain

$$R(m) \le cm + \frac{2}{m} \sum_{m/2}^{m-1} R(i)$$

$$\le cm + \frac{8c}{m} \sum_{m/2}^{m-1} i$$

$$< 4cm$$

If m is odd then

$$R(m) \le cm + \frac{2}{m} \sum_{(m+1)/2}^{m-1} R(i)$$

$$\le cm + \frac{8c}{m} \sum_{(m+1)/2}^{m-1} i$$

$$< cm$$

Since, $T_A(n) \le R(n)$, it follows that $T_A(n) \le 4cn$ and so $T_A(n)$ is $O(n)$.
□

The space needed by select is $O(1)$.

By choosing the partitioning element v more carefully, we can obtain a selection algorithm with worst case complexity $O(n)$. In order to obtain such an algorithm, v must be chosen such that at most some fraction of the elements will be smaller than v and at most some (other) fraction of elements will be greater than v. Such a selection of v may be made using the median of medians (mm) rule. In this rule the n elements are divided into $\lfloor n/r \rfloor$ groups of r elements each (for some r, $r > 1$). The remaining $n - r \lfloor n/r \rfloor$ elements are not used. The median m_i of each of these $\lfloor n/r \rfloor$ groups is found. Then, the median mm of the m_i's, $1 \le i \le \lfloor n/r \rfloor$ is found. mm is used as the partitioning element. Figure 3.5 illustrates the m_i's and mm when $n = 35$ and $r = 7$. B_i, $1 \le i \le 5$ are the seven groups of elements. The five elements in each group have been arranged into nondecreasing order down the column. The middle elements are the m_i's. The columns have been arranged in nondecreasing order of m_i. Hence, the m_i corresponding to column 3 is mm.

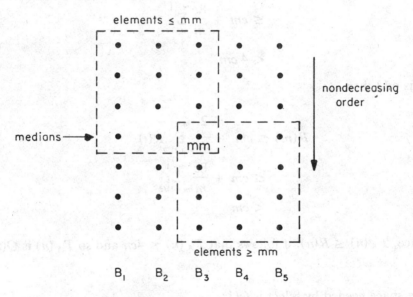

Figure 3.5   The median of medians when $r = 7$, $n = 35$

Since the median of r elements is the $\lceil r/2 \rceil$ smallest element, it follows (see Figure 3.5) that at least $\lceil \lfloor n/r \rfloor /2 \rceil$ of the m_i's are less than or equal to mm and at least $\lfloor n/r \rfloor - \lceil \lfloor n/r \rfloor /2 \rceil + 1 \geq \lceil \lfloor n/r \rfloor /2 \rceil$ m_i's are greater than or equal to mm. Hence, at least $\lceil r/2 \rceil$ $\lceil \lfloor n/r \rfloor /2 \rceil$ elements are less than or equal to (or greater than or equal to) mm. When $r = 5$, this quantity is at least $1.5 \lfloor n/5 \rfloor$. Thus, if we use the median of medians rule with $r = 5$ to select $v = mm$, we are assured that at least $1.5 \lfloor n/5 \rfloor$ elements will be greater than or equal to v. This in turn implies that at most $n - 1.5 \lfloor n/5 \rfloor < .7n + 1.5$ elements are less than v. Also, at most $.7 n + 1.5$ elements are greater than v. Thus, the median of medians rule satisfies our earlier requirement on v.

procedure $SELECT2$ (A, k, n)
   //find the kth smallest element in set A//
1.   divide A into $\lfloor n/r \rfloor$ subsets of size r each, ignore excess elements
2.   let M = $\{ m_1, m_2, \ldots, m_{\lfloor n/r \rfloor} \}$ be the set of medians of the above
     $\lfloor n/r \rfloor$ subsets.
3. $v \leftarrow SELECT2$ $(M, \lceil \lfloor n/r \rfloor /2 \rceil . \lfloor n/r \rfloor)$
4.   use PARTITION to partition A using v as the partitioning element
5.   assume v is position at j.
6.   **case**
     $:k = j:$ return (v)
     $:k < j:$ let S be the set of elements $A(1:j - 1)$
        return $(SELECT2$ $(S, k, j - 1))$
     :else: let R be the set of elements $A(j + 1:n)$
        return $(SELECT2$ $(R, k - j, n - j - 1))$
   endcase
end $SELECT2$

Algorithm 3.16 High level description of selection algorithm using
median of medians rule

The algorithm to select the kth smallest element uses the median of medians rule to determine a partitioning element. This element is computed by a recursive application of the selection algorithm. A high level description of the new selection algorithm appears as procedure SELECT2 (Algorithm 3.16). Procedure SELECT2 may now be analyzed for any given r. First, let us consider the case when $r = 5$ and all elements in A are distinct. Then, $|S|$ and $|R|$ (line 6) is at most $.7 n + 1.5$ which is no more than $3n/4$ for $n \geq 30$. Let $T(n)$ be the worst case time requirement of SELECT2. Steps

1, 2, 4 and 5 require at most $O(n)$ time (note that since $r = 5$ is fixed, each m_i (step 2) may be found in $O(1)$ time). The time for step 3 is $T(n/5)$ and that for step 6 is at most $T(3n/4)$ when $n \geq 30$. Hence, for $n \geq 30$ we obtain:

$$T(n) \leq T(n/5) + T(3n/4) + cn \qquad (3.8)$$

where c is chosen sufficiently large so that

$$T(n) \leq cn \quad \text{for} \quad n \leq 30$$

A proof by induction easily establishes that $T(n) \leq 20\,cn$ for $n \geq 1$. Procedure SELECT2 with $r = 5$ is a linear time algorithm for the selection problem on distinct elements! The exercises examine other values of r that also yield this behavior. Let us now see what happens when the elements of A are not all distinct. In this case, following a use of PARTITION (step 4) the size of S or R may be more than $.7n + 1.5$ as some elements equal to v may appear in both S and R. One way to handle the situation is to partition A into three sets U, S and R such that U contains all elements equal to v, S has all elements smaller than v and R has the remainder. Now step 6 is modified to:

case
   :$|S| \geq k$: **return** $(SELECT2 (S, k, |S|))$
   :$|S| + |U| \geq k$: **return** (v)
   :**else**: **return** $(SELECT2 (R, k - |S| - |U|, |R|))$
endcase

When this is done, the recurrence (3.8) is still valid as $|S|$ and $|R| \leq .7n + 1.5$. Hence, the new SELECT2 will be of linear complexity even when elements are not distinct.

Another way to handle the case of nondistinct elements is to use a different r. To see why a different r is needed, let us analyze SELECT2 with $r = 5$ and nondistinct elements. Consider the case when $.7n + 1.5$ elements are less than v and the remaining elements are equal to v. An examination of PARTITION reveals that at most half the remaining elements may be in S. We may verify that this is the worst case. Hence, $|S| \leq .7n + 1.5 + (.3n - 1.5)/2 = .85n + .75$. Similarly, $|R| \leq .85n + .75$.

Since, the total number of elements involved in the two recursive calls (step 3 and 6) is now $1.05n + .75 > n$, the complexity of SELECT2 is not $O(n)$. If we try $r = 9$ then, at least $2.5 \lfloor n/9 \rfloor$ elements will be less than or equal to v and at least this many will be greater than or equal to v. Hence, the size of S and R will be at most $n - 2.5 \lfloor n/9 \rfloor + \frac{1}{2}(2.5 \lfloor n/9 \rfloor) = n - 1.25 \lfloor n/9 \rfloor \le 31/36n + 1.25 \le 63n/72$ for $n \ge 90$. Hence, we obtain the recurrence:

$$T(n) \le \begin{cases} T(n/9) + T(63n/72) + c_1 n, & n \ge 90 \\ c_1 n, & n < 90 \end{cases}$$

where c_1 is a suitable constant.

An inductive argument shows that $T(n) \le 72c_1 n$, $n \ge 1$. Other suitable values of r are obtained in the exercises.

As far as the additional space needed by SELECT2 is concerned, we see that space is needed for the recursion stack. The recursive call from step 6 is easily eliminated as this call is the last statement executed in SELECT2. Hence, stack space is needed only for the recursion from step 3. The maximum depth of recursion is $\log n$. Hence, the recursion stack should be capable of handling this depth. As we shall see, in addition to this stack space, space is needed only for some simple variables.

Implementation of SELECT 2

Before attempting to write a SPARKS algorithm implementing procedure SELECT2, we need to decide (i) how the median of a set of size r is to be found and (ii) where we are going to store the $\lfloor n/r \rfloor$ medians of step 2. Since, we expect to be using a small r (say $r = 5$ or 9) an efficient way to find the median of r elements is to sort them using INSERTIONSORT (A, i, j). This algorithm is a modification of Algorithm 3.9 to sort $A(i:j)$. The median is now the middle element in $A(i:j)$. A convenient place to store these medians is at the front of the array. Thus, if we are finding the kth smallest element in $A(m:p)$ then the elements may be rearranged such that the medians are $A(m)$, $A(m + 1)$, $A(m + 2)$, etc. This makes it easy to implement step 3 as a selection on consective elements of A. Procedure SEL (Algorithm 3.17) results from the above discussion and the replacement of the recursive calls of step 6 by equivalent code to restart the algorithm (i.e. the calls are replaced by the **loop-repeat** of lines 3 and 18 and by code in lines 13-17). INTERCHANGE (X, Y) just interchanges the values of X and Y.

```
line    procedure SEL (A, m, p, k)
            //return i such that i ∈ [m, p] and A(i) is//
            //the kth smallest number in A(m:p). r is a global//
            //variable as described in the text//
1           global r
2           integer n, i, j
3           loop
4               n ← p - m + 1   //number of elements//
5                   for i ← 1 to ⌊n/r⌋ do   //compute medians//
6                       call INSERTIONSORT (A, m + (i - 1)*r, m + i*r - 1)
                        //collect medians in front part of A(m:p)//
7                   call INTERCHANGE (A(m + i - 1), A(m + (i - 1)*r
                        + ⌈r/2⌉ - 1))
8               repeat
9                   j ← SEL (A, m, m + ⌊n/r⌋ - 1, ⌈⌊n/r⌋ /2⌉)   //mm//
10                  call INTERCHANGE(A(m), A(j))         //set up partitioning//
                                                         //elements//
11                  j ← p
12                  call PARTITION (m, j)
13                  case
14                  :j - m + 1 = k: return (j)
15                  :j - m + 1 > k: p ← j - 1
16                  :else: m ← j + 1; k ← k - (j - m + 1)
17                  endcase
18              repeat
19          end SEL
```

Algorithm 3.17   SPARKS version of SELECT2

An alternative to moving the medians to the front of the array $A(m:p)$ (as in line 7) is to delete line 7 and use the fact that the medians are located at $m + (i - 1) r + ⌈r/2⌉ - 1, 1 ≤ i ≤ ⌊n/r⌋$. Hence, SEL, PARTITION and INSERTIONSORT need to be rewritten to work on arrays for which the interelement distance is $b, b ≥ 1$. At the start of the algorithm all elements are a distance of one apart i.e. $A(1), A(2), \ldots, A(n)$. On the first call from line 9 we wish to use only elements which are r apart starting with $A(⌈r/2⌉)$. At the next level of recursion, the elements will be r^2 apart and so on. This idea is developed further in the exercises. We shall refer to arrays with an inter-element distance of b as a b spaced array.

3.7 STRASSEN'S MATRIX MULTIPLICATION

Let A and B be two $n \times n$ matrices. The product matrix $C = AB$ is also an $n \times n$ matrix whose i, jth element is formed by taking the elements in the ith row of A and the jth column of B and multiplying them to give

$$C(i, j) = \sum_{1 \leq k \leq n} A(i, k) B(k, j) \qquad (3.9)$$

for all i and j between 1 and n. To compute $C(i, j)$ using this formula, we need n multiplications. As the matrix C has n^2 elements, the time for the resulting matrix multiplication algorithm, which we shall refer to as the "conventional" method is $\Theta(n^3)$.

The divide-and-conquer strategy suggests another way to compute the product of two $n \times n$ matrices. For simplicity we will assume that n is a power of 2, i.e. that there exists a nonnegative integer k such that $n = 2^k$. In case n is not a power of two then enough rows and columns of zeros may be added to both A and B so that the resulting dimensions are a power of two (see the exercises for more on this subject). Imagine that A and B are each partitioned into four square submatrices, each submatrix having dimensions $n/2 \times n/2$. Then the product AB can be computed by using the above formula for the product of 2×2 matrices, namely if AB is

$$\begin{bmatrix} A_{11} & A_{12} \\ A_{21} & A_{22} \end{bmatrix} \begin{bmatrix} B_{11} & B_{12} \\ B_{21} & B_{22} \end{bmatrix} = \begin{bmatrix} C_{11} & C_{12} \\ C_{21} & C_{22} \end{bmatrix} \qquad (3.10)$$

then

$$C_{11} = A_{11}B_{11} + A_{12}B_{21}$$
$$C_{12} = A_{11}B_{12} + A_{12}B_{22}$$
$$C_{21} = A_{21}B_{11} + A_{22}B_{21} \qquad (3.11)$$
$$C_{22} = A_{21}B_{12} + A_{22}B_{22}$$

If $n = 2$ then the above formulas are computed using a multiplication operation for the elements of A and B. These elements are typically floating point numbers. For $n > 2$ the elements of C can be computed using *matrix* multiplication and addition operations applied to matrices of size $n/2 \times n/2$. Since n is a power of 2, these matrix products can be recursively computed by the same algorithm we are using for the $n \times n$ case. This algorithm will continue applying itself to smaller size submatrices until n becomes suitably small ($n = 1$) so that the product is computed directly.

In order to compute AB using (3.11), we need to perform eight multiplications of $n/2 \times n/2$ matrices and four additions of $n/2 \times n/2$ matrices. Since two $n/2 \times n/2$ matrices may be added in time cn^2 for some constant c, the overall computing time, $T(n)$ of the resulting divide-and-conquer algorithm is given by the recurrence

$$T(n) = \begin{cases} b, & n \leq 2 \\ 8T(n/2) + cn^2, & n > 2 \end{cases}$$

where b and c are constants.

This recurrence may be solved in the same way as earlier recurrences to obtain $T(n) = O(n^3)$. Hence no improvement over the conventional method has been made. Since matrix multiplications are more expensive than matrix additions ($O(n^3)$ vs. $O(n^2)$) one may attempt to reformulate the equations for C_{ij} so as to have fewer multiplications and possibly more additions. Volker Strassen has discovered a way to compute the C_{ij}s of (3.11) using only 7 multiplications and 18 additions or subtractions. His method involves first computing the seven $n/2 \times n/2$ matrices P, Q, R, S, T, U, V as in (3.12). The the C_{ij}s are computed using the formulas in (3.13). As can be seen, P, Q, R, S, T, U, V may be computed using 7 matrix multiplications and 10 matrix additions or subtractions. The C_{ij}s require an additional 8 additions or subtractions.

$$\begin{aligned}
P &= (A_{11} + A_{22})(B_{11} + B_{22}) \\
Q &= (A_{21} + A_{22})B_{11} \\
R &= A_{11}(B_{12} - B_{22}) \\
S &= A_{22}(B_{21} - B_{11}) \\
T &= (A_{11} + A_{12})B_{22} \\
U &= (A_{21} - A_{11})(B_{11} + B_{12}) \\
V &= (A_{12} - A_{22})(B_{21} + B_{22})
\end{aligned} \tag{3.12}$$

$$\begin{aligned}
C_{11} &= P + S - T + V \\
C_{12} &= R + T \\
C_{21} &= Q + S \\
C_{22} &= P + R - Q + U
\end{aligned} \tag{3.13}$$

The resulting recurrence relation for $T(n)$ is

$$T(n) = \begin{cases} b, & n \le 2 \\ 7T(n/2) + a\,n^2, & n > 2 \end{cases} \qquad (3.14)$$

where a and b are constants.
Working with this formula we get

$$
\begin{aligned}
T(n) &= an^2(1 + 7/4 + (7/4)^2 + \ldots + (7/4)^{k-1}) + 7^k\,T(1) \\
&\le cn^2\,(7/4)^{\log_2 n} + 7^{\log_2 n}, \quad c \text{ a constant} \\
&= cn^{\log_2 4 + \log_2 7 - \log_2 4} + n^{\log_2 7} \\
&= O(n^{\log_2 7}) \approx O(n^{2.81})
\end{aligned}
$$

K. Glover has shown that there are exactly 36 different ways to compute the C_{ij}s of (3.11). All of these use 7 multiplications. The bound of $O(n^{2.81})$ may be further reduced if we could find a way to multiply two 2×2 matrices using less than 7 multiplications. But Hopcroft and Kerr have shown that 7 multiplications are necessary (see Chapter 10). Thus any further improvement can come only by considering higher dimensions such as 3×3 or 4×4 and using the recursive divide-and-conquer approach or by a totally different method. A new method by Victor Pan has improved the time to $O(n^{2.734})$.

Strassen's matrix multiplication algorithm has been programmed by Cohen and Roth in Algol and run on a PDP/10 computer. They have determined that Strassen's method is slightly faster than the conventional method when n is greater than about 40. However the difference in computing time remains small for values of n as large as 120. Another consideration is the space needed by the two methods. The conventional method needs only constant space in addition to that needed for A, B and C. In the divide-and-conquer approach space is needed for P, Q, R, S, T, U and V at each level of recursion. The total space needed is $7n^2(1/4 + 1/16 + 1/64 + \ldots) \le (7n^2/4)(4/3) = 7n^2/3$. By carefully reusing space which is no longer needed, some of this additional space may be saved.

Another question which researchers have investigated is how to store large matrices in a paging environment so that during the Strassen algorithm page fetches are minimized. Fischer and Probert give a "conversion" algorithm which permutes the elements of the two matrices in such a way that no more than $O(n^{2.81})$ page fetches are required.

At this point one may wonder why all this interest in matrix multiplication. As it turns out we can show that more typical matrix operations such as inverting a matrix and finding its determinant are directly related to matrix multiplication, in the sense that an efficient algorithm for one of these operations will immediately yield a similarly efficient algorithm for the other operations. Bunch and Hopcroft have shown that these other operations can be accomplished using no more than $O(n^{2.81})$ operations.

REFERENCES AND SELECTED READINGS

For a complete discussion of the maxmin problem see

"A sorting problem and its complexity", by I. Pohl, *CACM*, 15:6, 462–463.

For a more comprehensive discussion of mergesort and quicksort see

The art of computer programming: sorting and searching, Volume 3, by D. E. Knuth Sections 5.2.2 and 5.2.4

For more on FIND, SELECT, and QUICKSORT see

"Partition (Algorithm 63), Quicksort (Algorithm 64), and Find (Algorithm 65)", C. A. R. Hoare, *CACM*, vol. 4, no. 7, July 1961, 321–322.

Algorithm 489 (SELECT) by R. Floyd and R. Rivest, *CACM*, 18, (1975), 173.   3.

Quicksort, by R. Sedgewick, Computer science dept. Stanford technical report STAN-CS-75-492, May 1975

"Quicksort with equal keys", by R. Sedgewick, *SIAM J. Computing*, vol. 6 no. 2, June 1977, 240–267.

"Time bounds for selection", by M. Blum, R. Floyd, V. Pratt, R. Rivest and R. Tarjan, *J. CSS*, 7:4, (1972) pp. 448–461.

For an interesting way to merge files of unequal sizes see

"A simple algorithm for merging two disjoint linearly ordered sets", by F. K. Hwang and S. Lin, *SIAM J. Computing*, 1, (1972), 31–39.

For more information on the matrix multiplication problem see the following papers. Strassen's original method was given in

"Gaussian elimination is not optimal", by Volker Strassen *Numerische Mathematik*, 13, 354–356.

"On minimizing the number of multiplications necessary for matrix multiplication", by J. E. Hopcroft and L. R. Kerr, *SIAM J. App. Math.*, vol. 20, no. 1, Jan. 1971, 30–36.

"A note on Strassen's matrix multiplication method", by Keith Glover, Unpublished manuscript, Oxford University, England

"On obtaining upper bounds on the complexity of matrix multiplication", by Charles M. Fiduccia, *Proc. IBM Symposium on Complexity of Computations*, March 1972

"Fast matrix multiplication", by Charles M. Fiduccia *Proc. 3rd Annual ACM Symposium on Theory of Computing* 45-49, 1971

"On the implementation of Strassen's fast multiplication algorithm", by Jacques Cohen and Martin Roth, *Acta Informatica*, 6, 1976, 341-355.

"A note on matrix multiplication in a paging environment" by P. C. Fischer and R. L. Rivest, *Proc. ACM Annual Conf.* Oct. 1976, 17-21

"On the additive complexity of matrix multiplication" by R. L. Probert, SIAM J. *Computing*, (5, 2), June 1976, 187-203

"Further schemes for combining matrix algorithms" by P. C. Fischer, *Automata Languages and Programming -2nd Colloquium* ed. J. Loeckx, Springer Verlag, Berlin, 1974, 428-436.

"Triangular factorization and inversion by fast matrix multiplication", by James Bunch and John E. Hopcroft, *Math Comp.*, 28:125, 231-236.

"Duality in determining the complexity on noncommutative matrix multiplication", by John E. Hopcroft and Jean Musinski, *Proc. 5th Annual ACM Symposium on the Theory of Computing*, 73-87.

Also see

"Divide-and-conquer in multidimensional space", by John L. Bentley and Michael I. Shamos, *Proc. 8th Symposium on Theory of Computing*, ACM, May 1976, 220-230.

"On some generalizations of binary search" by David Dobkin and R. J. Lipton, *Proc. 6th Symposium on the Theory of Computing*, ACM, April, 1974, 310-316.

"Strassen's algorithm is not optimal" by Viktor Pan, *Proc. 19th Annual Symposium on the Foundations of Computer Science*, 1978.

EXERCISES

1. Solve the recurrence relation of formula (3.1) when

    (i) $g(n) = O(1)$ and $f(n) = O(n)$;
    (ii) $g(n) = O(1)$ and $f(n) = O(1)$.

2. Given the strategy for binary search as outlined in the beginning of section 3.2, write a recursive binary search program.

3. Using the result of exercise 2, run the recursive and iterative versions and compare the times. For appropriate sizes of n have each algorithm find every element in the set. Then try all $n + 1$ possible unsuccessful searches.

4. Devise a "binary" search algorithm which splits the set not into 2 sets of (almost) equal sizes, but into 2 sets of sizes one third and two thirds. How does this algorithm compare with binary search?

5. Devise a "ternary" search algorithm which first tests the element at position $n/3$ for equality with some value x and then possibly checks the element at $2n/3$ either discovering x or reducing the set size to one third of the original. Compare this with binary search.

6. (a) Prove that BINSRCH1 works correctly.
    (b) Verify that the following program segment correctly functions according to the specifications of binary search. Discuss its computing time.

    $low \leftarrow 1; high \leftarrow n$
    loop
    $mid \leftarrow (low + high)/2$
    if $x \geq A(mid)$
        then $low \leftarrow mid$
        else $high \leftarrow mid$
    endif
    until $low + 1 = high$ **repeat**

    Algorithm 3.19 A program segment

7. Using the transformations for removing recursion show the resulting iterative program that can be formed by starting with the result of exercise 2.

8. Prove the relationship $E = I + 2n$ for a binary tree with n internal nodes. E and I are the external and internal path length respectively.

9. Translate procedure MAXMIN into a computationally equivalent procedure which uses no recursion.

10. Test your iterative version of MAXMIN derived above against procedure STRAITMAXMIN. Count all comparisons.

11. There is an iterative program for finding the maximum and minimum which,

though not a divide-and-conquer based algorithm is probably more efficient than MAXMIN. It works by comparing consecutive pairs of elements and then comparing the larger one with the current maximum and the smaller one with the current minimum. Write out the algorithm completely and analyze the number of comparisons it requires.

12. Why is it necessary to have the auxiliary array B(low:high) in procedure MERGE. Give an example which shows why in place merging is inefficient.

13. The worst case time of procedure MERGESORT is $O(n \log n)$. What is its time in the best case? Can we say that the time for mergesort is $\Theta(n \log n)$?

14. A sorting method is said to be *stable* if at the end of the method identical elements occur in the same order as in the original unsorted set. Is mergesort a stable sorting method?

15. QUICKSORT is not a stable sorting algorithm. However if the key in $A(i)$ is changed to $A(i) * n + i - 1$ then the new keys are all distinct. After sorting, what transformation will restore the keys back to their original values?

16. In procedure PARTITION, Algorithm 3.12, discuss the merits or demerits of altering the statement "if $i < p$" to "if $i \leq p$". Simulate both algorithms on the data set (5, 4, 3, 2, 5, 8, 9) to see how they work differently.

17. Procedure QUICKSORT uses the output of procedure PARTITION, which gives the position where the partition element is placed. If equal keys are present then two elements may be properly placed instead of one. Show how you might change the output parameters of PARTITION so that QUICKSORT can take advantage of this situation.

18. Show how procedure QUICKSORT sorts the following sets of keys: (1, 1, 1, 1, 1, 1, 1) and (5, 5, 8, 3, 4, 3, 2).

19. There are many other ways to partition a set than procedure PARTITION. Consider modifying PARTITION so that i is incremented until $A(i) > v$ instead of $A(i) \geq v$. Rewrite PARTITION making all of the necessary changes to it and then compare it with PARTITION.

20. Compare the sorting methods MERGESORT1 with QUICKSORT2. Devise data sets which compare both the average and worst case times for these two algorithms.

21. Suppose $A(1:m)$ and $B(1:n)$ both contain sorted elements in nondecreasing

order. Write an algorithm which merges these items into $C(1:m + n)$. Your algorithm should be shorter than Algorithm 3.8 (MERGE) since you can now place a large value in $A(m + 1)$ and $B(n + 1)$.

22. Given a file of n records which are partially sorted as $x_1 \leq x_2 \leq \ldots \leq x_m$ and $x_{m+1} \leq \ldots \leq x_n$ is it possible to sort the entire file in time $O(n)$ using only a small fixed amount of additional storage?

23. Another way to sort a file of n records is to scan the file first merging consecutive pairs of size one, then merging pairs of size two, etc. Write a program which carries out this process. Show how your algorithm works on the data set keys (100, 300, 150, 450, 250, 350, 200, 400, 500).

24. (i) On what input data does QUICKSORT exhibit its worst case behavior?
    (ii) Answer (i) for the case when the partitioning element is selected according to the median of three rule.

25. With MERGESORT we included insertion sorting to eliminate the bookkeeping for small merges. How would you use this trick to improve QUICKSORT?

26. Take the iterative versions of MERGESORT and QUICKSORT and compare them for the same size data sets as was used in section 3.5.

27. A version of insertionsort is used by Algorithm 3.10 to sort small subfiles. However its parameters and intent are slightly different than the procedure INSERTIONSORT of Algorithm 3.9. Write a version of insertionsort which will work as Algorithm 3.10 expects.

28. Let u and v be two n bit numbers where for simplicity n is a power of 2. The traditional multiplication algorithm requires $O(n^2)$ operations. A divide-and-conquer based algorithm splits the numbers into two equal parts, computing the product as

$$uv = (a2^{n/2} + b)(c2^{n/2} + d)$$

(3.16)

$$= ac2^n + (ad + bc)2^{n/2} + bd$$

The multiplications ac, ad, bc, and bd are done using this algorithm recursively. Determine this algorithms computing time. What is the computing time if $ad + bc$ is computed as $(a + b)(c + d) - ac - bd$?

29. If k is a nonnegative constant then the solution to the recurrence

$$T(n) = \begin{cases} k, & n = 1 \\ 3T(n/2) + kn, & n > 1 \end{cases} \tag{3.17}$$

for n a power of 2 is

$$T(n) = 3kn^{\log_2 3} - 2kn \tag{3.18}$$

Prove this statement.

30. (i) Assume that SELECT2 is to be used only when all elements in A are distinct. Which of the following values of r guarantee $O(n)$ worst case performance? Prove your answers. $r = 3, 5, 7, 9, 11$.
    (ii) Do you expect the computing time of SELECT2 to increase or decrease if a larger (but still eligible) choice for r is made? Why?

31. Do exercise 30 for the case when A is not restricted to distinct elements. Answer (i) for $r = 7, 9, 11, 13, 15$. Also answer (ii).

32. Rewrite SEL, PARTITION, and INSERTIONSORT using the idea of b spaced arrays.

33. What test data would you use to determine worst case and average times for SELECT4?

34. Program SELECT1 and SELECT3. Determine when SELECT1 becomes better than SELECT3 on the average and also when SEL is better than SELECT3 for worst case performance.

35. Program SEL and determine optimal r values for worst case and average performance.

36. Section 3.6 describes an alternative way to handle the situation when A is not restricted to distinct elements. Using the partitioning element v, A is divided into three subsets. Write algorithms corresponding to SELECT1 and SELECT2 using this idea. Using your new version of SELECT2 show that the worst case computing time is $O(n)$ even when $r = 5$.

37. [Project] Programs the algorithms of exercise 36 as well as SELECT3 and SELECT4. Carry out a complete test along the lines discussed in section 3.6. Write a detailed report together with graphs explaining the data sets, test strategies and determination of $c_1, \ldots, c_4$. Write the final composite algorithms and give tables of computing times for these algorithms.

38. Write a SPARKS algorithm which multiplies two $n \times n$ matrices using $O(n^3)$ operations. Determine the precise number of multiplications, additions, and array element accesses.

39. Give a proof which shows that the recurrence relation $T(n) = mT(n/2) + an^2$ is satisfied by $T(n) = O(n^{\log m})$.

40. Verify by hand that equations (3.12) and (3.13) actually yield the correct values for C_{11}, C_{12}, C_{21} and C_{22}.

41. It is possible to consider the product of matrices of size $n \times n$ where n is a power of 3. Using divide-and-conquer the problem can be reduced to the multiplication of 3×3 matrices. The conventional method requires 27 multiplications. In how many multiplications must one be able to multiply 3×3 matrices so that the resultant computing time is smaller than $O(n^{2.81})$? Do the same for 4×4 matrix multiplication.

42. For any even integer n it is always possible to find integers m and k such that $n = m2^k$. To find the product of two $n \times n$ matrices Strassen suggests partitioning them into $2^k \times 2^k$ submatrices each having $m \times m$ elements. One then starts with Strassen's method to multiply the original matrices and uses the standard method for multiplying the required pairs of submatrices. Write a multiplication procedure for general n.

43. (Winograd) Let $n = 2p$, $V = (v_1, \ldots, v_n)$, $W = (w_1, \ldots, w_n)$. Then we can compute the vector product VW by the formula.

$$\sum_{1 \leq i \leq p} (v_{2i-1} + w_{2i})(v_{2i} + w_{2i-1}) - \sum_{1 \leq i \leq p} v_{2i-1} v_{2i} - \sum_{1 \leq i \leq p} w_{2i-1} w_{2i} \qquad (3.19)$$

which requires $3n/2$ multiplications. Show how to use this formula for the multiplication of two $n \times n$ matrices giving a method which requires $n^3/2 + n^2$ multiplications rather than the usual n^3 multiplications.

44. (Shamos) Let $X(1:n)$ and $Y(1:n)$ contain two sets of integers, each sorted in nondecreasing order. Write an algorithm which finds the median of the $2n$ combined elements. (Hint: use binary search)

45. Given two vectors $X = (x_1, \ldots, x_n)$, $Y = (y_1, \ldots, y_n)$, then $X < Y$ if there exists an i, $1 \leq i \leq n$ such that $x_j = y_j$ for $1 \leq j < i$ and $x_i < y_i$. Given m vectors each of size n, write an algorithm which determines the minimum vector. Analyze the time of your algorithm.

46. [Fiduccia]   The product of two 2×2 matrices can be rewritten as the matrix-vector product:

$$\begin{bmatrix} a_{11}\,a_{12} & 0 & 0 \\ a_{21}\,a_{22} & 0 & 0 \\ 0 & 0 & a_{11}\,a_{12} \\ 0 & 0 & a_{21}\,a_{22} \end{bmatrix} \begin{bmatrix} b_{11} \\ b_{21} \\ b_{12} \\ b_{22} \end{bmatrix}$$

the above matrix can be further decomposed into a product of three matrices:

$$\begin{bmatrix} 1 & 1 & 0 & 0 & 0 & 0 & 0 \\ 0 & -1 & 1 & 0 & 0 & 1 & 1 \\ -1 & 0 & 0 & -1 & 1 & 0 & -1 \\ 0 & 0 & -1 & 1 & 0 & 0 & 0 \end{bmatrix}$$

$$\begin{bmatrix} a-b & 0 & 0 & 0 & 0 & 0 & 0 \\ 0 & b & 0 & 0 & 0 & 0 & 0 \\ 0 & 0 & c-d & 0 & 0 & 0 & 0 \\ 0 & 0 & 0 & c & 0 & 0 & 0 \\ 0 & 0 & 0 & 0 & a+c & 0 & 0 \\ 0 & 0 & 0 & 0 & 0 & b+d & 0 \\ 0 & 0 & 0 & 0 & 0 & 0 & b+c \end{bmatrix} \begin{bmatrix} 1 & 0 & 0 & 0 \\ 1 & 1 & 0 & 0 \\ 0 & 0 & 0 & 1 \\ 0 & 0 & 1 & 1 \\ 1 & 0 & 1 & 0 \\ 0 & 1 & 0 & 1 \\ 1 & 0 & 0 & -1 \end{bmatrix}$$

Resolve the seven multiplication scheme implied by this matrix decomposition. Is it different from the one given in section 3.7?

47. *Testing*

In addition to SELECT1 and SEL, we can think of at least two more selection algorithms. The first of these is very straightforward and appears as Algorithm 3.18 (procedure SELECT3). The time complexity of SELECT3 is

$$O(n * min\{k, n - k + 1\})$$

Hence, it is very fast for values of k close to 1 or close to n. In the worst case, it complexity is $O(n^2)$. Its average complexity is also $O(n^2)$.

```
line    procedure SELECT3 (A, n, k)
            //return index i such that A(i) is the kth smallest//
            //element in A(1:n)//
1       integer i, j, l, min, max
2       case
3         :k ≤ n/2: for i ← 1 to k do   //find ith smallest element//
4         l ← i; min ← A(i)
5         for j ← i + 1 to n do
6         if A(j) < min then l ← j; min ← A(j)
7         endif
8         repeat
9         call INTERCHANGE (A(l); A(i))
10        repeat
11        :else: for i ← n to k by − 1 do   //find ith largest element//
12        l ← i; max ← A(i)
13        for j ← i − 1 to 1 by − 1 do
14        if A(j) > max then l ← j; max ← A(j)
15        endif
16        repeat
17        call INTERCHANGE (A(l), A(i)
18        repeat
19        endcase
20      end SELECT3
```

Algorithm 3.18   Straightforward selection algorithm

Another selection algorithm proceeds by first sorting the n elements into nondecreasing order and then picking out the kth element. A complete sort can be avoided by using a min-heap. The only k elements need to be removed from the heap. The time to set up the heap is $O(n)$. An additional $O(k \log n)$ time is needed to make k deletions. The total complexity is $O(n + k \log n)$. This basic algorithm can be improved further by using a max-heap when $k > n/2$ and deleting $n − k + 1$ elements. The complexity is now $O(n + \log n * \min\{k, n − k + 1\})$. Call the resulting algorithm SELECT4.

Now that we have four plausible selection algorithms, we would like to know which is best. Based upon the asymptotic analyses of the four selection algorithms, we can make the following qualitative statements about our expectations on the relative performance of the four algorithms.

i)   Because of overheads involved in SELECT1, SEL and SELECT4 and the relative simplicity of SELECT3, SELECT3 will be fastest both on the average and in the worst case for "small" values of n. It will also be fastest for large n and very small or very large k eg: $k = 1, 2, n, n − 1$.

ii) For larger values of n, SELECT1 will have best behavior on the average.

iii) As far as worst case behavior is concerned, SEL will outperform the others when n is suitably large. However, there will probably be a range of n for which SELECT4 will be faster than both SEL and SELECT3. We except this because of the relatively large overhead in SEL (i.e. the constant term in $O(n)$ is relatively large).

iv) As a result of (i)–(iii) it will be desirable to obtain composite algorithms for good average and worst case performance. The composite algorithm for good worst case performance will have the form of procedure SEL but will include line 4.1 as below

4.1 **case**
    $:n < c_1$: **return** ($SELECT3 (A, m, p, k)$)
    $:n < c_2$: **return** ($SELECT4 (A, m, p, k)$)
    endcase

Since the overhead in SELECT1 and SELECT4 is about the same, the constants associated with the average computing times will be about the same. Hence, SELECT1 may always be better than SELECT4 or there may be a small c_3 such that SELECT4 is better than SELECT1 for $n < c_3$. In any case, we expect there is a c_4, $c_4 > 0$ such that SELECT3 is faster than SELECT1 on the average for $n < c_4$.

In order to verify the preceding statements and determine c_1, c_2, c_3 and c_4, it is necessary to program the four algorithms in some programming language and run the four corresponding programs on a computer. Once the programs have been written, test data is needed to determine average and worst case computing times. So, let us now say something about the data needed to obtain computing times from which c_i, $1 \le i \le 4$ may be determined. Since, we would also like information regarding the average and worst case computing times of the resulting composite algorithms we need test data for this too. We shall limit out testing to the case of distinct elements.

To obtain worst case computing times for SELECT1, we shall change the algorithm slightly. This change will not affect its worst case computing time but will enable us to use a rather simple data set to determine this time for various values of n. We shall dispense with the RANDOM selection rule for PARTITION and instead use $A(m)$ as the partitioning element. It is easy to see that the worst case time is obtained with $A(i) = i$, $1 \le i \le n$ and $k = n$. As far as the average time for any given n is concerned, it is not easy to arrive at one data set and a k which exhibits this time. On the other hand, trying out all $n!$ different input permutations and $k = 1, 2, \ldots, n$ for each of these is not a feasible way to find the average. An approximation to the average computing time may be obtained by trying out a few (say 10) random permutations of the numbers $\{1, 2, \ldots, n\}$ and for each of these use a few (say 5) random values of k. The average of the times obtained may be used as an approximation to the average computing time. Of course, using more permutations and more k values with result in a better approximation. However, the number of permutations and k values we can use is limited by the amount of computational resources (in terms of time) we have available.

For SEL, the average time may be obtained in the same way as for SELECT1. For the worst case time we can either try and figure out an input permutation for which the number of elements less than the median of medians is always as large as possible and then use $k = 1$. A simpler approach is to just find an approximation to the worst case time. This can be obtained by taking the max of the computing times for all the tests done to obtain the average computing time. Since, the computing times for SEL vary with r, it will first be necessary to determine an r which yields optimum behavior. Note that the r's for optimum average and worst case behaviors may be different.

One may verify that the worst case data for SELECT3 is $A(i) = n + 1 - i$, $1 \leq i \leq n$ and $k = n/2$. The computing time for SELECT3 is relatively insensitive to the input permutation. This permutation affects only the number of times the 'then' clause of lines 6 (Algorithm 3.18) is executed. On the average, this will be done about half the time. This can be achieved by using $A(i) = n + 1 - i$, $1 \leq i \leq n/2$ and $A(i) = n + 1$, $n/2 < i \leq n$. The k value needed to obtain the average computing time is readily seen to be $n/4$.

An exercise examines how to obtain worst case and average times for SELECT4.

Computer Times

To verify the above qualitative statements, the four selection algorithms were programmed in FORTRAN by Elaine Frankowski and Warren Cartwright. The programs were run on a Cyber 74 computer and average and worst case times determined as described above. In programming algorithm SEL, b spaced arrays were used (thus eliminating line 7 of the algorithm). The value of r used was 5. In order to obtain accurate worst case times, the algorithms were made to perform the same selection on the same input sequence many times. The total time spent was divided by the number of times the selection was performed to obtain the time taken to solve the given problem instance. For average times (SELECT1 and SEL) for any fixed n many different input sequences and k were used. The total time spent was divided by the number of problem instances generated to obtain the average time. This approach was necessitated by the fact that the clock accuracy on the Cyber 74 is much higher than the time to solve one problem instance for small n. In all tests only distinct elements were used.

Table 3.5 gives the computing times obtained. There appear to be some "apparent" inconsistencies in the table. For example the worst case time for algorithm SEL with $n = 20$ is less than that when $n = 23$. This inconsistencies are easily explained by the fact that the worst case times are only the maximum time taken on any of the generated instances. This is only an approximation (hopefully a good one) to the actual worst case times. As can be seen, for worst case performance, SELECT3 is best for $n \leq 21$. For $n \geq 21$, SEL is fastest. SEL becomes faster than SELECT3 before SELECT4 does. So, $c_1 = 21$ and $c_2 = 0$. For average behavior, SELECT3 is fastest for $n \leq 11$ while SELECT1 is fastest when $n \geq 11$. Hence, $c_4 = 11$. SELECT4 is never faster than SELECT1. So, $c_3 = 0$.

One should remember that the values of $c_1 - c_4$ will in general be different if a different programming language or computer were used. The above values do however give "ball park" figures.

	SELECT1		SEL		SELECT3		SELECT4	
n	Average	Worse case	Average	Worst case	Average	Worst case	Average	Worst case
5	.2	.3	.3	.37	.12	.2	.3	.3
10	.3	.8	.64	.86	.32	.4	.8	.8
13	.4	1.0	.6	1.19	.50	.8	.9	1.1
15	.4	1.2	.9	1.28	.60	1.0	1.1	1.3
17	.5	1.5	1.0	1.36	.75	1.1	1.2	1.4
20	.5	1.9	1.27	1.77	1.1	1.6	1.6	1.9
23	.6	2.2	1.2	1.69	1.3	2.2	1.8	2.2
25	.6	2:6	1.5	2.01	1.5	2.4	1.9	2.4
50	1.3	7.6	3.1	4.32	5.5	9.7	4.0	5.5
75	1.5	15.0	4.9	5.86	11.0	19.0	7.0	8.5
100	2.0	26.0	6.5	12.0	17.0	31.0	9.0	12.0
300	10.0	60.0	34.0	41.0	422.0	765.0	45.0	66.0
1 000	19.0	2185.0	69.0	77.0			96.0	140.0
5 000	89.0	52000.02	356.0	375.0			557.0	843.0
10,000	175.0	> 2 minutes	717.0	759.0			1160.0	1745.0

Times in milliseconds
Table 3.5 Computing times for selection algorithms.
(Table prepared by Elaine Frankowski)

Chapter 4

THE GREEDY METHOD

4.1 THE GENERAL METHOD

The greedy method is perhaps the most straightforward design technique we shall be considering in this text, and whats more it can be applied to a wide variety of problems. Most, though not all, of these problems have n inputs and require us to obtain a subset that satisfies some constraints. Any subset that satisfies these constraints is called a *feasible* solution. We are required to find a feasible solution that either maximizes or minimizes a given *objective function*. A feasible solution that does this is called an *optimal solution*. There is usually an obvious way to determine a feasible solution, but not necessarily an optimal solution.

The greedy method suggests that one can devise an algorithm which works in stages, considering one input at a time. At each stage, a decision is made regarding whether or not a particular input is in an optimal solution. This is done by considering the inputs in an order determined by some selection procedure. If the inclusion of the next input into the partially constructed optimal solution will result in an infeasible solution, then this input is not added to the partial solution. The selection procedure itself is based on some optimization measure. This measure may or may not be the objective function. In fact, several different optimization measures may be plausible for a given problem. Most of these, however, will result in algorithms that generate suboptimal solutions.

We can describe the greedy method abstractly, but more precisely than above, by considering the following control abstraction.

procedure *GREEDY(A,n)*
  //*A*(1:*n*) contains the *n* inputs//
  solution ← φ //initialize the solution to empty//
  for *i* ← 1 **to** *n* **do**
    x ← *SELECT(A)*
    if *FEASIBLE(solution,x)*
      then *solution* ← *UNION(solution,x)*
    endif
  repeat
  return (*solution*)
end *GREEDY*

Algorithm 4.1   Greedy method control abstraction

The function SELECT selects an input from *A*, removes it and assigns its value to *x*. FEASIBLE is a Boolean-valued function which determines if *x* can be included into the solution vector. UNION actually combines *x* with solution and updates the objective function. Procedure GREEDY describes the essential way that a greedy based algorithm will look, once a particular problem is chosen and the procedures SELECT, FEASIBLE and UNION are properly implemented.

4.2 OPTIMAL STORAGE ON TAPES

There are *n* programs that are to be stored on a computer tape of length *L*. Associated with each program *i* is a length l_i, $1 \le i \le n$. Clearly, all programs can be stored on the tape if and only if the sum of the lengths of the programs is at most *L*. We shall assume that whenever a program is to be retrieved from this tape, the tape is initially positioned at the front. Hence, if the programs are stored in the order $I = i_1, i_2, \ldots, i_n$, the time t_j needed to retrieve program i_j is proportional to $\sum_{1 \le k \le j} l_{i_k}$. If all programs are retrieved equally often then the expected or *mean retrieval time* (MRT) is $(1/n)\sum_{1 \le j \le n} t_j$. In the optimal storage on tape problem, we are required to find a permutation for the *n* programs so that when they are stored on the tape in this order the MRT is minimized. Minimizing the MRT is equivalent to minimizing $D(I) = \sum_{1 \le j \le n} \sum_{1 \le k \le j} l_{i_k}$.

Example 4.1 Let $n = 3$ and $(l_1, l_2, l_3) = (5, 10, 3)$. There are $n! = 6$ possible orderings. These orderings and their respective D values are:

ordering I	$D(I)$
1,2,3	$5 + 5 + 10 + 5 + 10 + 3 = 38$
1,3,2	$5 + 5 + 3 + 5 + 3 + 10 = 31$
2,1,3	$10 + 10 + 5 + 10 + 5 + 3 = 43$
2,3,1	$10 + 10 + 3 + 10 + 3 + 5 = 41$
3,1,2	$3 + 3 + 5 + 3 + 5 + 10 = 29$
3,2,1	$3 + 3 + 10 + 3 + 10 + 5 = 34$

The optimal ordering is 3,1,2. $\square$

A greedy approach to building the required permutation would choose the next program based upon some optimization measure. One possible measure would be the D value of the permutation constructed so far. The next program to be stored on the tape would be one which minimizes the increase in D. If we have already constructed the permutation $i_1, i_2, \ldots, i_r$, then appending program j gives the permutation $i_1, i_2, \ldots, i_r, i_{r+1} = j$. This increases the D value by $\Sigma_{1 \le k \le r} l_{i_k} + l_j$. Since $\Sigma_{1 \le k \le r} l_{i_k}$ is fixed and independent of j, we trivially observe that the increase in D is minimized if the next program chosen is the one with the least length from among the remaining programs.

The greedy algorithm resulting from the above discussion is so simple that we won't bother to write it out. The greedy method simply requires us to store the programs in nondecreasing order of their lengths. This ordering can be carried out in $O(n \log n)$ time using an efficient sorting algorithm (e.g. heap sort from Chapter 2). Theorem 4.1 shows that the MRT is minimized when programs are stored in this order.

Theorem 4.1 If $l_1 \le l_2 \le \cdots \le l_n$ then the ordering $i_j = j$, $1 \le j \le n$ minimizes

$$\sum_{k=1}^{n} \sum_{j=1}^{k} l_{i_j}$$

over all possible permutations of the i_j.

Proof: Let $I = i_1, i_2, \ldots, i_n$ be any permutation of the index set $\{1, 2, \ldots, n\}$. Then

$$D(I) = \sum_{k=1}^{n} \sum_{j=1}^{k} l_{ij} = \sum_{1 \le k \le n} (n - k + 1) l_{ik}.$$

If there exist a, b such that $a < b$ and $l_{i_a} > l_{i_b}$ then interchanging i_a and i_b results in a permutation I' with

$$D(I') = (\sum_{\substack{k \\ k \ne a \\ k \ne b}} (n - k + 1) l_{ik}) + (n - a + 1) l_{i_b} + (n - b + 1) l_{i_a}.$$

Subtracting $D(I')$ from $D(I)$ we obtain:

$$D(I) - D(I') = (n - a + 1)(l_{i_a} - l_{i_b}) + (n - b + 1)(l_{i_b} - l_{i_a})$$

$$= (b - a)(l_{i_a} - l_{i_b})$$

$$> 0.$$

Hence, no permutation which is not in nondecreasing order of the l_i's can have minimum D. It is easy to see that all permutations in nondecreasing order of the l_i's have the same D value. Hence, the ordering defined by $i_j = j$, $1 \le j \le n$ minimizes the D value.   □

The tape storage problem can be extended to several tapes. If there are $m > 1$ tapes, $T_0, \ldots, T_{m-1}$, then the programs are to be distributed over these tapes. For each tape a storage permutation is to be provided. If I_j is the storage permutation for the subset of programs on tape j then $D(I_j)$ is as defined earlier. The *total retrieval time* (TD) is $\sum_{0 \le j \le m-1} D(I_j)$. The objective is to store the programs in such a way as to minimize TD.

The obvious generalization of the solution for the one tape case would be to consider the programs in nondecreasing order of l_i's. The program currently being considered is placed on the tape which results in the minimum increase in TD. This tape will be the one with the least amount of tape used so far. If there is more than one tape with this property then the one with smallest index can be used. If the jobs are initially ordered such that $l_1 \le l_2 \le \cdots \le l_n$ then the first m programs will be assigned to tapes $T_0, \ldots, T_{m-1}$ respectively. The next m programs will be assigned to tapes $T_0, \ldots, T_{m-1}$ respectively. The general rule is that program i is stored on tape $T_{i \bmod m}$. On any given tape the programs are stored in nondecreasing order of their lengths. Algorithm 4.2 presents this rule as a SPARKS program. It assumes that the programs are ordered as above. It has a computing time of $\theta(n)$ and does not need to know the actual program lengths. Theorem 4.2 proves that the resulting storage pattern is optimal.

```
procedure STORE(n, m)
  //n is the number of programs and m the number of tapes//
  integer m, n, j
  j ← 0   //next tape to store on//
  for i ← 1 to n do
    print ('append program', i, 'to permutation for tape', j)
    j ← (j + 1) mod m
  repeat
end STORE
```

Algorithm 4.2   Assigning programs to tapes

Theorem 4.2 If $l_1 \le l_2 \le \cdots \le l_n$ then Algorithm 4.2 generates an optimal storage pattern for m tapes.

Proof: In any storage pattern for m tapes, let r_i be one greater than the number of programs following program i on its tape. Then the total retrieval time TD is given by

$$TD = \sum_{i=1}^{n} r_i l_i.$$

In any given storage pattern, for any given n, there can be at most m programs for which $r_i = j$. From Theorem 4.1 it follows that TD is minimized if the m longest programs have $r_i = 1$, the next m longest programs have $r_i = 2$ and so on. When programs are ordered by length, i.e., $l_1 \le l_2 \le \cdots \le l_n$, then this minimization criteria is satisfied if $r_i = \lceil (n - i + 1)/m \rceil$. It is easy to see that Algorithm 4.2 results in a storage pattern with these r_i's. □

The above proof shows that there are actually many storage patterns that minimize TD. If we compute $r_i = \lceil (n - i + 1)/m \rceil$ for each program i, then so long as all programs with the same r_i are stored on different tapes and have $r_i - 1$ programs following them, the TD is the same. If n is a multiple of m then there are at least $(m!)^{n/m}$ storage patterns that minimize TD. Algorithm 4.2 produces one of these.

4.3 KNAPSACK PROBLEM

Now, let us try to apply the greedy method to solve a more complex problem. This problem is the knapsack problem. We are given n objects and a knapsack. Object i has a weight w_i and the knapsack has a capacity M. If a fraction x_i, $0 \le x_i \le 1$, of object i is placed into the knapsack then a profit of $p_i x_i$ is earned. The objective is to obtain a filling of the knapsack that maximizes the total profit earned. Since the knapsack capacity is M, we require the total weight of all chosen objects to be at most M. Formally, the problem may be stated as:

$$\text{maximize} \sum_{1 \le i \le n} p_i x_i \qquad (4.1)$$

$$\text{subject to} \sum_{1 \le i \le n} w_i x_i \le M \qquad (4.2)$$

$$\text{and} \quad 0 \le x_i \le 1, \quad p_i > 0, \quad w_i > 0, \quad 1 \le i \le n \qquad (4.3)$$

A feasible solution (or filling) is any set $(x_1, \ldots, x_n)$ satisfying (4.2) and (4.3) above. An optimal solution is a feasible solution for which (4.1) is maximum.

Example 4.2 Consider the following instance of the knapsack problem: $n = 3, M = 20, (p_1, p_2, p_3) = (25, 24, 15)$ and $(w_1, w_2, w_3) = (18, 15, 10)$. Four feasible solutions are:

	(x_1, x_2, x_3)	$\sum w_i x_i$	$\sum p_i x_i$
i)	(1/2, 1/3, 1/4)	16.5	24.25
ii)	(1, 2/15, 0)	20	28.2
iii)	(0, 2/3, 1)	20	31
iv)	(0, 1, 1/2)	20	31.5

Of these four feasible solutions, solution (iv) yields the maximum profit. As we shall soon see, this solution is optimal for the given problem instance. □

In case the sum of all the weights is $\le M$, then clearly $x_i = 1, 1 \le i \le n$ is an optimal solution. So, let us assume the sum of weights exceeds M. Now all the x_i's cannot be 1. Another observation to make is that all optimal solutions will fill the knapsack exactly. This is true because we can always increase by a fractional amount the contribution of some object i until the total weight is exactly M.

Several simply greedy strategies to obtain feasible solutions whose sum is identically M suggest themselves. First, we may try to fill the knapsack by including next the object with largest profit. If an object under consideration doesn't fit then a fraction of it is included to fill the knapsack. Thus each time an object is included (except possibly when the last object is included) into the knapsack we obtain the largest possible increase in profit value. Note that if only a fraction of the last object is included then it may be possible to get a bigger increase by using a different object. For example, if we have two units of space left and two objects with ($p_i = 4$, $w_i = 4$) and ($p_j = 3$, $w_j = 2$) remaining then using j is better than using half of i. Let us use this selection strategy on the data of Example 4.2.

Object one has the largest profit value ($p_1 = 25$). So, it is first placed into the knapsack. $x_1 = 1$ and a profit of 25 is earned. Only 2 units of knapsack capacity are left. Object two has the next largest profit ($p_2 = 24$). However, $w_2 = 15$ and it doesn't fit into the knapsack. Using $x_2 = 2/15$ fills the knapsack exactly with part of object 2 and the value of the resulting solution is 28.2. This is solution (ii) and it is readily seen to be suboptimal. The method used to obtain this solution is termed a "greedy method" because at each step (except possibly the last one) we chose to introduce that object which would increase the objective function value the most. However, this greedy method did not yield an optimal solution. Note that even if we change the above strategy so that in the last step the objective function increases by as much as possible, an optimal solution is not obtained for the instance of Example 4.2.

We can formulate at least two other greedy approaches attempting to obtain optimal solutions. From the preceding example we note that considering objects in order of nonincreasing profit values does not yield an optimal solution because even though the objective function value took on large increases at each step, the number of steps was few as the knapsack capacity was used up at a rapid rate. So, let us try to be greedy with capacity and use it up as slowly as possible. This would require us to consider the objects in order of nondecreasing weights w_i. Using Example 4.2, solution number (iii) is the resulting solution. This too is suboptimal. This time even though capacity was used slowly, profits weren't coming in rapidly enough. Thus, our next attempt will be an algorithm that strives to achieve a balance between the rate at which profit increases and the rate at which capacity is used. At each step we shall include that object which has the maximum profit per unit of capacity used. This means that objects will be considered in order of the ratio p_i/w_i. Solution (iv) of Example 4.2 will be produced by this strategy. If the objects have already been sorted into nonincreasing order of p_i/w_i then procedure GREEDY__KNAPSACK

(Algorithm 4.3) obtains solutions corresponding to this strategy. Note that solutions corresponding to the first two strategies can be obtained using this algorithm if the objects are initially in the appropriate order. Disregarding the time to initially sort the objects, each of the three strategies outlined above requires only $O(n)$ time.

```
procedure GREEDY_KNAPSACK(P, W, M, X, n)
    //P(1:n) and W(1:n) contain the profits and weights respectively of the n//
    //objects ordered so that P(i)/W(i) ≥ P(i + 1)/W(i + 1). M is the//
    //knapsack size and X(1:n) is the solution vector//
    real P(1:n), W(1:n), X(1:n), M, cu;
    integer i, n;
    X ← 0   //initialize solution to zero//
    cu ← M   //cu = remaining knapsack capacity//
    for i ← 1 to n do
        if W(i) > cu then exit endif
        X(i) ← 1
        cu ← cu - W(i)
    repeat
    if i ≤ n then X(i) ← cu/W(i) endif
end GREEDY_KNAPSACK
```

Algorithm 4.3 Algorithm for greedy strategies for the knapsack problem

We have seen that when one applies the greedy method to the solution of the knapsack problem there are at least three different measures one can attempt to optimize when determining which object to include next. These measures are total profit, capacity used and the ratio of accumulated profit divided by capacity used. Once an optimization measure has been chosen, the greedy method suggests choosing objects for inclusion into the solution in such a way that each choice optimizes the measure at that time. Thus a greedy method using profit as its measure will at each step choose an object that increases the profit the most. If the capacity measure is used, the next object included will increase this the least. For the last measure, the next object included will increase the ratio of profit/(capacity used) most or decrease it least (if no increase is possible). While greedy based algorithms using the first two measures do not guarantee optimal solutions for the knapsack problem, Theorem 4.3 shows that a greedy algorithm using the third strategy always obtains an optimal solution. This theorem is proved by comparing the greedy solution to any optimal solution. If the two solutions differ, then we find the first x_i at which they differ. Next, it is shown how to make the x_i in the optimal solution equal to that in the greedy solution without any loss in total value. Repeated use of this transformation shows that the greedy solution is optimal. This technique of proving solutions optimal will be used often in this text. Hence, you should master it at this time.

Theorem 4.3   If $p_1/w_1 \geq p_2/w_2 \geq \ldots \geq p_n/w_n$ then algorithm GREEDY__ KNAPSACK generates an optimal solution to the given instance of the knapsack problem.

Proof: Let $X = (x_1, \ldots, x_n)$ be the solution generated by GREEDY__ KNAPSACK. If all the x_i equal one then clearly the solution is optimal. So, let j be the least index such that $x_j \neq 1$. From the algorithm it follows that $x_i = 1$ for $1 \leq i < j$, $x_i = 0$ for $j < i \leq n$ and $0 \leq x_j < 1$. If X is not an optimal solution then there must exist another feasible solution $Y = (y_1, \ldots, y_n)$ such that $\Sigma p_i y_i > \Sigma p_i x_i$. Without loss of generality we may assume that $\Sigma w_i y_i = M$. Let k be the least index such that $y_k \neq x_k$. Clearly, such a k must exist. It also follows that $y_k < x_k$. To see this, consider the three possibilities: $k < j$, $k = j$ or $k > j$.

(i)   If $k < j$ then $x_k = 1$. But, $y_k \neq x_k$ and so $y_k < x_k$.
(ii)   If $k = j$ then since $\Sigma w_i x_i = M$ and $y_i = x_i$ for $1 \leq i < j$, it follows that either $y_k < x_k$ or $\Sigma w_i y_i > M$.
(iii) If $k > j$ then $\Sigma w_i y_i > M$ which is not possible.

Now suppose we increase y_k to x_k and decrease as many of $(y_{k+1}, \ldots, y_n)$ as is necessary so that the total capacity used is still M. This results in a new solution $Z = (z_1, \ldots, z_n)$ with $z_i = x_i$, $1 \leq i \leq k$ and $\Sigma_{k<i\leq n} w_i(y_i - z_i) = w_k(z_k - y_k)$. Then, for Z we have

$$\sum_{1 \leq i \leq n} p_i z_i = \sum_{1 \leq i \leq n} p_i y_i + (z_k - y_k) w_k p_k / w_k - \sum_{k < i \leq n} (y_i - z_i) w_i p_i / w_i$$

$$\geq \sum_{1 \leq i \leq n} p_i y_i + [(z_k - y_k) w_k - \sum_{k < i \leq n} (y_i - z_i) w_i] p_k / w_k$$

$$= \sum_{1 \leq i \leq n} p_i y_i$$

If $\Sigma p_i z_i > \Sigma p_i y_i$ then Y could not have been an optimal solution. If these sums are equal then either $Z = X$ and X is optimal or $Z \neq X$. In this latter case, repeated use of the above argument will either show that Y is not optimal or will transform Y into X, showing that X too is optimal. $\square$

4.4 JOB SEQUENCING WITH DEADLINES

We are given a set of n jobs. Associated with job i is an integer deadline $d_i \geq 0$ and a profit $p_i \geq 0$. For any job i the profit p_i is earned iff the job is completed by its deadline. In order to complete a job one has to process the job on a machine for one unit of time. Only one machine is available for processing jobs. A feasible solution for this problem is a subset, J, of jobs such that each job in this subset can be completed by its deadline. The value of a feasible solution J is the sum of the profits of the jobs in J or $\sum_{i \in J} p_i$. An optimal solution is a feasible solution with maximum value.

Example 4.3 Let $n = 4$, $(p_1, p_2, p_3, p_4) = (100, 10, 15, 27)$ and $(d_1, d_2, d_3, d_4) = (2, 1, 2, 1)$. The feasible solutions and their values are:

	feasible solution	processing sequence	value
(i)	(1, 2)	2, 1	110
(ii)	(1, 3)	1, 3 or 3, 1	115
(iii)	(1, 4)	4, 1	127
(iv)	(2, 3)	2, 3	25
(v)	(3, 4)	4, 3	42
(vi)	(1)	1	100
(vii)	(2)	2	10
(viii)	(3)	3	15
(ix)	(4)	4	27

Solution (iii) is optimal. In this solution only jobs 1 and 4 are processed and the value is 127. These jobs must be processed in the order: job 4 followed by job 1. Thus the processing of job 4 begins at time zero and that of job 1 is completed at time 2.   □

In order to formulate a greedy algorithm to obtain an optimal solution we must formulate an optimization measure to determine how the next job will be chosen. As a first attempt we can choose the objective function $\sum_{i \in J} p_i$ as our optimization measure. Using this measure, the next job to include will be the one that increases $\sum_{i \in J} p_i$ the most subject to the constraint that the resulting J is a feasible solution. This requires us to consider jobs in nonincreasing order of the p_is. Let us apply this criterion to the data of Example 4.3. We begin with $J = \phi$ and $\sum_{i \in J} p_i = 0$. Job 1 is added to J

as it has the largest profit and $J = \{1\}$ is a feasible solution. Next, job 4 is considered. $J = \{1, 4\}$ is also feasible. Next, job 3 is considered and discarded as $J = \{1, 3, 4\}$ is not feasible. Finally, job 2 is considered for inclusion into J. It is discarded as $J = \{1, 2, 4\}$ is not feasible. Hence, we are left with the solution $J = \{1, 4\}$ with value 127. This is the optimal solution for the given problem instance. Theorem 4.5 proves that the greedy algorithm just described always obtains an optimal solution to this sequencing problem.

Before attempting the proof let us first see how we may determine whether or not a given J is a feasible solution. One obvious way would be to try out all possible permutations of the jobs in J and check if the jobs in J can be processed in any one of these permutations (sequences) without violating the deadlines. For a given permutation $\sigma = i_1 i_2 i_3 \cdots i_k$ this is easy to do, as the earliest time job i_j, $1 \leq j \leq k$ will be completed is j. If $j > d_{i_j}$ then using σ, at least job i_j will not be completed by its deadline. However, if $|J| = i$ this requires checking $i!$ permutations. Actually, the feasibility of a set J can be determined by checking only one permutation of the jobs in J. This permutation is any one of the permutations in which jobs are ordered in nondecreasing order of deadlines.

Theorem 4.4 Let J be a set of k jobs and $\sigma = i_1, i_2, \ldots, i_k$ a permutation of jobs in J such that $d_{i_1} \leq d_{i_2} \leq \cdots \leq d_{i_k}$. J is a feasible solution iff the jobs in J can be processed in the order σ without violating any deadline.

Proof: Clearly, if the jobs in J can be processed in the order σ without violating any deadline then J is a feasible solution. So, we have only to show that if J is feasible then σ represents a possible order in which the jobs may be processed. If J is feasible then there exists $\sigma' = r_1, r_2, \ldots, r_k$ such that $d_{r_j} \geq j$, $1 \leq j \leq k$. Assume $\sigma' \neq \sigma$. Then let a be the least index such that $r_a \neq i_a$. Let $r_b = i_a$. Clearly, $b > a$. In σ' we can interchange r_a and r_b. Since $d_{r_a} \geq d_{r_b}$, the resulting permutation $\sigma'' = s_1, s_2, \ldots, s_k$ represents an order in which the jobs may be processed without violating a deadline. Continuing in this way, σ' can be transformed into σ without violating any deadline. Hence, the theorem is proved. $\square$

The above theorem is true even if the jobs have different processing times $t_i \geq 0$ (see the exercises).

Theorem 4.5 The greedy method described above always obtains an optimal solution to the job sequencing problem.

Proof: The proof technique used here is the same as that used in Theorems 4.3 and 4.4. Let (p_i, d_i), $1 \leq i \leq n$ define an instance of the job sequencing problem. Let $I = \{i_1, i_2, \ldots, i_k\}$ be the solution obtained by the greedy method. Let $J = \{j_1, j_2, \ldots, j_r\}$ be an optimal solution. We will show how J may be transformed into I without any loss in profit value. Hence, I must also be optimal.

Let us assume $I \neq J$. Without loss of generality, we may assume I and J to be ordered such that $p_{i_1} \geq p_{i_2} \geq \cdots \geq p_{i_k}$ and $p_{j_1} \geq p_{j_2} \geq \cdots \geq p_{j_r}$. Further, we may assume that in both I and J, jobs with equal profit value are in increasing order of index. Thus, if $p_{i_q} = p_{i_{q+1}}$ then $i_q < i_{q+1}$. We may also assume that the greedy method considers equal profit jobs in this order. Note that if $I \subsetneq J$ then, from the way the greedy algorithm works, J cannot be feasible. If $J \subsetneq I$ then J cannot be optimal. Hence, there exists a least index a such that $a \leq \min\{k, r\}$ and $i_a \neq j_a$. From the definition of the greedy method it follows that $p_{i_a} \geq p_{j_a}$. If $p_{i_a} > p_{j_a}$, $i_a \notin J$. If $p_{i_a} = p_{j_a}$ then from the ordering of equal valued jobs in I and J it follows that $i_a \notin J$. Hence, in both cases $i_a \notin J$.

Since J is feasible, it follows from Theorem 4.4 that the jobs in J can be processed in nondecreasing order of deadlines. Let R be the set of jobs processed by d_{i_a} in this order. Since each job is of unit time, $|R| = \min\{r, d_{i_a}\}$. If $|R| < d_{i_a}$ then $J \cup \{i_a\}$ is feasible and so J cannot be optimal. Hence, $|R| = d_{i_a}$. This together with the knowledge that $\{j_1, \ldots, j_{a-1}\} = \{i_1, \ldots, i_{a-1}\}$ implies R contains a job j_b with $b \geq a$. To see this, observe that otherwise, $R \subseteq \{j_1, \ldots, j_{a-1}\} \subsetneq \{i_1, \ldots, i_a\}$ and so $\{i_1, \ldots, i_a\}$ contains at least $d_{i_a} + 1$ jobs with deadline at most d_{i_a}. Hence, I cannot be feasible. This contradicts the assumption on I. Therefore, R contains a job j_b with $b \geq a$.

Let $J' = (J - \{j_b\}) \cup \{i_a\}$. From the selection of j_b and i_a, it follows that J' is feasible. Also, since $p_{i_a} \geq p_{j_a} \geq p_{j_b}$, it follows that the value of J' is no less than that of J. Repeating this replacement transformation, we can transform J' into I without loss of profit value. Hence, I is optimal. □

A high level description of the greedy algorithm just described appears as Algorithm 4.4. This algorithm constructs an optimal selection of jobs, J, to be processed by their due times. The selected jobs may be processed in the order given by Theorem 4.4.

line   procedure *GREEDY_JOB(D, J, n)*
         //J is an output variable. It is the set of jobs to be completed by//
         //their deadlines//
1        $j \leftarrow \{1\}$
2   **for** $i \leftarrow 2$ **to** n **do**
3   **if** all jobs in $J \cup \{i\}$ can be completed by their deadlines
              then $J \leftarrow J \cup \{i\}$
4   **endif**
5   **repeat**
6   **end** *GREEDY_JOB*

Algorithm 4.4   High level description of job sequencing algorithm

Now, let us see how to represent the set J and how to carry out the test of line 3. Theorem 4.4 tells us how to determine if all jobs in $J \cup \{i\}$ can be completed by their deadlines. We can avoid sorting the jobs in J each time by keeping the jobs in J ordered by deadlines. J itself may be represented by a one dimensional array $J(1:k)$ such that $J(r)$, $1 \leq r \leq k$ are the jobs in J and $D(J(1)) \leq D(J(2)) \leq \cdots \leq D(J(k))$. To test if $J \cup \{i\}$ is feasible, we have just to insert i into J preserving the deadline ordering and then verify that $D(J(r)) \leq r$, $1 \leq r \leq k + 1$. The insertion of i into J is simplified by the use of a fictitious job 0 with $D(0) = 0$ and $J(0) = 0$. Note also that if job i is to be inserted at position l then only the position of jobs $J(l)$, $J(l + 1)$, $\ldots$, $J(k)$ is changed after the insertion. Hence, it is necessary to verify only that these jobs (and also job i) do not violate their deadlines following the insertion. The algorithm which results from this discussion is procedure *JS* (Algorithm 4.5). The algorithm assumes that the jobs are already sorted such that $p_1 \geq p_2 \geq \ldots \geq p_n$. Further it assumes $n \geq 1$ and that the deadline $D(i)$ of job i is at least 1. Note that no job with $D(i) < 1$ can ever be finished by its deadline. Theorem 4.6 proves that *JS* is a correct implementation of the greedy strategy.

line   procedure *JS(D, J, n, k)*
        //$D(i) \geq 1, 1 \leq i \leq n$ are the deadlines, $n \geq 1$. The jobs are//
        //ordered such that $p_1 \geq p_2 \geq \ldots \geq p_n$. $J(i)$ is the ith job in//
        //the optimal solution, $1 \leq i \leq k$. Also, at termination $D(J(i))$//
        //$\leq D(J(i + 1)), 1 \leq i < k$.//
1   **integer** $D(0:n), J(0:n), i, k, n, r$
2      $D(0) \leftarrow J(0) \leftarrow 0$ //initialize//
3      $k \leftarrow 1; J(1) \leftarrow 1$ //include job 1//
4   **for** $i \leftarrow 2$ **to** n **do** //consider jobs in nonincreasing order of p_i//
        //Find position for i and check feasibility of insertion//
5         $r \leftarrow k$
6   **while** $D(J(r)) > D(i)$ **and** $D(J(r)) \neq r$ **do**
7            $r \leftarrow r - 1$
8   **repeat**
9   **if** $D(J(r)) \leq D(i)$ **and** $D(i) > r$ **then**
            //insert i into J//
10   **for** $l \leftarrow k$ **to** $r + 1$ **by** $- 1$ **do**
11            $J(l + 1) \leftarrow J(l)$
12   **repeat**
13         $J(r + 1) \leftarrow i; k \leftarrow k + 1$
14   **endif**
15   **repeat**
16   **end** *JS*

Algorithm 4.5 Greedy algorithm for sequencing unit time jobs with deadlines and profits

Theorem 4.6 Procedure *JS* is a correct implementation of the greedy based method described above.

Proof: Since $D(i) \geq 1$, the job with largest p_i will always be in the greedy solution. As the jobs are in nondecreasing order of the p_i's, line 3 includes the job with largest p_i. The loop of lines 4–15 considers the remaining jobs in the order required by the greedy method described earlier. At all times, the set of jobs already included in the solution is maintained in J. If $J(i)$, $1 \leq i \leq k$ is the set already included then J is such that $D(J(i)) \leq D(J(i + 1))$, $1 \leq i < k$. This allows for easy application of the feasibility test of Theorem 4.4. When job i is being considered, the loop of lines 6–8 determines where in J this job will have to be inserted. The use of a fictitious job 0 (line 2) allows easy insertion into position 1. Let q be such that $D(J(q)) \leq D(i)$ and $D(J(l)) > D(i)$, $q < l \leq k$. If job i is included into J then jobs $J(l)$, $q < l \leq k$ will have to be moved one position up in J (lines 10-12). From Theorem 4.4, it follows that such a move will retain feasibility of J iff $D(J(l)) \neq l$, $q < l \leq k$. This condition is verified in line 6. In addition, i may be inserted at position $q + 1$ iff $D(i) > q$. This is verified in line 9 (note $r = q$ upon exit from the **while** loop if $D(J(l)) \neq l$, $q < l \leq k$). The correctness of JS follows from these observations. $\square$

Complexity Analysis of Algorithm JS

For JS there are two possible parameters in terms of which its complexity may be measured. We can use n, the number of jobs and s, the number of jobs included in the solution J. The loop of lines 6-8 is iterated at most k times. Each iteration takes $O(1)$ time. If the conditional of line 9 is true then lines 10-13 are executed. These lines require $O(k - r)$ time to insert job i. Hence, the total time for each iteration of the loop of lines 4-15 is $O(k)$. This loop is iterated $n - 1$ times. If s is the final value of k i.e., s is the number of jobs in the final solution, then the total time needed by algorithm JS is $O(sn)$. Since $s \leq n$, the worst case time, as a function of n alone is $0(n^2)$. If we consider the job set $p_i = d_i = n - i + 1, 1 \leq i \leq n$ then algorithm JS takes $\theta(n^2)$ time to determine J. Hence, the worst case computing time for JS is $\theta(n^2)$. In addition to the space needed for D, JS needs $\theta(s)$ amount of space for J. Note that the profit values are not needed by JS. It is sufficient to know that $p_i \geq p_{i+1}, 1 \leq i < n$. $\square$

A Faster Implementation

The computing time of JS can be reduced from $O(n^2)$ to nearly $O(n)$ by using the disjoint set UNION and FIND algorithms (see Section 2.4) and using a different method to determine the feasibility of a partial solution. If J is a feasible subset of jobs then we can determine the processing times for each of the jobs using the rule: if job i hasn't been assigned a processing time then assign it to the slot $[\alpha - 1, \alpha]$ where α is the largest integer r such that $1 \leq r \leq d_i$ and the slot $[\alpha - 1, \alpha]$ is free. This rule simply delays the processing of job i as much as possible. Consequently, when J is being built up job by job, jobs already in J do not have to be moved from their assigned slots in order to accommodate the new job. If for the new job being considered there is no α as defined above then it cannot be included in J. The proof of the validity of this statement is left as an exercise.

Example 4.4 Let $n = 5$, $(p_1, \ldots, p_5) = (20, 15, 10, 5, 1)$ and $(d_1, \ldots, d_5) = (2, 2, 1, 3, 3)$. Using the above feasibility rule we have:

J	assigned slots	job being considered	action
ϕ	none	1	assign to [1, 2]
$\{1\}$	[1, 2]	2	assign to [0, 1]
$\{1, 2\}$	[0, 1], [1, 2]	3	cannot fit; reject
$\{1, 2\}$	[0, 1], [1, 2]	4	assign to [2, 3]
$\{1, 2, 4\}$	[0, 1], [1, 2], [2, 3]	5	reject.

The optimal solution is $J = \{1, 2, 4\}$. □

Since there are only n jobs and each job takes one unit of time, it is necessary only to consider the time slots $[i - 1, i]$, $1 \le i \le b$ such that $b = \min\{n, \max\{d_i\}\}$. One way to implement the above scheduling rule is to partition the time slots $[i - 1, i]$, $1 \le i \le b$ into sets. We shall use l to represent the time slot $[i - 1, i]$. For any slot i let n_i be the largest integer such that $n_i \le i$ and slot n_i is free. To avoid end conditions, we introduce a fictitious slot $[-1, 0]$ which is always free. Two slots i and j are in the same set iff $n_i = n_j$. Clearly, if i and j, $i < j$, are in the same set then i, $i + 1$, $i + 2$, $\ldots, j$ are in the same set. Associated with each set, k, of slots is a value $F(k)$. $F(k) = n_i$ for all slots i in set k. Using the set representation of Section 2.4, each set will be represented as a tree. The root node will identify the set. $F(\ )$ will be defined only for root nodes. Initially, all slots are free and we have $b + 1$ sets corresponding to the $b + 1$ slots $[i - 1, i]$, $0 \le i \le b$. At this time $F(i) = i$, $0 \le i \le b$. We shall use $P(l)$ to link slot i into its set tree. Using the conventions for the UNION and FIND algorithms of Section 2.4, $P(i) = -1$, $0 \le i \le b$ initially. If a job with deadline d is to be scheduled then we need to find the root of the tree containing the slot $\min\{n, d\}$. If this root is j then $F(j)$ is the nearest free slot provided $F(j) \ne 0$. Having used this slot, the set with root j should be combined with the set containing slot $F(j) - 1$.

Example 4.5 Using the problem instance of Example 4.4, the trees defined by the $P(i)$'s for the first three iterations, are:

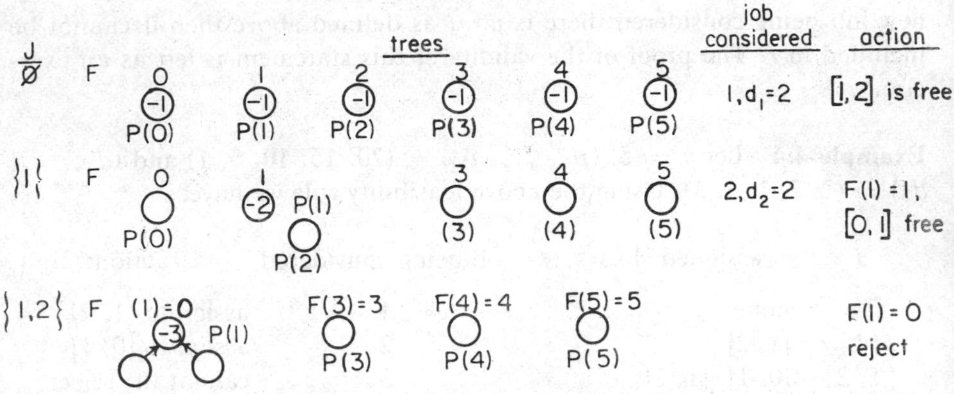

Figure 4.1 Fast job Scheduling

The faster algorithm appears as *FJS*. Its computing time is readily observed to be $O(n \, \alpha(2n, n))$ (recall that $\alpha(2n, n)$ is the inverse of Ackermann's function defined in Section 2.4). It needs an additional $2n$ words of space for F and P.

```
line   procedure FJS(D, n, J, k)
          //find an optimal solution J = J(1), ..., J(k)//
          //it is assumed that p₁ ≥ p₂ ≥ ... pₙ//
  1       integer D(n), J(n), F(0:n), P(0:n)
  2       for i ← 0 to n do   //initialize trees//
  3           F(i) ← i; P(i) ← −1
  4       repeat
  5       k ← 0   //initialize J//
  6       for i ← 1 to n do   //use greedy rule//
  7           j ← FIND(min(n, D(i))
  8           if F(j) ≠ 0 then k ← k + 1; J(k) ← i   //select job i//
  9                   l ← FIND(F(j) − 1); call UNION(l, j)
 10                   F(j) ← F(l)   //j may be new root//
 11           endif
 12       repeat
 13    end FJS
```

Algorithm 4.6 Faster algorithm for job sequencing

4.5 OPTIMAL MERGE PATTERNS

In Section 3.4 we saw that two sorted files containing n and m records respectively could be merged together to obtain one sorted file in time $O(n + m)$. When more than two sorted files are to be merged together the merge can be accomplished by repeatedly merging sorted files in pairs. Thus, if files $X1$, $X2$, $X3$ and $X4$ are to be merged we could first merge $X1$ and $X2$ to get a file $Y1$. Then we could merge $Y1$ and $X3$ to get $Y2$. Finally, $Y2$ and $X4$ could be merged to obtain the desired sorted file. Alternatively, we could first merge $X1$ and $X2$ getting $Y1$, then merge $X3$ and $X4$ getting $Y2$ and finally $Y1$ and $Y2$ getting the desired sorted file. Given n sorted files there are many ways in which to pairwise merge them into a single sorted file. Different pairings require differing amounts of computing time. The problem we shall address ourselves to now is that of determining an optimal (i.e. one requiring the fewest comparisons) way to pairwise merge n sorted files together.

Example 4.6 $X1$, $X2$ and $X3$ are three sorted files of length 30, 20 and 10 records each. Merging $X1$ and $X2$ requires 50 record moves. Merging the result with $X3$ requires another 60 moves. The total number of record moves required to merge the three files this way is 110. If instead, we first merge $X2$ and $X3$ (taking 30 moves) and then X1 (taking 60 moves), the total record moves made is only 90. Hence, the second merge pattern is faster than the first.   □

A greedy attempt to obtain an optimal merge pattern is easy to formulate. Since merging an n record file and an m record file requires possibly $n + m$ records moves, the obvious choice for a selection criterion is: at each step merge the two smallest size files together. Thus, if we have five files $(F_1, \ldots, F_5)$ with sizes (20, 30, 10, 5, 30) our greedy rule would generate the following merge pattern: merge F_4 and F_3 to get Z_1 ($|Z_1| = 15$); merge Z_1 and F_1 to get Z_2 ($|Z_2| = 35$); merge F_2 and F_5 to get Z_3 ($|Z_3| = 60$); merge Z_2 and Z_3 to get the answer Z_4. The total number of record moves is 205. One can verify that this is an optimal merge pattern for the given problem instance.

The merge pattern such as the one just described will be referred to as a 2-*way merge pattern* (each merge step involves the merging of two files). 2-way merge patterns may be represented by binary merge trees. Figure 4.2 shows a binary merge tree representing the optimal merge pattern obtained for the above five files. The leaf nodes are drawn as squares and represent the given five files. These nodes will be called external nodes. The remaining nodes are drawn circular and are called *internal* nodes. Each internal node has exactly two children and it represents the file obtained by merging the files represented by its two children. The number in each node is the length (i.e., the number of records) of the file represented by that node.

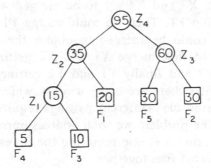

Figure 4.2   Binary merge tree representing a merge pattern

The external node F_4 is at a distance of 3 from the root node Z_4 (a node at level i is at a distance of $i - 1$ from the root). Hence, the records of file F_4 will be moved three times, once to get Z_1, once again to get Z_2 and finally one more time to get Z_4. If d_i is the distance from the root to the external node for file F_i and q_i the length of F_i then the total number of record moves for this binary merge tree is

$$\sum_{i=1}^{n} d_i q_i.$$

This sum is called the *weighted external path length* of the tree.

An optimal 2-way merge pattern corresponds to a binary merge tree with minimum weighted external path length. The procedure TREE of Algorithm 4.7 uses the greedy rule stated earlier to obtain a 2-way merge tree for n files. The algorithm has as input a list L of n trees. Each node in a tree has three fields, LCHILD, RCHILD and WEIGHT. Initially, each tree in L has exactly one node. This node is an external node and has LCHILD and RCHILD fields zero while the WEIGHT is the length of one of the n files to be merged. During the course of the algorithm, for any tree in L with root node T, WEIGHT(T) is the length of the merged file it represents (WEIGHT(T) equals the sum of the lengths of the external nodes in tree T). Procedure TREE uses three subalgorithms, GETNODE(T),

LEAST(*L*) and INSERT(*L*, *T*). GETNODE(*T*) provides a new node for use in building the tree. LEAST(*L*) finds a tree in *L* whose root has least WEIGHT. This tree is removed from *L*. INSERT(*L*, *T*) inserts the tree with root *T* into the list *L*. Theorem 4.7 below will show that the greedy procedure TREE (Algorithm 4.7) generates an optimal 2-way merge tree.

```
line   procedure TREE(L, n)
         //L is a list of n single node binary trees as described above//
1        for i ← 1 to n − 1 do
2          call GETNODE(T)    //merge two trees with//
3          LCHILD(T) ← LEAST(L)    //smallest lengths//
4          RCHILD(T) ← LEAST(L)
5          WEIGHT(T) ← WEIGHT(LCHILD(T)) + WEIGHT(RCHILD(T))
6          call INSERT(L, T)
7        repeat
8        return (LEAST(L))    //tree left in L is the merge tree//
9      end TREE
```

Algorithm 4.7   Algorithm to generate a 2-way merge tree

Example 4.7   Let us see how algorithm TREE works when *L* initially represents 6 files with lengths (2, 3, 5, 7, 9, 13). Figure 4.3 shows the list *L* at the end of each iteration of the **for** loop. The binary merge tree which results at the end of the algorithm can be used to determine which files are merged. Merging is performed on those files which are "lowest" (have the greatest depth) in the tree.

Analysis of Algorithm 4.7

The main loop is executed *n* − 1 times. If *L* is kept in nondecreasing order according to the WEIGHT value in the roots, then LEAST(*L*) requires only $O(1)$ time and INSERT(*L*, *T*) can be done in $O(n)$ time. Hence the total time taken is $O(n^2)$. In case *L* is represented as a min-heap where the root value is ≤ the values of its children (Section 2.3), then LEAST(*L*) and INSERT(*L*, *T*) can be done in $O(\log n)$ time. In this case the computing time for TREE is $O(n \log n)$. Some speed-up may be obtained by combining the INSERT of line 6 with the LEAST of line 4.

Theorem 4.7   If *L* initially contains *n* ≥ 1 single node trees with WEIGHT values $(q_1, q_2, \ldots, q_n)$ then algorithm TREE generates an optimal 2-way merge tree for *n* files with these lengths.

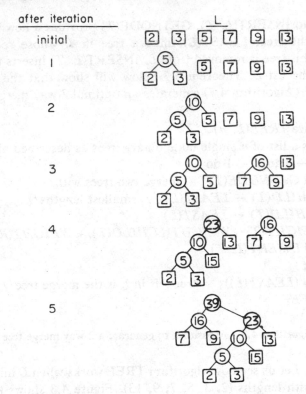

Figure 4.3   Trees in list L of procedure TREE for Example 4.7

Proof: The proof is by induction on n. For $n = 1$, a tree with no internal nodes is returned and this tree is clearly optimal. For the induction hypothesis, assume the algorithm generates an optimal 2-way merge tree for all $(q_1, q_2, \ldots, q_m)$, $1 \leq m < n$. We will show that the algorithm also generates optimal trees for all $(q_1, q_2, \ldots, q_n)$. Without loss of generality, we may assume $q_1 \leq q_2 \leq \cdots \leq q_n$ and that q_1 and q_2 are the values of the WEIGHT fields of the trees found by algorithm LEAST in lines 3 and 4 during the first iteration of the **for** loop. Now, the subtree T of Figure 4.4 is created. Let T' be an optimal 2-way merge tree for $(q_1, q_2, \ldots, q_n)$. Let P be an internal node of maximum distance from the root. If the children of P are not q_1 and q_2 then we may interchange the present children with q_1 and q_2 without increasing the weighted external path length of T'. Hence, T is also a subtree in an optimal merge tree. Now in T' if we replace T by an external node with weight $q_1 + q_2$ then the resulting tree T'' is an optimal merge tree for $(q_1 + q_2, q_3, \ldots q_n)$. From the induction hypothesis procedure TREE, after replacing T by the external node with value $q_1 + q_2$, proceeds to find an optimal merge tree for $(q_1 + q_2, q_3,$ $\ldots, q_n)$. Hence, TREE generates an optimal merge tree for $(q_1, q_2, \ldots, q_n)$. $\square$

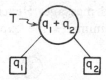

Figure 4.4   The simplest binary merge tree

The greedy method to generate merge trees also works for the case of k-ary merging. In this case the corresponding merge tree is a k-ary tree. Since all internal nodes must have degree k, for certain values of n there does not correspond a k-ary merge tree. For example when $k = 3$ there is no k-ary merge tree with $n = 2$ external nodes. Hence, it is necessary to introduce a certain number of "dummy" external nodes. Each dummy node is assigned a q_i of zero. This dummy value does not affect the weighted external path length of the resulting k-ary tree. Exercise 13 shows that a k-ary tree with all internal nodes having degree k exists only when the number of external nodes n satisfies the equality $n \bmod (k - 1) = 1$. Hence, at most $k - 2$ dummy nodes have to be added. The greedy rule to generate optimal merge trees is: at each step choose k subtrees with least length for merging. Exercise 14 proves the optimality of this rule.

Huffman Codes

Another application of binary trees with minimal weighted external path length is to obtain an optimal set of codes for messages $M_1, \ldots, M_{n+1}$. Each code is an binary string which will be used for transmission of the corresponding message. At the receiving end the code will be decoded using a decode tree. A decode tree is a binary tree in which external nodes represent messages. The binary bits in the code word for a message determine the branching needed at each level of the decode tree to reach the correct external node. For example, if we interpret a zero as a left branch and a one as a right branch, then the decode tree of Figure 4.5 corresponds to codes 000, 001, 01, and 1 for messages M_1, M_2, M_3 and M_4 respectively. These codes are called Huffman codes. The cost of decoding a code word is proportional to the number of bits in the code. This number is equal to the distance of the corresponding external node from the root node. If q_i is the relative frequency with which message M_i will be transmitted, then the expected decode time is $\Sigma_{1 \leq i \leq n+1} \, q_i d_i$ where d_i is the distance of the external node for message M_i from the root node. The expected decode time is minimized by choosing code words resulting in a decode tree with minimal weighted external path length! Note that $\Sigma_{1 \leq i \leq n+1} \, q_i d_i$ is also the expected length of a transmitted message. Hence the code which minimizes expected decode time also minimizes the expected length of a message.

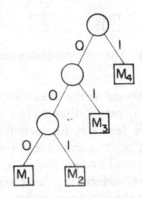

Figure 4.5   Huffman codes

4.6   MINIMUM SPANNING TREES

Definition   Let $G = (V, E)$ be an undirected connected graph. A subgraph $T = (V, E')$ of G is a *spanning tree* of G iff T is a tree.

Example 4.8   Figure 4.6 shows the complete graph on 4 nodes together with three of its spanning trees.   □

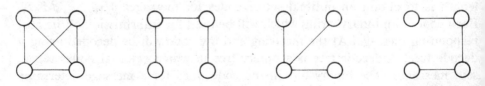

Figure 4.6   An undirected graph and three of its spanning trees

Spanning trees can be used to obtain an independent set of circuit equations for an electrical network. First, a spanning tree for the electrical network is obtained. Let B be the set of network edges not in the spanning tree. Adding an edge from B to the spanning tree creates a cycle. Different edges from B result in different cycles. Kirchoff's second law is used on each cycle to obtain a circuit equation. The cycles obtained in this way are independent (i.e., none of these cycles can be obtained by taking a linear combination of the remaining cycles) as each contains an edge from B which is not contained in any other cycle. Hence, the circuit equations so obtained are also independent. In fact, it may be shown that the cycles obtained by introducing the edges of B one at a time into the resulting spanning tree form a cycle basis and so all other cycles in the graph can be constructed by taking a linear combination of the cycles in the basis (see Harary in the references for further details).

It is not difficult to imagine other applications for spanning trees. One that is of interest arises from the property that a spanning tree is a minimal subgraph G' of G such that $V(G') = V(G)$ and G' is connected (by a minimal subgraph, we mean one with the fewest number of edges). Any connected graph with n vertices must have at least $n - 1$ edges and all connected graphs with $n - 1$ edges are trees. If the nodes of G represent cities and the edges represent possible communication links connecting 2 cities, then the minimum number of links needed to connect the n cities is $n - 1$. The spanning trees of G will represent all feasible choices.

In any practical situation, however, the edges will have weights assigned to them. These weights might represent the cost of construction, the length of the link, etc. Given such a weighted graph one would then wish to select for construction a set of communication links that would connect all the cities and have minimum total cost or be of minimum total length. In either case the links selected will have to form a tree (assuming all weights are positive). In case this is not so, then the selection of links contains a cycle. Removal of any one of the links on this cycle will result in a link selection of less cost connecting all cities. We are therefore interested in finding a spanning tree of G with minimum cost. (The cost of a spanning

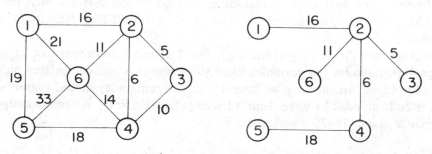

Figure 4.7 A graph and one of its minimum costs spanning trees

tree is the sum of the costs of the edges in that tree.) Figure 4.7 shows a graph and one of its minimum cost spanning trees.

A greedy method to obtain a minimum cost spanning tree would build this tree edge by edge. The next edge to include is chosen according to some optimization criteria. The simplest such criteria would be to choose an edge that results in a minimum increase in the sum of the costs of the edges so far included. There are two possible ways to interpret this criteria. In the first, the set of edges so far selected form a tree. Thus, if A is the set of edges so far selected then, A forms a tree. The next edge (u, v) to be included in A is a minimum cost edge not in A with the property that $A \cup \{(u, v)\}$ is also a tree. Exercise 17 shows that this selection criteria results in a minimum cost spanning tree. The corresponding algorithm is known as Prim's algorithm.

Example 4.9 Figure 4.8(b) shows the working of Prim's method on the graph of Figure 4.8(a). The spanning tree obtained has a cost of 105.   □

Having seen how Prim's method works, let us obtain a SPARKS algorithm to find a minimum spanning tree using this method. The algorithm will start with a tree that includes only a minimum cost edge of G. Then, edges will be added to this tree one by one. The next edge (i, j) to be added is such that i is a vertex already included in the tree, j is a vertex not yet included and the cost of (i, j), COST(i, j) is minimum among all edges (k, l) such that vertex k is in the tree and vertex l not in the tree. In order to determine this edge (i, j) efficiently, we shall associate with each vertex j not yet included in the tree a value NEAR(j). NEAR(j) is a vertex in the tree such that COST$(j,$ NEAR$(j))$ is minimum among all choices for NEAR(j). We shall define NEAR$(j) = 0$ for all vertices j that are already in the tree. The next edge to include is defined by the vertex j such that NEAR$(j) \neq 0$ (j not already in the tree) and COST$(j,$ NEAR$(j))$ is minimum.

In procedure PRIM (Algorithm 4.8), line 3 selects a minimum cost edge. Lines 4–10 initialize the variables so as to represent a tree comprising only the edge (k, l). In the loop of lines 11–21 the remainder of the spanning tree is built up edge by edge. Line 12 selects $(j,$ NEAR$(j))$ as the next edge to include. Lines 16–20 update NEAR( ).

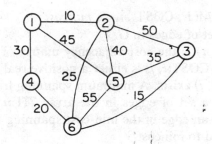

Figure 4.8(a)   Graph for Examples 4.9 and 4.10

Edge	Cost	Spanning tree
(1,2)	10	①—②
(2,6)	25	①—② ⑥
(3,6)	15	①—② ③ ⑥
(6,4)	20	①—② ④ ⑥ ③
(1,4)	reject	①—② ④ ⑥ ⑤—③
(3,5)	35	

Figure 4.8(b) . Stages in Prim's Algorithm

The time required by procedure PRIM is readily seen to be $\theta(n^2)$ where n is the number of vertices in the graph G. To see this note that line 3 takes $\theta(e)$ ($e = |E|$) time and line 4 takes $\theta(1)$ time. The loop of lines 6–9

line **procedure** PRIM(E, COST, n, T, $mincost$)
     //E is the set of edges in G//
     //COST(n, n) is the cost adjacency matrix of an n vertex graph//
     //such that COST(i, j) is either a positive real number or $+\infty$ if//
     //no edge (i, j) exists. A minimum spanning tree is computed and//
     //stored as a set of edges in the array $T(1{:}n - 1, 2)$. ($T(i, 1)$,//
     //$T(i, 2)$) is an edge in the min-cost spanning tree. The final cost//
     //is assigned to mincost//

```
1        real COST (n, n), mincost;
2        integer NEAR (n), n, i, j, k, l, T(1:n - 1, 2);
3        (k, l) ← edge with minimum cost
4        mincost ← COST(k, l)
5        (T(1, 1), T(1, 2)) ← (k, l)
6        for i ← 1 to n do //initialize NEAR//
7          if COST(i, l) < COST(i, k) then NEAR(i) ← 1
8                                      else NEAR(i) ← k endif
9        repeat
10       NEAR (k) ← NEAR (l) ← 0
11       for i ← 2 to n - 1 do   //find n - 2 additional edges for T//
12       let j be an index such that NEAR (j) ≠ 0 and COST(j, NEAR (j))
             is minimum
13       (T(i, 1), T(i, 2)) ← (j, NEAR (j))
14     mincost ← mincost + COST (j, NEAR (j)
15     NEAR (j) ← 0
16     for k ← 1 to n do   //update NEAR//
17       if NEAR (k) ≠ 0 and COST(k, NEAR(k)) > COST(k, j)
18         then NEAR (k) ← j
19       endif
20     repeat
21   repeat
22   if mincost ≥ ∞ then print ('no spanning tree') endif
23 end PRIM
```

     Algorithm 4.8 Prim's minimum spanning tree algorithm

takes $\theta(n)$ time. Line 12 and the loop of lines 16–20 require $\theta(n)$ time. So, each iteration of the loop of lines 11–21 takes $\theta(n)$ time. The total time for the loop of therefore $\theta(n^2)$. Hence, procedure PRIM has a time complexity that is $\theta(n^2)$.

The algorithm may be speeded a bit by making the observation that a minimum spanning tree includes for each vertex v a minimum cost edge incident to v. To see this, suppose T is a minimum cost spanning tree for $G = (V, E)$. Let v be any vertex in T. Let (v, w) be an edge with minimum cost among all edges incident to v. Assume $(v, w) \notin E(T)$ and that $COST(v, w) < COST(v, x)$ for all edges $(v, x) \in E(T)$. The inclusion of (v, w) into T creates a unique cycle. This cycle must include an edge (v, x), $x \neq w$. Removing (v, x) from $E(T) \cup \{(v, w)\}$ breaks this cycle without disconnecting the graph $(V, E(T) \cup \{(v, w)\})$. Hence, $(V, E(T) \cup \{(v, w)\} - \{(v, x)\}$ is also a spanning tree. Since $COST(v, w) < COST(v, x)$ this spanning tree has lesser cost than T. This contradicts the assumption that T is a minimum cost spanning tree of G. So, T includes minimum cost edges as stated above.

From this observation it follows that we can actually start the algorithm with a tree consisting of any arbitrary vertex and no edge. Then edges may be added one by one. The changes needed are to lines 3–11. These lines may be replaced by the lines

```
3'      mincost ← 0
4'      for i ← 2 to n do   //vertex 1 is initially in T//
5'          NEAR (i) ← 1
6'      repeat
7'          NEAR (1) ← 0
8'-11'  for i ← 1 to n - 1 do   //find n - 1 edges for T//
```

The overall complexity remains $\theta(n^2)$.

There is a second possible interpretation of the optimization criteria mentioned earlier where the edges of the graph are considered in nondecreasing order of cost. This interpretation is that the set T of edges so far selected for the spanning tree be such that it is possible to *complete* T into a tree. Thus T may not be a tree at all stages in the algorithm. In fact, it will generally only be a forest since the set of edges T can be completed into a tree iff there are no cycles in T. We shall show in Theorem 4.7 that this interpretation of the greedy method also results in a minimum cost spanning tree. This method is due to Kruskal.

Example 4.10 Consider the graph of Figure 4.8(a). Using Kruskal's method the edges of this graph are considered for inclusion in the minimum cost spanning tree in the order $(1, 2)$, $(3, 6)$, $(4, 6)$, $(2, 6)$, $(1, 4)$, $(3, 5)$, $(2, 5)$, $(1, 5)$, $(2, 3)$, and $(5, 6)$. This corresponds to the cost sequence 10, 15, 20, 25, 30, 35, 40, 45, 50, 55. The first four edges are included in T. The next edge to be considered is $(3, 4)$. This edge connects two vertices already connected in T and so it is rejected. Next, the edge $(3, 5)$ is selected and that completes the spanning tree. Figure 4.9

shows the forest represented by T during the various stages of this computation. The spanning tree obtained has a cost of 105.   □

Edge	Cost	Spanning Forest
(1,2)	10	
(3,6)	15	
(4,6)	20	
(2,6)	25	
(1,4)	30	(reject)
(3,5)	35	

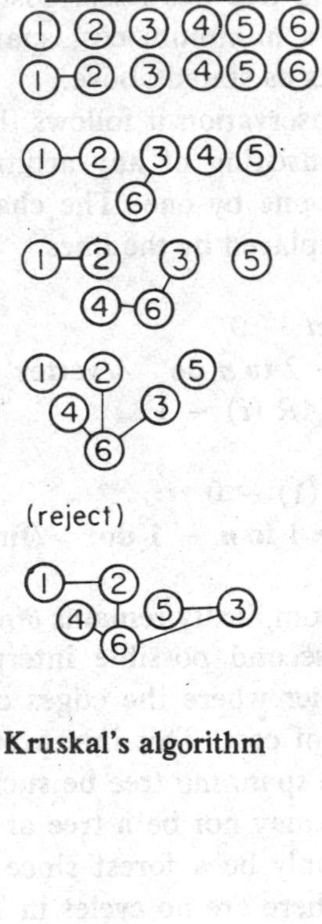

Figure 4.9   Stages in Kruskal's algorithm

For clarity, Kruskal's algorithm is written out more formally in Algorithm 4.9. Initially E is the set of all edges in G. The only functions we wish to perform on this set are: (i) determine an edge with minimum cost (line 3), and (ii) delete this edge (line 4). Both these functions can be performed efficiently if the edges in E are maintained as a sorted sequential list. Actually, it is not essential to sort all the edges so long as the next edge for line 3 can be determined easily. If the edges are maintained as a min-heap then the next edge to consider can be obtained in $O(\log e)$ time if G has e edges. The construction of the heap itself takes $O(e)$ time.

```
1    T ← φ
2    while T contains less than n − 1 edges do
3        choose an edge (v, w) from E of lowest cost
4        delete (v, w) from E
5        if (v, w) does not create a cycle in T
6            then add (v, w) to T
7            else discard (v, w)
8        endif
9    repeat
```

Algorithm 4.9 Early form of minimum spanning tree algorithm due to Kruskal

In order to be able to perform steps 5 and 6 efficiently, the vertices in G should be grouped together in such a way that one may easily determine if the vertices v and w are already connected by the earlier selection of edges. In case they are, then the edge (v, w) is to be discarded. If they are not, then (v, w) is to be added to T. One possible grouping is to place all vertices in the same connected component of T into a set (all connected components of T will also be trees). Then, two vertices v, w are connected in T iff they are in the same set. For example, when the edge $(2, 6)$ is to be considered, the sets would be $\{1, 2\}$, $\{3, 4, 6\}$, and $\{5\}$. Vertices 2 and 6 are in different sets so these sets are combined to give $\{1, 2, 3, 4, 6\}$ and $\{5\}$. The next edge to be considered is $(1, 4)$. Since vertices 1 and 4 are in the same set, the edge is rejected. The edge $(3, 5)$ connects vertices in different sets and results in the final spanning tree. Using the set representation of Section 2.4 and the UNION and FIND algorithm of that section we can obtain an efficient (almost linear) implementation of lines 5 and 6. The computing time is, therefore, determined by the time for lines 3 and 4 which in the worst case is $O(e \log e)$.

If the representations discussed above are used then the procedure of Algorithm 4.10 results. In line 3 an initial heap of edges is constructed. In line 4 each vertex is assigned to a distinct set (and hence to a distinct tree). T is the set of edges to be included in the minimum cost spanning tree while i is the number of edges in T. T itself may be represented as a sequential list using a two dimensional array $T(1:n − 1, 2)$. Edge (u, v) may be added to T by the assignments $T(i, 1) ← u$ and $T(i, 2) ← v$. In the loop of lines 6–14 edges are removed from the heap one by one in nondecreasing order of cost. Line 8 determines the sets containing u and v.

If $j \neq k$ then vertices u and v are in different sets (and so in different trees) and edge (u, v) is included into T. The sets containing u and v are combined (line 12). If $u = v$ the edge (u, v) is discarded as its inclusion into T will create a cycle. Line 15 determines whether a spanning tree was found. It follows that $i \neq n - 1$ iff the graph G is not connected. One may verify that the computing time is $O(e \log e)$ where e is the number of edges in G ($e = |E|$).

```
line   procedure KRUSKAL (E, COST, n, T, mincost)
       //E is the set of edges in G. G has n vertices. COST (u, v) is the//
       //cost of edge (u, v). T is the set of edges in the minimum span-//
       //ning tree and mincost is its cost//
1      real mincost, COST (1:n, 1:n)
2      integer PARENT (1:n), T (1:n - 1, 2), n
3      construct a heap out of the edge costs using HEAPIFY
4      PARENT ← -1 //each vertex is in a different set//
5      i ← mincost ← 0
6      while i < n - 1 and heap not empty do
7          delete a minimum ocst edge (u, v) from the heap and reheapify
           using ADJUST
8          j ← FIND (u); k ← FIND (v)
9          if j ≠ k then i ← i + 1
10                      T (i, 1) ← u; T (i, 2) ← v
11                      mincost ← mincost + COST (u, v)
12                      call UNION (j, k)
13         endif
14     repeat
15     if i ≠ n - 1 then print ('no spanning tree') endif
16     return
17 end KRUSKAL
```

Algorithm 4.10 Kruskal's Algorithm

Theorem 4.8 Kruskal's algorithm generates a minimum cost spanning tree for every connected undirected graph G.

Proof: Let G be any undirected connected graph. Let T be the spanning tree for G generated by Kruskal's algorithm. Let T' be a minimum cost spanning tree for G. We shall show that both T and T' have the same cost. Let $E(T)$ and $E(T')$ respectively be the edges in T and T'. If n is the number of vertices in G then both T and T' have $n - 1$ edges. If $E(T) =$

$E(T')$ then T is clearly of minimum cost. If $E(T) \neq E(T')$ then let e be a minimum cost edge such that $e \in E(T)$ and $e \notin E(T')$. Clearly, such an e must exist. The inclusion of e into T' creates a unique cycle (Exercise 20). Let $e, e_1, e_2, \ldots, e_k$ be this unique cycle. At least one of the e_i's, $1 \leq i \leq k$ is not in $E(T)$ as otherwise T will also contain the cycle $e, e_1, e_2, \ldots, e_k$. Let e_j be an edge on this cycle such that $e_j \notin E(T)$. If e_j is of lesser cost than e then Kruskal's algorithm would consider e_j before e and include e_j into T. To see this note that all edges in $E(T)$ of cost less than the cost of e are also in $E(T')$ and do not form a cycle with e_j. So $c(e_j) \geq c(e)$ ($c(\cdot)$ is the edge-cost function).

Now, reconsider the graph with edge set $E(T') \cup \{e\}$. Removal of any edge on the cycle $e, e_1, e_2, \ldots, e_k$ will leave behind a tree T'' (Exercise 20). In particular, if we delete the edge e_j then the resulting tree T'' will have a cost no more than the cost of T' (as $c(e_j) \geq c(e)$). Hence, T'' is also a minimum cost tree.

By repeatedly using the transformation described above, tree T' can be transformed into the spanning tree T without any increase in cost. Hence, T is a minimum cost spanning tree. $\square$

4.7 SINGLE SOURCE SHORTEST PATHS

Graphs may be used to represent the highway structure of a state or country with vertices representing cities and edges representing sections of highway. The edges may then be assigned weights which might be either the distance between the two cities connected by the edge or the average time to drive along that section of highway. A motorist wishing to drive from city A to city B would be interested in answers to the following questions:

(i) Is there a path from A to B?
(ii) If there is more than one path from A to B, which is the shortest path?

The problems defined by (i) and (ii) above are special cases of the path problem we shall be studying in this section. The length of a path is now defined to be the sum of the weights of the edges on that path. The starting vertex of the path will be referred to as the *source* and the last vertex the *destination*. The graphs will be digraphs to allow for one way streets. In the problem we shall consider, we are given a directed graph $G = (V, E)$, a weighting function $c(e)$ for the edges of G and a source vertex v_0. The problem is to determine the shortest paths from v_0 to *all* the remaining vertices of G. It is assumed that all the weights are positive.

Example 4.11 Consider the directed graph of Figure 4.10(a). The numbers on the edges are the weights. If v_0 is the source vertex, then the shortest path from v_0 to v_1 is $v_0 v_2 v_3 v_1$. The length of this path is $10 + 15 + 20 = 45$. Even though there are three edges on this path, it is shorter than the path $v_0 v_1$ which is of length 50. There is no path from v_0 to v_5. Figure 4.10(b) lists the shortest paths from v_0 to v_1, v_2, v_3 and v_4. The paths have been listed in nondecreasing order of path length.   □

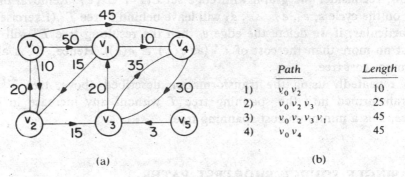

	Path	Length
1)	$v_0 v_2$	10
2)	$v_0 v_2 v_3$	25
3)	$v_0 v_2 v_3 v_1$	45
4)	$v_0 v_4$	45

(a)   (b)

Figure 4.10 Graph and shortest paths from v_0 to all destinations

In order to formulate a greedy based algorithm to generate the shortest paths, we must conceive of a multistage solution to the problem and also conceive of an optimization measure. One possibility is to build the shortest paths one by one. As an optimization measure we can use the sum of the lengths of all paths so far generated. In order for this measure to be minimized, each individual path must be of minimum length. Using this optimization measure, if we have already constructed i shortest paths then the next path to be constructed should be the next shortest minimum length path. The greedy way (and also a systematic way) to generate the shortest paths from v_0 to the remaining vertices would be to generate these paths in nondecreasing order of path length. First, a shortest path to the nearest vertex is generated. Then a shortest path to the second nearest vertex is generated and so on. For the graph of Figure 4.10(a) the nearest vertex to v_0 is v_2 ($c(v_0, v_2) = 10$). The path $v_0 v_2$ will be the first path generated. The second nearest vertex to v_0 is v_3 and the distance between v_0 and v_3 is 25. The path $v_0 v_2 v_3$ will be the next path generated. In order to generate the shortest paths in this order, we need to be able to determine (i) the next vertex to which a shortest path must be generated and (ii) a shortest path to this vertex. Let S denote the set of vertices (including v_0) to which the shortest paths have already been generated. For w not in S, let DIST(w) be the length of the shortest path starting from v_0 going through only those vertices which are in S and ending at w. We observe that:

(i)   If the next shortest path is to vertex u, then the path begins at v_0, ends at u and goes through only those vertices which are in S. To prove this we must show that all of the intermediate vertices on the shortest path to u must be in S. Assume there is a vertex w on this path that is not in S. Then, the v_0 to u path also contains a path from v_0 to w which is of length less than the v_0 to u path. By assumption the shortest paths are being generated in nondecreasing order of path length, and so the shorter path v_0 to w must already have been generated. Hence, there can be no intermediate vertex which is not in S.

(ii) The destination of the next path generated must be that vertex u which has the minimum distance, DIST(u), among all vertices not in S. This follows from the definition of DIST and observation (i). In case there are several vertices not in S with the same DIST, then any of these may be selected.

(iii) Having selected a vertex u as in (ii) and generated the shortest v_0 to u path, vertex u becomes a member of S. At this point the length of the shortest paths starting at v_0, going through vertices only in S and ending at a vertex w not in S may decrease. I.e., the value of DIST(w) may change. If it does change, then it must be due to a shorter path starting at v_0 going to u and then to w. The intermediate vertices on the v_0 to u path and the u to w path must all be in S. Further, the v_0 to u path must be the shortest such path, otherwise DIST(w) is not defined properly. Also, the u to w path can be chosen so as to not contain any intermediate vertices. Therefore, we may conclude that if DIST(w) is to change (i.e., decrease), then it is because of a path from v_0 to u to w where the path from v_0 to u is the shortest such path and the path from u to w is the edge (u, w). The length of this path is DIST(u) + $c(u, w)$.

The above observations lead to a simple algorithm (Algorithm 4.11) for the single source shortest path problem. This algorithm (known as Dijkstra's algorithm) actually only determines the lengths of the shortest paths from v_0 to all other vertices in G. The actual generation of the paths requires a minor extension to this algorithm and is left as an exercise. In procedure SHORTEST__PATHS (Algorithm 4.11) it is assumed that the n vertices of G are numbered 1 through n. The set S is maintained as a bit array with $S(i) = 0$ if vertex i is not in S and $S(i) = 1$ if it is. It is assumed that the graph itself is represented by its cost adjacency matrix with COST(i, j) being the weight of the edge (i, j). COST(i, j) will be set to some large number, $+\infty$, in case the edge (i, j) is not in $E(G)$. For $i = j$, COST(i, j) may be set to any nonnegative number without affecting the outcome of the algorithm.

```
    procedure SHORTEST-PATHS(v, COST, DIST, n)
        //DIST(j), 1 ≤ j ≤ n is set to the length of the shortest path//
        //from vertex v to vertex j in a digraph G with n vertices.//
        //DIST(v) is set to zero. G is represented by its cost adjacency//
        //matrix, COST(n, n)//
        boolean S(1:n); real COST(1:n, 1:n), DIST(1:n)
        integer u, v, n, num, i, w
1       for i ← 1 to n do    //initialize set S to empty//
2           S(i) ← 0; DIST(i) ← COST(v, i)
3       repeat
4       S(v) ← 1; DIST(v) ← 0       //put vertex v in set S//
5       for num ← 2 to n − 1 do    //determine n − 1 paths from vertex v//
6           choose u such that DIST(u) = min{DIST(w)}
                                           S(w) = 0
7           S(u) ← 1,   //put vertex u in set S//
8           for all w with S(w) = 0 do    //update distances//
9               DIST(w) ← min(DIST(w), DIST(u) + COST(u, w))
10          repeat
11      repeat
12      end SHORTEST-PATHS
```

Algorithm 4.11   Greedy algorithm to generate shortest paths

Analysis of Algorithm SHORTEST-PATHS

From our earlier discussion, it is easy to see that the algorithm is correct. The time taken by the algorithm on a graph with n vertices is $O(n^2)$. To see this note that the for loop of line 1 takes $\theta(n)$ time. The for loop of line 5 is executed $n - 2$ times. Each execution of this loop requires $O(n)$ time at line 6 to select the next vertex and again at lines 8–10 to update DIST. So the total time for this loop is $O(n^2)$. In case a list T of vertices currently not in S is maintained, then the number of nodes on this list would at any time be $n - num$. This would speed up lines 6 and 8–10, but the asymptotic time would remain $O(n^2)$. This and other variations of the algorithm are explored in the exercises.

Any shortest path algorithm must examine each edge in the graph at least once since any of the edges could be in a shortest path. Hence, the minimum possible time for such an algorithm would be $O(e)$. Since cost adjacency matrices were used to represent the graph, it takes $O(n^2)$ time just to determine which edges are in G and so any shortest path algorithm using this representation must take $O(n^2)$. For this representation then, algorithm SHORTEST-PATHS is optimal to within a constant factor. Even if a change to adjacency lists is made, only the overall time for the **for** loop of lines 8–10 can be brought down to $O(e)$ (since the DIST can change only for vertices adjacent from u). The total time for line 6 remains $O(n^2)$.

Example 4.12 Consider the 8 vertex digraph of Figure 4.11(a) with cost adjacency matrix as in 4.11(b). The values of DIST and the vertices selected at each iteration of the **while** loop of line 5 for finding all the shortest paths from Boston are shown in Figure 4.12. Note that the algorithm terminates when only seven of the eight vertices are in S. By the definition of DIST, the distance of the last vertex, in this case Los Angeles, is correct as the shortest path from Boston to Los Angeles can go through only the remaining six vertices. □

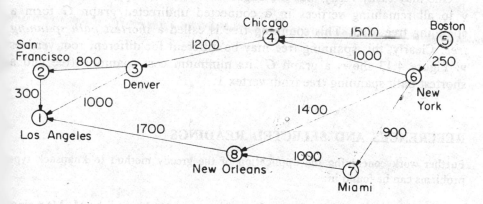

Figure 4.11 (a) Directed graph from a map

	1	2	3	4	5	6	7	8
1	0							
2	300	0						
3	1000	800	0					
4			1200	0				
5				1500	0	250		
6				1000		0	900	1400
7							0	1000
8	1700							0

Figure 4.11(b) Cost adjacency matrix for Figure 4.11(a). All entries not shown are $+\infty$

		Vertex		LA	SF	D	C	B	NY	M	NO
Iteration	S	Selected	DIST	(1)	(2)	(3)	(4)	(5)	(6)	(7)	(8)
Initial		—		$+\infty$	$+\infty$	$+\infty$	1500	0	250	$+\infty$	$+\infty$
1	5	6		$+\infty$	$+\infty$	$+\infty$	1250	0	250	1150	1650
2	5,6	7		$+\infty$	$+\infty$	$+\infty$	1250	0	250	1150	1650
3	5,6,7	4		$+\infty$	$+\infty$	$+\infty$	1250	0	250	1150	1650
4	5,6,7,4	8		$+\infty$	$+\infty$	2450	1250	0	250	1150	1650
5	5,6,7,4,8	3		3350	$+\infty$	2450	1250	0	250	1150	1650
6	5,6,7,4,8,3	2		3350	3250	2450	1250	0	250	1150	1650
	5,6,7,4,8,3,2			3350	3250	2450	1250	0	250	1150	1650

Figure 4.12 Action of SHORTEST_PATHS

One may easily verify that the edges on the shortest paths from a vertex *v* to all remaining vertices in a connected undirected graph *G* form a spanning tree of *G*. This spanning tree is called a *shortest path spanning tree*. Clearly, this spanning tree may be different for different root vertices *v*. Figure 4.13 shows a graph *G*, its minimum cost spanning tree and a shortest path spanning tree from vertex 1.

REFERENCES AND SELECTED READINGS

Further work concerning the application of the greedy method to knapsack type problems can be found in:

"When the greedy solution solves a class of knapsack problems," by M. Magazine G. Nemhauser and L. Trotter, *Operations Research*, 23(2), pp. 207–217 (1975).

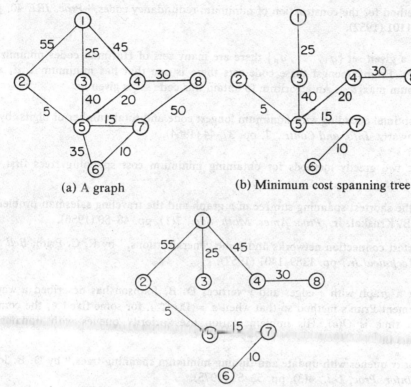

(a) A graph

(b) Minimum cost spanning tree

(c) Shortest path spanning tree from vertex 1.

Figure 4.13 Graphs and spanning trees

"Canonical coin changing and greedy solutions," by L. Chang and J. Korsh, *JACM*, 23(3), pp. 412–422 (1976).

The greedy method developed here to optimally store programs on tapes was first devised for a machine scheduling problem. In this problem n jobs have to be scheduled on m processors. Job i takes t_i amount of time. The time at which a job finishes is the sum of the job times for all jobs preceding and including job i. The average finish time corresponds to the mean access time for programs on tapes. The $(m!)^{n/m}$ schedules referred to in Theorem 4.2 are known as SPT schedules (shortest processing time). The rule to generate SPT schedules as well as the rule of exercise 9 first appeared in:

"Various optimizers for single-state production," by W. E. Smith, *Nav. Res. Log. Quart.*, 3(1), March (1956).

The greedy algorithm for generating optimal merge trees is due to D. Huffman and first appeared in:

"A method for the construction of minimum-redundancy codes," *Proc. IRE* 40, pp. 1098–1101 (1952).

For a given set $\{q_1, \ldots, q_n\}$ there are many sets of Huffman codes minimizing $\sum q_i d_i$. From amongst these code sets there is one that has minimum $\sum d_i$ and minimum $\max\{d_i\}$. An algorithm to obtain this code set is given in:

"An optimal encoding with minimum longest code and total number of digits, by E. S. Schwartz, *Info. and Contr.*, 7, pp. 37–44 (1964).

The two greedy methods for obtaining minimum cost spanning trees first appeared in:

"On the shortest spanning subtree of a graph and the traveling salesman problem," by J. B. Kruskal, Jr., *Proc. Amer. Math. Soc.*, 7(1), pp. 48–50 (1956).

"Shortest connection networks and some generalizations," by R. C. Prim, *Bell System Technical Jr.*, pp. 1389–1401 (1957).

For a graph with e edges and v vertices D. B. Johnson has described a way to implement Prim's method so that when $e = \Omega(v^{1+\epsilon})$, for some fixed ϵ, the computation time is $O(e)$. His implementation uses priority queues with updates. It appears in:

"Priority queues with update and finding minimum spanning trees," by D. B. Johnson, *Infor. Proc. Let.*, 4(3), pp. 53–57 (1975).

An $O(e \log\log v)$ spanning tree algorithm is given in:

"An $O(|E| \log\log |V|)$ algorithm for finding minimum spanning trees," by A. C. Yao, *Infor. Proc. Letters*, 4(1), pp. 21–23 (1975).

A study of several spanning tree algorithms appears in:

"Finding Minimum Spanning Trees," by D. Cheriton and R. Tarjan, *SIAM Jr. on Computing*, 5(4), pp. 724–742 (1976).

The shortest path algorithm of the text is from:

"A note on two problems in connexion with graphs," by E. W. Dijkstra, *Numerische Mathematik*, 1, pp. 269–271 (1959).

A better algorithm for graphs having few edges appears in:

"Efficient algorithms for shortest paths in sparse networks," by D. B. Johnson, *J. ACM*, 24(1), pp. 1–13 (1977).

Algorithms to update a minimum spanning tree or shortest path following either the addition or deletion of a vertex or edge can be found in:

"On finding and updating spanning trees and shortest paths," by P. M. Spira and A. Pan, *SIAM Jr. on Computing,* 4(3), pp. 375-380 (1975).

The relationship between greedy methods and matroids is discussed in:

Combinatorial optimization by E. Lawler, Holt, Reinhart and Winston, 1976.

"Matroids and the greedy algorithm," by J. Edmonds, *Math. Prog.,* 1, pp. 127-136 (1971).

"A greedy algorithm for solving a certain class of linear programmes," by F. D. J. Dunstan and D. J. A. Welsh, *Math. Prog.,* 5, pp. 338-353 (1973).

"Optimal assignments in an ordered set: an application of Matroid Theory," by D. Gale, *Jr. of Combin. Theo.,* 4, pp. 176-180 (1968).

EXERCISES

1. a) Find an optimal solution to the knapsack instance $n = 7$, $M = 15$, $(p_1, p_2, \ldots, p_7) = (10, 5, 15, 7, 6, 18, 3)$ and $(w_1, w_2, \ldots, w_7) = (2, 3, 5, 7, 1, 4, 1)$?

    b) Let $\hat{F}(I)$ be the value of the solution generated by GREEDY__KNAPSACK on problem instance I when the objects are input in nonincreasing order of the p_i's. Let $F^*(I)$ be the value of an optimal solution for this instance. How large can the ratio $F^*(I)/\hat{F}(I)$ get?

    c) Answer b) for the case when the input is in nondecreasing order of the w_i's.

2. [Coin changing] Let $A_n = \{a_1, a_2, \ldots, a_n\}$ be a finite set of distinct coin types (e.g., $a_1 = 50¢$, $a_2 = 25¢$, $a_3 = 10¢$ etc). We may assume each a_i is integer and that $a_1 > a_2 > \cdots > a_n$. Each type is available in unlimited quantity. The coin changing problem is to make up an exact amount C using a minimum total number of coins. C is an integer > 0.

    a) Show that if $a_n \neq 1$ then there exists a finite set of coin types and a C for which there is no solution to the coin changing problem.

    b) Show that there is always a solution when $a_n = 1$.

    c) When $a_n = 1$ a greedy solution to the problem will make change by using the coin types in the order $a_1, a_2, \ldots, a_n$. When coin type a_i is being considered, as many coins of this type as possible will be given. Write an algorithm based on this strategy. Show that this algorithm doesn't necessarily generate solutions that use the minimum total number of coins.

    d) Show that if $A_n = \{k^{n-1}, k^{n-2}, \ldots, k^0\}$ for some $k > 1$ then the greedy method of c) above always yields solutions with a minimum number of coins.

3. Let $P_1, P_2, \ldots, P_n$ be a set of n programs that are to be stored on a tape of length L. Program P_i requires a_i amount of tape. If $\Sigma a_i \leq L$ then clearly all the programs can be stored on the tape. So, assume $\Sigma a_i > L$. The problem is to select a maximum subset Q of the programs for storage on the tape. A maximum subset is one with the maximum number of programs in it. A greedy algorithm for this problem would build the subset Q by including programs in nondecreasing order of a_i.

a) Assume the P_i are ordered such that $a_1 \leq a_2 \leq \cdots \leq a_n$. Write a SPARKS algorithm for the above strategy. Your algorithm should output an array $S(1:n)$ such that $S(i) = 1$ if P_i is in Q and $S(i) = 0$ otherwise.

b) Show that this strategy always finds a maximum subset Q such that $\Sigma_{P_i \in Q} a_i \leq L$.

c) Let Q be the subet obtained using the above greedy strategy. How small can the tape utilization ratio $(\Sigma_{P_i \in Q} a_i)/L$ get?

d) Suppose the objective now is to determine a subset of programs that maximizes the tape utilization ratio. A greedy approach now would be to consider programs in nonincreasing order of a_i. If there is enough space left on the tape for P_i then it is included in Q. Assume the programs are ordered such that $a_1 \geq a_2 \geq \cdots \geq a_n$. Write a SPARKS algorithm incorporating this strategy. What is its time and space complexity?

e) Show that the strategy of (c) doesn't necessarily yield a subset that maximizes $(\Sigma_{P_i \in Q} a_i)/L$. How small can this ratio get? Prove your bound.

4. [0/1 Knapsack]   Consider the knapsack problem discussed in Section 4.3. We add the requirement that $x_i = 1$ or $x_i = 0$, $1 \leq i \leq n$. I.e. an object is either included or not included into the knapsack. We wish to solve the problem:

$$\max \sum_1^n p_i x_i$$

$$\text{subject to } \sum_1^n w_i x_i \leq M$$

$$x_i = 0 \text{ or } 1, \qquad 1 \leq i \leq n$$

One greedy strategy is: consider the objects in order of nonincreasing density p_i/w_i; add the object into the knapsack if it fits. Show that this strategy doesn't necessarily yield optimal solutions.

5. [Set Cover] You are given a family S of m sets S_i, $1 \le i \le m$. Denote by $|A|$ the size of set A. Let $|S_i| = j_i$, i.e. $S_i = \{S_1, S_2, \ldots, S_{ji}\}$. A subset $T = \{T_1, T_2, \ldots, T_k\}$ of S is a family of sets such that for each i, $1 \le i \le k$, $T_i = S_r$ for some r, $1 \le r \le m$. T is a *cover* of S iff $\cup T_i = \cup S_i$. The size of T, $|T|$, is the number of sets in T. A minimum cover of S is a cover of smallest size. Consider the following greedy strategy: build T iteratively; at the k'th iteration $T = \{T_1, \ldots, T_{k-1}\}$; now add to T a set S_j from S that contains the largest number of elements not already in T; stop when $\cup T_i = \cup S_i$.

a) Assume that $\cup S_i = \{1, 2, \ldots, n\}$ and that $m < n$. Using the strategy outlined above write an algorithm to obtain set covers. How much time and space does your algorithm require?

b) Show that the greedy strategy above doesn't necessarily obtain a minimum set cover.

c) Suppose now that a minimum cover is defined to be one for which $\sum_{i=1}^{k} |T_i|$ is minimum. Does the above strategy always find a minimum cover?

6. [Node Cover] Let $G = (V, E)$ be an undirected graph. A node cover of G is a subset U of the vertex set V such that every edge in E is incident to at least one vertex in U. A minimum node cover is one with the fewest number of vertices. Consider the following greedy algorithm for this problem:

```
procedure COVER(V, E)
  U ← φ
  loop
    let v∈ V be a vertex of maximum degree
    U ← U ∪ {v}; V ← V − {v}
    E ← E − {(u, w) such that u = v or w = v}
  until E = φ repeat
  return (U)
end COVER
```

Does this algorithm always generate a minimum node cover?

7. You are given a set of n jobs. Associated with each job, i, is a processing time t_i and a deadline d_i by which it must be completed. A feasible schedule is a permutation of the jobs such that if the jobs are processed in that order then each job finishes by its deadline. Define a greedy schedule to be one in which the jobs are processed in nondecreasing order of deadlines. Show that if there exists a feasible schedule then all greedy schedules are feasible.

8. [Optimal Assignment] Assume there are n workers and n jobs. Let v_{ij} be the

value of assigning worker i to job j. An assignment of workers to jobs corresponds to the assignment of 0 or 1 to the variables x_{ij}, $1 \leq i, j \leq n$. $x_{ij} = 1$ means worker i is assigned to job j; $x_{ij} = 0$ means that worker i is not assigned to job j. A valid assignment is one in which each worker is assigned to exactly one job and exactly one worker is assigned to any one job. The value of an assignment is $\Sigma_i \Sigma_j v_{ij} \cdot x_{ij}$. An optimal assignment is a valid assignment of maximum value. Write algorithms for two different greedy assignment schemes. One of these assigns a worker to the best possible job. The other assigns to a job the best possible worker. Show that neither of these schemes is guaranteed to yield optimal assignments. Is either scheme always better than the other? Assume $v_{ij} > 0$.

9. Assume n programs of lengths $l_1, l_2, \ldots, l_n$ are to be stored on a tape. Program i is to be retrieved with frequency f_i. If the programs are stored in the order $i_1, i_2, \ldots, i_n$, the *expected retrieval time* (ERT) is

$$[\sum_j (f_{ij} \sum_{k=1}^{j} l_{i_k})]/\Sigma f_i.$$

a) Show that storing the programs in nondecreasing order of l_i does not necessarily minimize the ERT.

b) Show that storing the programs in nonincreasing order of f_i does not necessarily minimize the ERT.

c) Show that the ERT is minimized when the programs as stored in nonincreasing order of f_i/l_i.

10. Consider the tape storage problem of Section 4.2. Assume that 2 tapes $T1$ and $T2$, are available and we wish to distribute n given programs of lengths $l_1, l_2, \ldots, l_n$ onto these two tapes in such a manner that the maximum retrieval time is minimized. I.e. if A and B are the sets of programs on the tapes $T1$ and $T2$ respectively then we wish to choose A and B such that $\max\{\Sigma_{i \in A} l_i, \Sigma_{i \in B} l_i\}$ is minimized. A possible greedy approach to obtaining A and B would be to start with A and B initially empty. Then consider the programs one at a time. The program currently being considered is assigned to set A if $\Sigma_{i \in A} l_i = \min\{\Sigma_{i \in A} l_i, \Sigma_{i \in B} l_i\}$, otherise it is assigned to B. Show that this does not guarantee optimal solutions even if $l_1 \leq l_2 \leq \cdots \leq l_n$. Show that the same is true if we require $l_1 \geq l_2 \geq \cdots \geq l_n$.

11. a) What is the solution generated by Algorithm 4.5 when $n = 7$, $(p_1, p_2, \ldots, p_7) = (3, 5, 20, 18, 1, 6, 30)$ and $(d_1, d_2, \ldots, d_7) = (1, 3, 4, 3, 2, 1, 2)$?

b) Show that Theorem 4.4 is true even if jobs have different processing requirements. Associated with job i is a profit $p_i > 0$, a time requirement $t_i > 0$ and a deadline $d_i \geq t_i$.

c) Show that for the situation of a), the greedy method of Section 4.4 doesn't necessarily yield an optimal solution.

12. a) For the job sequencing problem of Section 4.4 show that the subset J represents a feasible solution iff the jobs in J can be processed according to the rule: if job i in J hasn't been assigned a processing time then assign it to the slot $[\alpha - 1, \alpha]$ where α is the least interger r such that $1 \le r \le d_i$ and the slot $[\alpha - 1, \alpha]$ is free.

   b) For the problem instance of Exercise 11(a) draw the trees and give the values of $F(i)$, $0 \le i \le n$ after each iteration of the loop of lines 6-13 of Algorithm 4.6.

13. a) Show that if all internal nodes in a tree have degree k then the number of external nodes n is such that $n \bmod (k - 1) = 1$.

   b) Show that for every n such that $n \bmod (k - 1) = 1$ there exists a k-ary tree T with n external nodes (in a k-ary tree all nodes have degree at most k). Moreover, all internal nodes of T have degree k.

14. a) Show that if $n \bmod (k - 1) = 1$ then the greedy rule described following Theorem 4.7 generates an optimal k-ary merge tree for all $(q_1, q_2, \ldots, q_n)$.

   b) Draw the optimal 3-way merge tree obtained using this rule when $(q_1, q_2, \ldots, q_{11}) = (3, 7, 8, 9, 15, 16, 18, 20, 23, 25, 28)$.

15. Obtain a set of optimal Huffman codes for the seven messages $(M_1, \ldots, M_7)$ with relative frequencies $(q_1, \ldots q_7) = (5, 2, 10, 3, 20, 90, 9)$. Draw the decode tree for this set of codes.

16. Let T be a decode tree. An optimal decode tree minimizes $\Sigma q_i d_i$. For a given set of q's let D denote all the optimal decode trees. For any tree $T \in D$ let $L(T) = \max\{d_i\}$ and let $SL(T) = \Sigma d_i$. Schwartz has shown that there exists a tree $T^* \in D$ such that $L(T^*) = \min_{T \in D}\{L(T)\}$ and $SL(T^*) = \min_{T \in D}\{SL(T)\}$.

   a) For $(q_1, \ldots, q_8) = (1, 1, 2, 2, 4, 4, 4, 4)$ obtain trees $T1$ and $T2 \in D$ such that $L(T1) > L(T2)$.

   b) Using the data of a) obtain $T1$ and $T2 \in D$ such that $L(T1) = L(T2)$ but $SL(T1) > SL(T2)$.

   c) Show that if the subalgorithm LEAST used in algorithm TREE is such that in case of a tie it returns the tree with least depth, then TREE generates a tree with the properties of T^*.

17. Prove that Prim's method of Section 4.6 generates minimum cost spanning trees.

18. a) Rewrite Prim's algorithm under the assumption that the graphs are repre-
         sented by adjacency lists.
     b) Program and run the above version of Prim's algorithm against Algorithm
         4.9. Compare the two on a representative set of graphs.
     c) Analyze precisely the computing time and space requirements of your new
         version of Prim's algorithm using adjacency lists.

19. Program and run Kruskal's algorithm as described in Algorithm 4.11. You
     will have to modify procedures HEAPIFY and ADJUST of Chapter 2. Use the
     same test data you devised to test Prim's algorithm in Exercise 18.

20. a) Show that if T is a spanning tree for the undirected graph G, then the
         addition of an edge e, $e \notin E(T)$ and $e \in E(G)$, to T creates a unique cycle.
     b) Show that if any one of the edges on this unique cycle is deleted from
         $E(T) \cup \{e\}$ then the remaining edges form a spanning tree of G.

21. By considering the complete graph with n vertices, show that the number of
     spanning trees in an n vertex graph can be greater than $2^{n-1} - 2$.

22. Use algorithm SHORTEST-PATHS to obtain in nondecreasing order the
     lengths of the shortest paths from vertex 1 to all remaining vertices in the
     digraph of Figure 4.14.

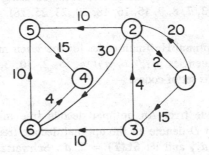

Figure 4.14   Directed graph

23. Using the directed graph of Figure 4.15 explain why SHORTEST-PATH will
     not work properly. What is the shortest path between vertices v_1 and v_7?

24. Rewrite algorithm SHORTEST-PATHS under the following assumptions:
     (i) G is represented by its adjacency lists. The head nodes are HEAD(1), $\cdots$
          HEAD(n) and each list node has three fields: VERTEX, COST, and
          LINK. COST is the length of the corresponding edge and n the number
          of vertices in G.
     (ii) Instead of representing S, the set of vertices to which the shortest paths

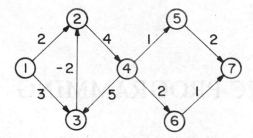

Figure 4.15 Directed graph

have already been found, the set $T = V(G) - S$ is represented using a
a linked list.

What can you say about the computing time of your new algorithm relative to that of SHORTEST-PATHS?

25. Modify algorithm SHORTEST-PATHS so that it obtains the shortest paths in addition to the lengths of these paths. What is the computing time of your algorithm?

26. [Traveling Salesperson] Let G be a complete directed graph with n vertices. Let *length* $(\langle u, v \rangle)$ be the length of the edge $\langle u, v \rangle$. A path starting at a given vertex v_0, going through every other vertex exactly once and finally returning to v_0 will be called a *tour*. The length of a tour is the sum of lengths of the edges on the path defining the tour. We are concerned with finding a tour of minimum length. A greedy way to construct such a tour would be: let (P, v) represent the path so far constructed, it starts at v_0 and ends at v. Initially P is empty and $v = v_0$; if all vertices in G are on P then include the edge $\langle v, v_0 \rangle$ and stop otherwise include an edge $\langle v, w \rangle$ of minimum length among all edges from v to a vertex w not on P. Show that this greedy method doesn't necessarily generate a minimum length tour.

Chapter 5

DYNAMIC PROGRAMMING

5.1 THE GENERAL METHOD

Dynamic Programming is an algorithm design method that can be used when the solution to a problem may be viewed as the result of a sequence of decisions. In earlier chapters we have seen many problems that can be viewed this way. Some examples are:

Example 5.1 [Knapsack] The solution to the knapsack problem (Section 4.3) may be viewed as the result of a sequence of decisions. We have to decide the values of x_i, $1 \leq i \leq n$. First we may make a decision on x_1, then on x_2, then on x_3 etc. An optimal sequence of decisions will maximize the objective function $\Sigma\, p_i x_i$. (It will also satisfy the constraints $\Sigma\, w_i x_i \leq M$ and $0 \leq x_i \leq 1$.) □

Example 5.2 [Optimal Merge Patterns] This problem was discussed in Section 4.4. An optimal merge pattern tells us which pair of files should be merged at each step. As a decision sequence, the problem calls for us to decide which pair of files should be merged first; which pair second; which pair third, etc. An optimal sequence of decisions is a least cost sequence. □

Example 5.3 [Shortest Path] One way to find a shortest path from vertex i to vertex j in a directed graph G is to decide which vertex should be the second vertex, which the third, which the fourth; etc. until vertex j is reached. An optimal sequence of decisions is one which results in a path of least length. □

For some of the problems that may be viewed in this way, an optimal sequence of decisions may be found by making the decisions one at a time and never making an erroneous decision. This is true for all problems solvable by the greedy method. For many other problems, it is not possible to make stepwise decisions (based only on local information) in such a manner that the sequence of decisions made is optimal.

Example 5.4 [Shortest Path] Suppose we wish to find a shortest path from vertex i to vertex j. Let A_i be the vertices adjacent from vertex i. Which of the vertices in A_i should be the second vertex on the path? There is no way to make a decision at this time and guarantee that future decisions may be made leading to an optimal sequence. If on the other hand we wish to find a shortest path from vertex i to all other vertices in G then at each step, a correct decision can be made (see Section 4.7).   □

One way to solve problems for which it is not possible to make a sequence of stepwise decisions leading to an optimal decision sequence is to try out all possible decision sequences. We could enumerate all decision sequences and then pick out the best. Dynamic programming often drastically reduces the amount of enumeration by avoiding the enumeration of some decision sequences that cannot possibly be optimal. In dynamic programming an optimal sequence of decisions is arrived at by making explicit appeal to the *Principle of Optimality*. This principle states that *an optimal sequence of decisions has the property that whatever the initial state and decision are, the remaining decisions must constitute an optimal decision sequence with regard to the state resulting from the first decision.* Thus, the essential difference between the greedy method and dynamic programming is that in the greedy method only one decision sequence is ever generated. In dynamic programming, many decision sequences may be generated. However, sequences containing suboptimal subsequences cannot be optimal (if the principal of optimality holds) and so will not (as far as possible) be generated.

Example 5.5 [Shortest Path] Consider the shortest path problem of Example 5.3. Assume that $i, i_1, i_2, \ldots, i_k, j$ is a shortest path from i to j. Starting with the initial vertex i, a decision has been made to go to vertex i_1. Following this decision, the problem state is defined by vertex i_1 and we need to find a path from i_1 to j. It is clear that the sequence $i_1, i_2, \ldots, i_k, j$ must constitute a shortest i_1 to j path. If not, let $i_1, r_1, r_2, \ldots, r_q, j$ be a shorter i_1 to j path. Then $i, i_1, r_1, \ldots, r_q, j$ is an i to j path which is shorter than the path $i, i_1, i_2, \ldots, i_k, j$. Therefore the principle of optimality applies for this problem.   □

Example 5.6 [0/1 Knapsack] The 0/1 knapsack problem is similar to the knapsack problem of Section 4.3 except that the x_i's are restricted to have a value either 0 or 1. Using KNAP(l, j, Y) to represent the problem

$$\text{maximize } \sum_{l \leq i \leq j} p_i x_i$$

$$\text{subject to } \sum_{l \leq i \leq j} w_i x_i \leq Y \tag{5.1}$$

$$x_i = 0 \text{ or } 1, \quad l \leq i \leq j$$

the 0/1 knapsack problem is KNAP(1, n, M). Let $y_1, y_2, \ldots, y_n$ be an optimal sequence of 0/1 values for $x_1, x_2, \ldots, x_n$ respectively. If $y_1 = 0$ then $y_2, y_3, \ldots, y_n$ must constitute an optimal sequence for the problem KNAP(2, n, M). If it does not then $y_1, y_2, \ldots, y_n$ is not an optimal sequence for KNAP(1, n, M). If $y_1 = 1$ then $y_2, \ldots, y_n$ must be an optimal sequence for the problem KNAP(2, n, $M - w_1$). If it isn't, then there is another 0/1 sequence $z_2, z_3, \ldots, z_n$ such that $\sum_{2 \leq i \leq n} w_i z_i \leq M - w_1$ and $\sum_{2 \leq i \leq n} p_i z_i > \sum_{2 \leq i \leq n} p_i y_i$. Hence, the sequence $y_1, z_2, z_3, \ldots, z_n$ is a sequence for (5.1) with greater value. Again the principle of optimality applies.   □

Let S_0 be the initial problem state. Assume that n decisions d_i, $1 \leq i \leq n$ have to be made. Let $D_1 = \{r_1, r_2, \ldots, r_j\}$ be the set of possible decision values for d_1. Let S_i be the problem state following the choice of decision r_i, $1 \leq i \leq j$. Let Γ_i be an optimal sequence of decisions with respect to the problem state S_i. Then, when the principle of optimality holds, an optimal sequence of decisions with respect to S_0 is the best of the decision sequences $r_i \Gamma_i$, $1 \leq i \leq j$.

Example 5.7 [Shortest Path] Let A_i be the set of vertices adjacent from vertex i. For each vertex $k \in A_i$ let Γ_k be a shortest path from k to j. Then, a shortest i to j path is the shortest of the paths $\{i, \Gamma_k | k \in A_i\}$.   □

Example 5.8 [0/1 Knapsack] Let $g_j(y)$ be the value of an optimal solution to KNAP($j + 1, n, y$). Clearly, $g_0(M)$ is the value of an optimal solution to KNAP(1, n, M). The possible decisions for x_1 are 0 and 1 ($D_1 = \{0, 1\}$). From the principle of optimality it follows that:

$$g_0(M) = \max\{g_1(M), g_1(M - w_1) + p_1\} \tag{5.2}$$ □

While the principle of optimality has been stated only with respect to the initial state and decision, it may be applied equally well to intermediate states and decisions. The next two examples show how this can be done.

Example 5.9 [Shortest Path] Let k be an intermediate vertex on a shortest i to j path $i, i_1, i_2, \ldots, k, p_1, p_2 \cdots j$. The paths $i, i_1, \ldots, k$ and $k, p_1, \ldots, j$ must respectively be shortest i to k and k to j paths.   □

Example 5.10 [0/1 Knapsack] Let $y_1, y_2, \ldots, y_n$ be an optimal solution to KNAP(1, n, M). Then, for each j, $1 \le j \le n$, $y_1, \ldots, y_j$ and $y_{j+1}, \ldots, y_n$ must be optimal solutions to the problems KNAP(1, j, $\sum_{1 \le i \le j} w_i y_i$) and KNAP($j + 1$, n, $M - \sum_{1 \le i \le j} w_i y_i$) respectively. This observation allows us to generalize (5.2) to:

$$g_i(y) = \max\{g_{i+1}(y), g_{i+1}(y - w_{i+1}) + p_{i+1}\} \qquad (5.3) \quad □$$

The recursive application of the optimality principle results in a recurrence relation of the type (5.3). Dynamic programming algorithms solve this recurrence to obtain a solution to the given problem instance. The recurrence (5.3) may be solved using the knowledge $g_n(y) = 0$ for all y. From $g_n(y)$ one may obtain $g_{n-1}(y)$ using (5.3) with $i = n - 1$. Then, using $g_{n-1}(y)$ one may obtain $g_{n-2}(y)$. Repeating in this way, one can determine $g_1(y)$ and finally $g_0(M)$ using (5.3) with $i = 0$.   □

In formulating the dynamic programming recurrence relation(s) that has (have) to be solved, one may use one of two different approaches: forward, or backward. Let $x_1, x_2, \ldots, x_n$ be the variables for which a sequence of decisions has to be made. In the *forward approach*, the formulation for decision x_i is made in terms of optimal decision sequences for $x_{i+1}, \ldots, x_n$. In the *backward approach* the formulation for decision x_i is in terms of optimal decision sequences for $x_1, \ldots, x_{i-1}$. Thus, in the forward approach formulation we "look" ahead on the decision sequence $x_1, x_2, \ldots, x_n$. In the backward formulation we "look" backwards on the decision sequence $x_1, x_2, \ldots, x_n$. Both examples 5.8 and 5.9 correspond to the forward approach. Examples 5.11 and 5.12 correspond to the backward approach.

Example 5.11 [Shortest Path] Let P_j be the set of vertices adjacent to vertex j (i.e. $k \in P_j$ iff $< k, j > \in E(G)$). For each $k \in P_j$ let Γ_k be a shortest i to k path. The principle of optimality holds and a shortest i to j path is the shortest of the paths $\{\Gamma_k, j \mid k \in P_j\}$.

To obtain this formulation, we started at vertex j and looked at the last decision made. The last decision was to use one of the edges $\langle k, j \rangle$, $k \in P_j$. In a sense, we are looking backwards on the i to j path. $\square$

Example 5.12 [0/1 Knapsack] Looking backwards on the sequence of decisions $x_1, x_2, \ldots, x_n$ we see that:

$$f_j(y) = \max\{f_{j-1}(y), f_{j-1}(y - w_j) + p_j\} \tag{5.4}$$

where $f_j(y)$ is the value of an optimal solution to KNAP$(1, j, y)$.

The value of an optimal solution to KNAP$(1, n, M)$ is $f_n(M)$. (5.4) may be solved by beginning with $f_0(y) = 0$ for all y, $y \geq 0$ and $f_0(y) = -\infty$, $y < 0$. From this, $f_1, f_2, \ldots, f_n$ may be successively obtained. $\square$

While at this point one may be skeptical about the virtue of the backward approach vis a vis the forward approach, future examples will show that, in many instances, it is easier to obtain the recurrence relations using the backward approach. It is also worth noting that if the recurrence relations are formulated using the forward approach then the relations are solved backwards (i.e. beginning with the last decision). On the other hand if the relations are formulated using the backward approach they are solved forwards. This is illustrated in Examples 5.10 and 5.12.

The solution method outlined in Examples 5.10 and 5.12 may indicate that one has to look at all possible decision sequences in order to obtain an optimal decision sequence using dynamic programming. Actually, this is not the case. Because of the use of the principle of optimality, decision sequences containing subsequences that are suboptimal are *not* considered. While the total number of different decision sequences is exponential in the number of decisions (if there are d choices for each of the n decisions to be made then there are d^n possible decision sequences), dynamic programing algorithms often have a polynomial complexity.

Another important feature of the dynamic programming approach is that optimal solutions to subproblems are retained so as to avoid recomputing their values. The use of these tabulated values makes it natural to recast the recursive equations into an iterative program. Most of the dynamic programming algorithms in this chapter will be expressed in this way.

Remaining sections of this chapter apply dynamic programming to a variety of problems. These examples should help you to understand the method better and also to realize the advantage of dynamic programming over explicitly enumerating all decision sequences.

5.2 MULTISTAGE GRAPHS

A multistage graph $G = (V, E)$ is a directed graph in which the vertices
are partitioned into $k \geq 2$ disjoint sets V_i, $1 \leq i \leq k$. In addition, if $\langle u, v \rangle$
is an edge in E then $u \in V_i$ and $v \in V_{i+1}$ for some i, $1 \leq i < k$. The sets
V_1 and V_k are such that $|V_1| = |V_k| = 1$. Let s and t respectively be the
vertex in V_1 and V_k. s is the *source* and t the *sink*. Let $c(i, j)$ be the cost
of edge $\langle i, j \rangle$. The cost of a path from s to t is the sum of the costs of the
edges on the path. The *multistage graph problem* is to find a minimum
cost path from s to t. Each set V_i defines a stage in the graph. Because of
the constraints on E, every path from s to t starts in stage 1, goes to stage
2, then to stage 3, then to stage 4 etc. and eventually terminates in stage k.
Figure 5.1 shows a 5 stage graph. A minimum cost s to t path is indicated
by the dark edges.

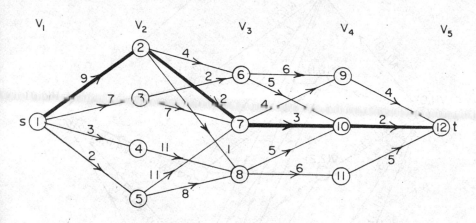

Figure 5.1 A 5 stage graph

Many problems can be formulated as multistage graph problems. We
shall give only one example. Consider a resource allocation problem in
which n units of resource are to be allocated to r projects. If j, $0 \leq j \leq n$
units of the resource are allocated to project i then the resulting net profit
is $N(i, j)$. The problem is to allocate the resource to the r projects in such
a way as to maximize total net profit. This problem may be formulated as
an $r + 1$ stage graph problem as follows. Stage i, $1 \leq i \leq r$ represents
project i. There are $n + 1$ vertices $V(i, j)$, $0 \leq j \leq n$ associated with stage
i, $2 \leq i \leq r$. Stages 1 and $r + 1$ each have one vertex $V(1, 0) = s$ and
$V(r + 1, n) = t$ respectively. Vertex $V(i, j)$, $2 \leq i \leq r$ represents the state
in which a total of j units of resource have been allocated to projects 1, 2,

..., $i - 1$. The edges in G are of the form $\langle V(i, j), V(i + 1, l)\rangle$ for all $j \leq l$ and $1 \leq i < r$. The edge $\langle V(i, j), V(i + 1, l)\rangle, j \leq l$ is assigned a weight or cost of $N(i, l - j)$ and corresponds to allocating $l - j$ units of resource to project i, $1 \leq i < r$. In addition, G has edges of the type $\langle V(r, j), V(r + 1, n)\rangle$. Each such edge is assigned a weight of $\max_{0 \leq p \leq n-j}\{N(r, p)\}$. The resulting graph for a three project problem with $n = 4$ is shown in Figure 5.2. It should be easy to see that an optimal allocation of resources is defined by a maximum cost s to t path. This is easily converted into a minimum cost problem by changing the sign of all the edge costs.

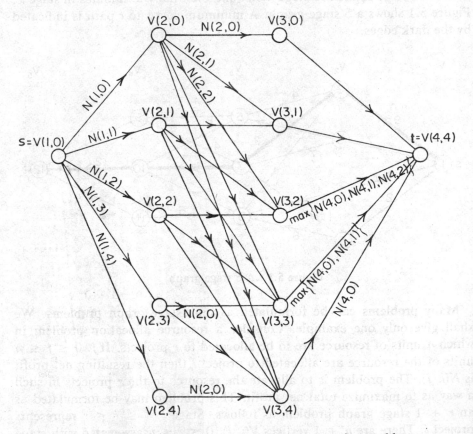

Figure 5.2 4 stage graph corresponding to a 3 project problem

A dynamic programming formulation for a k stage graph problem is obtained by first noticing that every s to t path is a result of a sequence of

$k - 2$ decisions. The ith decision involves determining which vertex in V_{i+1}, $1 \le i \le k - 2$, is to be on the path. It is easy to see that the principle of optimality holds. Let $P(i, j)$ be a minimum cost path from vertex j in V_i to vertex t. Let COST(i, j) be the cost of this path. Then, using the forward approach, we obtain:

$$\text{COST}(i, j) = \min_{\substack{l \in V_{i+1} \\ \langle j, l \rangle \in E}} \{c(j, l) + \text{COST}(i + 1, l)\} \tag{5.5}$$

Since, COST$(k - 1, j) = c(j, t)$ if $\langle j, t \rangle \in E$ and COST$(k - 1, j) = \infty$ if $\langle j, t \rangle \notin E$, (5.5) may be solved for COST$(1, s)$ by first computing COST$(k - 2, j)$ for all $j \in V_{k-2}$, then COST$(k - 3, j)$ for all $j \in V_{k-3}$, etc., and finally COST$(1, s)$. Trying this out on the graph of Figure 5.1, we obtain the following values:

$$\text{COST}(3, 6) = \min\{6 + \text{COST}(4, 9), 5 + \text{COST}(4, 10\}$$
$$= 7$$
$$\text{COST}(3, 7) = \min\{4 + \text{COST}(4, 9), 3 + \text{COST}(4, 10)\}$$
$$= 5$$
$$\text{COST}(3, 8) = 7$$
$$\text{COST}(2, 2) = \min\{4 + \text{COST}(3, 6), 2 + \text{COST}(3, 7), 1 + \text{COST}(3, 8)\}$$
$$= 7$$
$$\text{COST}(2, 3) = 9$$
$$\text{COST}(2, 4) = 18$$
$$\text{COST}(2, 5) = 15$$
$$\text{COST}(1, 1) = \min\{9 + \text{COST}(2, 2), 7 + \text{COST}(2, 3), 3 + \text{COST}(2, 4),$$
$$2 + \text{COST}(2, 5)\}$$
$$= 16$$

Thus, a minimum cost s to t path has a cost of 16. This path can be determined easily if we record the decision made at each state (vertex). Let $D(i, j)$ be the value of l which minimizes $c(j, l) + \text{COST}(i + 1, l)$ (see Eq. (5.5)). For Figure 5.1 we obtain.

$$D(3, 6) = 10; D(3, 7) = 10; D(3, 8) = 10;$$
$$D(2, 2) = 7; D(2, 3) = 6; D(2, 4) = 8; D(2, 5) = 8;$$
$$D(1, 1) = 2;$$

Let the minimum cost path be $s = 1, v_2, v_3, \ldots, v_{k-1}, t$. It is easy to see that $v_2 = D(1, 1) = 2; v_3 = D(2, D(1, 1)) = 7$ and $v_4 = D(3, D(2, D(1, 1))) = D(3, 7) = 10$.

Before writing an algorithm to solve (5.5) for a general k stage graph, let us impose an ordering on the vertices in V. This ordering will make it easier to write the algorithm. We shall require that the n vertices in V are indexed 1 through n. Indices are assigned in order of stages. First, s is assigned index 1, then vertices in V_2 are assigned indices, then vertices from V_3 and so on. t has index n. Hence, indices assigned to vertices in V_{i+1} are bigger than those assigned to vertices in V_i (see Figure 5.1). As a result of this indexing scheme, COST and D may be computed in the order $n - 1, n - 2, \ldots, 1$. The first subscript in COST, P and D only identifies the stage number and is omitted in the algorithm. The resulting algorithm is procedure FGRAPH.

```
line  procedure FGRAPH(E, k, n, P)
         //The input is a k stage graph with n vertices indexed in order//
         //of stages. E is a set of edges and c(i, j) is the cost of ⟨i, j⟩.//
         //P(1:k) is a minimum cost path//
1        real COST(n), integer D(n − 1), P(k), r, j, k, n
2        COST(n) ← 0
3        for j ← n − 1 to 1 by − 1 do   //compute COST(j)//
4          let r be a vertex such that ⟨j, r⟩ ∈ E and c(j, r) + COST(r) is
             minimum
5          COST(j) ← c(j, r) + COST(r)
6          D(j) ← r
7        repeat
         //find a minimum cost path//
8        P(1) ← 1; P(k) ← n
9        for j ← 2 to k − 1 do   //find jth vertex on path//
10         P(j) ← D(P(j − 1))
11       repeat
12     end FGRAPH
```

Algorithm 5.1 Multistage graph algorithm corresponding to forward approach

The complexity analysis of procedure FGRAPH is fairly straightforward. If G is represented by its adjacency lists, then r in line 4 may be found in time proportional to the degree of vertex j. Hence, if G has e edges then the time for the **for** loop of lines 3 to 7 is $\theta(n + e)$. The time for the **for** loop of lines 9 to 11 is $\theta(k)$. Hence, the total time in $\theta(n + e)$. In addition to the space needed for the input, space is needed for COST, D and P.

The multistage graph problem can also be solved using the backward approach. Let $BP(i, j)$ be a minimum cost path from vertex s to a vertex j in V_i. Let $BCOST(i, j)$ be the cost of $BP(i, j)$. From the backward approach we obtain:

$$BCOST(i, j) = \min_{\substack{l \in V_{i-1} \\ \langle l,j \rangle \in E}} \{BCOST(i - 1, l) + c(l, j)\} \qquad (5.6)$$

Since $BCOST(2, j) = c(1, j)$ if $\langle 1, j \rangle \in E$ and $BCOST(2, j) = \infty$ if $\langle 1, j \rangle \notin E$, $BCOST(i, j)$ may be computed using (5.6) by first computing BCOST for $i = 3$, then for $i = 4$ etc. For the graph of Figure (5.1) we obtain

$$BCOST(3, 6) = \min\{BCOST(2, 2) + 4, BCOST(2, 3) + 2\}$$
$$= 9$$
$$BCOST(3, 7) = 11$$
$$BCOST(3, 8) = 10$$
$$BCOST(4, 9) = 15$$
$$BCOST(4, 10) = 14$$
$$BCOST(4, 11) = 16$$
$$BCOST(5, 12) = 16$$

The corresponding algorithm to obtain a minimum cost $s - t$ path is procedure BGRAPH. The first subscript on BCOST, P and D are omitted for the same reasons as before. This algorithm has the same complexity as FGRAPH provided G is now represented by its inverse adjacency lists (i.e. for each vertex v we have a list of vertices w such that $\langle w, v \rangle \in E$).

```
procedure BGRAPH(E, k, n, P)
  //same function as FGRAPH//
  real BCOST(n); integer D(n - 1), P(k), r, j k, n
  BCOST(1) ← 0
  for j ← 2 to n do   //compute BCOST(j)//
    let r be a vertex such that ⟨r, j⟩ ⊂ E and BCOST(r) + c(r, j) is min-
      imum
    BCOST(j) ← BCOST(r) + c(r, j)
    D(j) ← r
  repeat
  //find a minimum cost path//
  P(1) ← 1; P(k) ← n
  for j ← k - 1 to 2 by - 1 do   //find jth vertex on path//
    P(j) ← D(P(j + 1))
  repeat
end BGRAPH
```

Algorithm 5.2 Multistage graph algorithm corresponding to backward approach

It should be easy to see that both FGRAPH and BGRAPH work correctly even on a more generalized version of multistage graphs. In this generalization, the graph is permitted to have edges $\langle u, v \rangle$ such that $u \in V_i$, $v \in V_j$ and $i < j$.

5.3 ALL PAIRS SHORTEST PATHS

Let $G = (V, E)$ be a directed graph with n vertices. Let C be a cost adjacency matrix for G such that $C(i, i) = 0$, $1 \leq i \leq n$, $C(i, j)$ is the length (or cost) of edge $\langle i, j \rangle$ if $\langle i, j \rangle \in E(G)$ and $C(i, j) = \infty$ if $i \neq j$ and $\langle i, j \rangle \notin E(G)$. The *all pairs shortest path problem* is to determine a matrix A such that $A(i, j)$ is the length of a shortest path from i to j. The matrix A may be obtained by solving n single source problems using the procedure SHORTEST__PATHS of Section 4.5 Since each application of this procedure requires $O(n^2)$ time, the matrix A may be obtained in $O(n^3)$ time. We shall obtain an alternate $O(n^3)$ solution to this problem using the principle of optimality. Our alternate solution will require a weaker restriction on edge costs than required by SHORTEST__PATHS. Rather than require all $C(i, j) \geq 0$, we shall only require that G have no cycles with negative length. Note that if we allow G to contain a cycle of negative length then the shortest path between any two vertices on this cycle will have length $-\infty$.

Let us examine a shortest i to j path in G, $i \neq j$. This path originates at vertex i and goes through some intermediate vertices (possibly none) and terminates at vertex j. We may assume that this path contains no cycles for if there is a cycle then this may be deleted without increasing the path length (no cycle has negative length). If k is an intermediate vertex on this shortest path then the subpaths from i to k and from k to j must be shortest paths from i to k and k to j respectively. Otherwise, the i to j path is not of minimum length. So, the principle of optimality holds. This alerts us to the prospect of using dynamic programming. If k is the intermediate vertex with highest index then the i to k path is a shortest i to k path in G going through no vertex with index greater than $k - 1$. Similarly the k to j path is a shortest k to j path in G going through no vertex of index greater than $k - 1$. We may regard the construction of a shortest i to j path as first requiring a decision as to which is the highest indexed intermediate vertex k. Once this decision has been made, we need to find two shortest paths. One from i to k and the other from k to j. Neither of these may go through a vertex with index greater than $k - 1$. Using $A^k(i, j)$ to represent the length of a shortest path from i to j going through no vertex of index greater than k, we obtain

$$A(i, j) = \min \{ \min_{1 \le k \le n} \{A^{k-1}(i, k) + A^{k-1}(k, j)\}, C(i, j)\} \qquad (5.7)$$

Clearly, $A^0(i, j) = C(i, j)$, $1 \le i \le n$, $1 \le j \le n$. We can obtain a recurrence for $A^k(i, j)$ using an argument similar to that used before. A shortest path from i to j going through no vertex higher than k either goes through vertex k or it does not. If it does, $A^k(i, j) = A^{k-1}(i, k) + A^{k-1}(k, j)$. If it does not then no intermediate vertex has index greater than $k - 1$. Hence $A^k(i, j) = A^{k-1}(i, j)$. Combining, we get

$$A^k(i, j) = \min\{A^{k-1}(i, j), A^{k-1}(i, k) + A^{k-1}(k, j)\}, \quad k \ge 1 \qquad (5.8)$$

The following example shows that (5.8) is not true for graphs with cycles of negative length.

Example 5.13 Figure 5.3 shows a digraph together with its matrix A^0. For this graph $A^2(1, 3) \ne \min\{A^1(1, 3), A^1(1, 2) + A^1(2, 3)\} = 2$. Instead we see that $A^2(1, 3) = -\infty$ as the length of the path

$$1, 2, 1, 2, 1, 2, \ldots, 1, 2, 3$$

can be made arbitrarily small. This is so because of the presence of the cycle 1 2 1 which has a length of -1. □

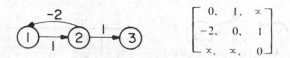

Figure 5.3 Graph with Negative Cycle

Recurrence (5.8) may be solved for A^n by first computing A^1, then A^2, then A^3, etc. Since there is no vertex in G with index greater then n, $A(i, j) = A^n(i, j)$. Procedure ALL_PATHS computes $A^n(i, j)$. The computation is done in-place so the superscript on A is not needed. The reason this computation can be carried out in-place is that $A^k(i, k) = A^{k-1}(i, k)$ and $A^k(k, j) = A^{k-1}(k, j)$. Hence, when A^k is formed, the kth column and row do not change. Consequently, when $A^k(i, j)$ is computed in line 9, $A(i, k) = A^{k-1}(i, k) = A^k(i, k)$ and $A(k, j) = A^{k-1}(k, j) = A^k(k, j)$. So, the old values upon which the new values are based do not change on this iteration.

```
      procedure ALL_PATHS(COST, A, n)
      //COST(n, n) is the cost adjacency matrix of a graph with n ver-//
      //tices; A(i, j) is the cost of a shortest path from vᵢ to vⱼ//
      //COST(i,i) = 0, 1 ≤ i ≤ n//
      integer i, j, k, n; real COST(n, n), A(n, n)
1     for i ← 1 to n do
2        for j ← 1 to n do
3           A(i, j) ← COST(i, j)   //copy COST into A//
4        repeat
5     repeat
6     for k ← 1 to n do   //for a path with highest vertex index k//
7        for i ← 1 to n do   //for all possible pairs of vertices//
8           for j ← 1 to n do
9              A(i, j) ← min{A(i, j), A(i, k) + A(k, j)}
10          repeat
11       repeat
12    repeat
13    end ALL_PATHS
```

Algorithm 5.3 Procedure to compute lengths of shortest paths

Example 5.14 The graph of Figure 5.4(a) has the cost matrix of Figure 5.4(b). The initial A matrix, $A^{(0)}$ plus its values after 3 iterations $A^{(1)}$, $A^{(2)}$, $A^{(3)}$ are given in Figure 5.5.   □

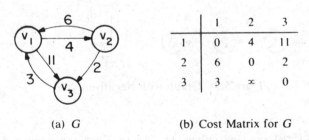

(a) G   (b) Cost Matrix for G

Figure 5.4 Directed graph and its cost matrix

Let $M = \max\{COST(i, j) | \langle i, j \rangle \in E(G)\}$. It is easy to see that $A^n(i, j) \le (n - 1)*M$. From the working of procedure ALL_PATHS, it is clear that if $\langle i, j \rangle \notin E(G)$ and $i \ne j$ then we may initialize $COST(i, j)$ to any number greater than $(n - 1)*M$ (rather than ∞). If at termination $A(i, j) > (n - 1)*M$ then there is no directed path from i to j in G.

$A^{(0)}$	1	2	3
1	0	4	11
2	6	0	2
3	3	∞	0

$A^{(1)}$	1	2	3
1	0	4	11
2	6	0	2
3	3	7	0

$A^{((2)}$	1	2	3
1	0	4	6
2	6	0	2
3	3	7	0

$A^{(3)}$	1	2	3
1	0	4	6
2	5	0	2
3	3	7	0

Figure 5.5 Matrices A^k produced by ALL__PATHS for the digraph of Figure 5.4

The time needed by procedure ALL__PATHS is especially easy to determine because the looping is independent of the data in the matrix A. Line 9 is iterated n^3 times and so the time for procedure ALL__PATHS is $\theta(n^3)$. An exercise examines the extensions needed to actually obtain the i to j paths with these lengths. Some speed-up can be obtained by noticing that the innermost for loop need be executed only when $A(i, k)$ and $A(k, j)$ are not equal to ∞.

5.4 OPTIMAL BINARY SEARCH TREES

Definition A *binary search tree* T is a binary tree; either it is empty or each node in the tree contains an identifier and
(i) all identifiers in the left subtree of T are less (numerically or alphabetically) than the identifier in the root node T;
(ii) all identifiers in the right subtree are greater than the identifier in the root node T;
(iii) the left and right subtrees of T are also binary search trees.

Note that the definition of a binary search tree requires that all identifiers in the tree be distinct. For a given set of identifiers, several different binary search trees are possible. Figure 5.6 shows two possible binary search trees for a subset of the reserved words of SPARKS.

To determine whether an identifier X is present in a binary search tree, X is compared with the root. If X is less than the identifier in the root, then the search continues in the left subtree; if X equals the identifier in the root, the search terminates successfully; otherwise the search continues in the right subtree. This is formalized in procedure SEARCH.

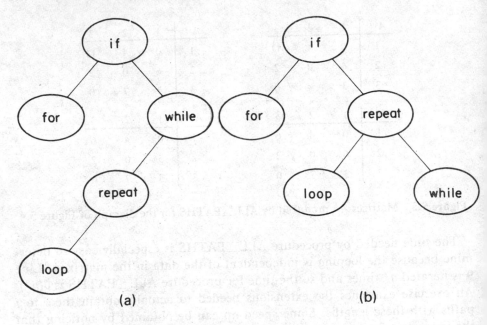

Figure 5.6   Two possible binary search trees

```
        procedure SEARCH(T, X, i)
          //Search the binary search tree T for X. Each node of the tree has/.
          //fields LCHILD, IDENT, RCHILD. If X is not in T then set i = /.
          //0. Otherwise, set i such that IDENT(i) = X.//
1           i ← T
2           while i ≠ 0 do
3             case
4               :X < IDENT(i): i ← LCHILD(i)   //search left subtree//
5               :X = IDENT(i): return
6               :X > IDENT(i): i ← RCHILD(i)   //search right subtree//
7             endcase
8           repeat
9         end SEARCH
```

Algorithm 5.4   Searching a binary search tree

Given a fixed set of identifiers, we wish to create a binary search tree organization. We may expect different binary search trees for the same identifier set to have different performance characteristics. The tree of Figure 5.6(a), in the worst case, requires four comparisons to find an identifier, while the tree of 5.6(b) requires only three. On the average the two trees need 12/5 and 11/5 comparisons respectively. This calculation assumes that each identifier is searched for with equal probability and that no searches for an identifier not in T are ever made.

In a general situation, we may expect different identifiers to be searched for with different frequencies (or probabilities). In addition, we may expect unsuccessful searches (i.e. searches for identifiers not in the tree) also to be made. Let us assume that the given set of identifiers is $\{a_1, a_2, \ldots, a_n\}$ with $a_1 < a_2 < \cdots < a_n$. Let $P(i)$ be the probability with which we shall be searching for a_i. Let $Q(i)$ be the probability that the identifier X being searched for is such that $a_i < X < a_{i+1}$, $0 \le i \le n$ (assume $a_0 = -\infty$ and $a_{n+1} = +\infty$). Then, $\sum_{0 \le i \le n} Q(i)$ is the probability of an unsuccessful search. Clearly, $\sum_{1 \le i \le n} P(i) + \sum_{0 \le i \le n} Q(i) = 1$. Given this data, we wish to construct an optimal binary search tree for $\{a_1, a_2, \ldots, a_n\}$. First, of course, we must be precise about what we mean by an optimal binary search tree.

In obtaining a cost function for binary search trees, it is useful to add a fictitious node in place of every empty subtree in the search tree. Such nodes are called external nodes and are drawn square in Figure 5.7. All other nodes are internal nodes. If a binary search tree represents n identifiers then there will be exactly n internal nodes and $n + 1$ (fictitious) external nodes. Every internal node represents a point where a successful search may terminate. Every external node represents a point where an unsuccessful search may terminate.

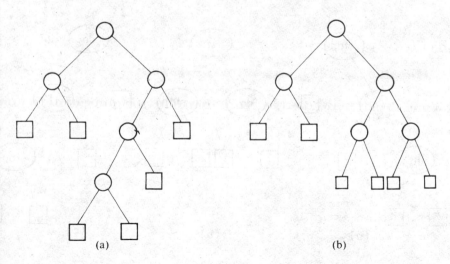

(a)   (b)

Figure 5.7 Binary search trees of Figure 5.6 with external nodes added

If a successful search terminates at an internal node at level l then l iterations of the loop of lines 2–7 (Algorithm 5.4) are needed. Hence, the expected cost contribution from the internal node for a_i is $P(i)*\text{level}(a_i)$.

Unsuccessful searches terminate with $i = 0$ (i.e. at an external node) in algorithm SEARCH. The identifiers not in the binary search tree may be partitioned into $n + 1$ equivalence classes E_i, $0 \le i \le n$. E_0 contains all identifiers X such that $X < a_1$. E_i contains all identifiers X such that $a_i < X < a_{i+1}$, $1 \le i < n$. E_n contains all identifiers X, $X > a_n$. It is easy to see that for all identifiers in the same class E_i, the search terminates at the same external node. For identifiers in different E_i the search terminates at different external nodes. If the failure node for E_i is at level l then only $l - 1$ iterations of the **while** loop are made. Hence, the cost contribution of this node is $Q(i)*(\text{level}(E_i) - 1)$.

The preceding discussion leads to the following formula for the expected cost of a binary search tree:

$$\sum_{1 \le i \le n} P(i)*\text{level}(a_i) + \sum_{0 \le i \le n} Q(i)*(\text{level}(E_i) - 1) \qquad (5.9)$$

We shall define an optimal binary search tree for the identifier set $\{a_1, a_2, \ldots, a_n\}$ to be a binary search tree for which (5.9) is minimum.

Example 5.15 The possible binary search trees for the identifier set $(a_1, a_2, a_3) = (\textbf{do}, \textbf{if}, \textbf{stop})$ are:

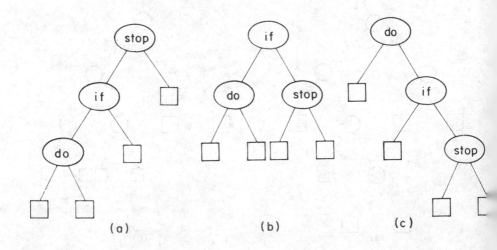

(a)   (b)   (c)

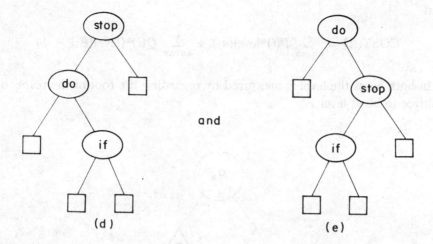

(d)   and   (e)

With equal probabilities $P(i) = Q(i) = 1/7$ for all i and j, we have

$$\text{cost(tree } a) = 15/7; \quad \text{cost(tree } b) = 13/7$$
$$\text{cost(tree } c) = 15/7; \quad \text{cost(tree } d) = 15/7$$
$$\text{cost(tree } e) = 15/7.$$

As expected, tree b is optimal. With $P(1) = .5$, $P(2) = .1$, $P(3) = .05$, $Q(0) = .15$, $Q(1) = .1$, $Q(2) = .05$ and $Q(3) = .05$ we have

$$\text{cost(tree } a) = 2.65; \quad \text{cost(tree } b) = 1.9$$
$$\text{cost(tree } c) = 1.5; \quad \text{cost(tree } d) = 2.05$$
$$\text{cost(tree } e) = 1.6$$

Tree c is optimal with this assignment of Ps and Qs. ☐

In order to apply dynamic programming to the problem of obtaining an optimal binary search tree we need to view the construction of such a tree as the result of a sequence of decisions and then observe that the principle of optimality holds when applied to the problem state resulting from a decision. A possible approach to this would be to make a decision as to which of the a_i's be assigned to the root node of T. If we choose a_k then it is clear that the internal nodes for $a_1, a_2, \ldots a_{k-1}$ as well as the external nodes for the classes $E_0, E_1, \ldots, E_{k-1}$ will lie in the left subtree, L, of the root. The remaining nodes will be in the right subtree, R. Define

$$\text{COST}(L) = \sum_{1 \le i < k} P(i)*\text{level}(a_i) + \sum_{0 \le i < k} Q(i)*(\text{level}(E_i) - 1)$$

and

$$\text{COST}(R) = \sum_{k<i\le n} P(i)*\text{level}(a_i) + \sum_{k\le i\le n} Q(i)*(\text{level}(E_i) - 1)$$

In both cases the level is measured by regarding the root of the respective subtree to be at level 1.

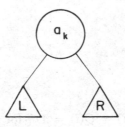

Figure 5.8   An optimal binary search tree with root a_k

Using $W(i, j)$ to represent the sum $Q(i) + \sum_{i+1}^{j} (Q(l) + P(l))$ we obtain the following as the expected cost of the search tree T (Figure 5.8)

$$P(k) + \text{COST}(L) + \text{COST}(R) + W(0, k - 1) + W(k, n) \qquad (5.10)$$

If T is optimal then Equation (5.10) must be minimum. Hence, COST(L) must be minimum over all binary search trees containing $a_1, a_2, \ldots, a_{k-1}$ and $E_0, E_1, \ldots, E_{k-1}$. Similarly COST($R$) must be minimum. If we use $C(i, j)$ to represent the cost of an optimal binary search tree, T_{ij}, containing $a_{i+1}, \ldots, a_j$ and $E_i, \ldots, E_j$ then for T to be optimal, we must have COST(L) = $C(0, k - 1)$ and COST(R) = $C(k, n)$. In addition, k must be chosen such that

$$P(k) + C(0, k - 1) + C(k, n) + W(0, k - 1) + W(k, n)$$

is minimum. Hence, for $C(0, n)$ we obtain:

$$C(0, n) = \min_{1\le k\le n} \{C(0, k - 1) + C(k, n) + P(k) + W(0, k - 1) + W(k, n)\}$$

$$(5.11)$$

We may generalize (5.11) to obtain for any $C(i, j)$

$$C(i, j) = \min_{i < k \le j} \{C(i, k - 1) + C(k, j) + P(k) + W(0, k - 1) + W(k, j)\}$$

$$= \min_{i < k \le j} \{C(i, k - 1) + C(k, j)\} + W(i, j) \tag{5.12}$$

Equation (5.12) may be solved for $C(0, n)$ by first computing all $C(i, j)$ such that $j - i = 1$ (note $C(i, i) = 0$ and $W(i, i) = Q(i), 0 \le i \le n)$. Next we can compute all $C(i, j)$ such that $j - i = 2$, then all $C(i, j)$ with $j - i = 3$ etc. If during this computation we record the root $R(i, j)$ of each tree T_{ij} then an optimal binary search tree may be constructed from these $R(i, j)$. Note that $R(i, j)$ is the value of k that minimizes (5.12).

Example 5.16 Let $n = 4$ and $(a_1, a_2, a_3, a_4) = ($**do, if, read,** while). Let $P(1:4) = (3, 3, 1, 1)$ and $Q(0:4) = (2, 3, 1, 1, 1)$. The Ps and Qs have been multiplied by 16 for convenience. Initially, we have $W(i, i) = Q(i)$, $C(i, i) = 0$ and $R(i, i) = 0, 0 \le i \le 4$. Using eq (5.12) and the observation $W(i, j) = P(j) + Q(j) + W(i, j - 1)$ we get:

$$W(0, 1) = P(1) + Q(1) + W(0, 0) = 8$$
$$C(0, 1) = W(0, 1) + \min\{C(0, 0) + C(1, 1)\} = 8$$
$$R(0, 1) = 1$$
$$W(1, 2) = P(2) + Q(2) + W(1, 1) = 7$$
$$C(1, 2) = W(1, 2) + \min\{C(1, 1) + C(2, 2)\} = 7$$
$$R(0, 2) = 2$$
$$W(2, 3) = P(3) + Q(3) + W(2, 2) = 3$$
$$C(2, 3) = W(2, 3) + \min\{C(2, 2) + C(3, 3)\} = 3$$
$$R(2, 3) = 3$$
$$W(3, 4) = P(4) + Q(4) + W(3, 3) = 3$$
$$C(3, 4) = W(3, 4) + \min\{C(3, 3) + C(4, 4)\} = 3$$
$$R(3, 4) = 4$$

Knowing $W(i, i + 1)$ and $C(i, i + 1), 0 \le i < 4$ we can again use equation (5.12) to compute $W(i, i + 2), C(i, i + 2), R(i, i + 2), 0 \le i < 3$. This process may be repeated until $W(0, 4), C(0, 4)$ and $R(0, 4)$ are obtained. The table of Figure 5.9 shows the results of this computation. The box in row i and column j shows the values of $W(j, j + i), C(j, j + i)$ and $R(j, j + i)$ respectively. The computation is carried out row wise from row 0 to row 4. From the table we see that $C(0, 4) = 32$ is the minimum cost of a binary search tree for (a_1, a_2, a_3, a_4). The root of tree T_{04} is a_2. Hence, the left subtree is T_{01} and the right subtree T_{24}. T_{01} has root a_1 and subtrees T_{00} and T_{11}. T_{24} has root a_3; its left subtree is therefore T_{22}

and right subtree T_{34}. Thus, with the data in the table it is possible to re-construct T_{04}. Figure 5.10 shows T_{04}.   □

row ↓	column → 0	1	2	3	4
0	2, 0, 0	3, 0, 0	1, 0, 0	1, 0, 0	1, 0, 0
1	8, 8, 1	7, 7, 2	3, 3, 3	3, 3, 4	
2	12, 19, 1	9, 12, 2	5, 8, 3		
3	16, 25, 2	11, 19, 2			
4	16, 32, 2				

Figure 5.9   Computation of C(0, 4), W(0, 4) and R(0, 4)

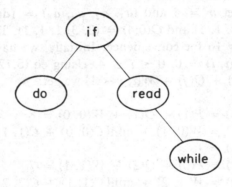

Figure 5.10   Optimal search tree for Example 5.16

The above example illustrates how Equation (5.12) may be used to determine the Cs and Rs and also how to reconstruct T_{on} knowing the Rs. Let us examine the complexity of this procedure to evaluate the Cs and Rs. The evaluation procedure described in the above example requires us to compute $C(i, j)$ for $(j - i) = 1, 2, \ldots, n$ in that order. When $j - i = m$ there are $n - m + 1$ $C(i, j)$s to compute. The computation of each of these $C(i, j)$s requires us to find the minimum of m quantities (see Equation (5.12)). Hence, each such $C(i, j)$ can be computed in time $O(m)$. The total time for all $C(i, j)$s with $j - i = m$ is therefore $O(nm - m^2)$. The total time to evaluate all the $C(i, j)$s and $R(i, j)$s is therefore

$$\Sigma_{1 \le m \le n} (nm - m^2) = O(n^3).$$

Actually we can do better than this using a result due to D. E. Knuth which shows that the optimal k is Equation (5.12) may be found by limiting the search to the range $R(i, j - 1) \leq k \leq R(i + 1, j)$. In this case the computing time becomes $O(n^2)$ (see exercises). Procedure OBST (Algorithm 5.5) uses this result to obtain in $O(n^2)$ time the values of $W(i, j)$, $R(i, j)$ and $C(i, j)$, $0 \leq i \leq j \leq n$. The actual tree T_{on} may be constructed from the values of $R(i, j)$ in $O(n)$ time. The algorithm for this is left as an exercise.

procedure *OBST*(P, Q, n)
   //Given n distinct identifiers $a_1 < a_2 < \ldots < a_n$ and probabilities//
   //$P(i)$, $1 \leq i \leq n$ and $Q(i)$, $0 \leq i \leq n$ this algorithm computes the cost//
   //$C(i, j)$ of optimal binary search trees T_{ij} fo identifiers $a_{i+1}, \ldots, a_j$.//
   //It also computes $R(i, j)$, the root of T_{ij}. $W(i, j)$ is the weight of T_{ij}//
   real $P(n)$, $Q(0{:}n)$, $C(0{:}n, 0{:}n)$, $W(0{:}n, 0{:}n)$
   integer $R(0{:}n, 0{:}n)$
   for $i \leftarrow 0$ **to** $n - 1$ **do**
     $(W(i, i), R(i, i), C(i, i)) \leftarrow (Q(i), 0, 0)$ //initialize//
     $(W(i, i + 1), R(i, i + 1), C(i, i + 1)) \leftarrow (Q(i) + Q(i + 1) + P(i + 1),$
       $i + 1, Q(i) + Q(i + 1) + P(i + 1))$ //optimal trees with one node//
   repeat
   $(W(n, n), R(n, n), C(n, n)) \leftarrow (Q(n), 0, 0)$
   for $m \leftarrow 2$ **to** n **do**   //find optimal trees with m nodes//
     for $i \leftarrow 0$ **to** $n - m$ **do**
      $j \leftarrow i + m$
      $W(i, j) \leftarrow W(i, j - 1) + P(j) + Q(j)$
      $k \leftarrow$ a value of l in the range $R(i, j - 1) \leq l \leq R(i + 1, j)$ that
        minimizes $\{C(i, l - 1) + C(l, j)\}$ //solve (5.12) using Knuth's
                                   //result//
      $C(i, j) \leftarrow W(i, j) + C(i, k - 1) + C(k, j)$
      $R(i, j) \leftarrow k$
     repeat
   repeat
end *OBST*

Algorithm 5.5   Finding a minimum cost binary search tree

5.5 0/1—KNAPSACK

The terminology and notation used in this section is the same as in section 5.1. A solution to the knapsack problem may be obtained by making a sequence of decisions on the variables $x_1, x_2, \ldots, x_n$. A decision on variable x_i involves deciding which of the values 0 or 1 is to be assigned to it. Let us assume that decisions on the x_i are made in the order $x_n, x_{n-1}, \ldots, x_1$. Following a decision on x_n we may be in one of two possible states: the capacity remaining in the knapsack is M and no profit has accrued or the capacity remaining is $M - w_n$ and a profit of p_n has accrued. It is clear that the remaining decisions $x_{n-1}, \ldots, x_1$ must be optimal with respect to the problem state resulting from the decision on x_n. Otherwise, $x_n, \ldots, x_1$ will not be optimal. Hence, the principle of optimality holds.

Let $f_j(X)$ be the value of an optimal solution to KNAP$(1, j, X)$. Since the principle of optimality holds, we obtain

$$f_n(M) = \max\{f_{n-1}(M), f_{n-1}(M - w_n) + p_n\} \tag{5.15}$$

For arbitrary $f_i(X)$, $i > 0$, Equation (5.13) generalizes to

$$f_i(X) = \max\{f_{i-1}(X), f_{i-1}(X - w_i) + p_i\} \tag{5.14}$$

Equation (5.14) may be solved for $f_n(M)$ by beginning with the knowledge $f_0(X) = 0$ for all X and $f_i(x) = -\infty, x < 0. f_1, f_2, \ldots, f_n$ may be successively computed using (5.14).

Example 5.17 Consider the knapsack instance $n = 3$, $(w_1, w_2, w_3) = (2, 3, 4)$, $(p_1, p_2, p_3) = (1, 2, 5)$ and $M = 6$. Figure 5.11 graphically displays f_1, f_2 and f_3. The first column of graphs gives the function $f_{i-1}(X - w_i) + p_i$. It is obtained by shifting $f_{i-1}(X)$ w_i units right on the X axis and then adding p_i to it. The second column gives the functions $f_i(X)$ obtained by using Equation (5.14). $f_3(6) = 6$. $\square$

From Figure 5.11 one sees that each f_i is completely specified by the pairs (P_j, W_j) where W_j is a value of X at which f_i takes a jump. $P_j = f_i(W_j)$. If there are r jumps then we need to know r pairs (P_j, W_j), $1 \leq j \leq r$. For convenience we introduce the pair $(P_0, W_0) = (0, 0)$. If we assume $W_j < W_{j+1}$, $0 \leq j < r$ then from (5.14) it follows that $P_j < P_{j+1}$. Further, $f_i(X) = f_i(W_i)$ for all X such that $W_j \leq X < W_{j+1}$, $0 \leq j < r. f_i(X) = f_i(W_r)$ for all X, $X \geq W_r$. If S^{i-1} is the set of all pairs for f_{i-1} (including $(0, 0)$) then the set S_1^i of all pairs for $g_i(X) = f_{i-1}(X - w_i) + p_i$ is obtained by adding to each pair in S^{i-1} the pair (p_i, w_i).

$$S_1^i = \{(P, W) | (P - p_i, W - w_i) \in S^{i-1}\} \tag{5.15}$$

S^i may now be obtained by merging together S^{i-1} and S_1^i. This merge corresponds to taking the maximum of the two functions $f_{i-1}(X)$ and $f_{i-1}(X$

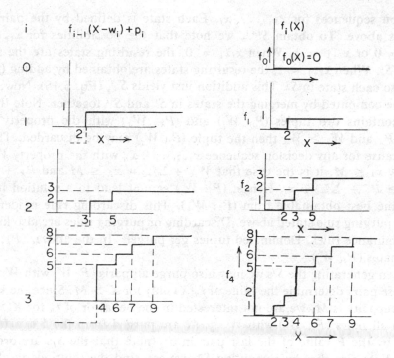

Figure 5.11 Knapsack values

$- w_i) + p_i$ in Equation (5.14). Thus, if one of S^{i-1} and $S_1{}^i$ has a pair (P_j, W_j) and the other has a pair (P_k, W_k) and $P_j \leq P_k$ while $W_j \geq W_k$ then the pair (P_j, W_j) is discarded. This is required by (5.14). $f_i(W_j) = \max\{P_j, P_k\} = P_k$.

Example 5.18 For the data of Example 5.17 we have

$S^0 = \{(0, 0)\}; S_1{}^1 = \{(1, 2)\}$
$S^1 = \{(0, 0), (1, 2)\}, S_1{}^2 = \{(2, 3), (3, 5)\}$
$S^2 = \{(0, 0), (1, 2), (2, 3), (3, 5)\}; S_1{}^3 = \{(5, 4), (6, 6), (7, 7), (8, 9)\}$
$S^3 = \{(0, 0), (1, 2), (2, 3), (5, 4), (6, 6), (7, 7), (8, 9)\}.$

Note that the pair (3, 5) has been eliminated from S^3 as a result of the purging rule stated above.   ☐

The above computation procedure for S^i, $0 \leq i \leq n$ may also be arrived at using a different line of reasoning. Suppose we attempt to solve the knapsack problem by explicitly enumerating all 2^n possibilities for $x_1, x_2, \ldots, x_n$. Then each S^i represents the possible states resulting from the 2^i

decision sequences for $x_1, \ldots, x_i$. Each state is defined by the pair (P_j, W_j) as above. To obtain S^{i+1}, we note that the possibilities for x_{i+1} are $x_{i+1} = 0$ or $x_{i+1} = 1$. When $x_{i+1} = 0$, the resulting states are the same as for S^i. When $x_{i+1} = 1$, the resulting states are obtained by adding (p_{i+1}, w_{i+1}) to each state in S^i. This addition just yields S_1^i, (Eq. 5.15). Now, S^{i+1} may be computed by merging the states in S^i and S_1^i together. Note that if S^{i+1} contains two tuples (P_j, W_j) and (P_k, W_k) with the property that $P_j \le P_k$ and $W_j \ge W_k$ then the tuple (P_j, W_j) may be discarded. This is so because for any decision sequence $x_{i+2}, \ldots, x_n$ with the property $W_j + \sum_{i+2}^n w_l x_l \le M$, it is the case that $W_k + \sum_{i+2}^n w_l x_l \le M$ and $P_k + \sum_{i+2}^n p_l x_l \ge P_j + \sum_{i+2}^n p_l x_l$. Hence, (P_j, W_j) cannot lead to a solution better than the best obtainable from (P_k, W_k). This discarding rule is identical to the purging rule stated above. Discarding or purging rules are also known as dominance rules. Dominated tuples get purged. In the above, (P_k, W_k) dominates (P_j, W_j).

When generating the S^is we may also purge all paris (P, W) with $W > M$ as these pairs determine the value of $f_n(X)$ only for $X > M$. Since the knapsack capacity is M, we are not interested in the behavior of f_n for $X > M$. When all pairs (P_j, W_j) with $W_j > M$ are purged from the S^is, $f_n(M)$ is given by the P value of the last pair in S^n (note that the S^is are ordered sets). Note also that by computing S^n, we can find the solutions to all the knapsack problems $\text{KNAP}(1, n, X), 0 \le X \le M$ and not just $\text{KNAP}(1, n, M)$. Since, we want only a solution to $\text{KNAP}(1, n, M)$, we may dispense with the computation of S^n altogether. The solution to $\text{KNAP}(1, n, M)$ is given by the last tuple (P, W) in S^n and only this has to be computed. The last tuple in S^n is either the last tuple in S^{n-1} or it is $(P_j + p_n, W_j + w_n)$ where $(P_j, W_j) \in S^{n-1}$ and W_j is the largest jump point in S^{n-1} such that $W_j + w_n \le M$.

If $(P1, W1)$ is the last tuple in S^n, a set of $0/1$ values for the x_is such that $\sum p_i x_i = P1$ and $\sum w_i x_i = W1$ may be determined by carrying out a search through the S^is. We may set $x_n = 0$ if $(P1, W1) \in S^{n-1}$. If $(P1, W1) \notin S^{n-1}$ then $(P1 - p_n, W1 - w_n) \in S^{n-1}$ and we may set $x_n = 1$. This leaves us to determine how either $(P1, W1)$ or $(P1 - p_n, W1 - w_n)$ was obtained in S^{n-1}. This may be done by using the argument used to determine x_n.

Example 5.19 With $M = 6$, the value of $f_3(6)$ is given by the tuple $(6, 6)$ in S^3 (Example 5.18). $(6, 6) \notin S^2$ and so we must set $x_3 = 1$. The pair $(6, 6)$ came from the pair $(6 - p_3, 6 - w_3) = (1, 2)$. Hence $(1, 2) \in S_2$. $(1, 2) \in$

S_1 and so we may set $x_2 = 0$. Since $(1, 2) \notin S^0$, we obtain $x_1 = 1$. Hence an optimal solution is $(x_1, x_2, x_3) = (1, 0, 1)$. □

We may sum up all we have said so far in the form of an informal algorithm procedure DKP (Algorithm 5.6). In order to be able to evaluate the complexity of the algorithm we need to specify how the sets S^i and $S_1{}^i$ are to be represented. An algorithm to merge S^i and $S_1{}^i$ is needed. This algorithm must purge pairs as needed. In addition, we need to specify an algorithm which will trace through S^{n-1}, ..., S^1 and determine a set of 0/1 values for x_n, ..., x_1.

line   **procedure** $DKP(p, w, n, M)$
1       $S^0 \leftarrow \{(0, 0)\}$
2   **for** $i \leftarrow 1$ **to** $n - 1$ **do**
3           $S_1{}^i \leftarrow \{(P1, W1) | (P1 - p_i, W1 - w_i) \in S^{i-1}$ and $W1 \leq M\}$
4           $S^i \leftarrow MERGE\_PURGE(S^{i-1}, S_1{}^i)$
5   **repeat**
6       $(PX, WX) \leftarrow$ last tuple in S^{n-1}
7       $(PY, WY) \leftarrow (P1 + p_n, W1 + w_n)$ where $W1$ is the largest W in
            any tuple in S^{n-1} such that $W + w_n \leq M$
            //trace back for $x_n, x_{n-1}, ..., x_1$//
8   **if** $PX > PY$ **then** $x_n \leftarrow 0$
9   **else** $x_n \leftarrow 1$
10   **endif**
11   trace back for $x_{n-1}, ..., x_1$
12 **end** DKP

Algorithm 5.6   Informal knapsack algorithm

Implementation of DKP

We can use two one dimensional arrays P and W to represent all the pairs $(P1, W1)$. The $P1$ values will be stored in P and the $W1$ values in W. Sets $S^0, S^1, ..., S^{n-1}$ may be stored adjacent to each other. This will require the use of pointers $F(i)$, $0 \leq i \leq n$ with $F(i)$ being the location of the first element in S^i, $0 \leq i < n$ and $F(n)$ being one more than the location of the last element in S^{n-1}.

Example 5.20 Using the representation above, the sets S^0, S^1 and S^2 of Example 5.18 will appear as:

	1	2	3	4	5	6	7
P	0	0	1	0	1	2	3
W	0	0	2	0	2	3	5
	↑	↑		↑			↑
	$F(0)$	$F(1)$		$F(2)$			$F(3)$ □

The merging and purging of S^{i-1} and $S_1{}^i$ may be carried out at the same time that $S_1{}^i$ is generated. Since the pairs in S^{i-1} are in increasing order of P and W, the pairs for S^i will be generated in this order. If the next pair generated for $S_1{}^i$ is (PQ, WQ) then we may merge into S^i all pairs from S^{i-1} with W value $\leq WQ$. The purging rule may be used to decide whether any pairs get purged. Hence, no additional space is needed in which to explicitly store $S_1{}^i$.

Procedure DKNAP generates S^i from S^{i-1} in this way. The S^is are generated in the loop of lines 4-29. At the start of each iteration $l = F(i - 1)$ and h is the index of the last pair in S^{i-1}. Hence $h = next - 1$. k points to the next tuple in S^{i-1} that has to be merged into S^i. Line 6 sets u such that for all W_j, $h \geq j > u$, $W_j + w_i > M$. Thus these pairs are not even generated in $S_1{}^i$. The pairs for $S_1{}^i$ are therefore all pairs $(P(j) + p_i, W(j) + w_i)$, $1 \leq j \leq u$. The loop of lines 7-22 generates these pairs. Each time a pair (pp, ww) is generated, all pairs (p, w) in S^{i-1} with $w < ww$ not yet purged or merged into S^i are merged into S^i. Note that none of these may be purged. Lines 13-14 handle the case when the next pair in S^{i-1} has a w value equal to ww. In this case the pair with lesser p value gets purged. In case $pp > P(next - 1)$ then the pair (pp, ww) gets purged. Otherwise, (pp, ww) is added to S^i. Lines 19-21 purge all unmerged pairs in S^{i-1} that can be purged at this time. Finally, following the merging of $S_1{}^i$, into S^i there may be pairs remaining in S^{i-1} to be merged into S^i. This is taken care of in lines 23-26. Note that because of lines 19-21, none of these pairs can be purged. Procedure PARTS (line 29) implements lines 8-9 of procedure DKP (Algorithm 5.6). This is left as an exercise.

line   **procedure** $DKNAP(p, w, n, M, m)$
        real $p(n), w(n), P(m), W(m), pp, ww, M$
        integer $F(0:n), l, h, u, i, j, p, next$
1       $F(0) \leftarrow 1; P(1) \leftarrow W(1) \leftarrow 0$ //S^0//
2       $l \leftarrow h \leftarrow 1$ //start and end of S^0//
3       $F(1) \leftarrow next \leftarrow 2$ //next free spot in P and W//
4   **for** $i \leftarrow 1$ **to** $n - 1$ **do**   //generate S^i//
5          $k \leftarrow l$
6          $u \leftarrow largest\ k, l \leq k \leq h,$ such that $W(k) + w_i \leq M$
7   **for** $j \leftarrow l$ **to** u **do**   //generate S_1^i and merge//
8             $(pp, ww) \leftarrow (P(j) + p_i, W(j) + w_i)$ //next element in S_1^i//
9   **while** $k \leq h$ **and** $W(k) \leq ww$ **do**   //merge in from S^{i-1}//
10               $P(next) \leftarrow P(k); W(next) \leftarrow W(k)$
11               $next \leftarrow next + 1; k \leftarrow k + 1$
12   **repeat**
13   **if** $k \leq h$ **and** $W(k) = ww$ **then** $pp \leftarrow \max(pp, P(k))$
14                                       $k \leftarrow k + 1$
15   **endif**
16   **if** $pp > P(next - 1)$ **then** $(P(next), W(next)) \leftarrow (pp, ww)$
17                                       $next \leftarrow next + 1$
18   **endif**
19   **while** $k \leq h$ **and** $P(k) \leq P(next - 1)$ **do**   //purge//
20               $k \leftarrow k + 1$
21   **repeat**
22   **repeat**
           //merge in remaining terms from S^{i-1}//
23   **while** $k \leq h$ **do**
24            $(P(next), W(next)) \leftarrow (P(k), W(k))$
25            $next \leftarrow next + 1; k \leftarrow k + 1$
26   **repeat**
           //initialize for S^{i+1}//
27         $l \leftarrow h + 1; h \leftarrow next - 1; F(i + 1) \leftarrow next$
28   **repeat**
29   **call** $PARTS$
30   **end** $DKNAP$

Algorithm 5.7   Algorithm for 0/1 knapsack problem

Analysis of Procedure DKNAP

If $|S^i|$ is the number of pairs in S^i then the arrays P and W should have a minimum dimension of $m = \Sigma_{0 \le i \le n} |S^i|$. Since it is not possible to predict the exact space needed, it will be necessary to test for $next > m$ each time $next$ is incremented. Since each S^i, $i > 0$, is obtained by merging S^{i-1} and S_1^i and $|S_1^i| \le |S^{i-1}|$, it follows that $|S^i| \le 2|S^{i-1}|$. In the worst case no pairs will get purged and

$$\sum_{0 \le i \le n-1} |S^i| = \sum_{0 \le i \le n-1} 2^i = 2^n - 1.$$

The time needed to generate S^i from S^{i-1} is $\theta(|S^{i-1}|)$. Hence, the time needed to compute all the S^is, $0 \le i < n$ is $\theta(\Sigma|S^{i-1}|)$. Since $|S^i| \le 2^i$, the time needed to compute all the S^is is $O(2^n)$. If the p_js are integer then each pair (P, W) in S^i has integer P and $P \le \Sigma_{1 \le j \le i} p_j$. Similarly, if the w_js are integer, each W is integer and $W \le M$. In any S^i the pairs have distinct W values and also distinct P values. Hence,

$$|S^i| \le 1 + \sum_{1 \le j \le i} p_j$$

when the p_js are integer and

$$|S^i| \le 1 + \min\{\sum_{1 \le j \le i} w_j, M\}$$

when the w_js are integer. When both the p_js and w_js are integer the time and space complexity of DKNAP (excluding the time for PARTS) is $O(\min\{2^n, n\Sigma_{1 \le i \le n} p_i, nM\})$. In this bound $\Sigma_{1 \le i \le n} p_i$ may be replaced by $\Sigma_{1 \le i \le n} p_i/\gcd(p_1, \ldots, p_n)$ and M by $\gcd(w_1, w_2, \ldots, w_n, M)$ (see exercises). The exercises indicate how PARTS may be implemented so as to have a space complexity $O(1)$ and a time complexity $O(n^2)$.

While the above analysis may seem to indicate that DKNAP requires too much computational resource to be practical for large n, in practice many instances of this problem can in fact be solved in a "reasonable" amount of time. This happens because usually, all the ps and ws are integer and M is much smaller than 2^n. The purging rule is effective in purging most of the tuples that would otherwise remain in the S^is.

Procedure DKNAP may be speeded by the use of heuristics. Let L be an estimate on the value of an optimal solution such that $f_n(M) \ge L$. Let $\text{PLEFT}(i) = \Sigma_{i < j \le n} p_j$. If S^i contains a tuple (P, W) such that $P + \text{PLEFT}(i) < L$ then (P, W) may be purged from S^i. To see this, observe that (P, W) can contribute at best the pair $(P + \Sigma_{i < j \le n} p_j, W + \Sigma_{i < j \le n} w_j)$ to S_1^n. Since $P + \Sigma_{i < j \le n} p_j = P + \text{PLEFT}(i) < L$, it follows that this pair cannot lead to a pair with value at least L and so cannot determine an optimal solution. A simple way to estimate L such that $L \le f_n(M)$ is to consider the last pair (P, W) in S^i. Then, $P \le f_n(M)$. A better estimate is obtained by adding to (P, W) some of the remaining objects. Example 5.21 illustrates this. Heuristics for the knapsack problem will be discussed in greater detail in the chapter on branch-and-bound. The exercises explore a divide and conquer approach to speed DKNAP so that the worst case time is $O(2^{n/2})$.

Example 5.21 Consider the following instance of the knapsack problem: $n = 6$; $(p_1, p_2, p_3, p_4, p_5, p_6) = (w_1, w_2, w_3, w_4, w_5, w_6) = (100, 50, 20, 10, 7, 3)$ and $M = 165$. Attempting to fill the knapsack using objects in the order 1, 2, 3, 4, 5 and 6, we see that objects 1, 2, 4 and 6 fit in yielding a profit of 163 and a capacity utilization of 163. We may thus begin with $L = 163$ as a value with the property $L \le f_n(M)$. Since $p_i = w_i$, every pair $(P, W) \in S^i$, $0 \le i \le 6$ has $P = W$. Hence, each pair may be replaced by the singleton P or W. PLEFT(0) = 190; PLEFT(1) = 90; PLEFT(2) = 40; PLEFT(3) = 20; PLEFT(4) = 10; PLEFT(5) = 3 and PLEFT(6) = 0. Eliminating from each S^i any singleton P such that P + PLEFT(i) $< L$ we obtain:

$$S^0 = \{0\}; S_1^1 = \{100\}$$
$$S^1 = \{100\}; S_1^2 = \{150\}$$
$$S^2 = \{100, 150\}; S_1^3 = \{120\}$$
$$S^3 = \{150\}; S_1^4 = \{160\}$$
$$S^4 = \{160\}; S_1^5 = \phi$$
$$S^5 = \{160\}$$

The singleton 0 is deleted from S^1 as 0 + PLEFT(1) < 163. S_1^3 does not contain the singleton $150 + 20 = 170$ as $M < 170$. S^3 does not contain the 100 or the 120 as each is less than L − PLEFT(3) etc. F_6 (165) may be determined from S^5. In this example, the value of L did not change. In general, L will change if a better estimate is obtained as a result of the computation of some S^i. If the heuristic wasn't used then the computation would have proceeded as:

$$S^0 = \{0\}$$
$$S^1 = \{0, 100\}$$
$$S^2 = \{0, 50, 100, 150\}$$
$$S^3 = \{0, 20, 50, 70, 100, 120, 150\}$$
$$S^4 = \{0, 10, 20, 30, 50, 60, 70, 80, 100, 110, 120, 130, 150, 160\}$$
$$S^5 = \{0, 7, 10, 17, 20, 27, 30, 37, 50, 57, 60, 67, 70, 77, 80, 87, 100,$$
$$107, 110, 117, 120, 127, 130, 137, 150, 157, 160\}$$

f_6 (165) may now be determined from S^5 using the knowledge $(p_6, w_6) = (3, 3)$.   □

5.6 RELIABILITY DESIGN

In this section we look at an example of how to use dynamic programming to solve a problem with a multiplicative optimization function. The problem is to design a system which is composed of several devices connected in series (Figure 5.12). Let r_i be the reliability of device D_i (i.e. r_i is the probability that device i will function properly). Then, the reliability of the entire system is Πr_i. Even if the individual devices are very reliable (the r_i's are very close to one), the reliability of the system may not be very good. For example, if $n = 10$ and $r_i = .99$, $1 \le i \le 10$ then $\Pi r_i = .895$. Hence, it is. desirable to duplicate devices. Multiple copies of the same device type are connected in parallel (Figure 5.13) through the use of switching circuits. The switching circuits determine which devices in any given group are functioning properly. They then make use of one such device at each stage.

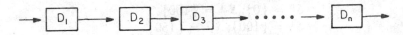

Figure 5.12 n devices D_i, $1 \le i \le n$ connected in series

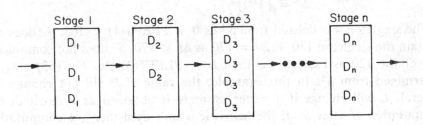

Figure 5.13   Multiple devices connected in parallel in each stage

If stage i contains m_i copies of device D_i then the probability that all m_i have a malfunction is $(1 - r_i)^{m_i}$. Hence the reliability of stage i becomes $1 - (1 - r_i)^{m_i}$. Thus, if $r_i = .99$ and $m_i = 2$ the stage reliability becomes 9999. In any practical situation, the stage reliability will be a little less than $1 - (1 - r_i)^{m_i}$ because the switching circuits themselves are not fully reliable. Also, failures of copies of the same device may not be fully independent (e.g. if failure is due to design defect). Let us assume that the reliability of stage i is actually given by a function $\phi_i(m_i)$, $1 \le i \le n$. (It is quite conceivable that $\phi_i(m_i)$ may decrease after a certain value of m_i). The reliability of the system of stages is $\Pi_{1 \le i \le n} \phi_i(m_i)$.

Our problem is to use device duplication to maximize reliability. This maximization is to be carried out under a cost constraint. Let c_i be the cost of each unit of device i and let c be the maximum allowable cost of the system being designed. We wish to solve the following maximization problem:

$$\text{maximize} \prod_{1 \le i \le n} \phi_i(m_i)$$

$$\text{subject to} \sum_{1 \le i \le m} c_i m_i \le c \qquad (5.16)$$

$$m_i \ge 1 \text{ and integer, } 1 \le i \le n$$

A dynamic programming solution may be obtained in a manner similar to that used for the knapsack problem. Since, we may assume each $c_i > 0$, each m_i must be in the range $1 \le m_i \le u_i$ where

$$u_i = \left\lfloor (c + c_i - \sum_1^n c_j)/c_i \right\rfloor$$

The upper bound u_i follows from the observation that $m_j \ge 1$. An optimal solution $m_1, m_2, \ldots, m_n$ is the result of a sequence of decisions, one decision for each m_i. Let $f_i(x)$ represent the maximum value of $\sum_{1 \le j \le i} \emptyset_j(m_j)$ subject to the constraints $\sum_{1 \le j \le i} c_j m_j \le x$ and $1 \le m_j \le u_j$, $1 \le j \le i$. Then, the value of an optimal solution is $f_n(c)$. The last decision made requires one to choose m_n from one of $\{1, 2, 3, \ldots, u_n\}$. Once a value for m_n has been chosen, the remaining decisions must be such as to use the remaining funds $c - c_n m_n$ in an optimal way. The principal of optimality holds and

$$f_n(c) = \max_{1 \le m_n \le u_n} \{\phi_n(m_n) f_{n-1}(c - c_n m_n)\} \qquad (5.17)$$

For any $f_i(x)$, $i \ge 1$, this equation generalizes to

$$f_i(x) = \max_{1 \le m_i \le u_i} \{\phi_i(m_i) f_{i-1}(c - c_i m_i)\} \qquad (5.18)$$

Clearly, $f_0(x) = 1$ for all x, $0 \le x \le c$. Hence, (5.18) may be solved using an approach similar to that used for the knapsack problem. Let S^i consist of tuples of the form (f, x) where $f = f_i(x)$. There is at most one tuple for each different x that results from a sequence of decisions on $m_1, m_2, \ldots, m_i$. The dominance rule (f_1, x_1) dominates (f_2, x_2) iff $f_1 \ge f_2$ and $x_1 \le x_2$ holds for this problem too. Hence, dominated tuples may be discarded from S^i.

Example 5.23   We are to design a three stage system with device types D_1, D_2 and D_3. The costs are \$30, \$15 and \$20 respectively. The cost of the system is to be no more than \$105. The reliability of each device type is .9, .8 and .5 respectively. We shall assume that if stage i has m_i devices of type i in parallel then $\emptyset_i(m_i) = 1 - (1 - r_i)^{m_i}$. In terms of the notation used earlier, $c_1 = 30$; $c_2 = 15$; $c_3 = 20$; $c = 105$; $r_1 = .9$; $r_2 = .8$; $r_3 = .5$; $u_1 = 2$; $u_2 = 3$ and $u_3 = 3$.

We shall use S^i to represent the set of all undominated tuples (f, x) that may result from the various decision sequences for $m_1, m_2, \ldots, m_i$. Hence, $f(x) = f_i(x)$. Beginning with $S^0 = \{(1, 0)\}$ we may obtain each S^i from S^{i-1} by trying out all possible values for m_i and combining the resulting tuples together. Using S_j^i to represent all tuples obtainable from S^{i-1} by choosing $m_i = j$ we obtain: $S_1^1 = \{(.9, 30)\}$ and $S_2^1 = \{(.9, 30), (.99, 60)\}$. $S_1^2 = \{(.72, 45), (.792, 75)\}$; $S_2^2 = \{(.864, 60)\}$. Note that the tuple (.9504, 90) which comes from (.99, 60) has been eliminated from S_2^2 as this leaves only \$10. This is not enough to allow $m_3 = 1$. $S_3^2 = \{(.8928, 75)\}$. Combining, we get $S^2 = \{(.72, 45), (.864, 60), (.8928, 75)\}$ as the tuple (.792, 75) is dominated by (.864, 60). $S_1^3 = \{(.36, 65), (.432, 80), (.4464, 95)\}$; $S_2^3 = \{(.54, 85), (.648, 100)\}$; $S_3^3 = \{(.63, 105)\}$. Combining, we get $S^3 = \{(.36, 65); (.432, 80); (.648, 100); (.63, 105)\}$.

The best design has a reliability of .63 and a cost of 105. Tracing back through the S^is we determine that $m_1 = 1$, $m_2 = 1$ and $m_3 = 3$.   □

As in the case of the knapsack problem, a complete dynamic programming algorithm for the reliability problem will use heuristics to reduce the size of the S^is. As noted in Example 5.23 there is no need to retain any tuple (f, x) in S^i with x value greater that $c - \Sigma_{i \le j \le n} c_j$ as such a tuple will not leave adequate funds to complete the system. In addition, we may devise a simple heuristic to determine the best reliability obtainable by completing a tuple (f, x) in S^i. If this is less than a heuristically determined lower bound on the optimal system reliability then (f, x) may be eliminated from S^i.

5.7 THE TRAVELING SALESPERSON PROBLEM

We have seen how to apply dynamic programming to a subset selection problem (0/1 knapsack). Now we turn our attention to a permutation problem. Note that permutation problems will usually be much harder to solve than subset problems as there are $n!$ different permutations of n objects while there are only 2^n different subsets of n objects ($n! > O(2^n)$). Let $G = (V, E)$ be a directed graph with edge costs c_{ij}. c_{ij} is defined such that $c_{ij} > 0$ for all i and j and $c_{ij} = \infty$ if $< i, j > \notin E$. Let $|V| = n$ and assume $n > 1$. A *tour* of G is a directed cycle that includes every vertex in V. The cost of a tour is the sum of the cost of the edges on the tour. The *traveling salesperson problem* is to find a tour of minimum cost.

The traveling salesperson problem finds application in a variety of situations. Suppose we have to route a postal van to pick up mail from mail boxes located at n different sites. An $n + 1$ vertex graph may be used to represent the situation. One vertex represents the post office from which the postal van starts and to which it must return. Edge $< i, j >$ is assigned a cost equal to the distance from site i to site j. The route taken by the postal van is a tour and we are interested in finding a tour of minimum length.

As a second example, suppose we wish to use a robot arm to tighten the nuts on some piece of machinery on an assembly line. The arm will start from its initial position (which is over the first nut to be tightened), successively move to each of the remaining nuts and return to the initial position. The path of the arm is clearly a tour on a graph in which vertices represent the nuts. A minimum cost tour will minimize the time needed for the arm to complete its task (note that only the total arm movement time is variable; the nut tightening time is independent of the tour).

Our final example is from a production environment in which several commodities are manufactured on the same set of machines. The manufacture proceeds in cycles. In each production cycle, n different commodities are produced. When the machines are changed from production of commodity i to commodity j, a change over cost c_{ij} is incurred. It is desired to find a sequence in which to manufacture these commodities. This sequence should minimize the sum of change over costs (the remaining production costs are sequence independent). Since the manufacture proceeds cyclically, it is necessary to include the cost of starting the next cycle. This is just the change over cost from the last to the first commodity. Hence, this problem may be regarded as a traveling salesperson problem on an n vertex graph with edge cost c_{ij} being the changeover cost from commodity i to commodity j.

In the following discussion we shall, without loss of generality, regard a tour to be a simple path that starts and ends at vertex 1. Every tour consists of an edge $<1, k>$ for some $k \in V - \{1\}$ and a path from vertex k to vertex 1. The path from vertex k to vertex 1 goes through each vertex in $V - \{1, k\}$ exactly once. It is easy to see that if the tour is optimal then the path from k to 1 must be a shortest k to 1 path going through all vertices in $V - \{1, k\}$. Hence, the principle of optimality holds. Let $g(i, S)$ be the length of a shortest path starting at vertex i, going through all vertices in S and terminating at vertex 1. $g(1, V - \{1\})$ is the length of an optimal salesperson tour. From the principal of optimality it follows that:

$$g(1, V - \{1\}) = \min_{2 \le k \le n} \{c_{1k} + g(k, V - \{1, k\})\} \qquad (5.19)$$

Generalizing (5.19) we obtain

$$g(i, S) = \min_{j \in S} \{c_{ij} + g(j, S - \{j\})\} \qquad (5.20)$$

(5.19) may be solved for $g(1, V - \{1\})$ if we know $g(k, V - \{1, k\})$ for all choices of k. The g values may be obtained by using (5.20). Clearly, $g(i, \phi) = c_{i,1}, 1 \le i \le n$. Hence, we may use (5.20 to obtain $g(i, S)$ for all S of size 1. Then we can obtain $g(i, S)$ for S with $|S| = 2$ etc. When $|S| < n - 1$, the values of i and S for which $g(i, S)$ is needed are such that $i \ne 1; 1 \notin S$ and $i \notin S$.

Example 5.23 Consider the directed graph of Figure 5.14(a). The edge lengths are given by the matrix c of Figure 5.14(b).

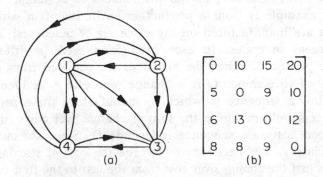

Figure 5.14 Directed graph and edge length matrix c

$$g(2, \phi) = c_{21} = 5; g(3, \phi) = c_{31} = 6 \text{ and } g(4, \phi) = c_{41} = 8.$$

Using (5.20) we obtain

$$g(2, \{3\}) = c_{23} + g(3, \emptyset) = 15; \qquad g(2, \{4\}) = 18$$
$$g(3, \{2\}) = 18; \qquad\qquad\qquad g(3, \{4\}) = 20$$
$$g(4, \{2\}) = 13; \qquad\qquad\qquad g(4, \{3\}) = 15$$

Next, we compute $g(i, S)$ with $|S| = 2$ and $i \neq 1$ and $1 \notin S$ and $i \notin S$.

$$g(2, \{3, 4\}) = \min\{c_{23} + g(3, \{4\}), c_{24} + g(4, \{3\})\} = 25$$
$$g(3, \{2, 4\}) = \min\{c_{32} + g(2, \{4\}), c_{34} + g(4, \{2\})\} = 25$$
$$g(4, \{2, 3\}) = \min\{c_{42} + g(2, \{3\}), c_{43} + g(3, \{2\})\} = 23$$

Finally, from (5.19) we obtain

$$g(1, \{2, 3, 4\}) = \min\{c_{12} + g(2, \{3, 4\}), c_{13} + g(3, \{2, 4\}), c_{14} + g(4, \{2, 3\})\}$$
$$= \min\{35, 40, 43\}$$
$$= 35$$

An optimal tour of the graph of Figure 5.14(a) has length 35. A tour of this length may be constructed if we retain with each $g(i, S)$ the value of j that minimizes the right hand side of (5.21). Let $J(i, S)$ be this value. Then, $J(1, \{2, 3, 4\}) = 2$. Thus the tour starts from 1 and goes to 2. The remaining tour may be obtained from $g(2, \{3, 4\})$. $J(2, \{3, 4\}) = 4$. Thus the next edge is $\langle 2, 4 \rangle$. The remaining tour is for $g(4, \{3\})$. $J(4, \{3\}) = 3$. The optimal tour is 1, 2, 4, 3, 1.   ☐

Let N be the number of $g(i, S)$s that have to be computed before (5.19) may be used to compute $g(1, V - \{1\})$. For each value of $|S|$ there are $n - 1$ choices for i. The number of distinct sets S of size k not including 1 and i is $\binom{n - 2}{k}$.

Hence

$$N = \sum_{k=0}^{n-2} (n - 1)\binom{n - 2}{k} = (n - 1)2^{n-2}.$$

An algorithm that proceeds to find an optimal tour by making use of (5.19) and (5.20) will require $\theta(n^2 2^n)$ time as the computation of $g(i, |S|)$ with $|S| = k$ requires $k - 1$ comparisons when solving (5.20). This is better than enumerating all $n!$ different tours to find the best one. The most serious drawback of this dynamic programming solution is the space needed. The space needed in $O(n2^n)$. This is too large even for modest values of n.

5.8   FLOW SHOP SCHEDULING

Often, the processing of a job requires the performance of several distinct tasks. Computer programs run in a multiprogramming environment are input, then executed. Following the execution, the job is queued for output and the output eventually printed. In a general flow shop we may have n jobs each requiring m tasks T_{1i}, T_{2i}, ..., T_{mi}, $1 \le i \le n$ to be performed. Task T_{ji} is to be performed on processor P_j, $1 \le j \le m$. The time required to complete task T_{ji} is t_{ji}. A schedule for the n jobs is an assignment of tasks to time intervals on the processors. Task T_{ji} must be assigned to processor P_j. No processor may have more than one task assigned to it in any time interval. Additionally, for any job i the processing of task T_{ji}, $j > 1$ cannot be started until task $T_{j-1,i}$ has been completed.

Example 5.24   Two jobs have to be scheduled on three processors. The task times are given by the matrix $\mathfrak{I}$:

$$\mathfrak{I} = \begin{bmatrix} 2 & 0 \\ 3 & 3 \\ 5 & 2 \end{bmatrix}$$

Two possible schedules for the jobs are shown in Figure 5.15.   ☐

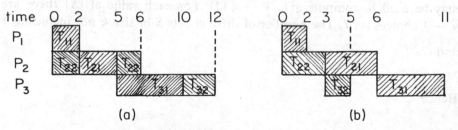

Figure 5.15   Two possible schedules for Example 5.24

A *non-preemptive* schedule is a schedule in which the processing of a task on any processor is not terminated until the task is complete. A schedule for which this need not be true is called *preemptive*. The schedule of Figure 5.15(a) is a preemptive schedule. Figure 5.15(b) shows a nonpreemptive schedule. The *finish time*, $f_i(S)$, of job i is the time at which all tasks of job i have been completed in schedule S. In Figure 5.15(a), $f_1(S) = 10$ and $f_2(S) = 12$. In Figure 5.15(b), $f_1(S) = 11$ and $f_2(S) = 5$. The finish time, $F(S)$, of a schedule S is given by

$$F(S) = \max_{1 \le i \le n}\{f_i(S)\} \tag{5.21}$$

The *mean flow time*, MFT(S), is defined to be

$$\text{MFT}(S) = \frac{1}{n} \sum_{1 \le i \le n} f_i(S) \tag{5.22}$$

An optimal finish time (OFT) schedule for a given set of jobs is a non-preemptive schedule S for which $F(S)$ is minimum over all nonpreemptive schedules S. A preemptive optimal finish time (POFT) schedule, optimal mean finish time schedule (OMFT) and preemptive optimal mean finish (POMFT) schedules are defined in the obvious way.

While the general problem of obtaining OFT and POFT schedules for $m > 2$ and of obtaining OMFT schedules is computationally difficult (see chapter 11), dynamic programming leads to an efficient algorithm to obtain OFT schedules for the case $m = 2$. In this section we consider this special case.

For convenience, we shall use a_i to represent t_{1i}, and b_i to represent t_{2i}. For the two processor case one may readily verify that nothing is to be gained by using different processing orders on the two processors (this is not true for $m > 2$). Hence, a schedule is completely specified by providing a permutation of the jobs. Jobs will be executed on each processor in this order. Each task will be started at the earliest possible time. The schedule of Figure 5.16 is completely specified by the permutation (5, 1, 3, 2, 4). We shall make the simplifying assumption that $a_i \ne 0$, $1 \le i \le n$. Note that if jobs with $a_i = 0$ are allowed then an optimal schedule may be constructed by first finding an optimal permutation for all jobs with $a_i \ne 0$ and then adding all jobs with $a_i = 0$ (in any order) in front of this permutation (see the exercises).

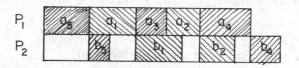

Figure 5.16   A schedule

It is easy to see that an optimal permutation (schedule) has the property that given the first job in the permutation, the remaining permutation is optimal with respect to the state the two processors are in following the completion of the first job. Let $\sigma_1, \sigma_2, \ldots, \sigma_k$ be a permutation prefix defining a schedule for jobs $T_1, T_2, \ldots, T_k$. For this schedule let f_1 and f_2 be the time at which the processing of jobs $T_1, T_2, \ldots, T_k$ is completed on processors P_1 and P_2 respectively. Let $t = f_2 - f_1$. The state of the processors following the sequence of decisions $T_1, T_2, \ldots, T_k$ is completely characterized by t. Let $g(S, t)$ be the length of an optimal schedule for the subset of jobs S under the assumption that processor 2 is not available until time t. The length of an optimal schedule for the job set $\{1, 2, \ldots, n\}$ is $g(\{1, 2, \ldots, n\}, 0)$.

Since the principle of optimality holds, we obtain

$$g(\{1, 2, \ldots, n\}, 0) = \min_{1 \le i \le n}\{a_i + g(\{1, 2, \ldots, n\} - \{i\}, b_i)\} \quad (5.23)$$

Equation (5.23) generalizes to (5.24) for arbitrary S and t. This generalization requires that $g(\phi, t) = \max\{t, 0\}$ and that $a_j \ne 0, 1 \le i \le n$.

$$g(S, t) = \min_{i \in S}\{a_i + g(S - \{i\}, b_i + \max\{t - a_i, 0\}) \quad (5.24)$$

The term $\max\{t - a_i, 0\}$ comes into (5.24) as task T_{2i} cannot start until $\max\{a_i, t\}$ (P_2 is not available until time t). Hence $f_2 - f_1 = b_i + \max\{a_i, t\} - a_i = b_i + \max\{t - a_i, 0\}$. We may solve for $g(S, t)$ using an approach similar to that used to solve (5.20). However, it turns out that (5.24) may be solved algebraically obtaining a very simple rule to generate an optimal schedule.

Consider any schedule R for a subset of jobs S. Assume that P_2 is not available until time t. Let i and j be the first two jobs in this schedule. Then, from (5.24) we obtain

$$g(S, t) = a_i + g(S - \{i\}, b_i + \max\{t - a_i, 0\})$$

$$= a_i + a_j + g(S - \{i, j\}, b_j + \max\{b_i + \max\{t - a_i, 0\} - a_j, 0\}$$

$$(5.25)$$

(5.25) may be simplified using the following result

$$t_{ij} = b_j + \max\{b_i + \max\{t - a_i, 0\} - a_j, 0\}$$
$$= b_j + b_i - a_j + \max\{\max\{t - a_i, 0\}, a_j - b_i\}$$
$$= b_j + b_i - a_j + \max\{t - a_i, a_j - b_i, 0\}$$
$$= b_j + b_i - a_j - a_i + \max\{t, a_i + a_j - b_i, a_i\} \qquad (5.26)$$

If jobs i and j are interchanged in R then the finish time $g'(S, t)$ will be

$$g'(S, t) = a_i + a_j + g(S - \{i, j\}, t_{ji})$$

where

$$t_{ji} = b_j + b_i - a_j - a_i + \max\{t, a_i + a_j - b_j, a_j\}$$

Comparing $g(s, t)$ and $g'(s, t)$ we see that if (5.27) below hold then $g(s, t) \le g'(s, t)$.

$$\max\{t, a_i + a_j - b_i, a_i\} \le \max\{t, a_i + a_j - b_j, a_j\} \qquad (5.27)$$

In order for (5.27) to hold for all values of t, we need

$$\max\{a_i + a_j - b_i, a_i\} \le \max\{a_i + a_j - b_j, a_j\}$$

or

$$a_i + a_j + \max\{-b_i, -a_j\} \le a_i + a_j + \max\{-b_j, -a_i\}$$

or

$$\min\{b_i, a_j\} \ge \min\{b_j, a_i\} \qquad (5.28)$$

From (5.28) we can conclude that there exists an optimal schedule in which for every pair (i, j) of adjacent jobs, $\min\{b_i, a_j\} \ge \min\{b_i, a_i\}$. Exercise 26 shows that all schedules with this property have the same length. Hence, it suffices to generate any schedule for which (5.28) holds for every pair of adjacent jobs. We can obtain a schedule with this property by making the following observations resulting from (5.28). If $\min\{a_1, a_2, \ldots, a_n, b_1, b_2, \ldots, b_n\}$ is a_i then job i should be the first job in an optimal schedule. If $\min\{a_1, a_2, \ldots, a_n, b_1, b_2, \ldots, b_n\}$ is b_j then job j should be the last job in an optimal schedule. This enables us to make a decision as to the positioning of one of the n jobs. (5.28) may now be used on the remaining $n - 1$ jobs to correctly position another job etc. The scheduling rule resulting from (5.28) is therefore

i) sort all the a_i s and b_i s into nondecreasing order.

ii) consider this sequence in this order. If the next number in the sequence is a_j and job j hasn't yet been scheduled, schedule job j at the left most available spot. If the next number is b_j and job j hasn't yet been scheduled, schedule job j at the right most available spot. If j has already been scheduled go to the next number in the sequence.

Note that the above rule also correctly positions jobs with $a_i = 0$. Hence these jobs need not be considered separately.

Example 5.25   Let $n = 4$, $(a_1, a_2, a_3, a_4) = (3, 4, 8, 10)$ and (b_1, b_2, b_3, b_4) $= (6, 2, 9, 15)$. The sorted sequence of a's and b's is $(b_2, a_1, a_2, b_1, a_3, b_3,$ $a_4, b_4) = (2, 3, 4, 6, 8, 9, 10, 15)$. Let $\sigma_1, \sigma_2, \sigma_3, \sigma_4$, be the optimal schedule. Since, the smallest number is b_2, we set $\sigma_4 = 2$. The next number is a_1 and we set $\sigma_1 = a_1$. The next smallest number is a_2. Job 2 has already been scheduled. The next number is b_1. Job 1 has already been scheduled. a_3 is the next and so we set $\sigma_2 = 3$. This leaves σ_3 free and job 4 unscheduled. Thus, $\sigma_3 = 4$. $\square$

The scheduling rule above may be implemented to run in time $O(n \log n)$. (see exercises). Solving (5.23) and (5.24) directly for $g(\{1, 2, \ldots, n\}, 0)$ for the optimal schedule will take at least $O(2^n)$ time as there are this many different S's for which $g(S, t)$ will be computed.

REFERENCES AND SELECTED READINGS

Two classic references on dynamic programming are:

Introduction to Dynamic Programming by G. Nemhauser, John Wiley and Sons, Inc., 1966

Applied Dynamic Programming by R. E. Bellman and S. E. Dreyfus, Princeton University Press, 1962.

The dynamic programming formulation for the shortest paths problem appears in:

"Algorithm 97: shortest path," by R. Floyd, *C.ACM*, 5(6), p. 345, 1962.

An all pairs shortest path algorithm with average behavior $O(n^2 \log n)$ appears in:

"A new algorithm for finding all shortest paths in a graph of positive arcs in average time $O(n^2 \log n)$," by P. Spira, *SIAM Jr. on Computing*, 2, pp. 28-32, 1973.

The construction of optimal binary search trees using dynamic programming is described in:

The Art of Programming: Sorting and Searching, Vol. 3, by D. E. Knuth, Addison Wesley, 1973.

"Optimum binary search trees," by D. E. Knuth, *Acta informatica*, 1, pp. 14-25, 1971.

A fast heuristic to generate nearly optimal binary search trees appears in:

"Nearly optimal binary search trees," by K. Melhorn, *Acta Informatica*, 5, pp. 287-295, 1975.

The set generation approach to solving the 0/1 Knapsack problem may be found in the papers:

"Discrete dynamic programming and capital allocation", by G. Nemhauser and Z. Ullman, *Management Science*, 15(9), pp. 494-505 (1969).

"Computing partitions with applications to the knapsack problem", by E. Horowitz and S. Sahni, *J. ACM*, 21, pp. 277-292 (1974).

The paper by Horowitz and Sahni extends this approach to include a divide and conquer scheme so that the recurrence (5.15) may be solved in time $O(2^{n/2})$ (exercise 13). Extensive experimentally observed computing times comparing various algorithms for the knapsack problem are also presented.

Dynamic programming recurrences similar to (5.15) can be obtained for many kinds of scheduling problems. Some references are:

"A functional equation and its application to resource allocation and sequencing problems," by E. Lawler and J. Moore, *Management Science*, 16(1), pp. 85-103 (1969).

"Algorithms for scheduling independent tasks," by S. Sahni, *J. ACM*, 23(1), pp. 114-127 (1976).

"Exact and approximate algorithms for scheduling nonidentical processors," by E. Horowitz and S. Sahni, *J. ACM*, 23(2), pp. 317-327 (1976).

Solutions to many of the exercises may be found in the above three papers. Our discussion on reliability design and flow shop scheduling is from the book by Bellman and Dreyfus. The rule of exercise 20 was derived by Bellman and Dreyfus and may be found in their book. Many other interesting examples are contained here. The flow shop scheduling rule was originally obtained by S. Johnson using a non dynamic programming approach. His original derivation may be found in:

"Optimal two- and three-stage production schedules with set-up times included," by S. Johnson, *Nav. Res. Log. Quat.*, 1, pp. 61–68 (1954).

The dynamic programming formulation for the traveling salesperson problem is due to M. Held and R. Karp and may be found in:

"A dynamic programming approach to sequencing problems," by M. Held and R. Karp, *J. Soc. Ind. and Appl. Math.*, 10(2), 1962.

R. Bellman obtained a similar solution to the traveling salesperson problem. His work appears in:

"Dynamic programming treatment of the traveling salesman problem," *J. ACM*, 9, pp. 61–63 (1962).

The dynamic programming solution to the matrix product chain problem (exercises 7 and 8) is due to S. Godbole and appears in:

"On efficient computation of matrix chain products," by S. Godbole, *IEEE Trans. on Computers*, C-22(9), pp. 864–866, 1973.

EXERCISES

1.   i)   Does the recurrence (5.8) hold for the following graph? Why?

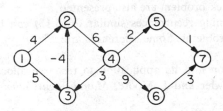

      ii)   Why does eq. (5.8) not hold for graphs with cycles of negative length?
2.   Modify procedure ALL__PATHS so that a shortest path is output for each pair of vertices (i, j). What are the time and space complexities of the new algorithm?

3.   Let A be the adjacency matrix of a directed graph G. Define the transitive closure, A^+, of A to be a matrix with the property $A^+(i, j) = 1$ iff G has a

directed path, containing at least one edge, from vertex i to vertex j. $A^+(i, j)$ = 0 otherwise. The reflexive transitive closure, A^*, is a matrix with the property $A^*(i, j) = 1$ iff G has a path, containing zero or more edges, from i to j. $A^*(i, j) = 0$ otherwise.

i)   Obtain A^+ and A^* for the following directed graph:

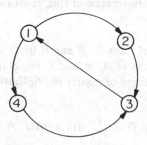

ii)   Let $A^k(i, j) = 1$ iff there is a path with zero or more edges from i to j going through no vertex of index greater than k. Define A° in terms of the adjacency matrix A.

iii)   Obtain a recurrence between A^k and A^{k-1} similar to (5.9). Use the logical operators **or** and **and** rather than **min** and $+$.

iv)   Write an algorithm, using the recurrence of (iii), to find A^*. Your algorithm can use only $O(n^2)$ space. What is its time complexity?

v)   Show that $A^+ = A \times A^*$ where matrix multiplication is defined as $A^+(i, j) = V_{k=1}^n (A^*(i, k) \wedge A^*(k, j))$. V is the logical **or** operation and $\wedge$ the logical **and** operation. Hence A^+ may be computed from A^*.

4.   Using algorithm OBST compute $W(i, j)$, $R(i, j)$ and $C(i, j)$, $0 \le i < j \le 4$ for the identifier set $(a_1, a_2, a_3, a_4) =$ (**end, goto, print, stop**) with $P(1) = 1/20$, $P(2) = 1/5$, $P(3) = 1/10$, $P(4) = 1/20$, $Q(0) = 1/5$, $Q(1) = 1/10$, $Q(2) = 1/5$, $Q(3) = 1/20$, $Q(4) = 1/20$. Using the $R(i, j)$s construct the optimal binary search tree.

5.   (a)   Show that the computing time of algorithm OBST is $O(n^2)$.
     (b)   Write an algorithm to construct the optimal binary search tree T given the roots $R(i, j)$, $0 \le i < j \le n$. Show that this can be done in time $O(n)$.

6.   Since, often only the approximate values of the Ps and Qs are known, it is perhaps just as meaningful to find a binary search tree that is nearly optimal i.e. its cost, eq. 5.9, is almost minimal for the given Ps and Qs. This exercise explores an $O(n \log n)$ algorithm that results in nearly optimal binary search trees. The search tree heuristic we shall study is:

Choose the root k such that $|W(0, k - 1) - W(k, n)|$

is as small as possible. Repeat this procedure to find the left and right sub-trees of the root.

(a) Using this heuristic obtain the resulting binary search tree for the data of exercise 4. What is its cost?

(b) Write a SPARKS algorithm implementing the above heuristic. Your algorithm should have a time complexity of at most $O(n \log n)$.

An analysis of the performance of this heuristic may be found in the paper by Melhorn.

7. [Matrix Product Chains] Let A, B and C be three matrices such that $C = A \times B$. Let the dimensions of A, B and C respectively be $m \times n$, $n \times p$ and $m \times p$. From the definition of matrix multiplication,

$$C(i, j) = \sum_{k=1}^{n} A(i, k)*B(k, j).$$

a) Write an algorithm to compute C directly using the above formula. Show that the number of multiplications needed by your algorithm is mnp.

b) Let $M_1 \times M_2 \times \cdots \times M_r$ be a chain of matrix products. This chain may be evaluated in several different ways. Two possibilities are $(\ldots((M_1 \times M_2) \times M_3) \times M_4) \times \cdots) \times M_r$, and $(M_1 \times (M_2 \times (\cdots \times (M_{r-1} \times M_r) \cdots)$. The *cost* of any computation of $M_1 \times M_2 \times \cdots \times M_r$ is the number of multiplications used. Consider the case $r = 4$ and matrices M_1 through M_4 with dimensions 100×1, 1×100, 100×1 and 1×100 respectively. What is the cost of each of the five ways to compute $M_1 \times M_2 \times M_3 \times M_4$? Show that the optimal way has a cost of 10,200 while the worst way has a cost of 1,020,000. Assume that all matrix products are computed using the algorithm of (a).

c) Let M_{ij} denote the matrix product $M_i \times M_{i+1} \times \cdots \times M_j$. Thus, $M_{ii} = M_i$, $1 \le i \le r$. $S = p_1, p_2, \ldots, p_{r-1}$ is a *product sequence* computing M_{1r}, iff each product p_k is of the form $M_{ij} \times M_{j+1,q}$ where M_{ij} and $M_{j+1,q}$ have been computed either by an earlier product p_l, $l < k$ or represent an input matrix M_{tt}. Note that $M_{ij} \times M_{j+1,q} = M_{iq}$. Also note that every valid computation of M_{1r} using only pairwise matrix products at each step is defined by a product sequence. Two product sequences $S_1 = p_1, p_2, \ldots, p_{r-1}$ and $S_2 = u_1, u_2, \ldots, u_{r-1}$ are *different* if $p_i \ne u_i$ for some i. Show that the number of different product sequences is $(r - 1)!$.

d) While there are $(r - 1)!$ different product sequences, many of these are essentially the same in the sense that the same pairs of matrices are multiplied. For example, the sequences $S_1 = (M_1 \times M_2), (M_3 \times M_4), (M_{12} \times M_{34})$ and $S_2 = (M_3 \times M_4), (M_1 \times M_2), (M_{12} \times M_{34})$ are different under the definition of c). However, the same pairs of matrices are multiplied in both S_1 and S_2. Show that if we consider only those product sequences that differ from each other in at least one matrix product then the number of different sequences is equal to the number of different binary trees having exactly $r - 1$ nodes.

e) Show that the number of different binary trees with n nodes is

$$\frac{1}{n + 1}\binom{2n}{n}$$

8. [Matrix Product Chains]   In the preceding exercise it was established that the number of different ways to evaluate a matrix product chain is very large even when r is relatively small (say 10 or 20). In this exercise we shall develop an $O(r^3)$ algorithm to find an optimal product sequence (i.e. one of minimum cost). Let $D(i)$, $0 \le i \le r$ represent the dimensions of the matrices, i.e. M_i has $D(i - 1)$ rows and $D(i)$ columns. Let $C(i, j)$ be the cost of computing M_{ij} using an optimal product sequence for M_{ij}. Observe that $C(i, i) = 0$, $1 \le i \le r$ and that $C(i, i + 1) = D(i - 1)*D(i)*D(i + 1)$, $1 \le i < r$.

   a)   Obtain a recurrence relation for $C(i, j)$, $j > i$. This recurrence relation will be similar to Equation (5.13).

   b)   Write an algorithm to solve the recurrence relation of a) for $C(1, r)$. Your algorithm should be of complexity $O(r^3)$.

   c)   What changes are needed in the algorithm of b) to determine an optimal product sequence. Write an algorithm to determine such a sequence. Show that the overall complexity of your algorithm remains $O(r^3)$.

   d)   Work through your algorithm (by hand) for the product chain of part (b) of the previous exercise. What are the values of $C(i, j)$, $1 \le i \le r$ and $j \ge i$? What is an optimal way to compute M_{14}?

9. Generate the sets S^i of jump points in $f_i(x)$, $0 \le i \le 4$ (eq. 5.15) when $(w_1, w_2, w_3, w_4) = (10, 15, 6, 9)$ and $(p_1, p_2, p_3, p_4) = (2, 5, 8, 1)$.

10. Write an algorithm, PARTS to determine an optimal solution $x_1, x_2, \ldots, x_n$ to the knapsack problem. Assume that S^i, $0 \le i < n$ have already been computed as in procedure DKNAP. Knowing $F(i)$ and $F(i + 1)$ one can use a binary search to determine if $(p', w') \in S^i$. Hence, the time complexity of your algorithm should be no more than $O(n \max_i\{\log|S^i|\}) \le O(n^2)$.

11. Give an example of a set of knapsack instances for which $|S^i| = 2^i$, $0 \le i \le n$. Your set should include one instance for each n.

12. (i)   Show that if the p_j's are integer then the size of each S^i, $|S^i|$, in the knapsack problem is no more than $1 + \sum_{1 \le i \le j} p_j/gcd(p_1, p_2, \ldots, p_n)$ where $gcd(p_1, p_2, \ldots, p_n)$ is the greatest common divisor of the p_i's.

   (ii)   Show that when the w_j's are integer then $|S^i| \le 1 + \min\{\sum_{1 \le j \le i} w_j, M\}/gcd(w_1, w_2, \ldots, w_n, M)$.

13. Using a divide-and-conquer approach coupled with the set generation approach of the text, show how to obtain an $O(2^{n/2})$ algorithm for the 0/1 knapsack problem.

14. Write an algorithm similar to DKNAP to solve the recurrence 5.18. What are the time and space requirements of your algorithm?

15. a) Obtain a data representation for the values $g(i, S)$ of the traveling salesperson problem. Your representation should allow for easy access to the value of $g(i, S)$ given i and S. (i) How much space does your representation need for an n vertex graph? (ii) How much time is needed to retrieve or update the value of $g(i, S)$?
    b) Using the representation of a) write a SPARKS algorithm corresponding to the dynamic programming solution of the traveling salesperson problem.

16. [W. Miller] Show that BGRAPH1 computes shortest paths for directed, acyclic graphs represented by adjacency lists (instead of inverse adjacency lists used by BGRAPH).

```
procedure BGRAPH1(E, n)
  real BCOST(n); integer j, n
  BCOST(1) ← 0
  for j ← 2 to n do BCOST(j) ← ∞ repeat
  for j ← 1 to n − 1 do
    for all ⟨ j, r ⟩ ∈ E do
      BCOST(r) ← min(BCOST(r), BCOST(j) + c(j, r))
    repeat
  repeat
end BGRAPH1
```

17. Consider the integer knapsack problem obtained by replacing the 0/1 constraint in (5.1) by $x_i \geq 0$ and integer. Generalize $f_i(x)$ to this problem in the obvious way.
    i) Obtain the dynamic programming recurrence relation corresponding to (5.14).
    ii) Show how to transform this problem into a 0/1 knapsack problem.
       (Hint: introduce new 0/1 variables for each x_i. If $0 \leq x_i < 2^j$ then introduce j variables, one for each bit in the binary representation of x_i.)

18. There are two warehouses W_1 and W_2 from which supplies are to be shipped to destinations D_i, $1 \leq i \leq n$. Let d_i be the demand at D_i and let r_i be the inventory at W_i. Assume $r_1 + r_2 = \Sigma d_i$. Let $c_{ij}(x_{ij})$ be the cost of shipping x_{ij} units from warehouse W_i to destination D_j. The warehouse problem is to find nonnegative integers x_{ij}, $1 \leq i \leq 2$ and $1 \leq j \leq n$ such that $x_{1j} + x_{2j} = d_j$,

$1 \leq j \leq n$ and $\Sigma_{i,j} \; c_{ij}(x_{ij})$ is minimized. Let $g_i(x)$ be the cost incurred when W_1 has an inventory of x and supplies are sent to D_j, $1 \leq j \leq i$, in an optimal manner (the inventory at W_2 is $\Sigma_{1 \leq j \leq i} \; d_j - x$). The cost of an optimal solution to the warehouse problem is $g_n(r_1)$.

i) Use the optimality principle to obtain a recurrence relation for $g_i(x)$.

ii) Write an algorithm to solve this recurrence and obtain an optimal sequence of values for x_{ij}, $1 \leq i \leq 2$, $1 \leq j \leq n$.

19. We are given a warehouse with a storage capacity of B units and an initial stock of v units. Let y_i be the quantity sold in each month i, $1 \leq i \leq n$. P_i is the per unit selling price in month i. Let x_i be the quantity purchased in month i. The buying price is c_i per unit. At the end of each month, the stock in hand must be no more than B. i.e.

$$v + \sum_{1 \leq i \leq j} (x_i - y_i) \leq B, \quad 1 \leq j \leq n$$

The amount sold in each month cannot be more than the stock at the end of the previous month (new stock arrives only at the end of a month) i.e.

$$y_i \leq v + \sum_{1 \leq j < i} (x_j - y_j), \quad 1 \leq i \leq n$$

Also, we require x_i and y_i to be non-negative integers. The total profit derived is

$$P_n' = \sum_{j=1}^{n} (p_j y_j - c_j x_j)$$

The problem is to determine x_j, y_j such that P_n is maximized. Let $f_i(v_i)$ represent the maximum profit that can be earned in months $i + 1$, $i + 2$, ..., n starting with v_i units of stock at the end of month i. Then $f_0(v)$ is the maximum value of P_n.

i) Obtain the dynamic programming recurrence for $f_i(v_i)$ in terms of $f_{i+1}(v_i)$.

ii) What is $f_n(v_i)$?

iii) Solve (i) analytically to obtain the formula

$$f_i(v_i) = a_i x_i + b_i v_i$$

for some constants a_i and b_i.

iv) Show that an optimal P_n is obtained by using the following strategy:

1. if $p_i \geq c_i$ and
   (a) $b_{i+1} \geq c_i$ then $y_i = v_i$ and $x_i = B$
   (b) $b_{i+1} \leq c_i$ then $y_i = v_i$ and $x_i = 0$

2. if $c_i \geq p_i$ and
    (a) $b_{i+1} \geq c_i$ then $y_i = 0$ and $x_i = B - v_i$
    (b) $b_{i+1} \leq p_i$ then $y_i = v_i$ and $x_i = 0$
    (c) $p_i \leq b_{i+1} \leq c_i$ then $y_i = 0$ and $x_i = 0$
v) Use the following p_i, c_i and obtain an optimal decision sequence from (iv).

i	1	2	3	4	5	6	7	8
p_i	8	8	2	3	4	3	2	5
c_i	3	6	7	1	4	5	1	3

Assume the warehouse capacity to be 100 and the initial stock to be 60.

vi) From (iv) conclude that an optimal set of values for x_i and y_i will always lead to the following policy: Do no buying or selling for the first k months (k may be zero) and then oscillate between a full and an empty warehouse for the remaining months.

20. Assume that n programs are to be stored on two tapes. Let l_i be the length of tape needed to store the ith program. Assume that $\Sigma \, l_i \leq L$ where L is the length of each tape. A program may be stored on either of the two tapes. If $S1$ is the set of programs on tape 1 then the worst case access time for a program is proportional to $\max\{\Sigma_{i \in S_1} l_i, \Sigma_{i \notin S_1} l_i\}$. An optimal assignment of programs to tapes minimizes the worst case access times. Formulate a dynamic programming approach to determine the worst case access time of an optimal assignment. Write an algorithm to determine this time. What is the complexity of your algorithm?

21. Redo problem 20 making the assumption that programs will be stored on tape 2 using a different tape density than used on tape 1. If l_i is the tape length needed by program i when stored on tape 1 then $a \cdot l_i$ is the tape length needed on tape 2.

22. N jobs are to be processed. Two machines A and B are available. If job i is processed on machine A then a_i units of processing time are needed. If it is processed on machine B then b_i units of processing time are needed. Because of the peculiarities of the jobs and the machines, it is quite possible that $a_i \geq b_i$ for some i while $a_j < b_j$ for some j, $j \neq i$. Obtain a dynamic programming formulation to determine the minimum time needed to process all the jobs. Note that jobs cannot be split between machines. Indicate how you would go about solving the recurrence relation obtained. Do this on an example of your choice. Also indicate how you would determine an optimal assignment of jobs to machines.

23. N jobs have to be scheduled for processing on one machine. Associated with job i is a 3-tuple (p_i, t_i, d_i). t_i is the processing time needed to complete job i. If job i is completed by its deadline d_i then a profit p_i is earned. If not then nothing is earned. From chapter 4 we know that J is a subset of jobs that can all be completed by their deadlines iff the jobs in J can be processed in nondecreasing order of deadlines without violating any deadline. Assume $d_i \leq d_{i+1}$, $1 \leq i < n$. Let $f_i(x)$ be the maximum profit that can be earned from a subset J of jobs when $n = i$. $f_n(d_n)$ is the value of an optimal selection of jobs J. $f_0(x) = 0$. Show that for $x \leq t_i$,

$$f_i(x) = \max\{f_{i-1}(x), \ f_{i-1}(x - t_i) + p_i\}$$

24. Let I be any instance of the 2 processor flow shop problem.
    (a) Show that the length of every POFT schedule for I is the same as the length of every OFT schedule for I. Hence, the algorithm of section 5.8 also generates a POFT schedule.
    (b) Show that there exists an OFT schedule for I in which jobs are processed in the same order on both processors.
    (c) Show that there exists an OFT schedule for I defined by some permutation σ of the jobs (see (b)) such that all jobs with $a_i = 0$ are at the front of this permutation. Further, show that the order in which these jobs appear at the front of the permutation is not important.

25. Let I be any instance of the two processor flow shop problem. Let $\sigma = \sigma_1 \sigma_2 \cdots \sigma_n$ be a permutation defining an OFT schedule for I.
    (a) Use (5.28) to argue that there exists and OFT σ such that $\min\{b_i, a_j\} \geq \min\{b_j, a_i\}$ for every i and j such that $i = \sigma_k$ and $j = \sigma_{k+1}$ (i.e. i and j are adjacent).
    (b) For a σ satisfying the conditions of a) show that $\min\{b_i, a_j\} \geq \min\{b_j, a_i\}$ for every i and j such that $i = \sigma_k$ and $j = \sigma_r$, $k < r$.
    (c) Show that all schedules corresponding to σ's satisfying the conditions of a) have the same finish time. (Hint: use b) to transform one of two different schedules satisfying a) into the other without increasing the finish time.)

26. The principle of optimality does not hold for every problem whose solution may be viewed as the result of a sequence of decisions. Find two problems for which the principle does not hold. Explain why the principle does not hold for these problems.

Chapter 6

BASIC SEARCH AND TRAVERSAL TECHNIQUES

6.1 THE TECHNIQUES

The solution to many problems involves the manipulation of binary trees, trees or graphs. Often, this manipulation requires us to determine a vertex (node) or a subset of vertices in the given data object that satisfies a given property. For example, we may wish to find all vertices in a binary tree with a data value less than X or we may wish to find all vertices in a given graph G that can be reached from another given vertex v. The determination of this subset of vertices satisfying a given property can be carried out by systematically examining the vertices of the given data object. This often takes the form of a search in the data object. When the search necessarily involves the examination of every vertex in the object being searched, it is called a *traversal*.

We have already seen an example of a problem whose solution required a search of a binary tree. In Section 5.4 we presented an algorithm to search a binary search tree for an identifier X. This algorithm is not a traversal algorithm as it does not examine every vertex in the search tree. Sometimes, we may wish to traverse a binary search tree (e.g. when we wish to list out all the identifiers in the tree). Algorithms for this will be studied in this chapter.

The techniques to be discussed in this section are divided into three categories. The first two categories include techniques applicable only to binary trees and trees respectively. As described, these techniques will involve examining every node in the given data object instance. Hence, these techniques are referred to as traversal methods. The third category includes techniques applicable to graphs (and hence also to trees and binary trees). These search strategies may not examine all vertices and so are referred to only as search methods. During a search (or traversal) the fields of a node may be made use of several times. It may be necessary to distinguish certain uses of the fields of a node. During these uses, the node is said to be *visited*. Visiting a node may involve printing out its data field, evaluating the operation specified by the node in case of a binary tree representing an expression; setting a mark bit to one or zero etc. Since we are describing search and traversals of trees and graphs independent of the application, we use the term *visited* rather than state the specific function performed on the node at this time.

6.1.1. BINARY TREE TRAVERSAL

There are many operations that we often want to perform on binary trees. One notion that arises frequently is the idea of traversing a tree or visiting each node in the tree exactly once. A full traversal produces a linear order for the information in a tree. This linear order may be familiar and useful. When traversing a binary tree we want to treat each node and its subtrees in the same fashion. If we let L, D, R stand for moving left, printing the data, and moving right when at a node then there are six possible combinations of traversal: LDR, LRD, DLR, DRL, RDL, and RLD. If we adopt the convention that we traverse left before right then only three traversals remain: LDR, LRD and DLR. To these we assign the names inorder, post-order and preorder. We will define these three traversals and show how they work on the binary tree of Figure 6.1.

Inorder Traversal: informally this calls for moving down the tree towards the left until you can go no farther. Then you "visit" the node, move one

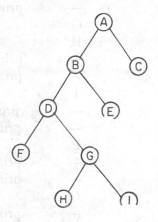

Figure 6.1   A binary tree

node to the right and continue again. If you cannot move to the right, go back one more node. A precise and elegant way to describe this traversal is to write it as a recursive procedure. Algorithm 6.1 is the result. In sub-algorithm VISIT, we perform whatever function needs to be performed at the time a node is visited.

procedure *INORDER(T)*
　　//*T* is a binary tree. Each node of *T* has three fields//
　　//LCHILD, DATA, RCHILD//
　　if *T* ≠ 0 **then call** *INORDER(LCHILD(T))*
　　　　　　　　call *VISIT(T)*
　　　　　　　　call *(INORDER(RCHILD(T))*
　　endif
end *INORDER*

　　　Algorithm 6.1　Recursive formulation of inorder traversal

Figure 6.2 traces how INORDER works on the binary tree of Figure 6.1. This trace assumes that visiting a node requires only the printing of its DATA field. The output resulting from this traversal is FDHGIBEAC.

Call of INORDER	value in root	Action
MAIN	A	
1	B	
2	D	
3	F	
4	—	print ('F')
4	—	print ('D')
3	G	
4	H	
5	—	print ('H')
5	—	print ('G')
4	I	
5	—	print ('I')
5	—	print ('B')
2	E	
3	—	print ('E')
3	—	print ('A')
1	C	
2	—	print ('C')
2	—	

Figure 6.2　Inorder traversal of binary tree of Figure 6.1 with **call** VISIT(*T*)
replaced by **print** (DATA(*T*))

The recursive procedures corresponding to preorder and postorder appear in Algorithms 6.2 and 6.3.

```
procedure PREORDER (T)
    //T is a binary tree. Each node in T has three fields LCHILD, DATA,//
    //RCHILD//
    if T ≠ 0 then call VISIT(T)
                call PREORDER(LCHILD(T))
                call PREORDER(RCHILD(T))
    endif
end PREORDER
```

Algorithm 6.2   Preorder traversal

```
procedure POSTORDER(T)
    //T is a binary tree. Each node in T has three fields LCHILD, DATA,//
    //RCHILD//
    if T ≠ 0 then call POSTORDER(LCHILD(T))
                call POSTORDER (RCHILD(T))
                call VISIT(T)
    endif
end POSTORDER
```

Algorithm 6.3   Postorder traversal

With **call** VISIT(T) replaced by **print**(DATA(T)) the application of Algorithms 6.2 and 6.3 to the binary tree of Figure 6.1 results in the outputs ABDFGHIEC and FHIGDEBCA respectively.

Theorem 6.1   Let $t(n)$ and $s(n)$ respectively represent the maximum time and space needed by any one of the traversal algorithms when the input tree T has $n \geq 0$ nodes. If the time and space needed to visit a node is $\Theta(1)$ then $t(n) = \Theta(n)$ and $s(n) = \Theta(n)$.

Proof: The work done by each traversal algorithm is made up of two components: (i) work done on this level of recursion and (ii) work done due to recursive invocation of the algorithm from this level. The time required for the first of these is bounded by a constant c_1. If the number of nodes in the left subtree of T is n_1 then $t(n)$ is given by the recursion:

$$t(n) = \max_{n_1}\{t(n_1) + t(n - n_1 - 1) + c_1\}, \qquad n \geq 1.$$

Note that $t(0) \leq c_1$. A proof by induction establishes that $t(n) \leq c_2 n +$

c_1 where c_2 is a constant such that $c_2 \geq 2c_1$. This inequality clearly holds when $n = 0$. Assume it holds for all n, $0 \leq n < m$. We shall show it is true when $n = m$. Let T be an m node tree. Let n_1 be the number of nodes in the left subtree of T. Then

$$
\begin{aligned}
t(m) &= \max\{t(n_1) + t(n - n_1 - 1) + c_1\} \\
&\leq \max\{c_2 n_1 + c_1 + c_2(n - n_1 - 1) + c_1 + c_1\} \\
&= \max\{c_2 n + 3c_1 - c_2\} \\
&\leq c_2 n + c_1
\end{aligned}
$$

It is easy to see that there exist c_1' and c_2' such that $t(n) \geq c_2'n + c_1'$. Hence, $t(n) = \Theta(n)$. The only additional space needed is for saving the values of local variables on recursive calls. If T has depth d then this space is clearly $\Theta(d)$. For an n node binary tree $d \leq n$ and so $s(n) = \Theta(n)$. □

While the recursive traversal algorithms can be used directly, the overhead of recursion may make it desirable to recode the algorithms first into nonrecursive versions. Standard rules for obtaining a nonrecursive equivalent of a recursive algorithm were given in Chapter 1. These rules generally result in inelegant algorithms. However, using the standard translation rules has the virture that given a correct recursive algorithm the nonrecursive version is guaranteed to be correct. Let us attempt to directly write a nonrecursive algorithm for inorder traversal. If T is the root of a binary tree then its left subtree (if nonempty) must be traversed before T can be visited. Thus, we may put T on a stack and proceed to traverse its left subtree. The stack will be maintained such that when the left subtree has been traversed, T is at the top of the stack.

Consider the binary tree of Figure 6.3. Node A has a left subtree B and so it is stacked. We then proceed to traverse B. Node B has a left subtree D so B gets stacked and we traverse D. D's left subtree is empty and so node D may be visited. Now, we have to traverse D's right subtree. This requires us to visit node G. At this time we have completed traversing the left subtree of B. Node B is on the top of the stack. B is removed and visited. We now continue with B's right subtree. Since B has an empty right subtree, the traversal of the subtree B which is the left subtree of A has been completed. A is at the top of the stack. In general, the stack will contain only those nodes whose left subtrees haven't yet been traversed. Whenever the traversal of a subtree which is a left subtree of some node

Q is completed, Q will be at the top of the stack. Thus, when the subtree with root D has been traversed, B will be the topmost node on the stack; when the traversal of tree B is completed A will be on top; when tree A has been traversed, the stack will be empty.

The formal algorithm is procedure INORDER1 (Algorithm 6.4.). The variable P traverses the binary tree T and at the start of the loop of lines 4–19, P points to the root of a subtree to be traversed. In lines 5–11 the roots of all left subtrees starting from P get stacked. On exit from this loop, P points to a node with empty left subtree and so P is now to be visited. At the start of the loop of lines 12–18, P points to a node that is now to be visited (i.e. its left subtree, if nonempty, has been traversed). Following the visiting of node P, its right subtree, if nonempty, is to be traversed. In case P has an empty right subtree then we have completed the traversal of a left subtree and we must now move to the parent of this completed left subtree. The parent is the topmost node on the stack (lines 16–17). It is easy to see that if Q is the root of the left subtree of R then when the traversal of Q is completed R is the node at the top of the stack. Whenever a node is visited it is removed from the stack. All nodes in Q must be visited before the traversal of Q is complete. Hence all nodes stacked after R is stacked must be deleted before the traversal of Q is complete.

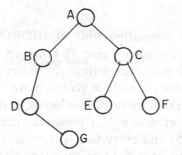

Figure 6.3   A binary tree

```
         procedure INORDER1 (T)
         //a nonrecursive version using a stack of size m//
1            integer STACK(m), i, m
2            if T = 0 then return   //T empty//
3            P ← T; i ← 0  //P traverses T; i is top of stack//
4            loop
5               while LCHILD(P) ≠ 0 do   //traverse left subtree//
6                  i ← i + 1
7                  if i > m then print ('stack overflow')
8                              stop
9                  endif
10                 STACK(i) ← P; P ← LCHILD(P)
11              repeat
12              loop
13                 call VISIT(P)  //left subtree of P has been traversed//
14                 P ← RCHILD(P)
15                 if P ≠ 0 then exit   //traverse right subtree//
16                 if i = 0 then return
17                 P ← STACK(i); i ← i - 1
18              repeat  //visit a parent node//
19           repeat
         end INORDER1
```

Algorithm 6.4   Nonrecursive algorithm for inorder traversal

Analysis of INORDER1

We shall analyze the computing time of INORDER1 in terms of the number of nodes, n, in the binary tree T. On each iteration of the **while** loop of lines 5-11, a node gets stacked (line 10). Every node that gets stacked gets visited (line 13). Since no node is visited more than once, the loop of lines 5-11 cannot be iterated more than n times in the entire execution of the algorithm. Actually, at most $n - 1$ nodes can get stacked as leaf nodes don't get stacked (line 5) and every tree with $n \geq 1$ has at least one leaf node. The total time for lines 5-11 is therefore $O(n)$. On each iteration of the loop of lines 12-18 a node gets visited. Since each node in T is visited exactly once and nodes are not visited anywhere else in the algorithm, this loop is iterated a total of n times in the algorithm. The total time needed for this loop is therefore $\Theta(n)$. Hence, the time complexity of INORDER1 is $\Theta(n)$.

As far as the stack space is concerned, we see that only nodes with a nonempty left subtree can be stacked. The worst case occurs when T is a left skewed binary tree (Figure 6.4(b)). In a *left skewed binary tree* every node except the leaf has a nonempty left subtree and an empty right subtree. In this case, a stack of size $n - 1$ is needed. The best case is when every node has an empty left subtree and all nodes other than the leaf have a nonempty right subtree. Such a binary tree is a *right skewed binary tree* (Figure 6.4(a)). In this case, no nodes get stacked. A more useful statement of the stack space needed is in terms of the depth of T. One may verify that if T has depth d then the stack space needed is $O(d)$.

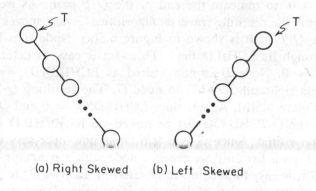

(a) Right Skewed   (b) Left Skewed

Figure 6.4   Skewed binary trees

At this point we may ask the question: can we do any better? Clearly, all traversal algorithms must visit each node and so the computing time must be at least $\Theta(n)$. The only improvement we can expect then is a reduction in the additional space required (i.e., the stack space). Is it possible to traverse binary trees in $\Theta(n)$ time and $\Theta(1)$ space?

Binary Tree Traversal in $\Theta(n)$ time and $\Theta(1)$ space

If each node has a PARENT field linking to its parent then, Exercise 4–6 examine how traversals may be accomplished in $\Theta(n)$ time and $\Theta(1)$ space. We will address ourselves here to the problem of obtaining a similarly behaved algorithm for the case when no PARENT fields exist. The presence of parent fields allows one to go from any node P to the root node. In obtaining a $\Theta(1)$ space algorithm we will achieve this effect by reversing the direction of links from the root node to the node currently being examined. Thus, if P points to the node in tree T that is currently being examined and Q points to its parent then we will maintain a path from Q to the root T. This path will be called the Q-T path and will be built by linking together all nodes on the path from T to Q. If U, V, and W are three nodes on this path such that U is the parent of V and V the parent of W, then V will be linked to U through its RCHILD field if W is the RCHILD of V. Otherwise, V will be linked to U through its LCHILD field.

Let us see how this works on the tree T of Figure 6.3. Initially, P is at the root A and Q is also at A indicating an empty Q-T path. Next, P moves to node B and the Q-T path contains only the root node A. LCHILD(A) is set to T since P is LCHILD(A) and this field is to be used to link A into the empty Q-T path list. We shall use LCHILD(A) = A rather than LCHILD(A) = 0 to indicate the end of the Q-T path. As we shall see, this will simplify the resulting traversal algorithms. P next moves to node D. The resulting Q-T path is shown in Figure 6.5(a). Node B is linked into this path through its LCHILD field. This fact is easy to determine since RCHILD(B) = 0. Node D is now visited as LCHILD(D) = 0. P next advances to its right subtree, i.e. to node G. The resulting Q-T path list is shown in Figure 6.5(b). Again, since LCHILD(Q) = 0 and Q is not the last node on the Q-T list, Q must be linked via its RCHILD field. Node G can now be visited. Since G is a leaf, it is now necessary to back up along the Q-T path list until we reach a node with a nonempty right subtree. From G it is easy to back up to D resetting RLINK(D) to point to D. This results in the situation of Figure 6.5(a). From D we back up to B resetting LCHILD(B) to D. Since we have returned from B's left subtree, it is time to visit B. B's right subtree is empty and we must back up to node A. At this time it is necessary to be able to determine whether B was the left or right child of A. Since neither LCHILD(A) = 0 nor RCHILD(A) = 0, the test used at nodes B and D cannot be used here. However, since LCHILD(A) = A, we know that B must be the left subtree of A. So, LCHILD(A) is set to B and node A visited. Now, we move P to node C and then to E getting the configuration of Figure 6.5(c). Backing up from E to C, we are faced with the problem of determining whether E is C's left or right child. Neither LCHILD(C) = 0 nor RCHILD(C) = 0. With the information we have at present, there is no way to determine whether E is C's left or right child. More information is needed. A TAG field in each node would be useful (see exercise). However, such a field is not available for use. We shall explicitly keep track of the last node R such that LCHILD(R) $\neq$ 0 and RCHILD(R) $\neq$ 0 and a move to R's right subtree was made. This will be done through variable LR. Initially, LR = 0. During P's traversal in A's left subtree LR remains zero. As a result, when we wish to back up from B to A, since $LR \neq A$ it follows that B was A's left subtree. When P moves to C, LR is updated to A. When backing up from E, $LR = A \neq C$ and so E was C's left child. Moving from C to F requires updating LR to C. Since the old value of LR will be needed once we have finished traversing the subtree C, it is necessary to save the values of LR on a stack. This stack can also be built in place making use of leaf nodes in T. Since both LCHILD and RCHILD fields of leaf nodes are zero, LCHILD can be used to retain the value of LR and RCHILD to link to the remainder of the stack. This is shown in Figure 6.5(d). The remaining details of the algorithm are spelled out in INORDER2 (Algorithm 6.5).

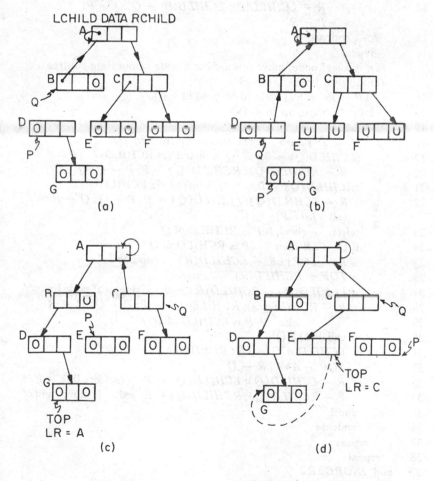

Figure 6.5 Traversing a binary tree in $\Theta(1)$ space

```
line    procedure INORDER2(T)
        //inorder traversal of binary tree T using a fixed amount of additional//
        //space//
1       if T = 0 then return endif   //empty binary tree//
2       TOP ← LR ← 0; Q ← P ← T   //initialize//
3       loop
4           loop   //move down as far as possible//
5               case
6               :LCHILD(P) = 0 and RCHILD(P) = 0:
                                //can't move down//
7                   call VISIT(P); exit
8               :LCHILD(P) = 0:   //move to RCHILD(P)//
9                   call VISIT(P)
10                  R ← RCHILD(P); RCHILD(P) ← Q
                    Q ← P; P ← R
11              :else:   //move to LCHILD(P)//
12                  R ← LCHILD(P); LCHILD(P) ← Q; Q ← P;
                    P ← R
13              endcase
14          repeat
            //P is a leaf node, move upwards to a node whose right subtree//
            //hasn't yet been examined//
15          AV ← P   //leaf node to be used in stack//
16          loop   //move up from P//
17              case
18              :P = T: return   //can't move up from root//
19              :LCHILD(Q) = 0:   //Q is linked via RCHILD//
20                  R ← RCHILD(Q); RCHILD(Q) ← P; P ← Q; Q ← R
21              :RCHILD(Q) = 0:   //Q is linked via LCHILD//
22                  R ← LCHILD(Q); LCHILD(Q) ← P; P ← Q; Q ← R;
                    call VISIT(P)
23              :else:   //check if P is RCHILD of Q//
24              if Q = LR then   //P is RCHILD of Q//
25                  R ← TOP; LR ← LCHILD(R)   //update LR//
26                  TOP ← RCHILD(R)   //unstack//
27                  LCHILD(R) ← RCHILD(R) ← 0   //reset leaf node links//
28                  R ← RCHILD(Q); RCHILD(Q) ← P; P ← Q; Q ← R
29                       else   //P is LCHILD of Q//
30                  call VISIT(Q)
31                  LCHILD(AV) ← LR; RCHILD(AV) ← TOP
32                  TOP ← AV; LR ← Q
33                  R ← LCHILD(Q); LCHILD(Q) ← P   //restore link to P//
34                  P ← RCHILD(Q); RCHILD(Q) ← R; exit   //move right//
35              endif
36              endcase
37          repeat
38      repeat
39      end INORDER2
```

Algorithm 6.5 Procedure to traverse a binary tree in $\Theta(1)$ time and $\Theta(1)$ space

Analysis of INORDER2

Let n_0, n_1 and n_2 be the number of nodes of degree 0, 1 and 2 respectively. Let $n = n_0 + n_1 + n_2$. It is clear that P points to a node of degree zero exactly once, i.e. when the node is reached during a downward move in the loop of lines 4-14. P will reach a node with one child exactly two times, once during a downward move and once again during an upward move from its child (lines 16-37). A node with two children will be reached by P exactly three times, once during a downward move (lines 4-14) and twice during upward moves from its two children (lines 16-37). Hence, the total number of changes in P's value is $n_0 + 2n_1 + 3n_2$. In every iteration of the loop of lines 4-14 P's value changes if P is not a leaf. If P is a leaf then an exit is made and P's value changes in the loop of lines 16-37. Each iteration of this loop necessarily changes P's value. Hence, the total number of iterations of the loops of lines 4-14 and 16-37 together is $2n_0 + 2n_1 + 3n_2$. An iteration of either of these loops takes $\Theta(1)$ time. The total time for the loops of lines 3-38 is therefore $\Theta(2n_0 + 2n_1 + 3n_2) = \Theta(n)$.

Lines 1 and 2 contribute $\Theta(1)$ and so the total time taken is $\Theta(n)$. The additional space needed is $\Theta(1)$ as this space is needed only for simple variables such as P, Q, AV, LR, TOP, R and $LR1$. One may readily verify that the algorithm on termination leaves the tree T in its original form. $\square$

There are several other traversal algorithms for binary trees. Some of these are examined in the exercises.

Empirical Comparison of Inorder Algorithms

We have seen three different algorithms for inorder traversal. These are INORDER, INORDER1 and INORDER2. We shall abbreviate these names to IN, IN1 and IN2 respectively. When traversing an n node binary tree T of depth d, each of these algorithms takes $\Theta(n)$ time. IN1 and IN2 require $0(d)$ additional space while IN3 requires only $\Theta(1)$ additional space. Since it is pretty clear that both IN and IN1 will run faster than IN2, IN2 is to be used only when $0(d)$ space is not available for IN and IN1 to operate in. When space is not at a premium, the choice is reduced to one between IN and IN1. We would expect IN1 to run faster than IN (because of the over-head of recursion). However, we do not know by how much IN1 will be faster than IN. This will depend on the programming language used. When the programming language does not support recursion (e.g. FORTRAN), only IN1 can be used.

To get a feel for the "cost" of recursion, IN and IN1 were programmed in PASCAL. It is easy to see that the time needed by IN to traverse an n node binary tree is relatively insensitive to the shape of the tree. For each node, two recursive calls are made. Hence, a total of $2n$ recursive calls will be made while traversing T. The time needed by IN1, however, depends on the shape of the n node binary tree being traversed. To see this, note that only nodes that have a left child get stacked (lines 5-11). Hence if no node in the tree being traversed has a left child then no nodes will get stacked. Hence, none will get unstacked either. IN1 will work fast on such a tree. If every node in the binary tree has a left child and no right child then $n - 1$ nodes will get stacked (and also unstacked). IN1 will take maximum time when T is a left skewed tree. On the average, half the nodes will have a left child and the other half will not. This case is represented by a full binary tree.

Since, IN1 is only an iterative version of IN, we programmed another inorder algorithm IN3 (Algorithm 6.6) which is obtained from IN by removing only the second recursive call. The three algorithms IN, IN1 and IN3 were programmed in PASCAL and run on a CDC Cyber 74 computer. The observed computing times are shown in Table 6.1. For comparison purposes, IN2 was also programmed in PASCAL and run. In addition to carrying out the comparison tests just described, IN1 and IN2 were also programmed in FORTRAN and run on the same computer. The computing times for the FORTRAN programs are also given in Table 6.1.

```
procedure IN3(T)
    while T ≠ 0 do
        call IN3(LCHILD(T))    //recursively traverse left subtree//
        call VISIT(T)
        T ← RCHILD(T)    //traverse right subtree//
    repeat
end IN3
```

Algorithm 6.6 Another inorder algorithm

The data of Table 6.1 indicates that in PASCAL recursion does not have an excessive overhead. In fact, algorithm IN takes less time than IN1 on left skewed binary trees. Algorithm IN3 took less time than IN on all data sets. It was faster than IN1 on left skewed and full binary trees. It is slower than IN1 only on right skewed binary trees. By comparison, IN2 takes between 1.5 to 3 times as much time as IN1. For PASCAL, IN3 is

	PASCAL				FORTRAN	
n	IN	IN1	IN2	IN3	IN1	IN2
31	1.15	0.75	1.85	0.85	0.3	1.2
63	2.15	1.25	4.0	1.7	0.5	2.2
127	4.3	2.55	7.5	3.5	1.0	4.45
225	8.75	5.05	15.3	7.05	2.25	8.8
511	17.75	10.4	30.85	14.3	4.35	17.3
1023	34.3	20.6	61.25	28.05	8.55	36.15
2047	70.7	40.65	124.85	55.2	17.5	70.45
4095	138.8	81.75	242.6	112.25	34.45	139.85

(a) Right skewed binary tree

	PASCAL				FORTRAN	
n	IN	IN1	IN2	IN3	IN1	IN2
31	1.15	1.3	2.1	0.9	0.75	1.15
63	2.15	2.5	4.15	1.8	1.6	2.25
127	4.35	5.1	8.4	3.65	2.85	4.85
255	8.8	10.15	16.6	7.35	6.3	9.5
511	17.05	20.6	33.35	13.05	12.05	19.2
1023	34.95	41.2	66.3	28.15	23.95	38.1
2047	69.5	82.15	133.65	56.95	48.2	75.5
4095	139.3	162.4	204.6	111.9	96.1	152.1

(b) Left skewed binary tree

	PASCAL				FORTRAN	
n	IN	IN1	IN2	IN3	IN1	IN2
31	1.05	0.95	2.5	0.9	0.45	1.35
63	2.2	1.85	5.0	1.85	1.0	2.85
127	4.3	4.0	10.05	3.7	2.05	5.65
255	8.8	7.85	20.1	6.9	3.95	10.65
511	17.15	15.7	41.1	13.85	7.95	21.6
1023	34.7	30.3	80.8	27.35	16.35	44.3
2047	70.25	61.55	162.75	55.4	32.55	89.45
4095	139.8	122.35	327.2	112.15	65.25	175.1

(c) Full binary tree

Table 6.1 Computing times for IN, IN1, IN2 and IN3. All times are in milliseconds.
(Tables prepared by N. R. Venkatesh)

the best inorder algorithm (provided enough space is available). The FORTRAN versions of IN1 and IN2 took considerably less time than the corresponding PASCAL programs.

6.1.2 TREE TRAVERSAL

For trees we can define traversal methods analogous to the ones defined for binary trees. While the subtrees of a tree are not ordered, our traversal methods will assume that some ordering exists for the subtrees. This makes it meaningful to talk of the first, second, third subtrees, etc., of a node. Since a tree is just a forest with one tree and the removal of the root from a tree creates a forest, it is convenient to define tree traversals recursively in terms of forest traversal. The names of the traversal methods for trees have been chosen so that they correspond to those for binary trees. F is a forest. The traversal methods are:

Tree Preorder (F)
 (i)   if F is empty then return;
 (ii)   visit the root of the first tree of F;
 (iii)   traverse the subtrees of the first tree of F in tree preorder;
 (iv)   traverse the remaining trees of F in tree preorder.

Tree Inorder (F)
 (i)   if F is empty then return;
 (ii)   traverse the subtrees of the first tree of F in tree inorder;
 (iii)   visit the root of the first tree of F;
 (iv)   traverse the remaining trees of F in tree inorder.

and *Tree Postorder* (F)
 (i)   if F is empty then return;
 (ii)   traverse the subtrees of the first tree of F in tree postorder;
 (iii)   traverse the remaining trees of F in tree postorder;
 (iv)   visit the root of the first tree of F.

Since trees are usually represented by their corresponding (or associated) binary trees, we shall not attempt to write detailed traversal algorithms for trees. In later sections, we shall see examples of the use of postorder traversal of a tree. In these examples however, the tree will be generated as needed. The whole tree being traversed will not reside in memory at any one given time. This situation is typical of most tree applications in which the corresponding binary tree is not used (see Chapters 7 and 8).

In chapter 2, we defined the corresponding binary tree T of a forest F. Preorder and inorder traversals of the corresponding binary tree T of a forest F have a natural correspondence with traversals on F. Preorder traversal of T is equivalent to visiting the nodes of F in *tree preorder*. Inorder traversal of T is equivalent to visiting the nodes of F in *tree inorder*. There is no natural analog for postorder traversal of the corresponding binary tree of a forest.

6.1.3 SEARCH AND TRAVERSAL TECHNIQUES FOR GRAPHS

A fundamental problem concerning graphs is the path problem. In its simplest form it requires us to determine whether or not there exists a path in the given graph $G = (V, E)$ such that this path starts at vertex v and ends at u. A more general form would be to determine for a given starting vertex $v \in V$ all vertices u such that there is a path from v to u. This latter problem can be solved by starting at vertex v and systematically searching the graph G for vertices that can be reached from v. We shall describe two search methods for this.

Breadth First Search and Traversal

In breadth first search we start at a vertex v and mark it as having been reached (visited). The vertex v will at this time be said to be unexplored. A vertex will be said to have been explored by an algorithm when the algorithm has visited all vertices adjacent from it. All unvisited vertices adjacent from v are visited next. These are new unexplored vertices. Vertex v has now been explored. The newly visited vertices haven't been explored and are put onto the end of a list of unexplored vertices. The first vertex on this list is the next to be explored. Exploration continues until no unexplored vertex is left. The list of unexplored vertices operates as a queue and may be represented using any of the standard queue representations. Procedure BFS (Algorithm 6.7) describes the details of the search. It makes use of two algorithms DELETEQ(v, Q) which deletes a vertex from the queue Q and returns, in v, the index and the vertex deleted and ADDQ(v, Q) which adds vertex v to the rear of queue Q.

Let us try out the algorithm on the undirected graph of Figure 6.6(a). If the graph is represented by its adjacency lists as in Figure 6.6(b) then the vertices get visited in the order 1, 2, 3, 4, 5, 6, 7, 8. A breadth first search of the directed graph of Figure 6.6(c) starting at vertex 1 will result in only the vertices 1, 2 and 3 being visited. Vertex 4 cannot be reached from 1.

line **procedure** *BFS(v)*
    //A breadth first search of *G* is carried out beginning at vertex *v*.//
    //All vertices visited are marked as VISITED(*i*) = 1. The graph//
    //*G* and array VISITED are global and VISITED is initialized to//
    //zero.//
1   *VISITED(v)* ← 1; *u* ← *v*
2   initialize *Q* to be an empty queue   //*Q* is a queue of unex-//
                                            //plored vertices//
3   **loop**
4   **for** all vertices w adjacent from u **do**
5   **if** *VISITED(w)* = 0 **then call** *ADDQ(w, Q)*   //w is unex-//
                                                    //plored//
6   *VISITED(w)* ← 1
7   **endif**
8   **repeat**
9   **if** *Q* is empty **then return**   //no unexplored vertex//
10   **call** *DELETEQ(u, Q)*   //get first unexplored vertex//
11   **repeat**
12 **end** *BFS*

Algorithm 6.7   Algorithm for breadth first search

Theorem 6.2   Algorithm BFS visits all vertices reachable from *v*.

Proof: Let $G = (V, E)$ be a graph (directed or undirected) and let $v \in V$. We shall prove the theorem by induction on the length of the shortest paths from *v* to all reachable vertices $w \in V$. The length (i.e. number of edges) of the shortest path from *v* to a reachable vertex *w* will be denoted by $d(v, w)$. Clearly, all vertices *w* with $d(v, w) \leq 1$ get visited. Now assume that all vertices *w* with $d(v, w) \leq r$ get visited. We will show that all vertices *w* with $d(v, w) = r + 1$ also get visited. Let *w* be a vertex in *V* such that $d(v, w) = r + 1$. Let *u* be a vertex that immediately precedes *w* on a shortest *v* to *w* path. Then $d(v, u) = r$ and so *u* gets visited by BFS. We may assume $u \neq v$ and $r \geq 1$. Hence, immediately before *u* gets visited, it is placed on the queue *Q* of unexplored vertices. The algorithm doesn't terminate until the *Q* becomes empty. Hence, *u* is removed from the *Q* at some time and all unvisited vertices adjacent from it get visited in the loop of lines 4–8. Hence, *w* gets visited.   □

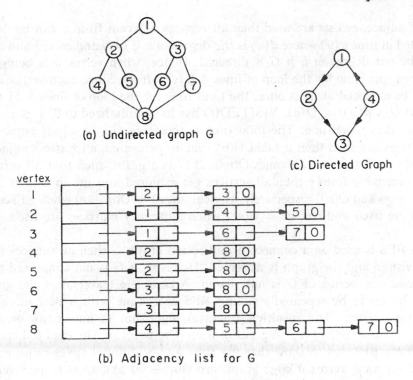

(a) Undirected graph G

(c) Directed Graph

(b) Adjacency list for G

Figure 6.6 Example graphs and adjacency lists

Theorem 6.3 Let $t(n, e)$ and $s(n, e)$ be the maximum time and maximum additional space taken by algorithm BFS on any graph G with n vertices and e edges. $t(n, e) = \Theta(n + e)$ and $s(n, e) = \Theta(n)$ if G is represented by its adjacency lists. If G is represented by its adjacency matrix then $t(n, e) = \Theta(n^2)$ and $s(n, e) = \Theta(n)$.

Proof: Vertices get added to the queue only in line 5. A vertex w can get onto the queue only if VISITED(w) = 0. Immediately following w's addition to the queue VISITED(w) is set to 1 (line 6). Hence, each vertex can get onto the queue at most once. Vertex v never gets onto the queue and so at most $n - 1$ additions are made. The queue space needed is at most $n - 1$. The remaining variables take 0(1) space. Hence $s(n, e) = 0(n)$. If G is an n vertex graph with v connected to the remaining $n - 1$ vertices then all $n - 1$ vertices adjacent from v will be on the queue at the same time. Furthermore, $\Theta(n)$ space is needed for the array VISITED. Hence $s(n, e) = \Theta(n)$. This result is independent of whether adjacency matrices or lists are used.

If adjacency lists are used then all vertices adjacent from u can be determined in time $d(u)$ where $d(u)$ is the degree of u if G is undirected and $d(u)$ is the out degree of u if G is directed. Hence, when vertex u is being explored, the time for the loop of lines 4–8 is $\Theta(d(u))$. Since each vertex in G can be explored at most once, the total time for the loop of lines 3–11 is at most $O(\Sigma\, d(u)) = O(e)$. VISITED(i) has to be initialized to 0, $1 \le i \le n$. This takes $O(n)$ time. The total time is therefore $O(n + e)$. If adjacency matrices are used then it takes $\Theta(n)$ time to determine all vertices adjacent from u and the time becomes $O(n^2)$. If G is a graph such that all vertices are reachable from v then all vertices get explored and the time is at least $O(n + e)$ and $O(n^2)$ respectively. Hence, $t(n, e) = \Theta(n + e)$ when adjacency lists are used and $t(n, e) = \Theta(n^2)$ when adjacency matrices are used.   □

If BFS is used on a connected undirected graph G then all vertices in G get visited and the graph is traversed. However, if G is not connected then at least one vertex of G is not visited. A complete traversal of the graph can be made by repeatedly calling BFS each time with a new unvisited starting vertex. The resulting traversal algorithm is known as breadth first traversal (BFT) (see Algorithm 6.8). The proof of Theorem 6.3 can be used for BFT too to show that the time and additional space required by BFT on an n vertex e edge graph are $\Theta(n + e)$ and $\Theta(n)$ respectively if adjacency lists are used. If adjacency matrices are used then the bounds are $\Theta(n^2)$ and $\Theta(n)$ respectively.

```
procedure BFT(G, n)
   //breadth first traversal of G//
      declare VISITED(n)
      for i ← 1 to n do   //mark all vertices unvisited//
         VISITED(i) ← 0
      repeat
      for i ← 1 to n do   //repeatedly call BFS//
         if VISITED(i) = 0 then call BFS(i) endif
      repeat
end BFT
```

Algorithm 6.8   Breadth first graph traversal

If G is a connected undirected graph then all vertices of G will get visited on the first call to BFS. If G is not connected then at least two calls to BFS will be needed. Hence, BFS can be used to determine whether or not G is connected. Furthermore, all newly visited vertices on a call to BFS from

BFT represent the vertices in a connected component of G. Hence the connected components of a graph can be obtained using BFT. For this, BFS can be modified so that all newly visited vertices are put onto a list. Then the subgraph formed by the vertices on this list together with their adjacency lists form a connected component. Hence, if adjacency lists are used, a breadth first traversal will obtain the connected components in $\Theta(n + e)$ time. BFT can also be used to obtain the reflexive transitive closure matrix of an undirected graph G. If A^* is this matrix then $A^*(i,j) = 1$ iff either $i = j$ or $i \neq j$ and i and j are in the same connected component. We can set up in $O(n)$ time an array CONNEC(i) such that CONNEC(i) is the index of the connected component containing vertex i, $1 \leq i \leq n$. Hence, we can determine whether $A^*(i,j)$, $i \neq j$ is 1 or 0 by simply seeing if CONNEC(i) = CONNEC(j). The reflexive transitive closure matrix of an undirected graph G with n vertices and e edges can therefore be computed in $\Theta(n^2)$ time and $\Theta(n)$ space using either adjacency lists or matrices (the space count does not include the space needed for A^* itself).

As a final application of breadth first search, consider the problem of obtaining a spanning tree for an undirected graph G. G has a spanning tree iff G is connected. Hence, BFS easily determines the existence of a spanning tree. Furthermore, consider the set of edges (u, w) used in lines 4–8 of algorithm BFS to reach unvisited vertices w. These edges are called *forward edges*. Let T denote this set of forward edges. We claim that if G is connected then T is a spanning tree of G. For the graph of Figure 6.6(a) the set of edges T will be all edges in G except (5, 8), (6, 8) and (7, 8) (see Figure 6.7(a)). Spanning trees obtained using breadth first searches are called *breadth first spanning trees*.

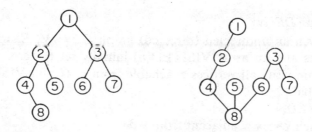

Figure 6.7   BFS and DFS spanning trees for graph of Figure 6.6(a)

Theorem 6.4   Modify algorithm BFS by adding on the statements $T \leftarrow \phi$ and $T \leftarrow T \cup \{(u, w)\}$ to lines 1 and 6 respectively. Call the resulting algorithm BFS*. If BFS* is called such that v is any vertex in a connected undirected graph G, then on termination, the edges in T form a spanning tree of G.

Proof: We have already seen that if G is a connected graph on n vertices then all n vertices will get visited. Also, each of these, except the start vertex v, will get onto the queue once (line 5). Hence, T will contain exactly $n - 1$ edges. All of these edges are distinct. The $n - 1$ edges in T will therefore define an undirected graph on n vertices. This graph is connected since it contains a path from the start vertex v to every other vertex (and so there is a path between every pair of vertices). A simple proof by induction shows that every connected graph on n vertices with exactly $n - 1$ edges is a tree. Hence T is a spanning tree of G.   □

The exercises explore further applications of breadth first search. An important technique to solve optimization problems is based on breadth first search. This technique, called branch-and-bound, is the subject of Chapter 8.

Depth First Search and Traversal

A depth first search of a graph differs from a breadth first search in that the exploration of a vertex v is suspended as soon as a new vertex is reached. At this time the exploration of the new vertex u begins. When this new vertex has been explored, we continue to explore v. The search terminates when all reached vertices have been fully explored. This search process is best described recursively as in Algorithm 6.9.

```
line  procedure DFS(v)
          //Given an undirected (directed) graph G = (V, E) with n ver-//
          //tices and an array VISITED(n) initially set to zero, this algo-//
          //rithm visits all vertices reachable from v. G and VISITED are//
          //global.//
1         VISITED(v) ← 1
2         for each vertex w adjacent from v do
3             if VISITED(w) = 0 then call DFS(w) endif
4         repeat
5     end DFS
```

Algorithm 6.9 Depth first search of a graph

A depth first search of the graph of Figure 6.6(a) starting at vertex 1 and using the adjacency lists of Figure 6.6(b) results in the vertices being visited in the order 1, 2, 4, 8, 5, 6, 3, 7. A nonrecursive algorithm for DFS would use a stack to keep track of all partially explored vertices. One can easily prove that DFS visits all vertices reachable from vertex v. If $t(n, e)$ and $s(n, e)$ represent the maximum time and maximum additional space taken by DFS for an n vertex e edge graph then $s(n, e) = \Theta(n)$ and $t(n, e) = \Theta(n + e)$ if adjacency lists are used and $t(n, e) = \Theta(n^2)$ if adjacency matrices are used (see exercises).

A depth first traversal of a graph is carried out by repeatedly calling DFS each time with a new unvisited starting vertex. The algorithm for this (DFT) differs from BFT only in that the call to BFS(i) is replaced by a call to DFT(i). As in the case of BFT, the connected components of a graph can be obtained using DFT. Similarly, the reflexive transitive closure matrix of an undirected graph can be found using DFT. If DFS is modified by adding $T \leftarrow \phi$ and $T \leftarrow T \cup \{(v, w)\}$ to lines 1 and the **then** clause of line 3 respectively then, when DFS terminates, the edges in T define a spanning tree for the undirected graph G if G is connected. A spanning tree obtained in this manner is called a *depth first spanning tree*. For the graph of Figure 6.6(a) the spanning tree obtained will include all edges in G except for (2, 5), (8, 7) and (1, 3) (see Figure 6.7(b)). Hence, DFS and BFS are equally powerful for the search problems discussed so far. The exercises contain some problems that are solved best by BFS and others that are best solved by DFS. Later sections of this chapter also discuss graph problems solved best by DFS.

Epilogue

BFS and DFS are two fundamentally different search methods. In BFS a node is fully explored before the exploration of any other node begins. The next node to explore is the first unexplored node remaining. The exercises examine a search technique (*D*-search) that differs from BFS only in that the next node to explore is the most recently reached unexplored node. In DFS the exploration of a node is suspended as soon as a new unexplored node is reached. The exploration of this new node is immediately begun. While the implementaiton of both DFS and *D*-Search requires a stack mechanism, the two search methods are different. The search methods presented in this section may be used on a variety of problems. Some applications are explored in the remaining sections of this chapter.

6.2 CODE OPTIMIZATION

The function of a compiler is to translate programs written in some source language into an equivalent assembly language or machine language program. Thus, the PASCAL compiler on the CDC Cyber 74 translates PASCAL programs into the machine language of this machine. We shall look at the problem of translating arithmetic expressions in a language such as PASCAL into assembly language code. The translation will clearly depend on the particular assembly language (and hence machine) being used. To begin, we will assume a very simple machine model. We shall call this model machine A. This machine has only one register called the accumulator. All arithmetic has to be performed in this register. If $\odot$ represents a binary operator such as $+$, $-$, $*$, $/$ then the left operand of $\odot$ must be in the accumulator. For simplicity, we shall restrict ourselves to these four operators. The discussion will easily generalize to other operators. The relevent assembly language instructions are:

> LOAD X ... load accumulator with contents of memory location X
> STORE X ... store contents of accumulator into memory location X
> OP X ... OP may be ADD, SUB, MPY or DIV

The instruction OP X computes the operator OP using the contents of the accumulator as the left operand and that of memory location X as the right operand. As an example consider the arithmetic expression: $(a + b)/(c + d)$. Two possible assembly language versions of this expression are given in Figure 6.8. $T1$ and $T2$ are temporary storage areas in memory. In both cases the result is left in the accumulator. Code (a) is two instructions longer than code (b). If each instruction takes the same amount of time then code (b) will take 25% less time than code(a). For the expression $(a + b)/(c + d)$ and the given machine A, it is not too difficult to see that code(b) is optimal.

LOAD	a		LOAD	c
ADD	b		ADD	d
STORE	$T1$		STORE	$T1$
LOAD	c		LOAD	a
ADD	d		ADD	b
STORE	$T2$		DIV	$T1$
LQAD	$T1$			
DIV	$T2$			
	(a)			(b)

Figure 6.8 Two possible codes for $(a + b)/(c + d)$

Definition A *translation* of an expression E into the machine or assembly language of a given machine is *optimal* iff it has a minimum number of instructions.

Let us look at three more examples. Consider the expression $a + b*c$. Figure 6.9 shows two possible translations. At first sight, code(b) may appear incorrect since we require the left operand of $+$ to be in the accumulator and the right operand in memory. However, $x + y = y + x$ and so (b) is equivalent to (a).

LOAD	b	LOAD	b
MPY	c	MPY	c
STORE	$T1$	ADD	a
LOAD	a		
ADD	$T1$		
(a)		(b)	

Figure 6.9 Possible codes for $a + b*c$

Definition a binary operator $\odot$ is *commutative* in the domain D iff $a \odot b = b \odot a$ for all a and b in D.

The operators $+$ and $*$ are commutative over the integers and reals while $-$ and $/$ are not. Using the commutative property of certain operators can result in shorter code. Next, consider the expression $a*b + c*b$. Figure 6.10 shows two possible codes. Code(b) actually computes $(a + c)b$ which is equivalent to $a*b + c*b$.

LOAD	c	LOAD	a
MPY	b	ADD	c
STORE	$T1$	MPY	b
LOAD	a		
MPY	b		
ADD	$T1$		
(a)		(b)	

Figure 6.10 Possible codes for $a*b + c*b$

Definition A binary operator $\circledast$ is *left distributive* with respect to the binary operator $\oplus$ over a domain D iff for every a, b, c in D, $a \circledast (b \oplus$

$c) = (a \odot b) \oplus (a \odot c)$. $\odot$ is *right distributive* with respect to $\oplus$ iff for every a, b, c in D, $(a \oplus b) \odot c = (a \odot c) \oplus (b \odot c)$.

Over the domain of real numbers, $*$ is left and right distributive with respect to $+$ and $-$ as $a*(b + c) = (a*b) + (a*c)$, $a*(b + c) = (a*b) - (b*c)$, $(a + b)*c = (a*c) + (b*c)$ and $(a - b)*c = (a*c) - (b*c)$. / is not left distributive with respect to $+$ as $a/(b + c) \neq (a/b) + (a/c)$. However, / is right distributive over the reals. Note that / is not right distributive with respect to $+$ over the domain of integers as $(2 + 3)/5 = 1$ while $(2/5) + (3/5) = 0$ (note that $2/3 = 0$ and $3/5 = 0$ in integer arithmetic).

As a final example, consider the expression $a*(b*c) + d*c$. Figure 6.11 presents two possible codes. The code of Figure 6.11(b) uses the knowledge $(a*b)*c = a*(b*c)$.

LOAD	b		LOAD	a
MPY	c		MPY	b
STORE	$T1$		ADD	d
LOAD	a		MPY	c
MPY	$T1$			
STORE	$T1$			
LOAD	d			
MPY	c			
STORE	$T2$			
LOAD	$T1$			
ADD	$T2$			
(a)			(b)	

Figure 6.11   Two possible codes for $a*(b*c) + d*c$

Definition   A binary operator $\odot$ is *associative* over the domain D iff $a \odot (b \odot c) = (a \odot b) \odot c$ for all a, b and c in A.

$*$ is associative over the integers and reals. / is associative over the reals but not over the integers $((2/3)/3 = 0$ while $2/(3/3) = 2)$.

Using the associative, distributive and commutative properties of operators can result in shorter codes. Note, however, that even though $(a + c)*b = (a*b) + (c*b)$ for real numbers, the codes of Figures 6.10(a) and (b) may generate different answers. This comes about because of the finiteness of computer arithmetic that creates errors in computation. In our discussion, we shall ignore this factor and assume that the associative, commutative and distributive laws may be freely used when applicable.

Having seen that different codes are possible for a given expression, we address ourselves to the problem of obtaining optimal code. Initially, we shall restrict ourselves to the simple machine A. Later, we shall look at a more general machine model. The form in which we have seen expressions up to now is known as *infix form*. The operators appear in between their operands. This is the way we normally write arithmetic expressions. In generating optimal code, it is convenient to represent arithmetic expressions as binary trees. Each nonleaf node in the binary tree will represent an operator. A nonleaf node will be called an *internal* node. The left subtree of an internal node P will represent the binary tree form of the left operand of the operator represented at P while the right subtree will represent the right operand. A leaf node represents either a variable or a constant. Figure 6.12 shows the binary tree forms for several expressions. The exercises develop an algorithm to obtain the binary tree representation of an arithmetic expression presented in infix form. We shall refer to a binary tree representing an arithmetic expression as an *expression tree*.

In obtaining an algorithm to generate optimal code from an expression tree, we shall first assume that none of the operators are either commutative, distributive or associative. In addition, we shall not concern ourselves with the possibility of using algebraic transformations to simplify the expression. Thus, while $a + b - a - b$ has value zero, under the above assumption the optimal code will be LOAD a; ADD b; SUB a; SUB b. We shall also not be concerned with handling common subexpressions. All subexpressions will be assumed independent. Hence, the optimal code for $a*b*$ $(a*b - d)$ is the same as that for $a*b*(c*e - d)$. Under these assumptions, it is easy to see that if an expression has n operators then its code will have exactly n instructions of the type ADD, SUB, MPY, DIV. Instructions of this type will be called operator instructions. Only the number of accumulator loads and stores will vary. Thus, the codes of Figures 6.8(a) and (b) both have three operator instructions. Code(a) has three loads and two stores while code(b) has only two loads and one store. One may readily verify that in any code that has no redundant statements, each load instruction except the first must be preceded immediately by a store instruction. Hence, the number of loads is always one more than the number of stores. Consequently, it is sufficient to generate code that minimizes either the number of loads or the number of stores.

Let P be an internal node of any expression tree. Let L and R be its left and right subtrees respectively. Let $\odot$ be the operator at node P. Because of the assumptions on operators, the only way to compute $L \odot R$ is to compute L and R independently and then compute $L \odot R$. The codes for L and R must also be optimal. Once we have optimal codes for L and R,

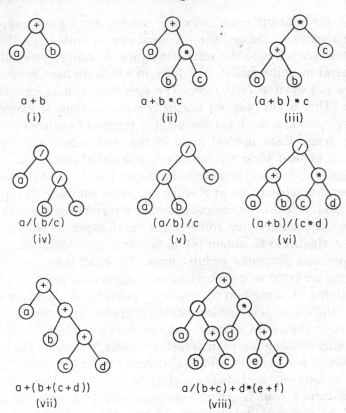

Figure 6.12   Binary tree forms for some infix expressions

several possibilities exist for the code for $L \odot R$. Let C_L and C_R represent optimal codes for the expression trees L and R respectively. Table 6.2 shows the different possibilities for the code for $L \odot R$. The "condition" column exhausts all possibilities for L and R and the order in which L and R are computed in case they are not leaves. In writing out the code, we have simply put $\odot$ a to represent an operator instruction. If $\odot$ is + then we mean ADD a. This change is easy to make. An examination of Table 6.2 reveals that in generating the code for $L \odot R$, we have a choice only when both L and R are internal nodes. When either is a leaf then (conditions (i), (ii) and (iii)) the code is unique (barring introduction of nonuseful statements). When L and R are internal nodes, the code for condition (v) is smaller than that for (iv) and so should be used. This leads to the observation that if R is an internal node then in the optimal code C_R precedes C_L; otherwise C_L precedes C_R.

	condition	*corresponding code*
i)	both L and R are leaves; variables are a and b respectively	LOAD a; $\odot\, b$
ii)	L is a leaf with variable a; R is not a leaf	C_R; STORE $T1$; LOAD a; $\odot\, T1$
iii)	R is a leaf with variable a; L is not a leaf	C_L; $\odot\, a$
iv)	neither L nor R are leaves. L is computed before R	C_L; STORE $T1$; C_R; STORE $T2$; LOAD $T1$; $\odot\, T2$
v)	neither L nor R are leaves. R is computed before L	C_R; STORE $T1$; C_L; $\odot\, T1$

Table 6.2 Possibilities for evaluating $L \odot R$

Note the similarity between the preceding discussion and one resulting from either divide-and-conquer or dynamic programming. Using divide-and-conquer we would obtain optimal code for L and R and then combine these optimal codes in some way to obtain optimal code for $L \odot R$. For dynamic programming, we could view code as the result of a sequence of decisions. At each step, a decision is made as to which subexpression is to be coded next. A subexpression $L \odot R$ may be coded next only if the codes for L and R have already been generated. It is easy to verify that the principle of optimality holds.

Table 6.2 leads to the recursive code generation procedure CODE1 (Algorithm 6.11). The algorithm uses procedures TEMP(i) and RETEMP(i). TEMP(i) gets a memory space for temporary storage while RETEMP(i) frees the temporary storage location i. It is assumed that the expression tree has a root node pointed at by T and that each node has three fields LCHILD, RCHILD and DATA. The DATA field for an internal node is an operator. For a leaf this field is an operand address. Furthermore, the algorithm assumes that $T \neq 0$. Note that the algorithm essentially carries out a traversal of the binary tree T. The traversal method however is not any of the three methods discussed in Section 6.1.1. Only internal nodes get visited. When a node gets visited, code for that node is generated. A node is visited only after the code for its two subtrees has been generated. This is similar to postorder traversal. However, in algorithm CODE1, a nontrivial right subtree is traversed before the corresponding left subtree (a trivial subtree is one with only a root node). If temporary storage is handled as a stack with TEMP and RETEMP respectively corresponding to deletion from and addition to the stack then Figure 6.13 shows the codes generated by CODE1 for some of the examples of Figure 6.12. From our earlier discussion it follows that the code generated by CODE1 is optimal for machine A. A more rigorous proof will be given when we study a generalization of machine A.

procedure *CODE*1 (*T*)
    //code generation for tree *T*. Assume *T* ≠ 0//
    if *T* is a leaf **then print** ("*LOAD*", *DATA*(*T*))
        return
    endif
    F ← 0   //*F* is set to 1 if RCHILD(*T*) is not a leaf//
    if *RCHILD*(*T*) is not a leaf **then**
        call *CODE*1 (*RCHILD*(*T*))   //generate C_R//
        call *TEMP*(*i*)
        print ("*STORE*", *i*)
        F ← 1
    endif
    call *CODE*1 (*LCHILD*(*T*))   //generate C_L//
    if *F* = 1 **then print** (*DATA*(*T*), *i*)
                call *RETEMP*(*i*)
            else print (*DATA*(*T*), *DATA*(*RCHILD*(*T*)))
    endif
end *CODE*1

Algorithm 6.10   Algorithm to generate code

LOAD	a	LOAD	b	LOAD	a
ADD	b	MPY	c	ADD	b
		STORE	T1	MPY	c
		LOAD	a		
		ADD	T1		
(i)		(ii)		(iii)	
LOAD	c	LOAD	e		
ADD	d	ADD	f		
STORE	T1	STORE	T1		
LOAD	b	LOAD	d		
ADD	T1	MPY	T1		
STORE	T1	STORE	T1		
LOAD	a	LOAD	b		
ADD	T1	ADD	c		
		STORE	T2		
		LOAD	a		
		DIV	T2		
		ADD	T1		

Figure 6.13   Code generated by CODE1 for some of the examples of Figure 6.12

Theorem 6.5 The code generated by CODE1 correctly evaluates the arithmetic expression represented by the expression tree T.

Proof: The proof is a simple induction on the depth of T and is left as and exercise. □

If we are allowed to use the commutative property of operators then, CODE1 does not generate optimal code for machine A. To see this, see example (ii) of Figure 6.12 and 6.13. The optimal code when + is commutative is LOAD b, MPY c, ADD a. Note that again, all nonredundant codes for a given expression will have the same number of operator instructions and that the number of loads will be one more than the number of stores. Let P be an internal node in an expression tree. Let L, R, C_L and C_R be as before. It is clear that the optimal code for $L \odot R$ will be made up of optimal codes for L and R. However, if $\odot$ is commutative then the possibilities for Table 6.2 increase. The modificiations needed to CODE1 so that it will generate optimal code taking into account commutative operators is left as an exercise.

We now generalize the machine A to another machine B. B has $N \geq 1$ registers in which arithmetic can be performed. There are four types of machine instructions for B:

1. LOAD   M, R
2. STORE   M, R
3. OP   R1, M, R2
4. OP   R1, R2, R3

These four instruction types perform the following functions:

1) LOAD M, R places the contents of memory location M into register R, $1 \leq R \leq N$
2) STORE M, R stores the contents of register R, $1 \leq R \leq N$, into memory location M.
3) OP $R1, M, R2$ computes contents($R1$) OP contents(M) and places the result in register $R2$. OP is any binary operator (e.g., $+$, $-$, $*$, $/$), $R1$ and $R2$ are registers, M is a memory location. $R1$ may equal $R2$.
4) OP $R1, R2, R3$ is similar to (3). $R1, R2$ and $R3$ are registers. Some or all of these registers may be the same.

In comparing the two machine models A and B, we note that when $N = 1$, instructions of types (1), (2) and (3) for model B are the same as the corresponding instructions for model A. Instructions of type (4) only allow trivial operations like $a + a$, $a - a$, $a*a$ and a/a to be performed without an additional memory access. This does not change the number of instructions in the optimal codes for A and B when $N = 1$. Hence, model A is in a sense identical to model B when $N = 1$. For model B, we see that the optimal code for a given expression E may be different for different values of N. Figure 6.14 shows the optimal code for expression (vi) of Figure 6.12. Two cases are considered, $N = 1$ and $N = 2$. Note that when $N = 1$, one store has to be made while when $N = 2$ no stores are needed. The registers are labeled $R1$ and $R2$. $T1$ is a temporary storage location in memory. Further note that the number of LOADs need no longer be exactly one more than the number of STOREs. Thus, it is no longer sufficient to optimize only either the number of LOADs or the number of STOREs. Their sum is to be minimized. To simplify the discussion, we begin by assuming that none of the operators are associative, commutative or distributive. Further, we assume that both the left and right operands of an operator have to be independently computed even if they are the same subexpressions. This restriction is extended to the case of expressions such as a OP a and we require that a reference to memory be made for both the left and right operands.

LOAD	$c, R1$		LOAD	$c, R1$
MPY	$R1, d, R1$		MPY	$R1, d, R1$
STORE	$R1, T1$		LOAD	$a, R2$
LOAD	$a, R1$		ADD	$R2, b, R2$
ADD	$R1, b, R1$		DIV	$R2, R1, R1$
DIV	$R1, T1, R1$			

(i) $N = 1$ (ii) $N = 2$

Figure 6.14 Optimal codes for $N = 1$ and $N = 2$

Given an expression E, the first question we may ask is: can E be evaluated without any STOREs? A closely related question is: what is the minimum number of registers needed to evaluate E without any stores? We answer these questions under the assumptions made above. We shall assume that the value of E is to be left in one of the N registers. Let E be represented by an expression tree T. If T has only one node then this node must be a leaf and clearly all that has to be done is load the value of the corresponding variable or constant into a register. Only one register is needed for this. If expression E has only one operator then it is of the form

$a \odot b$. One register ($R1$) is needed to load a into. Then we can use the instruction $\odot R1, b, R1$. Hence, for this case exactly one register is needed (Figure 6.15(ii)). When more than one operator is present then we have the situation of Figure 6.15(iii). Let l_1 and l_2 respectively be the minimum number of registers needed to independently evaluate the left (L) and right (R) operands of the root operator. Let l be the minimum number of registers needed to compute $L \odot R$. Since, under the assumptions we have made it is necessary that the values of both L and R be computed independently, it follows that $l \geq \max\{l_1, l_2\}$. If $l_1 > l_2$ then we can compute L first using l_1 registers. Then, leaving the register containing the value L untouched, we can compute R using the remaining $l_1 - 1 \geq l_2$ registers. Finally, with an instruction of type (4) we can compute $L \odot R$. Hence, when $l_1 > l_2$, $l = l_1$. Similarly, when $l_1 < l_2$, $l = l_2$. So, when $l_1 \neq l_2$ then $l = \max\{l_1, l_2\}$. When $l_1 = l_2$, we have two cases. First, if R is a leaf then $l = l_1$ as we just compute L using l_1 registers and then use an instruction of type (3) to compute $L \odot R$ placing the answer in one of the l_1 registers. If R is not a leaf then $l = l_1 + 1$ as no matter which of L and R is computed first, one register will have to be set aside to hold the value of the operand computed first and another l_1 registers needed to compute the second operand. The preceding discussion leads to the following theorem.

Theorem 6.6 Let P be a node in an expression tree T of depth at least 2. Define the function $MR(P)$ (Minimum Registers) as follows:

$$
MR(P) = \begin{cases}
0 & \text{if } P \text{ is a leaf and the right child of its parent} \\[1em]
1 & \text{if } P \text{ is a leaf and the left child of its parent} \\[1em]
\max\{l_1, l_2\} & \text{where } l_1 = MR(\text{LCHILD}(P)); l_2 = \\
 & \quad MR(\text{RCHILD}(P)) \text{ and } l_1 \neq l_2 \\[0.5em]
l_1 + 1 & \text{if } l_1, l_2 \text{ as above and } l_1 = l_2
\end{cases}
$$

$MR(P)$ for P an internal node is the minimum number of registers needed to compute the expression subtree with root P if no STOREs are permitted. □

The above theorem is true only under the stated assumptions about operators. For any expression tree T, the MR values of all nodes can be computed by a postorder traversal of T. Figure 6.16 gives the MR values

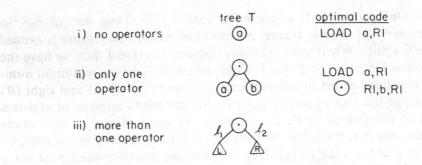

Figure 6.15 Figuring out the minimum number of registers

for all nodes of some expression trees. If the number N of registers available is greater than or equal to the MR value of the root T of the expression tree T then T can be evaluated without any STOREs. In this case an optimal code has to only minimize the number of LOADs. Because of the assumptions made, the number of instructions of types (2) and (3) is equal to the number of internal nodes. When $MR(T) > N$ then the code has to contain some STOREs and an optimal code will minimize the total number

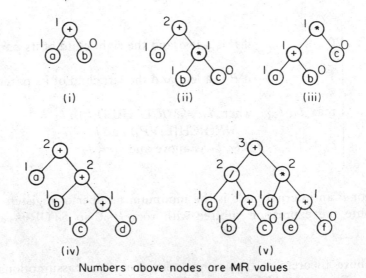

Numbers above nodes are MR values

Figure 6.16 MR values for nodes

of type (1) and type (2) instructions. The proof of Theorem 6.6 suggests a code generation algorithm (Algorithm 6.11). We shall show that CODE2 does in fact generate optimal code under the stated assumptions. First, let us make sure we understand the algorithm.

The algorithm assumes that each node in the expression tree T has four fields: LCHILD, RCHILD, DATA and MR. The MR values have been computed as defined by Theorem 6.6. CODE2 uses a subroutine TEMP. This is identical to that for CODE1. To generate the code for an expression tree T, CODE2 is called as **call** CODE2(T, 1). The total number of registers N is a global variable. It is assumed that $T \neq 0$, i.e. the expression is not null. On a call to CODE2(T, i), code is generated for the expression T using only registers $R_i, \ldots, RN$. The result is left in R_i. If T is a leaf and this is the initial call to CODE2 then only a load is to be performed. If T is a leaf and this is a recursive call from within lines 6–24 then T must be the left child of its parent (as lines 7–9 take care of a right child leaf) and again only a load is to be performed. When T is an internal node, the **case** statement (lines 6–24) is entered. L and R point to the left and right children of T respectively. Let $\odot$ be the operator at R. If R is a leaf then $MR(R) = 0$ and under the assumption made earlier, the optimal code for $L \odot R$ is the optimal code for L followed by the operation $\odot$. This is generated in lines 7–9. When both $MR(L)$ and $MR(R) \geq N$ then at least one store has to be made (Theorem 6.6). The optimal code for $L \odot R$ is now the optimal code for R followed by a store of the result from R, then the optimal code for L followed by the operation $\odot$ (lines 10–15). Note that this case can occur only when $MR(T) > N$ on the initial call. Since both the calls from lines 10 and 13 allow CODE2 to use registers $Ri, \ldots, RN$, it follows that $i = 1$ whenever $MR(L)$ and $MR(R) \geq N$. When at least one of $MR(R)$ and $MR(L)$ is less than N the code for T is generated in lines 16–23. Line 16 takes care of the case $MR(L) < MR(R)$. Since at least one of $MR(L)$ and $MR(R)$ is less than N, it follows that $MR(L) < N$. In this case, the optimal code is the optimal code for R using registers $Ri, \ldots, RN$ followed by the optimal code for L using registers $Ri + 1, \ldots, RN$ followed by the operation $\odot$. Note that if $MR(R)$ is not less than N then $i = 1$. Theorem 6.7 shows that whenever this section of the code is entered, $MR(L) \leq N - i$. Since following the computation of R, $N - i$ registers are free ($Ri + 1, \ldots, RN$), R can be computed with no stores. When $MR(L) \geq MR(R)$ (lines 20–23) then Theorem 6.7 shows that $MR(R) \leq N - i$ and so following the code generation for L, R can be computed with no stores using registers $Ri + 1, \ldots, RN$. Theorem 6.8 and 6.9 prove the correctness and optimality of the code generated by algorithm CODE2. If T has n nodes, then the time required by CODE2 is $\Theta(n)$ (see exercises).

```
line   procedure CODE2(T, i)
           //generate code for machine B with N registers using registers//
           //Ri, ..., RN only. Result is left in Ri. N is a global variable//
1          if T is a leaf then   //left child of parent//
2              print ('LOAD', DATA(T), 'R', i)
3              return
4          endif
           //T is an internal node//
5          L ← LCHILD(T); R ← RCHILD(T)
6          case
7              :MR(R) = 0:   //R is a leaf//
8                  call CODE2(L, i)
9                  print (DATA(T), 'R', i,', ', DATA(R), ', R', i)
10             :MR(L) ≥ N and MR(R) ≥ N: call CODE2(R, i)
11                                       call TEMP(S)
12                                       print ('STORE', 'R', i,', ', S)
13                                       call CODE2(L, i)
14                                       print (DATA(T), 'R', i',', S,
                                               ', R', i)
15                                       call RETEMP(S)
16             :MR(L) < MR(R):   //MR(L) < N, evaluate R first//
17                  call CODE2(R, i)
18                  call CODE2(L, i + 1)
19                  print (DATA(T), ', R', i + 1, ', R', i, ', R', i)
20             :else:   //MR(L) ≥ MR(R) and MR(R) < N, evaluate L first//
21                  call CODE2(L, i)
22                  call CODE2(R, i + 1)
23                  print(DATA(T), ', R', i,', R', i + 1, ', R', i)
24          endcase
25     end CODE2
```

Algorithm 6.11   Code generator for machine B

Theorem 6.7   The following are true for CODE2:

(i) $i = 1$ whenever lines 10–15 are executed

(ii) $MR(L) \leq N - i$ whenever lines 16–19 are executed

(iii) $MR(R) \leq N - i$ whenever lines 20–23 are executed

(iv) $i = 1$ whenever $MR(T) \geq N$.

Proof: The proof is a simple induction on the depth of recursion and is left as an exercise. □

Theorem 6.8 CODE2 generates correct code for every expression tree T.

Proof: Simple induction on the depth of T. □

Figure 6.17 shows the code generated by CODE2 for some of the expressions of Figure 6.16. $R1$, $R2$ and $R3$ are registers while $T1$ is a temporary storage location generated by TEMP( ).

| LOAD | $a, R1$ |
| ADD | $R1, b, R1$ |

$N = 1$

(i)

LOAD	$b, R1$
MPY	$R1, c, R1$
STORE	$R1, T1$
LOAD	$R1, a$
ADD	$R1, T1, R1$

$N = 1$

(ii) (a)

LOAD	$a, R1$
LOAD	$b, R2$
MPY	$R2, c, R2$
ADD	$R1, R2, R1$

$N = 2$

(ii) (b)

LOAD	$d, R1$
LOAD	$e, R2$
ADD	$R2, f, R2$
MPY	$R1, R2, R1$
STORE	$R1, T1$
LOAD	$a, R1$
LOAD	$b, R2$
ADD	$R2, c, R2$
DIV	$R1, R2, R1$
ADD	$R1, T1, R1$

$N = 2$

(v) (a)

LOAD	$a, R1$
LOAD	$b, R2$
ADD	$R2, c, R2$
DIV	$R1, R2, R1$
LOAD	$d, R2$
LOAD	$e, R3$
ADD	$R3, f, R3$
MPY	$R2, R3, R2$
ADD	$R1, R2, R1$

$N = 3$

(v) (b)

Figure 6.17 Code generated by CODE2 for trees (i), (ii) and (v) of Figure 6.16

We now proceed to show that CODE2 generates optimal code. It is necessary to distinguish two types of nodes in an expression tree.

Definition: Given a number of registers N, a node is *major* iff both its children have an MR value at least N. A node is *minor* iff it is either a leaf with no parent or it is a leaf and the left child of its parent.

Lemma 6.1 Let n be the number of major nodes in an expression tree T. At least n STOREs are needed to evaluate T when the expression T has no commutative operators and when there are no relationships among operators and operands (this disallows associative and distributive operators as well as common subexpressions).
Proof: Can be proved by induction on the number of nodes in T.   □

Lemma 6.2 For any expression tree T, the number of STOREs in the code generated by CODE2 is equal to the number of major nodes in an expression tree T.
Proof: This follows from the observation that line 12 is the only place in CODE2 that a store is generated. Line 12 is executed exactly once for each major node in T.   □

Lemma 6.3 Let m be the number of minor nodes in T. Under the assumptions of Lemma 6.1, every code to evaluate T must have at least m LOAD instructions.
Proof: Can be proved by induction on the number of minor nodes in any expression tree T.   □

Lemma 6.4 For any expression tree T, the number of LOAD instructions in the code generated by CODE2 is equal to the number of minor nodes in T.
Proof: Line 2 is the only line generating a LOAD. It is visited exactly once for each minor node in T.   □

Theorem 6.9 Under the conditions of Lemma 6.1, algorithm CODE2 generates optimal code.
Proof: Follows from Lemmas 6.1-6.4 and the observation that under the given assumptions the number of instructions of types (3) and (4) equals the number of internal nodes (or operators) in the expression tree T in all valid codes for T.   □

If commutative and associative operators are allowed then several different expression trees may compute the same expression. Figure 6.18(a) shows an expression tree equivalent to that of Figure 6.16 (ii) when + is commutative. Figure 6.18(b) shows one equivalent to that of Figure 6.16 (iv) when + is associative. Note that CODE2 generates codes for (a) and (b) using one register only while two registers were needed for the corresponding trees of Figure 6.16. Moreover, the codes have fewer instructions when $N = 1$. Hence, if the assumption of noncommutativity and nonassociativity o operators is removed, Theorem 6.9 is no longer true. However, if $\mathfrak{I}$ is the class of equivalent expression trees corresponding to an expression E that has commutative and associative operators then all trees in $\mathfrak{I}$ have the same number of internal (operator) nodes. This follows from the observation that neither commutative nor associative transformations reduce the number of operators in E. From Lemmas 6.1-6.4 it follows that the optimal code for E now corresponds to the code generated by CODE2 using as input a tree in $\mathfrak{I}$ for which the sum of major and minor nodes is minimum. When E has commutative operators but no associative operators then such a tree can be easily obtained from any expression tree T for E. Commutativity only allows one to exchange the left and right operands of a commutative operator. The sum of major and minor nodes is minimized if every left child of a commutative operator is an internal node (unless both children are leaves). Thus given any tree T we can obtain an optimal tree T' for use in CODE2 by simply examining all internal nodes that have exactly one leaf child and making this child the right child in case the parent operator is commutative (see exercise). The exercises develop algorithms for the case when E has both commutative and associative operators.

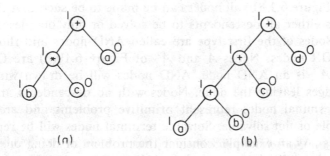

Figure 6.18   Equivalent trees for trees (ii) and (iv) of figure 6.16

When the assumption that the left and right operands of an operator have to be computed independently is dropped, the "expression tree" corresponding to an expression becomes a graph (as the expression may have common subexpressions). Obtaining optimal code for expressions with common subexpressions is computationally very difficult. The problem is

NP-Hard (see chapter 11). In fact, even determining *MR*(*E*) is *NP*-Hard. This change in complexity from a tree to a graph is typical of many optimization problems. Problems that are efficiently solvable on trees often become very hard on graphs.

6.3 AND/OR GRAPHS

Many complex problems can be broken down into a series of subproblems such that the solution of all or some of these results in the solution of the original problem. These subproblems may be broken down further into sub-subproblems and so on until the only problems remaining are sufficiently primitive as to be trivially solvable. This breaking down of a complex problem into several subproblems can be represented by a directed graph like structure in which nodes represent problems and descendents of a node represent the subproblems associated with it. For example the graph of Figure 6.19(a) represents a problem *A* that can be solved by either solving both the subproblems *B* and *C* or the single subproblems *D* or *E*. Groups of subproblems that must be solved in order to imply a solution to the parent node are joined together by an arc going across the respective edges (as the arc across the edges $\langle A, B \rangle$ and $\langle A, C \rangle$). By introducing dummy nodes as in Figure 6.19(b) all nodes can be made to be such that their solution requires either all descendents to be solved or only one descendent to be solved. Nodes of the first type are called AND nodes and those of the latter type OR nodes. Nodes *A* and *A''* of Figure 6.19(b) are OR nodes while node *A'* is an AND node. AND nodes will be drawn with an arc across all edges leaving the node. Nodes with no descendents are termed terminal. Terminal nodes represent primitive problems and are marked either solvable or not solvable. Solvable terminal nodes will be represented by rectangles. As an example, consider the problem of doing one's weekly laundry. Figure 6.20 shows a possible AND/OR graph, which is actually a tree, for this problem. The original problem is divided into five subproblems: collect clothes, wash clothes, dry, iron and fold and stack washed clothes. Each of these has to be done in order to complete the task. To wash the clothes we may either hand wash or wash by machine. The node representing hand wash has no descendents and is not a square node either. Hence, hand wash is not possible for this graph. While, to most minds, the laundry problem described above will be simple enough that a solution can be obtained without constructing the AND/OR tree of Figure 6.20 there are many other problems for which this is not the case. Breaking down a problem into several subproblems is known as problem reduction.

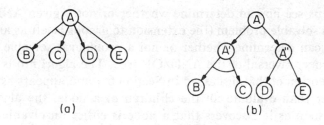

(a)   (b)

Figure 6.19   Graphs representing problems

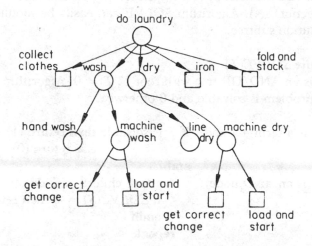

Figure 6.20   AND/OR graph corresponding to the laundry problem

Problem reduction has been used on such problems as theorem proving, symbolic integration and analysis of industrial schedules.

When problem reduction is used, two different problems may generate a common subproblem. In this case it may be desirable to have only one node representing this subproblem (this would imply that the subproblem is to be solved only once). Figure 6.21 shows an AND/OR graph for a case where this is done. Note that the graph is no longer a tree. Furthermore, such graphs may have directed cycles as in Figure 6.21(b). The presence of a directed cycle does not in itself imply the unsolvability of the problem. In fact, problem A of Figure 6.21(b) can be solved by solving the primitive problems G, H and I. This leads to the solution of D and E and hence of B and C. A *solution graph* is a subgraph of solvable nodes that shows that the problem is solved. The solution graphs for the graphs of Figure 6.21 are shown by heavy edges.

First, let us see how to determine whether or not a given AND/OR tree represents a solvable problem (the extension to graphs is left as an exercise). Clearly, we can determine whether or not a problem is solvable. This calls for a postorder traversal of the AND/OR tree. The algorithm is a straight-forward extension of that discussed in Section 6.1 and appears as Algorithm 6.12. Rather than evaluate all the children of a node, the algorithm terminates as soon as it discovers that a node is either unsolvable (line 6) or solvable (line 13). This reduces the amount of work being done by the algorithm without affecting the outcome. A similar modification to post-order is made in Section 6.4 when implementing an alph-beta search (to be defined in Section 6.4). Algorithm SOLVE can easily be modified so as to identify a solution subtree.

line	procedure $SOLVE(T)$
	//T is an AND/OR tree with root T. $T \neq 0$. Algorithm returns 1//
	//if problem is solvable and 0 otherwise//
1	**case**
2	: T is a terminal node: **if** T is solvable **then return** (1)
3	**else return** (0)
4	**endif**
5	: T is an *AND* node: **for** each child S of T **do**
6	**if** $SOLVE(S) = 0$ **then return** (0)
7	**endif**
8	**repeat**
9	**return** (1)
10	:**else**: **for** each child S of T **do** //OR node//
11	**if** $SOLVE(S) = 1$ **then return** (1) **endif**
12	**repeat**
13	**return** (0)
14	**endcase**
15	**end** $SOLVE$

Algorithm 6.12   Algorithm to determine if the AND/OR tree T is solvable

Often, the AND/OR tree corresponding to a given problem is available only implicitly. We are given a function F that generates all the children of a node already generated. In this case, given the root node we have to determine a solution tree (if one exists) for the problem. The nodes of the tree can be generated either in breadth first or depth first order. Since it is possible for an AND/OR tree to have infinite depth, a depth first generation of the tree may start generating all the nodes on an infinite path

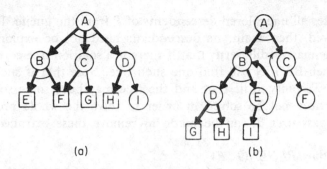

Figure 6.21 Two AND/OR graphs that are not trees

from the root and hence never determine a solution subtree (even when one exists). This can be overcome by restricting the depth first search to the generation of the AND/OR tree only to a certain depth d. Nonterminal nodes at depth d are labeled unsolvable. In this case a depth first search is guaranteed to find a solution subtree provided there is one of depth no more than d. Breadth first search (or generation) does not suffer from this drawback. Since each node can have only a finite number of children, no level in the AND/OR tree can have an infinite number of nodes. Hence, a breadth first generation of the AND/OR tree is guaranteed to find a solution subtree if one exists. Moreover, such a generation procedure would generate a solution subtree of minimum depth.

Algorithm BFGEN(T, F) generates a breadth first solution tree (if one exists) of the AND/OR tree obtained by applying the child generation function F starting with node T. If no solution subtree exists then BFGEN may not terminate. This happens only if the AND/OR tree has infinite depth. The algorithm can be made to terminate by restricting the depth of the desired solution tree. BFGEN makes use of a subalgorithm ASOLVE(T). ASOLVE(T) is similar to algorithm SOLVE. It makes a postorder traversal of the partially generated AND/OR tree T and labels the nodes as either solved, unsolvable or maybe solvable. Since T is not a complete AND/OR tree it has three kinds of leaf nodes. The first kind is a nonterminal leaf node. A nonterminal leaf node may or may not be solvable. It is an unexplored node. The other two kinds are terminal leaf nodes and have already been marked either solvable or unsolvable. If a nonleaf node is an AND node then it is unsolvable if any one of its children is unsolvable. A nonleaf node which is an OR node is solvable if it has at least one child which is marked solvable. Any nodes found to be unsolvable may be discarded from T (line 7). Further, there is no need to explore any descendent of an unsolvable node P as even if this descendent is solvable, P cannot be solved.

Line 9 deletes all unexplored descendents of P from the queue. If a node is already solved, then again, its descendents need not be explored further (line 9). One may readily verify that if there is a solution tree corresponding to (T, F) then BFGEN will find one such tree. Note that if such a tree is found then T points to its root and the tree may have some solvable leaf nodes that need not be solved in order to solve the whole problem. An additional pass over T can be made to remove these extraneous nodes.

```
line    procedure BFGEN(T, F)
            //F generates the children of nodes in T; T is the root//
            //node. At termination T is the root of the solution//
            //subtree if any.//
1           initialize Q to be an empty queue; V ← T
2           loop
3               use F to generate the children of V   //explore V//
4               if V has no children then lable V unsolvable
                                else (i)   put all children of V that are not
                                           leaf nodes onto Q and label the
                                           leaf nodes solvable or unsolvable.
                                     (ii)  add all the children of V to tree T
5               endif
6               call ASOLVE(T)
7               delete from tree T all nodes labeled unsolvable
8               if the root node T is labeled solvable then return (T) endif
9               delete from Q all nodes that had or have an ancestor in T
                    labeled either unsolvable or solved
10              if Q is empty then stop   //no solution// endif
11              delete first node on Q; let this node be V
12          repeat
13      end BFGEN
```

Algorithm 6.13   Breadth first generation of a solution tree

The exercises further explore AND/OR trees and graphs. We shall see more of AND/OR trees and graphs in Chapter 11.

6.4   GAME TREES

An interesting application of trees is the playing of games such as tic-tac-toe, chess, nim, kalah, checkers, go, etc. As an example, let us consider the game of nim. This game is played by two players A and B. The game itself is described by a board which initially contains a pile of n tooth-picks. The players A and B make moves alternately with A making the first move. A *legal move* consists of removing either 1, 2 or 3 of the tooth-picks from the pile. However, a player cannot remove more toothpicks than there are on the pile. The player who removes the last toothpick loses the game and the other player wins. The *board configuration* at any time is completely specified by the number of toothpicks remaining in the pile. At any time the game status is determined by the board configuration to-gether with the player whose turn it is to make the next move. A *terminal board configuration* is one which represents either a *win*, *lose* or *draw* situation. All other configurations are *nonterminal*. In nim there is only one terminal configuration: there are no toothpicks in the pile. This configura-tion is a win for player A if B made the last move, otherwise it is a win for B. The game of nim cannot end in a draw.

A sequence $C_1, \ldots, C_m$ of board configurations is said to be *valid* if:

(i) C_1 is the starting configuration of the game;
(ii) $C_i, 0 < i < m$, are nonterminal configurations;
(iii) C_{i+1} is obtained from C_i by a legal move made by player A if i is odd and by player B if i is even. It is assumed that there are only finitely many legal moves.

A valid sequence $C_1, \ldots, C_m$ of board configurations with C_m a terminal configuration is an *instance* of the game. The *length* of the sequence C_1, $C_2, \ldots, C_m$ is m. A *finite game* is one in which there are no valid sequences of infinite length. All possible instances of a finite game may be represented by a *game tree*. The tree of Figure 6.22 is the game tree for nim with $n =$ 6. Each node of the tree represents a board configuration. The root node represents the starting configuration C_1. Transitions from one level to the next are made via a move of A or B. Transitions from an odd level repre-sent moves made by A. All other transitions are the result of moves made by B. Square nodes have been used in Figure 6.22 to represent board con-figurations when it was A's turn to move. Circular nodes have been used for other configurations. The edges from level 1 nodes to level 2 nodes and from level 2 nodes to level 3 nodes have been labeled with the move made by A and B respectively (for example, an edge labeled 1 means 1 tooth-pick is to be removed). It is easy to figure out the labels for the remaining edges of the tree. Terminal configurations are represented by leaf nodes. Leaf nodes have been labeled by the name of the player who wins when that configuration is reached. By the nature of the game of nim player A can win only at leaf nodes on odd levels while B can win only at leaf nodes on even levels. The degree of any node in a game tree is at most equal to the number of distinct legal moves. In nim there are at most 3 legal moves from any configuration. By definition, the number of legal moves from any configuration is finite. The *depth* of a game tree is the length of a longest instance of the game. The depth of the nim tree of Figure 6.22 is 7. Hence, from start to finish this game involves at most 6 moves. It is not difficult to see how similar game trees may be constructed for other finite games such as chess, tic-tac-toe, kalah, etc. (Strictly speaking, chess is not a finite game as it is possible to repeat board configurations in the game. We can view chess as a finite game by disallowing this possibility. We could, for instance, define the repetition of a board configuration as resulting in a draw.)

Now that we have seen what a game tree is, the next question is "of what use are they?" Game trees are useful in determining the next move a player should make. Starting at the initial configuration represented by the root of Figure 6.22 player A is faced with the choice of making any one of three possible moves. Which one should he make? Assuming that player A wants to win the game, he should make the move that maximizes his chances of winning. For the simple tree of Figure 6.22 this move is not too difficult to determine. We can use an evaluation function $E(X)$ which assigns a numeric value to the board configuration X. This function is a measure of the value or worth of configuration X to player A. So, $E(X)$ is high for a configuration from which A has a good chance of winning and low for a configuration from which A has a good chance of losing. $E(X)$ has its maximum value for configurations that are either winning terminal configurations for A or configurations from which A is guaranteed to win regardless of B's countermoves. $E(X)$ has its minimum value for configurations from which B is guaranteed to win.

For a game such as nim with $n = 6$, whose game tree has very few nodes, it is sufficient to define $E(X)$ only for terminal configurations. We could define $E(X)$ as:

$$E(X) = \begin{cases} 1 & \text{if } X \text{ is a winning configuration for } A \\ -1 & \text{if } X \text{ is a losing configuration for } A \end{cases}$$

Using this evaluation function we wish to determine which of the configurations b, c, d player A should move the game into. Clearly, the choice is the one whose value is max $\{ V(b), V(c), V(d) \}$ where $V(x)$ is the value of configuration x. For leaf nodes x, $V(x)$ is taken to be $E(x)$. For all other nodes x let $d \geq 1$ be the degree of x and let $c_1, c_2, \ldots, c_d$ be the configurations represented by the children of x. Then $V(x)$ is defined by:

$$V(x) = \begin{cases} \max_{1 \leq i \leq d} \{V(c_i)\} & \text{if } x \text{ is a square node} \\ \\ \min_{1 \leq i \leq d} \{V(c_i)\} & \text{if } x \text{ is a circular node} \end{cases} \qquad (6.1)$$

The justification for (6.1) is fairly simple. If x is a square node, then it is at an odd level and it will be A's turn to move from here if the game ever reaches this node. Since A wants to win he will move to a child node with maximum value. In case x is a circular node it must be on an even level and if the game ever reaches this node, then it will be B's turn to move. Since B is out to win the game for himself, he will (barring mistakes) make a move that will minimize A's chances of winning. In this case the next configuration will be $\min_{1 \leq i \leq d} \{V(c_i)\}$. Equation (6.1) defines the *minimax* procedure to determine the value of configuration x.

This is illustrated on the hypothetical game of Figure 6.23. P_{11} represents an arbitrary board configuration from which A has to make a move. The values of the leaf nodes are obtained by evaluating the function $E(x)$. The value of P_{11} is obtained by starting at the nodes on level 4 and computing their values using eq. (6.1). Since level 4 is a level with circular nodes all unknown values on this level may be obtained by taking the minimum of the children values. Next, values on levels 3, 2 and 1 may be computed in that order. The resulting value for P_{11} is 3. This means that starting from P_{11} the best A can hope to do is reach a configuration of value 3. Even though some nodes have value greater than 3, these nodes will not be reached, as B's countermoves will prevent the game from reaching any such configuration (assuming B's countermoves are optimal for B with respect to A's evaluation function). For example, if A made a move to P_{21}, hoping to win the game at P_{31}, A would indeed be surprised by B's countermove to P_{32} resulting in a loss to A. Given A's evaluation function and the game tree of Figure 6.23 the best move for A to make is to configuration P_{22}. Having made this move, the game may still not reach configuration P_{52} as B would, in general, be using a different evaluation function, which might give different values to various board configurations. In any case, the *minimax* procedure can be used to determine the best move a player can make given his evaluation function. Using the minimax procedure on the game tree for nim (Figure 6.22) we see that the value of the root node is $V(a) = 1$. Since $E(X)$ for this game was defined to be 1 iff A was guaranteed to win,

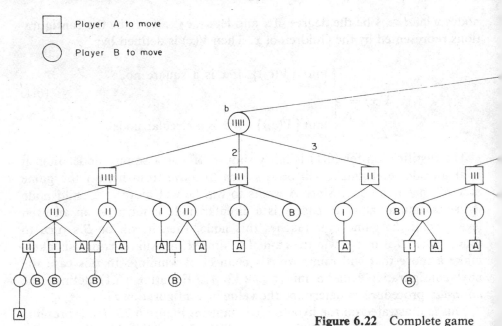

Figure 6.22   Complete game

this means that if *A* makes the optimal move from node *a* then no matter what *B*'s countermove is *A* will win. The optimal move is to node *b*. One may readily verify that from *b* *A* can win the game independent of *B*'s countermove!

For games such as nim with $n = 6$, the game trees are sufficiently small that it is possible to generate the whole tree. Thus, it is a relatively simple matter to determine whether or not the game has a winning strategy. Moreover, for such games it is possible to make a decision on the next move by looking ahead all the way to terminal configurations. Games of this type are not very interesting since assuming no errors are made by either player, the outcome of the game is predetermined and both players should use similar evaluation functions i.e., $E_A(X) = 1$ for X a winning configuration and $E_A(X) = -1$ for X a losing configuration for A; $E_B(X) = -E_A(X)$.

Of greater interest are games such as chess where the game tree is too large to be generated in its entirety. It is estimated that the game tree for chess has more than 10^{100} nodes. Even using a computer which is capable of generating 10^{11} nodes a second, the complete generation of the game tree for chess would require more than 10^{80} years. In games with large game trees the decision as to which move to make next can be made only by looking at the game tree for the next few levels. The evaluation function $E(X)$ is used to get the values of the leaf nodes of the subtree generated and then

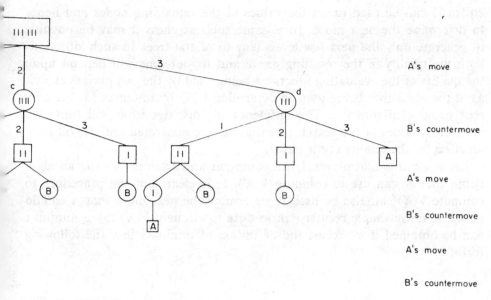

tree for Nim with $n = 6$

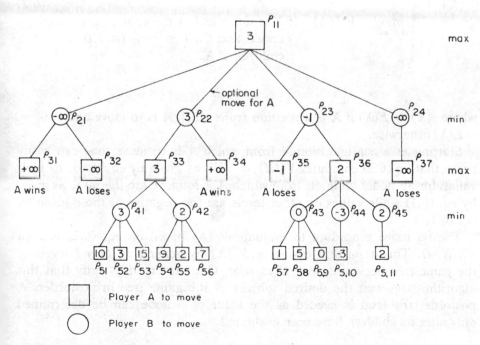

Figure 6.23 Portion of game tree for a hypothetical game. The value of terminal nodes is obtained from the evaluation function $E(x)$ for player A

eq. (6.1) can be used to get the values of the remaining nodes and hence to determine the next move. In a game such as chess it may be possible to generate only the next few levels (say 6) of the tree. In such situations both the quality of the resulting game and its outcome will depend upon the quality of the evaluating functions being used by the two players as well as of the algorithm being used to determine $V(X)$ by minimax for the current game configuration. The efficiency of this algorithm will limit the number of nodes of the search tree that can be generated and so will have an effect on the quality of the game.

Let us assume that player A is a computer and attempt to write an algorithm that A can use to compute $V(X)$. It is clear that the procedure to compute $V(X)$ can also be used to determine the next move that A should make. A fairly simple recursive procedure to evaluate $V(X)$ using minimax can be obtained if we recast the definition of minimax into the following form:

$$V'(X) = \begin{cases} e(X) & \text{if } X \text{ is a leaf of the subtree generated} \\[2ex] \max_{1 \le i \le d}\{-V'(c_i)\} & \text{If } X \text{ is not a leaf of the subtree generated and } C_i, \ 1 \le i \le d \text{ are the children of } X. \end{cases}$$
(6.2)

where $e(X) = E(X)$ if X is a position from which A is to move and $e(X) = -E(X)$ otherwise.

Starting at a configuration X from which A is to move, one can easily prove that eq (6.2) computes $V'(X) = V(X)$ as given by eq. (6.1). In fact, values for all nodes on levels from which A is to move are the same as given by eq. (6.1) while values on other levels are the negative of those given by eq. (6.1).

The recursive procedure to evaluate $V'(X)$ based on eq. (6.2) is then $VE(X, l)$. This algorithm evaluates $V'(X)$ by generating only l levels of the game tree beginning with X as root. One may readily verify that this algorithm traverses the desired subtree of the game tree in postorder. A postorder traversal is needed as the value of a node can be determined only after its children have been evaluated.

procedure $VE(X, l)$
  //compute $V'(X)$ by looking at most l moves ahead. $e(X)$ is the evaluation
  //function for player A. For convenience, it is assumed that starting//
  //from any board configuration X the legal moves of the game permit//
  //a transition only to the configurations $C_1, C_2, \ldots, C_d$ if X is not a//
  //terminal configuration.//
  if X is terminal **or** $l = 0$ **then return** $e(X)$ **endif**
  $ans \leftarrow - VE(C_1, l - 1)$ //traverse the first subtree//
  for $i \leftarrow 2$ **to** d **do**   //traverse the remaining subtrees//
    $ans \leftarrow \mathbf{max}(ans, - VE(C_i, l - 1))$
  repeat
  return (ans)
end VE

Algorithm 6.14 Postorder evaluation of a game tree

An initial call to algorithm VE with $X = P_{11}$ and $l = 4$ for the hypothetical game of Figure 6.23 would result in the generation of the complete game tree. The values of various configurations would be determined in the order: $P_{31}, P_{32}, P_{21}, P_{51}, P_{52}, P_{53}, P_{41}, P_{54}, P_{55}, P_{56}, P_{42}, P_{33}, \ldots, P_{37}, P_{24}, P_{11}$. It is possible to introduce, with relative ease, some heuristics into algorithm VE that will in general result in the generation of only a portion of the possible configurations while still computing $V'(X)$ accurately.

Consider the game tree of Figure 6.23. After $V(P_{41})$ has been computed, it is known that $V(P_{33})$ is at least $V(P_{41}) = 3$. Next, when $V(P_{55})$ is determined to be 2, then we know that $V(P_{42})$ is at most 2. Since P_{33} is a max position, $V(P_{42})$ cannot affect $V(P_{33})$. Regardless of the values of the remaining children of P_{42}, the value of P_{33} is not determined by $V(P_{42})$ as $V(P_{42})$ cannot be more than $V(P_{41})$. This observation may be stated more formally as the following rule: The *alpha* value of a max position is defined to be the minimum possible value for that position. *If the value of a min position is determined to be less than or equal to the alpha value of its parent, then we may stop generation of the remaining children of this min position.* Termination of node generation under this rule is known as *alpha cutoff*. Once $V(P_{41})$ in Figure 6.23 is determined, the alpha value of P_{33} becomes 3. $V(P_{55}) \le$ alpha value of P_{33} implies that P_{56} need not be generated.

A corresponding rule may be defined for min positions. The *beta* value
of a min position is the maximum possible value for that position. *If the
value of a max position is determined to be greater than or equal to the
beta value of its parent node, then we may stop generation of the remaining
children of this max position.* Termination of node generation under the
rule is called *beta cutoff*. In Figure 6.23, once $V(P_{35})$ is determined, the
beta value of P_{23} becomes -1. Generation of P_{57}, P_{58}, P_{59} gives $V(P_{43}) = 0$.
Thus, $V(P_{43})$ is greater than or equal to the beta value of P_{23} and we may
terminate the generation of the remaining children of P_{36}. The two rules
stated above may be combined together to get what is known as *alpha-
beta pruning*. When alpha-beta pruning is used on Figure 6.23 the subtree with root P_{36} is not generated at all! This is so because when the value
of P_{23} is being determined the alpha value of P_{11} is 3. $V(P_{35})$ is less than
the alpha value of P_{11} and so an alpha cutoff takes place. It should be
emphasized that the alpha or beta value of a node is a dynamic quantity.
Its value at any time during the game tree generation depends upon which
nodes have so far been generated and evaluated.

In actually introducing alpha-beta pruning into algorithm *VE* it is necessary to restate this rule in terms of the values defined by eq. (6.2). Under
eq. (6.2) all positions are max positions since the values of the min positions
of eq. (6.1) have been multiplied by -1. The alpha-beta pruning rule now
reduces to the following rule: let the *B*-value of a position be the minimum
value that position can have. *For any position X, let B be the B-value of
its parent and $D = -B$. Then, if the value of X is determined to be greater
than or equal to D, we may terminate generation of the remaining children
of X.* Incorporating this rule into algorithm *VE* is fairly straightforward
and results in algorithm *VEB*. This algorithm has the additional parameter
D which is the negative of the *B* value of the parent of *X*.

procedure *VEB* (X, l, D)
    //determine $V'(X)$ as in eq. (6.2) using the *B*-rule and looking//
    //only l moves ahead. Remaining assumptions and notation are//
    //the same as for algorithm *VE*.//
    if X is terminal **or** $l = 0$ **then return** $e(x)$ **endif**
    $ans \leftarrow -VEB(C_1, l - 1, \infty)$ //current lower bound on $V'(x)$//
    for $i \leftarrow 2$ **to** d **do**
        if $ans \geq D$ **then return** (ans) **endif**   //use *B*-rule//
        $ans \leftarrow \max(ans, -VEB(C_i, l - 1, -ans))$
    repeat
    return (ans)
end *VEB*

    Algorithm 6.15 Postorder evaluation of a game tree using alpha-beta pruning

If Y is a position from which A is to move, then the initial call VEB(Y, l, ∞) correctly computes $V'(Y)$ with an l move look ahead. Further pruning of the game tree may be achieved by realizing that the B-value of a node X places a lower bound on the value grandchildren of X must have in order to affect X's value. Consider the subtree of Figure 6.24(a). If $V'(GC(X)) \leq B$ then $V'(C(X)) \geq -B$. Following the evaluation of $C(X)$, the B-value of X is max $\{B, - V'(C(X))\} = B$ as $V'(C(X)) \geq -B$. Hence unless $V'(GC(X)) > B$, it cannot affect $V'(X)$ and so B is a lower bound on the value $GC(X)$ should have. Incorporating this lowerbound into algorithm VEB yields algorithm AB. The additional parameter LB is a lowerbound on the value X should have.

```
procedure AB(X, l, LB, D)
    //same as algorithm VEB. LB is a lowerbound on V'(X)//
    if X is terminal or l = 0 then return e(X) endif
    ans ← LB   //current lowerbound on V'(X)//
    for i ← 1 to d do
        if ans ≥ D then return (ans) endif
        ans ← max (ans, − AB(Cᵢ, l − 1, D, − ans))
    repeat
    return (ans)
end AB
```

Algorithm 6.16   Postorder evaluation of a game tree using deep alpha beta pruning

One may easily verify that the initial call $AB(Y, l - \infty, \infty)$ gives the same result as the call $VE(Y, l)$. With the addition of LB, the search algorithm is known as deep alpha beta pruning.

Figure 6.24(b) shows a hypothetical game tree in which the use of algorithm AB results in greater pruning than achieved by algorithm VEB. Let us first trace the action of VEB on the tree of Figure 6.24(b). We assume the initial call to be VEB(P_1, l, ∞) where l is the depth of the tree. After examining the left subtree of P_1, the B value of P_1 is set to 10 and nodes P_3, P_4, P_5 and P_6 are generated. Following this, $V'(P_6)$ is determined to be 9 and then the B-value of P_5 becomes -9. Using this, we continue to evaluate the node P_7. In the case of AB however, since the B-value of P_1 is 10, the lowerbound for P_4 is 10 and so the effective B-value of P_4 becomes 10. As a result the node P_7 is not generated since not matter what its value, $V'(P_5) \geq -9$ and this will not enable $V'(P_4)$ to reach its lower bound.

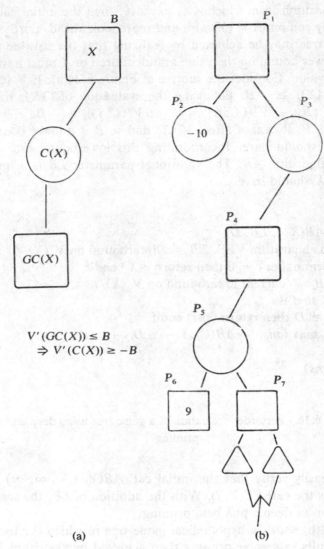

$$V'(GC(X)) \leq B$$
$$\Rightarrow V'(C(X)) \geq -B$$

(a)   (b)

Figure 6.24   Game trees showing lower bounding

Analysis of Procedures VEB and AB

Analyzing procedure AB to determine what fraction of nodes in a game tree will be generated is exceedingly difficult. Knuth and Moore have analyzed procedure VEB for certain kinds of game trees. Some of their results are stated below without proof.

Definition: A *uniform* game tree of degree d and height h is a game tree is which every node at levels $1, 2, \ldots, h - 1$ has exactly d children. In addition, every node at level h is terminal. A *random* uniform game tree is a uniform game tree in which the terminal nodes have independent random values.

Theorem 6.10 [Knuth and Moore] The expected number, $T(d, h)$ of terminal positions examined by the alpha-beta procedure without deep cut-offs (i.e. procedure VEB), in a random uniform game tree of degree d and height h is less than $c(d) r(d)^h$. $r(d)$ is the largest eigenvalue of the matrix M_d whose terms $M_d(i, j)$ are given by

$$M_d(i, j) = 1 \bigg/ \sqrt{\binom{i - 1 + (j - 1)/d}{i - 1}} \qquad 1 \le i \le d \text{ and } 1 \le j \le d.$$

$c(d)$ is an appropriate constant. □

Note that since procedure AB is at least as good as procedure VEB, the bound of Theorem 6.10 is also a bound for AB. Using Theorem 6.10, the following theorem may be proved:

Theorem 6.11 [Knuth and Moore] $T(d, h)$ for a random uniform game tree of degree d and height $h + 1$ satisfies the equality

$$\lim_{h \to \infty} T(d, h)^{1/h} = r(d)$$

where

$$c_1 \frac{d}{\log d} \le r(d) \le c_2 \frac{d}{\log d}$$

for some positive constants c_1 and c_2. □

Knuth and Moore have also analyzed the alpha-beta cutoff procedure on a different tree model.

Definition: A game tree is totally dependent if for every pair p_i and p_j, $i \ne j$ of nonterminal positions either all terminal children of p_i have greater value than the terminal children of p_j, or they all have lesser value.

Theorem 6.12 [Knuth and Moore] The expected number of terminal positions examined by procedure AB (i.e. with deep cutoffs), in a random totally dependent uniform game tree of degree d and height $h + 1$, is

$$\frac{d - H_d}{d - H_d^2} (d^{\lceil h/2 \rceil} + H_d d^{\lfloor h/2 \rfloor} - H_d^{h+1} - H_d^h) + H_d^h$$

where $H_d = 1 + 1/2 + \cdots + 1/d$. For $d \geq 3$, this bound is within a constant factor of the minimum number of terminal positions that must be examined by any algorithm which evaluates a uniform game tree of degree d and height $h + 1$. $\square$

6.5 BICONNECTED COMPONENTS AND DEPTH FIRST SEARCH

In this section, by a graph we shall always mean an undirected graph. A vertex v in a connected graph G is an *articulation point* iff the deletion of vertex v together with all edges incident to v disconnects the graph into two or more nonempty components. In the connected graph of Figure 6.25(a) vertex 2 is an articulation point as the deletion of vertex 2 and edges (1, 2), (2, 3), (2, 5), (2, 7) and (2, 8) leaves behind two disconnected nonempty components (Figure 6.25(b)). Graph G of Figure 6.25(a) has only two other articulation points: vertex 5 and vertex 3. Note that if any of the remaining vertices is deleted from G then exactly one component remains.

A graph G is *biconnected* iff it contains no articulation point. The graph of Figure 6.25(a) is not biconnected. The graph of Figure 6.26 is biconnected. The presence of articulation points in a connected graph can be an undesirable feature in many cases. For example, if G represents a communication network with the vertices representing communication stations and the edges communication lines then the failure of a communication station i which is an articulation point would result in loss of communication to points other than i too. On the other hand, if G has no articulation point then if any station i fails, we can still communicate between every pair of stations not including station i.

In this section we shall develop an efficient algorithm to test if a connected graph is biconnected. For the case of graphs that are not biconnected, this algorithm will identify all the articulation points. Once it has been determined that a connected graph G is not biconnected, it may be desirable to determine a set of edges whose inclusion will make the graph biconnected. Determining such a set of edges is facilitated if we know the maximal subgraphs of G that are biconnected. $G' = (V', E')$ is a maximal biconnected subgraph of G iff G has no biconnected subgraph $G'' = (V'', E')$ such

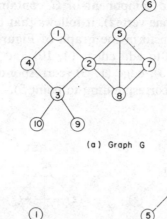

(a) Graph G

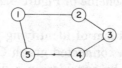

(b) Result of deleting vertex 2

Figure 6.25   An example graph

that $V' \subseteq V''$ and $E' \subset E''$. A maximal biconnected subgraph is a *biconnected component*.

The graph of Figure 6.26 has only one biconnected component (i.e. the entire graph). The biconnected components of the graph of Figure 6.25(a) are shown in Figure 6.27.

It is relatively easy to show that two biconnected components can have at most one vertex in common and that this vertex is an articulation point. Hence, no edge can be in two different biconnected components (as this would require two common vertices). The graph G may be transformed into a biconnected graph using the edge addition scheme of Figure 6.28.

Figure 6.26   A biconnected graph

Since every biconnected component of G contains at least two vertices (unless G itself has only one vertex), it follows that the v_i of step E3 exists. Using this scheme to transform the graph of Figure 6.25(a) into a biconnected graph requires us to add edges (4, 10) and (10, 9) (corresponding to the articulation point 3); edge (1, 5) (corresponding to the articulation point 2) and edge (6, 7) (corresponding to point 5).

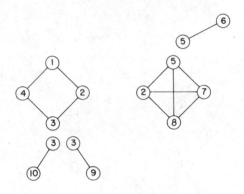

Figure 6.27   Biconnected components of graph of Figure 6.25(a)

$E1$:   **for each** articulation point a **do**
$E2$:   let $B_1, B_2, \ldots, B_k$ be the biconnected components containing vertex a
$E3$:   let v_i, $v_i \neq a$ be a vertex in B_i, $1 \leq i \leq k$
$E4$:   add to G the edges (v_i, v_{i+1}), $1 \leq i < k$
$E5$:   **repeat**

Figure 6.28   Scheme to construct a biconnected graph

Note that once the edges (v_i, v_{i+1}) of step $E4$ (Figure 6.28) are added vertex a is no longer an articulation point. Hence following the addition of the edges corresponding to all articulation points, G has no articulation points and so is biconnected. If G has p articulation points and b biconnected components then the scheme of Figure 6.28 introduces exactly $b - p$ new edges into G.

Now, let us attack the problem of identifying the articulation points and biconnected components of a connected graph G with $n \geq 2$ vertices. The problem is efficiently solved by considering a depth first spanning tree of G.

Figures 6.29(a) and (b) show a depth first spanning tree of the graph of Figure 6.25(a). In each figure there is a number outside each vertex. These numbers correspond to the order in which a depth first search visits these vertices. This number will be referred to as the *depth first number* (DFN) of the vertex. Thus, DFN(1) = 1, DFN(4) = 2 and DFN(6) = 8. In Figure 6.29(b) solid edges form the depth first spanning tree. These edges are called *tree edges*. Broken edges (i.e. all remaining edges) are called *back edges*.

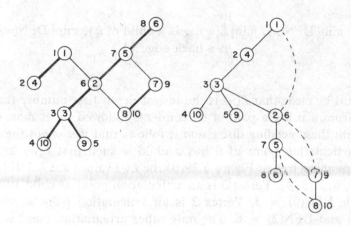

Figure 6.29   A depth first spanning tree of the graph of Figure 6.25(a)

Depth first spanning trees have a property that is very useful in identifying articulation points and biconnected components. This property is that if (u, v) is any edge in G then relative to the depth first spanning tree T either u is an ancestor of v or v is an ancestor of u. So, there are no cross edges relative to a depth first spanning tree $((u, v)$ is a *cross* edge relative to T iff neither u is an ancestor of v nor v an ancestor of u). To see this, assume that $(u, v) \in E(G)$ and (u, v) is a cross edge. (u, v) cannot be a tree edge as otherwise u is the parent of v or vice versa. So, (u, v) must be a back edge. Without loss of generality, we may assume DFN$(u) >$ DFN(v). Since vertex u is visited first, its exploration cannot be complete until vertex v is visited. From the definition of depth first search, it follows that u is an ancestor of all vertices visited until u is completely explored. Hence u is an ancestor of v in T and (u, v) cannot be a cross edge.

We next observe that the root node of a depth first spanning tree is an articulation point iff it has at least two children. Furthermore, if u is any other vertex then it is not an articulation point iff from every child w of u it is possible to reach an ancester of u using only a path made up of descendents of w and a back edge. Note that if this cannot be done for some child w of u then the deletion of vertex u will leave behind at least two nonempty components (one containing the root and the other containing vertex w). This observation leads to a simple rule to identify articulation points. For each vertex u define $L(u)$ as follows:

$$L(u) = \min\{ \text{DFN}(u), \min\{L(w)\,|\,w \text{ is a child of } u\}, \min\{ \text{DFN}(w)\,|\,(u, w) \text{ is a back edge }\}\}$$

It should be clear that $L(u)$ is the lowest depth first number that can be reached from u using a path of descendents followed by at most one back edge. From the preceding discussion it follows that if u is not the root then u is an articulation point iff u has a child w such that $L(w) \geq \text{DFN}(u)$. For the spanning tree of Figure 6.29(b) the $L(\ )$ values are $L(1:10) = (1, 1, 1, 1, 6, 8, 6, 7, 5, 4)$. Vertex 3 is an articulation point as child 10 has $L(10) = 4$ while $\text{DFN}(3) = 3$. Vertex 2 is an articulation point as child 5 has $L(5) = 6$ and $\text{DFN}(2) = 6$. The only other articulation point is vertex 5; child 6 has $L(6) = 8$ while $\text{DFN}(5) = 7$.

$L(u)$ can be easily computed if the vertices of the depth first spanning tree are visited in postorder. Thus, to determine the articulation points, it will be necessary to perform a depth first search of the graph G and visit the nodes in the resulting depth first spanning tree in postorder. It is possible to do both these functions in parallel. Procedure ART (Algorithm 6.17) carries out a depth first search of G. During this search each newly visited vertex gets assigned its depth first number. At the same time, $L(i)$ is computed for each vertex in the tree. This algorithm assumes that the connected graph G and the arrays DFN and L are global. In addition, it is assumed that the variable *num* is also global. It is clear from the algorithm that when vertex u has been explored and a return made from line 9 then $L(u)$ has been correctly computed. Note that in line 5 if $w \neq v$ then either (u, w) is a back edge or $\text{DFN}(w) > \text{DFN}(u) \geq L(u)$. In either case, $L(u)$ is correctly updated. The initial call to ART is **call** ART $(1, 0)$. DFN is initialized to zero before invoking ART.

line   **procedure** $ART(u, v)$
                //u is a start vertex for depth first search. v is its parent//
                //if any in the depth first spanning tree. It is assumed//
                //that the global array DFN is initialized to zero//
                //and that the global variable num is initialized to 1. n is//
                //the number of vertices in G//
                global $DFN(n), L(n), num, n$
  1             $DFN(u) \leftarrow num; L(u) \leftarrow num; num \leftarrow num + 1$
  2   **for** each vertex w adjacent from u **do**
  3   **if** $DFN(w) = 0$ **then call** $ART(w, u)$ //w is unvisited//
  4                            $L(u) \leftarrow \min (L(u), L(w))$
  5   **else if** $w \neq v$ **then** $L(u) \leftarrow \min (L(u), DFN(w))$
  6   **endif**
  7   **endif**
  8   **repeat**
  9   **end** ART

Algorithm 6.17   Algorithm to compute DFN and L

Once $L(1:n)$ has been computed the articulation points can be identified in $O(n)$ time. Since ART has a complexity $O(n + e)$ where e is the number of edges in G, the articulation points of G can be determined in $O(n + e)$ time.

Now, what needs to be done to determine the biconnected components of G? If following the call to ART (line 3) $L(w) \geq L(u)$ then we know that u is either the root or an articulation point. Regardless of whether u is not the root or is the root and has either one or more children, the edge (u, w) together with all edges (both tree and back) encountered during this call to ART (except for edges in other biconnected components contained in subtree w) form a biconnected component. A formal proof of this statement appears in the proof of Theorem 6.13. The changes needed to ART to obtain the biconnected components are:

  (i)   introduce a global stack S to hold edges.
  (ii) add the line
        2.1 **if** $v \neq w$ **and** $DFN(w) < DFN(u)$ **then** add (u, w) to top of S
            endif
        between lines 2 and 3. Note that (u, w) has already been stacked iff
        either v = w or DFN(w) > DFN(u).

(iii) between lines 3 and 4 add the lines:
    3.1 **if** $L(w) \geq DFN(u)$ **then print** (*'new biconnected component'*)
    3.2   **loop**
    3.3   delete an edge from the top of stack S
    3.4   let this edge be (x, y)
    3.5   **print** ('(', x, ', ', y, ') ')
    3.6   **until** $((x, y) = (u, w)$ **or** $(x, y) = (w, u))$ **repeat**
    3.7 **endif**

One may verify that following these additions to ART, its computing time remains $O(n + e)$. The following theorem establishes the correctness of the algorithm.

Theorem 6.13 Algorithm ART with lines 2.1 and 3.1–3.7 added correctly generates the biconnected components of the connected graph G when G has at least 2 vertices.

Proof: Note that when G has only one vertex, it has no edges so the algorithm generates no output. In this case G does have a biconnected component namely its single vertex. This case can be handled separartely.

When $n \geq 2$ the algorithm works correctly. This can be shown by induction on the number of biconnected components in G. Clearly, for all biconnected graphs G the root u of the depth first spanning tree has only one child w. Futhermore, w is the only vertex for which $L(w) \geq DFN(u)$ in line 3.1. By the time w has been explored all edges in G have been output as one biconnected component.

Now assume the algorithm works correctly for all connected graphs G with at most m biconnected components. We shall show that it also works correctly for all connected graphs with $m + 1$ biconnected components. Let G be any such graph. Consider the first time that $L(w) \geq DFN(u)$ in line 3.1. At this time no edges have been output and so all edges in G incident to the descendents of w are on the stack and are above the edge $(u\ w)$. Since none of the descendents of u is an articulation point and u is one, it follows that the set of edges above (u, w) on the stack forms a biconnected component together with the edge (u, w). Once these edges have been deleted from the stack and output, the algorithm behaves essentially as it would on the graph G' obtained by deleting from G the biconnected component just output. The behavior of the algorithm on G differs from that on G' only in that during the completion of the exploration of vertex u, some edges (u, r) such that (u, r) is in the component just output may be considered. However, for all such edges, DFN(r) $\neq$ 0 and DFN(r) $>$ $DFN(u)$

$\geq L(u)$. Hence, these edges only result in a vacuous iteration of the loop of lines 2-8 and do not materially affect the algorithm.

One may easily establish that G' has at least 2 vertices. Since in addition G' has exactly m biconnected components, it follows from the induction hypothesis that the remaining components are correctly generated. ☐

It should be noted that the algorithm described above will work with any spanning tree relative to which the given graph has no cross edges. Unfortunately, graphs can have cross edges relative to breadth first spanning trees. Hence, algorithm ART cannot be adapted to BFS.

REFERENCES AND SELECTED READINGS:

Algorithm INORDER2 is due to J. M. Robson and appears in:

"An improved algorithm for traversing binary trees without auxiliary stack," by J. M. Robson, *Info. Proc. Let.*, 2, pp 12-14 (1973).

Algorithms for other kinds of traversals without using stacks appear in:

"Simple algorithms for traversing a tree without an auxiliary stack," by B. Dwyer, *Info. Proc. Let.*, 2, pp 143-145 (1974).

"Scanning list structures without stacks or tag bits," by G. Lindstrom, *Info. Proc. Let.*, 2, pp 47-51 (1973).

Two of Dwyer's algorithms are developed in exercises 15 and 16.

Traversal and search algorithms for threaded trees, AVL trees, B-trees etc. may be found in:

Fundamentals of Data Structures, by E. Horowitz and S. Sahni, Computer Science Press, Potomac, Maryland (1976).

The Art of Computer Programming, Vol. 3, by D. E. Knuth, Addison Wesley, Reading, Mass. (1973).

Our discussion of code optimization for a multiregister machine (i.e. machine model B) is based on:

"The generation of optimal code for arithmetic expressions," by R. Sethi and J. Ullman, *JACM*, 17(4), pp 715-728 (1970).

Early work on code generation was done by Anderson, Floyd, Nakata and Redziejowski. The references are:

"A note on some compiling algorithms," by J. Anderson, *Comm. ACM*, 7(3), pp 149–150 (1964).

"An algorithm for coding efficient arithmetic operations," by R. Floyd, *Comm. ACM*, 4(1), pp 42–51 (1961).

"On compiling algorithms for arithmetic expressions," by I. Nakata, *Comm. ACM*, 10(8), pp 492–494 (1967).

"On arithmetic expressions and trees," by R. Redziejowski, *Comm. ACM*, 12(2), pp 81–84 (1969).

Further references on code optimization appear in chapter 11. A good discussion of state space search techniques, techniques for AND/OR graphs and game trees appears in Nilsson's book. This book also provides many applications of these techniques. Further applications are discussed in Slagle's book. The references are:

Problem Solving Methods in Artificial Intelligence, by N. Nilsson, McGraw Hill, New York, (1971).

Artificial Intelligence: The Heuristic Programming Approach, by J. Slagle, McGraw Hill, New York (1971).

Our discussion of alpha-beta cutoffs is from

"An analysis of alpha-beta cutoffs," by D. Knuth, *Artificial Intelligence*, 6, pp. 293–326 (1975).

The above paper contains proofs for Theorems 6.10, 6.11 and 6.12. Many other results are also presented. Further analysis of this pruning process may be found in:

"The efficiency of the alpha-beta search on trees with branch-dependent terminal node scores," by M. Newborn, School of Computer Science, McGill University, Montreal, Canada (1976).

"An analysis of the full alpha-beta pruning algorithm," by G. Baudet, *Proc. 10th Ann. ACM Symp. on Theo. of Comput.*, San Diego, 1978, pp. 296–313.

An extension of the minimax rule from trees to graphs is discussed in:

"Applying the minimax rule over graphs which are not trees," by T. Doffey, *Info. Proc. Let.*, 2, pp 79–81 (1973).

Several applications of depth first search to graph problems are given in:

"Depth first search and linear graph algorithms," by R. Tarjan *SIAM Jr. on Comput.*, 1(2), pp. 146–160 (1972).

The $O(n + e)$ depth first algorithm for biconnected components is due to R. Tarjan and appears in the above paper. This paper also contains an $O(n + e)$ algorithm to find the strongly connected components of a directed graph. An $O(n + e)$ depth first algorithm to find triconnected components can be found in:

"Dividing a graph into triconnected components," by J. Hopcroft and R. Tarjan, *SIAM Jr. on Comput.*, 2(3), pp. 135-158 (1973).

Some other references to efficient graph algorithms using depth first search are:

"Efficient planarity testing," by J. Hopcroft and R. Tarjan, *JACM*, 21(4), pp 549-568 (1974).

"Efficient algorithms for graph manipulation," by J. Hopcroft and R. Tarjan, *CACM*, 16(6), pp. 372-378 (1973).

"Finding all the elementary circuits of a directed graph," by D. Johnson, *SIAM Jr. on Comput.*, 4(1), pp 77-84 (1975).

"Finding dominators in directed graphs," by R. Tarjan, *Proc. 7th Annual Princeton Conference on Information Sciences and Systems*, pp 414-418 (1973).

"Testing Flow Graph Reducibility," by R. Tarjan, Proc. *5th Annual ACM Symp. on Th. of Comput.*, pp 96-107 (1973).

"A fast and usually linear algorithm for global flow analysis," by S. Graham and M. Wegman, *JACM*, 23(1), pp 172-202 (1976).

The breadth first search algorithms for exercises 37-38 may be found in:

"Finding spanning trees with differing cost functions," by E. Horowitz and S. Sahni (1976).

EXERCISES

Unless otherwise stated all binary trees are represented using nodes with three fields: LCHILD, DATA and RCHILD.

1. Give an algorithm to count the number of leaf nodes in a binary tree T. What is its computing time?

2. Write an algorithm SWAPTREE(T) which takes a binary tree and swaps the left and right children of every node. For example, if T is the binary tree

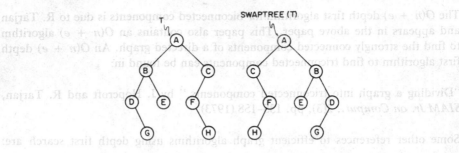

Use one of the three traversal methods discussed in Section 6.1.1.

3. Use one of the three traversal methods discussed in Section 6.1.1 to obtain an algorithm EQUIV(*T*, *U*) that determines whether or not the binary trees *T* and *U* are equivalent. Two binary trees *T*, *U* are equivalent iff they are structurally equivalent and if the data in corresponding nodes of *T* and *U* are the same.

4. Show that

   i)   the inorder and postorder sequences of a binary tree uniquely define the binary tree.
   ii) the inorder and preorder sequences of a binary tree uniquely define the binary tree.
   iii) the preorder and postorder sequences of a binary tree do not uniquely define the binary tree.

5. Write an algorithm to construct the binary tree with a given inorder sequence *I* and a given postorder sequence *P*. Use GETNODE(*X*) to get a new node. What is the complexity of your algorithm?

6. Do exercise 5 for a given inorder and preorder sequence.

7. Show that if *T* has *n* nodes then Theorem 6.1 holds even for algorithm INORDER1.

8. Write a nonrecursive algorithm for preorder traversal of a binary tree *T*. Your algorithm may use a stack. What are the time and space requirements of your algorithm?

9. Do problem 8 for postorder traversal.

10. Write a nonrecursive algorithm for inorder traversal of a binary tree T. Each node has four fields: LCHILD, DATA, PARENT, RCHILD. Your algorithm should take no more than $O(1)$ additional space and $O(n)$ time for a n node tree. Show that this is true for your algorithm.

11. Do problem 10 for preorder traversal.

12. Do problem 10 for postorder traversal.

13. Using the idea of algorithm INORDER2 write an $O(1)$ space and $O(n)$ time algorithm for preorder traversal of a binary tree T with n nodes. Each node has three fields: LCHILD, DATA, RCHILL.

14. Do problem 13 for postorder traversal.

15. Write a $\Theta(n)$ time and $\Theta(1)$ space algorithm for inorder traversal of a binary tree in which each node has a one bit TAG field in addition to the three fields: LCHILD, DATA, RCHILD. (Hint: Use the link reversal idea of INORDER2 but not the LR scheme. Use the TAG bit to distinguish between moves to left and right subtrees).

16. Do exercise 15 for preorder traversal.

17. Do exercise 15 for postorder traversal.

18. [Right threaded binary tree] In a right threaded binary tree, each node has four fields: LCHILD, DATA, RCHILD and TAG. The TAG of every node that has a nonempty right subtree is 1. A node with an empty right subtree has a TAG of 0 and its RCHILD field points to its inorder successor. Such a pointer is called a thread. Every threaded binary tree will have a head node. An empty binary tree will be represented by a headnode as:

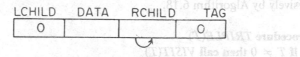

A nonempty binary tree will appear as the left subtree of its headnode. The headnode will also be the inorder successor of the binary tree's last node in inorder. The figure below shows a binary tree and the corresponding right threaded binary tree.

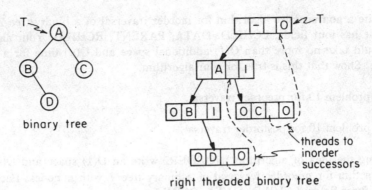

binary tree

right threaded binary tree

threads to inorder successors

The conventions for the headnode will simplify the traversal algorithms.

a)   Write an algorithm INSUC(P) to find the inorder successor of an arbitrary node P in a right threaded binary tree. Note that only $\Theta(1)$ additional space is needed and no link reversals are necessary. What is the worst case time complexity of your algorithm if the tree has n nodes?

b)   Is it possible to obtain an INSUC(P) algorithm for an unthreaded binary tree? Why?

c)   Using INSUC(P) of part a) obtain an inorder traversal algorithm for a binary tree T. Again, note that only $\Theta(1)$ additional space is needed. No link reversals are to be used. Show that the time taken for the traversal is $\Theta(n)$ if T has n nodes.

19. Do parts a), b) and c) of exercise 18 with inorder replaced by preorder. Note that a thread is still a pointer to the inorder successor.

20. Do parts a), b) and c) of exercise 18 with inorder replaced by postorder. Note that a thread is still a pointer to the inorder successor.

21. [Triple order traversal]   A triple order traversal of a binary tree T is defined recursively by Algorithm 6.18.

```
procedure TRIPLE(T)
  if T ≠ 0 then call VISIT(T)
    call TRIPLE(LCHILD(T))
    call VISIT(T)
    call TRIPLE(RCHILD(T))
    call VISIT(T)
  endif
end TRIPLE
```

Algorithm 6.18   Triple order traversal

B. Dwyer has given a very simple nonrecursive algorithm for such a traversal (Algorithm 6.19). In this algorithm P, Q, R point respectively to the present node, previously visited node and next node to visit. The algorithm assumes that $T \neq 0$ and that an empty subtree of node P is represented by a link to P rather than a zero.

```
line    procedure TRIP(T)
          //it is assumed that all LCHILD and RCHILD fields are > 0//
1         P ← T; Q ← -1
2         while P ≠ -1 do
3           call VISIT(P)
4           R ← LCHILD(P); LCHILD(P) ← RCHILD(P)
5           RCHILD(P) ← Q; Q ← P; P ← R
6         repeat
7       end TRIP
```

Algorithm 6.19 Dwyer's algorithm for triple order traversal

a) Prove that Dwyer's algorithm is correct. (Hint. Associated with each node S are three links, LCHILD, RCHILD and one from its parent. Each time S is visited, the links are rotated anticlockwise and so after three visits they are restored to the original configuration and the algorithm backs up the tree.)

b) Show that the time and space complexity of algorithm TRIP is $\Theta(n)$ and $\Theta(1)$ respectively. n is the number of nodes in T.

22. Binary trees are often stored such that the children of a node are higher indexed nodes than the parent. I.e., LCHILD(P) and RCHILD(P) $> P$ or equal to 0. Assume that if P has no left(right) child then LCHILD(P) (RCHILD(P)) $= P$. For this representation and procedure TRIP (Algorithm 6.19) show that

a) If line 3 is replaced by

> **if** $RCHILD(P) < P$ **then call** $VISIT(p)$ **endif**

then algorithm TRIP traverses T in inorder.

b) If line 3 is replaced by

> **if** $Q < P$ **then call** $VISIT(P)$ **endif**

then the algorithm traverses T in preorder.

c) If line 3 is replaced by

> **if** $LCHILD(P) < P$ **then call** $VISIT(P)$ **endif**

then a postorder traversal results.

23. Rewrite algorithm INORDER2 assuming the binary tree T is stored as in exercise 22. You can now dispense with LR and the stack of nodes from which a move to a right subtree has been made.

24. [Level order traversal]   In a level order traversal of a binary tree T all nodes on level i are visited before any node on level $i + 1$ is visited. Within a level, nodes are visited left to right. In level order the nodes of the tree of Figure 6.4 will be visited in the order $A\ B\ C\ D\ E\ F\ G$. Write an algorithm LEVEL(T) to traverse the binary tree T in level order. How much time and space are needed by your algorithm? Assume each node has three fields: LCHILD, DATA and RCHILD.

25. Show that if a tree of degree k is represented using nodes with k child fields each then $n(k - 1) + 1$ of the total nk child fields present in an n node tree will be zero.

26. Prove that traversing a tree in tree preorder gives the same results as traversing the corresponding binary tree in preorder (i.e. the nodes are visited in the same order).

27. Prove that traversing a tree in tree inorder gives the same results as traversing the corresponding binary tree in inorder (i.e. the nodes are visited in the same order).

28. Show that if a tree is traversed in tree postorder then the nodes may be visited in a different order than when the corresponding binary tree is traversed in postorder.

29. Write a nonrecursive algorithm $TI(T, k)$ for tree inorder. The tree T is of degree k and node P has k child fields CHILD(P, i), $1 \le i \le k$. What are the time and space requirements of your algorithm?

30. Do exercise 29 for tree preorder.

31. Do exercise 29 for tree inorder.

32. Assume tree T is represented as in exercise 29. Write an algorithm LEVEL(T, k) to traverse T by levels. Within each level nodes are to be visited left to right assuming the subtree ordering CHILD(P, i) is to the left of CHILD($P, i + 1$). What are the time and space requirements of your algorithm?

33. Show that for any undirected graph $G = (V, E)$ a call to BFS(v) with $v \in$ results in the visiting of all vertices in the connected component containing v

34. Rewrite BFS and BFT so that all the connected components of the undirected graph G get printed out. Assume that G is input in adjacency list form with HEAD(i) the headnode for the adjacency list for vertex i.

35. Write an algorithm using the idea of BFS to find a shortest (directed) cycle containing a given vertex v. Prove that your algorithm finds a shortest cycle. What are the time and space requirements of your algorithm?

36. Prove that if G is a connected undirected graph with n vertices and $n - 1$ edges then G is a tree.

37. a) The *radius* of a tree is its depth. Show that the forward edges used in BFS(v) define a spanning tree with root v having minimum radius amongst all spanning trees, for the undirected connected graph G, having root v.
    b) Using the result of a) write an algorithm to find a minimum radius spanning tree for G. What are the time and space requirements of your algorithm?

38. The *diameter* of a tree is the maximum distance between any two vertices. Let d be the diameter of a minimum diameter spanning tree for an undirected connected graph G. Let r be the radius of a minimum radius spanning tree for G.

    a) Show that $2r - 1 \le d \le 2r$.
    b) Write an algorithm to find a minimum diameter spanning tree for G. (Hint: Use breadth first search followed by some local modification.)
    c) Prove that your algorithm is correct.
    d) What are the time and space requirements of your algorithm?

39. Show that DFS visits all vertices in G reachable from v.

40. Prove that the bounds of Theorem 6.3 hold for DFS.

41. A *bipartite graph* $G = (V, E)$ is an undirected graph whose vertices can be partitioned into two disjoint sets V_1 and $V_2 = V - V_1$ with the properties (i) no two vertices in V_1 are adjacent in G and (ii) no two vertices in V_2 are adjacent in G. The graph G of Figure 6.6(a) is bipartite. A possible partitioning of V is: $V_1 = \{1, 4, 5, 6, 7\}$ and $V_2 = \{2, 3, 8\}$. Write an algorithm to determine whether a graph G is bipartite. In case G is bipartite your algorithm should obtain a partitioning of the vertices into two disjoint sets V_1 and V_2 satisfying properties (i) and (ii) above. Show that if G is represented by its adjacency lists, then this algorithm can be made to work in time $O(n + e)$ where $n = |V|$ and $e = |E|$.

42. It is easy to see that for any graph G, both DFS and BFS will take almost the same amount of time. However the space requirements may be considerably different.

   a) Give an example of an n vertex graph for which the depth of recursion of DFS starting from a particular vertex v is $n - 1$ whereas the queue of BFS will have at most 1 vertex at any given time if BFS is started from the same vertex v.

   b) Give an example of an n vertex graph for which the queue of BFS will have $n - 1$ vertices at one time whereas the depth of recursion of DFS is at most one. Both searches are started from the same vertex.

43. Another way to search a graph is D-search. This method differs from BFS in that the next vertex to explore is the vertex most recently added to the list of unexplored vertices. Hence, this list operates as a stack rather than a queue.

   a) Write an algorithm for D-search.

   b) Show that D-search starting from vertex v visits all vertices reachable from v.

   c) What are the time and space requirements of your algorithm?

   d) Modify your algorithm so that it produces a spanning tree for an undirected connected graph.

44. Write an algorithm to find the reflexive transitive closure matrix, A^*, of a directed graph G. Show that if G has n vertices and e edges and if G is represented by its adjacency lists then this can be done in time $\Theta(n^2 + ne)$. (Hint: use either BFS or DFS). How much space does your algorithm take in addition to that needed for G and A^*?

45. Write an algorithm to evaluate an arithmetic expression represented as a binary tree T. Assume that the only operators are binary $+$, $-$, $*$ and $/$. Each node in the binary tree has three fields LCHILD, DATA and RCHILD. If P is a leaf node then DATA(P) is the address in memory corresponding to the variable or constant represented by P. VAL(DATA(P)) is the current value of that variable or constant. What is the computing time of your algorithm?

46. The postfix representation of an infix arithmetic expression $L \odot R$ is defined recursively to be the postfix representation of L followed by the postfix representation of R followed by $\odot$. L and R are respectively the left and right operands of $\odot$. Consider some examples:

Infix	Postfix
i) $a + b$	$a\ b\ +$
ii) $(a + b)*c$	$a\ b\ +\ c\ *$
iii) $(a - b/(c*d)$	$a\ b\ -\ cd\ *\ /$

In postfix form there are no parenthesis.

a) What is the postfix form of the following expressions:

i) $(a + b*c)/(c - d)$

ii) $a + (b - c)*(b + c) + d/(e - f)$

iii) $a/(b + c) + d*(e - f)$

b) Write an algorithm to evaluate a postfix expression E. Assume E is presented as a string and that there exists an algorithm NEXT__TOKEN(E) that returns the next token (i.e. operator or operand) in E. When all tokens in E have been extracted, NEXT__TOKEN(E) returns ∞. Assume that the only operators in E are binary $+$, $-$, $*$ and $/$. (Hint: make a left to right scan of E using a stack to store operands and results. Whenever an operator is seen in E, the top two operands on the stack are its right and left operands.) What is the complexity of your algorithm?

c) Write an algorithm to obtain the postfix form of an infix expression E. Again assume E has only the binary operators $+$, $-$, $*$ and $/$. (Hint: make a left to right scan of E using a stack to store operators until both the left and right operands of an operator have been output in postfix form.) Note that E may contain parenthesis. What is the complexity of your algorithm?

47. Write an algorithm to obtain a binary expression tree for the postfix expression E. Assume E has the same operators as in the above exercise. You may use an algorithm GETNODE(X) to get a new node X. Each node has three fields: LCHILD, DATA and RCHILD. What is the complexity of your algorithm?

48. Prove Theorem 6.5.

49. Complete Table 6.2 to incude all possibilities for the code of an expression containing some commutative operators.

50. Modify algorithm CODE1 so that it generates optimal code even when the expression T contains some commutative operators. Show that your algorithm generates optimal code.

51. Do exercise 50 for the case when T contains some associative operators.

52. For the following expression obtain an expression tree. Label the nodes with their MR value and obtain the optimal code generated by CODE2 for the two cases $N = 1$ and $N = 2$. Assume that no operator is either commutative or associative.

i) $(a + b)*(c + d*(e + f)/(g + h))$

ii) $a*b*c/(e - f + g*(h - k)*(l + m))$

iii) $a*(b - c)*(d + f)/(g*(h + j) - k*l)$

53. Write an algorithm to compute MR(P) for each node P in a binary expression tree T. See Theorem 6.6 for the definition of MR(P). Assume each node P has four fields LCHILD, DATA, MR and RCHILD.

54. Prove Theorem 6.7.

55. Prove Theorem 6.8.

56. Show that the time complexity of CODE2 is $\Theta(n)$ where n is the number of nodes in T.

57. Show that if $MR(T) \leq N$ then CODE2 generates code using the minimum possible number of registers when no stores are allowed.

58. Prove Lemma 6.1.

59. The number of memory references needed to evaluate a code of length l for an expression E is l (to fetch the instructions) plus one reference for each LOAD, STORE and instruction of type OP R1, M, R2. Show that if the expression tree for E has n nodes and every code for E has at least s STOREs then the minimum number of memory references needed to evaluate any code for E is at least $l + n + 3s$. Show that the code generated by CODE2 requires exactly this many references.

60. Write an algorithm FLIP(T) to interchanges left and right subtrees of nodes in the expression tree T representing commutative operators. The resulting tree should be such that the sum of major and minor nodes is minimum for every given N. N is the number of registers. What is the complexity of FLIP?

61. Extend CODE2 to account for associative operators.

62. Write an algorithm to determine whether or not a given AND/OR graph G represents a solvable problem. Devise a suitable representation for the graph G.

63. Modify Algorithm 6.12 so that it identifies a solution subtree of T.

64. Write out the algorithm ASOLVE used in algorithm BFGEN.

65. Write an algorithm PRUNE to remove from the solution tree T generated by BFGEN, all nodes that need not be solved. I.e., the output tree is one in which all nodes must be solved in order to solve the whole problem.

66. Consider the hypothetical game tree:

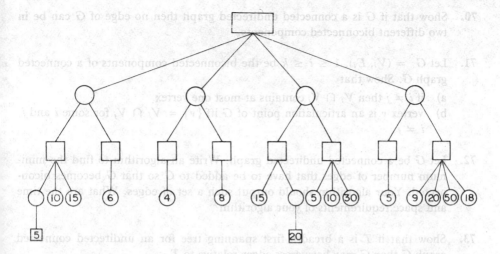

5

20

a) Using the minimax technique (eq. (6.1)) obtain the value of the root node.
b) What move should player A make?
c) List the nodes of this game tree in the order in which their value is computed by algorithm VE.
d) Using eq. (6.2) compute $V'(X)$ for every node X in the tree.
e) Which nodes of this tree are not evaluated during the computation of the value of the root node using algorithm AB with X = root, $l = \infty$, $LB = -\infty$ and $D = \infty$?

67. Show that $V'(X)$ computed by eq. (6.2) is the same as $V(X)$ computed by eq. (6.1) for all nodes on levels from which A is to move. For all other nodes show that $V(X)$ computed by eq. (6.1) is the negative of $V'(X)$ computed by eq. (6.2).

68. Show that algorithm AB when initially called with $LB = -\infty$ and $D = \infty$ yields the same results as VE does for the same X and l.

69. For the following graphs identify the articulation points and draw the biconnected components.

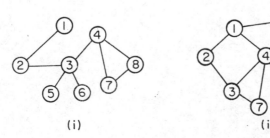

(i)   (ii)

70. Show that if G is a connected undirected graph then no edge of G can be in two different biconnected components.

71. Let $G_i = (V_i, E_i)$, $1 \leq i \leq k$ be the biconnected components of a connected graph G. Show that
    a) if $i \neq j$ then $V_i \cap V_j$ contains at most one vertex
    b) vertex v is an articulation point of G iff $\{v\} = V_i \cap V_j$ for some i and j, $i \neq j$.

72. Let G be a connected undirected graph. Write an algorithm to find the minimum number of edges that have to be added to G so that G becomes biconnected. Your algorithm should output such a set of edges. What are the time and space requirements of your algorithm?

73. Show that if T is a breadth first spanning tree for an undirected connected graph G then G may have cross edges relative to T.

74. Prove that u is an articulation point iff $L(w) \geq u$ for some child w of u.

75. Prove that when the additions 2.1 and 3.1–3.6 are made to algorithm ART then if either $v = w$ or DFN$(w) >$ DFN(u) then edge (u, w) is either already on the stack of edges or has been output as part of a biconnected component.

76. Write an algorithm of time complexity $\Theta(n^2)$ to find the transitive closure matrix A^+ of an undirected graph G.

77. Write an algorithm, using DFS, to find the transitive closure matrix A^+ of a directed graph G. Show that this can be done in time $O(n^2 + ne)$.

Chapter 7

BACKTRACKING

7.1 THE GENERAL METHOD

In the search for fundamental principles of algorithm design, backtracking represents one of the most general techniques. Many problems which deal with searching for a set of solutions or which ask for an optimal solution satisfying some constraints can be solved using the backtracking formulation. The name backtrack was first coined by D. H. Lehmer in the 1950's. Early workers who studied the process were R. J. Walker who gave an algorithmic account of it in 1960 and Golomb and Baumert who presented a very general description of backtracking coupled with a variety of applications. (See the references for further details).

In order to apply the backtrack method, the desired solution must be expressible as an n-tuple $(x_1, \ldots, x_n)$ where the x_i are chosen from some finite set S_i. Often the problem to be solved calls for finding one vector which maximizes (or minimizes or satisfies) a *criterion function* $P(x_1, \ldots, x_n)$. Sometimes it seeks all such vectors which satisfy P. For example, sorting the integers in $A(1:n)$ is a problem whose solution is expressible by an n-tuple where x_i is the index in A of the ith smallest element. The criterion function P is the inequality $A(x_i) \leq A(x_{i+1})$ for $1 \leq i < n$. The set S_i is finite and includes the integers 1 through n. Though sorting is not usually one of the problems solved by backtracking, it is one example of a familiar problem whose solution can be formulated as an n tuple. In this chapter we will study a collection of problems whose solution is best viewed using backtracking.

Suppose m_i is the size of set S_i. Then there are $m = m_1 m_2 \cdots m_n$ n-tuples which are possible candidates for satisfying the function P. The *brute force approach* would be to form all of these n-tuples and evaluate each one with P, saving those which yield the optimum. The backtrack algorithm has as its virtue the ability to yield the same answer with far fewer than m trials. Its basic idea is to build up the same vector one component at a time and to use modified criterion functions $P_i(x_1, \ldots, x_i)$ (sometimes called bounding functions) to test whether the vector being formed has any chance of success. The major advantage of this method is this: if it is realized that the partial vector $(x_1, x_2, \ldots, x_i)$ can in no way lead to an optimal solution, then $m_{i+1} \cdots m_n$ possible test vectors may be ignored entirely.

Many of the problems we shall solve using backtracking require that all the solutions satisfy a complex set of constraints. For any problem these constraints may be divided into two categories: explicit and implicit. *Explicit constraints* are rules which restrict each x_i to take on values only from a given set. Common examples of explicit constraints are

$$x_i \geq 0 \quad \text{or} \quad S_i = \{\text{all nonnegative real numbers}\}$$
$$x_i = 0 \text{ or } 1 \quad \text{or} \quad S_i = \{0, 1\}$$
$$l_i \leq x_i \leq u_i \quad \text{or} \quad S_i = \{a : l_i \leq a \leq u_i\}$$

The explicit constraints may or not depend on the particular instance I of the problem being solved. All tuples that satisfy the explicit constraints define a possible *solution space* for I. The *implicit constraints* determine which of the tuples in the solution space of I actually satisfy the criterion function. Thus implicit constraints describe the way in which the x_i must relate to each other.

Example 7.1 (8-queens) A classic combinatorial problem is to place eight queens on an 8×8 chessboard so that no two "attack", that is so that no two of them are on the same row, column or diagonal. Let us number the rows and columns of the chessboard 1 through 8 (figure 7.1). The queens may also be numbered 1 through 8. Since each queen must be on a different row, we can without loss of generality assume queen i is to be placed on row i. All solutions to the 8-queens problem can therefore be represented as 8-tuples $(x_1, \ldots, x_8)$ where x_i is the column on which queen i is placed. The explicit constraints using this formulation are $S_i = \{1, 2, 3, 4, 5, 6, 7, 8\}$, $1 \leq i \leq n$. Therefore the solution space consists of 8^8 8-tuples. The implicit constraints for this problem are that no two x_i's can be the same (i.e. all queens must be on different columns) and no two queens can be on the same diagonal. The first of these two constraints implies that all solutions are permutations of the 8-tuple (1, 2, 3, 4, 5, 6, 7, 8). This realization reduces the size of the solution space from 8^8 tuples to 8! tuples. We shall see later how to formulate the second constraint in terms of the x_i. Expressed as an 8-tuple, the solution in figure 7.1 is (4, 6, 8, 2, 7, 1, 3, 5).   □

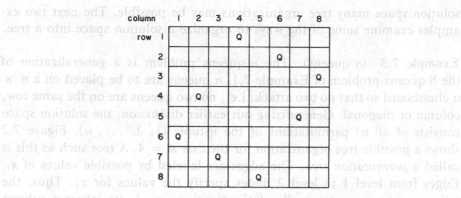

Figure 7.1 One solution to the 8-queens problem

Example 7.2 (Sum of subsets) Given $n + 1$ positive numbers: w_i, $1 \leq i \leq n$ and M, this problem calls for finding all subsets of the w_i whose sum is M. For example, if $n = 4$, $(w_1, w_2, w_3, w_4) = (11, 13, 24, 7)$ and $M = 31$ then the desired subsets are $(11, 13, 7)$ and $(24, 7)$. Rather than represent the solution vector by the w_i which sum to M, we could represent the solution vector by giving the indices of these w_i. Now the two solutions are described by the vectors $(1, 2, 4)$ and $(3, 4)$. In general, all solutions are k-tuples $(x_1, x_2, \ldots, x_k)$, $1 \leq k \leq n$ and different solutions may have different size tuples. The explicit constraints require $x_i \in \{j \mid j$ is an integer and $1 \leq j \leq n\}$. The implicit constraints require that no two be the same and that the sum of the corresponding w_i be M. Since we wish to avoid generating multiple instances of the same subset (e.g. $(1, 2, 4)$ and $(1, 4, 2)$ represent the same subset), another implicit constraint which is imposed is that $x_i < x_{i+1}$, $1 \leq i < n$.

In another formulation of the sum of subsets problem, each solution subset is represented by an n-tuple $(x_1, x_2, \ldots, x_n)$ such that $x_i \in \{0, 1\}$, $1 \leq i \leq n$. $x_i = 0$ if w_i is not chosen and $x_i = 1$ if w_i is chosen. The solutions to the above instance are $(1, 1, 0, 1)$ and $(0, 0, 1, 1)$. This formulation expresses all solutions using a fixed size tuple. Thus we conclude that there may be several ways to formulate a problem so that all solutions are tuples that satisfy some constraints. One may verify that for both of the above formulations, the solution space consists of 2^n distinct tuples. $\square$

Backtracking algorithms determine problem solutions by systematically searching the solution space for the given problem instance. This search is facilitated by using a *tree organization* for the solution space. For a given solution space many tree organizations may be possible. The next two examples examine some of the ways to organize a solution space into a tree.

Example 7.3 (*n*-queens)   The *n*-queens problem is a generalization of the 8-queens problem of Example 7.1. *n* queens are to be placed on a *n* × *n* chessboard so that no two attack, i.e., no two queens are on the same row, column or diagonal. Generalizing our earlier discussion, the solution space consists of all *n*! permutations of the *n*-tuple (1, 2, ..., *n*). Figure 7.2 shows a possible tree organization for the case *n* = 4. A tree such as this is called a *permutation tree*. The edges are labeled by possible values of x_i. Edges from level 1 to level 2 nodes specify the values for x_1. Thus, the leftmost subtree contains all solutions with x_1 = 1; its leftmost subtree contains all solutions with x_1 = 1 and x_2 = 2, etc. Edges from level *i* to level *i* + 1 are labeled with the values of x_i. The solution space is defined by all paths from the root node to a leaf node. There are 4! = 24 leaf nodes in the tree of figure 7.2.   □

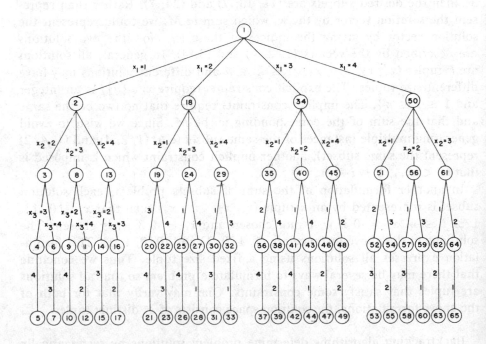

Figure 7.2   Tree organization of the 4-queens solution space.
Nodes are numbered as in depth first search.

Example 7.4 (Sum of subsets) In Example 7.2 we gave two possible formulations of the solution space for the sum of subsets problem. Figures 7.3 and 7.4 show a possible tree organization for each of these formulations for the case $n = 4$. The tree of Figure 7.3 corresponds to the variable tuple size formulation. The edges are labeled such that an edge from a level i node to a level $i + 1$ node represents a value for x_i. At each node, the solution space is partitioned into subsolution spaces. The solution space is defined by all paths from the root node to any node in the tree. The possible paths are ( ) (this corresponds to the empty path from the root to itself); (1), (1, 2); (1, 2, 3); (1, 2, 3, 4); (1, 2, 4); (1, 3, 4); (2); (2, 3); etc. Thus, the left-most subtree defines all subsets containing w_1, the next subtree defines all subsets containing w_2 but not w_1; etc.

The tree of Figure 7.4 corresponds to the fixed tuple size formulation. Edges from level i nodes to level $i + 1$ nodes are labeled with the value of x_i which is either zero or one. All paths from the root to a leaf node define the solution space. The left subtree of the root defines all subsets containing w_1 while the right subtree defines all subsets not containing w_1 etc. Now there are 2^4 leaf nodes which represent 16 possible tuples. □

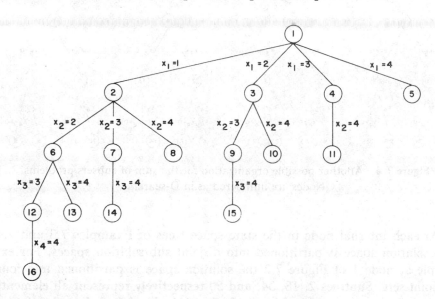

Figure 7.3 A possible solution space organization for the sum of subsets problem. Nodes are numbered as in breadth first search.

At this point it is useful to develop some terminology regarding tree organizations of solution spaces. Each node in this tree defines a *problem state*. All paths from the root to other nodes define the *state space* of the problem. *Solution states* are those problem states S for which the path from the root to S defines a tuple in the solution space. In the tree of Figure 7.3 all nodes are solution states while in the tree of Figure 7.4 only leaf nodes are solution states. *Answer states* are those solution states S for which the path from the root to S defines a tuple which is a member of the set of solutions (i.e., it satisfies the implicit constraints) of the problem. The tree organization of the solution space will be referred to as the *state space tree*.

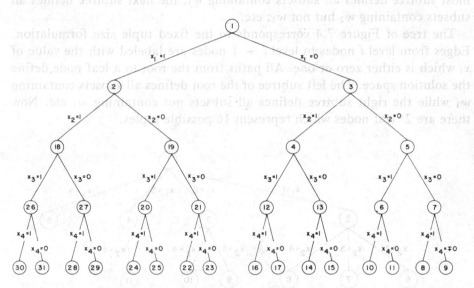

Figure 7.4 Another possible organization for the sum of subsets problems.
Nodes are numbered as in D-search.

At each internal node in the state space trees of Examples 7.3 and 7.4 the solution space is partitioned into disjoint sub-solution spaces. For example at node 1 of Figure 7.2 the solution space is partitioned into four disjoint sets. Subtrees 2, 18, 34, and 50 respectively represent all elements of the solution space with $x_1 = 1, 2, 3$ and 4. At node 2 the sub-solution space with $x_1 = 1$ is further partitioned into three disjoint sets. Subtree 3 represents all solution space elements with $x_1 = 1$ and $x_2 = 2$. For all of the state space trees we shall be studying in this chapter, the solution space will be partitioned into disjoint sub-solution spaces at each internal node. It should be noted that this is not a requirement on a state space tree. The only requirement is that every element of the solution space be represented by at least one node in the state space tree.

The state space tree organizations described in example 7.4 will be called *static trees*. This terminology follows from the observation that the tree organizations are independent of the problem instance being solved. For some problems it is advantageous to use different tree organizations for different problem instances. In this case the tree organization is determined dynamically as the solution space is being searched. Tree organizations that are problem instance dependent are called *dynamic trees*. As an example, consider the fixed tuple size formulation for the sum of subsets problem (example 7.4). Using a dynamic tree organization one problem instance with $n = 4$ may be solved using the organization given in figure 7.4 while another problem instance with $n = 4$ may be solved using a tree in which at level 1 the partitioning corresponds to $x_2 = 1$ and $x_2 = 0$. At level 2 the partitioning could correspond to $x_1 = 1$ and $x_1 = 0$ while at level 3 it could correspond to $x_3 = 1$ and $x_3 = 0$, and so on. We shall see more of dynamic trees in sections 7.6 and 8.3.

Once a state space tree has been conceived of for any problem, this problem may be solved by systematically generating the problem states, determining which of these are solution states and finally determining which solution states are answer states. There are two fundamentally different ways in which to generate the problem states. Both of these begin with the root node and generate other nodes. A node which has been generated and all of whose children have not yet been generated is called a *live node*. The live node whose children are currently being generated is called the E-node (node being expanded). A *dead node* is a generated node that is either not to be expanded further or one for which all of its children have been generated. In both methods of generating problem states we will have a list of live nodes. In the first of these two methods as soon as a new child, C, of the current E-node, R, is generated, this child will become the new E node. R will become the E-node again when the subtree C has been fully explored. This corresponds to a depth first generation of the problem states. In the second state generation method, the E-node remains the E-node until it is dead. In both methods, *bounding functions* will be used to kill live nodes without generating all their children. This will be done carefully enough so that at the conclusion of the process at least one answer node is always generated, or all answer nodes are generated if the problem requires us to find all solutions. Depth first node generation with bounding functions is called *backtracking*. State generation methods in which the E-node remains the E-node until it is dead lead to *branch-and-bound* methods. The branch-and-bound technique is discussed in chapter 8.

The nodes of Figure 7.2 have been numbered in the order they would be generated in a depth first generation process. The nodes in Figures 7.3 and 7.4 have been numbered according to two generation methods in which the E-node remains the E-node until it is dead. In Figure 7.3 each new node is placed into a queue. When all of the children of the current E-node have been generated, the next node at the front of the queue becomes the new E-node. In Figure 7.4 new nodes are placed into a stack instead of a queue. Current terminology is not uniform when referring to these two alternatives. Typically the queue method is called breadth first generation while the stack method is called D-search (depth search).

Example 7.5 (4-queens) Let us see how backtracking works on the 4-queens problem of Example 7.3. As a bounding function we will use the obvious criteria that if $(x_1, x_2, \ldots, x_i)$ is the path to the current E-node then all children nodes with parent-child labelings x_{i+1} are such that $(x_1, \ldots, x_{i+1})$ represents a chessboard configuration in which no two queens are attacking. We start with the root node as the only live node. This becomes the E-node and the path is ( ). We generate one child. Let us assume that children are generated in ascending order. Thus, node number 2 of Figure 7.2 is generated and the path is now (1). This corresponds to placing queen 1 on column 1. Node 2 becomes the E-node. Node 3 is generated and immediately killed. The next node generated is node 8 and the path becomes (1, 3). Node 8 becomes the E-node. However, it gets killed as all of its children represent board configurations that cannot lead to an answer node. We backtrack to node 2 and generate another child, node 13. The path is now (1, 4). Figure 7.5 shows the board configurations as backtracking proceeds. Figure 7.5 shows graphically the steps that the backtracking algorithm goes through as it tries to find a solution. The dots indicate placements of a queen which were tried and rejected because another queen was attacking. In (b) the second queen is placed on columns 1, 2 and finally settles on column 3. In (c) the algorithm tries all four columns and is unable to place the next queen on a square. Backtracking now takes place. In (d) the second queen is moved to the next possible column, column 4 and the third queen is placed on column 2. The boards in Figure 7.5 (e, f, g, h) show the remaining steps that the algorithm goes through until a solution is found.

Figure 7.6 shows the part of the tree of Figure 7.2 that is actually generated. Nodes are numbered in the order in which they are generated. A node that gets killed as a result of the bounding function has a B under it. Contrast this tree with Figure 7.2 which contains 31 nodes.   □

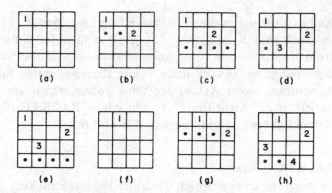

Figure 7.5   Example of a backtrack solution to the four queens problem

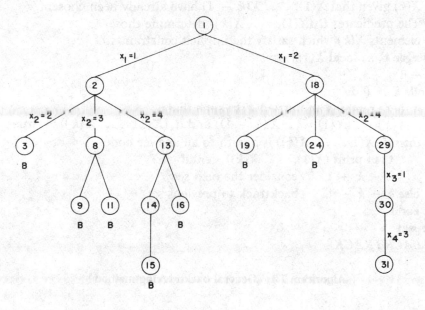

Figure 7.6   Portion of tree of Figure 7.2 that is generated during backtracking

With this example completed, we are now ready to present a precise formulation of the backtracking process. We will continue to treat back-tracking in a general way. We shall assume that all answer nodes are to be found and not just one. Let $(x_1, x_2, \ldots, x_i)$ be a path from the root to a node in a state space tree. Let $T(x_1, x_2, \ldots, x_i)$ be the set of all possible values for x_{i+1} such that $(x_1, x_2, \ldots, x_{i+1})$ is also a path to a problem state. We shall assume the existence of bounding functions B_{i+1} (expressed as predicates) such that $B_{i+1}(x_1, x_2, \ldots, x_{i+1})$ is false for a path $(x_1, x_2, \ldots, x_{i+1})$ from the root node to a problem state only if the path cannot be extended to reach an answer node. Thus the candidates for position $i + 1$ of the solution vector $X(1:n)$ are those values which are generated by T and satisfy B_{i+1}. Algorithm 7.1, procedure BACKTRACK, is the general backtracking schema making use of T and B_{i+1}.

procedure *BACKTRACK(n)*
    //This is a program schema which describes the backtracking process.//
    //All solutions are generated in $X(1:n)$ and printed as soon as they are//
    //determined. $T(X(1), \ldots, X(k - 1))$ gives all possible values of//
    //$X(k)$ given that $X(1), \ldots, X(k - 1)$ have already been chosen.//
    //The predicates $B_k(X(1), \ldots, X(k))$ determine those//
    //elements $X(k)$ which satisfy the implicit constraints.//
    integer k, n; **local** $X(1:n)$
    $k \leftarrow 1$
    while $k > 0$ **do**
      if there remains an untried $X(k)$ such that
        $X(k) \in T(X(1), \ldots, X(k - 1))$ **and** $B_k(X(1), \ldots, X(k)) =$ **true**
      then if $(X(1), \ldots, X(k))$ is a path to an answer node
          then print $(X(1), \ldots, X(k))$ **endif**
          $k \leftarrow k + 1$ //consider the next set//
      else $k \leftarrow k - 1$ //backtrack to previous set//
      endif
    repeat
end *BACKTRACK*

Algorithm 7.1   General backtracking method

Note that $T( )$ will yield the set of all possible values which can be placed as the first component, $X(1)$, of the solution vector. $X(1)$ will take on those values for which the bounding function $B_1(X(1))$ is true. Also note how the elements are generated in a depth first manner. k is continually incremented and a solution vector is grown until either a solution is found or no untried value of $X(k)$ remains. When k is decremented, the algorithm must resume the generation of possible elements for the kth position which have not yet been tried. Therefore one must develop a procedure which generates these values in some order. If only one solution is desired, **a return** after the **print** will suffice.

Algorithm 7.2 presents a recursive formulation of the backtracking algorithm. It is natural to describe backtracking in this way since it is essentially a postorder traversal of a tree (see section 6.1). This recursive version is initially invoked by

call *RBACKTRACK*(1)

procedure *RBACKTRACK(k)*
    //This is a program schema which describes the backtracking process//
    //using recursion. On entering, the first $k - 1$ values $X(1), \ldots, X(k - 1)$//
    //of the solution vector $X(1{:}n)$ have been assigned.//
    global n, $X(1{:}n)$
    for each $X(k)$ such that
        $X(k) \in T(X(1), \ldots, X(k - 1))$ **and** $B_k(X(1), \ldots, X(k)) = $ **true do**
      if $(X(1), \ldots, X(k))$ is a path to an answer node
        then print $(X(1), \ldots, X(k))$ **endif**
      call *RBACKTRACK(k + 1)*
    repeat
end *RBACKTRACK*

Algorithm 7.2   Recursive backtracking algorithm

The solution vector $(x_1, \ldots, x_n)$ is treated as a global array $X(1{:}n)$. All of the possible elements for the kth position of the tuple which satisfy B_k are generated, one by one, and adjoined to the current vector $(X(1), \ldots, X(k - 1))$. Each time $X(k)$ is attached a check is made to determine if a solution has been found. Then the algorithm is recursively invoked. When the **for** loop is exited, no more values for $X(k)$ exist and the current copy of RBACKTRACK ends. The last unresolved call now resumes, namely the one which continues to examine the remaining elements assuming only $k - 1$ values have been set.

Note that when k exceeds n, $T(X(1), \ldots, X(k - 1))$ returns the empty set and hence the **for** loop is never entered. Note also that this program causes *all* solutions to be printed and assumes that tuples of various sizes may comprise a solution. If only a single solution is desired, then a flag may be added as a parameter to indicate the first occurrence of success.

Efficiency

The efficiency of both of the backtracking programs we've just seen depends very much upon 4 factors: (i) the time to generate the next

$X(k)$; (ii) the number of $X(k)$ satisfying the explicit constraints; (iii) the time for the bounding functions B_i; and (iv) the number of $X(k)$ satisfying the B_i for all i. Bounding functions are regarded as good if they substantially reduce the numer of nodes that are generated. However there is usually a trade off in that bounding functions that are good also take more time to evaluate. What is desired is a reduction in the overall computing time and not just a reduction in the number of nodes generated. For many problems, the size of the state space tree is too large to permit the generation of all nodes. Bounding functions must be used and hopefully at least one solution will be found in a reasonable time span. Yet for many problems (e.g. n-queens) no sophisticated bounding methods are known.

One general principle of efficient searching is called *rearrangement*. For many problems the sets S_i can be taken in any order. This suggests that all other things being equal, it is more efficient to make the next choice from the set with the fewest elements. This strategy doesn't pay off for the n-queens problem and examples can be constructed which prove this principle won't always work. But from an information-theoretic point of view, it can be shown that on the average a choice from the smallest set is more efficient. The potential value of this heuristic is exhibited in Figure 7.7 by the two backtracking search trees for the same problem. If we are able to remove a node on level one of Figure 7.7(a) then we are effectively removing twelve possible 4-tuples from consideration. Whereas if we remove a node from level one of the tree in Figure 7.7(b) then only eight tuples are eliminated. More sophisticated rearrangement strategies will be studied in conjunction with dynamic state space trees.

As stated previously, there are four factors that determine the time required by a backtracking algorithm. Once a state space tree organization is selected, the first three of these are relatively independent of the problem instance being solved. Only the fourth, the number of nodes generated, varies from one problem instance to another. A backtracking algorithm on one problem instance might generate only $O(n)$ nodes while on a different (and even closely related) instance it might generate almost all the nodes in the state space tree. If the number of nodes in the solution space is 2^n or $n!$ the worst case time for a backtracking algorithm will generally be $O(p(n)2^n)$ or $O(q(n)n!)$ respectively. $p(n)$ and $q(n)$ are polynomials in n. The importance of backtracking lies in its ability to solve some instances with large n in a very small amount of time. The only difficulty is in predicting the behavior of a backtracking algorithm for the problem instance we wish to solve.

We can estimate the number of nodes that will be generated by a backtracking algorithm working on a certain instance I by using Monte Carlo

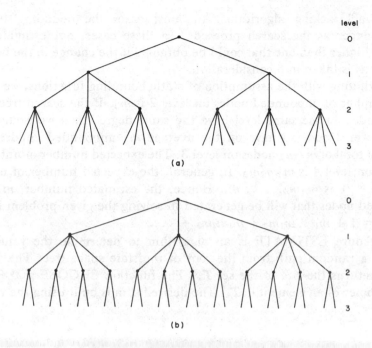

level

0

1

2

3

(a)

0

1

2

3

(b)

Figure 7.7   Rearrangement

methods. The general idea in the estimation method is to generate a random path in the state space tree. Let X be a node on this random path. Assume that X is at level i of the state space tree. The bounding functions are used at node X to determine the number, m_i, of its children that do not get bounded. The next node on the path is obtained by randomly selecting one of these m_i children that do not get bounded. The path generation terminates at a node which is either a leaf or at a node all of whose children get bounded. Using these m_is we can estimate the total number, m, of nodes in the state space tree that will not get bounded. This number is particularly useful when all answer nodes are to be searched for. In this case all unbounded nodes need to be generated. When only a single solution is desired, m may not be such a good estimate for the number of nodes generated as the backtracking algorithm may arrive at a solution by generating only a small fraction of the m nodes. To estimate m from the m_is we need to make an assumption on the bounding functions. We shall assume that these functions are static. I.e. the backtracking algorithm does not change its bounding functions as it gathers information during its execution. Moreover, exactly the same function is used for all nodes on the same level of the state space tree. This assumption is not true of most backtracking algorithms. In most cases the bounding functions get stronger as the search proceeds. In these cases, our estimate for m will be higher than one that could be obtained if the change in the bounding functions is taken into consideration.

Continuing with the assumption of static bounding functions, we see that the number of unbounded nodes on level 2 is m_1. If the search tree is such that nodes on the same level have the same degree then we would expect each level 2 node to have on the average m_2 unbounded children. This yields a total of $m_1 m_2$ nodes on level 3. The expected number of unbounded nodes on level 4 is $m_1 m_2 m_3$. In general, the expected number of nodes on level $i + 1$ is $m_1 m_2, \ldots, m_i$. Hence, the estimated number, m, of unbounded nodes that will be generated in solving the given problem instance I is $m = 1 + m_1 + m_1 m_2 + m_1 m_2 m_3 + \ldots$.

Procedure ESTIMATE is an algorithm to determine the value m. It selects a random path from the root of the state space tree. The function SIZE returns the size of the set T_k. The function CHOOSE makes a random choice of an element in T_k. The desired sum is built using the variables m and r.

procedure *ESTIMATE*
//This procedure follows a random path in a state space tree//
//and produces an estimate of the number of nodes in the tree.//
    $m \leftarrow 1; r \leftarrow 1; k \leftarrow 1$
    loop
        $T_k \leftarrow \{X(k): X(k) \in T(X(1), \ldots, X(k - 1)) \text{ and } B_k(X(1), \ldots, X(k))\}$
        if $SIZE(T_k) = 0$ **then exit endif**
        $r \leftarrow r * \text{size}(T_k)$
        $m \leftarrow m + r$
        $X(k) \leftarrow CHOOSE(T_k)$
        $k \leftarrow k + 1$
    repeat
    return(m)
end *ESTIMATE*

Algorithm 7.3   Estimating the efficiency of backtracking

We will use this estimator in later sections as we examine backtracking solutions to various problems.

A better estimate of the number of unbounded nodes that will be generated by a backtracking algorithm can be obtained by selecting several different random paths (typically no more that 20) and determining the average of these values.

7.2 THE 8-QUEENS PROBLEM

Now we are ready to tackle the 8-queens problem via a backtracking solution. In fact we will trivially generalize the problem and consider an $n \times n$ chessboard and try to find all ways to place n nonattacking queens. We observed from the 4-queens problem that we can let $(x_1, \ldots, x_n)$ represent a solution where x_i is the column of the ith row where the ith queen is placed. The $x_i s$ will all be distinct since no two queens can be placed in the same column. Now how do we test if two queens are on the same diagonal?

If we imagine the squares of the chessboard being numbered as the indices of the two dimensional array $A(1:n, 1:n)$ then we observe that for every element on the same diagonal which runs from the upper left to the lower right, each element has the same "row − column" value. Also, every element on the same diagonal which goes from the upper right to the lower left has the same "row + column" value. Suppose two queens are placed at positions (i, j) and (k, l). Then by the above they are on the same diagonal only if

$$i - j = k - l \quad \text{or} \quad i + j = k + l.$$

The first equation implies

$$j - l = i - k$$

while the second implies

$$j - l = k - i.$$

Therefore two queens lie on the same diagonal if and only if $|j - l| = |i - k|$.

Procedure PLACE(k) returns a boolean value which is true if the kth queen can be placed at the current value of $X(k)$. It tests both if $X(k)$ is distinct from all previous values $X(1), \ldots, X(k - 1)$ and also if there is no other queen on the same diagonal. Its computing time is $O(k - 1)$.

procedure *PLACE*(*k*)
  //returns **true** if a queen can be placed in *k*th row and//
  //*X*(*k*)th column. Otherwise it returns **false**.//
  //*X* is a global array whose first *k* values have been set.//
  //ABS(*r*) returns the absolute value of *r*//
  global *X*(1: *k*); **integer** *i, k*
  i ← 1
  while *i* < *k* **do**
    if *X*(*i*) = *X*(*k*)   //two in the same column//
      or *ABS*(*X*(*i*) −. *X*(*k*)) = *ABS*(*i* − *k*)   //in the same diagonal//
      then return(**false**)
    endif
    i ← *i* + 1
  repeat
  return(**true**)
end *PLACE*

Algorithm 7.4   Can a new queen be placed?

Using procedure PLACE we can now refine the general backtracking method as given by Algorithm 7.1 and give a precise solution to the *n*-queens problem.

procedure *NQUEENS*(*n*)
  //using backtracking this procedure prints all possible placements of//
  //*n* queens on an *n* × *n* chessboard so that they are nonattacking//
  integer *k, n, X*(1:*n*)
  X(1) ← 0; *k* ← 1   //*k* is the current row; *X*(*k*) the current column//
  while *k* > 0 **do**   //for all rows do//
    X(*k*) ← *X*(*k*) + 1   //move to the next column//
    while *X*(*k*) ≤ *n* **and not** *PLACE*(*k*) **do**   //can this queen be placed?//
      X(*k*) ← *X*(*k*) + 1
    repeat
    if *X*(*k*) ≤ *n*   //a position is found//
      then if *k* = *n*   //is a solution complete?//
        then print(*X*)   //yes, print the array//
        else *k* ← *k* + 1; *X*(*k*) ← 0   //go to the next row//
      endif
      else *k* ← *k* − 1   //backtrack//
    endif
  repeat
end *NQUEENS*

Algorithm 7.5   All solutions to the *n*-queens problem

At this point we might wonder how effective procedure NQUEENS is over the brute force approach. For an 8×8 chessboard there are $\binom{64}{8}$ possible ways to place 8 pieces or approximately 4.4 billion 8-tuples to examine. However by only allowing placements of queens on distinct rows and columns we require the examination of at most 8! or only 40,320 8-tuples.

We may use procedure ESTIMATE to estimate the number of nodes that will be generated by NQUEENS. Note that the assumptions which are needed for procedure ESTIMATE do hold for NQUEENS. The bounding function is static. No change is made to the function as the search proceeds. In addition, all nodes on the same level of the state space tree have the same degree. In Figure 7.8 we see five 8×8 chessboards which were created as a result of procedure ESTIMATE. As required the placement of each queen on the chessboard was chosen randomly. With each choice we kept track of the number of columns a queen could legitimately be placed on. These numbers are listed in the vector beneath each chessboard. The number following the vector represents the value that procedure ESTIMATE would produce from these sizes. The average of these five trials is 1625. The total number of nodes in the 8-queens state space tree is

$$1 + \sum_{j=0}^{7} \left(\sum_{i=0}^{j} (8 - i) \right) = 69,281.$$

So the estimated number of unbounded nodes is only about 2.34% of the total number of nodes in the 8-queens state space tree. (See the exercises for more ideas about the efficiency of NQUEENS.)

7.3 SUM OF SUBSETS

Suppose we are given n distinct positive numbers (usually called weights) and we desire to find all combinations of these numbers whose sum is M. This is called the *sum of subsets* problem. Examples 7.2 and 7.4 showed how we could formulate this problem using either fixed or variable size tuples. We will consider a backtracking solution using the fixed tuple size strategy. In this case the element $X(i)$ of the solution vector is either one or zero depending upon whether the weight $W(i)$ is included or not.

The children of any node in Figure 7.4 are easily generated. For a node at level i the left child corresponds to $X(i) = 1$ and the right to $X(i) = 0$.

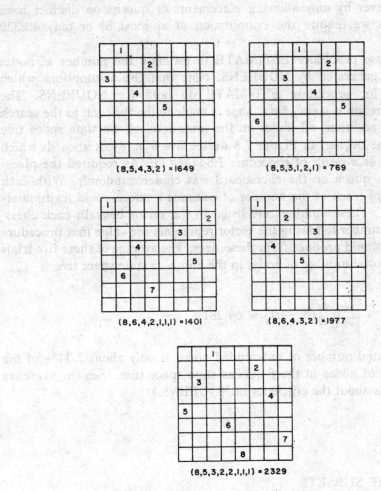

Figure 7.8 Five walks through the 8 queens problem plus estimates of the tree size

A simple choice for the bounding functions is $B_k(X(1), \ldots, X(k)) = $ true iff

$$\sum_{i=1}^{k} W(i)X(i) + \sum_{i=k+1}^{n} W(i) \geq M$$

Clearly $X(1), \ldots, X(k)$ cannot lead to an answer node if this condition is not satisfied. The bounding functions may be strengthened if we assume the $W(i)$s are initially in nondecreasing order. In this case $X(1), \ldots, X(k)$ cannot lead to an answer node if

$$\sum_{i=1}^{k} W(i)X(i) + W(k+1) > M$$

The bounding functions we shall use are therefore:

$$B_k(X(1), \ldots, X(k)) = \textit{true} \text{ iff} \left(\sum_{i=1}^{k} W(i)X(i) + \sum_{i=k+1}^{n} W(i) \geq M \right.$$

$$\left. and \ \sum_{i=1}^{k} W(i)X(i) + W(k+1) \leq M \right) \tag{7.1}$$

Since our algorithm will not make use of B_n, we need not be concerned by the appearance of $W(n+1)$ in this function. While we have now specified all that is needed to directly use either of the backtracking schemas, a simpler algorithm results if we tailor either of these schemas to the problem at hand. This simplification results from the realization that if $X(k) = 1$ then

$$\sum_{i=1}^{k} W(i)X(i) + \sum_{i=k+1}^{n} W(i) > M$$

For simplicity we shall refine the recursive schema. The resulting algorithm is SUMOFSUB.

procedure *SUMOFSUB(s, k, r)*

//find all subsets of $W(1:n)$ that sum to M. The values of//

//$X(j)$, $1 \le j < k$ have already been determined. $s = \sum_{j=1}^{k-1} W(j)X(j)$//

//and $r = \sum_{j=k}^{n} W(j)$ The $W(j)$s are in nondecreasing order.//

//It is assumed that $W(1) \le M$ and $\sum_{i=1}^{n} W(i) \ge m$.//

```
1    global integer M, n; global real W(1:n); global boolean X(1:n)
2    real r, s; integer k, j
     //generate left child. Note that s + W(k) ≤ M because B_{k-1} = true//
3    X(k) ← 1
4    if s + W(k) = M then    //subset found//
5        print(X(j), j ← 1 to k)
         //there is no recursive call here as W(j) > 0 1 ≤ j ≤ n//
6               else
7            if s + W(k) + W(k + 1) ≤ m then   //B_k = true//
8                call SUMOFSUB(s + W(k), k + 1, r − W(k))
9            endif
10   endif
     //generate right child and evaluate B_k//
11   if s + r − W(k) ≥ M and s + W(k + 1) ≤ M   //B_k = true//
12      then X(k) ← 0
13          call SUMOFSUB(s, k + 1, r − W(k))
14   endif
15   end SUMOFSUB
```

Algorithm 7.6   Recursive backtracking algorithm for sum of subsets problem

Procedure SUMOFSUB avoids computing $\sum_{i=1}^{k} W(i)X(i)$ and $\sum_{i=k+1}^{n} W(i)$ each time by keeping these values in variables s and r respectively. The algorithm assumes $W(1) \le M$ and $\sum_{i=1}^{n} W(i) \ge M$. The initial call is **call** SUMOFSUB$(0, 1, \sum_{i=1}^{n} W(i))$. It is interesting to note that the algorithm does not explicitly use the test $k > n$ to terminate the recursion. This test is not needed as on entry to the algorithm $s \ne M$ and $s + r \ge M$. Hence, $r \ne 0$ and so k can be no greater than n. Also note that in line 7, since $s + W(k) < M$ and $s + r \ge M$ it follows that $r \ne W(k)$ and hence $k + 1 \le n$. Observe also that if $s + W(k) = M$ (line 4) then $X(k + 1), \ldots,$ $X(n)$ must be zero. These zeros are omitted from the output of line 5. In

line 7 we do not test for $\sum_{i=1}^{k} W(i)X(i) + \sum_{i=k+1}^{n} W(i) \geq M$ as we already know
$s + r \geq M$ and $X(k) = 1$.

Example 7.6 Figure 7.9 shows the portion of the state space tree generated
by procedure SUMOFSUB while working on the instance $n = 6$, $M = 30$
and $W(1:6) = (5, 10, 12, 13, 15, 18)$. The rectangular nodes list the values
of s, k, r on each of the calls to SUMOFSUB. Circular nodes represent
points at which a subset with sum M is printed out. At nodes A, B and C
the output is respectively $(1, 1, 0, 0, 1)$, $(1, 0, 1, 1)$ and $(0, 0, 1, 0, 0, 1)$.
Note that the tree of Figure 7.9 contains only 23 rectangular nodes. The
full state space tree for $n = 6$ contains $2^6 - 1 = 63$ nodes from which
calls could be made (this count excludes the 64 leaf nodes as no call need
be made from a leaf). □

7.4 GRAPH COLORING

Let G be a graph and m be a given positive integer. We want to discover
if the nodes of G can be colored in such a way that no two adjacent nodes
have the same color yet only m colors are used. This is termed the *m-
colorability decision* problem and it is discussed again in Chapter 11. The
m-colorability optimization problem asks for the smallest integer m for
which the graph G can be colored. This integer is referred to as the
chromatic number of the graph.

A graph is said to be *planar* iff it can be drawn in a plane in such a way
that no two edges cross each other. A famous special case of the *m*-color-
ability decision problem is the 4-color problem for planar graphs. This
problem asks the following question: given any map, can the regions be
colored in such a way that no two adjacent regions have the same color yet
only four colors are needed. This turns out to be a problem where graphs
are very useful, because a map can easily be transformed into a graph.
Each region of the map becomes a node and if two regions are adjacent
then the corresponding nodes are joined by an edge. Figure 7.10 shows
a map with 5 regions and its corresponding graph. This map requires 4
colors. For many years it was known that 5 colors were sufficient to color
any map, but no map had ever been found which required more than 4
colors. After several hundred years this problem has just recently been
solved (to most peoples satisfaction) by a group of mathematicians with the
help of a computer. They showed that in fact 4 colors are sufficient. In
this section we consider not only graphs which are produced from maps

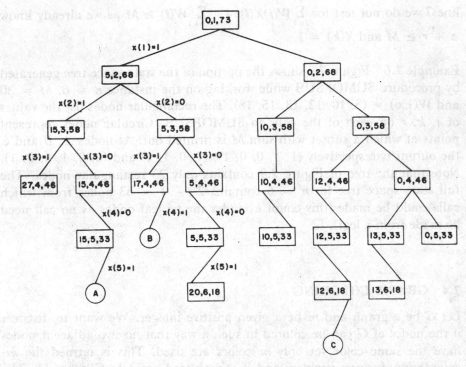

Figure 7.9 Portion of state space tree generated by SUMOFSUB

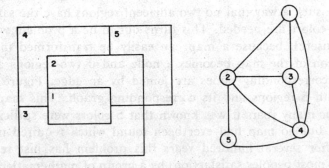

Figure 7.10   A map and its planar graph representation

but all graphs. We are interested in determining all the different ways in which a given graph may be colored using at most m colors.

Suppose we represent a graph by its adjacency matrix GRAPH(1:n, 1:n), where GRAPH(i, j) = true if (i, j) is an edge of G and otherwise GRAPH (i, j) = false. We prefer to use Boolean values since the algorithm will only be interested in whether or not an edge exists. The colors will be represented by the integers 1, 2, ..., m and the solutions will be given by the n-tuple ($X(1), ..., X(n)$) where $X(i)$ is the color of node i. Using the recursive back-tracking formulation as given in Algorithm 7.2 the resulting program is MCOLORING. The underlying state space tree used is a tree of degree m and height $n + 1$. Each node at level i has m children corresponding to the m possible assignments to $X(i)$, $1 \le i \le n$. Nodes at level $n + 1$ are leaf nodes. Figure 7.11 shows the state space tree when $n = 3$ and $m = 3$.

procedure MCOLORING(k)
//This program was formed using the recursive backtracking schema.//
//The graph is represented by its boolean adjacency matrix GRAPH(1://
//n, 1:n)). All assignments of 1, 2, ..., m to the vertices of the graph//
//such that adjacent vertices are assigned distinct integers are printed.//
//k is the index of the next vertex to color//
global integer m, n, $X(1:n)$ **boolean** GRAPH(1:n, 1:n)
integer k
loop   //generate all legal assignments for $X(k)$//
   call NEXTVALUE(k)   //assign to $X(k)$ a legal color//
   if $X(k) = 0$ **then exit endif**   //no new color possible//
   if $k = n$
      then print(X)   //at most m colors are assigned to n vertices//
      else call MCOLORING(k + 1)
   endif
repeat
end MCOLORING

Algorithm 7.7   Finding all m-colorings of a graph

Procedure MCOLORING is begun by first assigning the graph to its adjacency matrix, setting the array X to zero, and then invoking the statement **call** MCOLORING(1).

Notice the similarity between this algorithm and the general form of the recursive backtracking procedure of Algorithm 7.2. Procedure NEXT-VALUE produces the possible colors for $X(k)$ after $X(1)$ through $X(k - 1)$

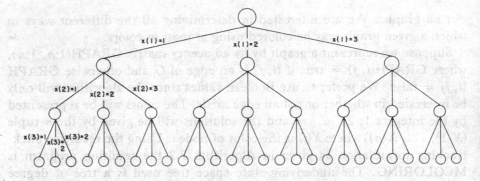

Figure 7.11 State space tree for MCOLORING when $n = 3$ and $m = 3$

have been defined. The main loop of MCOLORING repeatedly picks an element from the set of possibilities, assigns it to $X(k)$, and then calls MCOLORING recursively.

procedure *NEXTVALUE*(*k*)
//$X(1), \ldots, X(k - 1)$ have been assigned integer values in the range//
//$[1, m]$ such that adjacent vertices have distinct intergers. A value for//
//$X(k)$ is determined in the range $[0, m]$. $X(k)$ is assigned the next//
//highest numbered color while maintaining distinctness from the//
//adjacent vertices of vertex k. If no such color exists then $X(k) \leftarrow 0$.//
global integer $m, n, X(1:n)$ **boolean** *GRAPH*(1:*n*, 1:*n*)
integer *j, k*
loop
  $X(k) \leftarrow (X(k) + 1) \bmod (m + 1)$ //next highest color//
  if $X(k) = 0$ **then return endif** //all colors have been exhausted//
  for $j \leftarrow 1$ **to** *n* **do** //check if this color is distinct from adjacent colors//
    if *GRAPH*(*k, j*) **and** //if (k, j) is an edge//
      $X(k) = X(j)$ //and if adjacent vertices have identical colors//
      then exit endif
  repeat
  if $j = n + 1$ **then return endif** //new color found//
  repeat //otherwise try to find another color//
end *NEXTVALUE*

Algorithm 7.8 Generating a next color

An upper bound on the computing time of Algorithm 7.7 may be arrived at by noticing that the number of internal nodes in the state space tree is $\sum_{i=0}^{n-1} m^i$. At each internal node, $O(mn)$ time is spent by NEXTVALUE to determine the children corresponding to legal colorings. Hence, the total time is bounded by $\sum_{i=1}^{n} m^i n = n (m^{n+1} - 1) / (m - 1) = O(nm^n)$.

Figure 7.12 shows a simple graph containing four nodes. Below that is the tree which is generated by procedure MCOLORING. Each path to a leaf represents a coloring using at most 3 colors. Note that only twelve solutions exist with *exactly* 3 colors.

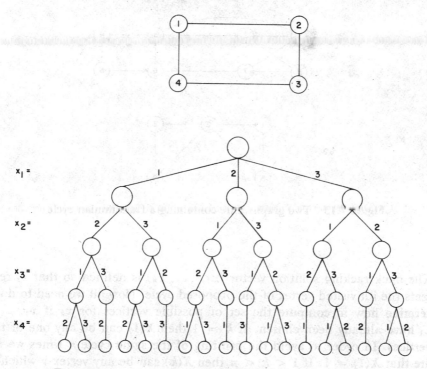

Figure 7.12　A 4 node graph and all possible 3 colorings

7.5 HAMILTONIAN CYCLES

Let $G = (V, E)$ be a connected graph with n vertices. A Hamiltonian cycle (suggested by Sir William Hamilton) is a round trip path along n edges of G which visits every vertex once and returns to its starting position. In other words if a Hamiltonian cycle begins at some vertex $v_1 \in G$ and the vertices of G are visited in the order $v_1, v_2, \ldots, v_{n+1}$ then the edges (v_i, v_{i+1}) are in E, $1 \le i \le n$ and the v_i are distinct except for v_1 and v_{n+1} which are equal.

The graph $G1$ of Figure 7.13 contains the Hamiltonian cycle 1, 2, 8, 7, 6, 5, 4, 3, 1. The graph $G2$ of Figure 7.13 contains no Hamiltonain cycle. There seems to be no easy way to determine if a given graph contains a Hamiltonian cycle. We shall now look at a backtracking algorithm which finds all the Hamiltonian cycles in a graph. The graph may either be directed or undirected. Only distinct cycles will be output.

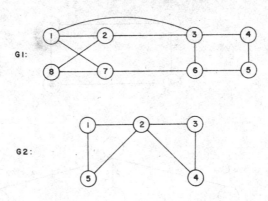

Figure 7.13   Two graphs, one containing a Hamiltonian cycle

The backtracking solution vector $(x_1, \ldots, x_n)$ is defined so that x_i represents the ith visited vertex of the proposed cycle. Now all we need to do is determine how to compute the set of possible vertices for x_k if $x_1, \ldots, x_{k-1}$ have already been chosen. If $k = 1$ then $X(1)$ can be any one of the n vertices. In order to avoid the printing of the same cycle n times we require that $X(1) = 1$. If $1 < k < n$ then $X(k)$ can be any vertex v which is distinct from $X(1), X(2), \ldots, X(k - 1)$ and v is connected by an edge to $X(k - 1)$. $X(n)$ can only be the one remaining vertex and it must be connected to both $X(n - 1)$ and $X(1)$. We begin by presenting procedure NEXTVALUE(k) which determines a possible next vertex for the proposed cycle.

procedure *NEXTVALUE*(k)

//$X(1), \ldots, X(k - 1)$ is a path of $k - 1$ distinct vertices. If $X(k) = 0$//
//then no vertex has as yet been assigned to $X(k)$. After execution $X(k)$//
//is assigned to the next highet numbered vertex which (i) does not//
//already appear in $X(1), \ldots, X(k - 1)$; (ii) is connected by an edge//
//to $X(k - 1)$. Otherwise $X(k) = 0$. If $k = n$ then in addition $X(k)$//
//is connected to $X(1)$.//

global integer n, $X(1:n)$, **boolean** GRAPH($1:n$, $1:n$)
integer k, j
loop
   $X(k) \leftarrow (X(k) + 1) \bmod (n + 1)$ //next vertex//
   if $X(k) = 0$ **then return endif**
   if $GRAPH(X(k - 1), X(k))$ //is there an edge//
      then for $j \leftarrow 1$ **to** $k - 1$ **do** //check for distinctness//
         if $X(j) = X(k)$
           then exit //exit this for loop//
         endif
      repeat
      if $j = k$ //if true then the vertex is distinct//
         then if $k < n$ **or** ($k = n$ **and** $GRAPH(X(n), 1)$) **then return**
           endif
      endif
   endif
repeat
end *NEXTVALUE*

Algorithm 7.9 Generating a next vertex

Using procedure NEXTVALUE we can particularize the recursive backtracking schema to find all Hamiltonian cycles.

procedure *HAMILTONIAN*(*k*)
   //This procedure uses the recursive formulation of backtracking//
   //to find all the Hamiltonian cycles of a graph. The graph//
   //is stored as a boolean adjacency matrix in GRAPH(1:*n*, 1:*n*). All//
   //cycles begin at vertex 1.//
   global integer $X(1:n)$
   local integer k, n
   loop   //generate values for $X(k)$//
      call *NEXTVALUE*(*k*)   //assign a legal next vertex to $X(k)$//
      if $X(k) = 0$ **then return endif**
      if $k = n$
         then print $(X, \text{'1'})$ //a cycle is printed//
         else call *HAMILTONIAN*(*k* + 1)
      endif
   repeat
end *HAMILTONIAN*

Algorithm 7.10   Finding all Hamiltonian cycles

This procedure is started by first initializing the adjacency matrix GRAPH
$(1:n, 1:n)$, then setting $X(2:n) \leftarrow 0$, $X(1) \leftarrow 1$ and then executing **call**
HAMILTONIAN(2).

Recall from section 5.8 the traveling salesperson problem which asked
for a "tour" which has minimum cost. This tour is a Hamiltonian cycle.
For the simple case of a graph all of whose edge costs are identical, procedure HAMILTONIAN will find a minimum cost tour if a tour exists.
If the common edge cost is c, the cost of a tour is cn since there are n
edges in a Hamiltonian cycle.

7.6   KNAPSACK PROBLEM

In this section we reconsider a problem which was defined and solved by a
dynamic programming algorithm in Chapter 5, the zero-one knapsack
optimization problem. Given n positive weights w_i, n positive profits p_i,
and a positive number M which is the knapsack capacity, this problem
calls for choosing a subset of the weights such that

$$\sum_{1 \le i \le n} w_i x_i \le M \quad \text{and} \quad \sum_{1 \le i \le n} p_i x_i \text{ is maximized} \tag{7.2}$$

The x's constitute a zero-one valued vector.

The solution space for this problem consists of the 2^n distinct ways to assign zero or one values to the x's. Thus the solution space is the same as that for the sum of subsets problem. Two possible tree organizations are possible. One corresponds to the fixed tuple size formulation (Figure 7.4) and the other to the variable tuple size formulation (Figure 7.3). Backtracking algorithms for the knapsack problem may be arrived at using either of these two state space trees. Regardless of which is used, bounding functions are needed to help kill some live nodes without actually expanding them. A good bounding function for this problem is obtained by using an upper bound on the value of the best feasible solution obtainable by expanding the given live node and any of its descendants. If this upper bound is not higher than the value of the best solution determined so far then that live node may be killed.

We shall continue the discussion using the fixed tuple size formulation. If at node Z the values of x_i, $1 \leq i \leq k$ have already been determined, then an upper bound for Z can be obtained by relaxing the requirement $x_i = 0$ or 1 to $0 \leq x_i \leq 1$ for $k + 1 \leq i \leq n$ and using the greedy algorithm of section 4.3 to solve the relaxed problem. Procedure BOUND (p, w, k, M) determines an upper bound on the best solution obtainable by expanding any node Z at level $k + 1$ of the state space tree. The object weights and profits are $W(i)$ and $P(i)$. $p = \Sigma_{i=1}^{k} P(i)X(i)$ and it is assumed that $P(i)/W(i) \geq P(i + 1)/W(i + 1)$, $1 \leq i < n$.

```
procedure BOUND(p, w, k, M)
  //p, the current profit total//
  //w, the current weight total//
  //k, the index of the last removed item//
  //M, the knapsack size//
  //the result is a new profit//
  global n, P(1:n), W(1:n)
  integer k, i; real b, c, p, w, M
  b ← p; c ← w
  for i ← k + 1 to n do
    c ← c + W(i)
    if c < M then b ← b + P(i)
             else return(b + (1 − (c − M)/W(i))*P(i))
    endif
  repeat
  return(b)
end BOUND
```

Algorithm 7.11   A bounding function

From Algorithm 7.11 it follows that the bound for a feasible left child of a node Z is the same as that for Z. Hence, the bounding function need not be used whenever the backtracking algorithm makes a move to the left child of a node. Since the backtracking algorithm will attempt to make a left child move whenever given a choice between a left and right child, we see that the bounding function need be used only after a series

```
procedure BKNAP1(M, n, W, P, fw, fp, X)
  //M, the size of the knapsack//
  //n, the number of weights and profits//
  //W(1:n), the weights//
  //P(1:n), the corresponding profits; P(i)/W(i) ≥ P(i + 1)/W(i + 1)//
  //fw, the final weight of the knapsack//
  //fp, the final maximum profit//
  //X(1:n), either zero or one. X(k) = 0 if W(k) is not in the knapsack//
  //else X(k) = 1//
1  integer n, k, Y(1:n), i, X(1:n); real M, W(1:n), P(1:n), fw, fp, cw, cp;
2  cw ← cp ← 0; k ← 1; fp ← −1 //cw = current weight, cp = cur-//
                                                        //rent profit//
3  loop
4      while k ≤ n and cw + W(k) ≤ M do   //place k into knapsack//
5          cw ← cw + W(k); cp ← cp + P(k); Y(k) ← 1; k ← k + 1
           //place W(k) in the knapsack//
6      repeat
7      if k > n then fp ← cp; fw ← cw; k ← n; X ← Y //update so-//
                                                          //lution//
8          else Y(k) ← 0   //M is exceeded so object k does not fit//
9      endif
10     while BOUND(cp, cw, k, M) ≤ fp do   //after fp is set above,//
                                                       //BOUND = fp//
11         while k ≠ 0 and Y(k) ≠ 1 do
12             k ← k − 1   //find the last weight included in the knapsack//
13         repeat
14         if k = 0 then return endif   //the algorithm ends here//
15         Y(k) ← 0; cw ← cw − W(k); cp ← cp − P(k) //remove the kth//
                                                            //item//
16     repeat
17     k ← k + 1
18     repeat
19 end BKNAP1
```

Algorithm 7.12   Backtracking solution to the 0/1 knapsack problem of successful left child moves (i.e. moves to feasible left children). The resulting algorithm is procedure BKNAP1 (Algorithm 7.12). It was obtained from the iterative backtracking schema.

When $fp \neq -1$, $X(i)$, $1 \le i \le n$ is such that $\sum_{i=1}^{n} W(i)X(i) = fp$. In the while loop of lines 4–6 successive moves are made to feasible left children. $Y(i)$. $1 \le i \le k$ is the path to the current node. $cw = \sum_{i=1}^{k-1} W(i)Y(i)$ and $cp = \sum_{i=1}^{k-1} P(i)Y(i)$. If at line 7, $k > n$ then $cp > fp$ as otherwise the path to this leaf would have been terminated the last time the bounding function was used. If $k \le n$ then $W(k)$ does not fit and a right child move has to be made. So, $Y(k)$ is set to 0 in line 8. If in line 10, BOUND $\le fp$, then the present path may be terminated as it cannot lead to a better solution than the best found so far. In lines 11–13 we trace back along the path to the most recent node from which an as yet untried move may be made. If there is no such node then the algorithm terminates in line 14. Otherwise $Y(k)$, cw and cp are appropriately updated to correspond to a right child move. The bound for this new node is computed. The back-up process of lines 10–16 continues until a move is made to a right child from which there is a possibility of obtaining a solution with value greater than fp. Note that the bounding function of line 10 is not static as fp changes as more of the tree is searched. Hence the bounding function gets stronger dynamically.

Example 7.7 Consider the following instance of the knapsack problem: $P = (11, 21, 31, 33, 43, 53, 55, 65)$, $W = (1, 11, 21, 23, 33, 43, 45, 55)$, $M = 110$, $n = 8$

Figure 7.14 shows the tree that gets generated as various choices are made for the vector Y. The ith level of the tree corresponds to an assignment of one or zero to $Y(i)$, either including or excluding the weight $W(i)$. The two numbers contained in a node are the weight (cw) and profit (cp) (reading downwards), given the assignments down to the level of the node. Nodes containing no numbers imply that the weight and profit is the same as their parent. The number outside each right child and outside the root is the bound corresponding to that node. The bound for a left child is the same as that for its parent. The variable fp of Algorithm 7.12 is updated at each of the nodes A, B, C and D. Each time fp is updated, X is also updated. On termination $fp = 159$ and $X = (1, 1, 1, 0, 1, 1, 0, 0)$. Of the $2^9 - 1 = 511$ nodes in the state space tree only 33 are generated. This number could have been reduced to 26 by noticing that since all the $P(i)$'s

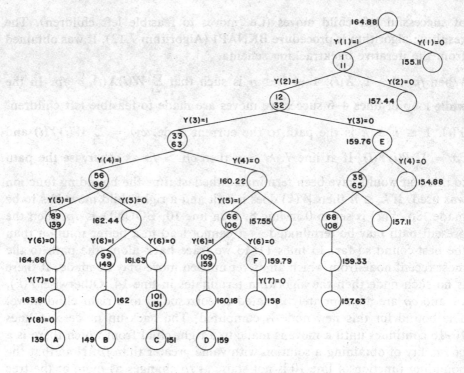

Figure 7.14   Tree generated by Algorithm 7.12

are integer, the value of all feasible solutions is also integer. Hence a better upper bound is $\lfloor \text{BOUND}(p, w, k, M) \rfloor$. Consequently the nodes E and F need not be expanded. $\square$

Algorithm BKNAP1 can be improved further by realizing that the loop of lines 4 to 6 is essentially executed each time a call to BOUND is made in line 10. Hence, there should be no need to redo this work. To avoid the work done in lines 4 to 6 of BKNAP1 we need to change BOUND to a function with side effects. The new algorithms BOUND1 and BKNAP2 appear as Algorithms 7.13 and 7.14. All variables have the same meanings as in Algorithms 7.11 and 7.12.

procedure $BOUND1(p, w, k, M, pp, ww, i)$
  //pp and ww are the profit and weight corresponding to the last left//
  //child move. i is the index of the first object that does not fit.//
  //It is $n + 1$ if no objects remain.//
  global $n, P(1:n), W(1:n), Y(1:n)$
  integer k, i; **real** p, w, pp, ww, M, b
  $pp \leftarrow p; ww \leftarrow w$
  for $i \leftarrow k + 1$ **to** n **do**
    if $ww + W(i) \leq M$ **then** $ww \leftarrow ww + W(i); pp \leftarrow pp + P(i); Y(i) \leftarrow 1$
                         else return $(pp + (M - ww)*P(i)/W(i))$
    endif
  repeat
  return(pp)
end $BOUND1$

Algorithm 7.13 Generating a bound

procedure $BKNAP2(M, n, W, P, fw, fp, X)$
  //same as BKNAP1//
  integer $n, k, Y(1:n), i, j, X(1:n)$
  real $W(1:n), P(1:n), M, fw, fp, pp, ww, cw, cp$
  $cw \leftarrow cp \leftarrow k \leftarrow 0; fp \leftarrow -1$
  loop
    while $BOUND1(cp, cw, k, M, pp, ww, j) \leq fp$ **do**
    while $k \neq 0$ **and** $Y(k) \neq 1$ **do**
    $k \leftarrow k - 1$
    repeat
    if $k = 0$ **then return endif**
    $Y(k) \leftarrow 0; cw \leftarrow cw - W(k); cp \leftarrow cp - P(k)$
    repeat
    $cp \leftarrow pp; cw \leftarrow ww; k \leftarrow j$ //equivalent to loop of lines 4-6 in//
                                           //BKNAP1//
    if $k > n$ **then** $fp \leftarrow cp; fw \leftarrow cw; k \leftarrow n; X \leftarrow Y$
           else $Y(k) \leftarrow 0$
    endif
  repeat
end $BKNAP2$

Algorithm 7.13 Modified knapsack algorithm

So far, all our backtracking algorithms have worked on a static state space tree. We shall now see how a dynamic state space tree may be used for the knapsack problem. One method for dynamically partitioning the solution space is based upon trying to obtain an optimal solution using the greedy algorithm of section 4.3. We first replace the integer constraint $x_i = 0$ or 1 by the constraint $0 \le x_i \le 1$. This yields the relaxed problem

$$\max \sum_{1 \le i \le n} p_i x_i$$
$$\text{subject to} \sum_{1 \le i \le n} w_i x_i \le M \qquad (7.3)$$
$$0 \le x_i \le 1, \qquad 1 \le i \le n$$

If the solution generated by the greedy method has all x_is equal to zero or one, then it is also an optimal solution to the original zero-one knapsack problem. If this is not the case then exactly one x_i will be such that $0 < x_i < 1$. We shall partition the solution space of (7.2) into two subspaces. In one $x_i = 0$ and in the other $x_i = 1$. Thus the left subtree of the state space tree will correspond to $x_i = 0$ and the right to $x_i = 1$. In general, at each node Z of the state space tree the greedy algorithm will be used to solve (7.3) under the added restrictions corresponding to the assignments already made along the path from the root to this node. In case the solution is all integer then an optimal solution for this node has been found. If not then there is exactly one x_i such that $0 < x_i < 1$. The left child of Z corresponds to $x_i = 0$ and the right to $x_i = 1$.

The justification for this partitioning scheme is that the noninteger x_i is what prevents the greedy solution from being a feasible solution to the zero-one knapsack problem. So, we would expect to reach a feasible greedy solution quickly by forcing this x_i to be integer. Choosing left branches to correspond to $x_i = 0$ rather than $x_i = 1$ is also justifiable. Since the greedy algorithm requires $p_j/w_j \ge p_{j+1}/w_{j+1}$, we would expect most objects with low index (i.e. small j and hence high density) to be in an optimal filling of the knapsack. When x_i is set to zero, we are not preventing the greedy algorithm from using any of the objects with $j < i$ (unless x_j has already been set to zero). On the other hand, when x_i is set to 1, some of the x_js with $j < i$ will not be able to get into the knapsack. Therefore we expect to arrive at an optimal solution with $x_i = 0$. So we wish the backtracking algorithm to try this alternative first. Hence the left subtree corresponds to $x_i = 0$.

Example 7.8 Let us try out a backtracking algorithm and the above dynamic partitioning scheme on the data of Example 7.7. The greedy solution corresponding to the root node (i.e. Equation (7.3)) is $x = (1, 1, 1, 1, ,1,$ $21/45, 0, 0)$. Its value is 164.88. The two subtrees of the root correspond to $x_6 = 0$ and $x_6 = 1$ respectively (Figure 7.15). The greedy solution at node 2 is $x = (1, 1, 1, 1, 1, 0, 21/45, 0)$. Its value is 164.66. The solution space at node 2 is partitioned using $x_7 = 0$ and $x_7 = 1$. The next E-node is node 3. The solution here has $x_8 = 21/55$. The partitioning now is with $x_8 = 0$ and $x_8 = 1$. The solution at node 4 is all integer so there is no need to expand this node further. The best solution found so far has value 139 and $x = (1, 1, 1, 1, 1, 0, 0, 0)$. Node 5 is the next E-node. The greedy solution for this node is $X = (1, 1, 1, 22/23, 0, 0, 0, 1)$. Its value is 159.56. The partitioning is now with $x_4 = 0$ and $x_4 = 1$. The greedy solution at node 6 has value 156.66 and $x_5 = 2/3$. Next, node 7 becomes the E-node. The solution here is $(1, 1, 1, 0, 0, 0, 0, 1)$. Its value is 128. Node 7 is not expanded as the greedy solution here is all integer. At node 8 the greedy solution has value 157.71 and $x_3 = 4/7$. The solution at node 9 is all integer and has value 140. The greedy solution at node 10 is $(1, 0, 1, 0, 1, 0, 0, 1)$. Its value is 150. The next E-node is node 11. Its value is 159.52 and $x_3 = 20/21$. The partitioning is now on $x_3 = 0$ and $x_3 = 1$. The remainder of the backtracking process on this knapsack instance is left as an exercise □

Experimental work cited in the references indicates that backtracking algorithms for the knapsack problem generally work in less time when using a static tree than when using a dynamic tree. The dynamic partitioning scheme is, however, very useful in the solution of integer linear programs. The general integer linear program is mathematically stated in (7.4)

$$\text{minimize } \sum_{1 \le j \le n} c_j x_j$$
$$\text{subject to } \sum_{1 \le j \le n} a_{ij} x_j \le b_i, \qquad 1 \le i \le m \qquad (7.4)$$

and x_js are nonnegative integers

If the integer constraints on the x_is in (7.4) are replaced by the constraint $x_i \ge 0$ then we obtain a linear program whose optimal solution has a value at least as large as the value of an optimal solution to (7.4). Linear programs may be solved using the simplex method (see the references). If the solution is not all integer then a noninteger x_i is chosen to partition the solution space. Let us assume that the value of x_i in the optimal solution to the linear program corresponding to any node Z in the state space is v and v is not an integer. The left child of Z corresponds to $x_i \le \lfloor v \rfloor$ while the right child of Z corresponds to $x_i \ge \lceil v \rceil$. Since the resulting state space tree has a potentially infinite depth (note that on the path from

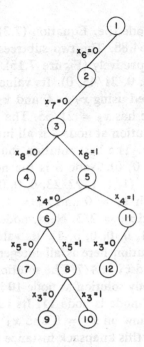

Figure 7.15   Part of the dynamic state space tree generated in Example 7.7

the root to a node Z the solution space can be partitioned on one x_i many times as each x_i can have as value any nonnegative integer) it is almost always searched using a branch-and-bound method (see chapter 8).

Testing

Algorithm BKNAP1 was programmed in Pascal by N. R. Venkatesh and run on a CDC Cyber 74 Computer. The objective of the experiment was to determine how the computing time required by BKNAP1 varied with changes in the profits and weights and also with a change in n. The number of data sets one can design is potentially infinite. We shall report the results of the experiment for the following data sets:

(i)   random weights and profits in the range [1, 1000]
(ii)   random weights and profits in the range [1, 100]
(iii)   random weights in the range [1, 100] and $p_i = w_i + 10$
(iv)   random weights in the range [1, 100] and $p_i = 1.1w_i$.

In each of the above data sets M was set to be half the sum of the weights. For each n chosen, 10 different problem instances from each data set were generated. Table 7.1 gives the average and maximum times as well as the standard deviation in the times. These figures are reported only for selected values of n. For data set (iii) more than 2 minutes were needed to solve ten instances for each n, $n > 40$. As is readily observable the computing times for any fixed n are very much dependent on the actual weights and profits.

In another test conducted by N. R. Venkatesh it was determined that the backtracking algorithm using a variable tuple size formulation required between 8%-12% less time than BKNAP1.

Table 7.2 presents corresponding computing times for the dynamic programming algorithm discussed in chapter 5. This algorithm was modified to include the heuristics described at the end of section 5.6. It was found that the addition of these heuristics reduced the time for DKNAP by more than 50% on data sets (i), (ii) and (iv). While there was a decrease in computing time for data set (iii), it wasn't quite as significant. In general, the dynamic programming algorithm performed worse than BKNAP1. This observation should be contrasted with the findings of an independent test conducted by Horowitz and Sahni (see the references). Their tests show that the divide-and-conquer dynamic programming algorithm discussed in the exercises of chapter 5 is superior to BKAP1. The exercises explore the relative efficiency of BKNAP2 as well as strengthening of the bounding function.

REFERENCES AND SELECTED READINGS

An early modern account of backtracking is given in

"An enumerative technique for a class of combinatorial problems" by R. J. Walker, *Proceedings of Symposia in Applied Mathematics*, vol. X, American Mathematical Society, Providence, R. I., 1960.

Another description of the method plus a set of applications can be found in

"Backtrack programming" by S. Golomb and L. Baumert, *J. ACM*, vol. 12, (1965), 516-524.

Table 7.1 Computing times for BKNAP1 on Cyber 74 (Times in milliseconds)
(Table prepared by N. R. Venkatesh)

Data set	(i)			(ii)			(iii)			(iv)		
n	avg	max	std	avg	max	std	avg	max	std	avg	max	std
10	2.15	5	1.1	2.2	4	0.81	7.6	14	4.14	8.3	28	7.1
20	7.45	15	3.22	7.2	13	2.93	46.3	261	59.34	7.8	26	5.68
30	14.5	42	9.02	11.3	25	4.64	217.8	1026	300.12	8.1	13	2.53
40	16.05	28	4.71	15.85	27	4.67	1286.25	11954	2736.21	10.25	20	4.55
75	44.8	68	11.18	41.5	60	8.53				21.0	52	8.69
100	81.5	174	32.62	64.95	111	13.5				31.7	73	11.12
125	107.9	291	47.17	106.9	163	26.12				39	57	7.69
150	166.85	426	70.02	126.3	187	23.97				53.4	86	11.11
175	191.5	338	54.06	185.6	262	30.25				62.45	72	4.5
190	227.6	413	70.44	211.0	333	48.48				73.9	95	7.51

Table 7.2 Computing times for dynamic programming algorithm (Times in milliseconds) (table prepared by N. R. Venkatesh)

Data Set n	(i)			(ii)			(iii)			(iv)		
	avg	max	std	avg	max	std	avg	max	std	avg	max	std
10	5.15	8	1.06	5.4	10	1.62	19.4	27	2.8	12.75	22	4.13
20	26.4	51	8.2	26.3	54	8.98	170.15	245	27	134	195	34.85
30	67.5	93	14.8	66.6	94	13.68	528.6	658	69.6	423.4	571	77.7
40	147.4	244	32.3	135.5	199	27.8	989.5	1146	95.2	788.4	989	102.4
75	823.7	1468	249.6	689.1	1273	190.6	Excessive storage needed					
100	Excessive storage needed											

A set of backtrack programs in FORTRAN is presented in

Combinatoral Algorithms by A. Nijenhuis and H. S. Wilf, Academic Press, New York, 1975.

and a method for improving the efficiency of backtracking using assembly language macros is given in

"Backtrack programming techniques" by J. R. Bitner and E. M. Reingold, *C.ACM*, vol. 18, (1975), 651-656.

The technique for estimating the efficiency of a backtrack program was first proposed in

"Combinatorial analysis and computers" by M. Hall and D. E. Knuth, *American Mathematical Monthly*, vol. 72, Part II, Feb. 1965, 21-28.

and was later published in

"Estimating the efficiency of backtrack programs" by D. E. Knuth, *Mathematics of Computation*, vol. 29, (1975), 121-136.

The dynamic partitioning scheme for the zero-one knapsack problem was proposed by Greenberg and Hegerich. Their algorithm appears in

"A branch-and-search algorithm for the knapsack problem" by H. Greenberg and R. Hegerich, *Manag. Sci*, 16(5), 327-332 (1970).

Experimental results showing static trees to be superior for this problem may be found in

"Computing partitions with applications to the knapsack problem" by E. Horowitz and S. Sahni, *J.ACM*, 21(2), 277-292 (1974).

Data presented in the above paper by Horowitz and Sahni shows that the divide-and-conquer dynamic programming algorithm for the knapsack problem is superior to BKNAP1.

A good reference for the use of dynamic state space trees in the solution of integer linear programs is:

"*Integer Programming*" by R. Garfinkel and G. Nemhauser, John Wiley, 1973.

A discussion of the simplex method for solving linear programs may be found in:

"*Linear Programming*," by S. Gass, McGraw Hill, New York, 1969.

EXERCISES

1. Change the two backtracking control abstractions, Algorithms 7.1 and 7.2 so that they find only a single solution rather than all solutions.

2. Using the rules given in section 1.3, translate the recursive backtracking algorithm, Algorithm 7.2, into an equivalent iterative one. Then apply all of the simplifications you can think of and compare the result to Algorithm 7.1.

3. Procedure NQUEENS can be made more efficient by redefining procedure PLACE(k) so that it either returns the next legitimate column on which to place the kth queen or an illegal value. Rewrite both procedures so they implement this alternative strategy.

4. For the n-queens problem we observe that some solutions are simply reflections or rotations of others. For example when $n = 4$ the two solutions given below are equivalent under reflection.

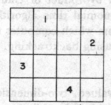   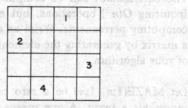

Figure 7.16 Equivalent solutions to the 4-queens problem

Observe that for finding inequivalent solutions the algorithm need only set $X(1) = 2, 3, \ldots, \lceil n/2 \rceil$. Modify procedure NQUEENS so that only inequivalent solutions are computed.

5. Run the n-queens algorithm devised above for $n = 8, 9, 10$. Tabulate the number of solutions your program finds for each value of n.

6. Given an $n \times n$ chessboard, a knight is placed on an arbitrary square with coordinates (x, y). The problem is to determine $n^2 - 1$ knight moves such

that every square of the board is visited once if such a sequence of moves exists. Write an algorithm to solve this problem.

7.   Suppose you are given n men and n women and two $n \times n$ arrays P and Q such that $P(i, j)$ is the preference of man i for woman j and $Q(i, j)$ is the preference of woman i for man j. Give an algorithm which finds a pairing of men and women such that the sum of the product of the preferences is maximized.

8.   Prove that the size of the set of all subsets of n elements is 2^n.

9.   Let $A(1:n, 1:n)$ be an $n \times n$ matrix. The *determinant* of A is the number

$$\det(A) = \sum_s \text{sgn}(s) a_{1, s(1)} a_{2, s(2)} \cdots a_{n, s(n)}$$

where the sum is taken over all permutations $s(1), \ldots, s(n)$ of $\{1, 2, \ldots, n\}$ and $\text{sgn}(s)$ is $+1$ or -1 according to whether s is an even or odd permutation. The *permanent* of A is defined as

$$\text{per}(A) = \sum_s a_{1, s(1)} a_{2, s(2)} \cdots a_{n, s(n)}$$

The determinant can be computed as a byproduct of Gaussian elimination requiring $O(n^3)$ operations, but no polynomial time algorithm is known for computing permanents. Write an algorithm which computes the permanent of a matrix by generating the elements of s using backtracking. Analyze the time of your algorithm.

10.   Let MAZE$(1:n, 1:n)$ be a zero or one valued, two-dimensional array which represents a maze. A one means a blocked path while a zero stands for an open position. You are to develop an algorithm which begins at MAZE$(1, 1)$ and tries to find a path to position MAZE(n, n). Once again backtracking will be necessary here. See if you can analyze the time of your algorithm.

11.   The *assignment problem* is usually stated in this way: there are n people to be assigned to n jobs. The cost of assigning the ith man to the jth job is COST (i, j). You are to develop an algorithm which assigns every job to a person and at the same time minimizes the total cost of the assignment.

12.   Let $W = (5, 7, 10, 12, 15, 18, 20)$ and $M = 35$. Find all possible subsets of W which sum to M. Do this using SUMOFSUB. Draw the portion of the state space tree which is generated.

13.   Run procedure SUMOFSUB on the data $M = 35$ and (i) $W = (5, 7, 10, 12,$

15, 18, 20), (ii) $W = (20, 18, 15, 12, 10, 7, 5)$, and (iii) $W = (15, 7, 20, 5, 18, 10, 12)$. Are there any discernible differences in the computing times?

14. Write a backtracking algorithm for the sum of subsets problem using the state space tree corresponding to the variable tuple size formulation.

15. [Programming Project] Write a program for the sum of subsets problem. Use backtracking and a fixed tuple size formulation and assume the objects are in nonincreasing order of weights. Program algorithm SUMOFSUB. Design several data sets to compare the performance of the two programs (see section 7.6). Obtain computing times for the two programs. What conclusions can you draw?

16. Run Algorithm 7.7, MCOLORING using as data the complete graphs of size $n = 2, 3, 4, 5, 6$ and 7. Let the desired number of colors be $k = n$ and $k = n/2$. Tabulate the computing times for each value of n and k.

17. Determine the order of magnitude of the worst case computing time for the backtracking procedure which finds all Hamiltonian cycle.

18. Draw the portion of the state space tree generated by Algorithm 7.10 for the graph G1 of Figure 7.13

19. Generalize procedure HAMILTONIAN so that it processes a graph whose edges have costs associated with them and finds a Hamiltonian cycle with minimum cost. You may assume that all edge costs are positive.

20. (i) Write a backtracking program for solving the knapsack optimization problem using the variable size tuple formulation.
    (ii) Draw the portion of the state space tree your algorithm will generate when solving the knapsack instance of Example 7.6.

21. Complete the state space tree of Figure 7.13.

22. Write a backtracking algorithm for the knapsack problem using the dynamic state space tree discussed in section 7.6.

23. [Programming project] (i) Program the knapsack algorithms BKNAP1, BKNAP2 and the algorithms of exercises 19 and 21. Run these four algorithms using the same data as in section. 7.6. Determine average times, maximum times and standard deviations as in Table 7.1. Which algorithm is expected to perform best?

    (ii) Now program the dynamic programming algorithm of chapter 5 for the knapsack problem. Use the heuristics suggested at the end of section 5.6.

Obtain computing times and compare this algorithm with the backtracking algorithms.

24.   (i) Obtain a knapsack instance for which more nodes are generated by the backtracking algorithm using a dynamic tree than when using a static tree.

  (ii) Obtain a knapsack instance for which more nodes are generated by the backtracking algorithm using a static tree than when a dynamic tree is used.

  (iii) Strengthen the heuristic used in the backtracking algorithms of (i) by first building on array MINW(i) with the property that MINW(i) is the index of the object which has least weight amongst objects $i, i + 1, \ldots, n$. Now any E-node at which decision for $x_1, \ldots, x_{i-1}$ have been made and at which the unutilized knapsack capacity is less than $W(\text{MINW}(i))$ may be terminated provided the profit earned up to this node is no more than the maximum determined as far. Incorporate this into your programs of (i). Rerun the new programs on the same data sets and see what (if any) improvements result. This strengthening of the heuristic is due to Antonio Albano and Renzo Orsini and appears in their paper: "A tree search approach to the M-Partition and Knapsack Problem," Instituto di Scienze dell' Informazione, Pisa, Italy, 1977.

25.   This problem is called the postage stamp problem. Envision a country which issues n different denominations of stamps but allows no more than m stamps on a single letter. For given values of m and n write an algorithm which computes the greatest consecutive range of postage values, from one on up, and all possible sets of denominations that realize that range. For example for $n = 4$ and $m = 5$ the stamps with values (1, 4, 12, 21) allow the postage values 1 through 71. Are there any other denominations of four stamps which have the same range?

26.   Here is a game one can buy in most toy stores. Its called Hi-Q. Thirty two pieces are arranged on a board as shown in Figure 7.17. Only the center position is unoccupied. A piece is only allowed to move by jumping over one of its neighbors into an empty space. When a piece is jumped it is removed from the board. Write an algorithm which determines a series of jumps so that all of the pieces except one are eventually removed, and that final piece ends up at the center position.

27.   Imagine a set of 12 plane figures each composed of five equal-sized squares. Each figure differs in shape from the others but together they can be arranged to make different size rectangles. In Figure 7.18 there is a picture of 12 pentominoes which are joined to create a 6 × 10 rectangle. Write an algorithm which finds all possible ways to place the pentominoes so that a 6 × 10 rectangle is formed.

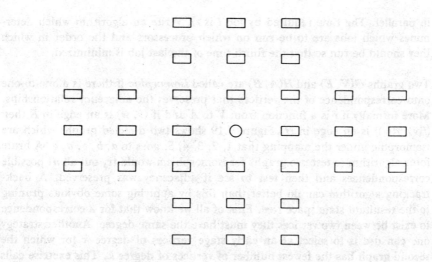

Figure 7.17   A Hi-Q board in its initial state

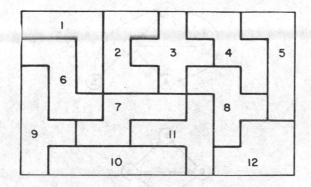

Figure 7.18   A pentominoe configuration

28. Suppose a set of electrical components such as transistors are to be placed on a circuit board. We are given a connection matrix CONN where CONN(i, j) equals the number of connections between component i and component j and a matrix DIST where DIST(r, s) is the distance between position r and position s on the circuit board. The "wiring" of the board consists of placing each of n components at some location. The cost of a wiring is the sum of the products of CONN(i, j)*DIST(r, s) where component i is placed at location r and component j is placed at location s. Compose an algorithm which finds an assignment of components to locations which minimizes the total cost of the wiring.

29. Suppose there are n jobs to be executed but only k processors which can work

in parallel. The time required by job i is t_i. Write an algorithm which determines which jobs are to be run on which processors and the order in which they should be run so that the finish time of the last job is minimized.

30. Two graphs $G(V, E)$ and $H(A, B)$ are called *isomorphic* if there is a one-to-one onto correspondence of the vertices that preserves the adjacency relationships. More formally if f is a function from V to A and if (v, w) is an edge in E then $(f(v), f(w))$ is an edge in H. Figure 7.19 shows two directed graphs which are isomorphic under the mapping that 1, 2, 3, 4, 5, goes to a, b, c, d, e. A brute force algorithm to test two graphs for isomorphism would try out all $n!$ possible correspondences and then test to see if adjacency was preserved. A backtracking algorithm can do better than this by applying some obvious pruning to the resultant state space tree. First of all we know that for a correspondence to exist between two vertices they must have the same degree. Another strategy one can use is to select at an early stage vertices of degree k for which the second graph has the fewest number of vertices of degree k. This exercise calls for devising an isomorphism algorithm which is based on backtracking that makes use of these ideas.

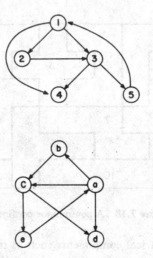

Figure 7.19 Two isomorphic graphs

31. A graph is called *complete* if all of its vertices are connected to all of the other vertices in the graph. A maximal complete subgraph of a graph is called a *clique*. By maximal we mean that this subgraph is contained within no other subgraph which is also complete. A clique of size k has $\binom{k}{i}$ subcliques of size i, $1 \le i \le k$. This implies that any algorithm which looks for a maximal clique must be careful about generating each subclique the fewest number of times that is possible. One way to generate the cliques is to extend a clique

of size m to size $m + 1$ and to continue this process by trying out all possible vertices. But this strategy will generate the same clique many times and this can be avoided by using the following rules. Given a clique X suppose node v is the first node which is added to produce a clique of size one greater. After the backtracking process examines all possible cliques which are produced from X and v, then no vertex which is adjacent to v need be added to X and examined. Let X and Y be cliques where X is properly contained in Y. If all cliques containing X and vertex v have been generated, then all cliques with Y and v can be ignored. Write a backtracking algorithm which generates the maximal cliques of a directed graph and makes use of these last rules for pruning the state space tree.

32. Define the following terms: state space, tree organization, rearrangement, explicit constraints, implicit constraints, permutation tree, problem state, solution states, answer states, static trees, dynamic trees, live node, E-node, dead node, bounding functions.

Chapter 8

BRANCH-AND-BOUND

8.1 THE METHOD

This chapter makes extensive use of terminology defined in Section 7.1. The reader is urged to review this section before proceeding.

The term branch-and-bound refers to all state space search methods in which all children of the E-node are generated before any other live node can become the E-node. We have already seen two graph search strategies, BFS and D-search, in which the exploration of a new node cannot begin until the node currently being explored is fully explored. Both of these generalize to branch-and-bound strategies. In branch-and-bound terminology, a BFS-like state space search will be called FIFO (First In First Out) search as the list of live nodes is a first-in-first-out list (or queue). A D-search-like state space search will be called LIFO (Last In First Out) search as the list of live nodes is a last-in-first-out list (or stack). As in the case of backtracking, bounding functions are used to help avoid the generation of subtrees that do not contain an answer node.

Example 8.1 (4-queens) Let us see how a FIFO branch-and-bound algorithm would search the state space tree (Figure 7.2) for the 4-queens problem. Initially, there is only one live node, node 1. This represents the case when no queen has been placed on the chessboard. This node becomes the E-node. It is expanded and its children, nodes 2, 18, 34 and 50 are generated. These nodes represent a chessboard with queen 1 in row 1 and columns 1, 2, 3 and 4 respectively. The only live nodes now are nodes 2, 18, 34 and 50. If the nodes were generated in this order, then the next E-node is node 2. It is expanded and nodes 3, 8 and 13 are generated. Node 3 is immediately killed using the bounding function of example 7.5. Nodes 8 and 13 are added to the queue of live nodes. Node 18 becomes the next E-node. Nodes 19, 24 and 29 are generated. Nodes 19 and 24 are killed as a result of the bounding functions. Node 29 is added to the queue of live nodes. The next E-node is node 34. Figure 8.1 shows the portion of the tree of Figure 7.2 that is generated by a FIFO branch-and-bound search. Nodes that get killed as a result of the bounding functions have a B under them. Numbers inside the node correspond to the numbers in figure 7.2. Numbers outside the node give the order in which the nodes are generated by FIFO branch-and-bound. At the time the answer node, node 31, is reached the only live nodes remaining are nodes 38 and 54. A comparison of figures 7.6 and 8.1 indicates that backtracking is a superior search method for this problem. ☐

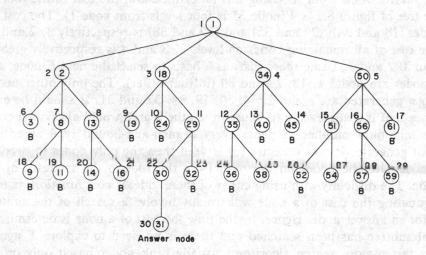

Figure 8.1 Portion of 4-queens state space tree generated by FIFO branch-and-bound

LC-Search

In both LIFO and FIFO branch-and-bound the selection rule for the next E-node is rather rigid and in a sense "blind". The selection rule for the next E-node does not give any preference to a node that has a very good chance of getting the search to an answer node quickly. Thus, in example 8.1 when node 30 is generated, it should have become obvious to the search algorithm that this node will lead to an answer node in one move. However, the rigid FIFO rule requires first the expansion of all live nodes generated before node 30 was generated.

The search for an answer node can often be speeded by using an "intelligent" ranking function, $\hat{c}(\cdot)$, for live nodes. The next E-node is selected on the basis of this ranking function. If in the 4-queens example we use a ranking function that assigns node 30 a better rank than all other live nodes, then node 30 will become the E-node following node 29. The remaining live nodes will never become E-nodes as the expansion of node 30 results in the generation of an answer node (node 31).

The ideal way to assign ranks would be on the basis of the additional computational effort (or cost) needed to reach an answer node from the live node. For any node X, this cost could be (i) the number of nodes in the subtree X that need to be generated before an answer node is generated or more simply, (ii) it could be the number of levels the nearest answer node (in the subtree X) is from X. Using this latter measure, the cost of the root of the tree of figure 8.1 is 4 (node 31 is four levels from node 1). The cost of nodes (18 and 34); (29 and 35) and (30 and 38) is respectively 3, 2 and 1. The cost of all remaining nodes on levels 2, 3 and 4 is respectively greater than 3, 2 and 1. Using these costs as a basis to select the next E-node, the E-nodes are nodes 1, 18, 29 and 30 (in that order). The only other nodes to get generated are nodes 2, 34, 50, 19, 24, 32 and 31. It should be easy to see that if cost measure (i) is used then the search would always generate the minimum number of nodes every branch-and-bound type algorithm must generate. If cost measure (ii) is used then the only nodes to become E-nodes are the nodes on the path from the root to the nearest answer node. The difficulty with using either of these "ideal" cost functions is that computing the cost of a node will usually involve a search of the subtree X for an answer node. Hence, by the time the cost of a node is determined, that subtree has been searched and there is no need to explore X again. For this reason, search algorithms usually rank nodes based only on an estimate, $\hat{g}(\cdot)$, of their cost.

Let $\hat{g}(X)$ be an estimate of the additional effort needed to reach an answer node from X. Node X is assigned a rank using a function $\hat{c}(\cdot)$ such that $\hat{c}(X) = f(h(X)) + \hat{g}(X)$ where $h(X)$ is the cost of reaching X from the root and $f(\ )$ is any nondecreasing function. At first, we may doubt the usefullness of using an $f(\ )$ other than $f(h(X)) = 0$ for all $h(X)$. We can "justify" such an $f(\ )$ on the grounds that the effort already expended in reaching the live nodes cannot be reduced and all we are concerned with now is minimizing the additional effort we will be spending to find an answer node. Hence, the effort already expended need not be considered.

Using $f(\ ) \equiv 0$ usually biases the search algorithm to make deep probes into the search tree. To see this note that we would normally expect $\hat{g}(Y) \le \hat{g}(X)$ for Y a child of X. Hence, following X, Y will become the E-node; then one of Y's children will become the E-node; next one of Y's grandchildren will become the E-node and so on. Nodes in subtrees other than the subtree X will not get generated until the subtree X is fully searched. This would be no cause for concern if $\hat{g}(X)$ was the true cost of X. Then, we would not wish to explore the remaining subtrees in any case (as X is guaranteed to get us to an answer node quicker than any other existing live node). However, $\hat{g}(X)$ is only an estimate of the true cost. So, it is quite possible that for two nodes W and Z, $\hat{g}(W) < \hat{g}(Z)$ and Z is actually much closer to an answer node than W. It is therefore desirable not to over bias the search algorithm in favor of deep probes. By using $f(\cdot) \neq 0$ we can force the search algorithm to favor a node Z close to the root over a node W which is many levels below Z. This would reduce the possibility of deep and fruitless searches into the tree.

A search strategy that uses a cost function $\hat{c}(X) = f(h(x)) + \hat{g}(X)$ to select the next E-node would always choose for its next E-node a live node with least $\hat{c}(\cdot)$. Hence, such a search strategy is called an LC-search (Least Cost search). It is interesting to note that BFS and D-search are special cases of LC-search. If we use $\hat{g}(X) \equiv 0$ and $f(h(x)) =$ level of node X then an LC-search generates nodes by levels. This is essentially the same as a BFS search. If $f(h(x)) \equiv 0$ and $\hat{g}(X) < \hat{g}(Y)$ whenever Y is a child of X then the search is essentially a D-search. An LC-search coupled with bounding functions will be called an LC branch-and-bound search.

In discussing LC-searches we will sometimes make reference to a cost function $c(\cdot)$ defined as follows: if X is an answer node then $c(X)$ is the cost (level, computational difficulty etc.) of reaching X from the root of the state space tree. If X is not an answer node then $c(X) = \infty$ if the subtree X contains no answer node otherwise $c(X)$ equals the cost of a minimum cost answer node in the subtree X. It should be easy to see that $\hat{c}(\cdot)$ with $f(h(X)) = h(X)$ is an approximation to $c(\ )$. From now on $c(X)$ will be referred to as the cost of X.

The 15-puzzle—An Example

The 15-puzzle (invented by Sam Loyd in 1878) consists of 15 numbered tiles on a square frame with a capacity of 16 tiles (Figure 8.2). We are given an initial arrangement of the tiles and the objective is to transform this arrangement into the goal arrangement of Figure 8.3(b) through a series of legal moves. The only legal moves are ones in which a tile adjacent to the empty spot (ES) is moved to ES. Thus from the initial arrangement of Figure 8.2(a), four moves are possible. We can move any one of the tiles numbered 2, 3, 5 or 6 to the empty spot. Following this move, other moves can be made. Each move creates a new arrangement of the tiles. These arrangements will be called the *states* of the puzzle. The initial and goal arrangements are called the initial and goal states. A state is reachable

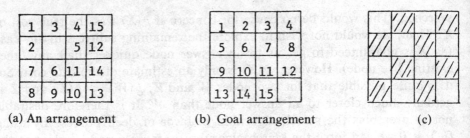

(a) An arrangement   (b) Goal arrangement   (c)

Figure 8.2   15-puzzle arrangements

from the initial state iff there is a sequence of legal moves from the initial state to this state. The state space of an initial state consists of all states that can be reached from the initial state. The most straightforward way to solve the puzzle would be to search the state space for the goal state and use the path from the initial state to the goal state as the answer. It is easy to see that there are 16! (16! $\approx 20.9 \times 10^{12}$) different arrangements of the tiles on the frame. Of these only one half are reachable from any given initial state. Indeed, the state space for the problem is very large. Before attempting to search this state space for the goal state, it would be worthwhile to determine whether or not the goal state is reachable from the initial state. There is a very simple way to do this. Let us number the frame positions 1–16. Position i is the frame position containing tile numbered i in the goal arrangement of Figure 8.2(b). Position 16 is the empty spot. Let POSITION(i) be the position number in the initial state of the tile numbered i. POSITION(16) will denote the position of the empty spot. For any state let LESS(i) be the number of tiles j such that $j < i$ and POSITION(j) > POSITION(i). For the state of Figure 8.2(a) we have, for example, LESS(1) = 0, LESS(4) = 1 and LESS(12) = 6. Let $X = 1$ if in the initial state, the empty spot is at one of the shaded positions of Figure 8.2(c) and $X = 0$ if it is at one of the remaining positions. Then, we have the following theorem:

Theorem 8.1 The goal state of Figure 8.2(b) is reachable from the initial state iff $\sum_{i=1}^{16} \text{LESS}(i) + X$ is even.

Proof: Left as an exercise.   □

Theorem 8.1 may be used to determine whether or not the goal state is in the state space of the initial state. If it is, then we may proceed to determine a sequence of moves leading to the goal state. In order to carry out this search, the state space may be organized into a tree. The children of each node X in this tree represent the states reachable from state X by one legal move. It is convenient to think of a move as actually involving a move of the empty space rather than a move of a tile. The empty space, on each move, moves either up, right, down or left. Figure 8.3(a) shows the first three levels of the state space tree of the 15-puzzle beginning with the initial state shown in the root. Parts of levels 4 and 5 of the tree are also shown. The tree has been pruned a little. No node P has a child state that is the same as P's parent. The subtree eliminated in this way is already present in the tree and has root PARENT(P). As can be seen, there is an answer node at level 4.

A depth first generation of the state space tree will generate the subtree of Figure 8.3(b) when next moves are attempted in the order: move the empty space up, right, down, left. It is clear from successive board configurations that each move gets us farther from the goal rather than closer. The search of the state space tree is blind. It will take the leftmost path from the root regardless of the starting configuration. As a result, an answer node may never be found (unless the left most path ends in such a node). In a FIFO search of the tree of Figure 8.3(a), the nodes will be generated in the order numbered. A breadth first search will always find a goal node nearest to the root. However, such a search is also "blind" in the sense that no matter what the initial configuration, the algorithm attempts to make the same sequence of moves. A FIFO search always generates the state space tree by levels.

What we would like, is a more "intelligent" search method. One that seeks out an answer node and adapts the path it takes through the state space tree to the specific problem instance being solved. With each node X in the state space tree we can associate a cost $c(X)$. $c(X)$ is the length of a path from the root to a nearest goal node (if any) in the subtree with root X. Thus, in Figure 8.3(a), $c(1) = c(4) = c(10) = c(23) = 3$. When such a cost function is available, a very efficient search can be carried out. We begin with the root as the E-node and generate a child node with $c(\ )$ value the same as the root. Thus children nodes 2, 3 and 5 are eliminated and only node 4 becomes a live node. This becomes the next E-node. Its first child, node 10, has $c(10) = c(4) = 34$. The remaining children are not generated. Node 4 dies and node 10 becomes the E-node. In generating node 10's children, node 22 is killed immediately as $c(22) > 3$. Node 23 is generated next. It is a goal node and the search terminates. In this search strategy, the only nodes to become E-nodes are nodes on the path from the root to a nearest goal node. Unfortunately, this is an impractical strategy as it is not possible to easily compute the function $c(\cdot)$ specified above.

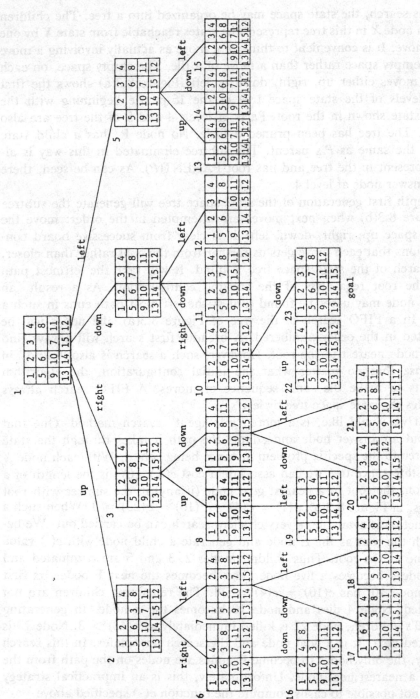

Figure 8.3(a)   Part of the state space tree for the 15-puzzle
edges are labeled according to the direction in which the empty space moves

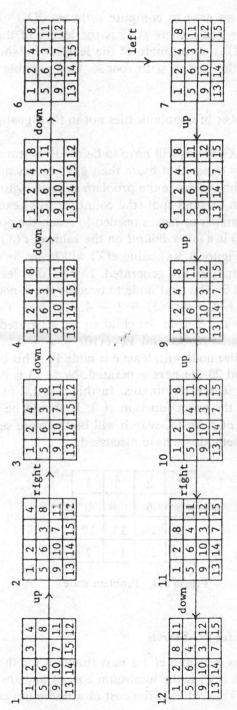

Figure 8.3(b) First ten steps in a depth first search

We can arrive at an easy to compute estimate $\hat{c}(X)$ of $c(X)$. We can write $\hat{c}(X) = f(X) + \hat{g}(X)$ where $f(X)$ is the length of the path from the root node X and $\hat{g}(X)$ is an estimate of the length of a shortest path from X to a goal node in the subtree with root X. One possible choice for $\hat{g}(X)$ is:

$$\hat{g}(X) = \text{number of nonblank tiles not in their goal position}$$

Clearly, at least $\hat{g}(X)$ moves will have to be made to transform state X to a goal state. It is easy to see that more than $\hat{g}(X)$ moves may be needed to achieve this. To see this, examine the problem state of Figure 8.4. $\hat{g}(X) = 1$ as only tile 7 is not in its final spot (the count for $\hat{g}(X)$ excludes the blank tile). However, the number of moves needed to reach the goal state is many more than $\hat{g}(X)$. $\hat{c}(X)$ is a *lower bound* on the value of $\hat{c}(X)$.

An LC search of Figure 8.3(a) using $\hat{c}(X)$ will begin by using node 1 as the E-node. All its children are generated. Node 1 dies leaving behind the live nodes 2, 3, 4 and 5. The next node to become the E-node is a live node with least $\hat{c}(X)$. $\hat{c}(2) = 1 + 4$, $\hat{c}(3) = 1 + 4$, $\hat{c}(4) = 1 + 2$ and $\hat{c}(5) = 1 + 4$. Node 4 becomes the E-node. Its children are generated. The live nodes at this time are 2, 3, 5, 10, 11 and 12. $\hat{c}(10) = 2 + 1$, $\hat{c}(11) = 2 + 3$, $\hat{c}(12) = 2 + 3$. The live node with least $\hat{c}$ is node 10. This becomes the next E-node. Nodes 22 and 23 are next generated. Node 23 is determined to be a goal node and the search terminates. In this case LC-search was almost as efficient as using the exact function $c( )$. It should be noted that with a suitable choice for $\hat{c}( )$, an LC-search will be far more selective than any of the other search methods we have discussed.

1	2	3	4
5	6		8
9	10	11	12
13	14	15	7

Figure 8.4   Problem state

Control Abstractions for LC-Search

Let T be a state space tree and $c( )$ a cost function for the nodes in T. If X is a node in T then $c(X)$ is the minimum cost of any answer node in the subtree with root X. Thus, $c(T)$ is the cost of a minimum cost answer node in T. As remarked earlier, it will usually not be possible to find an easily computable function $c(\ )$ as defined above. Instead, a heuristic $\hat{c}(\ )$ that estimates $c(\ )$ will be used. This heuristic should be easy to compute and will generally have the property that if X is either an answer node or a leaf node then $c(X) = \hat{c}(X)$. Procedure LC (Algorithm 8.1) uses $\hat{c}$ to find an answer node. The algorithm uses two subalgorithms LEAST(X) and ADD(X) to respectively delete and add a live node from or to the list of live nodes. LEAST(X) finds a live node with least $\hat{c}(\ )$. This node is deleted from the list of live nodes and returned in variable X. ADD(X) adds the new live node X to the list of live nodes. The list of live nodes will usually be implemented as a min-heap (Section 2.3). Procedure LC outputs the path from the answer node it finds to the root node T. This is easy to do if with each node X that becomes live, we associate a variable PARENT(X) which gives the parent of node X. When an answer node G is found, the path from G to T can be determined by following a sequence of PARENT values starting from the current E-node (which is the parent of G) and ending at node T.

The correctness of algorithm LC is easy to establish. Variable E always points to the current E-node. By definition of LC-search, the root node is

line   procedure $LC\ (T, \hat{c})$
          //search T for an answer node. It is assumed that T is not//
          //an answer node//
1       $E \leftarrow T$ //E-node//
2   initialize the list of live nodes to be empty
3   **loop**
4   **for** each child X of E **do**
5   **if** X is an answer node **then** output the path from X to T
6   **return**
7   **endif**
8   **call** $ADD(X)$ //X is a new live node//
9               $PARENT(X) \leftarrow E$ //pointer for path to root//
10   **repeat**
11   **if** there are no more live nodes **then print** ('no answer node')
12   **stop**
13   **endif**
14   **call** $LEAST(E)$
15   **repeat**
16   **end** LC

Algorithm 8.1 LC-search

the first E-node (line 1). Line 2 initializes the list of live nodes. At any time during the execution of LC, this list contains all live nodes except the E-node. Thus, initially this list should be empty (line 2). The **for** loop of lines 4–10 examines all the children of the E-node. If one of the children is an answer node then the algorithm outputs the path from X to T and terminates. If a child of E is not an answer node then it becomes a live node. It is added to the list of live nodes (line 8) and its PARENT field set to E. When all the children of E have been generated, E becomes a dead node and line 11 is reached. This happens only if none of E's children is an answer node. So, the search must continue further. In case there are no live nodes left then the entire state space tree has been searched and no answer nodes found. The algorithm terminates in line 12. Otherwise, LEAST(X), by definition correctly chooses the next E-node and the search continues from here.

From the preceding discussion, it is clear that LC terminates only when either an answer node is found or when the entire state space tree has been generated and searched. Thus, termination is guaranteed only for finite state space trees. Termination can also be guaranteed for infinite state space trees that have at least one answer node provided a "proper" choice for the cost function, $\hat{c}(\ )$, is made. This is the case, for example, when $\hat{c}(X) > \hat{c}(Y)$ for every pair of nodes X and Y such that the level number of X is "sufficiently" higher than that of Y. For infinite state space trees with no answer nodes, LC will not terminate. Thus, it is advisable to restrict the search to find answer nodes with a cost no more than a given bound C.

One should note the similarity between algorithm LC and algorithms for a breadth first search and D-search of a state space tree. If the list of live nodes is implemented as a queue with LEAST(X) and ADD(X) being algorithms to delete an element from and add an element to the queue then LC will be transformed to a FIFO search schema. If the list of live nodes is implemented as a stack with LEAST(X) and ADD(X) being algorithms to delete and add elements to the stack then LC will carry out a LIFO search of the state space tree. Thus, the algorithms for LC, FIFO and LIFO search are essentially the same. The only difference is in the implementation of the list of live nodes. This is to be expected as the three search methods differ only in the selection rule used to obtain the next E-node.

Properties of LC-Search

Let us explore some properties of procedure LC. In many applications it is desirable to find an answer node that has minimum cost among all answer

nodes. Does LC necessarily find an answer node G with minimum cost
$c(G)$? The answer to this is no. Consider the state space tree of Figure 8.5.
Square leaf nodes are answer nodes. Associated with each node is a pair of
numbers. The upper number is the value of c and the lower the estimate
$\hat{c}$. Thus, $c(\text{root}) = 10$ and $\hat{c}(\text{root}) = 0$. It is clear that LC will first generate
the two children of the root and then the node with $\hat{c}(\ ) = 2$ will become
the E-node. The expansion of this node leads us to the answer node G
with $\hat{c}(G) = c(G) = 20$ and the algorithm terminates. The minimum cost
answer node G has cost $c(G) = 10$. The reason LC did not get to the minimum cost answer node is that the function $\hat{c}$ is such that there exist two
nodes X and Y such that $\hat{c}(X) < \hat{c}(Y)$ while $c(X) > c(Y)$. As a result LC
will choose node X as an E-node before node Y and possibly terminate
finding an answer node which is a descendent of X. If $\hat{c}(X) < \hat{c}(Y)$ for
every pair of nodes X, Y such that $c(X) < c(Y)$ then, one may show that
LC always finds a minimum cost answer node in a finite state space tree
that has at least one answer node.

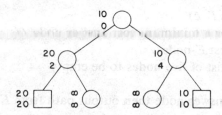

Figure 8.5   LC-search

Theorem 8.2   For every node X in a finite state space tree T let $\hat{c}(X)$ be an
estimate of $c(X)$ such that for every pair of nodes Y, Z, $\hat{c}(Y) < \hat{c}(Z)$ iff
$c(Y) < c(Z)$. Algorithm LC using $\hat{c}(\ )$ as an estimator for $c(\ )$ reaches a
minimum cost answer node and terminates.

Proof: We have already stated that when T is finite, LC finds an answer
node if T has such a node. So, assume LC terminates at an answer node G
such that $c(G) > c(G')$ where G' is a minimum cost answer node. Let R
be the nearest ancestor of G such that the subtree R includes a minimum
cost answer node (Figure 8.6). Let $R, \alpha_1, \alpha_2, \ldots, \alpha_k, G'$ be the path from
R to G' and let $R, \beta_1, \beta_2, \ldots, \beta_j, G$ be the path from R to G. By definition of R, $\alpha_1 \neq \beta_1$ and the subtree β_1 has no answer node with cost $c(G')$.
In order for the search to reach node G, R must become an E-node at
some time. At this time its children (including α_1 and β_1) become live

nodes. From the definition of $c(\ )$, it follows that $c(R) = c(\alpha_1) = c(\alpha_2) = \cdots = c(G')$ and $c(\beta_1), c(\beta_2), \ldots, c(G) > c(R)$. Hence, from the condition on $\hat{c}(\ )$ it follows that $\hat{c}(\alpha_1), \hat{c}(\alpha_2), \ldots, \hat{c}(\alpha_k) < \hat{c}(\beta_1)$ and so β_1 cannot become an E-node until $\alpha_i 1 \le i \le k$ become E-nodes and G' is reached. $\square$

This theorem is easily extended to infinitite state space trees in which each node is of finite degree. It is usually not possible to obtain an easily computable $\hat{c}(\ )$ that meets the requirement of Theorem 8.2. We can often only find a $\hat{c}(\ )$ that is easy to compute and has the property that for each node X, $\hat{c}(X) \le c(X)$. In this case, algorithm LC does not necessarily find a minimum cost answer node (Figure 8.5). When $\hat{c}(X) \le c(X)$ for every node X and $\hat{c}(X) = c(X)$ for X an answer node, a slight modification to LC results in a search algorithm that terminates when a minimum cost answer node is reached. In this modification, the search continues until an answer node becomes the E-node. The new algorithm is LC1 (Algorithm 8.2).

```
line    procedure LC1 (T, ĉ)
        //search T for a minimum cost answer node.//
1         E ← T   //first E-node//
2         initialize the list of live nodes to be empty
3         loop
4           if E is an answer node then output path from E to T
5                                    return
6           endif
7           for each child X of E do
8             call ADD(X); PARENT(X) ← E
9           repeat
10          if there are no more live nodes then print ('no answer node')
11                                    stop
12          endif
13          call LEAST(E)
14        repeat
15      end LC1
```

Algorithm 8.2   LC – search for least cost answer node

Theorem 8.3   Let $\hat{c}(\cdot)$ be such that $\hat{c}(X) \le c(X)$ for every node X in a state space tree T and $\hat{c}(X) = c(X)$ for every answer node X in T. If algorithm LC1 terminates in line 5 then the answer node found is of minimum cost.

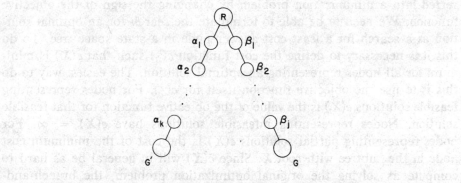

Figure 8.6 Infinite state space tree

Proof: At the time the E-node E is an answer node, $\hat{c}(E) \le \hat{c}(L)$ for every live node L on the list of live nodes. By assumption, $\hat{c}(E) = c(E)$ and $\hat{c}(L) \le c(L)$ for every live node L. Hence $c(E) \le c(L)$ and so E is a minimum cost answer node. $\square$

Bounding

A branch-and-bound method searches a state space tree using any search mechanism in which all the children of the E-node are generated before another node becomes the E-node. We shall assume that each answer node X has a cost $c(X)$ associated with it and that a minimum cost answer node is to be found. Three common search strategies are FIFO, LIFO and LC. (Another method, Heuristic search, is discussed in the exercises.) A cost function $\hat{c}(\cdot)$ such that $\hat{c}(X) \le c(X)$ is used to provide lower bounds on solutions obtainable from any node X. If U is an upper bound on the cost of a minimum cost solution then all live nodes X with $\hat{c}(X) > U$ may be killed as all answer nodes reachable from X have cost $c(X) \ge \hat{c}(X) > U$. In case an answer node with cost U has already been reached then all live nodes with $\hat{c}(X) \ge U$ may be killed. The starting value for U may be obtained by some heuristic or may be set to ∞. Clearly, so long as the initial value for U is no less than the cost of a minimum cost answer node, the above rules to kill live nodes will not result in the killing of a live node that can reach a minimum cost answer node. Each time a new answer node is found, the value of U may be updated.

Let us see how these ideas may be used to arrive at branch-and-bound algorithms for optimization problems. In this section we shall deal directly only with minimization problems. A maximization problem is easily converted into a minimization problem by changing the sign of the objective function. We need to be able to formulate the search for an optimal solution as a search for a least cost answer node in a state space tree. To do this it is necessary to define the cost function $c(\cdot)$ such that $c(X)$ is minimum for all nodes representing an optimal solution. The easiest way to do this is to use the objective function itself for $c(\cdot)$. For nodes representing feasible solutions $c(X)$ is the value of the objective function for that feasible solution. Nodes representing infeasible solutions have $c(X) = \infty$. For nodes representing partial solutions $c(X)$ is the cost of the minimum cost node in the subtree with root X. Since $c(X)$ will in general be as hard to compute as solving the original optimization problem, the branch-and-bound algorithm will use an estimate $\hat{c}(X)$ such that $\hat{c}(X) \leq c(X)$ for all X. In general then, the $\hat{c}(\cdot)$ function used in the branch-and-bound solution to optimization functions will estimate the objective function value and not the computational difficulty of reaching an answer node. In addition, to be consistent with the terminology used in connection with the 15-puzzle, any node representing a feasible solution (a solution node) will be an answer node. However, only minimum cost answer nodes will correspond to an optimal solution. Thus, answer nodes and solution nodes are indistinguishable.

As an example optimization problem, consider the job sequencing with deadlines problem introduced in section 4.4. We shall generalize this problem to allow jobs with different processing times. We are given n jobs and one processor. Each job i has associated with it a three tuple (p_i, d_i, t_i). Job i requires t_i units of processing time. If its processing is not completed by the deadline d_i then a penalty p_i is incurred. The objective is to select a subset J of the n jobs such that all jobs in J can be completed by their deadlines. Hence, a penalty can be incurred only on those jobs not in J. J should be a subset such that the penalty incurred is minimum among all possible subsets J. Such a J is optimal.

Consider the following instance: $n = 4$; $(p_1, d_1, t_1) = (5, 1, 1)$; $(p_2, d_2, t_2) = (10, 3, 2)$; $(p_3, d_3, t_3) = (6, 2, 1)$ and $(p_4, d_4, t_4) = (3, 1, 1)$. The solution space for this instance consists of all possible subsets of the job index set $\{1, 2, 3, 4\}$. The solution space may be organized into a tree using either of the two formulations used for the sum of subsets problem (example 7.3). Figure 8.7 corresponds to the variable tuple size formulation while Figure 8.8 corresponds to the fixed tuple size formulation. In both figures square nodes represent infeasible subsets. In Figure 8.7 all nonsquare nodes are answer nodes. Node 9 represents an optimal solution and is the only minimum cost answer node. For this node $J = \{2, 3\}$ and the penalty (cost) is 8. In Figure 8.8 only nonsquare leaf nodes are answer nodes. Node 25 represents the optimal solution and is also a minimum cost answer node. This node corresponds to $J = \{2, 3\}$ and a penalty of 8. The costs of the answer nodes of Figure 8.8 is given below the nodes.

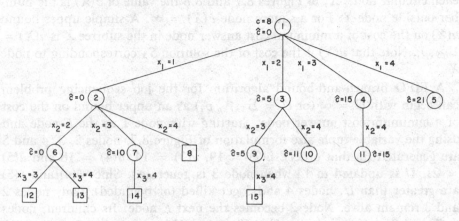

Figure 8.7 State space tree corresponding to variable tuple size formulation

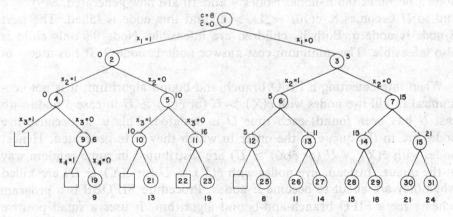

Figure 8.8 State space tree corresponding to fixed tuple size formulation

We can define a cost function $c(\ )$ for the state space formulations of Figures 8.7 and 8.8. For any circular node X, $c(X)$ is the minimum penalty corresponding to any node in the subtree with root X. $c(X) = \infty$ for a square node. In the tree of Figure 8.7, $c(3) = 8$, $c(2) = 9$ and $c(1) = 8$. In the tree of Figure 8.8, $c(1) = 8$, $c(2) = 9$, $c(5) = 13$ and $c(6) = 8$. Clearly, $c(1)$ is the penalty corresponding to an optimal selection J.

A bound $\hat{c}(X)$ such that $\hat{c}(X) \le c(X)$ for all X is easy to obtain. Let S_X be the subset of jobs selected for J at node X. If $m = \max\{i \,|\, i \in S_X\}$ then $\hat{c}(X) = \sum\limits_{\substack{i < m \\ i \notin S_X}} p_i$ is an estimate for $c(X)$ with the property $\hat{c}(X) \le c(X)$. For each circular node, X, in Figures 8.7 and 8.8 the value of $\hat{c}(X)$ is the number outside node X. For a square node $\hat{c}(X) = \infty$. A simple upper bound $u(X)$ on the cost of a minimum cost answer node in the subtree X is $u(X) = \sum_{i \notin S_X} p_i$. Note that $u(X)$ is the cost of the solution S_X corresponding to node X.

A FIFO branch-and-bound algorithm for the job sequencing problem can begin with $U = \infty$ (or $U = \sum_{1 \le i \le n} p_i$) as an upper bound on the cost of a minimum cost answer node. Starting with node 1 as the E-node and using the variable tuple size formulation of Figure 8.7, nodes 2, 3, 4 and 5 are generated (in that order). $u(2) = 19$, $u(3) = 14$, $u(4) = 18$ and $u(5) = 21$. U is updated to 14 when node 3 is generated. Since $\hat{c}(4)$ and $\hat{c}(5)$ are greater than U, nodes 4 and 5 get killed (or bounded). Only nodes 2 and 3 remain alive. Node 2 becomes the next E-node. Its children, nodes 6, 7, and 8 are generated. $u(6) = 9$ and so U is updated to 9. $\hat{c}(7) = 10 > U$ and node 7 gets killed. Node 8 is infeasible and so it is killed. Next, node 3 becomes the E-node. Nodes 9 and 10 are now generated. $u(9) = 8$ and so U becomes 8. $\hat{c}(10) = 11 > U$ and this node is killed. The next E-node is node 6. Both its children are infeasible. Node 9's only child is also infeasible. The minimum cost answer node is node 9. It has a cost of 8.

When implementing a FIFO branch-and-bound algorithm, it is not economical to kill live nodes with $\hat{c}(X) > U$ (or $\hat{c}(X) \ge U$ in case a node with cost U has been found) each time U is updated. This is so because live nodes are in the queue in the order in which they were generated. Hence, nodes with $\hat{c}(X) > U$ (or $\hat{c}(X) \ge U$) are distributed in some random way in the queue. Instead, live nodes with $\hat{c}(X) > U$ (or $\hat{c}(X) \ge U$) are killed when they are about to become E-nodes. Procedure FIFOBB is a program schema for a FIFO branch-and-bound algorithm. It uses a small positive constant ϵ such that if for any two feasible nodes X and Y $u(X) < u(Y)$, then $u(X) < u(X) + \epsilon < u(Y)$. This ϵ is needed to distinguish between the case when a solution with cost $u(X)$ has been found and the case when such a solution has not been found. If the latter is the case then U is updated to $\min\{U, u(X) + \epsilon\}$. When U is updated in this way, live nodes Y with $u(Y) \ge U$ may be killed. This does not kill the node that promised to lead to a solution with value $\le U$. We may dispense with this use of ϵ if every feasible node X that is generated defines a feasible solution and $u(X) = $ cost of X. This is true, for example, for Figure 8.7 with $u(\cdot)$

as defined above. FIFOBB also uses the subalgorithms ADDQ(X) and DELETEQ(X). These algorithms respectively add a node to a queue and delete a node from a queue. For every solution node X in the state space tree $COST(X)$ is the cost of the solution corresponding to node X. FIFOBB assumes $\hat{c}(X) = \infty$ for infeasible nodes and $\hat{c}(X) \le c(X) \le u(X)$ for feasible nodes.

```
line   procedure FIFOBB (T, ĉ, u, ε, cost)
         //Search T for a least cost answer (solution) node. It is//
         //assumed that T contains at least one solution node and//
         //ĉ(X) ≤ c(X) ≤ u(X).//
  1        E ← T; PARENT(E) ← 0;
  2        if T is a solution node then U ← min(cost(T), u(T) + ε); ans ← T
  3                             else U ← u(T) + ε; ans ← 0
  4        endif
  5        initialize queue to be empty
  6        loop
  7          for each child X of E do
  8            if ĉ(X) < U then call ADDQ(X); PARENT(X) ← E
  9                        case
 10                          :X is a solution node and cost(X) < U:
 11                            U ← min (cost(X), u(X) + ε)
 12                            ans ← X
 13                          :u(X) + ε < U:U ← u(X) + ε
 14                        endcase
 15            endif
 16          repeat
 17          loop   //get next E-node//
 18            if queue is empty then print ('least cost =', U)
 19              while ans ≠ 0 do
 20                print (ans)
 21                ans ← PARENT(ans)
 22              repeat
 23            endif
 24            call DELETEQ(X)
 25            if ĉ(X) < U then exit   //kill nodes with ĉ(X) ≥ U//
 26          repeat
 27        repeat
 28      end FIFOBB
```

Algorithm 8.3 FIFO branch-and-bound to find minimum cost answer node

LC Branch-and-Bound

An LC branch-and-bound search of the tree of Figure 8.7 will begin with $U = \infty$ and node 1 as the first E-node. When node 1 is expanded, nodes 2, 3, 4 and 5 are generated in that order. As in the case of FIFO branch-and-bound, U is updated to 14 when node 3 is generated and nodes 4 and 5 are killed as $u(4) > U$ and $u(5) > U$. Node 2 is the next E-node as $\hat{c}(2) = 0$ while $\hat{c}(3) = 5$. Nodes 6, 7 and 8 are generated. U is updated to 9 when node 6 is generated. So, node 7 is killed as $\hat{c}(7) = 10 > U$. Node 8 is infeasible and so killed. The only live nodes now are nodes 3 and 6. Node 6 is the next E-node as $\hat{c}(6) = 0 < \hat{c}(3)$. Both its children are infeasible. Node 3 becomes the next E-node. When node 9 is generated U is updated to 8 as $u(9) = 8$. So, node 10 with $\hat{c}(10) = 11$ is killed upon generation. Node 9 becomes the next E-node. Its only child is infeasible. No live nodes remain. The search terminates with node 9 representing the minimum cost answer node. An LC branch-and-bound algorithm may also terminate when the next E-node E has $\hat{c}(E) \geq U$.

The control abstraction for LC branch-and-bound is LCBB. It operates under the same assumptions as FIFOBB. ADD and LEAST are algorithms to respectively add a node to a min-heap and delete a node from a min-heap.

```
line   procedure LCBB (T, ĉ, u, ∈, cost)
          //search T for a least cost answer (solution) node. It is assumed//
          //that T contains at least one solution node and ĉ(X) ≤ c(X) ≤//
          //u(X).//
1          E ← T; PARENT(E) ← 0
2          if T is a solution node then U ← min(cost(T), u(T) + ∈); ans ← T
3                                 else U ← u(T) + ∈; ans ← 0
4          endif
5          initialize the list of live nodes to be empty
6          loop
7             for each child X of E do
8                if ĉ(X) < U then call ADD(X)
9                              PARENT(X) ← E
10                             case
11                                :X is a solution node and cost(X) < U:
12                                  U ← min(cost (X), u(X) + ∈)
13
14                                :u(X) + ∈ < U: U ← u(X) + ∈
15                             endcase
16               endif
17            repeat
18            if there are no more live nodes or the next E-node
19            has ĉ ≥ U then print ('least cost =', U)
20               while ans ≠ 0 do
21                  print (ans)
22                  ans ← PARENT(ans)
23               repeat
24            endif
25            call LEAST(E)
26         repeat
27      end LCBB
```

Algorithm 8.4 LC branch-and-bound to find minimum cost answer node

8.2 ZERO-ONE KNAPSACK PROBLEM

In order to use the branch-and-bound technique to solve any problem, it is first necessary to conceive of a state space tree for the problem. We have already seen two possible state space tree organizations for the knapsack problem (Section 7.6). Still, we cannot directly apply the techniques of Section 8.1 since these were discussed with respect to minimization problems whereas the knapsack problem is a maximization problem. This difficulty is easily overcome by replacing the objective function $\Sigma\ p_i x_i$ by the function $-\Sigma p_i x_i$. Clearly, $\Sigma p_i x_i$ is maximized iff $-\Sigma p_i x_i$ is minimized. This modified knapsack problem is stated as (8.1).

$$\text{minimize} -\sum_{i=1}^{n} p_i x_i$$

$$\text{subject to } \sum_{i=1}^{n} w_i x_i \le M \tag{8.1}$$

$$x_i = 0 \text{ or } 1, \qquad 1 \le i \le n$$

We continue the discussion assuming a fixed tuple size formulation for the solution space. The discussion is easily extended to the variable tuple size formulation. Every leaf node in the state space tree representing an assignment for which $\Sigma_{1 \le i \le n}\ w_i x_i \le M$ is an answer (or solution) node. All other leaf nodes are infeasible. In order for a minimum cost answer node to correspond to any optimal solution, we need to define $c(X) = -\Sigma_{1 \le i \le n}\ p_i x_i$ for every answer node X. $c(X) = \infty$ for infeasible leaf nodes. For nonleaf nodes, $c(X)$ is recursively defined to be $\min\{c(\text{LCHILD}(X)), c(\text{RCHILD}(X))\}$.

We now need two functions $\hat{c}(X)$ and $u(X)$ such that $\hat{c}(X) \le c(X) \le u(X)$ for every node X. $\hat{c}(\cdot)$ and $u(\cdot)$ satisfying this requirement may be obtained as follows. Let X be a node at level j, $1 \le j \le n + 1$. At node X assignments have already been made to x_i, $1 \le i < j$. The cost of these assignments is $-\Sigma_{1 \le i < j} p_i x_i$. So, $c(X) \le -\Sigma_{1 \le i < j} p_i x_i$ and we may use $u(x) = -\Sigma_{1 \le i < j} p_i x_i$. If $q = -\Sigma_{1 \le i < j} p_i x_i$ then an improved upper bound function $u(X)$ is $u(X) = \text{UBOUND}(q, \Sigma_{1 \le i < j} w_i x_i, j - 1, M)$ where UBOUND is defined by Algorithm 8.5. As for $c(X)$, it is clear that $-\text{BOUND}(-q, \Sigma_{1 \le i < j} w_i x_i, j - 1, M) \le c(X)$ where BOUND is Algorithm 7.10.

procedure UBOUND (p, w, k, m)

    $//p, w, k$ and m have the same meaning as in Algorithm 7.10$//$

    $//W(i)$ and $P(i)$ are respectively the weight and profit of the ith object$//$

    global $W(1:n), P(1:n)$; **integer** i, k, n

    $b \leftarrow p; c \leftarrow w$

    for $i \leftarrow k + 1$ **to** n **do**

      if $c + W(i) \leq m$ **then** $c \leftarrow c + W(i); b \leftarrow b - P(i)$ **endif**

    repeat

    return (b)

end UBOUND

Algorithm 8.5 Function $u(\ \ )$ for knapsack problem

LC Branch-and-Bound Solution

Example 8.2 (LCBB) Consider the knapsack instance: $n = 4$; $(p_1, p_2, p_3, p_4) = (10, 10, 12, 18)$; $(w_1, w_2, w_3, w_4) = (2, 4, 6, 9)$ and $M = 15$. Let us trace the working of an LC branch-and-bound search using $\hat{c}(\ )$ and $u(\ )$ as defined above. We shall continue to use the fixed tuple size formulation. The search begins with the root as the E-node. For this node, node 1 of Figure 8.9, we have $\hat{c}(1) = -38$ and $u(1) = -32$. Since this is not a solution node, procedure LCBB sets $ans = 0$ and $U = -32 + \epsilon$. The E-node is expanded and its two children, nodes 2 and 3 generated. $\hat{c}(2) = -38, \hat{c}(3) = -32, u(2) = -32$ and $u(3) = -27$. Both nodes are put onto the list of live nodes. Node 2 is the next E-node. It is expanded and nodes 4 and 5 generated. Both nodes get added to the list of live nodes. Node 4 is the live node with least $\hat{c}$ value and becomes the next E-node. Nodes 6 and 7 are generated. Assuming node 6 is generated first, it gets onto the list of live nodes. Next node 7 gets onto this list and U is updated to $-38 + \epsilon$. The next E-node will be one of nodes 6 and 7. Let us assume it is node 7. Its two children are nodes 8 and 9. Node 8 is a solution node, U is updated to -38 and node 8 is put onto the live nodes list. Node 9 has $\hat{c}(9) > U$ and is killed immediately. Nodes 6 and 8 are two live nodes with least $\hat{c}$. Regardless of which becomes the next E-node, $\hat{c}(E) \geq U$ and the search terminates with node 8 the answer node. At this time, the value -38 together with the path 8, 7, 4, 2, 1 is printed out and the algorithm terminates. From the path one cannot figure out the assignment of values to the x_i's such that $\Sigma p_i x_i = U$. Hence, a proper implementation of procedure LCBB will have to keep additional information from which the values of the x_i's may be extracted. One way is to associate with each node a one bit field, TAG. The sequence of TAG bits from the answer node to the root give the x_i values. Thus, we will have TAG(2) = TAG(4) = TAG(6) = TAG(8) = 1 and TAG(3) = TAG(5) = TAG(7) = TAG(9) = 0. The TAG sequence for the path 8, 7, 4, 2, 1 is 1 0 11 and so $x_4 = 1$, $x_3 = 0$, $x_2 = 1$ and $x_1 = 1$.   □

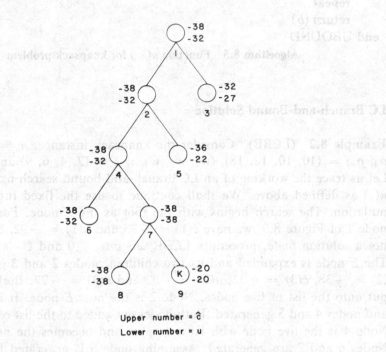

Upper number = $\hat{c}$
Lower number = u

Figure 8.9   LC Branch-and-bound tree for Example 8.2

In order to use procedure LCBB (Algorithm 8.5) to solve the knapsack problem, we need to specify (i) the structure of nodes in the state space tree being searched, (ii) how to generate the children of a given node; (iii) how to recognize a solution node; (iv) a representation of the list of live nodes and subalgorithms ADD and LEAST. The node structure needed will depend on which of the two formulations for the state space tree is being used. Let us continue with a fixed size tuple formulation. Each node X that is generated and put onto the list of live nodes must have a PARENT field. In addition, as noted in Example 8.2, each node should have a one bit TAG field. This field is needed to output the x_i values corresponding to an optimal solution. In order to be able to generate X's children, we shall need to know the level of node X in the state space tree. For this we shall use a field LEVEL. The left child of X is obtained by setting $x_{\text{LEVEL}(X)}$ = 1 and the right child by setting $x_{\text{LEVEL}(X)}$ = 0. In order to determine the feasibility of the left child, we need to know the amount of knapsack space available at node X. This can be determined either by following the path from node X to the root or by explicitly retaining this value in the node. We choose to retain this value in a field CU (capacity unused). The evaluation of $\hat{c}(X)$ and $u(X)$ requires knowledge of the profit $\sum_{1 \leq i < \text{LEVEL}(X)} p_i x_i$ earned by the filling corresponding to node X.

This may be computed by following the path from X to the root. Alternatively, this value may be explicitly retained in a field PE. Finally, in order to determine the live node with least $\hat{c}$ value or to insert nodes properly into the list of live nodes, we need to know $\hat{c}(X)$. Again, we have a choice. $\hat{c}(X)$ may be stored explicitly in a field UB or may be computed when needed. Assuming all information is kept explicitly, we need nodes with six fields each: PARENT, LEVEL, TAG, CU, PE and UB.

Using this six field node structure, the children of any live node X may be easily determined. The left child, Y, is feasible iff $CU(X) \geq w_{\text{LEVEL}(X)}$. In this case, $PARENT(Y) = X$; $LEVEL(Y) = LEVEL(X) + 1$; $CU(Y) = CU(X) - w_{\text{LEVEL}(X)}$; $PE(Y) = PE(X) + p_{\text{LEVEL}(X)}$; $TAG(Y) = 1$ and $UB(Y) = UB(X)$. The right child may be generated similarly. Solution nodes are easily recognized too. Node X is a solution node iff $LEVEL(X) = n + 1$.

We are now left with the task of specifying the representation of the list of live nodes. The functions we wish to perform on this list are: a) test if the list is empty b) add nodes and c) delete a node with least UB. We have seen a data structure that allows us to perform these three functions efficiently: a min-heap. If there are m live nodes then function a) can be carried out in $\theta(1)$ time while b) and c) require only $O(\log n)$ time.

While the preceding discussion together with procedure LCBB result in a complete specification of an LC branch-and-bound algorithm for the knapsack problem, some improvement in algorithm efficiency results if we tailor LCBB to this specific problem. First, our tailored algorithm will compute $-\hat{c}$ and $-u$, which are nonnegative quantities, rather than $\hat{c}$ and u. In addition, we shall retain $L = -U$ rather than U. Also, for any live node X, $UB(X) = -\hat{c}(X)$. These changes only result in minor changes in procedure LCBB. These changes are:

   i)   The conditional of line 8 becomes **if** $UB(X) > L$ **then**

   ii) the conditional of line 11 becomes :$LEVEL(X) = n + 1$ **and** $PE(X) > L$:

iii)   line 12 becomes $L \leftarrow PE(X)$
iv)   line 14 becomes $: -u(X) - \epsilon > L:$ $L \leftarrow -u(X) - \epsilon$
v)   the conditional of line 19 becomes $UB(X) \le L$
vi)   in line 25 the next E node is the live node with maximum UB.

While these changes do not materially affect the running time of the resulting algorithm, they result in an algorithm that mirrors the "maximization" formulation of the problem rather than the "minimization" formulation (8.1). Thus L is a *l*ower bound on the value of an optimal filling and $UB(X)$ is an *u*pper *b*ound on the maximum filling obtainable from any solution node in the subtree with root X. The remaining changes we shall make will reduce the running time of the search algorithm. The final algorithm is procedure LCKNAP.

LCKNAP makes use of the subalgorithms LUBOUND (Algorithm 8.6); NEWNODE (Algorithm 8.7(a)); FINISH (Algorithm 8.7(b)), INIT and GETNODE. LUBOUND computes $-\hat{c}(\cdot)$ and $-u(\cdot)$. NEWNODE creates a new six field node, sets the fields appropriately and adds this node to the list of live nodes. Procedure FINISH prints out the value of the optimal solution as well as the objects with $x_i = 1$ in an optimal solution. INIT initializes the list of available nodes and also the list of live nodes. Since nodes are never freed by the algorithms, nodes may be used sequentially *i.e.* nodes 1 through m may be assigned in the order 1, 2, ..., m. GETNODE gets a free node. In accordance with conventions established in Section 8.1, L will be the larger of the value of the best solution found so far and the highest lower bound computed by LUBOUND less ϵ. ϵ is a "small" positive number.

The parameters to LCKNAP are P, W, M and N. N is the number of objects. $P(i)$ and $W(i)$, $1 \le i \le N$ are the profits and weights respectively. The objects are indexed such that $P(i)/W(i) \ge P(i + 1)/W(i + 1)$, $1 \le i < N$. M is the capacity of the knapsack. Lines 1-5 initialize the list of free nodes and the root node of the search tree. This root node E is the first E-node. The loop of lines 6-24, successively examines each of the live nodes generated. The loop terminates either when there are no live nodes remaining (line 22) or when the next node, E, selected for expansion (the next E-node) is such that $UB(E) \le L$ (line 24). The termination at line 24 is valid as the node selected to be the next E-node is a live node with maximum $UB(E)$. Hence, for all other live nodes X, $UB(X) \le UB(E) \le L$ and none of them can lead to a solution node with value greater than L. Within this loop, the new E-node E is examined. This node is either a leaf node ($LEVEL(E) = n + 1$) or it has exactly two children. In case it is a leaf, then it is a solution node and may be a new candidate for the answer node. Lines 9-11 determine this. In case E is not a leaf node, its two children are generated.

The left child, X, corresponds to $x_i = 1$ and the right, Y, to $x_i = 0$ where $i = \text{LEVEL}(E)$. The left child is feasible (i.e. can lead to a solution node) iff there is enough space left in the knapsack to accommodate x_i (cap $\geq W(i)$). In case this child is feasible and from the way the upper bound is computed by LUBOUND, it follows that $\text{UB}(X) = \text{UB}(E)$. Since $\text{UB}(E) > L$ (line 24) or $L = \text{LBB} - \epsilon < \text{UBB}$ (line 5) it follows that X is to be added to the list of live nodes. Note that there is no need to recompute the lower and upper bound values for this node. They are the same as for E! The right child R is always feasible since E is feasible. For this node the lower and upper bound values may differ from those of node E. Hence, a call to LUBOUND is made (line 16). $\text{UB}(R) = \text{UBB}$. Node R may be killed if $\text{UB}(R) \leq L$. Line 18 adds R to the list of live nodes when R is not be killed. Line 19 updates the value of L.

procedure $LUBOUND(P, W, rw, cp, N, k, LBB, UBB)$
  //rw is the remaining capacity and cp is the profit already earned//
  //objects $k, \ldots, N$ have yet to be considered//
  //$\text{LBB} = -u(X)$ and $\text{UBB} = -\hat{c}(X)$//
  $LBB \leftarrow cp; c \leftarrow rw$
  for $i \leftarrow k$ **to** N **do**
    if $c < W(i)$ **then** $UBB \leftarrow LBB + c * P(I)/W(I)$
                for $j \leftarrow i + 1$ **to** N **do**
                  if $c \geq W(i + 1)$ **then** $c \leftarrow c - W(i + 1)$
                                    $LBB \leftarrow LBB + P(i + 1)$
                  endif
                repeat
                return
    endif
    $c \leftarrow c - W(i); LBB \leftarrow LBB + P(i)$
  repeat
  $UBB \leftarrow LBB$
end $LUBOUND$

Algorithm 8.6   Algorithm to compute lower and upper bounds

procedure $NEWNODE$ $(par, lev, t, cap, prof, ub)$
  //create a new node I and add it to the list of live nodes.//
  call $GETNODE(I)$
  $PARENT(I) \leftarrow par; LEVEL(I) \leftarrow lev; TAG(I) \leftarrow t$
  $CU(I) \leftarrow cap; PE(I) \leftarrow prof; UB(I) \leftarrow ub$
  call $ADD(I)$
end $NEWNODE$

Algorithm 8.7 (a)   Creating a new node

procedure *FINISH*(*L*, *ANS*, *N*)
  //print solution//
  real *L*; **global** *TAG*, *PARENT*
  print ('*VALUE OF OPTIMAL FILLING IS*', *L*)
  print ('*OBJECTS IN KNAPSACK ARE*')
  for *j* ← *N* **to** 1 **by** − 1 **do**
    if *TAG(ANS)* = 1 **then print**(*j*) **endif**
    ANS ← *PARENT(ANS)*
  repeat
end *FINISH*

Algorithm 8.7 (b)   Printing the answer

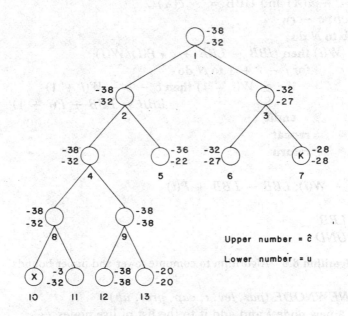

Figure 8.10   FIFO branch-and-bound tree for example 8.3

line **procedure** *LCKNAP*(*P, W, M, N,* ε)

//least cost branch-and-bound algorithm for the 0/1 knapsack//
//problem. A fixed tuple size formulation is used. It is assumed//
//that $P(1)/W(1) \geq P(2)/W(2) \geq \ldots \geq P(N)/W(N)$//
real *P(N), W(N), M, L, LBB, UBB, cap, prof*
integer *ANS, X, N*

1   **call** *INIT* //initialize list of available nodes and list of live nodes//
2   **call** *GETNODE(E)* //root node//
3   *PARENT(E)* ← 0; *LEVEL(E)* ← 1; *CU(E)* ← *M*; *PE(E)* ← 0
4   **call** *LUBOUND* (*P, W, M, N,* 0, 1, *LBB, UBB*)
5   *L* ← *LBB* − ε; *UB(E)* ← *UBB*
6   **loop**
7   *i* ← *LEVEL(E)*; *cap* ← *CU(E)*; *prof* ← *PE(E)*
8   **case**
9   :*i* = *N* + 1: //solution node//
10   **if** *prof* > *L* **then** *L* ← *prof*; *ANS* ← *E*
11   **endif**
12   :**else**: //*E* has two children//
13   **if** *cap* ≥ *W(i)* **then** //feasible left child//
14   **call** *NEWNODE(E, i* + 1, 1, *cap* − *W(i), prof* + *P(I)UB(E))*
15   **endif**
                //see if right child is to live//
16   **call** *LUBOUND* (*P, W, cap, prof, N, i* + 1, *LBB, UBB*)
17   **if** *UBB* > *L* **then** //right child is to live//
18   **call** *NEWNODE(E, i* + 1, 0, *cap, prof, UBB)*
19   *L* ← **max** (*L, LBB* − ε)
20   **endif**
21   **endcase**
22   **if** there are no more live nodes **then exit endif**
23   **call** *LARGEST(E)* //next *E*-node is node with largest *UB*(·)//
24   **until** *UB(E)* ≤ *L* **repeat**
25   **call** *FINISH(L, ANS, N)*
26 **end** *LCKNAP*

Algorithm 8.8 LC-branch-and-bound algorithm for **knapsack** problem

FIFO Branch-and-Bound Solution

Example 8.3 (FIFOBB) Now, let us trace through procedure FIFOBB
(Algorithm 8.3) using the same knapsack instance as in Example 8.2 and
using the knapsack formulation (8.1). Initially the root node, node 1 of
Figure 8.10, is the E-node and the queue of live nodes is empty. Since this
is not a solution node, U is initialized to $u(1) + \epsilon = -32 + \epsilon$. We shall
assume the children of a node are generated left to right. Nodes 2 and 3
are generated and added to the queue (in that order). The value of U remains unchanged. Node 2 becomes the next E-node. Its children, nodes
4 and 5, are generated and added to the queue. Node 3, the next E-node,
is expanded. It's children nodes are generated. Node 6 gets added to the
queue. Node 7 is immediately killed as $\hat{c}(7) \geq U$. Node 6 is next expanded.
Nodes 8 and 9 are generated and added to the queue. U is updated to
$u(9) + \epsilon = -38 + \epsilon$. Nodes 5 and 6 are the next two nodes to become
E-nodes. Neither is expanded as for each, $\hat{c}( ) \geq U$. Node 8 is the next
E-node. Nodes 10 and 11 are generated. Node 10 is infeasible and so killed.
Node 11 has $\hat{c}(11) \geq U$ and so is also killed. Node 9 is next expanded.
When node 12 is generated U and *ans* are updated to -38 and 12 respectively. Node 12 joins the queue of live nodes. Node 13 is killed before
it can get onto the queue of live nodes as $\hat{c}(13) > U$. The only remaining
live node is node 12. It has no children and the search terminates. The
value of U and the path from node 12 to the root is output. As in the case
of Example 8.2 additional information is needed to determine the x_i values
on this path.   □

As in the case of LCKNAP, we shall tailor the FIFO branch-and-bound
algorithm, FIFOKNAP to the problem at hand as well as to the state space
tree formulation chosen. Since nodes will be generated and examined (i.e.
become E-nodes) by levels, it is possible to keep track of the level of a node
by the use of an end of level marker, '#', on the queue of live nodes. This
leaves us with five fields per node: *CU*, *PE*, *TAG*, *UB* and *PARENT*. Procedure NNODE (Algorithm 8.9) generates a new live node, sets the fields
and adds it to the queue of live nodes.

procedure *NNODE*(*par*, *t*, *cap*, *prof*, *ub*)
  //create a new live node X and add it to the queue of live nodes//
  call *GETNODE*(*I*)
  PARENT(*I*) ← *par*; *TAG*(*I*) ← *t*
  CU(*I*) ← *cap*; *PE*(*I*) ← *prof*; *UB*(*E*) ← *ub*
  call *ADDQ*(*X*)
end *NNODE*

Algorithm 8.9 Creating a new node

Algorithm FIFOKNAP works with the maximization formulation of the knapsack problem. L represents a lower bound on the value of an optimal solution. Since no solution nodes can be reached until nodes at level N + 1 are generated, we can dispense with ϵ as used in LCKNAP. Lines 3–6 initialize the list of free nodes, the root node E, L and the queue of live nodes. This queue initially contains the root node E and the end of level marker '#'. i is the level counter. During the algorithm, i will have as value the level number corresponding to the current E-node. Initially, $i = 1$. In each iteration of the main while loop (lines 7–26), all live nodes at level i are removed from the queue. In the loop of lines 8–23, nodes are removed from the queue one by one. In case the end of level marker is removed then the loop is exited (line 11). Otherwise, node E is expanded only if $UB(E) \geq L$. Lines 13–21 generate the left and right children of node E and are similar to the corresponding code in procedure LCKNAP. When we exit from the while loop, the only live nodes on the queue are nodes at level N + 1. Each of these is a solution node. A node with maximum PE value is an answer node. Such a node may be easily found by examining the PE values of the remaining live nodes one by one. Procedure FINISH (Algorithm 8.7) prints out the value of an optimal solution as well as the objects that must be included into the knapsack in order to obtain this profit.

```
    procedure FIFOKNAP(P, W, M, N)
      //same function and assumptions as LCKNAP//
1     real P(N), W(N), M, L, LBB, UBB, E, prof, cap
2     integer ANS, X, N
3     call INIT; i ← 1
4     call LUBOUND(P, W, M, 0, N, 1, L, UBB)
5     call NNODE(0, 0, M, 0, UBB)   //root node//
6     call ADDQ('#')   //level marker//
7     while i ≤ N do   //for all live nodes on level i//
8       loop
9         call DELETEQ(E)
10        case
11          :E = '#': exit   //end of level i.Exit to line 24//
12          :UB(E) ≥ L:   //E is to live//
13            cap ← CU(E); prof ← PE(E)
14            if cap ≥ W(i) then   //feasible left child//
15              call NNODE(E, 1, cap - W(i), prof + P(i), UB(E))
16            endif
17            call LUBOUND(P, W, cap, prof, N, i + 1, LBB, UBB)
18            if UBB ≥ L then   //right child is to live//
19              call NNODE(E, 0, cap, prof, UBB)
20              L ← max(L, LBB)
21            endif
22        endcase
23      repeat
24      call ADDQ('#')   //end of level//
25      i ← i + 1
26    repeat
27    ANS ← live node X with PE(X) = L
28    call FINISH(L, ANS, N)
29  end FIFOKNAP
```

Algorithm 8.10   FIFO branch-and-bound knapsack algorithm

At first, we may be tempted to discard FIFOKNAP in favor of LCKNAP. Our intuition leads us to believe that LCKNAP will examine fewer nodes in its quest for an optimal solution. However, we should keep in mind that insertions into and deletions from a heap are far more expensive (proportional to the logarithm of the heap size) than the corresponding operations on a queue ($\theta(1)$). Consequently, the work done for each E-node is more in LCKNAP than in FIFOKNAP. Unless LCKNAP uses far fewer E-nodes than FIFOKNAP, FIFOKNAP will outperform (in terms of real computation time) LCKNAP.

We have now seen four different approaches to solving the knapsack problem: dynamic programming; backtracking; LC branch-and-bound and FIFO branch-and-bound. If we compare the dynamic programming algorithm DKNAP (Algorithm 5.7) and FIFOKNAP we see that there is a correspondence between generating the $S^{(i)}$s and generating nodes by levels. $S^{(i)}$ contains all pairs (P, W) corresponding to nodes on level $i + 1, 0 \leq i \leq n$. Hence, both algorithms generate the state space tree by levels. The dynamic programming algorithm, however, keeps the nodes on each level ordered by their profit earned (P) and capacity used (W) values. No two tuples have the same P or W value. In FIFOKNAP we may have many nodes on the same level with the same P or W value. It is not easy to implement the dominance rule of Section 5.5 into FIFOKNAP as nodes on a level are not ordered by their P or W values. However, the bounding rules can easily be incorporated into DKNAP. Towards the end of Section 5.5 we discussed some simple heuristics to determine if a pair $(P, W) \in S^{(i)}$ should be killed. These heuristics are readily seen to be bounding functions of the type discussed here. Let the algorithm resulting from the inclusion of the bounding functions into DKNAP be DKNAP1. DKNAP1 is expected to be superior to FIFOKNAP as it uses the dominance rule in addition to the bounding functions. In addition, the overhead incurred each time a node is generated is less.

To determine which of the knapsack algorithms is best, it is necessary to program them and obtain real computing times for different data sets. Since the effectiveness of the bounding functions and the dominance rule is highly data dependent, we expect a wide variation in the computing time for different problem instances having the same number of objects n. In order to get representative times, it is necessary to generate many problem instances for a fixed n and obtain computing times for these instances. The generation of these data sets and the problem of conducting the tests is discussed in a programming project at the end of this chapter. The results of some tests may be found in the references to this chapter.

Before closing our discussion of the knapsack problem, we briefly discuss a very effective heuristic to reduce a knapsack instance with large n to an equivalent one with smaller n. This heuristic, REDUCE, actually uses some of the ideas developed for the branch-and-bound algorithm. It classifies the objects $\{1, 2, \ldots, n\}$ into one of three categories $I1, I2,$ and $I3$. $I1$ is a set of objects for which x_i must be 1 in every optimal solution. $I2$

is a set for which x_i must be 0. $I3$ is $\{1, 2, \ldots, n\} - I1 - I2$. Once $I1$, $I2$, and $I3$ have been determined only the reduced knapsack instance:

$$\text{maximize} \sum_{i \in I3} p_i x_i$$

$$\text{subject to} \sum_{i \in I3} w_i x_i \le M - \sum_{i \in I1} w_i x_i \qquad (8.2)$$

$$x_i = 0 \text{ or } 1$$

has to be solved. From the solution to (8.2) an optimal solution to the original knapsack instance is obtained by setting $x_i = 1$ if $i \in I1$ and $x_i = 0$ if $i \in I2$.

Procedure REDUCE makes use of two functions UBB($I1$, $I2$) and LBB ($I1$, $I2$). UBB($I1$, $I2$) is an upper bound on the value of an optimal solution to the given knapsack instance with the added constraints $x_i = 1$ if $i \in I1$ and $x_i = 0$ if $i \in I2$. LBB($I1$, $I2$) is a lower bound under the constraints of $I1$ and $I2$. Note that UBB($I1$, $I2$) and LBB($I1$, $I2$) are the same as UBB and LBB of LUBOUND provided they are computed at a node X representing the assignment $x_i = 1$ if $i \in I1$ and $x_i = 0$ if $i \in I2$. Procedure REDUCE needs no further explanation. It should be clear that $I1$ and $I2$ are such that from an optimal solution to (8.2) we can easily obtain an optimal solution to the original knapsack problem.

procedure *REDUCE* $(P, W, n, M, I1, I2)$
    //variables are as described above. $P(i)/W(i) \ge P(i + 1)/W(i + 1)$,//
    //$1 \le i < n$//
    $I1 \leftarrow I2 \leftarrow \phi$
    $L \leftarrow LBB(\phi, \phi)$
    $k \leftarrow$ largest j such that $\sum_{1 \le i \le j} W(i) < M$
    for $i \leftarrow 1$ **to** k **do**   //determine $I1$//
        case
            : $UBB(\phi, \{i\}) < L : I1 \leftarrow I1 \cup \{i\}$
            : $LBB(\phi, \{i\}) > L : L \leftarrow LBB(\phi, \{i\})$
        endcase
    repeat
    for $i \leftarrow k + 1$ **to** n **do**   //determine $I2$//
        case
            : $UBB(\{i\}, \phi) < L : I2 \leftarrow I2 \cup \{i\}$
            : $LBB(\{i\}, \phi) > L : L \leftarrow LBB(\{i\}, \phi)$
        endcase
    repeat
end *REDUCE*

Algorithm 8.11   Reduction algorithm for knapsack problem

The time complexity of REDUCE is $O(n^2)$. Because the reduction procedure is very much like the heuristics used in DKNAP1, LCKNAP, BKNAP1 and BKNAP2, the use of REDUCE does not decrease the overall computing time by as much as may be expected by the reduction in number of objects. These algorithms do dynamically what REDUCE does. The exercises explore the value of REDUCE further.

8.3   TRAVELING SALESPERSON

An $O(n^2 2^n)$ dynamic programming algorithm for the traveling salesperson problem was arrived at in Section 5.7. We shall now investigate branch-and-bound algorithms for this problem. While the worst case complexity of these algorithms will not be any better than $O(n^2 2^n)$, the use of good bounding functions will enable these branch-and-bound algorithms to solve some problem instances in much less time than required by the dynamic programming algorithm.

Let $G = (V, E)$ be a directed graph defining an instance of the traveling salesperson problem. Let c_{ij} be the cost of edge $\langle i, j \rangle$, $c_{ij} = \infty$ if $\langle i, j \rangle \notin E$ and let $|V| = n$. Without loss of generality, we may assume that every tour starts and ends at vertex 1. So, the solution space S is given by $S = \{1, \pi, 1 | \pi$ is a permutation of $(2, 3, \ldots, n)\}$. $|S| = (n - 1)!$. The size of S may be reduced by restricting S so that $(1, i_1, i_2, \ldots, i_{n-1}, 1) \in S$ iff $\langle i_j, i_{j+1} \rangle \in E$, $0 \le j \le n - 1$, $i_0 = i_n = 1$. S may be organized into a state space tree similar to that for the n-queens problem (see Figure 7.2). Figure 8.11 shows the tree organization for the case of a complete graph with $|V| = 4$. Each leaf node L is a solution node and represents the tour defined by the path from the root to L. Node 14 represents the tour $i_0 = 1, i_1 = 3, i_2 = 4, i_3 = 2$ and $i_4 = 1$.

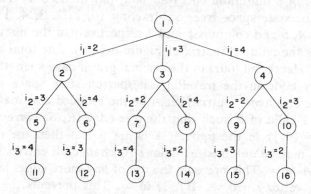

Figure 8.11   State space tree for the traveling salesperson problem with $n = 4$ and $i_0 = i_4 = 1$

In order to use LC-branch-and-bound to search the traveling salesperson state space tree, we need to define a cost function $c(\cdot)$ and two other functions $\hat{c}(\cdot)$ and $u(\cdot)$ such that $\hat{c}(R) \leq c(R) \leq u(R)$ for all nodes R. $c(\cdot)$ is such that the solution node with least $c(\cdot)$ corresponds to a shortest tour in G. One choice for $c(\cdot)$ is:

$$c(A) = \begin{cases} \text{length of tour defined by the path from the root to } A \text{ if } A \text{ is a leaf} \\ \text{cost of a minimum cost leaf in the subtree } A \text{ if } A \text{ is not a leaf} \end{cases}$$

A simple $\hat{c}(\cdot)$ such that $\hat{c}(A) \leq c(A)$ for all A is obtained by defining $\hat{c}(A)$ to be the length of the path defined at node A. For example, the path defined at node 6 of Figure 8.11 is $i_0, i_1, i_2 = 1, 2, 4$. It consists of the edges $\langle 1, 2 \rangle$ and $\langle 2, 4 \rangle$. A better $\hat{c}(\cdot)$ may be obtained by using the reduced cost matrix corresponding to G. A row (column) is said to *reduced* iff it contains at least one zero and all remaining entries are non-negative. A matrix is *reduced* iff every row and column is reduced. As an example of how to reduce the cost matrix of a given graph G, consider the matrix of Figure 8.12(a). This corresponds to a graph with five vertices. Since every tour on this graph includes exactly one edge $\langle i, j \rangle$ with $i = k$, $1 \leq k \leq 5$ and exactly one edge $\langle i, j \rangle$ with $j = k$, $1 \leq k \leq 5$, subtracting a constant t from every entry in one column or one row of the cost matrix reduces the length of every tour by exactly t. A minimum cost tour remains a minimum cost tour following this subtraction operation. If t is chosen to be the minimum entry in row i (column j), then subtracting it from all entries in row i (column j) will introduce a zero into row i (column j). Repeating this as often as needed, the cost matrix may be reduced. The total amount subtracted from all the columns and rows is a lower bound on the length of a minimum cost tour and may be used as the $\hat{c}$ value for the root of the state space tree. Subtracting 10, 2, 2, 3, 4, 1 and 3 from rows 1, 2, 3, 4, 5 and columns 1 and 3 respectively of the matrix of Figure 8.12(a) yields the reduced matrix of Figure 8.12(b). The total amount subtracted is 25. Hence, all tours in the original graph have a length at least 25.

With every node in the traveling salesperson state space tree we may associate a reduced cost matrix. Let A be the reduced cost matrix for node R. Let S be a child of R such that the tree edge (R, S) corresponds to including edge $\langle i, j \rangle$ in the tour. If S is not a leaf then the reduced cost matrix for S may be obtained as follows (i) change all entries in row i and column j of A to ∞. This prevents the use of any more edges leaving vertex i or entering vertex j. (ii) set $A(j, 1)$ to ∞. This prevents the use of edge $\langle j, 1 \rangle$. (iii) reduce all rows and columns in the resulting matrix except for

$$\begin{bmatrix} \infty & 20 & 30 & 10 & 11 \\ 15 & \infty & 16 & 4 & 2 \\ 3 & 5 & \infty & 2 & 4 \\ 19 & 6 & 18 & \infty & 3 \\ 16 & 4 & 7 & 16 & \infty \end{bmatrix} \qquad \begin{bmatrix} \infty & 10 & 17 & 0 & 1 \\ 12 & \infty & 11 & 2 & 1 \\ 0 & 3 & \infty & 0 & 2 \\ 15 & 3 & 12 & \infty & 0 \\ 11 & 0 & 0 & 12 & \infty \end{bmatrix}$$

(a) Cost Matrix

(b) Reduced Cost
Matrix
L = 25

Figure 8.12 An example

rows and columns containing only ∞. Let the resulting matrix be B. Steps
(i) and (ii) are valid as no tour in the subtree S can contain edges of the
type $\langle i, k \rangle$ or $\langle k, j \rangle$ or $\langle j, 1 \rangle$ (except for edge $\langle i, j \rangle$). If r is the total
amount subtracted in step (iii) then $\hat{c}(S) = \hat{c}(R) + A(i, j) + r$. For leaf
nodes $\hat{c}(\cdot) = c(\ )$ is easily computed as each leaf defines a unique tour.
For the upper bound function u, we may use $u(R) = \infty$ for all nodes R.

Let us now trace the progress of the LC brand-and-bound algorithm,
LCBB(Algorithm 8.4), on the problem instance of Figure 8.12(a). We shall
use $\hat{c}$ and u as above. The initial reduced matrix is that of Figure 8.12(b)
and $U = \infty$. The portion of the state space tree that gets generated is
shown in Figure 8.13. Starting with the root node as the E-node, nodes
2, 3, 4, and 5 are generated (in that order). The reduced matrices corresponding to these nodes are shown in Figure 8.14. The matrix of Figure
8.14(b) is obtained from that of 8.12(b) by (i) setting all entries in row 1
and column 3 to ∞; (ii) the element at position (3, 1) is set to ∞; (iii)
column 1 is reduced by subtracting by 11. The $\hat{c}$ for node 3 is therefore
25 + 17 (cost of edge $\langle 1, 3 \rangle$ in reduced matrix) + 11 = 53. The matrices
and $\hat{c}$ values for nodes 2, 4, and 5 are obtained similarly. U is unchanged
and node 4 becomes the next E node. Its children 6, 7 and 8 are generated.
The live nodes at this time are nodes 2, 3, 5, 6, 7 and 8. Node 6 has least
$\hat{c}$ value and becomes the next E node. Nodes 9 and 10 are generated. Node
10 is the next E node. The solution node, node 11, is generated. The tour
length for this node is $\hat{c}(11) = 28$ and U is updated to 28. For the next
E-node, node 5, $\hat{c}(5) = 31 > U$. Hence, LCBB terminates with 1, 4, 2, 5,
3, 1 as the shortest length tour.

An exercise examines the implementation considerations for the algorithm
described above. A different LC branch-and-bound algorithm may be

arrived at by considering a different tree organization for the solution space. This organization is arrived at by regarding a tour as a collection of n edges. If $G = (V, E)$ has e edges then every tour contains exactly n of the e edges. However, for each i, $1 \le i \le n$ there is exactly one edge of the form $\langle i, j \rangle$ and one of the form $\langle j, i \rangle$ in every tour. A possible organization for the state space is a binary tree in which a left branch represents the inclusion of a particular edge while the right branch represents the exclusion of that edge. Figures 8.15(b) and (c) represent the first two levels of two possible state space trees for the three vertex graph of Figure 8.15(a). As is true of all problems, many state space trees are possible for a given problem formulation. Different trees differ in the order in which decisions are made. Thus, in Figure 8.15(b) we first decide the fate of edge $\langle 1, 3 \rangle$ while in Figure 8.15(c) we first decide the fate of edge $\langle 1, 2 \rangle$. Rather than use a static state space tree, we shall now consider a dynamic state space tree (see Section 7.1). This will also be a binary tree. However, the order in which edges will be considered will depend on the particular problem instance being solved. We shall compute $\hat{c}$ in the same way as we did using the earlier state space tree formulation.

As an example of how LCBB would work on the dynamic binary tree formulation, consider the cost matrix of Figure 8.12(a). Since a total of 25 needs to be subtracted from the rows and columns of this matrix in order

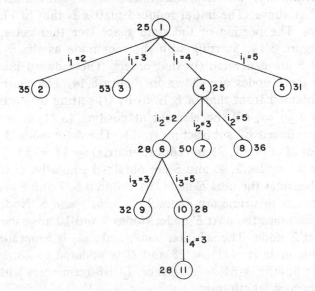

Numbers outside the node are $\hat{c}$ values

Figure 8.13   State space tree generated by procedure LCBB.

$$
\begin{bmatrix}
\infty & \infty & \infty & \infty & \infty \\
\infty & \infty & 11 & 2 & 0 \\
0 & \infty & \infty & 0 & 2 \\
15 & \infty & 12 & \infty & 0 \\
11 & \infty & 0 & 12 & \infty
\end{bmatrix}
\quad
\begin{bmatrix}
\infty & \infty & \infty & \infty & \infty \\
1 & \infty & \infty & 2 & 0 \\
\infty & 3 & \infty & 0 & 2 \\
4 & 3 & \infty & \infty & 0 \\
0 & 0 & \infty & 12 & \infty
\end{bmatrix}
\quad
\begin{bmatrix}
\infty & \infty & \infty & \infty & \infty \\
12 & \infty & 11 & \infty & 0 \\
0 & 3 & \infty & \infty & 2 \\
\infty & 3 & 12 & \infty & 0 \\
11 & 0 & 0 & \infty & \infty
\end{bmatrix}
$$

a) path 1,2; node 2 b) path 1,3; node 3 c) path 1,4; node 4

$$
\begin{bmatrix}
\infty & \infty & \infty & \infty & \infty \\
10 & \infty & 9 & 0 & \infty \\
0 & 3 & \infty & 0 & \infty \\
12 & 0 & 9 & \infty & \infty \\
\infty & 0 & 0 & 12 & \infty
\end{bmatrix}
\quad
\begin{bmatrix}
\infty & \infty & \infty & \infty & \infty \\
\infty & \infty & 11 & \infty & 0 \\
0 & \infty & \infty & \infty & 2 \\
\infty & \infty & \infty & \infty & \infty \\
11 & \infty & 0 & \infty & \infty
\end{bmatrix}
\quad
\begin{bmatrix}
\infty & \infty & \infty & \infty & \infty \\
1 & \infty & \infty & \infty & 0 \\
\infty & 1 & \infty & \infty & 0 \\
\infty & \infty & \infty & \infty & \infty \\
0 & 0 & \infty & \infty & \infty
\end{bmatrix}
$$

d) path 1,5; node 5 e) path 1,4,2; node 6 f) path 1,4,3; node 7

$$
\begin{bmatrix}
\infty & \infty & \infty & \infty & \infty \\
1 & \infty & 0 & \infty & \infty \\
0 & 3 & \infty & \infty & \infty \\
\infty & \infty & \infty & \infty & \infty \\
\infty & 0 & 0 & \infty & \infty
\end{bmatrix}
\quad
\begin{bmatrix}
\infty & \infty & \infty & \infty & \infty \\
\infty & \infty & \infty & \infty & \infty \\
\infty & \infty & \infty & \infty & 0 \\
\infty & \infty & \infty & \infty & \infty \\
0 & \infty & \infty & \infty & \infty
\end{bmatrix}
\quad
\begin{bmatrix}
\infty & \infty & \infty & \infty & \infty \\
\infty & \infty & \infty & \infty & \infty \\
0 & \infty & \infty & \infty & \infty \\
\infty & \infty & \infty & \infty & \infty \\
\infty & \infty & 0 & \infty & \infty
\end{bmatrix}
$$

g) path 1,4,5; node 8 h) path 1,4,2,3; node 9 i) path 1,4,2,5; node 10

Figure 8.14 Reduced cost matrices corresponding to nodes in Figure 8.13

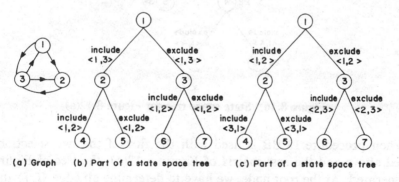

(a) Graph (b) Part of a state space tree (c) Part of a state space tree

Figure 8.15 An example

to obtain the reduced matrix of Figure 8.12(b), all tours have a length
at least 25. This fact is represented by the root of the state space tree of
Figure 8.16. Now, we must decide which edge to use to partition the solution
space into two subsets. If edge ⟨i, j⟩ is used then the left subtree of the
root will represent all tours including edge ⟨i, j⟩ and the right subtree

will represent all tours that do not include edge $\langle i, j \rangle$. If an optimal tour is included in the left subtree then only $n - 1$ edges remain to be selected. If all optimal tours lie in the right subtree then we have still to select n edges. Since the left subtree selects fewer edges, it should be easier to find an optimal solution in it than to find one in the right subtree. Consequently, we would like to choose as the partitioning edge an edge $\langle i, j \rangle$ that has highest probability of being in an optimal tour. Several heuristics for determining such an edge may be formulated. A selection rule that is commonly used is: select that edge which results in a right subtree that has highest $\hat{c}$ value. The logic behind this is that we will soon have right subtrees (perhaps at lower levels) for which the $\hat{c}$ value is higher than the length of an optimal tour. Another possibility is to choose an edge such that the difference in the $\hat{c}$ values for the left and right subtrees in maximum. Other selection rules are also possible.

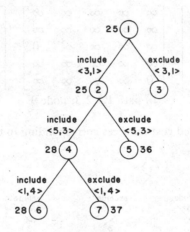

Figure 8.16 State space tree for Figure 8.12(a)

When procedure LCBB is used with the first of the two selection rules stated above and the cost matrix of Figure 8.12(a), the tree of Figure 8.16 is generated. At the root node, we have to determine an edge $\langle i, j \rangle$ that will maximize the $\hat{c}$ value of the right subtree. If we select an edge $\langle i, j \rangle$ whose cost in the reduced matrix (Figure 8.12(b)) is positive then the $\hat{c}$ value of the right subtree will remain 25. This is so as the reduced matrix, for the right subtree will have $B(i, j) = \infty$ and all other entries will be identical to those in Figure 8.12(b). Hence B will be reduced and $\hat{c}$ cannot increase. So, we must choose an edge with reduced cost 0. If we choose $\langle 1, 4 \rangle$ then $B(1, 4) = \infty$ and we need to subtract 1 from row 1 to obtain a reduced matrix. In this case $\hat{c}$ will be 26. If $\langle 3, 1 \rangle$ is selected then 11 needs to be subtracted from column 1 in order to obtain the reduced matrix for the right subtree. So, $\hat{c}$ will be 36. If A is the reduced cost matrix for node R then the selection of edge $\langle i, j \rangle$ $(A(i, j) = 0)$ as the next partitioning edge will increase the $\hat{c}$ of the right subtree by $\Delta = \min_{k \ne j}\{A(i, k)\} + \min_{k \ne 1}\{A(k j)\}$ as this much needs to be subtracted from row i and column j in order to introduce a zero into both. For edges $\langle 1, 4 \rangle$, $\langle 2, 5 \rangle$, $\langle 3, 1 \rangle$, $\langle 3, 4 \rangle$, $\langle 4, 5 \rangle$, $\langle 5, 2 \rangle$ and $\langle 5, 3 \rangle$, $\Delta = 1, 2, 11, 0, 3, 3$ and 11 respectively. So, either of the edges $\langle 3, 1 \rangle$ or $\langle 5, 3 \rangle$ may be used. Let us assume that LCBB selects edge $\langle 3, 1 \rangle$. $\hat{c}(2)$ (Figure 8.16) may be computed in a manner similar to that for the state space tree of Figure 8.13. In the corresponding reduced cost matrix all entries in row 3 and column 1 will be ∞. Moreover the entry $(1, 3)$ will also be ∞ as inclusion of this edge will result in a cycle. The reduced matrices corresponding to nodes 2 and 3 are given in Figures 8.17(a) and (b). The $\hat{c}$ values for nodes 2 and 3 (as well as for all other nodes) appears outside the respective node.

$$
\begin{bmatrix}
\infty & 10 & \infty & 0 & 1 \\
\infty & \infty & 11 & 2 & 0 \\
\infty & \infty & \infty & \infty & \infty \\
\infty & 3 & 12 & \infty & 0 \\
\infty & 0 & 0 & 12 & \infty
\end{bmatrix}
\qquad
\begin{bmatrix}
\infty & 10 & 17 & 0 & 1 \\
1 & \infty & 11 & 2 & 0 \\
\infty & 3 & \infty & 0 & 2 \\
4 & 3 & 12 & \infty & 0 \\
0 & 0 & 0 & 12 & \infty
\end{bmatrix}
\qquad
\begin{bmatrix}
\infty & 7 & \infty & 0 & \infty \\
\infty & \infty & \infty & 2 & 0 \\
\infty & \infty & \infty & \infty & \infty \\
\infty & 0 & \infty & \infty & 0 \\
\infty & \infty & \infty & \infty & \infty
\end{bmatrix}
$$

(a) node 2   (b) node 3   (c) node 4

$$
\begin{bmatrix}
\infty & 10 & \infty & 0 & 1 \\
\infty & \infty & 0 & 2 & 0 \\
\infty & \infty & \infty & \infty & \infty \\
\infty & 3 & 1 & \infty & 0 \\
\infty & 0 & \infty & 12 & \infty
\end{bmatrix}
\qquad
\begin{bmatrix}
\infty & \infty & \infty & \infty & \infty \\
\infty & \infty & \infty & \infty & 0 \\
\infty & \infty & \infty & \infty & \infty \\
\infty & 0 & \infty & \infty & \infty \\
\infty & \infty & \infty & \infty & \infty
\end{bmatrix}
\qquad
\begin{bmatrix}
\infty & 0 & \infty & \infty & \infty \\
\infty & \infty & \infty & 0 & 0 \\
\infty & \infty & \infty & \infty & \infty \\
\infty & 0 & \infty & \infty & 0 \\
\infty & \infty & \infty & \infty & \infty
\end{bmatrix}
$$

(d) node 5   (e) node 6   (f) node 7

Figure 8.17 Reduced cost matrices for Figure 8.16

Node 2 is the next E-node. Now, for edges $\langle 1, 4 \rangle$, $\langle 2, 5 \rangle$, $\langle 4, 5 \rangle$, $\langle 5, 2 \rangle$ and $\langle 5, 3 \rangle$, $\Delta = 3, 2, 3, 3$ and 11 respectively. Edge $\langle 5, 3 \rangle$ is selected and nodes 4 and 5 generated. The corresponding reduced matrices are given in Figures 8.17(c) and (d). $\hat{c}(4)$ becomes 28 as we need to subtract 3 from column 2 inorder to reduce this column. Note that entry $(1, 5)$ has been set to ∞ in Figure 8.17(c). This is necessary as the inclusion of edge $\langle 1, 5 \rangle$ to the collection $\{ \langle 3, 1 \rangle, \langle 5, 3 \rangle \}$ will result in a cycle. In addition, entries in column 3 and row 5 are set to ∞. Node 4 is the next E-node. The $\triangle$ values corresponding to edges $\langle 1, 4 \rangle$, $\langle 2, 5 \rangle$ and $\langle 4, 2 \rangle$ are 9, 2 and 0 respectively. Edge $\langle 1, 4 \rangle$ is selected and nodes 6 and 7 generated. The edge selection at node 6 is $\{ \langle 3, 1 \rangle, \langle 5, 3 \rangle, \langle 1, 4 \rangle \}$. This corresponds to the path 5, 3, 1, 4. So, entry $(4, 5)$ is set to ∞ in Figure 8.17(e). In general if edge $\langle i, j \rangle$ is selected then the entries in row i and column j are set to ∞ in the left sub-tree. In addition, one more entry needs to be set to ∞. This is an entry whose inclusion in the set of edges would create a cycle (an exercise examines how to determine this). The next E-node is node 6. At this time three of the five edges have already been selected. The remaining two may be selected directly. The only possibility is $\{ \langle 4, 2 \rangle, \langle 2, 5 \rangle \}$. This gives the path 5, 3, 1, 4, 2, 5 with length 28. U is updated to 28. Node 3 is the next E-node. LCBB terminates now as $\hat{c}(3) = 36 > U$.

In the preceding example, LCBB was modified slightly to handle nodes "close" to a solution node differently from other nodes. Node 6 is only two levels from a solution node. Rather than evaluate $\hat{c}$ at the children of 6 and then obtain their grandchildren, we just obtained an optimal solution for that subtree by a complete search with no bounding. We could have done something similar when generating the tree of Figure 8.13. Since node 6 is only two levels from the leaf nodes, we can simply skip computing $\hat{c}$ for the children and grandchildren of 6 and generate all of them, picking up the best. This works out to be quite efficient as it is easier to generate a subtree with a small number of nodes and evaluate all the solution nodes in it than it is to compute $\hat{c}$ for one of the children of 6. This latter state-ment is true of many applications of branch-and-bound. Branch-and-bound is used on large subtrees. Once a small subtree is reached (say one with 4 or 6 nodes in it) then that subtree is fully evaluated without using the bounding functions.

The exercises examine yet another LC branch-and-bound algorithm for the traveling salesperson problem. This algorithm also uses a dynamic state space tree. Associated with each node in the state space tree is a graph. Each node represents a subproblem requiring us to find a minimum length tour in the graph associated with that node. The original graph $G = (V, E)$ is associated with the root node. A lower bound $\hat{c}$ on the length of a shortest tour in the graph $H = (V, A)$ associated with any node X is obtained by solving the following *assignment problem*:

$$\text{minimize} \sum_{j=1}^{n} \sum_{i=1}^{n} c_{ij} x_{ij}$$

$$\text{subject to} \sum_{i=1}^{n} x_{ij} = 1, \ 1 \leq j \leq n$$

$$\sum_{j=1}^{n} x_{ij} = 1, \ 1 \leq i \leq n \qquad (8.2)$$

$$x_{ij} = 0 \ \text{ if } \ \langle i, j \rangle \notin A$$

$$x_{ij} = 0 \text{ or } 1, \qquad 1 \leq i \leq n, 1 \leq j \leq n$$

Note that $|V| = n$ and c_{ij} is the length of edge $\langle i, j \rangle$. $c_{ij} = \infty$ if $\langle i, j \rangle \notin E$. Algorithms to solve the assignment problem (8.2) are discussed in the texts: Linear Programming (pp. 227–228) by S. Gass, McGraw-Hill, New York, 1969 and Flows in Networks (pp. 111–112) by L. Ford and D. Fulkerson, Princeton University Press, 1962.

In case the solution to (8.2) is a tour then the length of a shortest tour in H has been obtained. Usually, however, the solution to (8.2) will be made up to several disjoint cycles. One of these cycles is used to partition the solution space of H. Let C be any one of the cycles in a solution to (8.2) (assume there are at least two cycles). Let $W = \{w_1, w_2, \ldots, w_r\}$ be the vertices in C. Define R_i and $\bar{R}_i$ as:

$$R_i = \{(w_i, j) \mid j \in W\}$$

$$\bar{R}_i = \{(w_i, j) \mid j \notin W\}$$

Now, define the edge sets:

$$E_1 = A - R_1$$
$$E_2 = A - \bar{R}_1 - R_2$$
$$E_3 = A - \bar{R}_1 - \bar{R}_2 - R_3$$
$$\vdots$$
$$E_r = A - \bar{R}_1 - \bar{R}_2 \ldots - R_r$$

The children of X correspond to the graphs (V, E_i), $1 \le i \le r$. The correctness of this partitioning rule follows from the following theorem:

Theorem 8.4 [Garfinkel] If T is a tour in H then T is a tour in exactly one of the graphs (V, E_i), $1 \le i \le r$.

Proof: Left as an exercise.   □

We have now seen several branch-and-bound strategies for the traveling salesperson problem. It is not possible to determine analytically which of these is best. The exercises describe computer experiments that determine empirically the relative performance of the strategies suggested.

8.4 EFFICIENCY CONSIDERATIONS

One can pose several questions concerning the performance characteristics of branch-and-bound algorithms that find least cost answer nodes. We might ask questions such as:

(i)   Will the use of a better starting value for U always decrease the number of nodes generated?

(ii)   Is it possible to decrease the number of nodes generated by actually expanding some nodes with $\hat{c}(\ ) > U$?

(iii) Will the use of a better $\hat{c}$ always result in a decrease in (or at least will not increase) the number of nodes generated? ($\hat{c}_2$ is better than $\hat{c}_1$ iff $\hat{c}_1(X) \le \hat{c}_2(X) \le c(X)$ for all nodes X).

(iv)   Does the use of dominance relations ever result in the generation of more nodes that will otherwise be generated?

In this section we shall answer these questions. While the answers to most of the questions examined will agree with our intuition, the answers to others will be contrary to intuition. However, even in cases where the answer does not agree with intuition we can expect the performance of the algorithm to generally agree with the intuitive expectations. All of the following theorems assume that the branch-and-bound algorithm is to find a minimum cost solution node. Consequently, $c(X) = $ cost of minimum cost solution node in subtree X.

Theorem 8.5 Let T be a state space tree. The number of nodes of T generated by FIFO, LIFO and LC branch-and-bound algorithms cannot be decreased by the expansion of any node X with $\hat{c}(X) \ge U$ where U is the current upper bound on the cost of a minimum cost solution node in T.

Proof: The theorem follows from the observation that the value of U cannot be decreased by expanding X(as $\hat{c}(X) \geq U$). Hence, such an expansion cannot affect the operation of the algorithm on the remainder of the tree.   □

Theorem 8.6   Let U_1 and U_2, $U_1 < U_2$ be two initial upper bounds on the cost of a minimum cost solution node in the state space tree T. FIFO, LIFO and LC branch-and-bound algorithms beginning with U_1 will generate no more nodes than they would if they started with U_2 as the initial upper bound.

Proof: Left as an exercise.   □

Theorem 8.7   The use of a better $\hat{c}$ function in conjunction with FIFO and LIFO branch-and-bound algorithms will not increase the number of nodes generated.

Proof: Left as an exercise.   □

Theorem 8.8   If a better $\hat{o}$ function is used in a LC branch and bound algorithm, the number of nodes generated may increase.

Proof: Consider the state space tree of Figure 8.18. All leaf nodes are solution nodes. The value outside each leaf is its cost. From these values it follows that $c(1) = c(3) = 3$ and $c(2) = 4$. Outside each of nodes 1, 2, and 3 is a pair of numbers $\begin{pmatrix} \hat{c}_1 \\ \hat{c}_2 \end{pmatrix}$. Clearly, $\hat{c}_2$ is a better function than $\hat{c}_1$.

However, if $\hat{c}_2$ is used, node 2 can become the E-node before node 3 (as $\hat{c}_2(2) = \hat{c}_2(3)$). In this case all 9 nodes of the tree will get generated. When $\hat{c}_1$ is used, nodes 4, 5 and 6 are not generated.   □

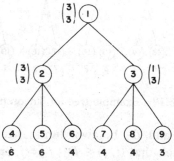

Figure 8.18   Example tree for Theorem 8.8

Now, let us look at the effect of dominance relations. Formally, a dominance relation D is given by a set of tuples, $D = \{(i_1, i_2), (i_3, i_4), (i_5, i_6) \ldots\}$. If $(i,j) \in D$ then node i is said to dominate node j. By this we mean that subtree i contains a solution node with cost no more than the cost of a minimum cost solution node in subtree j. Dominated nodes may be killed without expansion.

Since every node dominates itself, $(i, i) \in D$ for all i and D. The relation (i, i) should not result in the killing of node i. In addition, it is quite possible for D to contain tuples $(i_1, i_2), (i_2, i_3), (i_3, i_4) \cdots (i_n, i_1)$. In this case, the transitivity of D implies that each node i_k dominates all nodes i_j, $1 \le j \le n$. Care should be taken to leave at least one of the i_j's alive. A dominance relation D_2 is said to be *stronger* than another dominance relation D_1, iff $D_1 \subset D_2$. In the following theorems I will donote the identity relation $\{(i, i) \mid 1 \le i \le n\}$.

Theorem 8.9 The number of nodes generated during a FIFO or LIFO branch-and-bound search for a least cost solution node may increase when a stronger dominance relation is used.

Proof: Just consider the state space tree of Figure 8.19. The only solution nodes are leaf nodes. Their cost is written outside the node. For the remaining nodes the number outside each node is its $\hat{c}$ value. The two dom- D_2 is stronger than D_1 and fewer nodes are generated using D_1 rather than D_2. $I = \{(i, i) \mid i \in D\}$.   □

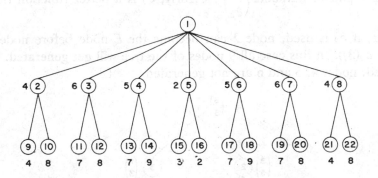

Figure 8.19 Example tree for Theorem 8.9

Theorem 8.10 Let D_1 and D_2 be two dominance relations. Let D_2 be stronger than D_1 and such that $(i, j) \in D_2$, $i \ne j$, implies $\hat{c}(i) < \hat{c}(j)$. An

LC branch-and-bound using D_1 generates the same number of nodes as one using D_2.

Proof: Left as an exercise. ☐

Theorem 8.11 If the condition $\hat{c}(i) < \hat{c}(j)$ in Theorem 8.10 is removed then an LC branch-and-bound using D_1 may generate fewer nodes than one using D_2.

Proof: Left as an exercise. ☐.

REFERENCES AND SELECTED READINGS

LC branch-and-bound algorithms have been extensively studied by researchers in areas such as artificial intelligence and operations research. Some of the more interesting general references are:

"Problem Solving Methods in Artificial Intelligence" by N. J. Nilsson, McGraw-Hill, New York, 1971.

"Integer Programming," by R. S. Garfinkel and G. L. Nemhauser, John Wiley and Sons, Inc., New York, 1972.

"Branch-and-bound methods: a survey," by E. L. Lawer and D. E. Wood, *Oper. Res.*, 14, pp. 699–719, 1966.

"Branch-and-bound methods: general formulation and properties," by L. Mitten, *Oper. Res.*, 18, pp. 24–34, 1970.

Branch-and-bound algorithms using dominance relations in a manner similar to that suggested by FIFOKNAP (resulting in DKNAP1) may be found in:

"A dynamic programming approach to sequencing problems," by M. Held and R. Karp, *Jr. of SIAM*, 10, pp. 196–210, 1962.

"Algorithms for scheduling independent tasks," by S. Sahni, *J. ACM*, 23(1), pp. 116–127, 1976.

"Exact and approximate algorithms for scheduling nonidentical processors," by E. Horowitz and S. Sahni, *J. ACM*, 23, pp. 317–327, 1976.

"General techniques for combinatorial approximation," by S. Sahni, *Oper. Res.*, 25(6), pp. 920–936, 1977.

"Branch-and-bound strategies for dynamic programming," by T. Morin and R. Marsten, *Oper. Res.*, 24, pp. 611–627, 1976.

The algorithms in the above five papers are very similar to dynamic programming type algorithms. Further branch-and-bound algorithms for scheduling problems appear in:

"Sequencing by enumerative methods," by J. Lenstra, *Math Centre. Tract 69*, Mathematisch Centrum, Amsterdam, 1976.

"Job-shop scheduling by implicit enumeration," by B. Lageweg, J. Lenstra and A. Rinnooy Kan, *Manag. Sci.*, 24(4), pp. 441–450, 1977.

"Application of the branch-and-bound technique to some flow-shop scheduling problems," by E. Ignall and L. Schrage, *Oper. Res.*, 13, pp. 400–412, 1965.

The reduction technique for the knapsack problem is due to Ingargiola and Korsh. It appears in:

"A reduction algorithm for zero-one single knapsack problems," by G. Ingargiola and J. Korsh, *Manag. Sci.*, 20(4), pp. 460–663, 1973.

A related reduction technique may be found in:

"A general algorithm for one dimensional knapsack problems," by G. Ingargiola and J. Korsh, *Oper. Res.*, 25(5), pp. 752–759, 1977.

Branch-and-bound algorithms for the traveling salesperson problem have been proposed by many researchers. A survey of these algorithms appears in:

"The traveling salesman problem: a survey," by M. Bellmore and G. Nemhauser, *Oper. Res.*, 16, pp. 538–558, 1968.

The reduced matrix technique to compute $\hat{c}$ is due to Little, Murty, Sweeny and Karel. It appears in the paper:

"An algorithm for the traveling salesman problem," by J. Little, K. Murty, D. Sweeny and C. Karel, *Oper Res.*, 11(6), pp. 972–989, 1963.

The above paper uses the dynamic state space tree approach. The partitioning scheme (8.3) is due to Garfinkel. His work is reported in:

"On partitioning the feasible set in a branch-and-bound algorithm for the asymmetric traveling salesman problem," by R. Garfinkel, *Oper. Res.*, 21(1), pp. 340–342, 1973.

A more efficient branch-and-bound algorithm for the traveling salesperson problem has been proposed by Held and Karp. Their algorithm can be used only when $c_{ij} = c_{ji}$ for all i and j. The following two papers describe the algorithm:

"The traveling salesman problem and minimum spanning trees," by M. Held and R. Karp, *Oper. Res.*, 18, pp. 1138–1162, 1970.

"The traveling salesman problem and minimum spanning trees: part II," by M. Held and R. Karp, *Math Prog.*, 1, pp. 6–25, 1971.

The results of section 8.4 are based on the work of Kohler, Steiglitz and Ibaraki. The relevent papers are:

"Characterization and theoretical comparison of branch-and-bound algorithms for permutation problems," by W. Kohler and K. Steiglitz, *J. ACM* 21(1), pp. 140–156, 1974.

"Computational efficiency of approximate branch-and-bound algorithms," by T. Ibaraki, *Math of Oper. Res.*, 1(3), pp. 287–298, 1976.

"Theoretical comparisons of search strategies in branch-and-bound algorithms," by T. Ibaraki, *Int. Jr. of Comp. and Info. Sci.*, 5(4), pp. 315–344, 1976.

"On the computational efficiency of branch-and-bound algorithms," by T. Ibaraki, *Jr. of the Oper. Res. Soc. of Japan*, 20(1), pp. 16–35, 1977.

"The power of dominance relations in branch-and-bound algorithms," by T. Ibaraki, *J. ACM*, 24(?), pp. 264 279, 1977.

The papers by T. Ibaraki cited above also contain a discussion of heuristic search. More ideas on heuristic search can be found in N. Nilsson's book which was cited earlier.

EXERCISES

1. Prove Theorem 8.1.

2. Write a program schema DFBB, for a LIFO branch-and-bound search for a least cost answer node.

3. Draw the portion of the state space tree generated by FIFOBB, LCBB and a LIFO branch-and-bound for the job sequencing with deadlines instance $n = 5$; $(p_1, p_2, \ldots, p_5) = (6, 3, 4, 8, 5)$; $(t_1, t_2, \ldots, t_5) = (2, 1, 2, 1, 1)$; $(d_1, d_2, \ldots, d_5) = (3, 1, 4, 2, 4)$. What is the penalty corresponding to an optimal solution? Use a variable tuple size formulation and $\hat{c}(\cdot)$ and $u(\cdot)$ as in Section 8.1.

4. Write a complete LC branch-and-bound algorithm for the job sequencing with deadlines problem. Use the fixed tuple size formulation.

5. Work out Example 8.2 using the variable tuple size formulation.

6. Work out Example 8.3 using the variable tuple size formulation.

7. Draw the portion of the state space tree generated by LCKNAP for the knap-sack instances:

   (i) $n = 5$, $(p_1, p_2, \ldots, p_5) = (10, 15, 6, 8, 4)$, $(w_1, w_2, \ldots, w_5) = (4, 6, 3, 4, 2)$ and $M = 12$.

   (ii) $n = 5$, $(p_1, p_2, p_3, p_4, p_5) = (w_1, w_2, w_3, w_4 w_5) = (4, 4, 5, 8, 9)$ and $M = 15$.

8. Do problem 7 using a LC branch-and-bound on a dynamic state space tree (see Section 7.6). Use the fixed tuple size formulation.

9. Write a LC branch-and-bound algorithm for the knapsack problem using the fixed tuple size formulation and the dynamic state space tree of Section 7.6.

10. [Programming Project] Program algorithms DKNAP, DKNAP1, LCKNAP and BKNAP2. Compare these algorithms empirically using randomly generated data as below:

    Data Set

    (i)   Random w_i and p_i, $w_i \in [1, 100]$, $p_i \in [1, 100]$, $M = \Sigma_1^n w_i/2$.
    (ii) Random w_i and p_i, $w_i \in [1, 100]$, $p_i \in [1, 100]$; $M = 2\max\{w_i\}$
    (iii) Random w_i, $w_i \in [1, 100]$; $p_i = w_i + 10$; $M = \Sigma_1^n w_i/2$
    (iv) Same as (iii) except $M = 2*\max\{w_i\}$
    (v)   Random p_i, $p_i \in [1, 100]$; $w_i = p_i + 10$; $M = \Sigma_1^n w_i/2$
    (vi) Same as (v) except $M = 2*\max\{w_i\}$

    Obtain computing times for $n = 5, 10, 20, 30, 40, \ldots$. For each n generate (say) 10 problem instances from each of the above data sets. Report average and worst case computing times for each of the above data sets. From these times can you say anything about the expected behavior of these algorithms? Now, generate problem instances with $p_i = w_i$, $1 \leq i \leq n$, $M = \Sigma w_i/2$ and $\Sigma w_i x_i \neq M$ for any 0, 1 assignment to the x_i's. Obtain computing times for your four programs for $n = 10, 20$ and 30.

    If you still have computer time available, then study the effect of changing the range to $[1, 1000]$ in data sets (i) through (vi). In sets (iii) to (vi) replace $p_i = w_i + 10$ by $p_i = w_i + 100$ and $w_i = p_i + 10$ by $w_i = p_i + 100$ respectively.

11. [Programming Project] (a) Program the reduction heuristic REDUCE of Section 8.2. Generate several problem instances from the data sets of Exercise 10 and determine the size of the reduced problem instances. Use $n = 100$, 200, 500 and 1000.

(b) Program DKNAP1 and the backtracking algorithm BKNAP2 for the knapsack problem. Compare the effectiveness of REDUCE by running several problem instances (as in Exercise 10). Obtain average and worst case computing times for DKNAP1 and BKNAP2 for the generated problem instances and also for the reduced instances. To the times for the reduced problem instances add the time required by REDUCE. What conclusions can you draw from your experiments?

12. a) Write a branch-and-bound algorithm for the job sequencing with deadlines problem using a dominance rule. Your algorithm should work with a fixed tuple size formulation and should generate nodes by levels. Nodes on each level should be kept in an order permitting easy use of your dominance rule.

b) Convert your algorithm into a computer program and using randomly generated problem instances, determine the worth of the dominance rule as well as the bounding functions. To do this, you will have to run four versions of your program: PROGA... bounding functions and dominance rules are removed; PROGB... dominance rule is removed; PROGC ... bounding function is removed and PROGD ... bounding functions and dominance rules are included. Determine both computing time figures as well as the number of nodes generated.

13. Consider the traveling salesperson instance defined by the cost matrix:

$$
\begin{bmatrix}
\infty & 7 & 3 & 12 & 8 \\
3 & \infty & 6 & 14 & 9 \\
5 & 8 & \infty & 6 & 18 \\
9 & 3 & 5 & \infty & 11 \\
18 & 14 & 9 & 8 & \infty
\end{bmatrix}
$$

a) Obtain the reduced cost matrix

b) Using a state space tree formulation similar to that of Figure 8.11 and $\hat{c}(\cdot)$ as described in Section 8.3, obtain the portion of the state space tree that will be generated by LCBB. Label each node by its $\hat{c}$ value. Write out the reduced matrices corresponding to each of these nodes.

c) Do part b) using the reduced matrix method and the dynamic state space tree approach discussed in Section 8.3.

d) Solve the above traveling salesperson instance using the assignment problem formulation. Draw the state space tree and describe the progress of the method from node to node.

e) Solve the given traveling salesperson problem using backtracking and the same $\hat{c}(\cdot)$ function as above. Use the static state space tree formulation.

f) Do part e) using a dynamic state space tree.

14. Do problem 13 using the following traveling salesperson cost matrix:

$$\begin{bmatrix} \infty & 11 & 10 & 9 & 6 \\ 8 & \infty & 7 & 3 & 4 \\ 8 & 4 & \infty & 4 & 8 \\ 11 & 10 & 5 & \infty & 5 \\ 6 & 9 & 5 & 5 & \infty \end{bmatrix}$$

15. a) Describe an efficient implementation for a LC branch-and-bound traveling salesperson problem using the reduced cost matrix approach and (i) a dynamic state space tree and (ii) a static tree as in Figure 8.11.

b) Are there any problem instances for which the LC branch-and-bound will generate fewer nodes using a static tree than using a dynamic tree? Prove your answer.

16. Consider the LC branch-and-bound traveling salesperson algorithm described using the dynamic state space tree formulation. Let A and B be nodes. Let B be a child of A. If the edge (A, B) represents the inclusion of edge $\langle i, j \rangle$ in the tour then in the reduced matrix for B all entries in row i and column j are set to ∞. In addition, one more entry is set to ∞. Obtain an efficient way to determine this entry.

17. [Programming Project]. Write computer programs for the following traveling salesperson algorithms:

i) the dynamic programming algorithm of chapter 5
ii) a backtracking algorithm using the static tree formulation of Section 8.3
iii) a backtracking algorithm using the dynamic tree formulation of Section 8.3
iv) a LC branch-and-bound algorithm corresponding to (ii)
v) a LC branch-and-bound algorithm corresponding to (iii)

Design data sets to be used to compare the efficiency of the above algorithms. Randomly generate problem instances from each of these data sets and obtain computing times for your programs. Obtain tables along the lines of those in Section 7.6. What conclusions can you draw from your computing times?

18. Prove theorem 8.4.

19. Prove theorem 8.6.

20. Prove theorem 8.7.

21. Prove theorem 8.10.

22. Prove theorem 8.11.

23. [Heuristic Search] Heuristic search is a generalization of FIFO, LIFO and LC search. A heuristic function $h(\cdot)$ is used to evaluate all live nodes. The next E-node is the live node with least $h(\cdot)$. Discuss the advantages of using a heuristic function $h(\cdot)$ different from $\hat{c}(\cdot)$ in the search for a least cost answer node. Consider the knapsack and traveling salesperson problems as two example problems. Also consider any other problems you wish to. For these problems devise "reasonable" functions $h(\cdot)$ (different from $\hat{c}(\cdot)$). Obtain problem instances on which heuristic search performs better than LC search.

Chapter 9

ALGEBRAIC SIMPLIFICATION AND TRANSFORMATION

9.1 THE GENERAL METHOD

In this chapter we shift our attention away from the problems we've dealt with previously to concentrate on methods for dealing with numbers and polynomials. Though computers have the ability already builtin to manipulate integers and reals, they are not directly equipped to manipulate symbolic mathematical expressions such as polynomials. One must determine a way to represent them and then write procedures which perform the desired operations. A system which allows for the manipulation of mathematical expressions, (usually including arbitrary precision integers, polynomials and rational functions), is called a *mathematical symbol manipulation* system. These systems have been fruitfully used to solve a variety of scientific problems for many years. The techniques we will study here have often led to efficient ways to implement the operations offered by these systems.

The first design technique we present is called algebraic transformation. Assume we have an input I which is a member of set S_1 and a function $f(I)$ which describes what must be computed. Usually the output $f(I)$ is also a member of S_1. Though a method may exist for computing $f(I)$ using operations on elements in S_1, this method may be inefficient. The *algebraic transformation* technique suggests that we alter the input into another form producing a member of set S_2. S_2 contains exactly the same elements as S_1 except it assumes a different representation for them. Why would we transform the input into another form? Because it may be easier to compute the function f for elements of S_2 than for elements of S_1. Once the answer in S_2 is computed an *inverse transformation* is performed to yield the result in set S_1.

For example let S_1 be the set of integers represented using decimal notation and S_2 the set of integers using binary notation. Given two integers from set S_1, plus any arithmetic operations to carry out on these numbers, todays computers will transform the numbers into elements of set S_2, perform the operations and transform the result back into decimal form. The algorithms for transforming the numbers are familiar to most students of computer science. To go from elements of set S_1 to set S_2 repeated division by 2 is used and from set S_2 to set S_1 repeated multiplication is used. The value of binary representation is the simplification which results in the internal circuitry of a computer.

For another example let S_1 be the set of n-degree polynomials ($n \geq 0$) with integer coefficients represented by a list of their coefficients, e.g.

$$A(x) = a_n x^n + \ldots + a_1 x + a_0.$$

The set S_2 consists of exactly the same set of polynomials but represented by their values at $2n + 1$ points, namely the $2n + 1$ pairs $(x_i, A(x_i))$, $1 \leq i \leq 2n + 1$ would represent the polynomial A. (At this stage we won't worry about what the values of x_i are, but for now you can consider them as consecutive integers.) The function f to be computed is the one which determines the product of two polynomials $A(x)$, $B(x)$ assuming the set S_1 representation to start with. Rather than forming the product directly using the conventional method, (which requires $O(n^2)$ operations where n is the degree of A and B and ignoring any possible growth in the size of the coefficients), we could transform the two polynomials into elements of set S_2. We do this by *evaluating* $A(x)$ and $B(x)$ at $2n + 1$ points. The product can now be computed simply, by multiplying the corresponding points together. The representation of $A(x)*B(x)$ in set S_2 is given by the tuples $(x_i, A(x_i)*B(x_i))$ $1 \leq i \leq 2n + 1$, and requires only $O(n)$ operations to compute. We may determine the product of $A(x)*B(x)$ in coefficient form by finding the polynomial which *interpolates* (or satisfies) these $2n + 1$ points. It is easy to show that there is a unique polynomial of degree $\leq 2n$ which goes through $2n + 1$ points.

Figure 9.1 describes these transformations in a graphical form indicating the two paths one may take to reach the coefficient product domain, either directly using conventional multiplication or by algebraic transformation. The transformation in one direction is affected by evaluation while the inverse transformation is accomplished by interpolation. The value of the scheme rests entirely on whether or not these transformations can be carried out efficiently.

The world of algebraic algorithms is so broad that we will only attempt to cover a few of the interesting topics. In Section 9.2 we discuss the question of polynomial evaluation at one or more points and the inverse opera-

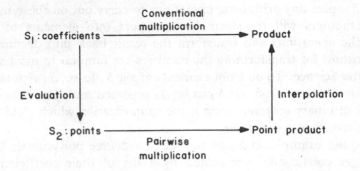

Figure 9.1   Transformation technique for polynomial products

tion of polynomial interpolation at n points. Then in Section 9.3 we discuss the same problems as in section 9.2 but this time assuming the n points are nth roots of unity. This is shown to be equivalent to computing the Fourier transform and in that section we show how the divide-and-conquer strategy leads to the *fast* Fourier transform algorithm. In Section 9.4 we shift out attention to integer problems, in this case the processes of modular arithmetic. Modular arithmetic can be viewed as a transformation scheme which is useful for speeding up large precision integer arithmetic operations. Moreover we will see that transformation into and out of modular form is a special case of evaluation and interpolation. Thus there is an algebraic unity to Sections 9.2, 9.3, and 9.4. Finally, in Section 9.5 we present the asymptotically best known algorithms for n-point evaluation and inter- polation.

9.2 EVALUATION AND INTERPOLATION

In this section we examine the operations on polynomials of evaluation and interpolation. As we search for efficient algorithms, we will see examples of another design strategy called algebraic simplification. When applied to algebraic problems, *algebraic simplification* refers to the process of re-ex- pressing computational formulas so that the required number of operations to compute these formulas is minimized. One issue we will ignore here is the numerical stability of the resulting algorithms. Though this is often an important consideration it is too far from our purposes. See the references for some pointers to the literature regarding numerical stability.

A univariate *polynomial* is generally written as

$$A(x) = a_n x^n + a_{n-1} x^{n-1} + \ldots + a_1 x + a_0$$

where x is an indeterminate and the a_i may be integers, floating point numbers or more generally elements of a commutative ring or a field. If $a_n \neq 0$ then n is called the *degree* of A.

When considering the representation of a polynomial by its coefficients, there are at least two alternatives. The first calls for storing the degree followed by degree + 1 coefficients:

$$(n, a_n, n - 1, a_{n-1}, \ldots, a_1, 1, a_0, 0).$$

This is termed the *dense* representation because it explicitly stores all coefficients whether or not they are zero. We observe that for a polynomial such as $x^{1000} + 1$ the dense representation is wasteful since it requires 1002 locations while there are only 2 nonzero terms.

The second representation calls for storing only each *nonzero* coefficient and its corresponding exponent e.g. if all the a_i are nonzero then

$$(n, a_n, n - 1, a_{n-1}, \ldots, 1, a_1, 0, a_0).$$

This is termed the *sparse* representation because the storage depends directly upon the number of nonzero terms and not on the degree. For a polynomial of degree n, all of whose coefficients are nonzero, this second representation requires roughly twice the storage of the first. However that is the worst case. For high degree polynomials with few nonzero terms, the second representation will be many times better than the first.

Secondarily we note that the terms of a polynomial will often be linked together rather than sequentially stored. However we will avoid this complication in the following programs and assume that we can access the ith coefficient by writing a_i.

Suppose we are given the polynomial $A(x) = a_n x^n + \ldots + a_0$ and we wish to evaluate it at a point v, i.e. compute $A(v)$. The straightforward or right-to-left method adds $a_1 v$ to a_0, $a_2 v^2$ to this sum and continues as described in Algorithm 9.1. The analysis of this algorithm is quite simple, namely $2n$ multiplications, n additions and $2n + 2$ assignments are made (excluding the **for** loop).

procedure $STRAITEVAL(A, n, v)$
  $s \leftarrow a_0; r \leftarrow 1$
  for $i \leftarrow 1$ **to** n **do**
    $r \leftarrow r * v$
    $s \leftarrow a_i * r + s$
  repeat
  return(s)
end $STRAITEVAL$

Algorithm 9.1 Straightforward evaluation

An improvement to this procedure was devised by Isaac Newton in 1711. The same improvement was used by W. G. Horner in 1819 to evaluate the coefficients of $A(x + c)$. The method came to be known as Horner's rule. They suggest rewriting the polynomial in the following way:

$$A(x) = (\ldots ((a_n x + a_{n-1})x + a_{n-2})x + \ldots + a_1)x + a_0.$$

This is our first and perhaps most famous example of algebraic simplification. The procedure for evaluation which is based on this formula is given in Algorithm 9.2.

```
procedure HORNER(A, n, v)
  s ← aₙ
  for i ← n − 1 to 0 by −1 do
    s ← s*v + aᵢ
  repeat
  return(s)
end HORNER
```

Algorithm 9.2   Horner's rule

Horner's rule requires n multiplications, n additions and $n + 1$ assignments (excluding the **for** loop). Thus we see that it is an improvement over the straightforward method by a factor of 2. In fact in Chapter 10 we shall see that Horner's rule yields the optimal way to evaluate an nth degree polynomial.

Now suppose we consider the sparse representation of a polynomial, $A(x) = a_m x^{e_m} + \ldots + a_1 x^{e_1}$ where the $a_i \neq 0$ and $e_m > e_{m-1} > \ldots > e_1 \geq 0$. The straightforward algorithm (Algorithm 9.1) when generalized to this sparse case is given in Algorithm 9.3.

```
procedure SSTRAITEVAL(A, m, v)
  //sparse straightforward evaluation. m is the number of nonzero terms//
  s ← 0
  for i ← 1 to m do
    s ← s + aᵢ*v↑eᵢ
  repeat
  return(s)
end SSTRAITEVAL
```

Algorithm 9.3   Sparse evaluation

Assuming that $v \uparrow e$ is computed by repeated multiplication with v, this operation requires $e - 1$ multiplications and Algorithm 9.3 requires $e_m + e_{m-1} + \ldots + e_1$ multiplications, m additions and $m + 1$ assignments. This is horribly inefficient and can easily be improved by an algorithm based on computing

$$v^{e1}, \; v^{e2-e1} * v^{e1}, \; v^{e3-e2} * v^{e2}, \; \ldots, \text{ etc.}$$

procedure $NSTRAITEVAL(A, m, v)$
  $s \leftarrow e_0 \leftarrow 0; t \leftarrow 1$
  for $i \leftarrow 1$ **to** m **do**
    $r \leftarrow v \uparrow (e_i - e_{i-1})$
    $s \leftarrow s + a_i * r * t$
    $t \leftarrow r$
  repeat
  return(s)
end $NSTRAITEVAL$

Algorithm 9.4   Evaluating a polynomial represented in coefficient exponent form

Algorithm 9.4 requires $e_m + m$ multiplications, $3m + 3$ assignments, m additions and m subtractions.

A more clever scheme is to generalize Horner's strategy yielding the revised formula,

$$A(x) = ((\ldots((a_m x^{e_m - e_{m-1}} + a_{m-1}) x^{e_{m-1} - e_{m-2}} + \ldots + a_2) x^{e_2 - e_1} + a_1) x^{e_1}$$

The program below is based on this formula.

procedure $SHORNER(A, m, v)$
  $s \leftarrow e_0 \leftarrow 0$
  for $i \leftarrow m$ **to** 1 **by** -1 **do**
    $s \leftarrow (s + a_i) * v \uparrow (e_i - e_{i-1})$
  repeat
  return(s)
end $SHORNER$

Algorithm 9.5   Horner's rule for a sparse representation

The number of required multiplications is

$$(e_m - e_{m-1} - 1) + \ldots + (e_1 - e_0 - 1) + m = e_m$$

which is the degree of A. In addition there are m additions, m subtractions and $m + 2$ assignments. Thus we see that Horner's rule is easily adapted to either the sparse or dense polynomial model and in both cases the number of operations is bounded and linear in the degree. With a little more work one can find an even better method, assuming a sparse representation, which requires only $m + \log_2 e_m$ multiplications. (See the exercises for a hint.)

Interpolation

Given n points (x_i, y_i) our task is to find the coefficients of the unique polynomial $A(x)$ of degree $\leq n - 1$ which goes through these n points. Mathematically the answer to this problem was given by Lagrange

$$A(x) = \sum_{1 \leq i \leq n} \left(\prod_{\substack{i \neq j \\ 1 \leq j \leq n}} \frac{(x - x_j)}{(x_i - x_j)} \right) y_i. \tag{9.1}$$

To verify that $A(x)$ does satisfy the n points we observe that

$$A(x_i) = \left(\prod_{\substack{i \neq j \\ 1 \leq j \leq n}} \frac{(x_i - x_j)}{(x_i - x_j)} \right) y_i = y_i \tag{9.2}$$

since every other term will become zero. The numerator of each term is a product of $n - 1$ factors and hence the degree of A is $\leq n - 1$.

We now give a program which produces the coefficients of $A(x)$ based upon this formula. We will need to perform some addition and multiplication of polynomials so we assume the existence of functions PADD(A, B) and PMULT(A, B) with the obvious interpretations.

procedure *LAGRANGE*(*X*, *Y*, *n*, *ANS*)
  //*X*, *Y* are one-dimensional arrays containing *n* points (x_i, y_i).//
  //*ANS* is a polynomial which interpolates these points//
  integer *den*, *n*; **polynomial** *POLY*, *ANS*; **real** *X*(1:*n*), *Y*(1:*n*);
  ANS ← 0
  for *i* ← 1 **to** *n* **do**
    POLY ← *den* ← 1
    for *j* ← 1 **to** *n* **do**
      if *i* ≠ *j*
      then *POLY* ← *PMULT*(*POLY*, *x* − *X*(*i*)) //*x* − *X*(*i*) is a degree//
                                  //one polynomial in *x*//
          den ← *den* ∗ (*X*(*i*) − *X*(*j*)) //*X*(*i*) − *X*(*j*) is a constant//
      endif
    repeat
    ANS ← *PADD*(*ANS*, *PMULT*(*Y*(*i*)/*den*, *POLY*))
  repeat
end *LAGRANGE*

Algorithm 9.6 Lagrange interpolation

An analysis of the computing time of LAGRANGE is instructive. The innermost **if** statement is executed n^2 times. The time to compute each new value of den is one subtraction and one multiplication, but the execution of PMULT requires more than constant time per call. Since the degree of $x - X(i)$ is one, the time for one execution of PMULT is proportional to the degree of POLY, which is at most $j - 1$ on the *j*th iteration.
Therefore the total cost of the polynomial multiplication step is

$$\sum_{1 \le i \le n} \sum_{1 \le j \le n} j - 1 = \sum_{1 \le i \le n} \left(\frac{n(n + 1)}{2} - n \right)$$

$$= n^2 (n + 1)/2 - n^2$$

$$= O(n^3). \tag{9.3}$$

This result is discouraging because it is so high. Perhaps we should search for a better method. Suppose we already have an interpolating polynomial $A(x)$ such that $A(x_i) = y_i$ for $1 \le i \le n$ and we want to add just one more point (x_{n+1}, y_{n+1}). How would we compute this new interpolating polynomial given the fact that $A(x)$ was already available? If we could solve this problem efficiently, then we could apply our solution *n* times to get an *n* point interpolating polynomial.

Let $G_{j-1}(x)$ interpolate $j - 1$ points (x_k, y_k) $1 \le k \le j$ such that $G_{j-1}(x_k)$ $= y_k$. Also let $D_{j-1}(x) = (x - x_1) \ldots (x - x_{j-1})$. Then we can compute $G_j(x)$ by the formula

$$G_j(x) = (y_j - G_{j-1}(x_j))(D_{j-1}(x)/D_{j-1}(x_j)) + G_{j-1}(x)$$

We observe that

$$G_j(x_k) = (y_j - G_{j-1}(x_j))(D_{j-1}(x_k)/D_{j-1}(x_j)) + G_{j-1}(x_k)$$

but $D_{j-1}(x_k) = 0$ for $1 \le k < j$ so

$$G_j(x_k) = G_{j-1}(x_k) = y_k$$

Also we observe that

$$G_j(x_j) = (y_j - G_{j-1}(x_j))(D_{j-1}(x_j)/D_{j-1}(x_j)) + G_{j-1}(x_j)$$

$$= y_j - G_{j-1}(x_j) + G_{j-1}(x_j)$$

$$= y_j$$

Having verified that this formula is correct, we present an algorithm for computing the interpolating polynomial which is based upon this formula. Notice that from the formula, two applications of Horner's rule are required, once for evaluating $G_{j-1}(x)$ at x_j and the other for evaluating $D_{j-1}(x)$ at x_j.

procedure *INTERP*(*X*, *Y*, *n*, *G*)
   //assume $n \ge 2$. $X(1{:}n)$, $Y(1{:}n)$ are the n pairs of points//
   //The coefficients of the unique interpolating polynomial//
   //of degree $< n$ is returned in *G*.//
   real $X(1{:}n)$, $Y(1{:}n)$, *num*, *denom*; **polynomial** *G*, *D*;
   $G \leftarrow Y(1)$ //*G* begins as a constant//
   $D \leftarrow x - X(1)$ //*D*(*x*) is a linear polynomial.//
   for $i \leftarrow 2$ **to** n **do**
      $denom \leftarrow HORNER(D, i - 1, X(i))$ //evaluate *D* at x_i//
      $num \leftarrow HORNER(G, i - 2, X(i))$ //evaluate *G* at x_i//
      $G \leftarrow PADD(PMULT((Y(i) - num)/denom, D), G)$
      $D \leftarrow PMULT(D, x - X(i))$
   repeat
end *INTERP*

Algorithm 9.7   Newtonian interpolation

On the ith iteration D has degree $i - 1$ and G has degree $i - 2$. Therefore the invocations of HORNER require

$$\sum_{1 \leq i \leq n-1} (i + i - 1) = n(n - 1) - (n - 1) = (n - 1)^2 \tag{9.4}$$

multiplications in total. The term $(Y(i) - num)/denom$ is a constant. Multiplying this constant by D requires $i + 1$ multiplications and multiplication of D by $x - X(i)$ requires $i + 1$ multiplications. The addition with G requires zero multiplications. Thus the remaining steps require

$$\sum_{1 \leq i \leq n-1} (2i + 2) = n(n - 1) + 2(n - 1) = (n - 1)(n + 2) \tag{9.5}$$

operations and so we see that the entire procedure INTERP requires $O(n^2)$ operations.

In conclusion we observe that for a dense polynomial of degree n, evaluation can be accomplished using $O(n)$ operations or for a sparse polynomial with m nonzero terms and degree n, evaluation can be done using at most $O(m + n) = O(n)$ operations. Also, given n points we can produce the interpolating polynomial in $O(n^2)$ time. In chapter 10 we will discuss the question of the optimality of Horner's rule for evaluation. Section 9.5 presents an even faster way to perform interpolation of n points as well as evaluation of a polynomial at n points.

9.3   THE FAST FOURIER TRANSFORM

If one is able to devise an algorithm which is an order of magnitude faster than any previous method, that is a worthy accomplishment. When the improvement is for a process which has many applications then that accomplishment will have a significant impact upon researchers and practitioners. This is the case of the fast Fourier transform. No algorithm improvement has had a greater impact in the recent past than this one. The Fourier transform is used by electrical engineers in a variety of ways including speech transmission, coding theory, and image processing. But before this fast algorithm was developed the use of this transform was considered inpractical.

The Fourier transform of a continuous function $a(t)$ is given by

$$A(f) = \int_{-\infty}^{\infty} a(t)e^{2\pi i f t} \, dt \tag{9.6}$$

while the inverse transform is

$$a(t) = 1/(2\pi) \int_{-\infty}^{\infty} A(f)e^{-2\pi i f t} df. \qquad (9.7)$$

The i in the above two equations stands for the square root of -1. The constant e is the base of the natural logarithm. The variable t is often regarded as time while f is taken to mean frequency and then the Fourier transform is interpreted as taking a function of time into a function of frequency.

Corresponding to this continuous Fourier transform is the *discrete* Fourier transform which handles sample points of $a(t)$, namely $a_0, a_1, \ldots, a_{N-1}$. The discrete Fourier transform is defined by

$$A_j = \sum_{0 \le k \le N-1} a_k e^{2\pi ijk/N}, \qquad 0 \le j \le N - 1 \qquad (9.8)$$

and the inverse is

$$a_k = (1/N) \sum_{0 \le j \le N-1} A_j e^{-2\pi ijk/N}, \qquad 0 \le j \le N - 1 \qquad (9.9)$$

In the discrete case a set of N sample points is given and a resulting set of N points is produced. An important fact to observe is the close connection between the discrete Fourier transform and polynomial evaluation. If we imagine the polynomial

$$a(x) = a_{N-1}x^{N-1} + a_{N-2}x^{N-2} + \ldots + a_1x + a_0$$

then the Fourier element A_j is the value of $a(x)$ at $x = w^j$ where $w = e^{2\pi i/N}$. Similarly for the inverse Fourier transform if we imagine the polynomial with the Fourier coefficients

$$A(x) = A_{N-1}x^{N-1} + A_{N-2}x^{N-2} + \ldots + A_1x + A_0$$

then each a_k is the value of $A(x)$ at $x = (w^{-1})^k$ where $w = e^{2\pi i/N}$. *Thus, the discrete Fourier transform corresponds exactly to the evaluation of a polynomial at N points*: $w^0, w^1, \ldots, w^{N-1}$.

From the preceding section we know that we can evaluate an Nth degree polynomial at N points using $O(N^2)$ operations. We apply Horner's rule once for each point. The *fast Fourier transform* (abbreviated as FFT) is an algorithm for computing these N values using only $O(N \log N)$ operations. This algorithm was popularized by Cooley and Tukey in 1965 and the long history of this method was traced by Cooley, Lewis and Welch (see the references).

A hint that the Fourier transform can be computed faster than by Horner's rule comes from observing that the evaluation points are not arbitrary, but are in fact very special. They are the N powers w^j for $0 \le j \le N - 1$ where $w = e^{2\pi i/N}$. The point w is a primitive Nth root of unity in the complex plane.

Definition: An element w in a commutative ring is called a *primitive Nth root of unity* if

(i) $w \ne 1$

(ii) $w^N = 1$

(9.10)

(iii) $\displaystyle\sum_{0 \le p \le N-1} w^{jp} = 0, \qquad 1 \le j \le N - 1$

We now present two simple properties of Nth roots from which we can see how the FFT algorithm can easily be understood.

Theorem 9.1 Let $N = 2n$ and suppose w is a primitive Nth root of unity. Then $-w^j = w^{j+n}$.

Proof: $(w^{j+n})^2 = (w^j)^2(w^n)^2 = (w^j)^2 w^{2n} = (w^j)^2$ since $w^N = 1$. Since the w^j are distinct we know that $w^j \ne w^{j+n}$ so we can conclude that $w^{j+n} = -w^j$. $\square$

Theorem 9.2 Let $N = 2n$ and w a primitive Nth root of unity. Then w^2 is a primitive nth root of unity.

Proof: Since $w^N = w^{2n} = 1$, $(w^2)^n = 1$ implying w^2 is a nth root of unity. In addition we observe that $(w^2)^j \ne 1$ for $1 \le j \le n - 1$ since otherwise we would have $w^k = 1$ for $1 \le k < 2n = N$ which would contradict the fact that w is a primitive Nth root of unity. Therefore w^2 is a primitive nth root of unity. $\square$

From this theorem we can conclude that if w^j, $0 < j \le N - 1$ are the primitive Nth roots of unity, $N = 2n$, then w^{2j}, $0 < j \le n - 1$ are primitive nth roots of unity. Using these two theorems we are now ready to show how to derive a divide-and-conquer algorithm for the Fourier transform.

The complexity of the algorithm is $O(N\log N)$, an order of magnitude faster than the $O(N^2)$ conventional algorithm which uses polynomial evaluation.

Again let $a_{N-1}, \ldots, a_0$ be the coefficients to be transformed and let $a(x) = a_{N-1}x^{N-1} + \ldots + a_1x + a_0$. We break up $a(x)$ into two parts, one which contains even numbered exponents and the other odd numbered exponents.

$$a(x) = a_{N-1}x^{N-1} + a_{N-3}x^{N-3} + \ldots + a_1x +$$

$$a_{N-2}x^{N-2} + \ldots + a_2x^2 + a_0$$

Letting $y = x^2$ we can rewrite $a(x)$ as a sum of two polynomials

$$a(x) = (a_{N-1}y^{n-1} + a_{N-3}y^{n-2} + \cdots + a_1)x$$
$$+ (a_{N-2}y^{n-1} + a_{N-4}y^{n-2} + \cdots + a_0)$$

$$= c(y)*x + b(y)$$

Recall that the values of the Fourier transform are $a(w^j)$, $0 \le j \le N - 1$. By the above the values of $a(x)$ at the points w^j, $0 \le j \le n - 1$ are now expressible as

$$a(w^j) = c(w^{2j})w^j + b(w^{2j})$$
$$a(w^{j+n}) = -c(w^{2j})w^j + b(w^{2j})$$

These two formulas are computationally valuable in the following way. They reveal how to take a problem of size N and transform it into 2 identical problems of size $n = N/2$. These subproblems are the evaluation of $b(y)$ and $c(y)$, each of degree $n - 1$, at the points $(w^2)^j$, $0 \le j \le n - 1$ and these points are primitive nth roots. This is an example of divide-and-conquer and we can apply the divide-and-conquer strategy again as long as the number of points remains even. This leads us to always choose N as a power of 2, $N = 2^m$, for then we can continue to carry out the splitting procedure until a trivial problem is reached, namely evaluating a constant polynomial.

Procedure FFT in Algorithm 9.8 combines all of these ideas into a recursive version of the fast Fourier transform algorithm.

procedure $FFT(N, a(x), w, A)$
//$N = 2^m$, $a(x) = a_{N-1}x^{N-1} + \ldots + a_0$, w is a//
//primitive N-th root of unity $A(0:N - 1)$ is set to//
//the values $a(w^j)$, $0 \le j \le N - 1$.//
integer N **real** $A(0:N - 1)$, $B(0:(N/2) - 1)$, $C(0:(N/2) - 1)$,
   $WP(-1:(N/2) - 1)$
if $N = 1$ **then** $A(0) \leftarrow a_0$
   else $n \leftarrow N/2$
      $b(x) \leftarrow a_{N-2}x^{n-1} + \ldots + a_2 x + a_0$ //divide the coefficients//
      $c(x) \leftarrow a_{N-1}x^{n-1} + \ldots + a_3 x + a_1$ //into 2 sets//
      call $FFT(n, b(x), w^2, B)$ //apply this algorithm again//
      call $FFT(n, c(x), w^2, C)$ //and again//
      $WP(-1) \leftarrow 1/w$
      for $j \leftarrow 0$ **to** $n - 1$ **do**
         $WP(j) \leftarrow w * WP(j - 1)$
         $A(j) \leftarrow B(j) + WP(j)*C(j)$
         $A(j + n) \leftarrow B(j) - WP(j)*C(j)$
      repeat
   endif
end FFT

Algorithm 9.8   Recursive fast Fourier transform

Now let us derive the computing time of FFT. Let $T(N)$ be the time for the algorithm applied to N inputs. Then we have

$$T(N) = 2T(N/2) + cN$$

where c is a constant and cN is a bound on the time needed to form $b(x)$, $c(x)$, A and B. Since $T(1) = d$, where d is another constant, we can repeatedly simplify this recurrence relation to get

$$
\begin{aligned}
T(2^m) &= 2T(2^{m-1}) + c2^m \\
&= \ldots = cm2^m + T(1)2^m \\
&= cN \log_2 N + dN \\
&= O(N \log_2 N)
\end{aligned}
$$

Suppose we return briefly to the problem considered at the beginning of this chapter, the multiplication polynomials. The transformation technique calls for evaluating $A(x)$ and $B(x)$ at $2N + 1$ points, computing the $2N + 1$ products $A(x_i) * B(x_i)$ and then finding the product $A(x)B(x)$ in coefficient form by computing the interpolating polynomial which satisfies these points. In Section 9.2 we saw that N point evaluation and interpolation required $O(N^2)$ operations, so that no asymptotic improvement is gained by using this transformation over the conventional multiplication algorithm. However, in this section we have seen that if the points are especially chosen to be the $N = 2^m$ distinct powers of an Nth root of unity, then evaluation and interpolation can be done using at most $O(N \log N)$ operations. Therefore by using the fast Fourier transform algorithm we can multiply two N-degree polynomials in $O(N \log N)$ operations.

The divide-and-conquer strategy plus some simple properties of primitive Nth roots of unity leads to a very nice conceptual framework for understanding the FFT. The above analysis shows that asymptotically it is better than the direct method by an order of magnitude. However the version we have produced may still not be faster! The reason for this is the considerable overhead that is required to implement the recursive calls. We need to study this algorithm more closely to eliminate this overhead. However uninterested readers may skip directly to Section 9.4.

An iterative version of the FFT

Recall that if we view the elements of the vector $(a_0, \ldots, a_{N-1})$ to be transformed as coefficients of a polynomial $a(x)$, then the Fourier transform is the same as computing $a(w^j)$ for $0 \le j < N$. This transformation is also equivalent to computing the remainder when $A(x)$ is divided by the linear polynomial $x - w^j$, for if $q(x)$ and c are the quotient and remainder such that

$$A(x) = (x - w^j)q(x) + c$$

then $A(w^j) = 0 * q(x) + c = c$. We could divide $A(x)$ by these N linear polynomials, but that would require $O(N^2)$ operations. Instead we are going to make use of the principle called *balancing* and compute these remainders with the help of a process which is structured like a binary tree.

Consider the product of the linear factors $(x - w^0) (x - w^1) \ldots (x - w^7) = x^8 - w^0$. All of the intermediate terms cancel leaving only exponents eight and zero with nonzero coefficients. If we select out from this product the even and odd degree terms a similar phenomenon occurs, namely

$(x - w^0) (x - w^2) (x - w^4) (x - w^6) = (x^4 - w^0)$ and $(x - w^1) (x - w^3)$ $(x - w^5) (x - w^7) = x^4 - w^4$. Continuing in a similar fashion we see in Figure 9.2 that the selected products have only two nonzero terms and we can continue this splitting until only linear factors are present.

Now suppose we want to compute the remainders of $A(x)$ by eight linear factors $(x - w^0), \ldots, (x - w^7)$. We begin by computing the remainder of $A(x)$ divided by the product $D(x) = (x - w^0) \ldots (x - w^7)$. If $A(x) = Q(x)D(x) + R(x)$ then $A(w^j) = R(w^j)$ $0 \le j \le 7$, since $D(w^j) = 0$ and the degree of $R(x)$ is less than the degree of $D(x)$ which equals 8. Now we divide $R(x)$ by $x^4 - w^0$ obtaining $S(x)$ and by $x^4 - w^4$ obtaining $T(x)$. $A(w^j) = R(w^j) = S(w^j)$ for $j = 0, 2, 4, 6$ and $A(w^j) = R(w^j) = T(w^j)$ for $j = 1, 3, 5, 7$ and the degrees of S and T are less than 4. Next we divide $S(x)$ by $x^2 - w^0$ and $x^2 - w^4$ obtaining remainders $U(x)$ and $V(x)$ where $A(w^j) = U(w^j)$ for $j = 0, 4$ and $A(w^j) = V(w^j)$ for $j = 2, 6$. Notice how each divisor has only two nonzero terms and so the division process will be fast. By continuing in this way we will eventually conclude with the eight values $A(x) \bmod (x - w^j)$ for $j = 0, 1, \ldots, 7$.

By carrying out successive divisions down the binary tree of Figure 9.2 we will eventually arrive at the appropriate coefficients of the Fourier transform. The order of these coefficients will be permuted in the same way the $x - w^i$ appear at the bottom of the tree, but this can be corrected at the end of the algorithm. Since this permutation caused the polynomials

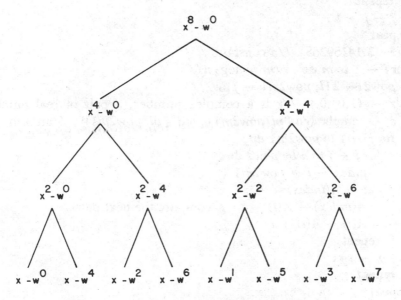

Figure 9.2   Divisors in the FFT algorithm of size 8

at each node of the tree to have such a simple form, the division at each stage is simple and the resulting computation time for the entire transform reduces to $O(N \log N)$. One can see this in a simple way by observing that the tree has $\log N$ levels, 2^i nodes on each level, where a dividend polynomial on level i has at most 2^{k-i} terms. Thus the work on the ith level is proportion to $2^i * 2^{k-i} = 2^k = N$ and hence $O(N \log N)$ bounds the time

```
procedure NFFT(A, m)
  //nonrecursive FFT algorithm where A(1:n) contains//
  //the input coefficients, n = 2↑m. The elements//
  //of the transform are computed in-place.//
  //Complex arithmetic is assumed and w = e^(2πi/j)//
  //is expressed in terms of sines and cosines.//
  integer i, j, k, l, m, n, ndiv2, pow2, pow2m1, index
  complex A(1:n), r, s, t
  n ← 2↑m; ndiv2 ← N/2; j ← 1
  for i ← 1 to n − 1 do   //permute the input//
    if i < j then t ← A(j); A(j) ← A(i); A(i) ← t
    endif
    k ← ndiv2
    while k < j do
      j ← j − k; k ← k/2
    repeat
    j ← j + k
  repeat
  pi ← 3.14159265   //a constant//
  for l ← 1 to m do   //m = log₂ n//
    pow2 ← 2↑l; pow2m1 ← pow2/2
    r ← (1.0, 0.)   //r is a complex number, a pair of real numbers//
    s ← cmplx (cos( pi/pow2m1), sin ( pi/pow2m1))   //an nth root//
    for j ← 1 to pow2m1 do
      for i ← j to n by pow2 do
        index ← i + pow2m1
        t ← A(index)*r
        A(index) ← A(i) − t   //compute the next pair//
        A(i) ← A(i) + t
      repeat
      r ← r*s
    repeat
  repeat
end NFFT
```
Algorithm 9.9   Nonrecursive FFF

for the entire algorithm. Algorithm 9.9 uses this point of view to produce an FFT algorithm which is iterative in nature.

Procedure NFFT is an in-place, iterative version of the fast Fourier transform. It begins by rearranging the input so that at the end of the algorithm the correct values are in their proper positions. Complex arithmetic is assumed and $w = e^{2\pi i/j}$ is expressed in terms of sines and cosines. To verify that the complexity of NFFT is truly $O(n \log n)$, assume $n = 2^m$ and examine the triply nested **for** loops. The statements contained in the innermost **for** loop require no more than constant time per iteration. The innermost **for** loop is executed no more than $\lceil n/2^l \rceil < 2^{m-l+1}$ times. This implies that the total time of NFFT is bounded by

$$\sum_{1 \le l \le m} \sum_{1 \le j \le 2^{l-1}} c2^{m-l+1} = \sum_{1 \le l \le m} c2^m = c2^m m = O(n \log n).$$

Now suppose we simulate the algorithm as it works on the particular case $n = 4$. We assume as inputs the symbolic quantities $A(1) = a_1$, $A(2) = a_2$, $A(3) = a_3$ and $A(4) = a_4$. Initially $m = 2$ and $n = 4$. After the first **for** loop is completed, the array contains the elements permuted as $A(1) = a_1, A(2) = a_3, A(3) = a_2, A(4) = a_4$. The main **for** loop is executed for $l = 1$ and $l = 2$. After the $l = 1$ pass is completed the array contains $A(1) = a_1 + a_3, A(2) = a_1 - a_3, A(3) = a_2 + a_4, A(4) = a_2 - a_4$. At this point one should observe in general that $w^{n/2} = -1$ or for this case $w^2 = -1$ and the complex number expressed as a 2-tuple, $(\cos \pi, \sin \pi)$ is equal to w. At the end of the algorithm the final values in the array A are $A(1) = a_1 + a_2 + a_3 + a_4, A(2) = a_1 + wa_2 + w^2a_3 + w^3a_4, A(3) = a_1 + w^2a_2 + a_3 + w^2a_4, A(4) = a_1 + w^3a_2 + w^2a_3 + wa_4.$

Some remaining points

Up to now we have been treating the value w as $e^{2\pi i/N}$. This is a complex number (it has an imaginary part) and its value cannot be represented exactly in a digital computer. Thus the arithmetic operations performed in the Fourier transform algorithm were assumed to be operations on complex numbers and this implies they are approximations to the actual values. When the inputs to be transformed are readings from a continuous signal, approximations of w do not cause any significant loss in accuracy. However there are occasions when one would prefer an exact result, for instance when one is using the FFT for polynomial multiplication in a mathematical symbol manipulation system. It is possible to circumvent the need for approximate, complex arithmetic by working in a finite field.

Let p be chosen such that it is a prime which is less than your computer's word size and such that the integers $0, 1, \ldots, p - 1$ contain a primitive nth root of unity. By doing all of the arithmetic of the fast Fourier transform modulo p, all of the results will be single precision. By choosing p to be a prime the integers $0, 1, \ldots, p - 1$ form a field and all arithmetic operations including division can be performed. If all values during the computation are bounded by $p - 1$ then the exact answer will be formed since $x \bmod p = x$ if $0 \leq x < p$. However if one or more values exceeds $p - 1$ the exact answer can still be produced by repeating the transform using several different primes followed by the Chinese Remainder Theorem as described in the next section. So the question which remains is, given an N can one find a sufficient number of primes of a certain size which contain Nth roots. From finite field theory $\{0, 1, \ldots, p - 1\}$ contains a primitive Nth root iff N divides $p - 1$. Therefore, to transform a sequence of size $N = 2^m$, primes of the form $p = 2^e k + 1$ where $m \leq e$ must be found. Call such a number a *Fourier* prime. J. Lipson has shown that there are more than $x/(2^{e-1} \ln x)$ Fourier primes less than x with exponent e and hence there are more than enough for any reasonable application. For example if the work size is 32 bits let $x = 2^{31}$ and $e = 20$. Then there are approximately 182 primes of the form $2^f k + 1$ where $f \geq 20$. Any of these Fourier primes would suffice to compute the FFT of a sequence of at most 2^{20}. See the exercises for more details.

9.4 MODULAR ARITHMETIC

Another example of a useful set of transformations is modular arithmetic. Modular arithmetic is useful in one context because it allows one to reformulate the way addition, subtraction, and multiplication are performed. This reformulation is one which exploits parallelism whereas the normal methods for doing arithmetic are serial in nature. The growth of special computers which make it desirable to perform parallel computation make modular arithmetic attractive. A second use of modular arithmetic is with systems which allow for symbolic mathematical computation. These software packages usually provide operations which permit arbitrarily large integers and rational numbers as operands. Modular arithmetic has been found to yield efficient algorithms for the manipulation of large numbers. Finally there is an intrinsic interest in finite field arithmetic (the integers $0, 1, \ldots, p - 1$ where p is a prime form a field) by number theorists and electrical engineers specializing in communications and coding theory. In this section we will study this subject from a computer scientists point of view, namely the development of efficient algorithms for the required operations.

The *mod* operator is defined as

$$x \bmod y = x - y(x/y), \qquad \text{if } y \neq 0$$

$$x \bmod 0 = x$$

Note that (x/y) corresponds to fixed point integer division which is commonly found on most current day computers.

We will denote the set of integers $\{0, 1, \ldots, p - 1\}$ where p is a prime by GF(p), (the Galois field with p elements), named after the mathematician Galois who studied and characterized the properties of these fields. Also we will assume that p is a single precision number for the computer you plan to execute on. It is, in fact, true that the set GF(p) forms a field under the following definitions of addition, subtraction, multiplication and division:

If $a, b \in$ GF(p), then

$$(a + b) \bmod p = \begin{cases} a + b & \text{if } a + b < p \\ \\ a + b - p & \text{if } a + b \geq p \end{cases}$$

$$(a - b) \bmod p = \begin{cases} a - b & \text{if } a - b \geq 0 \\ \\ a - b + p & \text{if } a - b < 0 \end{cases}$$

$(ab) \bmod p = r$ such that r is the remainder when the product ab is divided by p, $ab = qp + r$ where $0 \leq r < p$

$(a/b) \bmod p = (ab^{-1}) \bmod p = r$, the unique remainder when ab^{-1} is divided by p, $ab^{-1} = qp + r, 0 \leq r < p$

b^{-1} is the *multiplicative inverse* of b in GF(p). For every element b in GF(p) except zero there exists a unique element called b^{-1} such that $bb^{-1} \bmod p = 1$. We shall see how to compute this value very soon.

Now what are the computing times for these operations? We have assumed that p is a single precision integer, which implies that all $a, b \in$ GF(p) are also single precision integers. The time for addition, subtraction and multiplication mod p given the formulas above are easily seen to be $O(1)$.

But before we can determine the time for division we must develop an algorithm to compute the multiplicative inverse of an element $b \in GF(p)$.

By definition we know that to find $x = b^{-1}$ there must exist an integer $k, 0 \leq k < p$ such that $bx = kp + 1$. For example, if $p = 7$

$$
\begin{array}{llllllll}
b: & 1 & 2 & 3 & 4 & 5 & 6 & \text{(element)} \\
b^{-1}: & 1 & 4 & 5 & 2 & 3 & 6 & \text{(inverse)} \\
k: & 0 & 1 & 2 & 1 & 2 & 5 &
\end{array}
$$

An algorithm for computing the inverse of b in $GF(p)$ is provided by generalizing Euclid's algorithm for the computation of greatest common divisors (see Section 1.3). Recall that given two nonnegative integers a, b Euclid's algorithm computes their gcd. It does so by making use of the theorem that if $a > b \geq 0$ then $gcd(a, b) = gcd(b, a \bmod b)$ if b is nonzero and otherwise $gcd(a, 0) = a$. It is also possible to compute two more integers x, y such that $ax + by = gcd(a, b)$. Letting a be a prime p and $b \in GF(p)$, then the $gcd(p, b) = 1$ (since the only divisors of a prime are itself and one) and Euclid's generalization reduces to finding integers x, y such that $px + by = 1$. This implies that y is the multiplicative inverse of $b \bmod p$.

procedure $EXEUCLID(b, p)$
  $//b \in GF(p)$, p is a prime. EXEUCLID is a function$//$
  $//$whose result is the integer x such that $bx + kp = 1//$
  $//$The statement $(e, f) \leftarrow (g, \cdot h)$ is$//$
  $//$interpreted as $e \leftarrow g; f \leftarrow h//$
  $(c, d, x, y) \leftarrow (p, b, 0, 1)$ $//$initialize$//$
  while $d \neq 1$ **do**
    $q \leftarrow c/d$ $//$compute quotient$//$
    $e \leftarrow c - d*q$ $//$compute new remainder$//$
    $w \leftarrow x - y*q$
    $(c, d, x, y) \leftarrow (d, e, y, w)$
  repeat
  if $y < 0$ **then** $y \leftarrow y + p$
  return(y)
end $EXEUCLID$

Algorithm 9.10   Extended Euclidean algorithm

A close examination of EXEUCLID shows that Euclid's gcd algorithm is carried out by the steps $q \leftarrow c/d; e \leftarrow c - d*q; c \leftarrow d;$ and $d \leftarrow e$. The only other steps are the updating of x and y as the algorithm proceeds. In order to analyze the time for EXEUCLID we need to know the number of divisions Euclid's algorithm may require. This was answered in the worst case by Lame' in 1845.

Theorem 9.6 (*G. Lame', 1845*): For $n \geq 1$ let a, b be integers $a > b > 0$ such that Euclid's algorithm applied to a, b requires n division steps. Then $n \leq 5 \log_{10} b$.

Thus the **while** loop is executed no more than $O(\log_{10} p)$ times and this is the computing time for the extended Euclidean algorithm and hence for modular division. By *modular arithmetic* we will mean the operations of addition, subtraction, multiplication and division modulo p as previously defined.

Now lets see how we can use modular arithmetic as a transformation technique to help us work with integers. We begin by looking at how we can represent integers using a set of moduli, then how we perform arithmetic on this representation and finally how to produce the proper integer result.

Let a and b be integers and suppose that a is represented by the r-tuple $(a_1, \ldots, a_r)$ where $a_i = a \bmod p_i$ and b is represented as $(b_1, \ldots, b_r)$ where $b_i = b \bmod p_i$. The p_i are typicaly single precision primes. This is called a *mixed radix* representation which contrasts with the conventional representation of integers using a single radix such as 10 (decimal) or 2 (binary). The following rules for addition, subtraction and multiplication using a mixed radix representation are as follows:

$$(a_1, \ldots, a_r) + (b_1, \ldots, b_r) = ((a_1 + b_1) \bmod p_1, \ldots, (a_r + b_r) \bmod p_r),$$

$$(a_1, \ldots, a_r) * (b_1, \ldots, b_r) = (a_1 b_1 \bmod p_1, \ldots, a_r b_r \bmod p_r),$$

For example let the moduli be $p_1 = 3$, $p_2 = 5$, and $p_3 = 7$ and suppose we start with the integers 10 and 15.

$$10 = (10 \bmod 3, 10 \bmod 5, 10 \bmod 7) = (1, 0, 3)$$

$$15 = (15 \bmod 3, 15 \bmod 5, 15 \bmod 7) = (0, 0, 1)$$

Then

$$10 + 15 = (25 \bmod 3, 25 \bmod 5, 25 \bmod 7) = (1, 0, 4)$$

$$= (1 + 0 \bmod 3, 0 + 0 \bmod 5, 3 + 1 \bmod 7) = (1, 0, 4)$$

Also

$$15 - 10 = (5 \bmod 3, 5 \bmod 5, 5 \bmod 7) = (2, 0, 5)$$
$$= (0 - 1 \bmod 3, 0 - 0 \bmod 5, 1 - 3 \bmod 7) = (2, 0, 5)$$

Also

$$10*15 = (150 \bmod 3, 150 \bmod 5, 150 \bmod 7) = (0, 0, 3)$$
$$= (1*0 \bmod 3, 0*0 \bmod 5, 3*1 \bmod 7) = (0, 0, 3)$$

After we have performed some desired sequence of arithmetic operations using these r-tuples, we are left with some r-tuple $(c_1, \ldots, c_r)$. We now need some way of transforming back from modular form with the assurance that the resulting integer is the correct one. The ability to do this is guaranteed by the following theorem which was first proven in full generality by L. Euler in 1734.

Theorem 9.7 (Chinese Remainder Theorem): Let $p_1, \ldots, p_r$ be positive integers which are pairwise relatively prime (no two integers have a common factor). Let $p = p_1 \ldots p_r$ and let $b, a_1, \ldots, a_r$ be integers. Then, there is exactly one integer, a, which satisfies the conditions

$$b \le a < b + p, \text{ and } a = a_i \,(\bmod p_i) \text{ for } 1 \le i \le r.$$

Proof: Let x be another integer, different from a, such that $a = x(\bmod p_i)$ for $1 \le i \le r$. Then $a - x$ is a multiple of p_i for all i. Since the p_i are pairwise relatively prime it follows that $a - x$ is a multiple of p. Thus, there can be only one solution which satisfies the above relations. We will show how to construct this value in a moment.   □

A pictorial view of these transformations when applied to integer multiplication is given in Figure 9.3. Instead of using conventional multiplication, which requires $O((\log a)^2)$ operations $(a = \max(a, b))$ we choose a set of primes $p_1, \ldots, p_r$, compute $a_i = a \bmod p_i$, $b_i = b \bmod p_i$ and then $c_i = a_i b_i \bmod p_i$. These are all single precision operations and so they require $O(r)$ steps. r must be sufficiently large so that $ab < p_1, \ldots, p_r$. The precision of a is proportional to $\log a$ and hence the precision of ab is no more than $2 \log a = O(\log a)$. Thus $r = O(\log a)$ and the time for transforming into modular form and computing the r products is $O(\log a)$. Therefore the value of this method rests upon how fast we can perform the inverse transformation by the Chinese Remainder Algorithm.

Suppose we consider how to compute the value in the Chinese Remainder Theorem for only two moduli: Given $a\ mod\ p$ and $b\ mod\ q$ we wish to determine the unique c such that $c\ mod\ p = a$ and $c\ mod\ q = b$. The value for c which satisfies these two constraints is easily seen to be

$$c = (b - a)sp + a$$

where s is the multiplicative reciprocal of p mod q, i.e. an s which satisfies $ps\ mod\ q = 1$. To show that this formula is correct we note that

$$((b - a)sp + a)\ mod\ p = a$$

since the term $(b - a)sp$ has p as a factor. Secondly

$$
\begin{aligned}
((b - a)sp + a)\ mod\ q &= (b - a)sp\ mod\ q + a\ mod\ q \\
&= (b - a)\ mod\ q + a\ mod\ q \\
&= (b - a + a)\ mod\ q \\
&= b
\end{aligned}
$$

Procedure ONESTEPCRA below uses procedure EXEUCLID and arithmetic modulo p to compute the formula we've just described.

```
procedure ONESTEPCRA(a, p, b, q)
  //a, b are in GF(p), gcd(p, q) = 1//
  //returns a value c such that c mod p = a and c mod q = b.//
  integer a, b, p, q, t, pb, r, u
  t ← a mod q
  pb ← p mod q
  s ← EXEUCLID(pb, q)
  u ← (b - t) * s mod q
  return(u * p + a)
end ONESTEPCRA
```

Algorithm 9.11   One step Chinese Remainder Algorithm

The computing time is dominated by the call to EXEUCLID which requires $O(\log q)$ operations.

The simplest way to use this procedure to implement the Chinese Remainder Theorem for r moduli is to apply it $r - 1$ times in the following way. Given a set of congruences $a_i\ mod\ p_i$, $1 \le i \le r$ we let procedure

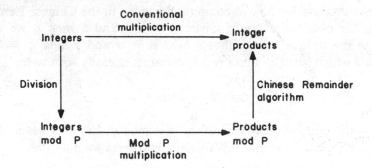

Figure 9.3   Integer multiplication by **mod** p transformations

ONESTEPCRA be called $r - 1$ times with the following set of values for the parameters.

	a	p	b	q	output
first time	a_1	p_1	a_2	p_3	c_1
second time	c_1	$p_1 p_2$	a_3	p_3	c_2
third time	c_2	$p_1 p_2 p_3$	a_4	p_4	c_3
...	...	...	.		...
r-1-st time	c_{r-2}	$p_1 p_2 \ldots p_{r-1}$	a_r	p_r	c_{r-1}

The final result c_{r-1} is an integer such that $c_{r-1} \bmod p_i = a_i$ for $1 \leq i \leq r$ and $c_{r-1} < p_1 \ldots p_r$. The total computing time is $O(r \log q) = O(r^2)$.

An example: Suppose we wish to take 4, 6, 8 and compute $4 + 8 \ddagger 6 = 52$. Let $p_1 = 7, p_2 = 11$.

$$4 = (4 \bmod 7, 4 \bmod 11) = (4, 4)$$

$$6 = (6 \bmod 7, 6 \bmod 11) = (6, 6)$$

$$8 = (8 \bmod 7, 8 \bmod 11) = (1, 8)$$

$$8*6 = (6*1 \bmod 7, 8*6 \bmod 11) = (6, 4)$$

$$4 + 8*6 = (4 + 6 \bmod 7, 4 + \bmod 11) = (3, 8)$$

So, we must convert the 2-tuple (3, 8) back to integer notation. Using procedure ONESTEPCRA with $a = 3, b = 8, p = 7, q = 11$ we get

1) $t \leftarrow a \bmod q = 3 \bmod 11 = 3$
2) $pb \leftarrow p \bmod q = 7 \bmod 11 = 7$
3) $s \leftarrow pb \bmod q = \ > s = 8; k = 5$
4) $u \leftarrow (b - t)s \bmod q = (8 - 3)8 \bmod 11 = 40 \bmod 11 = 7$
5) **return**$(u * p + a) = 7 * 7 + 3 = 52$

In conclusion we review the computing times for modular arithmetic. If $a, b \in \mathrm{GF}(p)$ where p is single precision then

Operation	Computing Time
$a + b$	$O(1)$
$a \cdot b$	$O(1)$
a / b	$O(\log p)$
$c \leftarrow (c_1, \dots, c_r)$ $c_i = c \bmod p_i$	$O(r \log c)$
$c \leftarrow (c_1, \dots, c_r)$	$O(r^2)$

9.5   EVEN FASTER EVALUATION AND INTERPOLATION

In this section we will study four problems

(1) from an n-precision integer compute its residues modulo n single precision primes;
(2) from an n-degree polynomial compute its values at n points;
(3) from n single precision residues compute the unique n-precision integer which is congruent to the residues;
(4) from n points compute the unique interpolating polynomial through those points;

We have seen in Sections 9.2 and 9.4 that the classical methods for problems (1)–(4) take $O(n^2)$ operations. Here we will show how to use the fast Fourier transform to speed up all four problems. In particular we will derive algorithms for problems (1) and (2) whose times are $O(n (\log n)^2)$ and for problems (3) and (4) whose time is $O(n (\log n)^3)$. These algorithms will rely on the fast Fourier transform as it is used to perform n-precision integer multiplication in time $O(n \log n \log \log n)$. This algorithm, developed by Schonhage and Strassen is the fastest known way to multiply. Because this algorithm is complex to describe and already appears in several places (see the references), we will simply assume its existence here. Moreover to simplify things somewhat we will assume that for n-precision integers and for n-degree polynomials the time to add or subtract is $O(n)$ and the time to multiply or divide is $O(n \log n)$. In addition we will assume that an extended gcd algorithm is available, (see Algorithm 9.10) for integers or polynomials whose computing time is $O(n (\log n)^2)$.

Now consider the binary tree as shown in Figure 9.4. As we "go down" the tree the level numbers increase, while the root of the tree is at the top at level 1. The ith level has 2^{i-1} nodes and a tree with k levels has a total of 2^k nodes. We will be interested in computing different functions at every node of such a binary tree. So for example an algorithm for moving up the tree is

procedure $MOVEUPATREE(T, n)$
    //$n = 2^{k-1}$ values are stored in $T(1:k, 1:n)$//
    //in locations $T(k \; 1), \ldots, T(k, n)$//
    //The algorithm causes the nodes of a binary tree to be//
    //visited such that at each node an abstract binary operation//
    //denoted by $*$ is performed. The resulting values are//
    //stored in the array T as indicated in Figure 9.4.//
    for $i \leftarrow k - 1$ **to** 1 **by** -1 **do**
      $p \leftarrow 1$
      for $j \leftarrow 1$ **to** $2\uparrow(i - 1)$ **do**
        $T(i, j) \leftarrow T(i + 1, p) \ddagger T(i + 1, p + 1)$
        $p \leftarrow p + 2$
      repeat
    repeat
end $MOVEUPATREE$

Algorithm 9.12   Moving up a tree

Subsequently we will be concerned about the cost of the operation $*$, which is denoted by $C(*)$. Given the value of $C(*)$ on the ith level and the above algorithm, the total time needed to compute every node in a tree is

$$\sum_{1 \leq i \leq k-1} 2^{i-1} C(*) \tag{9.17}$$

Similarly an algorithm which computes elements as we go down the tree would be

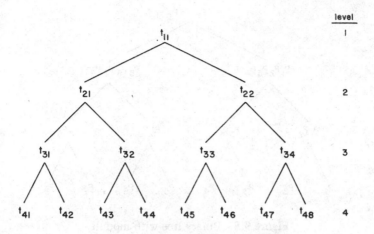

Figure 9.4 A binary tree

```
procedure MOVEDOWNATREE(S, T, n)
  //n = 2^(k-1) and T(1, 1) is given.//
  //Also S(1:n, 1:k) is given containing a binary tree of values //
  //The algorithm produces elements and stores them//
  //in the array T(1:k, 1:n) at the positions which//
  //correspond to the nodes of the binary tree in Figure 9.4.//
  for i ← 2 to k do
    p ← 1
    for j ← 1 to 2↑(i − 1) by 2 do
      T(i, j) ← S(i, j)*T(i − 1, p)
      T(i, j + 1) ← S(i, j + 1)*T(i − 1, p)
      p ← p + 1
    repeat
  repeat
end MOVEDOWNATREE
```

Algorithm 9.13 Moving down a tree

We now proceed to the specific problems.

Problem 1.   Let u be an n-precision integer and $p_1, \ldots, p_n$ single precision primes. We wish to compute the n residues $u_i = u \mod p_i$ which gives the mixed radix representation for u. We consider the binary tree in Figure 9.5.

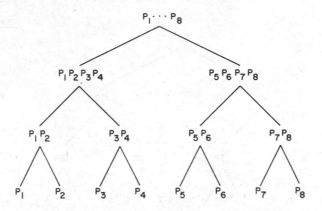

Figure 9.5 Binary tree with moduli

If $n = 2^{k-1}$ then products on the ith level have precision 2^{k-i}, $1 \le i \le k$. Using our fast integer multiplication algorithm we can compute the elements going up the tree. Therefore $C(*)$ at the ith level is $2^{k-i-1}(k - i - 1)$ and the total time to complete the tree is

$$\sum_{1 \le i \le k-1} 2^{i-1} 2^{k-i-1} (k - i - 1)$$

(9.18)

$$= 2^{k-2} \left\{ k^2 - \frac{k(k + 1)}{2} + 1 \right\} = O(n(\log n)^2)$$

Now to compute the n residues $u_i = u \bmod p_i$ we reverse direction and proceed to compute functions down the tree. Since u is n-precision and the primes are all near the maximum size of a single precision number we first compute $u \bmod p_1 \ldots p_n = ub$. Then the algorithm will continue by computing next

$$u_{2,1} = ub \bmod p_1 \ldots p_{n/2} \text{ and } u_{2,2} = ub \bmod p_{n/2+1} \ldots p_n.$$

Then we compute

$$u_{3,1} = u_{2,1} \bmod p_1 \ldots p_{n/4}, \, u_{3,2} = u_{2,1} \bmod p_{n/4+1} \ldots p_{n/2}$$

$$u_{3,3} = u_{2,2} \bmod p_{n/2+1} \ldots p_{3n/4}, \, u_{3,4} = u_{2,2} \bmod p_{3n/4+1} \ldots p_n$$

and so on down the tree until we have

$$u_{k,1} = u_1, \quad u_{k,2} = u_2, \quad \ldots, \quad u_{k,2\,1(k-1)} = u_n$$

A node on level i is computed using the previously computed product of primes at that position plus the element $u_{j,\,i-1}$ at the descendant node. The computation requires a division operation so $C(*)$ at the ith level is $2^{k-i+1}(k - i + 1)$ and the total time for problem 1 is

$$\sum_{1 \le i \le k} 2^{i-1}2^{k-i+1}(k - i + 1)$$

$$(9.19)$$

$$= 2^k\left\{k^2 - \frac{k(k - 1)}{2}\right\} = O(n(\log n)^2)$$

Problem 2.   Let $P(x)$ be an n-degree polynomial and $x_1, \ldots, x_n$ n single precision points. We wish to compute the n values $P(x_i)$ $1 \le i \le n$. We consider the binary tree in Figure 9.6.

If $n = 2^{k-1}$ the products on the ith level have degree 2^{k-i}. Using fast polynomial multiplication we compute the elements going up the tree. Therefore $C(*)$ on the ith level is $2^{k-i-1}(k - i - 1)$ and the total time to complete the tree is

$$\sum_{1 \le i \le k-1} 2^{i-1}2^{k-i-1}(k - i - 1)$$

$$(9.20)$$

$$= 2^{k-2}\left\{k^2 - \frac{k(k + 1)}{2} + 1\right\} = O(n(\log n)^2)$$

Note that this process shows how to compute the elementary symmetric functions of $x_1, \ldots, x_n$ in $O(n \log n)^2)$ operations.

Now to compute the n values $P(x_i)$ we reverse direction and proceed to compute functions down the tree. If $D(x) = (x - x_1) \ldots (x - x_n)$ then we can divide $P(x)$ by $D(x)$ obtaining a quotient and remainder as follows

$$P(x) = D(x)Q(x) + R_{11}(x)$$

where the degree of R_{11} is less than the degree of D. By substitution it follows that

$$P(x_i) = R_{11}(x_i), \quad 1 \le i \le n.$$

The algorithm would continue by next dividing $R_{11}(x)$ by the first $n/2$

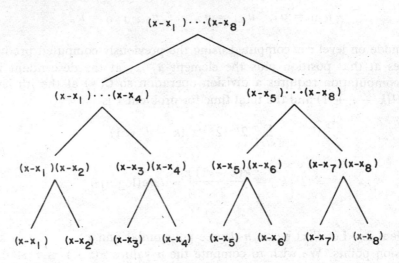

Figure 9.6   A binary tree with linear moduli

factors of $D(x)$ and then by the second $n/2$ factors. Calling these polynomials $D_1(x)$ and $D_2(x)$ we get the quotients and remainders

$$R_{11}(x) = D_1(x)Q_1(x) + R_{12}(x)$$

$$R_{11}(x) = D_2(x)Q_2(x) + R_{22}(x)$$

By the same argument we see that

$$P(x_i) = \begin{cases} R_{12}(x_i), & 1 \le i \le n/2 \\ \\ R_{22}(x_i), & n/2 + 1 \le i \le n \end{cases} \tag{9.21}$$

Eventually we will arrive at constants $R_{k1}, \ldots, R_{k,2^{(k-1)}}$ where $P(x_i) = R_{k,1}$ for $1 \le i \le n$. Since the time for multiplication and division of polynomials is the same, $C(*)$ on the ith level is $2^{k-i}(k - i)$ and the total for problem 2 is

$$\sum_{1 \le i \le k} 2^{i-1} 2^{k-i}(k - i)$$

$$\tag{9.22}$$

$$= 2^{k-1} \left\{ k^2 - \frac{k(k + 1)}{2} \right\} = O(n(\log n)^2)$$

Problem 3.   Given n residues u_i of n single precision primes p_i we wish to find the unique n-precision integer u such that $u \bmod p_i = u_i 1 \le i \le n$. It follows from the Chinese remainder theorem, Theorem 9.7, that this integer exists and is unique. For this problem as for problem 1 we will assume the binary tree in Figure 9.5 has already been computed. What we need to do is go up the tree at each node compute a new integer which is congruent to the product of the integers at the children nodes. For example, at the first level let $u_i = u_{k,i}$, $1 \le i \le n = 2^{k-1}$. Then for i odd we compute from $u_{k,i}$, $\bmod p_i$ and $u_{k,i+1} \bmod p_{i+1}$ the unique integer $u_{k-1,i} = u_{k,i} \bmod p_i$ and $u_{k-1,i} = u_{k,i+1} \bmod p_{i+1}$. Thus $u_{k-1,i}$ lies in the range $[0, p_i p_{i+1})$. Repeating this process up the tree we will eventually produce the integer u in the interval $[0, p_1 \ldots p_n)$. So we need to develop an algorithm which proceeds from level i to $i - 1$. But we already have such an algorithm, the one step Chinese remainder algorithm or procedure ONESTEPCRA. The time for this algorithm was shown to be dominated by the time for EXECULID. Using our assumption that EXECULID can be done in $O(n \log n)^2)$ operations, where n is the maximum precision of the moduli, then this is also the time for ONESTEPCRA. Note the difference between its use in this section and in Section 9.4. In the latter section only one of the moduli was growing.

We now apply this one step algorithm to an algorithm which proceeds up the tree of Figure 9.5. The total time for problem 3 is seen to be

$$\sum_{1 \le i \le k-1} 2^{i-1} 2^{k-i-1} (k - i - 1)^2$$

$$\tag{9.23}$$

$$= 2^{k-2} \sum_{1 \le i \le k-1} (k - i - 1)^2 = O(n(\log n)^3)$$

Problem 4.   Given n values $y_1, \ldots, y_n$ at $n = 2^{k-1}$ points $x_1, \ldots, x_n)$ we wish to compute the unique interpolating polynomial $P(x)$ of degree $\le n - 1$ such that $P(x_i) = y_i$. For this problem as for problem 2 we will assume that the binary tree in Figure 9.6 has already been computed. Again we need an algorithm which goes up the tree and at each node computes a new interpolating polynomial from its two ancestors. For example at level k we compute polynomials $R_{k1}(x), \ldots, R_{kn}(x)$ such that $R_{ki}(x_i) = y_i$. Then at level $k - 1$ we compute $R_{k-1,1}, \ldots, R_{k-1,n/2}$ such that

$$R_{k-1,i}(x_i) = y_i$$

$$R_{k-1,i}(x_{i+1}) = y_{i+1}$$

and so on until $R_{11}(x) = P(x)$. Therefore we need an algorithm which combines two interpolating polynomials to give a third which interpolates at both sets of points. This requires a generalization of procedure INTERP, Algorithm 9.7.

procedure *BALANCEDINTERP(U1, U2, Q1, Q2, m)*
    //*U1, U2, Q1, Q2* are all polynomials *n x* such that//
    //*U1* interpolates the points $x_1, \ldots, x_{m/2}$//
    //*U2* interpolates $x_{m/2+1}, \ldots, xm$//
    //*Q1* = $(x - x_1) \ldots (x - x_{m/2})$, *Q2* = $(x - x_{m/2+1}) \ldots (x - x_m)$//
    //*gcd(Q1, Q2)* = 1. A polynomial *U3(x)* is computed and returned.//
    //*U3(x_i)* = *U1(x_i)* for $1 \le i \le m/2$//
    //*U3(x_i)* = *U2(x_i)* for $m/2 + 1 \le i \le m$//
    //and the degree of *U3* is $\le m - 1$.//
    U1B ← *PMOD(U1, Q2)* //PMOD(*A, B*) computes the polynomial re-//
                                    //mainder//
    CB ← *PMOD(Q1, Q2)*   //of *A(x)* divided by *B(x)*//
    CB1 ← *EXEUCLID(CB, Q2)* //the extended Euclidean algorithm for//
                                    //polynomials//
    C ← *PMOD(CB1, Q2)*
    U3 ← *PADD(U1, PMUL(PMUL(PSUB(U2 − U1 B), C), Q1))*
end *BALANCEDINTERP*

Algorithm 9.14   Balanced interpolation

We note that steps one, two and three above imply that there exists quotients *C1, C2, C3* such that

$$U1 = Q2*C1 + U1B, \deg(U1B) < \deg(Q2) \quad \text{(a)}$$
$$Q1 = Q2*C2 + CB, \deg(CB) \quad\; < \deg(Q2) \quad \text{(b)}$$
$$C*CB + C3*Q2 = 1, \deg(C) < \deg(Q2) \quad\quad\quad \text{(c)}$$

C is the multiplicative inverse of *CB* modulo *Q2*. Therefore

$$U3 = U1 + (U2 − U1B)*C*Q1 \quad \text{(i)}$$

$$U3 = U1 + (U2 + Q2*C1 − U1)((1 − C3*Q2)/CB)*Q1 \quad \text{(ii)}$$

using (a) and (c). By (i) $U3(x_i) = U1(x_i)$ for $1 \le i \le m/2$ since $Q1(x)$ evaluated at those points is zero. By (ii) it is easy to see that $U3(x) = U2(x)$ at the points $x_{m/2+1}, \ldots, x_m$.

Now steps 1 and 2 take $O(m \log m)$ operations. In order to compute the multiplicative inverse of CB we use the extended gcd algorithm for polynomials which takes $O(m \log m)^2)$ operations. The time for step 4 is no more than $O(m \log m)$ so the total time for one step interpolation is $O(m (\log m)^2)$.

Applying this one step algorithm as we proceed up the tree gives a total computing time for problem 4 of

$$\sum_{1 \le i \le k-1} 2^{i-1} 2^{k-i-1} (k - i - 1)^2 = O(n(\log n)^3) \qquad (9.24)$$

The exercises show how one can further reduce the time for problems 3 and 4 using the idea of preconditioning.

REFERENCES AND SELECTED READINGS

The paper which presented the fast Fourier transform to a modern audience was

"An algorithm for the machine calculation of complex Fourier series" by J. M. Cooley and J. W. Tukey, *Math*. Comp, 19, 1965, 297-301.

Other papers of interest concerning this algorithm are

"History of the fast Fourier transform" by J. M. Cooley, P. A. Lewis, and P. D. Welch, *Proc. IEEE*, 55, 1967, 1675-1679.

"The fast Fourier transform: its role as an algebraic algorithm" by John D. Lipson, *Proc. XXth ACM Conf*, Houston, 436-441.

"Algebraic theory of finite Fourier transforms" by P. J. Nicholson, *J. Computer and System Sciences*, 5:5, 1971, 524-549.

"The fast Fourier transform on a finite field" by J. M. Pollard, *Math. Comp.*, 25, 114, April 1971, 365-374.

"Discrete Fourier transform when the number of data points is prime" by C. M. Rader, *Proc. IEEE*, 56, 1968, 1107-1108.

An even faster method for computing the Fourier transform has just recently appeared. A description of it can be found in

"On computing the discrete Fourier transform" by S. Winograd, IBM Research Report RC6291, Watson Research Center, Yorktown Heights, N.Y. December 1976.

For an interesting collection of papers which deal with evaluation, interpolation, and modular arithmetic see

"Evaluating polynomials at many points" by A. B. Borodin and I. Munro, *Information Processing Letters*, 1:2, 1971, 66–68.

The Computational Complexity of Algebraic and Numeric Problems, by Borodin, A. B., and I. Munro, American Elsevier, New York, 1975.

"Polynomial evaluation via the division algorithm—the fast Fourier transform revisited" by C. M. Fiduccia, *Proc. 4th Annual ACM Symposium on Theory of Computing*, 1972, 88–93.

"On decreasing the computing time for modular arithmetic" by L. E. Heindel and E. Horowitz, *Proc. IEEE 12th Annual Symposium on Switching and Automata Theory*, 1971, 126–128.

"A fast method for interpolation using preconditioning" by E. Horowitz, *Information Processing Letters*, 1:4, 1972, 157–163.

"A unified view of the complexity of evaluation and interpolation" by E. Horowitz, *Acta Informatica*, 3, 1974, 123–133.

"Chinese remainder and interpolation algorithms" by J. Lipson, *Proc. 2nd Symposium on Symbolic and Algebraic Manipulation*, 1971, 372–391.

"Fast modular transforms via division" by R. Moenck and A. B. Borodin, *Proc. IEEE 13th Annual Symposium on Switching and Automata Theory*, 1972, 90–96.

For more on mathematical symbol manipulation systems which allow for operations on mathematical expressions see

"Computer algebra of polynomials and rational functions" by G. E. Collins, *American Math. Monthly*, 80:7, 1973, 725–754.

ALTRAN Users Manual by W. S. Brown, 3rd edition, Bell laboratories, Murray Hill, New Jersey.

MACSYMA Users Manual by J. Moses et. al., M.I.T., Cambridge, Mass.

REDUCE Users Manual by A. Hearn, Computer science, University of Utah, Salt Lake City, Utah.

The use of the FFT plus modular arithmetic for multiplying large precision integers was originally given by

"Schnelle multiplikation grosser zahlen" by A. Schonhage and V. Strassen, *Computing*, 7, 1971, 281–292.

English accounts of the method, which requires $O(n \log n \log \log n)$ operations to multiply two n bit integers, can be found in

The Design and Analysis of Computer Algorithms by A. V. Aho, J. E. Hopcroft, and J. D. Ullman, Addison Wesley, Reading, Mass. 1974.

and

The Art of Computer Programming: Semi-Numerical Algorithms by D. E. Knuth, vol. 11, Addison Wesley, 1969.

EXERCISES

1. Devise an algorithm which accepts a number in decimal and produces the equivalent number in binary.

2. Devise an algorithm which performs the inverse transformation of exercise 1.

3. Show the tuples which would result by representing the polynomials $5x^2 + 3x + 10$ and $7x + 4$ at the values $x = 0, 1, 2, 3, 4, 5, 6$. What set of tuples are sufficient to represent the product of these two polynomials.

4. If $A(x) = a_n x^n + \ldots + a_1 x + a_0$ then the derivative of $A(x)$, $A'(x) = na_n x^{n-1} + \ldots + a_1$. Devise an algorithm which produces the value of a polynomial and its derivative at a point $x = v$. Determine the number of required arithmetic operations.

5. Devise a divide-and-conquer algorithm to evaluate a polynomial at a point. Analyze carefully the time for your algorithm. How does it compare to Horner's rule?

6. A polynomial of degree $n > 0$ has n derivatives, each one obtained by taking the derivative of the previous one. Devise an algorithm which produces the values of a polynomial and its n derivatives.

7. Assume that polynomials such as $A(x) = a_n x^n + \ldots + a_0$ are represented by an array POLY(0:n + 1) where $P(0) = n$ and $P(i) = a_{n-i+1}$ for $1 \le i \le n + 1$. Write a procedure PADD(R, S, T) which takes the polynomials in the arrays R and S and places their sum in the array T.

8. Using the same assumptions as for problem 7, write a procedure PMUL(R, S, T) which computes the product of the polynomials in R and S and places the result in T.

9. Let $A(x) = a_n x^n + \ldots + a_0$, $p = n/2$ and $q = \lceil n/2 \rceil$. Then a variation of Horner's rule states that

$$A(x) = (\ldots(a_{2p}x^2 + a_{2p-2})x^2 + \ldots)x^2 + a_0$$

$$+ ((\ldots(a_{2q-1}x^2 + a_{2q-3})x^2 + \ldots)x^2 + a_1)x$$

Show how to use this formula to evaluate $A(x)$ at $x = v$ and $x = -v$.

10. Given the polynomial $A(x)$ as above devise an algorithm which computes the coefficients of the polynomial $A(x + c)$ for some constant c.

11. Suppose the polynomial $A(x)$ has real coefficients but we wish to evaluate A at the complex number $x = u + iv$, u and v being real. Develop an algorithm to do this.

12. Suppose the polynomial $A(x) = a_m x^{em} + \ldots + a_1 x^{e1}$ where $a_i \neq 0$ and $em > em - 1 > \ldots > e1 \geq 0$ is represented by an array POLY(0:2m) where $P(0) = m$, $P(1) = e_m$, $P(2) = a_m$, $\ldots$, $P(2m - 1) = e_1$, $P(2m) = a_1$. Write a procedure PADD(R, S, T) which computes the sum of two such polynomials and stores the result in the array T.

13. Using the same assumptions as in exercise 9 write a procedure PMUL(R, S, T) which computes the product of the polynomials represented in R and S and places the result in T. What is the computing time of your algorithm?

14. Determine the polynomial of smallest degree with interpolates the points $(0, 1), (1, 2), (2, 3)$.

15. Given n points (x_i, y_i), $1 \leq i \leq n$ devise an algorithm which computes both the interpolating polynomial $A(x)$ and its derivative at the same time. How efficient is your algorithm?

16. Prove that the polynomial of degree $\leq n$ which interpolates $n + 1$ points is unique.

17. The binary method for exponentiation uses the binary expansion of the exponent, n, to determine when to square the temporary result and when to multiply it by x. Since there are $\lfloor \log n \rfloor + 1$ bits in n the algorithm requires $O(\log n)$ operations which is an order of magnitude faster than iteration. Algorithm 9.15 below describes the procedure precisely. Show how to use the binary method to evaluate a sparse polynomial in time $m + \log e_m$.

```
procedure EXPONENTIATE(x, n)
  //returns xⁿ for an integer n ≥ 0.//
  integer m, n real x
  m ← n; y ← 1; z ← x
  while m > 0 do
    while mod(m, 2) = 0 do
      m ← ⌊m/2⌋; z ← z*z
    repeat
    m ← m - 1; y ← y*z
  repeat
  return(y)
end EXPONENTIATE
```

Algorithm 9.15 Binary exponentiation

18. Show the result of applying the Fourier transform to the sequence $(a_0, \ldots, a_7)$.

19. The iterative version of the FFT, Algorithm 9.9, rests upon the fact that dividing a polynomial by $x^t - c$ can be done efficiently. Prove that if $P(x) = a_{2t-1}x^{2t-1} + \ldots + a_0$ then the remainder of $P(x)/(x^t - c)$ is the sum of $(a_j + ca_{j+t})x^j$ for $j = 0, \ldots, t - 1$.

20. Given the finite field $A = (0, 1, \ldots, p - 1)$ one of these elements x, is such that $x^0, x, x^2, \ldots, x^{p-2}$ is equal to all of the nonzero elements of A. x is called a primitve element. If x is a primitive element and n divides $p - 1$ then $x^{(p-1)/n}$ is a primitive nth root of unity. To find such a value x we use the fact that $x^{(p-1)/q} \neq 1$ for each prime factor q of $p - 1$. Use this fact to write an algorithm which, when given a, b and e finds the a largest Fourier primes less than or equal to b of the form $2^f k + 1$ with $f \geq e$. For example if $a = 10$, $b = 2^{31}$ and $e = 20$ the answer is

p	f	least primitive element
2130706433	24	3
2114977793	20	3
2113929217	25	5
2099249153	21	3
2095054849	21	11
2088763393	23	5
2077229057	20	3
2070937601	20	6
2047868929	20	13
2035286017	20	10

Table 9.1 Fourier primes

21. The Fourier transform can be generalized to k dimensions. For example the 2-dimensional transform takes the matrix $a(0:n - 1, 0:n - 1)$ and yields the transformed matrix

$$A(i,j) = \sum_{0 \le k \le n-1} \sum_{0 \le l \le n-1} a_{k,l} w^{-(ik+jl)/n} \qquad (9.25)$$

for an $n \times n$ matrix with elements in $GF(p)$. The inverse transformation is

$$a(i,j) = (1/n^2) \sum_{0 \le k \le n-1} \sum_{0 \le l \le n-1} A(k,l) w^{-(ik+jl)/n} \qquad (9.26)$$

Define the 2-dimensional convolution $C(i, j) = A(i, j)*B(i, j)$ and derive an efficient algorithm for computing it.

22. Investigate the problem of evaluating an nth degree polynomial at the n points $2^i, 0 \le i \le n - 1$. Note that $A(2^i)$ requires no multiplications, only n additions and n shifts.

23. Given the n points $(2^i, y_i)$, $0 \le i \le n - 1$ where y_i is an integer, determine an algorithm which produces the unique interpolating polynomial of degree $\le n$. Try to minimize the number of multiplications.

24. In Section 9.5 the time for the n value Chinese remainder algorithm and n point interpolation is shown to be $O(n(\log n)^3)$. However it is possible to get modified algorithms whose complexity is $O(n(\log n)^2)$ if we allow certain values to be computed in advance without cost. Assuming the moduli and the points are so known, what should be computed in advance to lower the complexity of these two problems?

25. [Diffie, Hellman, Rivest, Shamir, Adelman] Some people are connected to a computer network. They need a mechanism by which they can send messages to one another which can't be decoded by a third party (security) and in addition be able to prove that any particular message was actually sent by a given person (a signature). In short each person needs an encoding mechanism E and a decoding mechanism D such that $D(E(M)) = M$ for any message M. A signature feature is possible if the sender, A, first decodes his message, sends it and it is encoded by the receiver using As encoding scheme E, $(E(D(M)) = M)$. The E for all users is published in a public directory. The scheme to implement D and E proposed by the last three people above relies on the difficulty of factoring versus the simplicity of determining several large (100 digit) primes. Using modular arithmetic see if you can construct an encoding function which is invertible, but only if the factors of a number are known.

Chapter 10

LOWER BOUND THEORY

Lower Bound Techniques

In the previous nine chapters we have surveyed a broad range of problems and their algorithmic solution. Our main task for each problem has been to obtain a correct and efficient solution. If two algorithms for solving the same problem were discovered and if their times differed by an order of magnitude, then the one with the smaller order was generally regarded as superior. But still we are left with the question "is there a faster method". The purpose of this chapter is to expose you to some techniques that have been used to establish that a given algorithm is the most efficient possible. The way this is done is by discovering a function, $g(n)$, which is a lower bound on the time that *any* algorithm must take to solve the given problem. If we have an algorithm whose computing time is the same order as $g(n)$ then we know that asymptotically we can do no better.

Recall from chapter one that there is a mathematical notation for expressing lower bounds. If $f(n)$ is the time for some algorithm, then we write $f(n) = \Omega(g(n))$ to mean that $g(n)$ is a lower bound for $f(n)$. Formally this equation can be written if there exists positive constants c and n_0 such that $|f(n)| \geq c |g(n)|$ for all $n > n_0$. In addition to developing lower bounds to within a constant factor, we will also be concerned with determining more exact bounds whenever this is possible.

Deriving good lower bounds is often more difficult than devising efficient algorithms. Perhaps this is because a lower bound states a fact about *all* possible algorithms for solving a problem. Usually we cannot enumerate and analyze all of these algorithms, so lower bound proofs are often hard to obtain.

However, for many problems it *is* possible to easily observe that a lower bound identical to n exists, where n is the number of inputs (or possibly outputs) to the problem. For example consider all algorithms which find the maximum of an unordered set of n integers. Clearly every integer must be

461

examined at least once and so $\Omega(n)$ is a lower bound for any algorithm which solves this problem. Or, suppose we wish to find an algorithm which efficiently multiplies two $n \times n$ matrices. Then $\Omega(n^2)$ is a lower bound on any such algorithm since there are $2n^2$ inputs which must be examined and n^2 outputs to be computed. Bounds such as these are often referred to as *trivial* lower bounds because they are so easy to obtain. We know how to find the maximum of n elements by an algorithm which uses only $n - 1$ comparisons so there is no gap between the upper and lower bound for this problem. But for matrix multiplication the best known algorithm requires $O(n^{2+\epsilon})$* operations $\epsilon > 0$ and so there is no reason to believe that a better method cannot be found.

In section 10.1 we present the computational model called comparison trees. These are useful for determining lower bounds for sorting and searching problems. In section 10.2 we examine the technique for establishing lower bounds called an oracle and also we study a closely related method called an adversary argument. In section 10.3 we study some arguments which have been used to find lower bounds for the arithmetic and algebraic problems discussed in Chapter 9. Then in section 10.4 we examine some lower bound results assuming that more than one processor is available.

10.1 COMPARISON TREES FOR SORTING AND SEARCHING

In this section we will study the use of comparison trees for deriving lower bounds on problems which are collectively called sorting and searching. We will see how these trees are especially useful for modeling the way in which a large number of sorting and searching algorithms work. By appealing to some elementary facts about trees the lower bounds are obtained.

Suppose that we are given a set S of distinct values upon which an ordering relation "$<$" holds. The *sorting problem* calls for determining a permutation of the integers 1 to n, say $p(1)$ to $p(n)$ such that the n distinct values from S stored in $A(1:n)$ satisfy $A(p(1)) < A(p(2)) < \ldots < A(p(n))$. The *ordered searching problem* asks if a given element $x \in S$ occurs within the elements in $A(1:n)$ which are ordered so that $A(1) < \ldots < A(n)$. If x is in $A(1:n)$ then we are to determine an i between 1 and n such that $A(i) = x$. The *merging problem* assumes that two ordered sets of distinct inputs from S are given in $A(1:m)$ and $B(1:n)$ such that $A(1) < \ldots < A(m)$ and $B(1) < \ldots < B(n)$; these $m + n$ values are to be rearranged into an array $C(1:m + n)$ so that $C(1) < \ldots < C(m + n)$. For all of these problems we will restrict the class of algorithms we are considering to those which work solely by making comparisons between elements. No arithmetic

* see chapter 3 for more details

involving elements is permitted, though it is possible for the algorithm to
move elements around. This class of algorithms is referred to as *comparison
based* algorithms. We rule out algorithms such as radix sort which decom-
pose the values into subparts.

In obtaining the lower bound for the ordered searching problem, we
shall consider only those comparison based algorithms in which every comparison between two elements of S is of the type "compare x and $A(i)$".
Any searching algorithm which satisfies this restriction can be described
by an extended binary tree (see section 3.2 and 5.3). Each internal node
in this tree represents a comparison between x and an $A(i)$. There are
three possible outcomes of this comparison: $x < A(i)$, $x = A(i)$, and $x >
A(i)$. We may assume that if $x = A(i)$ then the algorithm terminates.
Hence the progress of the algorithm may be described by a binary tree in
which the left branch is taken if $x < A(i)$ and the right branch is taken if
$x > A(i)$. If the algorithm terminates following a left or right branch (but
before another comparison between x and $A(i)$) than no i has been found
such that $x = A(i)$ and the algorithm must declare the search unsuccessful.

Figure 10.1 shows two comparison trees, one modeling a linear search
algorithm and the other a binary search (see Algorithm 3.3). It should be
easy to see that the comparison tree for any search algorithm must contain
at least n internal nodes corresponding to the n different values of i for
which $x = A(i)$ and at least one external node corresponding to an unsuccessful search.

Theorem 10.1 Let $A(1:n)$, $n \geq 1$, contain n distinct elements, ordered so
that $A(1) < \ldots < A(n)$. Let FIND(n) be the minimum number of comparisons needed, in the worst case, by any comparison based algorithm to
recognize if $x \in A(1:n)$. Then FIND(n) $\geq \lceil \log (n + 1) \rceil$.

Proof: Consider all possible comparison trees which model algorithms
to solve the searching problem. FIND(n) is bounded below by the distance
of the longest path from the root to a leaf in such a tree. There must be
n internal nodes in all of these trees corresponding to the n possible successful occurrences of x in A. If all internal nodes of a binary tree are at
levels less than or equal to k, then there are at most $2^k - 1$ internal nodes.
Thus $n \leq 2^k - 1$ and FIND(n) $= k \geq \lceil \log (n + 1) \rceil$. $\square$

From the above theorem and theorem 3.2 we can conclude that binary
search is an optimal worst case algorithm for solving the searching problem.

Now lets consider the sorting problem. We can describe any sorting algorithm which satisfies the restrictions of the comparison tree model by an

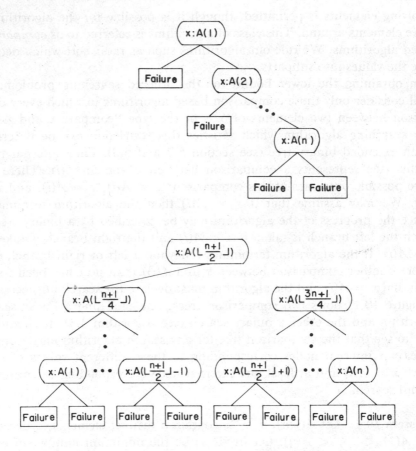

Figure 10.1 Comparison trees for two searching algorithms

extended binary tree. Since the keys are distinct, any comparison between $A(i)$ and $A(j)$ must result in one of two possibilities: either $A(i) < A(j)$ or $A(i) > A(j)$. Thus this tree will be a binary tree where the value of any internal node is the pair $i{:}j$ which represents the comparison $A(i)$ with $A(j)$. If $A(i)$ is less than $A(j)$ then the algorithm proceeds down the left branch of the tree and otherwise it proceeds down the right branch. The external nodes represent termination of the algorithm. Associated with every path from the root to an external node is a unique permutation. To see that this permutation is unique, note that the algorithms we allow are only permitted to move data and make comparisons. The data movement on any path from the root to an external node is the same no matter what the initial input values are. As there are $n!$ different possible permutations of n items, and any one of these might legitimately be the only correct answer for the sorting problem on a given instance, the comparison tree must have at least $n!$ external nodes.

Figure 10.2 shows a comparison tree for sorting 3 items. The first comparison is $A(1) : A(2)$. If $A(1)$ is less than $A(2)$ then the next comparison is $A(2)$ with $A(3)$. If $A(2)$ is less than $A(3)$ then the left branch leads to an external node containing 1,2,3. This implies that the original set was already sorted for $A(1) < A(2) < A(3)$. The other five external nodes correspond to the other possible orderings which could yield a sorted set.

We consider the worst case for all comparison based sorting algorithms. Let $T(n)$ be the minimum number of comparisons which are sufficient to sort n items in the worst case. Using our knowledge of binary trees once again, if all internal nodes are at levels less than k then there are at most 2^k external nodes, (one more than the number of internal nodes). Therefore, letting $k = T(n)$

$$n! \leq 2^{T(n)}$$

Since $T(n)$ is an integer we get the lower bound

$$T(n) \geq \lceil \log n! \rceil$$

By Stirling's approximation (see exercise 7) it follows that

$$\lceil \log n! \rceil = n \log n - n/\ln 2 + (1/2) \log n + O(1)$$

where $\ln 2$ refers to the natural logarithm of 2 while $\log n$ is the logarithm to the base 2 of n. This formula shows that $T(n)$ is of the order $n \log n$.

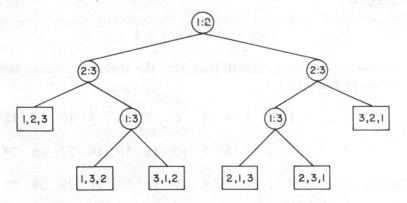

Figure 10.2 A comparison tree for sorting three items

Hence we say that no comparison based sorting algorithm can work in less than $\Omega(n \log n)$ *time.* (This bound can be shown to hold even when operations more complex than just comparisons are allowed, e.g. see in the references the paper by N. Friedman who considers operations such as addition, subtraction and in some cases arbitrary analytic functions).

How close do the known sorting methods get to this lower bound of $T(n)$? Consider the "bottom-up" version of mergesort which first orders consecutive pairs of elements, and then merges adjacent groups of size 2, 4, 8, ... until the entire sorted set is produced. The worst case number of comparisons required by this algorithm is bounded by

$$\sum_{1 \le i \le k} (n/2^i)(2^i - 1) \le n \log n - O(n) \qquad (10.1)$$

Thus we know at least one algorithm which requires slightly less than $n \log n$ comparisons. Is there still a better method?

The sorting strategy called *binary insertion sorting* works in the following way. The next unsorted item is chosen and a binary search (see Algorithm 3.3) is performed on the sorted set to determine where to place this new item. Then the sorted items are moved to make room for the new value. This algorithm will require $O(n^2)$ data movements to sort the entire set but far fewer comparisons. Let BISORT(n) be the number of comparisons it requires. Then by the results of section 3.2

$$\text{BISORT}(n) = \sum_{1 \le k \le n} \lceil \log_2 k \rceil \qquad (10.2)$$

which is equal to

$$\lceil \log n \rceil - 2^{\lceil \log n \rceil} + 1$$

Now suppose we compare BISORT(n) with the theoretical lower bound. This is done in Table 10.1.

n	1	2	3	4	5	6	7	8	9	10	11	12	13
$T(n)$	0	1	3	5	7	10	13	16	19	22	26	29	33
BISORT(n)	0	1	3	5	8	11	14	17	21	25	29	33	37

Table 10.1 Bounds for minimum comparison sorting

Scanning Table 10.1 we observe that for $n = 1, 2, 3$, and 4 the values are the same so binary insertion is optimal. But for $n = 5$ there is a difference of one and so we are left with the question of whether 7 or 8 is the minimum number of comparisons in the worst case needed to sort 5 items. This question has been answered by Lester Ford Jr. and Selmer Johnson who presented a sorting algorithm which requires even fewer comparisons than the binary insertion method. In fact their method requires exactly $T(n)$ comparisons for $1 \le n \le 11$ and $20 \le n \le 21$.

Merge insertion sorting

To see how the Ford-Johnson method works suppose we consider the sorting of 17 items which originally reside in SORTED(1:17). We begin by comparing consecutive pairs SORTED(1): SORTED(2), SORTED(3) : SOR-TED(4), ..., SORTED(15) : SORTED(16) placing the larger items into the array HIGH and the smaller items into the array LOW. SORTED(17) is placed into LOW(9). Then we sort the array HIGH using this algorithm recursively. When this is done we have that LOW(1) < HIGH(1) < ... < HIGH(8) and though LOW(2) through LOW(9) remain unsorted, we do know that LOW(i) $\le$ HIGH(i) for $2 \le i \le 8$. Now if we insert LOW(2) into the sorted set, that will possibly require two comparisons and at the same time cause the insertion of LOW(3) to possibly require 3 comparisons for a total of 5. A better approach is to first insert LOW(3) among the items LOW(1), HIGH(1), HIGH(2) using binary insertion followed by inserting LOW(2). Each insertion requires only 2 comparisons and the merged elements are stored back into the array SORTED. This gives us the new relationships SORTED(1) < SORTED(2) < ... < SORTED(6) < HIGH(4) < HIGH(5) < HIGH(6) < HIGH(7) < HIGH(8) and LOW(i) $\le$ HIGH(i), for $4 \le i \le 8$. Eleven items are now sorted while six remain to be merged. If we insert LOW(4) followed by LOW(5), 3 and 4 comparisons may be needed respectively. Once again it is more economical to first insert LOW(5) followed by LOW(4), each insertion requiring at most 3 comparisons. This gives us the new situation SORTED(1) < ... < SORTED(10) < HIGH(6) < HIGH(7) < HIGH(8) and LOW(i) < HIGH(i), $6 \le i \le 8$. If we insert LOW(7), which will require only four comparisons then LOW(8) will require 5 comparisons. However if we insert LOW(9) followed by LOW(8), LOW(7), and LOW(6) then each item will require at most four comparisons. We do the insertions in the order LOW(9) to LOW(6) yielding the completely sorted set of seventeen items.

A count of the total number of comparisons needed to sort the seventeen items is: 8 to compare SORTED(i) : SORTED($i + 1$), 16 to sort HIGH(1:8) using merge insertion recursively, 4 to insert LOW(3) and LOW(2), 6 to insert LOW(5) and LOW(4), and 16 to insert LOW(9) to LOW(6) requiring a total of 50. The value of $T(n)$ for $n = 17$ is 49 so merge insertion requires only one more comparison than the theoretical lower bound.

In general, merge insertion can be summarized as follows: Let SORTED(1 :n) contain the n items to be sorted. Make pairwise comparisons of SORTED(i) and SORTED($i + 1$) placing the larger items into an array HIGH and the smaller items into array LOW. If n is odd then the last item of SORTED is appended to LOW. Now apply merge insertion to the elements of HIGH. After that we know that HIGH(1) $\leq$ HIGH(2) $\leq \ldots \leq$ HIGH($\lfloor n/2 \rfloor$) and LOW(i) $\leq$ HIGH(i) for $1 \leq i \leq \lfloor n/2 \rfloor$. Now we insert the items of LOW into the HIGH array using binary insertion. However, the order in which we insert the LOW's is important. We want to select the maximum number of items in LOW such that the number of comparisons required to insert each one into the already sorted list is a constant j. As we have seen from our example the insertion will proceed in the order LOW(t_j), LOW($t_j - 1$), ..., LOW($t_{j-1} + 1$) where the t_j are a set of increasing integers. In fact t_j has the form $t_j = 2^j - t_{j-1}$ and in the exercises it is shown that this recurrence relation can be solved to give the formula $t_j = (2^{j+1} + (-1)^j)/3$. Thus items are inserted in the order LOW(3), LOW(2); LOW(5), LOW(4); LOW(11), LOW(10), LOW(9), LOW(8), LOW(7), LOW(6); etc.

It can be shown that the time for this algorithm is

$$\sum_{1 \leq k \leq n} \left\lceil \log_2 \left(\frac{3k}{4} \right) \right\rceil \qquad (10.3)$$

For $n = 1$ to 21 the values of this sum are

0, 1, 3, 5, 7, 10, 13, 16, 19, 22, 26, 30, 34, 38, 42, 46, 50, 54, 58, 62, 66

Comparing these values with the values of the lower bound $T(n)$, we see that merge insertion is truly optimal for $1 \leq n \leq 11$ and $n = 20, 21$.

Is it the case that the Ford-Johnson algorithm actualy requires the fewest number of comparisons needed to sort n items for all values n? Recently Glenn Manacher has exhibited an algorithm which uses fewer comparisons than the Ford-Johnson algorithm for infinitely many n. The smallest such value is $n = 189$. His algorithm makes use of a minimum comparison merging algorithm which we will see in the next section. For more on Manacher's result see his paper in the references.

Lower bounds on selection

From our previous discussion it should be clear that any comparison tree which models comparison based algorithms for finding the maximum of n elements has at least 2^{n-1} external nodes. This follows since each path from the root to an external node must contain at least $n - 1$ internal nodes implying at least $n - 1$ comparisons, for otherwise at least two of the input items never lose a comparison and the largest is not yet found.

Now suppose we let $L_k(n)$ denote a lower bound for the number of comparisons necessary for a comparison based algorithm to determine the largest, 2nd largest, ..., kth largest out of n elements, in the worst case. $L_1(n) = n - 1$ from above. Since the comparison tree must contain enough external nodes to allow for any possible permutation of the input it follows immediately that $L_k(n) \geq \lceil \log n(n - 1) \ldots (n - k + 1) \rceil$.

Theorem 10.2 $L_k(n) \geq n - k + \lceil \log n(n - 1) \ldots (n - k + 2) \rceil$ for all integers k, n where $1 \leq k \leq n$.

Proof: As before internal nodes of the comparison tree contain integers of the form $i{\cdot}j$ which imply a comparison between the input items $A(i)$ and $A(j)$. If $A(i) < A(j)$ then the algorithm proceeds down the left branch and otherwise it proceeds down the right branch. Now consider the set of all possible inputs and place inputs into the same equivalence class if their $k - 1$ largest values appear in the same positions. There will be $n(n - 1) \ldots (n - k + 2)$ equivalence classes which we denote by E_i. Now consider the external nodes for the set of inputs in the equivalence class E_i. The external nodes of the entire tree are also partitioned into classes called X_i. For all external nodes in X_i the positions of the largest, ..., $k - 1$st largest are identical. If we examine the subtree of the original comparison tree which defines the class X_i, then we observe that all comparisons are made on the position of the $n - k + 1$ smallest elements, in essence trying to determine the kth largest element. Therefore this subtree can be viewed as a comparison tree for finding the largest of $n - k + 1$ elements and therefore it has at least 2^{n-k} external nodes.

Therefore the original tree contains at least $n(n - 1) \ldots (n - k + 2)2^{n-k}$ external nodes and the theorem follows. $\square$

10.2   ORACLES AND ADVERSARY ARGUMENTS

One of the proof techniques which is useful for obtaining lower bounds consists of making use of an "oracle". The most famous oracle in history was called the Delphic oracle, located in Delphi, Greece. This oracle can still be found, situated in the side of a hill embedded in some rocks. In olden times people would approach the oracle and ask it a question. After some period of time elapsed, the oracle would reply and a caretaker would interpret the oracles answer.

A similar phenomenon takes place when we use an oracle to establish a lower bound. Given some model of computation such as comparison trees, the oracle tells us the outcome of each comparison. In order to derive a good lower bound, the oracle tries its best to cause the algorithm to work as hard as it might. It does this by choosing as the outcome of the next test, the result which causes the most work to be required to determine the final answer. And by keeping track of the work that is done a worst case lower bound for the problem can be derived.

Now we consider the merging problem. Given the sets $A(1:m)$ and $B(1:n)$ where the items in A and the items in B are sorted, we investigate lower bounds for algorithms which merge these two sets to give a single sorted set. As was the case for sorting we will assume that all of the $m + n$ elements are distinct and that $A(1) < A(2) < \ldots < A(m)$ and $B(1) < B(2) < \ldots < B(n)$. It is possible that after these two sets are merged, the n elements of B may be interleaved within A in every possible way. Elementary combinatorics tells us that there are $\binom{m+n}{m}$ ways that the A's and B's may merge together while still preserving the ordering within A and B. Thus if we use comparison trees as our model for merging algorithms, then there will be $\binom{m+n}{m}$ external nodes and therefore at least

$$\lceil \log \binom{m+n}{m} \rceil$$

comparisons are required by any comparison based merging algorithm. The conventional merging procedure which was given in section 3.4 (Algorithm 3.8) takes $m + n - 1$ comparisons. If we let MERGE(m, n) be the minimum number of comparisons need to merge m items with n items then we have the inequality

$$\left\lceil \log \binom{m + n}{m} \right\rceil \leq \text{MERGE}(m, n) \leq m + n - 1$$

The exercises show that these upper and lower bounds can get arbitrarily far apart as m gets much smaller than n. This should not be a surprise because the conventional algorithm is designed to work best when m and n are approximately equal. In the extreme case when $m = 1$ we observe that binary insertion would require the fewest number of comparisons needed to merge $A(1)$ into $B(1), \ldots, B(n)$.

When m and n are equal then the lower bound given by the comparison tree model is actually too low and the number of comparisons for the conventional merging algorithm can be shown to be optimal.

Theorem 10.3   MERGE$(m, m) = 2m - 1$, for $m \geq 1$.

Proof: Consider any algorithm which merges the two sets $A(1) < \ldots < A(m)$ and $B(1) < \ldots < B(m)$. We already have an algorithm which requires $2m - 1$ comparisons. If we can show that MERGE$(m, m) \geq 2m - 1$ then the theorem follows. Consider any comparison based algorithm for solving the merging problem and an instance for which the final result is $B(1) < A(1) < B(2) < A(2) < \ldots < B(m) < A(m)$, i.e. where the B's and A's alternate. Any merging algorithm must make each of the $2m - 1$ comparisons $B(1) : A(1)$, $A(1) : B(2)$, $B(2) : A(2)$, $\ldots$, $B(m) : A(m)$ while merging the given inputs. To see this suppose that a comparison of type $A(i):B(i)$ is not made for some i. Then the algorithm cannot distinguish between the previous ordering and the one where $B(1) < A(1) < \ldots < A(i - 1) < A(i) < B(i) < B(i + 1) < \ldots < B(m) < A(m)$. So the algorithm will not necessarily merge the A's and B's properly. If a comparison of type $A(i):B(i + 1)$ is not made, then the algorithm will not be able to distinguish between the cases when $B(1) < A(1) < B(2) < \ldots < B(m) < A(m)$ and when $B(1) < A(1) < B(2) < A(2) < \ldots < B(i) < A(i) < A(i + 1) < B(i + 1) < \ldots < B(m) < A(m)$. So any algorithm must make all $2m - 1$ comparisons to produce this final result. The theorem follows.   □

Theorem 10.3 shows us that the conventional merging procedure actually uses the minimum number of comparisons when $m = n$. Since it is known that this procedure gets worse as m gets small why not try to develop an algorithm which works well for small m. When $m = 1$ we have already observed that binary insertion would require the fewest number of comparisons. A hybrid algorithm which combines the merits of binary merging and conventional merging has been developed by F. K. Hwang and S. Lin.

procedure *BINARYMERGE(A, m, B, n, C)*
//*A*(1:*m*) and *B*(1:*n*) satisfy *A*(1) ≤ *A*(2) ≤ ... ≤ *A*(*m*) and//
//*B*(1) ≤ *B*(2) ≤ ... ≤ *B*(*n*). The result is to store the//
//items in *A* and *B* into *C* such that *C*(1) ≤ *C*(2) ≤ ... ≤ *C*(*m* + *n*).//
while *m* ≠ 0 **and** *n* ≠ 0 **do**
  if *m* ≤ *n*
    then *t* ← ⌊log *n*/*m*⌋
      if *A*(*m*) < *B*(*n* + 1 − 2**t)
        then *C* ← *B*(*n* + 1 − 2**t), ..., *B*(*n*)   //move 2^t items into
        C.//
          n ← *n* − 2**t
        else call *BINSRCH(B, n* + 1 − 2***t, n, A*(*m*), *k*)
        k is the greatest integer: *A*(*m*) > *B*(*k*)
        C ← *A*(*m*), *B*(*k* + 1), ..., *B*(*n*)   //Move *n* − *m* + 1//
        //items into *C*//
        m ← *m* − 1; *n* ← *k*
      endif
    else *t* ← ⌊log *m*/*n*⌋
      if *B*(*n*) < *A*(*m* + 1 − 2**t),
        then *C* ← *A*(*m* + 1 − 2**t), ..., *A*(*m*)   //move 2^t items//
        //into *C*//
          m ← *m* − 2**t
      else call *BINSRCH(A, m* + 1 − 2***t, m, B*(*n*), *k*)
      k is the greatest integer: *B*(*n*) > *A*(*k*)
      C ← *B*(*n*), *A*(*k* + 1), ..., *A*(*m*)   //move *m* − *n* + 1 items//
      //into *C*//
      n ← *n* − 1; *m* ← *k*
    endif
  endif
repeat
if *n* = 0 **then** *C* ← *A*(1), ..., *A*(*m*)
        else *C* ← *B*(1), ..., *B*(*n*)
endif
end *BINARYMERGE*

Algorithm 10.1 Minimum comparison merging

As one can see the algorithm is essentially symmetric in the sense that
the main **then else** clauses work in the same way only depending upon
whether *m* or *n* is greater. Procedure BINSRCH (see section 3.2) allows
for a lower and upper bound of an array to be specified and it returns an

index k which points to the largest item in the array which is less than the item to be inserted. The notation $C \leftarrow A(k), A(k + 1), \ldots$ means that everything to the right of the assignment statement is placed into the appropriate place in the output array C.

BINARYMERGE essentially works in the following way. Assuming that $m \leq n$, the last element in the smaller array, $A(m)$, is compared with an element of B which is near the high index end of the array, but not too near. Essentially it is as if the B array were segmented into $m + 1$ groups of $\lceil n/m \rceil$ elements each and the last element in the next to the last group is compared with $A(m)$. If $A(m) < B(k)$, then all of $B(k), B(k + 1), \ldots,$ $B(n)$ can be copied into the output. Otherwise $A(m)$ is inserted into the rightmost group using binary search. $A(m)$ and the values of B which are greater than $A(m)$ can then be inserted into the output. Then the algorithm continues in this way.

Table 10.2 shows an example of BINARYMERGE for $m = 21$ and $n = 3$. The three columns m, n, t show how these variables change throughout the algorithm. The next columns show the comparisons that are made and every time a call to binary search is executed the value of k is set. The output vector is C and you will notice that for this example more than one element is place there each time through the loop. The conventional merging algorithm would require 17 comparisons on this example while BINARYMERGE requires only 5.

The original input is $m = 21, n = 3$ and

$A = (100, 120, 140, 160, 180, 200, 220, 240, 260, 280, 300, 320, 340, 360, 380, 400, 420,$
$440, 460, 480, 500)$

$B = (170, 250, 370)$

m	n	t	comparisons	k	output
21	3	2	$B(3) < A(18)$		$C \leftarrow A(18), A(19), A(20), A(21)$
17	3	2	$B(3) > A(14)$	14	$C \leftarrow B(3), A(15), A(16), A(17)$
14	2	2	$B(2) < A(11)$		$C \leftarrow A(11), A(12), A(13), A(14)$
10	2	2	$B(2) > A(7)$	8	$C \leftarrow B(2), A(9), A(10)$
8	1	3	$B(1) > A(1)$	4	$C \leftarrow B(1), A(5), A(6), A(7), A(8)$
4	0				$C \leftarrow A(1), A(2), A(3), A(4)$

Table 10.2   An example of binary merging

For another example which we can solve using oracles, consider the problem of finding the largest and the 2nd largest elements out of a set of n. What is a lower bound on the number of comparisons required by any algorithm which finds these two quantities? Theorem 10.2 has already provided us with an answer using comparison trees. An algorithm which makes $n - 1$ comparisons to find the largest and then $n - 2$ to find the second largest gives an immediate upper bound of $2n - 3$. So a large gap still remains.

This problem was originally stated in terms of a tennis tournament where the values are called players and the largest value is interpreted as the winner, the second largest as the runner-up. Figure 10.3 shows a sample tournament among eight players. The winner of each match (which is the larger of the two vaues being compared) is promoted up the tree until the final round which, in this case, determines McMahon as the winner. Now, who are the candidates for second place? The runner-up must be someone who lost to McMahon but who did not lose to anyone else? In Figure 10.3 that means that either Daks, Guttag, Rosen, or Francez are the possible candidates for second place.

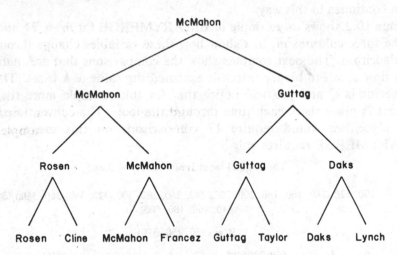

Figure 10.3   A tennis tournament

Figure 10.3 leads us to another algorithm for determining the runner-up once the winner of a tournament has been found. The players who have lost to the winner play a second tournament to determine the runner-up. This second tournament need only be replayed along the path that the winner, in this case McMahon, followed as he rose through the tree. For a tournament with n players there are $\lceil \log n \rceil$ levels and hence only $\lceil \log n \rceil - 1$ comparisons are required for this second tournament. This new algorithm, which was first suggested by J. Schreier in 1932, requires a total of $n - 2 + \lceil \log n \rceil$ comparisons. Therefore we have an identical agreement between the known upper and lower bounds for this problem.

Now we show how the same lower bound can be derived using an oracle.

Theorem 10.4 Any comparison based algorithm which computes the largest and second largest of a set of n unordered elements requires $n - 2 + \lceil \log n \rceil$ comparisons.

Proof: Assume that a tournament has been played obtaining the largest element and the second largest element by some method. Since we cannot determine the second largest element without having determined the largest element we see that at least $n - 1$ comparisons are necessary. Therefore all we need to show is that there is always some sequence of comparisons which forces the second largest to be found in $\lceil \log n \rceil - 1$ additional comparisons.

Suppose that the winner of the tournament has played x matches. Then there are x people who are candidates for the runner-up position. The runner-up has lost only once, to the winner, and the other $x - 1$ candidates must have lost to one other person. Therefore we produce an oracle which decides the results of matches in such a way that the winner plays $\lceil \log n \rceil$ other people.

In a match between a and b the oracle declares a as the winner if a is previously undefeated and b has lost at least once or if both a and b are undefeated but a has won more matches than b. In any other case the oracle can decide arbitrarily as long as it remains consistent.

Now, consider a tournament in which the outcome of each match is determined by the above oracle. Corresponding to this tournament imagine drawing a directed graph with n vertices. Each vertex corresponds to one of the n players. Draw a directed edge from vertex b to a, $b \neq a$ iff either player a has defeated b or a has defeated another player who has defeated b. It is easy to see by induction that any player who has played and won only x matches can have at most 2^{x-1} edges pointing into its corresponding node. Since for the overall winner there must be an edge from each of the remaining $n - 1$ vertices, it follows that the winner must have played at least $\lceil \log n \rceil$ matches. $\square$

Another technique for establishing lower bounds which is related to oracles is the state space description method. Often it is possible to describe any algorithm for solving a given problem by a set of n-tuples. A *state space description* is a set of rules which show the possible states (n-tuples) which an algorithm can assume from a given state and a single comparison. Once the state transitions are given it is possible to derive lower bounds by arguing that the finish state cannot be reached using any fewer transitions. As an example of the state space description method we consider a problem originally defined and solved in section 3.3, given n distinct items find the maximum and the minimum. Recall that the divide-and-conquer based solution required $\lceil 3n/2 \rceil - 2$ comparisons. We would like to show that this algorithm is indeed optimal.

Theorem 10.5 Any algorithm which computes the largest and smallest element of a set of n unordered elements requires $\lceil 3n/2 \rceil - 2$ comparisons.

Proof: The technique we use to establish a lower bound is to define an oracle by a state table. We consider the state of a comparison based algorithm as being described by a four tuple (a, b, c, d) where a is the number of items which have never been compared; b is the number of items which have won but never lost; c is the number of items which have lost but never won; and d is the number of items which have both won and lost. Originally the algorithm is in state $(n, 0, 0, 0)$ and concludes with $(0, 1, 1, n - 2)$. Then, after each comparison the tuple (a, b, c, d) can make progress only if it assumes one of five possible states:

$(a - 2, b + 1, c + 1, d)$ if $a \geq 2$ //two items from a are compared//

$(a - 1, b, c + 1, d)$ or $(a - 1, b + 1, c, d)$ if $a \geq 1$ //an item from a compared with one from b or c//

$(a, b - 1, c, d + 1)$ if $b \geq 2$ //two items from b are compared//

$(a, b, c - 1, d + 1)$ if $c \geq 2$ //two items from c are compared//

In order to get the state $(0, 1, 1, n - 2)$ from the state $(n, 0, 0, 0)$ it follows that $\lceil 3n/2 \rceil - 2$ comparisons are needed. To see this observe that the quickest way to get the a component to zero requires $n/2$ state changes yielding the tuple $(0, n/2, n/2, 0)$. Next the b and c components are reduced, requiring an additional $n - 2$ state changes.   □

We end this section by deriving another lower bound on the selection problem. We originally studied this problem in Chapter 3 where we presented several solutions. One of the algorithms presented there has a worst case complexity of $O(n)$ no matter what value is being selected. Therefore we know that asymptotically any selection algorithm requires $\Theta(n)$ time. Let $SEL_k(n)$ be the minimum number of comparisons needed for finding the kth element of an unordered set of size n. We have already seen that for $k = 1$ $SEL_1(n) = n - 1$ and for $k = 2$, $SEL_2(n) = n - 2 + \lceil \log n \rceil$. In the following paragraphs we present a state table which shows that $n - k + (k - 1) \lceil \log n/(k - 1) \rceil \le SEL_k(n)$. We continue to use the terminology which refers to an element of the set as a "player" and to a comparison between two players as a "match" which must be won by one of the players. A procedure for selecting the kth largest element is referred to as a tournament which finds the kth best player.

In order to derive this lower bound on the selection problem, an oracle will be constructed in the form of a state transition table which will cause any comparison based algorithm to make at least $n - k + (k - 1) \lceil \log n/(k - 1) \rceil$ comparisons. The tuple size for states in this case is two, (it was four for the max-min problem), and the components of a tuple, say (Map, Set), stand for the following: Map is an onto mapping from the integers $1, 2, \ldots, n$ to itself and Set is an ordered subset of the input. The inital state is the identity mapping and the empty set. At any time period t the oracle is assumed to be given two unordered elements from the input, say a and b, and the oracle acts as follows:

(i)   if a and b are both in Set at time t then a wins iff $a > b$. The tuple (Map, Set) remains unchanged.

(ii) If a is in Set and b is not in Set then a wins and the tuple (Map, Set) remains unchanged.

(iii) if a and b are both not in Set, then if $Map(a) > Map(b)$ at time t then a wins. If $Map(a) = Map(b)$ then it doesn't matter who wins as long as no inconsistency with any previous decision is made. If $Map(a) + Map(b) > n/(k - 1)$ at time t then Map is unchanged and the winner is inserted into Set as the new smallest value. Otherwise Set stays the same and Map(the loser) $\leftarrow 0$ at time $t + 1$ and Map(the winner) $\leftarrow Map(a) + Map(b)$ at time $t + 1$ and for all items w, $w \ne a$, $w \ne b$, $Map(w)$ stays the same.

Lemma 10.1 Using the oracle just defined, the $k - 1$ best players will have played at least $(k - 1) \lceil \log (n/(k - 1)) \rceil$ matches when the tournament is completed.

Proof: At time t the number of matches won by any player x is $\ge \lceil \log Map(x) \rceil$. The elements in Set are ordered so that $x_1 < \ldots < x_y$. Now for all w in the input $\Sigma(Map(w)) = n$. Let $W = \{ y : y$ is not in Set but

Map(y) > 0}. Since for all w in the input Map(w) $< n/(k - 1)$ it follows that the size of Set plus the size of W is $> k - 1$. However since the elements y in W can only be less than some x_i in Set, if the size of Set is $< k - 1$ at the end of the tournament then any player in Set or W is a candidate for the $k - 1$ best players. This is a contradiction so it follows that at the end of the tournament the $k - 1$ best players are ordered and in Set.　□

We are now in a position to establish the main theorem.

Theorem 10.6　[Hyafil]　The function $SEL_k(n)$ satisfies
$$n - k + (k - 1) \lceil \log n/(k - 1) \rceil \leq SEL_k(n).$$

Proof:　According to the lemma the $k - 1$ best players have played at least $(k - 1) \lceil \log n/(k - 1) \rceil$ matches. Any player who is not among the k best players has lost at least one match against a player which is not among $k - 1$ best. Thus there are $n - k$ additional matches which were not included in the count of the matches played by the $k - 1$ top players. Thus the statement of the proof follows.　□

10.3　TECHNIQUES FOR ALGEBRAIC PROBLEMS

In this section we will examine two methods, substitution and linear independence, for deriving lower bounds on arithmetic and algebraic problems. The algebraic problems we are considering here are operations on integers, polynomials and rational functions. Solutions to these problems were presented in Chapter 9. In addition we also include matrix multiplication and related operations which were discussed in Chapter 3.

The model of computation we will use is called a *straight line* program. It is called this because there are no branching instructions allowed. This implies that if we know a way of solving a problem for n inputs, then a *set* of straight line programs, one each for solving a different size n, can be given. The only statement in a straight line program is the assignment which has the form $s \leftarrow p$ op q. s, p, q are variables of bounded size and op is typically one of the arithmetic operations: addition, subtraction, multiplication or division. Moreover s is a variable which has not yet appeared in any previous step, while p and q are either constants, an input variable or a variable which has already appeared on the left of an assignment statement. For example one possible straight-line program which computes the value of a degree two polynomial has the form

$$v1 \leftarrow a_2 * x$$
$$v1 \leftarrow v1 + a_1$$
$$v1 \leftarrow v1 * x$$
$$\text{ans} \leftarrow v1 + a_0$$

In order to determine the complexity of a straight line program we assume that each instruction takes one unit of time and requires one unit of space. Then the time complexity of a straight line program is the number of assignments, or its length. A more realistic assumption takes into account the fact that an interger n requires $\lfloor \log n \rfloor + 1$ bits to represent it. But in this section we will assume that all operands are small enough to occupy a fixed size register and hence the unit cost assumption is appropriate.

Now we need to consider the class of constants we intend to allow. This requires some elementary definitions from algebra.

Definition   A *ring* is an algebraic structure containing a set of elements S and two binary operations denoted by $+$ and $*$. For each $a, b \in S$, $a + b$ and $a*b$ are also in S. Also the following properties hold:

$(a + b) + c = a + (b + c)$ and $(a*b)*c = a*(b*c)$ (associativity)

$\quad a + b = b + a$ (commutativity)

$(a + b)*c = a*c + b*c$ and $a*(b + c) = a*b + a*c$ (distributivity)
$\quad a + 0 = 0 + a = a$ (0 is the additive identity)

$\quad\quad a*1 = 1*a = a$ (1 is the multiplicative identity)

for each $a \in S$ there is an additive inverse denoted by $-a$ such that $a + (-a) = (-a) + a = 0$.
If multiplication is also commutative then the ring is called commutative.

Definition   A *field* is a commutative ring such that for each element $a \in S$ (other than 0) there is a multiplicative inverse denoted by a^{-1} which satisfies the equation $a*a^{-1} = 1$.

The real numbers form a field under the regular operations of additon and multiplication. Similarly for the complex numbers. However the integers with the operations $+$ and $*$ do not form a field since only plus or minus one have multiplicative inverses. Another field is the set of integers modulo a prime as discussed in Chapter 9. They form a finite field consisting of the integers $(0, 1, \ldots, p - 1)$.

Definition An *indeterminate* over an algebraic system is a symbol which does not occur in S. The *extension* of S by the indeterminates $x_1, \ldots, x_n$ is the smallest commutative ring which contains all combinations of the elements of S and the indeterminates. Such an extension is denoted by $S[x_1, \ldots, x_n]$. When an extension is made to a field which allows for quotients of combinations of elements of S and indeterminates then that is denoted by $S(x_1, \ldots, x_n)$.

The elements in an extension $S[x_1, \ldots, x_n]$ can be viewed as polynomials in the variables x_i with coefficients from the set S. The elements in an extension $S(x_1, \ldots, x_n)$ should be viewed as rational functions of the variables x_i with coefficients which are from S. The indeterminates are independent in the sense that no one can be expressed by the others and hence two such polynomials or rational functions are equal only if one can be transformed into the other using the laws of the ring or field.

The field of constants can make an important difference on the complexity of the algorithms for some problems. For example if we wish to examine programs for computing $x^2 + y^2$ where the field is the reals, then two multiplications are required. However if the field is the complex numbers, then only one complex multiplication is needed, namely $(x + iy)*(x - iy)$.

Theorem 10.7 Every algorithm for computing the value of a general nth degree polynomial which uses only $+$, $-$, $*$ requires n addition or subtractions.

Proof: Any straight line program which computes the value of $a_n x^n + \ldots + a_0$ can be transformed into a program to compute $a_n + \ldots + a_0$ given some field of constants F and indeterminates $(a_n, \ldots, a_0)$. This new program is produced by inserting the statement $s \leftarrow 1$ at the beginning and then replacing every occurrence of x by s. We now prove by induction that $a_n + \ldots + a_0$ requires n additions or subtractions. For $n = 1$ we need to compute $a_1 + a_0$ *as an element in* $F[a_1, a_0]$. If we disallow additions or subtractions then by the definition of extension only products of the a_i multiplied by constants from the field can be produced. Thus $a_1 + a_0$ requires one addition. Now suppose we have computed a sum or difference of at least two terms where each term is possibly a product of elements from the vector a and possibly a field element. Without a loss of generality assume that a_n appears in one of these terms. If we substitute zero for a_n then this eliminates the need for this first addition or subtraction since one of the arguments is zero. We are now computing $a_{n-1} + \ldots + a_0$ which by the induction hypotheses requires $n - 1$ additions or subtractions. Thus the theorem follows.   □

The basic idea of this proof is the substitution argument. Using the same technique one can derive a not much more complicated theorem which shows that Horner's rule is optimal with respect to multiplications or divisions.

Definition Suppose F and G are two fields such that F is contained in G and we are computing in $G(a_1, \ldots, a_n)$. The operation f op g where op is * or / is said to be *inactive* if one of the following hold: (i) $g \in F$; (ii) $f \in F$ and the operation is multiplication; (iii) $f \in G$ and $g \in G$.

Any multiplication or division which is not inactive is called *active*. So for example operations such as $x*x$ or $15*a_i$ are inactive while the operations $x*a_i$ or a_1*a_2 or $15/a_i$ are active.

Definition Let $a = (a_0, \ldots, a_n)$. Then $p_1(a), \ldots, p_u(a)$ is *linearly independent* if there does not exist a nontrivial set of constants $c_1, \ldots, c_n$ such that $\Sigma\, c_i p_i = $ a constant.

$P(a, x)$ can be thought of as a general polynomial in the sense that it is a function not only of x, but of the inputs a. We can write $P(a, x)$ as $\Sigma(p_i(a)x^i + r(x)$ where u of the p_i are linearly independent.

Theorem 10.8 [Borodin, Munro] If u active * or / are required to compute $P(a, x)$ then n active * or / are required to evaluate a general nth degree polynomial.

Proof: The proof proceeds by induction on u. Suppose $u = 1$. If there is no active * or / then it is only possible to form $p_i(a) + r(x)$ for some i. Now suppose $(p_i(a) + r_1(x))*(p_j(a) + r_2(x))$ is the first active multiplication in a straight line program which computes $P(a, x)$. Without loss of generality assume that $p_j(a) \neq$ a constant. Then, in the straight line program let $p_j(a) + r_2(x)$ be replaced by a constant d such that no illegal division by zero is caused. This can always be done for if p_j is a linear combination of constants c_i times a_i and since there must be exist a $j : c_j \neq 0$, then by setting

$$a_j = -\frac{1}{c_j}\left(\sum_{i, i \neq j} c_i a_i + r_2(x) - d\right)$$ (10.4)

it follows that $p_j(a) + r_2(x) = d$. Now consider $P(a, x)$ where the substitution of a_j has been made. P can be rewritten into the form

$$\sum_{0 \leq i \leq n} P_i{'}(x)\, x^i + r{'}(x)$$ (10.5)

Therefore by making the one replacement we can remove one active multiplication or division and we are now computing a new expression. If it can be shown that there are $u - 1$ linearly independent p_j then by the induction hypothesis there are at least $u - 1$ remaining active * or / and the theorem follows. This is a technical lemma and so we will skip its presentation here. It can be found in the exercises.

Corollary 10.1   Horner's rule is an optimal algorithm with respect to the number of multiplications and divisions necessary to evaluate a polynomial.

Proof: From the previous theorem and the result in the exercises that under substitution $u - 1$ linearly independent combinations remain and the fact that Horner's rule requires only n multiplications the theorem follows. $\square$

Another method of proof for deriving lower bounds for algebraic problems is to consider these problems in a matrix setting. Returning to polynomial evaluation we can express this problem in the following way: compute the $1 \times (n + 1)$ by $(n + 1) \times 1$ matrix product

$$[1, x, x^2, \ldots, x^n] \begin{bmatrix} a_0 \\ a_1 \\ \cdot \\ \cdot \\ \cdot \\ a_n \end{bmatrix} \tag{10.6}$$

which is the product of two vectors. Another problem is complex number multiplication. The product of $(a + ib) * (c + id) = ac - bd + (bc + ad)i$ can be written in terms of matrices as

$$\begin{bmatrix} a & -b \\ b & a \end{bmatrix} \begin{bmatrix} c \\ d \end{bmatrix} = \begin{bmatrix} ac - bd \\ bc + ad \end{bmatrix} \tag{10.7}$$

In more general terms we wish to consider problems which can be formulated as the product of a matrix times a vector

$$
\begin{bmatrix} a_{11}, & \cdots, & a_{1n} \\ \cdot & & \\ \cdot & & \\ \cdot & & \\ a_{m1}, & \cdots, & a_{mn} \end{bmatrix} \begin{bmatrix} x_1 \\ \cdot \\ \cdot \\ \cdot \\ x_n \end{bmatrix} \qquad (10.8)
$$

Definition   Let F be a field and $x_1, \ldots, x_n$ be indeterminates. Let $F^m[x_1, \ldots, x_n]$ stand for the m-dimensional space of vectors with components from $F[x_1, \ldots, x_n]$ and F^m stand for the m-dimensional space of vectors with components from F. A set of vectors $v_1, \ldots, v_k$ from $F^m[x_1, \ldots, x_n]$ is *linearly independent modulo* F^m if for $u_1, \ldots, u_k$ in F the sum $\Sigma(u_i v_i)$ $i = 1, k$ in F^m implies the u_i are all zero. If the v_i are not linearly independent then they are called linearly *dependent* modulo F^m. The *row rank* of a matrix A modulo F^r is the number of linearly independent rows modulo F^r. The *column rank* is the number of linearly independent columns.

We now state the main theorem of this section.

Theorem 10.9 Let A be an $r \times s$ matrix with elements from the extension field $F[x_1, \ldots, x_n]$ and $y = [y_1, \ldots y_s]$ a column vector containing s indeterminates.

(i)   if the row rank of A is v, then any computation of Ay requires at least v active multiplications;

(ii)   if the column rank of A is w, then any computation of Ay requires at least w active multiplications;

(iii)   If A contains a submatrix B of size $v \times w$ such that for any vectors $p \in F^v$, $q \in F^w$, $p^T B q \in F$ iff $p = 0$ or $q = 0$, then any computation of Ay requires $v + w - 1$ multiplications.

Proof: For a proof of part (i) see the paper by Winograd. For a proof of parts (ii) and (iii) see the papers by Fiduccia. Also see Aho, Hopcroft and Ullman.   □

Example 10.1   Reconsider the problem of multiplying two 2×2 matrices

$$\begin{bmatrix} a & b \\ c & d \end{bmatrix} \begin{bmatrix} e & f \\ g & h \end{bmatrix} = \begin{bmatrix} ae + bg, & af + bh \\ ce + dg, & cf + dh \end{bmatrix}$$

which by definition seemingly requires 8 multiplications. We can rephrase this computation in terms of a matrix-vector product as follows

$$\begin{bmatrix} a & b & 0 & 0 \\ c & d & 0 & 0 \\ 0 & 0 & a & b \\ 0 & 0 & c & d \end{bmatrix} \begin{bmatrix} e \\ g \\ f \\ h \end{bmatrix} = \left(\begin{bmatrix} a - b & 0 & 0 & 0 \\ 0 & 0 & 0 & 0 \\ a + b & 0 & 0 & 0 \\ 0 & 0 & 0 & 0 \end{bmatrix} \right.$$

$$+ \begin{bmatrix} b & b & 0 & 0 \\ -b & -b & 0 & 0 \\ 0 & 0 & 0 & 0 \\ 0 & 0 & 0 & 0 \end{bmatrix} + \begin{bmatrix} 0 & 0 & 0 & 0 \\ 0 & 0 & 0 & c - d \\ 0 & 0 & 0 & 0 \\ 0 & 0 & 0 & -c + d \end{bmatrix}$$

$$+ \begin{bmatrix} 0 & 0 & 0 & 0 \\ 0 & 0 & 0 & 0 \\ 0 & 0 & -c & -c \\ 0 & 0 & c & c \end{bmatrix} + \begin{bmatrix} 0 & 0 & 0 & 0 \\ 0 & 0 & 0 & 0 \\ a + c & 0 & a + c & 0 \\ 0 & 0 & 0 & 0 \end{bmatrix}$$

$$+ \begin{bmatrix} 0 & 0 & 0 & 0 \\ 0 & b + d & 0 & b + d \\ 0 & 0 & 0 & 0 \\ 0 & 0 & 0 & 0 \end{bmatrix} + \left. \begin{bmatrix} 0 & 0 & 0 & 0 \\ b + c & 0 & 0 & -b - c \\ -b - c & 0 & 0 & b + c \\ 0 & 0 & 0 & 0 \end{bmatrix} \right) \begin{bmatrix} e \\ g \\ f \\ h \end{bmatrix}$$

The first 2×2 matrix, say A, has been expanded as the 4×4 matrix

$$\begin{bmatrix} A & 0 \\ 0 & A \end{bmatrix}$$

This matrix is then further decomposed into a sum of 7 matrices, each of size 4×4. Both the row rank and the column rank of each matrix is one and hence by Theorem 10.11 we see that 7 multiplications are necessary.

Example 10.2   Given two complex numbers $a + ib$ and $c + id$, the product $(a + ib) * (c + id) = ac - bd + i(ad + bc)$ can be described by the matrix-vector computation

$$\begin{bmatrix} a & -b \\ b & a \end{bmatrix} \begin{bmatrix} c \\ d \end{bmatrix} = \begin{bmatrix} ac - bd \\ bc + cd \end{bmatrix} \qquad (10.9)$$

which seemingly requires 4 multiplications, but it can also be written as

$$\left(\begin{bmatrix} a + b & 0 \\ 0 & a - b \end{bmatrix} + \begin{bmatrix} -b & -b \\ b & b \end{bmatrix} \right) \begin{bmatrix} c \\ d \end{bmatrix} \qquad (10.10)$$

The row and column rank of the first matrix is 2 while the row and column rank of the second matrix is 1. Thus 3 multiplications are necessary. The product can be computed as

(i) $a * (d - c)$
(ii) $(a + b) * c$
(iii) $b * (c + d)$

Then (ii) $-$ (iii) $= ac - bd$ and (i) + (ii) $= ad + bc$.

Example 10.3   Equation 10.6 phrases the evaluation of an nth degree polynomials in terms of a matrix-vector product. The matrix has n linearly independent columns modulo the constant field F and thus by theorem 10.11, n multiplications are necessary.

Lower bounds on polynomials with preconditioning

In this section we've already seen that any algorithm which evaluates a general nth degree polynomial requres n multiplications or divisions and n additions or subtractions. This assertion was based on the assumption that the input to any algorithm was both the value of x plus the coefficients of the polynomial. We might take another view and consider how well one can do if the coefficients of the polynomial are known in advance and functions of these coefficients can be computed without cost before evalua- tion begins. This process of computing functions of the coefficients is re- ferred to as *preconditioning*.

Suppose we begin by considering the general 4th degree polynomial $A(x) = a_4x^4 + a_3x^3 + a_2x^2 + a_1x + a_0x^0$ and the scheme

$$y \leftarrow (x + c_0)x + c_1 \qquad A(x) \leftarrow ((y + x + c_2)y + c_3)c_4$$

Only three multiplications and five additions are required if we can deter- mine the values of the c_i in terms of the a_i. Expanding $A(x)$ in terms of x and the c_i we get

$$A(x) = c_4x^4 + (2c_0c_4 + c_4)x^3 + (c_0^2 + 2c_1 + c_0c_4 + c_2c_4)x^2 +$$
$$(2c_0c_1c_4 + c_1c_4 + c_0c_2c_4)x + (c_1^2c_4 + c_1c_2c_4 + c_3c_4)$$

and equating the above coefficients with the a_i we get that

$$c_4 = a_4; \quad c_0 = (a_3/a_4 - 1)/2$$
$$b = a_2/a_4 - c_0(c_0 + 1)$$
$$c_1 = a_1/a_4 - c_0b; \quad c_2 = b - 2c_1 \quad c_3 = a_0/a_4 - c_1(c_1 + c_2)$$

Applying the above method to the polynomial $A(x) = -x^4 + 3x^3 - 2x^2 + 2x + 1$ yields the straight line program

$$q \leftarrow x - 2$$
$$r \leftarrow q*x$$
$$y \leftarrow r - 2$$
$$s \leftarrow y + x$$
$$t \leftarrow s + 4$$
$$u \leftarrow t*y$$
$$v \leftarrow u + 3$$
$$p \leftarrow -1*v$$

which evaluates to $A(x)$ in just three multiplications.

In fact the following can be shown; for any polynomial $A(x)$ of degree $n \geq 3$ there exist real numbers c, d_i, e_i for $0 \leq i \leq \lceil n/2 \rceil - 1$ such that $A(x)$ can be evaluated in $\lfloor n/2 \rfloor + 2$ multiplications and n additions by the following scheme

$$y \leftarrow x + c; \quad w \leftarrow y*y$$

$$z \leftarrow (a_n y + d_0)y + e_0 \ (n \text{ even}); \quad z \leftarrow a_n y + e_0 \ (n \text{ odd})$$

$$z \leftarrow z(w - d_i) + e_i, \quad \text{for } i = 1, 2, \ldots, m;$$

answer $\leftarrow z$.

Now that we have a scheme which reduces the number of required multiplications by about one half, it is natural to ask how close we have come to the optimal. The lower bound we are about to present follows from the fact that any straight line program can be put into a "normal form" involving a limited number of constants. We will restrict our arguments here to programs without division, leaving the extension to interested readers.

Lemma 10.2 (Motzkin 1954) For any straight line program with k multiplications and a single input variable x, there exists an equivalent program using at most $2k$ constants.

Proof: Let s_i, $0 \leq i \leq k$ denote the result of the ith multiplication. We can rewrite the program as

$$s_0 \leftarrow x$$

$$s_i \leftarrow L_i * R_i, \quad 1 \leq i \leq k$$

$$A(x) \leftarrow L_{k+1}$$

where each L_i and R_i is a certain sum of a constant (which may accumulate other constants from the original program) and an earlier s_j (an s_j may appear several times in this sum). The first product $s1 \leftarrow (c_1 + m_1 x)*(c_2 + m_2 x)$ can be replaced by $s1 \leftarrow mx(x + c)$, where $m = m_1 m_2$ and $c = m_1 c_2 + m_2 c_1$, provided that later constants are suitably altered.   □

Lemma 10.3 (Belaga 1958) For any straight line program with k addition-subtractions and a single input variable x, there exists an equivalent program using at most $k + 1$ constants.

Proof: Let s_i, $0 \le i \le k$ be the result of the kth addition-subtraction. As in the previous proof we can rewrite the program as

$$s_0 \leftarrow x$$

$$s_i \leftarrow c_i p_i + d_i q_i, \quad 1 \le i \le k$$

$$A(x) \leftarrow c_{k+1} P_{k+1}$$

where each p_i and q_i is a product of earlier s_j. For $k = 1, 2, \ldots$ replace s_i by $s_i \leftarrow (c_i d_i^{-1}) p_i + q_i$, simultaneously replacing subsequent references to s_i by $d_i s_i$.   □

Theorem 10.10   (Motzkin, Belaga) A randomly selected polynomial of degree n has probability zero of being computable either with less then $\lceil (n + 1)/2 \rceil$ multiplications-divisions or with less than n addition-subtractions.

Proof sketch: If a given straight line program with the single input variable x has only a "few" operations, then we may assume that it has at most n constants. Each time these constants are set they determine a set of coefficients of the polynomial computed by the last operation of the program. Given $A(x)$ of degree n, the probability is zero that the program's n or fewer constants can be adjusted to align the computed polynomial with all $n + 1$ of the given polynomial coefficients. A formal proof here relies on showing that the subset of $(n + 1)$-dimensional space which can be so represented has Lebesque measure zero. It follows (because the set of straight line programs is enumerable if we identify programs differing only in their constants) that with only zero probability can the constants of any such short program be set so as to evaluate the polynomial.   □

The above theorem shows that the preconditioning method previously given comes very close to being optimal, but some room for improvement remains.

10.4   SOME LOWER BOUNDS ON PARALLEL COMPUTATION

In this section we will present just some of the recent lower bounds which have been developed under the assumption that a machine with many processors is available. We refer to this situation as *parallel computation*. The machine model which underlies all of the results to be presented here assumes that k independently programmable processors are available. Sometimes k is fixed, while other times the number may vary with the problem instance. Each processor can perform arithmetic and comparisons just like the single processor we have been assuming throughout this book. At each time period it is possible that all processors can be "working", but during this time period they can perform at most a constant number of operations. We will not consider whether the processors are working synchronously or asynchronously. We only wish to note that more control is necessary when the processors can act at varying speeds. There is a memory that is shared by all of the processors. Moreover, the assumption is made that at any time t all k processors can access this memory simultaneously. In practice this turns out to be a very unrealistic assumption. However from the perspective of obtaining lower bounds it does not invalidate the results. It only implies that any actual speed-up in computation time through the use of parallel processors will not be as great as the bounds presented here.

A *parallel algorithm* is an algorithm which is run on a parallel-processor, i.e. a machine which permits more than one processor to function on the same problem at the same time. Some of the algorithms which are typically described for a single processor machine are naturally converted to a many processor machine. Modular arithmetic as discussed in Chapter 9 is one such example. On the other hand many solutions to problems seem essentially sequential in nature and it looks as if no speed-up can be obtained by running such an algorithm on a parallel machine. Therefore many researchers have recently been investigating new algorithms which will best exploit the capabilities of a parallel processor. The complexity of a parallel algorithm is the worst case number of time periods needed for an algorithm to complete. Since at each time period k processors can be computing, the complexity of a parallel algorithm is usually less than for a one processor machine.

Information theoretic arguments

Consider the computation of x^n where $n = 2^m$. Information theory tells us that it is impossible to generate too much information about a problem in a given amount of time. For this problem that means that x^n cannot be computed in fewer than $\lceil \log n \rceil$ steps, or in particular that $x^2, x^4, x^8, \ldots,$ x^n requires m steps no matter how many processors are available. This result was first stated in more general terms by Kung.

Theorem 10.11 Let $A(x) = P(x)/Q(x)$ be a rational function, P and Q are relatively prime, and where n is the maximum of the degrees of P and Q. Then at least $\lceil \log n \rceil$ parallel time is needed to compute $A(x)$.

Proof The proof proceeds by induction on n. Suppose $n = 1$. Then $A(x)$ has the form $(ax + b)/(cx + d)$ where a, b, c, d are constants. Thus $A(x)$ can be computed in a constant amount of time which is bounded below by $\lceil \log n \rceil$. Suppose that the theorem is true for any rational function $A(x)$ where the maximum degree n is less than 2^m. By the induction hypothesis this implies that only m steps were needed to compute $A(x)$. At step $m + 1$ $A(x)$ can either be added to another rational function or multiplied by another rational functional, but in both cases the degree of the other argument can be no more than n. Therefore at time $m + 1$ the maximum degree of any result can be at most $2n = 2^{m+1}$. Since the $\lceil \log 2^{m+1} \rceil = m + 1$ the result follows. $\square$

Now lets turn our attention to the sorting problem. In Section 10.1 we observed that $\Omega(n \log n)$ was a lower bound for sorting on a sequential machine.

Theorem 10.12 Given $n = 2^m$ unordered elements it takes at least $\lceil \log n \rceil$ parallel time to sort these values.

Proof: Consider the comparison tree model defined for the sorting problem and presented in Section 10.1. There are $n!$ external nodes corresponding to the $n!$ possible permutations of the input. On any level of this comparison tree imagine that as many processors as one would like are available to determine the relationships on that level. Since the tests made on a given level depend upon the results of tests made on the previous level, we conclude that no parallel processor can work faster than the number of levels in the tree. As there are at least $\lceil \log n \rceil$ levels the theorem follows. $\square$

Evaluating arithmetic expressions

Theorem 10.13 [Munro and Paterson] Suppose the computation of an arithmetic expression requires n binary operations. Then the shortest parallel time which is needed to evaluate this expression using at most k processors is bounded below by $(n + 1)/k + \log k - 1$ for n sufficiently large.

Proof: Let P_{min} be the fewest number of parallel steps required by k processors to evaluate an expression. At the last time period at most one processor is needed to evaluate the final binary operator. Similarly, at the time period $P_{min} - 1$ at most 2 processors are needed, at time $P_{min} - 2$ at most

4 processors and in general at time $P_{min} - m$ at most 2^m processors are needed. During the time periods 1, 2, ..., $P_{min} - m - 1$ at most k processors can be used. Therefore we get a bound on n, namely

$$n \leq 1 + 2 + 2^2 + \ldots + 2^m + (P_{min} - m - 1)k$$

Solving for P_{min} one gets

$$(n - 2^{m+1} + 1)/k \leq P_{min} - m - 1$$

and letting $k = 2^m$ and simplifying we get

$$P_{min} \geq (n + 1)/k + \log k - 1 \qquad \square$$

It is interesting to review how close researchers have come to this lower bound. For expressions with $n - 1$ binary operators and k processors where every variable appears once and no division is allowed, Brent has given an algorithm which requires $2n/k + O(\log n)$ parallel steps and if division is allowed then $10n/k + O(\log n)$ parallel steps. Winograd has improved on these bounds somewhat by giving algorithms such that for expressions without division $3n/2k + O((\log n)^2)$ parallel time is required and if division is allowed than $5n/2k + O((\log n)^2)$. See the references for more details.

More on sorting and searching

Theorem 10.14 [Valiant] Given n unordered elements and $k = n$ processors, if MAX(n) is a lower bound on the worst case time needed to determine the maximum value in parallel time, then MAX(n) $\geq \log \log n - c$, where c is a constant.

Proof: Consider the information determined from the set of comparisons which can be made by time t for some parallel maximum finding algorithm. Some of the elements have been shown to be smaller than other elements and so they have been eliminated. The others form a set S which contains the correct answer. If at time t two elements not in S are compared then no progress is made decreasing set S. If an element in set S and one not in S are compared and if the larger element is in S then again no improvement has been made. Assume that the worst case holds which means that the only way to decrease the set S is to make comparisons between pairs of its elements.

Imagine a graph where the nodes represent the values in the input and a directed edge from a to b implies that b is greater than a. A subset of the nodes is said to be *stable* if no pair from it is connected by an edge. Then the size of S at time t can be expressed as

S at time $t \geq$ min(max(h : the graph contains a stable set of size h)
or G is a graph with the size of S nodes and n edges)

It has been shown by Turan in *On the theory of graphs*, Colloq. Math., 1954 that the size of S at time t is $\geq$ the size of S at time $t - 1$, squared divided by $2k$ + the size of S. We can solve this recurrence relation using the fact that initially the size of S equals n which shows that the size of S will be greater than one so long as $t < \log \log n - c$.   □

This lower bound on maximum finding may come as a surprise and a first reaction might be that is it unusually low. Even more surprising is the fact that Valiant has given an algorithm for finding the maximum which takes no more time than log log n + a constant. Though his algorithm assumes a great deal of overhead between each parallel step, this sort of result is of great interest. For more details see his paper as listed in the references.

Now what can we say about sorting on a parallel computer. The information theoretic lower bound says that $\Omega(\log n)$ is the best any parallel algorithm can do. An interesting method given by K. Batcher requires $O(n (\log n)^2)$ on a sequential machine, but on a parallel machine only $O((\log n)^2)$ parallel steps are required because at each time unit all comparisons are independent.

Procedure *BATCHER(A, n)*

  //sorts the values $A(1), \ldots, A(n)$ in-place, assuming $n \geq 2$//

  $t \leftarrow \lceil \log n \rceil$

  $i \leftarrow 2**(t - 1)$ //$2^{t-1} < n \leq 2^t$//

  while $i \geq 1$ **do**

    $q \leftarrow 2**(t - 1); r \leftarrow 0; d \leftarrow i$

  $L : j \leftarrow 0$

    while $j < n - d$ **and** $((j$ **and** $i) = r)$ **do**

      if $A(j + 1) > A(j + d + 1)$

        then *temp* $\leftarrow A(j + 1); A(j + 1) \leftarrow A(j + d + 1); A(j + d + 1)$

        $\leftarrow$ *temp*

      endif

      $j \leftarrow j + 1$

      repeat

      if $q \neq i$ **then** $d \leftarrow q - i; q \leftarrow q/2; r \leftarrow i;$ **go to** L

        else $i \leftarrow i/2$

      endif

  repeat

end *BATCHER*

Algorithm 10.2

Example 10.4 Suppose we take nine values and trace the algorithm as it sorts these values. The lines indicate comparisons and exchanges which are possibly made.

135, 382, 154, 72, 341, 422, 174, 243, 120   one exchange

120, 382, 154, 72, 341, 422, 174, 243, 135   no exchanges

120, 382, 154, 72, 341, 422, 174, 243, 135   one exchange

120, 382, 154, 72, 135, 422, 174, 243, 341   two exchanges

120, 72, 154, 382, 135, 243, 174, 422, 341   no exchange

120, 72, 154, 382, 135, 243, 174, 422, 341   two exchanges

120, 72, 135, 243, 154, 382, 174, 422, 341   one exchange

72, 120, 135, 243, 154, 382, 174, 422, 341   no exchanges

72, 120, 135, 243, 154, 382, 174, 422, 341   two exchanges

72, 120, 135, 174, 154, 341, 243, 422, 382   three exchanges

72, 120, 135, 154, 174, 243, 341, 382, 422

A proof that Batcher's method does actually sort in all cases can be found in Knuth, volume I♥. Also there one can find an account of how to use Batcher's algorithm on a parallel processor so that the time for transferring data as well as for performing logical operations remains bounded by $O((\log n)^2)$. The value of Batcher's method or any other parallel algorithm must wait until these machines are built and tested. At this point it seems that merely counting logical operations is insufficient to produce a truly efficient algorithm for a parallel processor and it is likely that data movement will also be an important parameter to measure to determine the real efficiency of any algorithm.

REFERENCES AND SELECTED READINGS

For a detailed account of lower bounds for sorting, merging and selection see Sections 5.3, 5.3.1, 5.3.2 and 5.3.3 in

The Art of Computer Programming, volume III sorting and searching by Donald Knuth, Addison-Wesley, 1973.

Another good source of material on lower bounds was circulated as a set of notes for a while

Cs230 notes by Richard Karp, Univ. of Calfornia-Berkeley, Fall quarter 1972 and spring quarter 1971

The sorting algorithm which requires the fewest known number of comparisons was originally presented in

"A tournament problem" by L. Ford Jr. and S. Johnson, *American Math Monthly*, 66, (1959), 387–389.

See also

"The Ford-Johnson algorithm is not optimal" by Glenn K. Manacher, Dept. of Information Engineering, Univ. of Illinois, Chicago, Ill. 60680.

The minimum comparison merging algorithm was presented in

"A simple algorithm for merging two disjoint linearly ordered sets" by F. K. Hwang and S. Lin, *SIAM J. Computing*, 1 (1972), 31-39.

The lower bound on the selection problem can be found in

"Bounds for selection", by Laurent Hyafil, *SIAM J. Computing*, vol. 5, no. 1, March 1976, 109-114.

Other relevant papers containing lower bound results includes

"Using comparison trees to derive lower bounds for selection problems" by Frank Fussenegger and Harold Gabow, *Proc. 17th Found. of C. S.*, IEEE, October, 1976, 178-182.

"Bounds on the complexity of the longest common subsequence problem" by A. Aho, D. S. Hirschberg and J. D. Ullman, *J. ACM*, vol. 23, no. 1, January 1976, 1-12.

"On the optimality of some set algorithms" by E. M. Reingold, *J. ACM*, vol. 19, no. 4, October 1972, 649-659.

In

"Computing the maximum and the median" by E. M. Reingold *Proc. 12th Symp. on Switching and Automata Theory*, IEEE, October 1971, 216-218

it is shown that the maximum of a set of n integers cannot be computed in fewer than $n - 1$ comparisons if comparisons of only linear functions of the integers are permitted, but in $\log n$ comparisons if exponential functions are allowed.

In

"Some results on the effect of arithmetics on comparison problems" by Nathan Friedman, *Proc. 13th Symp. on Switching and Automata Theory*, IEEE, October 1972, 139-143

it is shown that the $\Omega(n \log n)$ bound for sorting holds even if comparisons between arbitrary functions and analytic functions on output are permitted. Other results of interest are included.

The solution of exercise 17 can be found in

"On the complexity of computations under varying sets of primitives" by David Dobkin and Richard Lipton, *Automata theory and formal languages*, Springer-Verlag lecture notes in computer science 33.

"A lower bound of $(1/2)n^2$ on linear search programs for the knapsack problem" by David Dobkin and Richard Lipton, Research report 70, Yale University, New Haven, Conn.

Several related papers on lower bounds can be found in the single technical report

"Excursions into geometry" by David Dobkin, Richard Lipton and Reiss, Research report 71, Yale University, New Haven, Conn.

Many of the algebraic lower bounds can be found in the following two books

The computation complexity of algebraic and numeric problems, by A. Borodin and I. Munro, American Elsevier, New York, 1975.

The Design and Analysis of Computer Algorithms by A. Aho, J. E. Hopcroft and J. D. Ullman, Addison-Wesley, Reading, 1974.

A proof of part (i) of Theorem 10.11 can be found in

"On the number of multiplications necessary to compute certain functions" by S. Winograd, *Comm. Pure and Applied Math.*, vol. 23, 1970, 165-179.

A proof of part (ii) of Theorem 10.11 can be found in

"On obtaining upper bounds on the complexity of matrix multiplication" by C. Fiduccia, *Proc. IBM Symposium on complexity of computer computations*, March 1972.

A proof of part (iii) of Theorem 10.11 can be found in

"Fast matrix multiplication" by C. Fiduccia, *Proc. 3rd Annual ACM symposium on theory of computing*, (1971), 45-49.

For readings on parallel computation see the following papers plus their references

"The complexity of parallel evaluation of linear recurrences" by L. Hyafil and H. T. Kung, *J. ACM*, (24, 1) July 1977, 513-521.

"The parallel evaluation of general arithmetic expressions" by Richard P. Brent, *J. ACM*, (21, 2) April, 1974, 201–206.

"On the parallel evaluation of certain arithmetic expressions" by S. Winograd, *J. ACM*, (22, 4), October, 1975, 477–492.

"New algorithms and lower bounds for the parallel evaluation of certain rational expressions and recurrences" by H. T. Kung, *J. ACM*, (23, 2), April, 1976, 252–261.

"Optimal algorithms for parallel polynomial evaluation" by I. Munro and M. Paterson, *J. Comp. and Sys. Scis,* vol. 7, 1973, 189–198.

"Parallelism in comparison problems" by Leslie Valiant *SIAM J. Comp.*, (4, 3), September, 1975, 348–355.

and the book by Borodin and Munro cited above.

EXERCISES

1. Draw the comparison tree for sorting four elements.

2. Draw the comparison tree for sorting four elements which is produced by the binary insertion method.

3. When equality between keys is permitted there are thirteen possible permutations when sorting 3 elements. What are they?

4. When keys are allowed to be equal a comparison can have one of three results: $A(i) < A(j)$, $A(i) = A(j)$, $A(i) > A(j)$. Sorting algorithms can therefore be represented by extended ternary comparison trees. Draw an extended ternary tree for sorting 3 elements when equality is allowed.

5. Let $TE_{min}(n)$ be the minimum number of comparisons needed to sort n items and to determine all equalities between them. It is clear that $TE(n) \geq T(n)$ since the n items could be distinct. Show that $TE(n) = T(n)$.

6. Find a comparison tree for sorting six elements which has all external nodes on levels 10 and 11.

7. Stirling's approximation is $n! \sim \sqrt{2\pi n}\,(n/e)^{n(1+n/12)}$. Show how this approximation is used to show that $\lceil \log n! \rceil = n \log n - n/(\ln 2) + (1/2)\log n + O(1)$.

8. Prove that the closed form for BISORT$(n) = n \lceil \log n \rceil - 2^{\lceil \log n \rceil} + 1$ is correct.

9. Show that log $(n!)$ is approximately equal to $n \log n - n \log e + O(1)$ by using the fact that the function log k is monotonic and bounded below by $\log x \, dx$ from $k - 1$ to k.

10. Show that the sum $2^k - 2^{k-1} + 2^{k-2} + \ldots + (-1)^k 2^0 = (2^{k+1} + (-1)^k)/3$.

11. Let $m = \alpha n$. Then by Stirling's approximation $\log\binom{\alpha n + n}{\alpha n} = n((1 + \alpha) \log (1 + \alpha) - \alpha\log \alpha) - (1/2)\log n + O(1)$. Show that as $\alpha \to 0$ the difference between this formula and $m + n - 1$ gets arbitrarily large.

12. Let $F(n)$ be the minimum number of comparisons, in the worst case, needed to insert $B(1)$ into the ordered set $A(1) < A(2) < \ldots < A(n)$. Prove by induction that $F(n) \geq \lceil \log n + 1 \rceil$.

13. A *partial ordering* is a binary relation, denotes by "$\leq$", which satisfies (i) if $x \leq y$ and $y \leq z$ then $x \leq z$; and (ii) if $x \leq y$ and $y \leq x$ then $x = y$. A *total ordering* is a partial ordering which satisfies (iii) for all x, y either $x \leq y$ or $y \leq x$. How can a directed graph be used to model a partial ordering or a total ordering.

14. Consider the problem of determining a lower bound for the problem of multiplying an $m \times n$ matrix A by an $n \times 1$ vector. Show how to reexpress this problem using a different matrix formulation so that theorem 10.11 can be applied yielding the lower bound of mn multiplications.

15. [Reingold] Let $A(1{:}n)$ and $B(1{:}n)$ each contain n unordered elements. Show that if comparisons between pairs of elements of A or B are not allowed, then $O(n^2)$ operations are required to test if the elements of A are identical (though possibly a permutation) of the elements of B.

16. In the derivation of the Ford-Johnson sorting algorithm, the sequence t_j must be determined. Explain why $t_j + t_{j-1} = 2^j$. Then show how to derive the formula $t_j = (2^{j+1} + (-1)^j)/3$.

17. [Dobkin and Lipton]   A search program is a finite sequence of instructions of three types: (i) **if** $f(x)$ R 0 **then go to** $L1$ **else go to** $L2$ where R is either $<$, $>$, or $=$ and x is a vector; (ii) **accept**, (iii) **reject**. The sum of subsets problem asks for a subset I of the integers $1, 2, \ldots, n$ for the inputs $w_1, \ldots, w_n$ such

that $\Sigma(w_i) = b$, where b is a given number. Consider search programs where the function f is restricted so that it can only make comparisons of the form

$$\sum_{i \in i} w_i = b \qquad (10.11)$$

Using the adversary technique Dobkin and Lipton have shown that $\Omega(2^n)$ such operations are required to solve the sum of subsets problem $(w_1, \ldots, w_n, b)$. See if you can derive their proof.

18. Let A be an $n \times n$ symmetric matrix, $A(i, j) = A(j, i)$ for $1 \le i, j \le n$. Show that if p is the number of nonzero entries of $A(i, j)$, $i < j$ then $n + p$ multiplications are sufficient to compute Ax.

19. Show how an $n \times n$ matrix can be multiplied by two $n \times 1$ vectors using $(3n^2 + 5n)/2$ multiplications.

20. [W. Miller] (i) Let (N, R) denote the reflexive transitive closure of a directed graph (N, E). Thus $<u, v>$ is an edge in R if there is a path from u to v using zero or more edges in E. Show that R is a partial order on N iff (N, E) is acyclic. (ii) Prove that $(N, E \cup \langle u, v \rangle)$ is acyclic iff (N, E) is acyclic and there is no path from v to u using edges in E. (iii) Prove that if (N, E) is acyclic and if u, v are distinct elements of N, then one of $(N, E \cup \langle u, v \rangle)$ or $(N, \cup(E \langle v, u \rangle))$ is acyclic. (iv) Show that it is natural to think of an oracle as constructing an acyclic digraph on the set N of players. Interpret (ii) and (iii) as rules governing how the oracle may resolve matches.

21. [Valiant]   Devise a parallel algorithm which produces the maximum of n unordered elements in $\log \log n + c$ parallel time, where c is a constant.

22. [Valiant] For a number of processors $k = \sqrt{mn}$ and for $n \le m$, devise a parallel algorithm for merging two ordered sets of m and n elements which works in time $2 \log \log n + c$, where c is a constant.

23. [Valiant]   Use the idea of mergesort and the fast merging algorithm in the previous exercise to devise a parallel sorting algorithm which takes at most $2 \log n \log \log n + O(\log n)$ parallel time.

24. Write an exponentiation procedure which computes x^n using the low order to the high order bits of n.

25. Determine how fast the inner product $\Sigma a_i b_i$ of two vectors can be formed in parallel time.

26. Devise a parallel algorithm which computes the set of values $x^2, x^3, \ldots, x^n$ which requires less than $O(n)$ time.

27. [Kung]   Consider the recurrence relation $y_{i+1} = (1/2)(y_i + a/y_i)$ $i = 0,$ 1, 2, ..., $n - 1$ for approximating $a^{1/2}$. Show that evaluating y_n by any parallel algorithm requires $O(n)$ parallel time.

28. [Kung]   Given the recurrence $y_i = y_{i-1}b_i + a_{i+1}, i \geq 1$, show that a speed-up of at most $(2/3)k + 1/3$ is the best possible for evaluating y_n.

29. [Borodin Munro]   This exercise completes the proof of Theorem 10.9. Let $p_1(a_1, \ldots a_s), \ldots, p_u(a_1, \ldots, a_s)$ be u linearly independent functions of $a_1, \ldots, a_s$. Let $a_1 = p(a_2, \ldots, a_s)$. Then show that there are at lest $u - 1$ linearly independent $p_i' = p_i$ where a_1 is replaced by p.

30. Devise a parallel algorithm which computes the value of an nth degree polynomial in time $O(\log n)$.

31. Devise a parallel algorithm which merges two ordered sets of n elements in $O(\log n)$ time.

32. [W. Miller]   Show that the inner product of two n-vectors can be computed in $\lceil n/2 \rceil$ multiplications if separate preconditioning of the vector elements is not counted.

Chapter 11

NP-HARD AND NP-COMPLETE PROBLEMS

11.1 BASIC CONCEPTS

This chapter contains what is perhaps the most important theoretical development in algorithms research in the past decade. Its importance arises from the fact that the results have meaning for all researchers who are developing computer algorithms, not only computer scientists but electrical engineers, operations researchers, etc. Thus we believe that many people will turn immediately to this chapter. In recognition of this we have tried to make the chapter self-contained. Also, we have organized the later sections according to different areas of interest.

There are however some basic ideas which one should be familiar with before reading on. The first is the idea of analyzing apriori the computing time of an algorithm by studying the frequency of execution of its statements given various sets of data. A second notion is the concept of the order of magnitude of the time complexity of an algorithm and its expression by asymptotic notation. If $T(n)$ is the time for an algorithm on n inputs, then, we write $T(n) = O(f(n))$ to mean that the time is bounded *above* by the function $f(n)$, and $T(n) = \Omega(g(n))$ to mean that the time is bounded *below* by the function $g(n)$. Precise definitions and greater elaboration of these ideas can be found in Section 1.4.

Another important idea is the distinction between problems whose solution is by a polynomial time algorithm ($f(n)$ is a polynomial) and problems for which no polynomial time algorithm is known ($g(n)$ is larger than any polynomial). It is an unexplained phenomena that for many of the problems we know and study, the best algorithms for their solution have computing times which cluster into two groups. The first group consists of problems whose solution is bounded by a polynomial of small degree. Examples we have seen in this book include ordered searching which is $O(\log n)$, poly-

501

nomial evaluation is $O(n)$, sorting is $O(n \log n)$, and matrix multiplication which is $O(n^{2.81})$.

The second group contains problems whose best known algorithms are nonpolynomial. Examples we have seen include the traveling salesperson and the knapsack problem for which the best algorithms given in this text have a complexity $O(n^2 2^n)$ and $O(2^{n/2})$ respectively. In the quest to develop efficient algorithms, no one has been able to develop a polynomial time algorithm for any problem in the second group. This is very important because algorithms whose computing time is greater than polynomial (typically the time is exponential) very quickly require such vast amounts of time to execute that even moderate size problems cannot be solved. (See Section 1.4 for more details.)

The theory of NP-completeness which we present here does not provide a method of obtaining polynomial time algorithms for problems in the second group. Nor does it say that algorithms of this complexity do not exist. Instead, what we shall do is show that many of the problems for which there is no known polynomial time algorithm are computationally related. In fact, we shall establish two classes of problems. These will be given the names NP-hard and NP-complete. A problem which is NP-complete will have the property that it can be solved in polynomial time iff all other NP-complete problems can also be solved in polynomial time. If an NP-hard problem can be solved in polynomial time then all NP-complete problems can be solved in polynomial time. As we shall see all NP-complete problems are NP-hard but all NP-hard problems are not NP-complete.

While one can define many distinct problem classes having the properties stated above for the NP-hard and NP-complete classes, the classes we study are related to nondeterministic computations (to be defined later). The relationship of these classes to nondeterministic computations together with the "apparent" power of nondeterminism leads to the "intuitive" (though as yet unproved) conclusion that no NP-complete or NP-hard problem is polynomially solvable.

We shall see that the class of NP-hard problems (and the subclass of NP-complete problems) is very rich as it contains many interesting problems from a wide variety of disciplines. First, we formalize the preceding discussion of the classes.

Nondeterministic Algorithms

Up to now the notion of algorithm that we have been using has the property that the result of every operation is uniquely defined. Algorithms with this property are termed *deterministic algorithms*. Such algorithms agree with the way programs are executed on a computer. In a theoretical framework we can remove this restriction on the outcome of every operation. We can allow algorithms to contain operations whose outcome is not uniquely defined but is limited to a specified set of possibilities. The machine executing such operations is allowed to choose any one of these outcomes subject to a termination condition to be defined later. This leads to the concept of a *nondeterministic algorithm*. To specify such algorithms we introduce one new function and two new statements into SPARKS:

(i) **choice** (S)...arbitrarily chooses one of the elements of set S
(ii) **failure** ...signals an unsuccessful completion
(iii) **success** ...signals a successful completion.

The assignment statement $X \leftarrow$ **choice**$(1:n)$ could result in X being assigned any one of the integers in the range $[1, n]$. There is no rule specifying how this choice is to be made. The **failure** and **success** signals are used to define a computation of the algorithm. These statements are equivalent to a **stop** statement and cannot be used to effect a **return**. Whenever there is a set of choices that leads to a successful completion then one such set of choices is always made and the algorithm terminates successfully. *A nondeterministic algorithm terminates unsuccessfuly if and only if there exists no set of choices leading to a success signal.* The computing times for **choice**, **success**, and **failure** are taken to be $O(1)$. A machine capable of executing a nondeterministic algorithm in this way is called a *nondeterministic machine*. While nondeterministic machines (as defined here) do not exist in practice, we shall see that they will provide strong intuitive reasons to conclude that certain problems cannot be solved by "fast" deterministic algorithms.

Example 11.1 Consider the problem of searching for an element x in a given set of elements $A(1:n)$, $n \geq 1$. We are required to determine an index j such that $A(j) = x$ or $j = 0$ if x is not in A. A nondeterministic algorithm for this is

```
j ← choice(1:n)
if A(j) = x then print(j); success endif
print('0'); failure
```

From the way a nondeterministic computation is defined, it follows that the number '0' can be output if and only if there is no j such that $A(j) = x$.

The above algorithm is of nondeterministic complexity $O(1)$. Note that since A is not ordered, every deterministic search algorithm is of complexity $\Omega(n)$.   □

Example 11.2 [Sorting] Let $A(i)$, $1 \leq i \leq n$ be an unsorted set of positive integers. The nondeterministic algorithm NSORT(A, n) sorts the numbers into nondecreasing order and then outputs them in this order. An auxiliary array $B(1:n)$ is used for convenience. Line 1 initializes B to zero though any value different from all the $A(i)$ will do. In the loop of lines 2–6 each $A(i)$ is assigned to a position in B. Line 3 nondeterministically determines this position. Line 4 ascertains that $B(j)$ has not already been used. Thus, the order of the numbers in B is some permutation of the initial order in A. Lines 7 to 9 verify that B is sorted in nondecreasing order. A successful completion is achieved iff the numbers are output in nondecreasing order. Since there is always a set of choices at line 3 for such an output order, algorithm NSORT is a sorting algorithm. Its complexity is $O(n)$. Recall that all deterministic sorting algorithms must have a complexity $\Omega(n \log n)$.   □

```
      procedure  NSORT(A, n)
          //sort n positive integers//
          integer  A(n), B(n), n, i, j
  1          B ← 0   //initialize B to zero//
  2          for  i ← 1 to n do
  3              j ← choice(1:n)
  4                  if  B(j) ≠ 0 then failure endif
  5                  B(j) ← A(i)
  6              repeat
  7          for  i ← 1 to n − 1 do    //verify order//
  8              if  B(i) > B(i + 1) then failure endif
  9          repeat
  10         print(B)
  11         success
  12     end  NSORT
```

Algorithm 11.1 Nondeterministic sorting

A deterministic interpretation of a nondeterministic algorithm can be made by allowing unbounded parallelism in computation. Each time a choice is to be made, the algorithm makes several copies of itself. One copy is made for each of the possible choices. Thus, many copies are executing at the same time. The first copy to reach a successful completion terminates all other computations. If a copy reaches a failure completion then only that copy of the algorithm terminates. Recall that the **success** and **failure** signals are equivalent to **stop** statements in deterministic algorithms. They may not be used in place of **return** statements. While this interpretation may enable one to better understand nondeterministic algorithms, it is important to remember that a nondeterministic machine does not make any copies of an algorithm every time a choice is to be made. Instead, it has the ability to select a "correct" element from the set of allowable choices (if such an element exists) every time a choice is to be made. A "correct" element is defined relative to a shortest sequence of choices that leads to a successful termination. In case there is no sequence of choices leading to a successful termination, we shall assume that the algorithm terminates in one unit of time with output "unsuccessful computation." Whenever successful termination is possible, a nondeterministic machine makes a sequence of choices which is a shortest sequence leading to a successful termination. Since, the machine we are defining is fictitious, it is not necessary for us to concern ourselves with how the machine can make a correct choice at each step.

It is possible to construct nondeterministic algorithms for which many different choice sequences lead to a successful completion. Procedure NSORT of Example 11.2 is one such algorithm. If the numbers $A(i)$ are not distinct then many different permutations will result in a sorted sequence. If NSORT were written to output the permutation used rather than the $A(i)$'s in sorted order then its output would not be uniquely defined. We shall concern ourselves only with those nondeterministic algorithms that generate a unique output. In particular we shall consider only *nondeterministic decision algorithms*. Such algorithms generate only a zero or one as their output. A binary decision is made. A successful completion is made iff the output is '1'. A '0' is output iff there is no sequence of choices leading to a successful completion. The output statement is implicit in the signals **success** and **failure**. No explicit output statements are permitted in a decision algorithm. Clearly, our earlier definition of a nondeterministic computation implies that the output from a decision algorithm is uniquely defined by the input parameters and the algorithm specification.

While the idea of a decision algorithm may appear very restrictive at this time, many optimization problems can be recast into decision problems with the property that the decision problem can be solved in polynomial time iff the corresponding optimization problem can. In other cases, we can at least make the statement that if the decision problem cannot be solved in polynomial time then the optimization problem cannot either.

Example 11.3 [Max Clique] A maximal complete subgraph of a graph $G = (V, E)$ is a **clique**. The size of the clique is the number of vertices in it. The *max clique problem* is to determine the size of a largest clique in G. The corresponding decision problem is to determine if G has a clique of size at least k for some given k. Let DCLIQUE(G, k) be a deterministic decision algorithm for the clique decision problem. If the number of vertices in G is n, the size of a max clique in G can be found by making several applications of DCLIQUE. DCLIQUE is used once for each k, $k = n, n - 1, n - 2, \ldots$ until the output from DCLIQUE is 1. If the time complexity of DCLIQUE is $f(n)$ then the size of a max clique can be found in time $n*f(n)$. Also, if the size of a max clique can be determined in time $g(n)$ then the decision problem may be solved in time $g(n)$. Hence, the max clique problem can be solved in polynomial time iff the clique decision problem can be solved in polynomial time.   □

Example 11.4 [0/1-Knapsack] The knapsack decision problem is to determine if there is a 0/1 assignment of values to x_i, $1 \le i \le n$ such that $\Sigma p_i x_i \ge R$ and $\Sigma w_i x_i \le M$. R is a given number. The p_i's and w_i's are nonnegative numbers. Clearly, if the knapsack decision problem cannot be solved in deterministic polynomial time then the optimization problem cannot either.   □

Before proceeding further, it is necessary to arrive at a uniform parameter, n, to measure complexity. We shall assume that n is the length of the input to the algorithm. We shall also assume that all inputs are integer. Rational inputs can be provided by specifying pairs of integers. Generally, the length of an input is measured assuming a binary representation. I.e., if the number 10 is to be input then, in binary it is represented as 1010. Its length is 4. In general, a positive integer k has a length of $\lfloor \log_2 k \rfloor + 1$ bits when represented in binary. The length of the binary representation of 0 is 1. The size or length, n, of the input to an algorithm is the sum of the lengths of the individual numbers being input. In case the input is given using a different representation (say radix r), then the length of a positive number k is $\lfloor \log_r k \rfloor + 1$. Thus, in decimal notation, $r = 10$ and the number 100 has a length $\log_{10} 100 + 1 = 3$ digits. Since $\log_r k = \log_2 k / \log_2 r$, the length of any input using radix $r(r > 1)$ representation is $c(r) \cdot n$ where n is the length using a binary representation and $c(r)$ is a number which is fixed for a given r.

When inputs are given using the radix $r = 1$, we shall say the input is in *unary form*. In unary form, the number 5 is input as 11111. Thus, the length of a positive integer k is k. It is important to observe that the length of a unary input is exponentially related to the length of the corresponding r-ary input for radix r, $r > 1$.

Example 11.5 [Max Clique] The input to the max clique decision problem may be provided as a sequence of edges and an integer k. Each edge in $E(G)$ is a pair of numbers (i, j). The size of the input for each edge (i, j) is $\lfloor \log_2 i \rfloor + \lfloor \log_2 j \rfloor + 2$ if a binary representation is assumed. The input size of any instance is

$$n = \sum_{\substack{(i,j) \in E(G) \\ i<j}} (\lfloor \log_2 i \rfloor + \lfloor \log_2 j \rfloor + 2) + \lfloor \log_2 k \rfloor + 1.$$

Note that if G has only one connected component then $n \geq |V|$. Thus, if this decision problem cannot be solved by an algorithm of complexity $p(n)$ for some polynomial $p( )$ then it cannot be solved by an algorithm of complexity $p(|V|)$.   □

Example 11.6 [0/1 Knapsack] Assuming p_i, w_i, M and R are all integers, the input size for the knapsack decision problem is

$$m = \sum_{1 \leq i \leq n} (\lfloor \log_2 p_i \rfloor + \lfloor \log_2 w_i \rfloor) + \lfloor \log_2 M \rfloor + \lfloor \log_2 R \rfloor + 2n + 2.$$

Note that $m \geq n$. If the input is given in unary notation then the input size s is $\sum p_i + \sum w_i + M + R$. Note that the knapsack decision and optimization problems can be solved in time $p(s)$ for some polynomial $p( )$ (see the dynamic programming algorithm). However, there is no known algorithm with complexity $O(p(n))$ for some polynomial $p( )$.   □

We are now ready to formally define the complexity of a nondeterministic algorithm.

Definition The *time required by a nondeterministic algorithm* performing on any given input is the minimum number of steps needed to reach a successful completion if there exists a sequence of choices leading to such a completion. In case successful completion is not possible then the time required is $O(1)$. A nondeterministic algorithm is of complexity $O(f(n))$ if for all inputs of size, n, $n \geq n_0$, that result in a successful completion the time required is at most $c \cdot f(n)$ for some constants c and n_0.

In the above definition we assume that each computation step is of a fixed cost. In word oriented computers this is guaranteed by the finiteness of each word. When each step is not of a fixed cost it is necessary to consider the cost of individual instructions. Thus, the additon of two m bit numbers takes $O(m)$ time, their multiplication takes $O(m^2)$ time (using classical multiplication) etc. To see the necessity of this consider procedure SUM (Algorithm 11.2). This is a deterministic algorithm for the sum of subsets decision problem. It uses an $M + 1$ bit word S. The i'th bit in S is zero iff no subset of the integers $A(j)$, $1 \le j \le n$ sums to i. Bit 0 of S is always 1 and the bits are numbered 0, 1, 2, ..., M right to left. The function SHIFT shifts the bits in S to the left by $A(i)$ bits. The total number of steps for this algorithm is only $O(n)$. However, each step moves $M + 1$ bits of data and would really take $O(M)$ time on a conventional computer. Assuming one unit of time is needed for each basic operation for a fixed word size, the true complexity is $O(nM)$ and not $O(n)$.

```
procedure  SUM(A, n, M)
  integer  A(n), S, n, M
  S ← 1  //S is an M + 1 bit word. Bit zero is 1//
  for i ← 1 to n do
      S ← S or SHIFT(S, A(i))
  repeat
  if Mth bit in S = 0 then print ('no subset sums to M')
                      else print ('a subset sums to M')
  endif
end SUM
```

Algorithm 11.2 Deterministic sum of subsets

The virtue of conceiving of nondeterministic algorithms is that often what would be very complex to write down deterministically is very easy to write nondeterministically. In fact, it is very easy to obtain polynomial time nondeterministic algorithms for many problems that can be deterministically solved by a systematic search of a solution space of exponential size.

Example 11.7 [Knapsack decision problem] Procedure DKP (Algorithm 11.3) is a nondeterministic polynomial time algorithm for the knapsack decision problem. Lines 1 to 3 assign 0/1 values to $X(i)$, $1 \le i \le n$. Line 4 checks to see if this assignment is feasible and if the resulting profit is at least R. A successful termination is possible iff the answer to the decision problem is yes. The time complexity is $O(n)$. If m is the input length using a binary representation, the time is $O(m)$. □

```
       procedure  DKP(P, W, n, M, R, X)
          integer  P(n), W(n), R, X(n), n, M, i
1          for i ← 1 to n do
2             X(i) ← choice (0, 1)
3          repeat
4          if  Σ   (W(i)*X(i)) > M or  Σ   (P(i)*X(i)) < R then failure
              1≤i≤n                    1≤i≤n                      else success
5          endif
       end DKP
```

Algorithm 11.3 Nondeterministic Knapsack problem

Example 11.8 [Max Clique] Procedure DCK (Algorithm 11.4) is a nondeterministic algorithm for the clique decision problem. The algorithm begins by trying to form a set of k distinct vertices. Then it tests to see if these vertices form a complete subgraph. If G is given by its adjacency matrix and $|V| = n$, the input length m is $n^2 + \lfloor \log_2 k \rfloor + \lfloor \log_2 n \rfloor + 2$. Lines 2 to 6 can easily be implemented to run in nondeterministic time $O(n)$. The time for lines 7-10 is $O(k^2)$. Hence the overall nondeterministic time is $O(n + k^2) = O(n^2) = O(m)$. There is known polynomial time deterministic algorithm for this problem. □

```
       procedure  DCK (G, n, k)
1          S ← φ   //S is an initially empty set//
2          for i ← 1 to k do   //select k distinct vertices//
3             t ← choice (1:n)
4             if t ∈ S then failure endif
5             S ← S ∪ t   //add t to set S//
6          repeat
           //at this point S contains k distinct vertex indices//
7          for all pairs (i, j) such that i ∈ S, j ∈ S and i ≠ j do
8             if (i, j) is not an edge of the graph
9                then failure endif
10         repeat
11         success
       end DCK
```

Algorithm 11.4 Nondeterministic clique

Example 11.9 [Satisfiability] Let $x_1, x_2, \ldots,$ denote boolean variables (their value is either true or false). Let $\bar{x}_i$ denote the negation of x_i. A *literal* is either a variable or its negation. A formula in the propositional calculus is an expression that can be constructed using literals and the operations **and** and **or**. Examples of such formulas are $(x_1 \wedge x_2) \vee (x_3 \wedge \bar{x}_4); (x_3 \vee \bar{x}_4) \wedge (x_1 \vee \bar{x}_2)$. $\vee$ denotes **or** and $\wedge$ denotes **and**. A formula is in *conjunctive normal form* (CNF) iff it is represented as $\wedge_{i=1}^{k} c_i$ where the c_i are clauses each represented as $\vee\, l_{ij}$. The l_{ij} are literals. It is in *disjunctive normal form* (DNF) iff it is represented as $\vee_{i=1}^{k} c_i$ and each clause c_i is represented as $\wedge\, l_{ij}$. Thus $(x_1 \wedge x_2) \vee (x_3 \wedge \bar{x}_4)$ is in DNF while $(x_3 \vee \bar{x}_4) \wedge (x_1 \vee \bar{x}_2)$ is in CNF. The *satisfiability* problem is to determine if a formula is true for any assignment of truth values to the variables. *CNF-satisfiability* is the satisfiability problem for CNF formulas.

It is easy to obtain a polynomial time nondeterministic algorithm that terminates successfully if and only if a given propositional formula $E(x_1, \ldots, x_n)$ is satisfiable. Such an algorithm could proceed by simply choosing (nondeterministically) one of the 2^n possible assignments of truth values to $(x_1, \ldots, x_n)$ and verifying that $E(x_1, \ldots, x_n)$ is true for that assignment.

Procedure EVAL (Algorithm 11.5) does this. The nondeterministic time required by the algorithm is $O(n)$ to choose the value of $(x_1, \ldots, x_n)$ plus the time needed to deterministically evaluate E for that assignment. This time is proportional to the length of E. $\square$

```
procedure EVAL(E, n)
    //Determine if the propositional formula E is satisfiable. The variables//
    //are x_i, 1 ≤ i ≤ n//
    boolean x(n)
    for i ← 1 to n do   //choose a truth value assignment//
        x_i ← choice (true, false)
    repeat
    if E(x_1, ..., x_n) is true then success   //satisfiable//
                            else failure
    endif
end EVAL
```

Algorithm 11.5 Nondeterministic satisfiability

The Classes NP-hard and NP-complete

In measuring the complexity of an algorithm we shall use the input length as the parameter. An algorithm A is of *polynomial complexity* if there exists a polynomial $p(\ )$ such that the computing time of A is $O(p(n))$ for every input of size n.

Definition P is the set of all decision problems solvable by a deterministic algorithm in polynomial time. NP is the set of all decision problems solvable by a nondeterministic algorithm in polynomial time.

Since deterministic algorithms are just a special case of nondeterministic ones, we can conclude that $P \subseteq NP$. What we do not know, and what has become perhaps the most famous unsolved problem in computer science is whether $P = NP$ or $P \neq NP$.

Is it possible that for all of the problems in NP there exist polynomial time deterministic algorithms which have remained undiscovered? This seems unlikely, at least because of the tremendous effort which has already been expended by so many people on these problems. Nevertheless, a proof that $P \neq NP$ is just as elusive and seems to require as yet undiscovered techniques. But as with many famous unsolved problems, they serve to generate other useful results, and the $P \overset{?}{=} NP$ question is no exception.

In considering this problem S. Cook formulated the following question: Is there any single problem in NP such that if we showed it to be in P, then that would imply that $P = NP$. Cook answered his own question in the affirmative with the following theorem.

Theorem 11.1   (Cook)   Satisfiability is in P if and only if $P = NP$.

Proof: See Section 11.2   □

We are now ready to define the NP-hard and NP-complete classes of problems. First we define the notion of reducibility.

Definition   Let L_1 and L_2 be problems. L_1 *reduces to* L_2 (also written $L_1 \propto L_2$) if and only if there is a way to solve L_1 by a deterministic polynomial time algorithm using a deterministic algorithm that solves L_2 in polynomial time.

This definition implies that if we have a polynomial time algorithm for L_2 then we can solve L_1 in polynomial time. One may readily verify that $\propto$ is a transitive relation (i.e. if $L_1 \alpha L_2$ and $L_2 \alpha L_3$ then $L_1 \alpha L_3$).

Definition   A problem L is *NP-hard* if and only if satisfiability reduces to L (satisfiability $\propto L$). A problem L is *NP-complete* if and only if L is *NP-hard* and $L \in NP$.

It is easy to see that there are *NP*-hard problems that are not *NP*-complete. Only a decision problem can be NP-complete. However, an optimization problem may be NP-hard. Furthermore if L_1 is a decision problem and L_2 an optimization problem, it is quite possible that $L_1 \propto L_2$. One may trivially show that the knapsack decision problem reduces to the knapsack optimization problem. For the clique problem one may easily show that the clique decision problem reduces to the clique optimization problem. In fact, we can also show that these optimization problems reduce to their corresponding decision problems (see exercises). Yet, optimization problems cannot be NP-complete while decision problems can. There also exist NP-hard decision problems that are not NP-complete.

Example 11.10 As an extreme example of an NP-hard decision problem that is not NP-complete consider the halting problem for deterministic algorithms. The *halting problem* is to determine for an arbitrary deterministic algorithm A and an input I whether algorithm A with input I ever terminates (or enters an infinite loop). It is well known that this problem is undecidable. Hence, there exists no algorithm (of any complexity) to solve this problem. So, it clearly cannot be in NP. To show satisfiability $\propto$ halting problem simply construct an algorithm A whose input is a propositional formula X. If X has n variables then A tries out all 2^n possible truth assignments and verifies if X is satisfiable. If it is then A stops. If X is not satisfiable then A enters an infinite loop. Hence, A halts on input X iff X is satisfiable. If we had a polynomial time algorithm for the halting problem then we could solve the satisfiability problem in polynomial time using A and X as input to the algorithm for the halting problem. Hence, the halting problem is an NP-hard problem which is not in NP. ☐

Definition Two problems L_1 and L_2 are said to be *polynomially equivalent* iff $L_1 \propto L_2$ and $L_2 \propto L_1$.

In order to show that a problem, L_2 is NP-hard it is adequate to show $L_1 \propto L_2$ where L_1 is some problem already known to be NP-hard. Since $\propto$ is a transitive relation, it follows that if satisfiability $\propto L_1$ and $L_1 \propto L_2$ then satisfiability $\propto L_2$. *To show an NP-hard decision problem NP-complete we have just to exhibit a polynomial time nondeterministic algorithm for it.* Later sections will show many problems to be NP-hard. While we shall restrict ourselves to decision problems, it should be clear that the corresponding optimization problems are also NP-hard. The NP-completeness proofs will be left as exercises (for those problems that are NP-complete).

11.2 COOK'S THEOREM

Cook's theorem (Theorem 11.1) states that satisfiability is in P iff $P =$ NP. We shall now prove this important theorem. We have already seen that satisfiability is in NP (Example 11.9). Hence, if $P = $ NP then satisfiability is in P. It remains to be shown that if satisfiability is in P then $P = $ NP. In order to prove this latter statement, we shall show how to obtain from any polynomial time nondeterministic decision algorithm A and input I a formula $Q(A, I)$ such that Q is satisfiable iff A has a successful termination with input I. If the length of I is n and the time complexity of A is $p(n)$ for some polynomial $p(\ )$ then the length of Q will be $O(p^3(n) \log n) = O(p^4(n))$. The time needed to construct Q will also be $O(p^3(n) \log n)$. A deterministic algorithm Z to determine the outcome of A on any input I may be easily obtained. Z simply computes Q and then uses a deterministic algorithm for the satisfiability problem to determine whether or not Q is satisfiable. If $O(q(m))$ is the time needed to determine if a formula of length m is satisfiable then the complexity of Z is $O(p^3(n) \log n + q(p^3(n) \log n))$. If satisfiability is in P then $q(m)$ is a polynomial function of m and the complexity of Z becomes $O(r(n))$ for some polynomial $r(\ )$. Hence, if satisfiability is in P then for every nondeterministic algorithm A in NP we can obtain a deterministic Z in P. So, the above construction will show that if satisfiability is in P then $P = $ NP.

Before going into the construction of Q from A and I, we shall make some simplifying assumptions on our nondeterministic machine model and on the form of A. These assumptions will not in any way alter the class of decision problems in NP or P. The simplifying assumptions are:

i)   The machine on which A is to be executed is word oriented. Each word is w bits long. Multiplication, addition, subtraction etc. between numbers one word long take one unit of time. In case numbers are longer than a word then the corresponding operations take at least as many units as the number of words making up the longest number.

ii) A *simple expression* is an expression that contains at most one operator and all operands are simple variables (i.e., no array variables are used). Some sample simple expressions are $-B$, $B + C$, D or E, F.

We shall assume that all assignment statements in A are of one of the following forms:

a) (simple variable) ← (simple expression)
b) (array variable) ← (simple variable)
c) (simple variable) ← (array variable)
d) (simple variable) ← **choice** (S) where S may be a finite set $\{S_1, S_2, \ldots, S_k\}$ or S may be $l{:}u$. In the latter case the function chooses an integer in the range $[l{:}u]$.

Indexing within an array is done using a simple integer variable and all index values are positive. Only one dimensional arrays are allowed. Clearly, all assignment statements not falling into one of the above categories may be replaced by a set of statements of these types. Hence, this restriction does not alter the class NP.

iii) All variables in A are of type integer or boolean.

iv) A contains no **read** or **print** statements. The only input to A is via its parameters. At the time A is invoked all variables (other than the parameters) have value zero (or **false** if boolean).

v) A contains no constants. Clearly, all constants in any algorithm may be replaced by new variables. These new variables may be added to the parameter list of A and the constants associated with them can be part of the input.

vi) In addition to simple assignment statements, A is allowed to contain only the following types of statements:

a) **go to** k where k is an instruction number
b) **if** c **then go to** a **endif.** c is a simple boolean variable (i.e., not an array) and a is an instruction number
c) **success, failure, end**
d) A may contain type declaration and dimension statments. These are not used during execution of A and so need not be translated into Q. The dimension information is used to allocate array space. It is assumed that successive elements in an array are assigned to consective words in memory.

It is assumed that the instructions in A are numbered sequentially from 1 to l (if A has l instructions). Every statement in A has a number. The **go to** instructions in a) and b) use this numbering scheme to effect a branch. It should be easy to see how to rewrite 'while-repeat', 'repeat-until', 'case-endcase', 'for-repeat', etc. statements in terms of **go to** and **if** c **then go to** a **endif** statements. Also, note that the **go to** k statement can be replaced by the statement **if true then go to** k **endif**. So, this may also be eliminated.

vii) Let $p(n)$ be a polynomial such that A takes no more than $p(n)$ time units on any input of length n. Because of the complexity assumptions of (i), A cannot change or use more than $p(n)$ words of memory. We may assume that A uses some subset of the words indexed 1, 2, 3, ..., $p(n)$. This assumption does not restrict the class of decision problems in NP. To see this let $f(1), f(2), ..., f(k), 1 \leq k \leq p(n)$, be the distinct words used by A while working on input I. We can construct another polynomial time nondeterministic algorithm A' which uses $2p(n)$ words indexed 1, 2, ..., $2p(n)$ and solves the same decision problem as does A. A' simulates the behavior of A. However, A' maps the addresses $f(1), f(2), ..., f(k)$ onto the set $\{1, 2, ..., k\}$. The mapping function used is determined dynamically and is stored as a table in words $p(n) + 1$ through $2p(n)$. If the entry at word $p(n) + i$ is j then A' uses word i to hold the same value that A stored in word j. The simulation of A proceeds as follows· Let k be the number of distinct words referenced by A up to this time. Let j be a word referenced by A in the current step. A' searches its table to find word $p(n) + i, 1 \leq i \leq k$ such that the contents of this word is j. If no such i exists then A' sets $k \leftarrow k + 1, i \leftarrow k$ and word $p(n) + k$ is given the value j. A' makes use of the word i to do whatever A would have done with word j. Clearly, A' and A solve the same decision problem. The complexity of A' is $O(p^2(n))$ as it takes A' $p(n)$ time to search its table and simulate a step of A. Since $p^2(n)$ is also a polynomial in n, restricting our algorithms to use only consecutive words does not alter the classes P and NP.

Formula Q will make use of several boolean variables. We state the semantics of two sets of variables used in Q:

i) $B(i, j, t), 1 \leq i \leq p(n), 1 \leq j \leq w, 0 \leq t < p(n)$.

$B(i, j, t)$ represents the status of bit j of word i following t steps (or time units) of computation. The bits in a word are numbered from right to left. The rightmost bit is numbered 1. Q will be constructed such that in any truth assignment for which Q is true, $B(i, j, t)$ is true iff the corresponding bit has value 1 following t steps of some successful computation of A on input I.

ii) $S(j, t), 1 \leq j \leq l, 1 \leq t \leq p(n)$.

Recall that l is the number of instructions in A. $S(j, t)$ represents the instruction to be executed at time t. Q will be constructed such that in any truth assignment for which Q is true, $S(j, t)$ is true iff the instruction executed by A at time t is instruction j.

Q will be made up of six subformulas C, D, E, F, G and H. $Q = C \wedge D \wedge E \wedge F \wedge G \wedge H$. These subformulas will make the following assertions:

C: The initial status of the $p(n)$ words represents the input I. All non-input variables are zero.

D: Instruction 1 is the first instruction to execute.

E: At the end of the i'th step, there can be only one next instruction to execute. Hence, for any fixed i, at most one of the $S(j, i)$, $1 \leq j \leq l$ can be true.

F: If $S(j, i)$ is true then $S(j, i + 1)$ is also true if instruction j is a **success**, **failure** or **end** statement. $S(j + 1, i + 1)$ is true if j is an assignment statement. If j is a **go to** k statement then $S(k, i + 1)$ is true. The last possibility for j is the **if** c **then** a **endif** statement. In this case $S(a, i + 1)$ is true if c is true and $S(j + 1, i + 1)$ is true if c is false.

G: If the instruction executed at step t is not an assignment statement then the $B(i, j, t)$s are unchanged. If this instruction is an assignment and the variable on the left hand side is X, then only X may change. This change is determined by the right hand side of the instruction.

H: The instruction to be executed at time $p(n)$ is a **success** instruction. Hence the computation terminates successfully.

Clearly, if C through H make the above assertions, then $Q = C \wedge D \wedge E \wedge F \wedge G \wedge H$ is satisfiable iff there is a successful computation of A on input I. We now give the formulas C through H. While presenting these formulas we shall also indicate how each may be transformed into CNF. This transformation will increase the length of Q by an amount independent of n (but dependent on w and l). This will enable us to show that CNF-satisfiability is NP-complete.

1.   Formula C describes the input I. We have:

$$C = \bigwedge_{\substack{1 \leq i \leq p(n) \\ 1 \leq j \leq w}} T(i, j, 0)$$

$T(i, j, 0)$ is $B(i, j, 0)$ if the input calls for bit $B(i, j, 0)$ (i.e. bit j of word i) to be 1. $T(i, j, 0)$ is $\bar{B}(i, j, 0)$ otherwise. Thus, if there is no input then

$$C = \bigwedge_{\substack{1 \le i \le p(n) \\ 1 \le j \le w}} \bar{B}(i, j, 0).$$

Clearly, C is uniquely determined by I and is in CNF. Also, C is satisfiable only by a truth assignment representing the initial values of all variables in A.

2. $D = S(1, 1) \wedge \bar{S}(2, 1) \wedge \bar{S}(3, 1) \wedge \ldots \wedge \bar{S}(l, 1)$.

Clearly, D is satisfiable only by the assignment $S(1, 1) =$ true and $S(i, 1)$ $=$ false, $2 \le i \le l$. Using our interpretation of $S(i, 1)$, this means that D is true iff instruction 1 is the first to be executed. Note that D is in CNF.

3. $E = \bigwedge_{1 < t \le p(n)} E_t$.

Each E_t will assert that there is a unique instruction for step t. We may define E_t to be:

$$E_t = (S(1, t) \vee S(2, t) \vee \ldots \vee S(l, t)) \wedge (\bigwedge_{\substack{1 \le j \le l \\ 1 \le k \le l \\ j \ne k}} (\bar{S}(j, t) \vee \bar{S}(k, t))$$

One may verify that E_t is true iff exactly one of the $S(j, t)$s, $1 \le j \le l$ is true. Also, note that E is in CNF.

4. $F = \bigwedge_{\substack{1 \le i \le l \\ 1 \le t < p(n)}} F_{i,t}$.

Each $F_{i,t}$ asserts that either instruction i is not the one to be executed at time t, or if it is then the instruction to be executed at time $t + 1$ is correctly determined by instruction i. Formally, we have

$$F_{i,t} = \bar{S}(i, t) \vee L$$

where L is defined as follows:

i)   if instruction i is **success, failure** or **end** then L is $S(i, t + 1)$. Hence the program cannot leave such an instruction.

ii)   if instruction i is **go to** k then L is $S(k, t + 1)$.

iii) if instruction i is **if** X **then go to** k **endif** and variable X is repre-
sented by word j then L is $((B(j, 1, t - 1) \wedge S(k, t + 1)) \vee (\bar{B}(j, 1, t - 1) \wedge S(i + 1, t + 1)))$. This assumes that bit 1 of X is 1 iff X is
true.

iv)   if instruction i is not any of the above then L is $S(i + 1, t + 1)$.

The $F_{i,t}$s defined in cases (i), (ii) and (iv) above are in CNF. The $F_{i,t}$ in
case (iii) may be transformed into CNF using the boolean identity $a \vee (b \wedge c) \vee (d \wedge e) \equiv (a \vee b \vee d) \wedge (a \vee c \vee d) \wedge (a \vee b \vee e) \wedge (a \vee c \vee e)$.

5. $G = \bigwedge\limits_{\substack{1 \le i \le l \\ 1 \le t < p(n)}} G_{i,t}$.

Each $G_{i,t}$ asserts that at time t either (i) instruction i is not executed or
(ii) it is and the status of the $p(n)$ words after step t is correct with respect to the status before step t and the changes resulting from instruction i. Formally, we have

$$G_{i,t} = \bar{S}(i, t) \vee M$$

where M is defined as follows:

i)   if instruction i is a **go to**, **if—then go to—endif**, **success**, **failure**,
or **end** statement then M asserts that the status of the $p(n)$ words is
unchanged. I.e., $B(k, j, t - 1) = B(k, j, t)$, $1 \le k \le p(n)$ and
$1 \le j \le w$.

$$M = \bigwedge\limits_{\substack{1 \le k \le p(n) \\ 1 \le j \le w}} ((B(k, j, t - 1) \wedge B(k, j, t)) \vee (\bar{B}(k, j, t - 1) \wedge \bar{B}(kj, t))$$

In this case, $G_{i,t}$ may be rewritten as

$$G_{i,t} = \bigwedge\limits_{\substack{1 \le k \le p(n) \\ 1 \le j \le w}} (\bar{S}(i, t) \vee (B(k, j, t - 1) \wedge B(k, j, t)))$$

$$\vee (\bar{B}(k, j, t - 1) \wedge \bar{B}(k, j, t)))$$

Each clause in $G_{i,t}$ is of the form $z \vee (x \wedge s) \vee (\bar{x} \wedge \bar{s})$ where z is
$\bar{S}(i, t)$, x represents a $B(\ ,,\ t - 1)$ and s a $B(\ ,,\ t)$. Note that $z \vee (x \wedge s) \vee (\bar{x} \wedge \bar{s})$ is equivalent to $(x \vee \bar{s} \vee z) \wedge (\bar{x} \vee s \vee z)$. Hence,
$G_{i,t}$ may be transformed into CNF easily.

ii) if i is an assignment statement of type a) then M depends on the operator (if any) on the right hand side. We shall first describe the form of M for the case when instruction i is of the type $Y \leftarrow V + Z$. Let Y, V and Z be respectively represented in words y, v and z. We shall make the simplifying assumption that all numbers are non-negative. The exercises examine the case when negative numbers are allowed and 1's complement arithmetic is being used. In order to get a formula asserting that the bits $B(y, j, t)$, $1 \leq j \leq w$ represent the sum of $B(v, j, t - 1)$ and $B(z, j, t - 1)$ $1 \leq j \leq w$, we shall have to make use of w additional bits $C(j, t)$, $1 \leq j \leq w$. $C(j, t)$ will represent the carry from the addition of the bits $B(v, j, t - 1)$, $B(z, j, t - 1)$ and $C(j - 1, t)$, $1 < j \leq w$. $C(1, t)$ is the carry from the addition of $B(v, 1, t - 1)$ and $B(z, 1, t - 1)$. Recall that a bit is 1 iff the corresponding variable is true. Performing a bit wise addition of V and Z, we obtain $C(1, t) = B(v, 1, t - 1) \wedge B(z, 1, t - 1)$ and $B(y, 1, t) = B(v, 1, t - 1) \oplus B(z, 1, t - 1)$ where $\oplus$ is the exclusive or operation ($a \oplus b$ is true iff exactly one of a and b is true). Note that $a \oplus b \equiv (a \vee b) \wedge \overline{(a \wedge b)} \equiv (a \vee b) \wedge (\bar{a} \vee \bar{b})$. Hence, the right hand side of the expression for $B(y, 1, t)$ may be transformed into CNF using this identity. For the other bits of Y, one may verify that

$$B(y, j, t) = B(v, j, t - 1) \oplus (B(z, j, t - 1) \oplus C(j - 1, t))$$

and

$$C(j, t) = (B(v, j, t - 1) \wedge B(z, j, t - 1)) \vee (B(v, j, t - 1)$$
$$\wedge C(j - 1, t)) \vee (B(z, j, t - 1) \wedge C(j - 1, t)).$$

Finally, we require that $C(w, t) = \text{false}$. (i.e. there is no overflow). Let M' be the **and** of all the equations for $B(y, j, t)$ and $C(j, t)$, $1 \leq j \leq w$. M is given by

$$M = (\bigwedge_{\substack{1 \leq k \leq p(n) \\ k \neq y \\ 1 \leq j \leq w}} ((B(k, j, t - 1) \wedge B(k, j, t))$$
$$\vee (\bar{B}(k, j, t - 1) \wedge \bar{B}(k, j, t))) \wedge M'$$

$G_{i, t}$ may be converted into CNF using the idea of 5 (i). This transformation will increase the length of $G_{i, t}$ by a constant factor independent of n. We leave it to the reader to figure out what M is when instruction i is either of the form $Y \leftarrow V$; $Y \leftarrow V \text{\textcircled{op}} Z$ for $\text{\textcircled{op}}$ one of $-$, $/$, $*$, $<$, $>$, $\leq$, $=$, etc.

When i is an assignment statement of types b) or c) then it necessary to select the correct array element. Consider an instruction of type b): $R(m) \leftarrow X$. In this case the formula M may be written as:

$$M = W \wedge (\bigwedge_{1 \leq j \leq u} M_j)$$

where u is the dimension of R. Note that because of restriction (vii) on the algorithm A, $u \leq p(n) \cdot W$ asserts that $1 \leq m \leq u$. The specification of W is left as an exercise. Each M_j asserts that either $m \neq j$ or $m = j$ and only the jth element of R changes. Let us assume that the values of X and m are respectively stored in words x and m and that $R(1:u)$ is stored in words α, $\alpha + 1$, $\ldots$, $\alpha + u - 1$. M_j is given by:

$$M_j = \bigvee_{1 \leq k \leq w} T(m, k, t - 1) \vee Z$$

where T is B if the k'th bit in the binary representation of j is O and T is $\bar{B}$ otherwise. Z is defined as

$$Z = \bigwedge_{\substack{1 \leq k \leq w \\ 1 \leq r \neq p(n) \\ r \neq \alpha + j - 1}} ((B(r, k, t - 1) \wedge B(r, k, t)) \vee (\bar{B}(r, k, t - 1)$$

$$\wedge \bar{B}(r, k, t - 1)))$$

$$\bigwedge_{1 \leq k \leq w} ((B(\alpha + j - 1, k, t) \wedge B(x, k, t - 1))$$

$$\vee (\bar{B}(\alpha + j - 1, k, t) \wedge \bar{B}(x, k, t - 1)))$$

Note that the number of literals in M is $O(p^2(n))$. Since j is w bits long it can represent only numbers smaller than 2^w. Hence, for $u \geq 2^w$ we need a different indexing scheme. A simple generalization is to allow multiprecision arithmetic. The index variable j could use as many words as needed. The number of words used would depend on u. At most $\log (p(n))$ words are needed. This calls for a slight change in M_j but the number of literals in M remains $O(p^2(n))$. There is no need to explicitly incorporate multiprecision arithmetic as by giving the program access to individual words in a multiprecision index j we can require the program to simulate multiprecision arithmetic.

When i is an instruction of type c) the form of M is similar to that obtained for instructions of type b). Next, we describe how to construct M for the case i is of the form $Y \leftarrow$ choice (S) where S is either a set of the form $S = \{S_1, S_2, \ldots, S_k\}$ or S is of the form $r{:}u$. Assume Y is represented by word y. Is S is a set then we define

$$M = \bigvee_{1 \leq j \leq k} M_j.$$

M_j asserts that Y is S_j. This is easily done by choosing $M_j = a_1 \wedge a_2 \wedge \cdots \wedge a_w$ where $a_l = B(y, l, t)$ if bit l is 1 in S_l and $a_i = \bar{B}(y, l, t)$ if bit l is zero in S_l. If S is of the form $r{:}u$ then M is just the formula that asserts $r \leq Y \leq u$. This is left as an exercise. In both cases, $G_{i,t}$ may be transformed into CNF increasing the length of $G_{i,t}$ by at most a constant amount.

6. Let $i_1, i_2, \ldots, i_k$ be the statement numbers corresponding to the success statements in A. H is given by:

$$H = S(i_1, p(n)) \vee S(i_2, p(n)) \vee \cdots \vee S(i_k, p(n)).$$

One may readily verify that $Q = C \wedge D \wedge E \wedge F \wedge G \wedge H$ is satisfiable iff the computation of algorithm A with input I terminates successfully. Further, Q may be transformed into CNF as described above. Formula C contains $wp(n)$ literals, D contains l literals, E contains $O(l^2 p(n))$ literals, F contains $O(lp(n))$ literals, G contains $O(lwp^3(n))$ literals and H contains at most l literals. The total number of literals appearing in Q is $O(lwp^3(n)) = O(p^3(n))$ as lw is constant. Since, there are $O(wp^2(n) + lp(n))$ distinct literals in Q, each literal can be written down using $O(\log (wp^2(n) + lp(n))) = O(\log n)$ bits. The length of Q is therefore $O(p^3(n) \log n) = O(p^4(n))$ as $p(n)$ is at least n. The time to construct Q from A and I is also $O(p^3(n) \log n)$.

The above construction, shows that every problem in NP reduces to satisfiability and also to CNF-satisfiability. Hence, if either of these two problems is in P then NP $\subseteq P$ and so $P = $ NP. Also, since satisfiability is in NP, the construction of a CNF formula Q shows that satisfiability $\propto$ CNF-satisfiability. This together with the knowledge that CNF-satisfiability is in NP, implies that CNF-satisfiability is NP-complete. Note that satisfiability is also NP-complete as satisfiability α satisfiability and satisfiability is in NP.

11.3 NP-HARD GRAPH PROBLEMS

The strategy we shall adopt to show that a problem L_2 is NP-hard is:

i)   Pick a problem L_1 already known to be NP-hard.

ii)   Show how to obtain (in polynomial deterministic time) an instance I' of L_2 from any instance I of L_1 such that from the solution of I' we can determine (in polynomial deterministic time) the solution to instance I to L_1.

iii)   Conclude from (ii) that $L_1 \propto L_2$.

iv)   Conclude from (i), (iii) and the transitivity of $\propto$ that L_2 is NP-hard.

For the first few proofs we shall go through all the above steps. Later proofs will explicitly deal only with steps (i) and (ii). An NP-hard decision problem L_2 can be shown NP-complete by exhibiting a polynomial time nondeterministic algorithm for L_2. All the NP-hard decision problems we shall deal with here are also NP-complete. The construction of polynomial time nondeterministic algorithms for these problems is left as an exercise.

Clique Decision Problem (CDP)

The clique decision problem was introduced in Section 11.1. We shall show in Theorem 11.2 that CNF-satisfiability $\propto$ CDP. Using this result, the transitivity of $\propto$ and the knowledge that satisfiability $\propto$ CNF-satisfiability (Section 11.2) we can readily establish that satisfiability $\propto$ CDP. Hence, CDP is NP-hard. Since, CDP $\in$ NP, CDP is also NP-complete.

Theorem 11.2   CNF-satisfiability $\propto$ clique decision problem (CDP)

Proof: Let $F = \wedge_{1 \leq i \leq k} C_i$ be a propositional formula in CNF. Let x_i, $1 \leq i \leq n$ be the variables in F. We shall show how to construct from F a graph $G = (V, E)$ such that G will have a clique of size at least k iff F is satisfiable. If the length of F is m, then G will be obtainable from F in $O(m)$ time. Hence, if we have a polynomial time algorithm for CDP, then we can obtain a polynomial time algorithm for CNF-satisfiability using this construction.

For any F, $G = (V, E)$ is defined as follows: $V = \{\langle \sigma, i \rangle | \sigma$ is a literal in clause $C_i\}$; $E = \{(\langle \sigma, i \rangle, \langle \delta, j \rangle) | i \neq j$ and $\sigma \neq \bar{\delta}\}$. A sample construction is given in Example 11.11.

If F is satisfiable then there is a set of truth values for x_i, $1 \leq i \leq n$ such that each clause is true with this assignment. Thus, with this assignment there is at least one literal σ in each C_i such that σ is true. Let $S = \{\langle \sigma, i \rangle | \sigma$ is true in $C_i\}$ be a set containing exactly one $\langle \sigma, i \rangle$ for each i.

S forms a clique in G of size k. Similarly, if G has a clique $K = (V', E')$ of size at least k then let $S = \{\langle \sigma, i \rangle \mid \langle \sigma, i \rangle \in V'\}$. Clearly, $|S| = k$ as G has no clique of size more than k. Furthermore, if $S' = \{\sigma \mid \langle \sigma, i \rangle \in S$ for some $i\}$ then S' cannot contain both a literal δ and its complement $\bar{\delta}$ as there is no edge connecting $\langle \delta, i \rangle$ and $\langle \bar{\delta}, j \rangle$ in G. Hence by setting $x_i =$ true if $x_i \in S'$ and $x_i =$ false if $\bar{x}_i \in S'$ and choosing arbitrary truth values for variables not in S', we can satisfy all clauses in F. Hence, F is satisfiable iff G has a clique of size at least k. $\square$

Example 11.11 Consider $F = (x_1 \vee x_2 \vee x_3) \wedge (\bar{x}_1 \vee \bar{x}_2 \vee \bar{x}_3)$. The construction of Theorem 11.2 yields the graph:

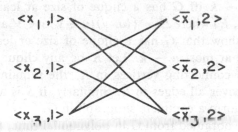

Figure 11.1 A sample graph and satisfiability

This graph contains six cliques of size two. Consider the clique with vertices $\{\langle x_1, 1 \rangle, \langle \bar{x}_2, 2 \rangle\}$. By setting $x_1 =$ true and $\bar{x}_2 =$ true (i.e. $x_2 =$ false) F is satisfied. x_3 may be set either to true or false. $\square$

Node Cover Decision Problem

A set $S \subseteq V$ is a *node cover* for a graph $G = (V, E)$ iff all edges in E are incident to at least one vertex in S. The size of the cover, $|S|$, is the number of vertices in S.

Example 11.12 Consider the graph:

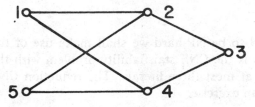

Figure 11.2 A sample graph and node cover

$S = \{2, 4\}$ is a node cover of size 2. $S = \{1, 3, 5\}$ is a node cover of size 3.   □

In the node cover decision problem (NCDP) we are given a graph G and an integer k. We are required to determine if G has a node cover of size at most k.

Theorem 11.3   Clique decision problem (CDP) ∝ node cover decision problem (NCDP)

Proof: Let $G = (V, E)$ and k define an instance of CDP. Assume that $|V| = n$. We shall construct a graph G' such that G' has a node cover of size at most $n - k$ iff G has a clique of size at least k. Graph G' is given by $G' = (V, \overline{E})$ where $\overline{E} = \{(u, v) | u \in V, v \in V \text{ and } (u, v) \notin E\}$.

Now, we shall show that G has a clique of size at least k iff G' has a node cover of size at most $n - k$. Let K be any clique in G. Since there are no edges in $\overline{E}$ connecting vertices in K, the remaining $n - |K|$ vertices in G' must cover all edges in $\overline{E}$. Similarly, if S is a node cover of G' then $V - S$ must form a complete subgraph in G.

Since G' can be obtained from G in polynomial time, CDP can be solved in polynomial deterministic time if we have a polynomial time deterministic algorithm for NCDP.   □

Note that since CNF-satisfiability ∝ CDP, CDP ∝ NCDP and ∝ is transitive, it follows that NCDP is NP-hard.

Chromatic Number Decision Problem (CN)

A coloring of a graph $G = (V, E)$ is a function $f : V \rightarrow \{1, 2, \ldots, k\}$ defined for all $i \in V$. If $(u, v) \in E$ then $f(u) \neq f(v)$. The *chromatic number decision problem* (CN) is to determine if G has a coloring for a given k.

Example 11.13   A possible 2-coloring of the graph of Figure 11.2 is: $f(1) = f(3) = f(5) = 1$ and $f(2) = f(4) = 2$. Clearly, this graph has no 1-coloring.   □

In proving CN to be NP-hard we shall make use of the NP-hard problem SATY. This is the CNF staisfiability problem with the restriction that each clause has at most three literals. The reduction CNF-satisfiability ∝ SATY is left as an exercise.

Theorem 11.4 Satisfiability with at most three literals per clause (SATY) $\propto$ chromatic number (CN)

Proof: Let F be a CNF formula having at most three literals per clause and having r clauses. Let x_i, $1 \le i \le n$ be the n variables in F. We may assume $n \ge 4$. If $n < 4$ then we can determine if F is satisfiable by trying out all eight possible truth value assignments to x_1, x_2 and x_3. We shall construct, in polynomial time, a graph G that is $n + 1$ colorable iff F is satisfiable. The graph $G = (V, E)$ is defined by:

$$V = \{x_1, x_2, \ldots, x_n\} \cup \{\bar{x}_1, \bar{x}_2, \ldots, \bar{x}_n\}$$
$$\cup \{y_1, y_2, \ldots, y_n\} \cup \{C_1, C_2, \ldots, C_r\}$$

and

$$E = \{(x_1, \bar{x}_1), 1 \le i \le n\} \cup \{(y_i, y_j) | i \ne j\} \cup \{(y_i, x_j) | i \ne j\}$$
$$\cup \{(y_i, \bar{x}_j) | i \ne j\} \cup \{(x_i, C_j) | x_i \notin C_j\} \cup \{\bar{x}_i, C_j) | \bar{x}_i \notin C_j\}$$

To see that G is $n + 1$ colorable iff F is satisfiable, we first observe that the y_i's form a complete subgraph on n vertices. Hence, each y_i must be assigned a distinct color. Without loss of generality we may assume that in any coloring of G y_i is given the color i. Since y_i is also connected to all the x_j's and $\bar{x}_j$'s except x_i and $\bar{x}_i$, the color i can be assigned to only x_i and $\bar{x}_i$. However $(x_i, \bar{x}_i) \in E$ and so a new color $n + 1$, is needed for one of these vertices. The vertex that is assigned the new color, $n + 1$, will be called the *false vertex*. The other vertex is a *true* vertex. The only way to color G using $n + 1$ colors is to assign color $n + 1$ to one of $\{x_i, \bar{x}_i\}$ for each i, $1 \le i \le n$.

Under what conditions can the remaining vertices be colored using no new colors? Since $n \ge 4$ and each clause has at most three literals, each C_i is adjacent to a pair of vertices x_j, $\bar{x}_j$ for at least one j. Consequently, no C_i may be assigned the color $n + 1$. Also, no C_i may be assigned a color corresponding to an x_j or $\bar{x}_j$ not in clause C_i. The last two statements imply that the only colors that can be assigned to C_i correspond to vertices x_j or $\bar{x}_j$ that are in clause C_i and are true vertices. Hence, G is $n + 1$ colorable iff there is a true vertex corresponding to each C_i. So, G is $n + 1$ colorable iff F is satisfiable. $\square$

Directed Hamiltonian Cycle (DHC)

A directed Hamiltonian cycle in a directed graph $G = (V, E)$ is a directed cycle of length $n = |V|$. So, the cycle goes through every vertex exactly once and then returns to the starting vertex. The DHC problem is to determine if G has a directed Hamiltonian cycle.

Example 11.14 1, 2, 3, 4, 5, 1 is a directed Hamiltonian cycle in the graph of Figure 11.3.

If the edge $\langle 5, 1 \rangle$ is deleted from this graph then it has no directed Hamiltonian cycle.

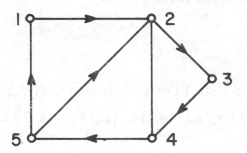

Figure 11.3 A sample graph and Hamiltonian cycle

Theorem 11.5 CNF-satisfiability $\propto$ directed hamiltonian cycle (DHC).
Proof: Let F be a propositional formula in CNF. We shall show how to construct a directed graph G such that F is satisfiable iff G has a directed Hamiltonian cycle. Since this construction can be carried out in time polynomial in the size of F, it will follow that CNF-satisfiability $\propto$ DHC. Understanding of the construction of G is greatly facilitated by the use of an example. The example we shall use is $F = C_1 \wedge C_2 \wedge C_3 \wedge C_4$ where

$$C_1 = x_1 \vee \bar{x}_2 \vee x_4 \vee \bar{x}_5$$
$$C_2 = \bar{x}_1 \vee x_2 \vee x_3$$
$$C_3 = \bar{x}_1 \vee \bar{x}_3 \vee x_5$$
$$C_4 = \bar{x}_1 \vee \bar{x}_2 \vee \bar{x}_3 \vee x_4 \vee \bar{x}_5$$

Assume that F has r clauses $C_1, C_2, \ldots, C_r$ and n variables $x_1, x_2, \ldots, x_n$. Draw an array with r rows and $2n$ columns. Row i will denote clause C_i. Each variable x_i will be represented by two adjacent columns, one for each of the literals x_i and $\bar{x}_i$. Figure 11.4 shows the array for the example formula. Insert a ⊛ into column x_i and row C_j iff x_i is a literal in C_j. Insert a ⊙ into column $\bar{x}_i$ and row C_j iff $\bar{x}_i$ is a literal in C_j. Between each pair of columns x_i and $\bar{x}_i$ introduce two vertices u_i and v_i: u_i at the top and v_i at the bottom of the column. For each i, draw two chains of edges upwards from v_i to u_i one connecting together all ⊙'s in column x_i and the other connecting all ⊙'s in column $\bar{x}_i$ (see Figure 11.4). Now, draw edges $\langle u_i, v_{i+1} \rangle$, $1 \leq i < n$. Introduce a box $\boxed{i}$ at the right end of each row C_i, $1 \leq i \leq r$. Draw the edges $\langle u_r, \boxed{1} \rangle$ and $\langle \boxed{r}, v_1 \rangle$. Draw edges $\langle \boxed{i}, \boxed{i+1} \rangle$, $1 \leq i < r$ (see Figure 11.4).

To complete the graph we shall replace each ⊛ and $\boxed{i}$ by a subgraph. Each ⊙ is replaced by the subgraph of Figure 11.5(a) (of course, unique vertex labelings are needed for each copy of the subgraph). Each box $\boxed{i}$ is replaced by the subgraph of Figure 11.6. In this subgraph A_i is an entrance node and B_i an exit node. The edges $\langle \boxed{i}, \boxed{i+1} \rangle$ referred to earlier are really $\langle B_i, A_{i+1} \rangle$. Edge $\langle u_r, \boxed{1} \rangle$ is $\langle u_r, A_1 \rangle$ and $\langle \boxed{r}, v_1 \rangle$ is $\langle B_r, v_1 \rangle$. i_j is the number of literals in clause C_i. In the subgraph of Figure 11.6 an edge

$$R_{i_a} \longrightarrow \text{⊙} \longrightarrow R_{i_{a+1}}$$

indicates a connection to a ⊙ subgraph in row C_i. R_{i_a} is connected to the "1" vertex of the ⊙ and $R_{i_{a+1}}$ (or R_{i_1} if $a = j$) is entered from the "3" vertex. Thus in the ⊙ subgraph

of Figure 11.5(b) w_1 and w_3 are the "1" and "3" vertices respectively. The incoming edge is $\langle R_{i_1}, w_1 \rangle$ and the outgoing edge is $\langle w_3, R_{i_2} \rangle$. This completes the construction of G.

If F is satisfiable then let S be an assignment of truth values for which F is true. A Hamiltonian cycle for G can start at v_1, go to u_1 then to v_2, then u_2, then v_3, then u_3, $\ldots$, u_r. In going from v_i up to u_i this cycle will use the column corresponding to x_i if x_i is true in S. Otherwise it will go up the column corresponding to $\bar{x}_i$. From u_r this cycle will go to A_1 and then through R_{1_1}, R_{1_2}, R_{1_3}, $\ldots$, R_{1_i}, B_1 to $A_2 \cdots$ to v_1. In going from R_{i_a} to $R_{i_{a+1}}$ in any subgraph $\boxed{i}$ a diversion will be made to a ⊙ subgraph in row i iff the vertices of that ⊙ subgraph are not already on the path from v_1 to R_{i_a}. Note that if C_i has i_j literals then the construction of $\boxed{i}$ allows a diversion to at most $i_j - 1$ ⊙ subgraphs. This is adequate as at least one ⊙ subgraph must already have been traversed in row C_i (as at least one such subgraph must correspond to a true literal). So, if F is satisfiable then G has a directed Hamiltonian cycle. It remains to show that if G has a directed Hamiltonian cycle then F is satisfiable. This may be seen by starting at vertex v_1 on any Hamiltonian cycle for G. Because of the construction of the ⊙ and $\boxed{i}$ subgraphs, such a cycle must proceed by going up exactly one column of each pair $(x_i, \bar{x}_i)$. In addition, this part of the cycle must traverse at least one ⊙ subgraph in each row. Hence the columns used in going from v_i to u_i, $1 \leq i \leq n$ define a truth assignment for which F is true.

We conclude that F is satisfiable iff G has a Hamiltonian cycle. The theorem now follows from the observation that G may be obtained from F in polynomial time.   □

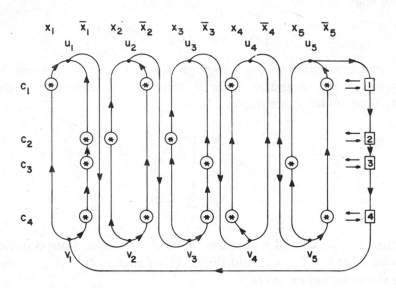

Figure 11.4   Array structure for formula in Theorem 11.5

Traveling Salesperson Decision Problem (TSP)

The traveling salesperson problem was introduced in Chapter 5. The corresponding decision problem is to determine if a complete directed graph $G = (V, E)$ with edge costs, $c(u, v)$, has a tour of cost at most M.

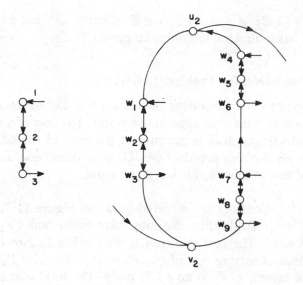

Figure 11.5 The ⊛ subgraph and its insertion into column 2

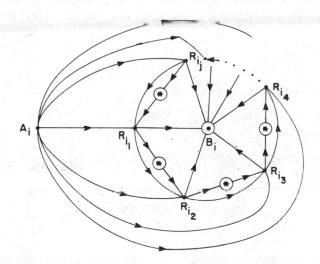

Figure 11.6 The $\boxed{i}$ subgraph

Theorem 11.6 Directed Hamiltonian cycle (DHC) $\propto$ traveling salesperson decision problem (TSP)

Proof: From the directed graph $G = (V, E)$ construct the complete directed graph $G' = (V, E')$, $E = \{\langle i, j \rangle \mid i \neq j\}$ and $c(i, j) = 1$ if $\langle i, j \rangle$

$\in E$; $c(i, j) = 2$ if $i \neq j$ and $\langle i, j \rangle \notin E$. Clearly, G' has a tour of cost at most n iff G has a directed hamiltonian cycle.   □

AND/OR Graph Decision Problem (AOG)

AND/OR graphs were introduced in Section 6.3. Let us assume that there is a cost associated with each edge in the graph. The *cost* of a solution graph H of an AND/OR graph G is the sum of the costs of the edges in H. The *AND/OR graph decision problem* (AOG) is to determine if G has a solution graph of cost at most k, for k a given input.

Example 11.15   Consider the directed graph of Figure 11.7. The problem to be solved is P_1. To do this, one may solve either nodes P_2, P_3 or P_7, as P_1 is an OR node. The cost incurred is then either 2, 2 or 8 (i.e., cost in addition to that of solving one of P_2, P_3 or P_7). To solve P_2, both P_4 and P_5 have to be solved, as P_2 is an AND node. The total cost to do this is 2. To solve P_3, we may solve either P_5 or P_6. The minimum cost to do this is 1. P_7 is free. In this example, then, the optimal way to solve P_1 is first solve P_6, then P_3 and finally P_1. The total cost for this solution is 3.   □

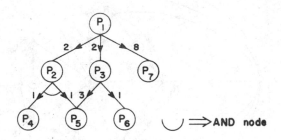

Figure 11.7   AND/OR graph

Theorem 11.7   CNF-satisfiability $\propto$ AND/OR graph decision problem

Proof: Let P be a propositional formula in CNF. We show how to transform a formula P in CNF into an AND/OR graph such that the AND/OR graph so obtained has a certain minimum cost solution iff P is satisfiable. Let

$$P = \bigwedge_{i=1}^{k} C_i, \quad C_i = \vee l_j,$$

where the l_j's are literals. The variables of P, $V(P)$ are $x_1, x_2, \ldots, x_n$. The AND/OR graph will have nodes as follows:

1. There is a special node, S, with no incoming arcs. This node represents the problem to be solved.
2. S is an AND node with descendent nodes $P, x_1, x_2, \ldots, x_n$.
3. Each node x_i represents the corresponding variable x_i in the formula P. Each x_i is an OR node with two descendents denoted Tx_i and Fx_i respectively. If Tx_i is solved, then this will correspond to assigning a truth value of "true" to the variable x_i. Solving node Fx_i will correspond to assigning a truth value of "false" to x_i.
4. The node P represents the formula P, and is an AND node. It has k descendents $C_1, C_2, \ldots, C_k$. Node C_i corresponds to the clause C_i in the formula P. The nodes C_i are OR nodes.
5. Each node of type Tx_i or Fx_i has exactly one descendent node which is terminal (i.e., has no edges leaving it). These terminal nodes shall be denoted $v_1, v_2, \ldots, v_{2n}$.

To complete the construction of the AND/OR graph, the following edges and costs are added:

1. From each node C_i an edge $\langle C_i, Tx_j \rangle$ is added if x_j occurs in clause C_i. An edge $\langle C_i, Fx_j \rangle$ is added if $\bar{x}_j$ occurs in the clause C_i. This is done for all variables x_j appearing in the clause C_i. C_i is designated an OR node.
2. Edges from nodes of type Tx_i or Fx_i to their respective terminal nodes are assigned a weight or cost 1.
3. All other edges have a cost 0.

In order to solve S, each of the nodes $P, x_1, x_2, \ldots, x_n$ must be solved. Solving nodes $x_1, x_2, \ldots, x_n$ costs n. To solve P, we must solve all the nodes $C_1, C_2, \ldots, C_k$. The cost of a node C_i is at most 1. However, if one of its descendent nodes was solved while solving the nodes $x_1, x_2, \ldots, x_n$, then the additional cost to solve C_i is 0, as the edges to its descendent nodes have cost 0 and one of its descendents has already been solved. I.e., a node C_i can be solved at no cost if one of the literals occurring in the clause C_i has been assigned a value "true." From this it follows that the entire graph (i.e., node S) can be solved at a cost n if there is some assignment of truth values to the x_i's such that at least one literal in each clause is true under that assignment, i.e., if the formula P is satisfiable. If P is not satisfiable, then the cost is more than n.

We have now shown how to construct an AND/OR graph from a formula P such that the AND/OR graph so constructed has a solution of cost n iff P is satisfiable. Otherwise the cost is more than n. The construction clearly takes only polynomial time. This completes the proof. ☐

Example 11.16 Consider the formula:

$$P = (x_1 \lor x_2 \lor x_3) \land (\bar{x}_1 \lor \bar{x}_2 \lor x_3) \land (\bar{x}_1 \lor x_2); \ V(P) = x_1, x_2, x_3; \ n = 3.$$

Figure 11.8 shows the AND/OR graph obtained by applying the construction of Theorem 11.7.

The nodes Tx_1, Tx_2, Tx_3 can be solved at a total cost of 3. The node P then costs nothing extra. The node S can then be solved by solving all its descendent nodes and the nodes Tx_1, Tx_2 and Tx_3. The total cost for this solution is 3 (which is n). Assigning the truth value "true" to the variables of P results in P being "true." ☐

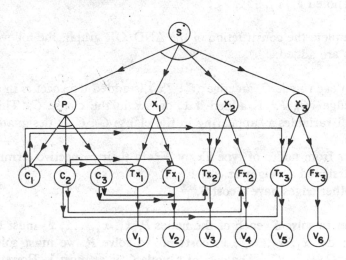

AND nodes marked ⌣
All other nodes are OR

Figure 11.8 AND/OR graph for Example 11.16

11.4 NP-HARD SCHEDULING PROBLEMS

To prove the results of this section we shall need to use the NP-hard problem called partition. This problem requires us to decide whether a given multiset $A = \{a_1, a_2, \ldots, a_n\}$ of n positive integers has a partition P such that $\Sigma_{i \in P} a_i = \Sigma_{i \notin P} a_i$. We can show this problem NP-hard by first showing the sum of subsets problem (Chapter 7) NP-hard. Recall that in the sum of subsets problem we have to determine if $A = \{a_1, a_2, \ldots, a_n\}$ has a subset S that sums to a given integer M.

Theorem 11.8 Exact cover $\propto$ sum of subsets.

Proof: The exact cover problem is shown NP-hard in the exercises. In this problem we are given a family of sets $F = \{S_1, S_2, \ldots, S_k\}$ and are required to determine if there is a subset $T \subseteq F$ of disjoint sets such that

$$\bigcup_{S_i \in T} S_i = \bigcup_{S_i \in F} S_i = \{u_1, u_2, \ldots, u_n\}.$$

From any given instance of this problem construct the sum of subset problem $A = \{a_1, \ldots, a_k\}$ with $a_j = \Sigma_{1 \le i \le n} \epsilon_{ji}(k + 1)^{i-1}$ where $\epsilon_{ji} = 1$ if $u_i \in S_j$ and $\epsilon_{ji} = 0$ otherwise and $M = \Sigma_{0 \le i < n} (k + 1)^i = ((k + 1)^n - 1)/k$. Clearly, F has an exact cover iff $A = \{a_1, \ldots, a_k\}$ has a subset with sum M. Since A and M may be constructed from F in polynomial time, exact cover $\propto$ sum of subsets. $\square$

Theorem 11.9 Sum of subsets $\propto$ partition

Proof: Let $A = \{a_1, \ldots, a_n\}$ and M define an instance of the sum of subsets problem. Construct the set $B = \{b_1, b_2, \ldots, b_{n+2}\}$ with $b_i = a_i$, $1 \le i \le n$, $b_{n+1} = M + 1$ and $b_{n+2} = (\Sigma_{1 \le i \le n} a_i) + 1 - M$. B has a partition iff A has a subset with sum M. Since B may be obtained from A and M in polynomial time, sum of subsets $\propto$ partition. $\square$

One may easily show Partition $\propto$ 0/1-Knapsack and Partition $\propto$ Job sequencing with deadlines. Hence, these problems are also NP-hard.

Scheduling Identical Processors

Let P_i, $1 \le i \le m$ be m identical processors (or machines). The P_i could for example be line printers in a computer output room. Let J_i, $1 \le i \le n$ be n jobs. Job J_i requires t_i processing time. A schedule S is an assignment of jobs to processors. For each job J_i, S specifies the time intervals and the processor(s) on which this job is to be processed. A job cannot be processed by more than one processor at any given time. Let f_i be the time at which the processing of job J_i is completed. The *mean finish time* (mft) of schedule S is:

$$\text{MFT}(S) = \frac{1}{n} \sum_{1 \leq i \leq n} f_i$$

Let w_i be a weight associated with each job J_i. The *weighted mean finish time* (wmft) of schedule S is:

$$\text{WMFT}(S) = \frac{1}{n} \sum_{1 \leq i \leq n} w_i f_i.$$

Let T_i be the time at which P_i finishes processing all jobs (or job segments) assigned to it. The *finish time* of S is:

$$\text{FT}(S) = \max_{1 \leq i \leq m} \{T_i\}.$$

S is a *non-preemptive schedule* iff each job J_i is processed continuously from start to finish on the same processor. In a *preemptive* schedule each job need not be processed continuously to completion on one processor.

At this point it is worth noting the similarity between the optimal tape storage problem of Section 4.2 and non-preemptive schedules. Mean retrieval time, weighted mean retrieval time and maximum retrieval time respectively correspond to mean finish time, weighted mean finish time and finish time. Minimum finish time schedules can therefore be obtained using the algorithm developed in Section 4.2. Obtaining minimum weighted mean finish time and minimum finish time non-preemptive schedules is NP-hard.

Theorem 11.10 Partition $\propto$ minimum finish time non-preemptive schedule

Proof: We shall prove this for $m = 2$. The extension to $m > 2$ is trivial. Let a_i, $1 \leq i \leq n$ be an instance of the partition problem. Define n jobs with processing requirements $t_i = a_i$, $1 \leq i \leq n$. There is a non-preemptive schedule for this set of jobs on two processors with finish time at most $\sum t_i/2$ iff there is a partition of the a_i's. □

Theorem 11.11 Partition $\propto$ minimum WMFT non-preemptive schedule

Proof: Once again we prove this for $m = 2$ only. The extension to $m > 2$

is trivial. Let a_i, $1 \leq i \leq n$ define an instance of the partition problem. Construct a two processor scheduling problem with n jobs and $w_i = t_i = a_i$, $1 \leq i \leq n$. For this set of jobs there is a non-preemptive schedule S with weighted mean flow time at most $1/2 \, \Sigma \, a_i^2 + 1/4 \, (\Sigma \, a_i)^2$ iff the a_i's have a partition. To see this let the weights and times of jobs on P_1 be $(\bar{w}_1, \bar{t}_1), \ldots, (\bar{w}_k, \bar{t}_k)$ and on P_2 be $(\bar{\bar{w}}_1, \bar{\bar{t}}_1), \ldots, (\bar{\bar{w}}_l, \bar{\bar{t}}_l)$. Assume this is the order in which the jobs are processed on their respective processors. Then, for this schedule S we have:

$$\text{WMFT}(S) = \bar{w}_1 \bar{t}_1 + \bar{w}_2(\bar{t}_1 + \bar{t}_2) + \ldots + \bar{w}_k(\bar{t}_1 + \ldots + \bar{t}_k)$$

$$+ \, \bar{\bar{w}}_1 \bar{\bar{t}}_1 + \bar{\bar{w}}_2(\bar{\bar{t}}_1 + \bar{\bar{t}}_2) + \cdots + \bar{\bar{w}}_l(\bar{\bar{t}}_1 + \cdots + \bar{\bar{t}}_l)$$

$$= \frac{1}{2} \, \Sigma \, w_i^2 + \frac{1}{2} \, (\Sigma \, \bar{w}_i)^2 + \frac{1}{2} \, (\Sigma \, w_i - \Sigma \, \bar{w}_i)^2.$$

Thus, $\text{WMFT}(S) \geq (1/2) \, \Sigma \, w_i^2 + (1/4) \, (\Sigma \, w_i^2)$. This value is obtainable iff the w_i's (and so also the a_i's) have a partition. $\square$

Flow Shop Scheduling

We shall use the flow shop terminology developed in Section 5.8. When $m = 2$, minimum finish time schedules can be obtained in $O(n \log n)$ time if n jobs are to be scheduled. When $m = 3$ obtaining minimum finish time schedules (whether preemptive or non-preemptive) is NP-hard. For the case of non-preemptive schedules this is easy to see (exercise 30). We shall prove the result for preemptive schedules. The proof we shall give is also valid for the non-preemptive case. However, a much simpler proof exists for the non-preemptive case.

Theorem 11.12 Partition $\propto$ minimum finish time preemptive flow shop schedule $(m > 2)$.

Proof: We shall use only three processors. Let $A = \{a_1, a_2, \ldots, a_n\}$ define an instance of the partition problem. Construct the following preemptive flow shop instance, FS, with $n + 2$ jobs, $m = 3$ machines and at most 2 nonzero tasks per job:

$$t_{1,i} = a_i; \; t_{2,i} = 0; \; t_{3,i} = a_i, \quad 1 \leq i \leq n$$

$$t_{1,n+1} = T/2; \; t_{2,n+1} = T; \; t_{3,n+1} = 0$$

$$t_{1,n+2} = 0; \; t_{2,n+2} = T; \; t_{3,n+2} = T/2$$

where

$$T = \sum_1^n a_i.$$

We now show that the above flow shop instance has a preemptive schedule with finish time at most $2T$ iff A has a partition.

(a) If A has a partition u then there is a non-preemptive schedule with finish time $2T$. One such schedule is shown in Figure 11.9.

(b) If A has no partition then all preemptive schedules for FS must have a finish time greater than $2T$. This can be shown by contradiction. Assume that there is a preemptive schedule for FS with finish time at most $2T$. We make the following observations regarding this schedule:

(i) task $t_{1,n+1}$ must finish by time T (as $t_{2,n+1} = T$ and cannot start until $t_{1,n+1}$ finishes)

(ii) task $t_{3,n+2}$ cannot start before T units of time have elapsed as $t_{2,n+2} = T$.

Observation (i) implies that only $T/2$ of the first T time units are free on processor one. Let V be the set of indices of tasks completed on processor 1 by time T (excluding task $t_{1,n+1}$). Then,

$$\sum_{i \in V} t_{1,i} < T/2$$

as A has no partition. Hence

$$\sum_{\substack{i \notin V \\ 1 \le i \le n}} t_{3,i} > T/2.$$

The processing of jobs not included in V cannot commence on processor 3 until after time T since their processor 1 processing is not completed until after T. This together with observation (ii) implies that the total amount of processing left for processor 3 at time T is

$$t_{3,n+2} + \sum_{\substack{i \notin V \\ 1 \le i \le n}} t_{3,i} > T.$$

The schedule length must therefore be more than $2T$.   □

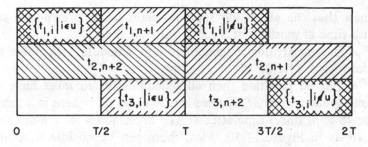

Figure 11.9 A possible schedule

Job Shop Scheduling

A job shop, like a flow shop, has m different processors. The n jobs to be scheduled require the completion of several tasks. The time of the jth task for job J_i is $t_{k,i,j}$. Task j is to be performed on processor P_k. The tasks for any job J_i are to be carried out in the order 1, 2, 3, ..., etc. Task j cannot begin until task $j - 1$ (if $j > 1$) has been completed. Note that it is quite possible for a job to have many tasks that are to be performed on the same processor. In a non-preemptive schedule, a task once begun is processed without interruption until it is completed. The definitions of FT(S) and MFT(S) extend to this problem in a natural way. Obtaining either a minimum finish time preemptive or minimum finish time non-preemptive schedule is NP-hard even when $m = 2$. The proof for the nonpreemptive case is very simple (use partition). We shall present the proof for the preemptive case. This proof will also be valid for the non-preemptive case but will not be the simplest proof for this case.

Theorem 11.13 Partition $\propto$ minimum finish time preemptive job shop schedule ($m > 1$).

Proof: We shall use only two processors. Let $A = \{a_1, a_2, ..., a_n\}$ define an instance of the partition problem. Construct the following job shop instance JS, with $n + 1$ jobs and $m = 2$ processors.

Jobs 1, ..., n: $t_{1,i,1} = t_{2,i,2} = a_i$ for $1 \le i \le n$
Job $n + 1$: $t_{2,n+1,1} = t_{1,n+1,2} = t_{2,n+1,3} = t_{1,n+1,4} = T/2$

where

$$T = \sum_1^n a_i$$

We show that the above job shop problem has a preemptive schedule with finish time at most $2T$ iff S has a partition.

a) If A has a partition u then there is a schedule with finish time $2T$ (see Figure 11.10).

b) If A has no partition then all schedules for JS must have a finish time greater than $2T$. To see this assume that there is a schedule S for JS with finish time at most $2T$. Then, job $n + 1$ must be scheduled as in Figure 11.10. Also, there can be no idle time on either P_1 or P_2. Let R be the set of jobs scheduled on P_1 in the interval $[0, T/2]$. Let R' be the subset of R representing jobs whose first task is completed on P_1 in this interval. Since the a_i's have no partition, $\sum_{j \in R'} t_{i,j,1} < T/2$. Consequently, $\sum_{j \in R'} t_{2,j,2} < T/2$. Since only the second tasks of jobs in R' may be scheduled on P_2 in the interval $[T/2, T]$, it follows that there is some idle time on P_2 in this interval. Hence, S must have finish time greater than $2T$. □

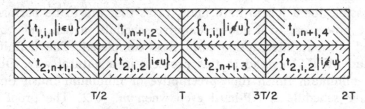

T/2   T   3T/2   2T

Figure 11.10 Another schedule

11.5   NP-HARD CODE GENERATION PROBLEMS

Code Generation With Common Subexpressions

When arithmetic expressions have common subexpressions they may be represented by a directed acyclic graph (dag). Every internal node (node with nonzero out-degree) in the dag represents an operator. Assuming the expression contains only binary operators, each internal node, P, has out-degree two. The two nodes adjacent from P will be called the left and right children of P respectively. The children of P are the roots of the dags for the left and right operands of P. P is the parent of its children. In case the expression contains no common subexpressions, its dag representation is identical to the tree representation of Section 6.2. Figure 11.11 shows some expressions and their dag representations.

Definition: A *leaf* is a node with out-degree zero. A *level one* node is a node both of whose children are leaves. A *shared node* is a node with more than one parent. A *leaf dag* is a dag in which all shared nodes are leaves. A *level one* dag is a dag in which all shared nodes are level one nodes.

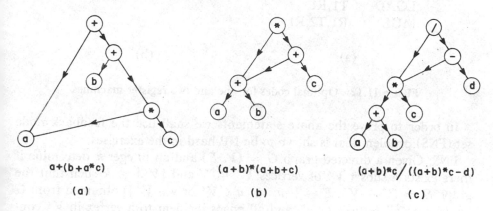

$$a+(b+a*c)$$

(a)

$$(a+b)*(a+b+c)$$

(b)

$$(a+b)*c/((a+b)*c-d)$$

(c)

Figure 11.11 Expressions and their dags

Example 11.17 The dag of Figure 11.11(a) is a leaf dag. Figure 11.11(b) is a level one dag. Figure 11.11(c) is neither a leaf dag nor a level one dag. □

A leaf dag results from an arithmetic expression in which the only common subexpressions are simple variables or constants. A level one dag results from an expression in which the only common subexpressions are of the form a ⓞ b where a and b are simple variables or constants and ⓞ is an operator.

The problem of generating optimal code for level one dags is NP-hard even when the machine for which code is being generated has only one register. Determining the minimum number of registers needed to evaluate a dag with no STOREs is also NP-hard. Note that both these problems can be solved in linear time when there are no common subexpressions (Section 6.2).

Example 11.18 The optimal codes for the dag of Figure 11.11(b) for one and two registers machines is given in Figure 11.12.

The minimum number of registers needed to evaluate this dag without any STOREs is 2. □

```
LOAD      a,R1              LOAD      a,R1
ADD       R1,b,R1           ADD       R1,b,R1
STORE     T1,R1             ADD       R1,c,R2
ADD       R1,c,R1           MUL       R1,R2,R1
STORE     T2,R1
LOAD      T1,R1
MUL       R1,T2,R1
```

(a)   (b)

Figure 11.12 Optimal codes for one and two register machines

In order to prove the above statements we shall use the feedback node set (FNS) problem that is shown to be NP-hard in the exercises.

FNS: Given a directed graph $G = (V, E)$ and an integer k determine if there exists a subset V' of vertices $V' \subseteq V$ and $|V'| \leq k$ such that the graph $H = (V - V', E - \{\langle u, v \rangle | u \in V' \text{ or } v \in V'\})$ obtained from G by deleting all vertices in V' and all edges incident to a vertex in V' contains no directed cycles.

We shall explicitly prove only that generating optimal code is NP-hard. Using the construction of this proof one can also show that determining the minimum number of registers needed to evaluate a dag with no STOREs is also NP-hard. The proof assumes that expressions may contain commutative operators and that shared nodes may be computed only once. It is easily extended to allow recomputation of shared nodes. Using an idea due to Ravi Sethi, the proof is easily extended to the case when only noncommutative operators are allowed (see Exercise 41).

Theorem 11.14 FNS $\propto$ optimal code generation for level one dags on a one register machine.

Proof: Let G, k be an instance of FNS. Let n be the number of vertices in G. We shall construct a dag A with the property that the optimal code for the expression corresponding to A has at most $n + k$ LOADs iff G has a feedback node set of size at most R.

The dag A consists of three kinds of nodes: leaf nodes, chain nodes and tree nodes. All chain and tree nodes are internal nodes representing commutative operators (e.g., '+'). Leaf nodes represent distinct variables. We shall use d_v to denote the out-degree of vertex v of G. Corresponding to each vertex v of G there is a directed chain of chain nodes $v_1, v_2, \ldots, v_{d_v+1}$ in A. Node v_{d_v+1} is the *head node* of the chain for v and is the parent of two leaf nodes v_L and v_R (see Example 11.19 and Figure 11.13). v_1 is the *tail* of the chain. From each of the chain nodes corresponding to vertex v, except the head node, there is one directed edge to the head node of one of the chains corresponding to a vertex w such that $\langle v, w \rangle$ is an edge in G. Each such edge goes to a distinct head. Note that as a result of the addition of these edges, each chain node now has out-degree two. Since each chain node represents a commutative operator, it does not matter which of its two children is regarded as the left child.

At this point we have a dag in which the tail of every chain has in-degree zero. We now introduce tree nodes to combine all the heads together so that we are left with only one node (the root) with in-degree zero. Since G has n vertices, we need $n - 1$ tree nodes (note that every binary tree with $n - 1$ internal nodes has n external nodes). These $n - 1$ nodes are connected together to form a binary tree (any binary tree with $n - 1$ nodes will do). In place of the external nodes we connect the tails of the n chains (see Figure 11.13(b)). This yields a dag A corresponding to an arithmetic expression.

It is easy to see that every optimal code for A will have exactly n LOADs of leaf nodes. Also, there will be exactly one instruction of type ⑱ for every chain node and tree node (we assume that a shared node is computed only once). Hence, the only variable is the number of LOADs and STOREs of chain and tree nodes. If G has no directed cycles then its vertices may be arranged in topological order (vertex u precedes vertex v in a topological ordering only if there is no directed path from u to v in G). Let $v_1, v_2, \ldots, v_n$ be a topological ordering of the vertices in G. The expression A can be computed using no LOADs of chain and tree nodes by first computing all nodes on the chain for v_n and storing the result tail node. Next, all nodes on the chain for v_{n-1} may be computed. In addition, we can compute any nodes on the path from the tail for v_{n-1} to the root for which both operands are available. Finally, one result needs to be stored. Next, the chain for v_{n-2} may be computed. Again, we can compute all nodes on the path from this chain tail to the root for which both operands are available. Continuing in this way, the entire expression may be computed.

If G contains at least one cycle: $v_1, v_2, \ldots, v_i, v_1$ then every code for A must contain at least one LOAD of a chain node on a chain for one of $v_1, v_2, \ldots, v_i$. Further, if none of these vertices is on any other cycle then all their chain nodes may be computed using only one load of a chain node. This argument is readily generalized to show that if the size of a minimum feedback node set is p then every optimal code for A contains exactly $n + p$ LOADs. The p LOADs correspond to a combination of tail nodes corresponding to a minimum feedback node set and the siblings of these tail nodes. In case we had used non-commutative operators for chain nodes and made each successor on a chain the left child of its parent then the p LOADs will correspond to the tails of the chains of any minimum feedback set. Furthermore, if the optimal code contains p LOADs of chain nodes then G has a feedback node set of size p.   □

Example 11.19   Figure 11.13(b) shows the dag A corresponding to the graph G of Figure 11.13(a). $\{r, s\}$ is a minimum feedback node set for G. The operator in each chain and tree node may be assumed to be '$+$'. Every code for A has a load corresponding to one of (p_L, p_R), (q_L, q_R), $\ldots$ and (u_L, u_R). The expression A can be computed using only two additional LOADs by computing nodes in the order $r_4, s_2, q_2, q_1, p_2, p_1, c, u_3, u_2, u_1, t_2, t_1, e, s_1, r_3, r_2, r_1, d, b, a$. Note that a LOAD is needed to compute s_1 and also to compute r_3.   □

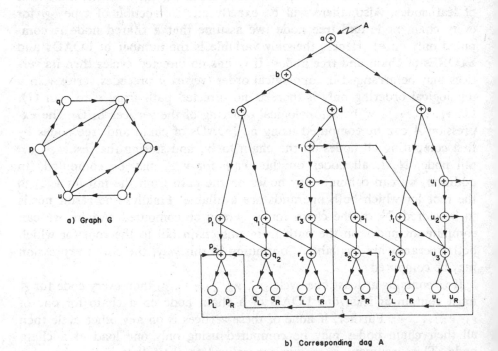

a) Graph G

b) Corresponding dag A

Figure 11.13   A graph and its corresponding dag.

Implementing Parallel Assignment Instructions

A SPARKS *parallel assignment* instruction has the format $(v_1, v_2, \ldots, v_n)$ $\leftarrow (e_1, e_2, \ldots, e_n)$ where the $v_i s$ are distinct variable names and the $e_i s$ are expressions. The semantics of this statement is that the value of v_i is updated to be the value of the expression e_i, $1 \le i \le n$. The value of the expression e_i is to be computed using the values the variables in e_i have before this instruction is executed.

Example 11.20

(i) $(A, B) \leftarrow (B, C)$ is equivalent to $A \leftarrow B; B \leftarrow C$

(ii) $(A, B) \leftarrow (B, A)$ is equivalent to $T \leftarrow A; A \leftarrow B; B \leftarrow T$

(iii) $(A, B) \leftarrow (A + B, A - B)$ is equivalent to $T1 \leftarrow A; T2 \leftarrow B;$ $A \leftarrow T1 + T2; B \leftarrow T1 - T2$ and also to $T1 \leftarrow A; A \leftarrow A + B;$ $B \leftarrow T1 - B.$ □

As the above example indicates, it may be necessary to store some of the $v_i s$ into temporary locations when executing a parallel assignment. These stores are needed only when some of the $v_i s$ appear in the expressions e_j, $1 \le j \le n$. A variable v_i is *referenced* by expression e_j iff v_i appears in e_j. It should be clear that only referenced variables need to be copied into temporary locations. Further, Examples 11.20 (ii) and (iii) show that not all referenced variables need to be copied.

An implementation of a parallel assignment statement is a sequence of instructions of types $T_j \leftarrow v_i$ and $v_i \leftarrow e'_i$ where e'_i is obtained from e_i by replacing all occurrences of a v_i that has already been updated with a reference to the temporary location in which the old value of v_i has been saved. Let $R = (\tau(1), \ldots, \tau(n))$ be a permutation of $(1, 2, \ldots, n)$. R is a *realization* of an assignment statement. It specifies the order in which statements of type $v_i \leftarrow e'_i$ appear in an implementation of a parallel assignment statement. The order is $v_{\tau(1)} \leftarrow e'_{\tau(1)}; v_{\tau(2)} \leftarrow e'_{\tau(2)};$ etc. The implementation also has statements of type $T_j \leftarrow v_i$ interspersed. Without loss of generality we may assume that the statement $T_j \leftarrow v_i$ (if it appears in the implementation) immediately precedes the statement $v_i \leftarrow e'_i$. Hence, a realization completely characterizes an implementation. The minimum number of instructions of type $T_j \leftarrow v_i$ for any given realization is easy to determine. This number is the cost of the realization. The *cost* $C(R)$ of a realization R is the number of v_i that are referenced by an e_j that corresponds to an instruction $v_j \leftarrow e'_j$ that appears after the instruction $v_i \leftarrow e'_i$.

Example 11.21   Consider the statement $(A, B, C) \leftarrow (D, A + B, A - B)$
The $3! = 6$ different realizations and their costs are:

R	$C(R)$
1, 2, 3	2
1, 3, 2	2
2, 1, 3	2
2, 3, 1	1
3, 1, 2	1
3, 2, 1	0

The realization 3, 2, 1 corresponding to the implementation $C \leftarrow A - B$;
$B \leftarrow A + B$; $A \leftarrow D$ needs no temporary stores ($C(R) = 0$).   □

An optimal realization for a parallel assignment statement is one with
minimum cost. When the expressions e_i are all variable names or constants,
an optimal realization can be found in linear time ($O(n)$). When the e_i
are allowed to be expressions with operators then finding an optimal realization is NP-Hard. We shall prove this latter statement using the feedback
node set problem.

Theorem 11.15   FNS $\propto$ minimum cost realization.

Proof: Let $G = (V, E)$ be any n vertex directed graph. Construct the
parallel assignment statement P: $(v_1, v_2, \ldots, v_n) \leftarrow (e_1, e_2, \ldots, e_n)$ where
the v_i's correspond to the n vertices in V and e_i is the expression $v_{i_1} + v_{i_2}$
$+ \cdots + v_{i_j}$. $\{v_{i_1}, v_{i_2}, \ldots, v_{i_j}\}$ is the set of vertices adjacent from v_i (i.e.
$\langle v_i, v_{i_l} \rangle \in E(G)$, $1 \leq l \leq j$). This construction requires at most $O(n^2)$
time.
   Let U be any feedback node set for G. Let $G' = (V', E') = (V - U, E$
$- \{\langle x, y \rangle | x \in U \text{ or } y \in U\})$ be the graph obtained by deleting vertex set
U and all edges incident to vertices in U. From the definition of a feedback
node set it follows that G' is acyclic. So, the vertices in $V - U$ may be
arranged in a sequence $s_1, s_2, \ldots, s_m$ where $m = |V - U|$ and E' con-
tains no edge $\langle s_j, s_i \rangle$ for any i, j, $1 \leq i < j \leq m$. Hence, an implementation of P in which variables corresponding to vertices in U are first stored
in temporary locations followed by the instructions $v_i \leftarrow e'_i$ corresponding
to $v_i \in U$, followed by the corresponding instructions for $s_1, s_2, \ldots, s_m$ (in
that order), will be a correct implementation. (e'_i is e_i with all occurrences
of $v_i \in U$ replaced by the corresponding temporary location). The realiza-
tion, R, corresponding to this implementation has $C(R) = |U|$. Hence,

if G has a feedback node set of size at most k then P has an optimal realization of cost at most k.

Suppose P has a realization R of cost k. Let U be the set of k variables that have to be stored in temporary locations and let $R = (q_1, q_2, \ldots, q_n)$. From the definition of $C(R)$ it follows that no e_{q_i} references a v_{q_j} with $j < i$ unless $v_{q_j} \in U$. Hence, the deletion of vertices in U from G leaves G acyclic. Thus, U defines a feedback node set of size k for G.

G has a feedback node set of size at most k iff P has a realization of cost at most k. Thus we can solve the feedback node set problem in polynomial time if we have a polynomial time algorithm that determines a minimum cost realization. $\square$

11.6 SOME SIMPLIFIED NP-HARD PROBLEMS

Once we have shown a problem L to be NP-hard we would be inclined to dismiss the possibility that L can be solved in deterministic polynomial time. At this point, however, one may naturally ask the question: Can a suitably restricted version (i.e., some subclass) of an NP-hard problem be solved in deterministic polynomial time? It should be easy to see that by placing enough restrictions on any NP-hard problem (or by defining a sufficiently small subclass) we can arrive at a polynomially solvable problem. As examples, consider the following:

i) CNF-satisfiability with at most three literals per clause is NP-hard. If each clause is restricted to have at most two literals then CNF-satisfiability is polynomially solvable.

ii) Generating optimal code for a parallel assignment statement is NP-hard. However, if the expressions e_i are restricted to be simple variables then optimal code can be generated in polynomial time.

iii) Generating optimal code for level one dags is NP-hard but optimal code for trees can be generated in polynomial time.

iv) Determining if a planar graph is three colorable is NP-hard. To determine if it is two colorable we only have to see if it is bipartite.

Since it is very unlikely that NP-hard problems are ploynomially solvable, it is important to determine the weakest restrictions under which we can solve a problem in polynomial time.

To narrow the gap between subclasses for which polynomial time algorithms are known and those for which such algorithms are not known, it is desirable to obtain as strong a set of restrictions under which a problem remains NP-hard or NP-complete.

We state without proof the severest restrictions under which certain problems are known to be NP-hard or NP-complete. We shall state these simplified or restricted problems as decision problems. For each problem we shall specify only the input and the decision to be made.

Theorem 11.16   The following decision problems are NP-complete:

1. **Node Cover**
   Input: An undirected graph G with node degree at most 3 and an integer k.
   Decision: Does G have a node cover of size at most k?

2. **Planar Node Cover**
   Input: A planar undirected graph G with node degree at most 6 and an integer k.
   Decision: Does G have a node cover of size at most k?

3. **Colorability**
   Input: A planar undirected graph G with node degree at most four.
   Decision: Is G 3-colorable?

4. **Undirected Hamiltonian Cycle**
   Input: An undirected graph G with node degree at most three.
   Decision: Does G have a Hamiltonian cycle?

5. **Planar Undirected Hamiltonian Cycle**
   Input: A planar undirected graph.
   Decision: Does G have a Hamiltonian cycle?

6. **Planar Directed Hamiltonian Path**
   Input: A planar directed graph G with in-degree at most 3 and out-degree at most 4.
   Decision: Does G have a directed Hamiltonian path?

7. **Unary Input Partition**
   Input: Positive integers a_i, $1 \le i \le m$, n, and B such that

$$\sum_{1 \le i \le m} a_i = nB, \frac{B}{4} < a_i < \frac{B}{2}, 1 \le i \le m \text{ and } m = 3n.$$

Input is in unary notation.
   Decision: Is there a partition $\{A_1, \ldots, A_n\}$ of the a_i's such that each A_i contains three elements and

$$\sum_{a \in A_i} a = B, \quad 1 \le i \le n?$$

8. **Unary Flow Shop**
   Input: Task times in unary notation and an integer T.
   Decision: Is there a two processor non-preemptive schedule with mean finish time at most T?

9. **Simple Max Cut**
   Input: A graph $G = (V, E)$ and an integer k.
   Decision: Does V have a subset V_1 such that there are at least k edges $(u, v) \in E$ with $u \in V_1$ and $v \notin V_1$?

10. **SAT2**
    Input: A propositional formula F in CNF. Each clause in F has at most two literals. An integer k.
    Decision: Can at least k clauses of F be satisfied?

11. **Minimum Edge Deletion Bipartite Subgraph**
    Input: An undirected graph G and an integer k.
    Decision: Can G be made bipartite by the deletion of at most k edges?

12. **Minimum Node Deletion Bipartite Subgraph**
    Input: An undirected graph G and an integer k.
    Decision: Can G be made bipartite by the deletion of at most k vertices.

13. **Minimum Cut Into Equal-Sized Subsets**
    Input: An undirected graph $G = (V, E)$, two distinguished vertices s and t and a positive integer W.
    Decision: Is there a partition $V = V_1 \cup V_2$, $V_1 \cap V_2 = \phi$, $|V_1| = |V_2|$, $s \in V_1$, $t \in V_2$ and $|\{(u, v)| u \in V_1, v \in V_2 \text{ and } (u, v) \in E\}| \le W$?

14. **Simple Optimal Linear Arrangement**
    Input: An undirected graph $G = (V, E)$ and an integer k. $|V| = n$.
    Decision: Is there a one to one function $f: V \rightarrow \{1, 2, \ldots, n\}$ such that

$$\sum_{(u, v) \in E} |f(u) - f(v)| \le k$$

REFERENCES AND SELECTED READINGS

A comprehensive treatment of NP-hard and NP-complete problems may be found in the book:

Computers and intractability: A guide to the theory of NP-Completeness, by M. Garey and D. Johnson, Freeman and Co., San Francisco, 1978.

Cook's theorem (Section 11.2) appears in:
"The complexity of theorem-proving procedures," by S. A. Cook, *Proc. of the Third ACM Symposium on Theory of Computing,* 1971, pp. 151–158.

The above paper also shows satisfiability $\propto$ clique. Cook's original proof is in terms of Turing machines. The proof given in the text was adapted by S. Sahni. We are grateful to R. Kain for pointing out an error in the original adaptation. J. Ullman has adapted Cook's proof to a somewhat different machine model.

Karp showed the importance of the class of NP-complete problems by exhibiting 21 problems that are NP-complete. His list of problems includes node cover, feedback arc set, feedback node set, Hamiltonian cycle, partition, sum of subsets, job sequencing with deadlines, max cut etc. Karp's work appears in:

"Reducibility among combinatorial problems," by R. Karp, *Complexity of Computer Computations,* R. E. Miller and J. W. Thatcher, eds., Plenum Press, New York, 1972, pp. 85–104. [exercises 6, 10, 11, 14, 19, 20, 21, 23, 24, 29, 37, 40].

Our proof satisfiability $\propto$ directed Hamiltonian cycle is from:

"On reducibility among combinatorial problems," by P. Hermann, MIT MAC Report TR-113, December 1973. [exercises 8, 9]

The proof satisfiability $\propto$ AND/OR Graphs is from:

"Computationally related problems," by S. Sahni, *SIAM Journal on Computing,* 3:4(1974), pp. 262–279. [exercises 18, 25, 35]

This paper also contains reductions to many network flow, n-person game theory and optimization problems. Theorem 11.11 is due to Bruno, Coffman and Sethi. It appears in the following paper:

"Scheduling independent tasks to reduce mean finishing-time," by J. Bruno, E. G. Coffman, Jr. and R. Sethi, *Comm. ACM,* 17:7, July 1974, pp. 382–387.

The proof used in the text for Theorem 11.11 is due to S. Sahni and appears in:

"Algorithms for scheduling independent tasks," by S. Sahni, *JACM*, 23, 1976, pp. 114–127.

Theorems 11.12 and 11.13 are due to Gonzalez and Sahni. The reference is:

"Flow shop and job shop schedules: complexity and approximation," by T. Gonzalez and S. Sahni, *Op. Res.*, 26(1), pp. 36–52, 1978.

The proof used in the text for Theorem 11.13 is due to D. Nassimi. Many other scheduling problems are known to be NP-hard. Some references are:

"Machine scheduling problems," by A. Rinnooy Kan, Ph.D. thesis, Mathematical Centrum, Amsterdam, 1976.

"Sequencing by enumerative methods," by J. K. Lenstra, Ph.D. thesis, Mathematisch Centrum, Amsterdam, 1976.

"Polynomial complete scheduling problems," by J. D. Ullman, *JCSS*, June 1975, pp. 384–393.

Computer and Job Shop Scheduling Theory, by E. G. Coffman, J. Wiley, New York 1976.

"The Complexity of Flowshop and Jobshop Scheduling," by M. Garey, D. Johnson, and R. Sethi, *Math. of Operations Research*, 1:2(1976), pp. 117–129 [exercises 30, 31].

"Complexity results for multiprocessor scheduling under resource constraints," by M. Garey and D. Johnson, *SIAM Journal on Computing*, 4:4(1975), pp. 397–411.

"On the complexity of a timetable and multicommodity flow problems," by S. Even, *SIAM Jr. on Computing*, 5, 691–703 (1976).

"Algorithms for minimizing mean flow time," by J. Bruno, E. G. Coffman, and R. Sethi, *Proc. IFIP Congr. 74*, 1974, pp. 504–510.

"On the complexity of mean flow time scheduling," by R. Sethi, *Math. of Op. Res.*, 2(4), 320–330 (1977).

"Open Shop Scheduling to Minimize Finish Time," by T. Gonzalez and S. Sahni, *JACM*, 23(4), pp. 665–679 (1976).

"Optimization and approximation in deterministic sequencing and scheduling: a survey," by R. Graham, E. Lawler, J. Lenstra and A. Rinnooy Kan, Department of Operations Research, Mathematisch Centrum, Amsterdam, Report #BW 82/77, 1977.

"Complexity of machine scheduling problems," by P. Brucker, J. Lenstra and A.

Rinnooy Kan, Math. Centrum, Amsterdam, Report #BW 43/75, 1975. [exercises 30, 31, 32, 33].

"Complexity of scheduling shops with no wait in process," by S. Sahni and Y. Cho, University of Minnesota, Technical Report #77-20, 1977 (to appear in Math. of Oper. Res.).

"Preemptive shop scheduling of independent job with release times," by Y. Cho and S. Sahni, University of Minnesota, Technical Report #78-5, 1978. [exercise 36].

The proof of Theorem 11.14 is an adapation of a proof that appears in:

"Code generation for expressions with common subexpressions," by A. Aho, S. Johnson and J. Ullman, *JACM*, 24(1), pp. 146–160 (1977). [exercise 41].

The fact that the code generation problem for one register machines is NP-hard was first proved by Bruno and Sethi in:

"Code generation for a one-register machine," by J. Bruno and R. Sethi, *J.ACM*, 23(3), pp. 502–510 (1976).

The result of the above paper is stronger than Theorem 11.14 as it applies even to expressions containing no commutative operators. Theorem 11.15 is due to R. Sethi. The reference is:

"A note on implementing parallel assignment instructions," by R. Sethi, *Info. Proc. Let.*, 2, pp. 91–95 (1973).

Further results on NP-Hard code generation problems appear in:

"Complete register allocation problems," by R. Sethi, *SIAM Jr. on Comp.*, 4(3), pp. 226–248 (1975).

"Code generation for short/long address machines," by E. Robertson, University of Wisconsin, MRC report #1779, August 1977.

The results stated in Section 11.6 may be found in:

"Some simplified NP-Complete graph problems," by M. Garey, D. Johnson and L. Stockmeyer, *Jr. Theo. Comp. Sci.*, 1, pp. 237–267 (1976).

"The planar Hamiltonian circuit problem is NP-Complete," by M. Garey, D. Johnson and R. Tarjan, *SIAM Jr. on Computing*, 5(4), pp. 704–714, 1976.

"The complexity of flowshop and jobshop scheduling," by M. Garey, D. Johnson and R. Sethi, *Math. of Oper. Res.*, 1(2), pp. 117–129 (1976).

Other interesting papers on NP-hard and NP-complete problems are:

"Some complexity results for the traveling salesman problem," by C. Papadimitriou and K. Steiglitz, *Proc. Eighth Annual ACM Symposium on Theory of Computing,* May 1976, pp. 1–9.

"On the computational complexity of combinatorial problems," by R. Karp, *Networks,* 5, 1975, pp. 45–68.

"Polynomially complete fault detection problems," by O. Ibarra and S. Sahni, *IEEE Trans. Comp.,* 24(3), pp. 242–249(1975). [exercises 26, 27].

"Generalizing NP-Completeness to permit different input measures," by M. Garey and D. Johnson, Bell Laboratories, New Jersey, 1976.

"Strong NP-Completeness results: motivation, examples and implications," by M. Garey and D. Johnson, Bell Laboratories, New Jersey, 1976.

"Constructing optimal binary decision trees is NP-Complete," by L. Hyafil and R. Rivest, *Info. Proc. Let.,* 5(1), pp. 15–17 (1976).

"Assignment commands with array references," by P. Downey and R. Sethi, *Proc. 17th Annual Symp. on Found. of Comp.,* pp. 57–66 (1976) (to appear in *JACM*).

"On the computational complexity of schema equivalence," by R. Constable, H. Hunt and S. Sahni, *8th Annual Princeton Conference on Information Sciences and Systems,* pp. 15–20 (1974).

"Complexity of trie index construction," by D. Comer and R. Sethi, *JACM,* 24(3), 1977, pp. 428–440.

"Combinatorial problems: reducibility and approximation," by S. Sahni and E. Horowitz, *Operations Research,* to appear.

"Complexity of decision problems based on finite two-person perfect-information games," by T. Schaefer, *Proc. Eighth Annual ACM Symposium on Theory of Computing,* May 1976, pp. 41–49.

"Some polynomial and integer divisibility problems are NP-Hard," by D. Plaisted, *Proc. 17th Annual Symp. on Found. of Comp.,* pp. 264–267 (1976).

"Traversal marker placement problems are NP-Complete," by S. Maheshwari, University of Colorado, Computer Science Technical Report #CU-CS-092-76, May 1976.

"A note on reductions to directed HC," by J. Seiferas, *8th Annual Princeton Conference on Information Sciences and Systems,* pp. 24–28, 1974.

"Two NP-complete problems in nonnegative integer programming," by G. Leuker, Princeton University Computer Science Laboratory, Technical Report TR-178, 1975. [exercise 44].

"The complexity of satisfiability problems," by T. Schaefer, *10th ACM Symposium on Theory of Computing*, pp. 216–226, 1978.

EXERCISES

1. Obtain a nondeterministic algorithm of complexity $O(n)$ to determine whether or not there is a subset of the n numbers a_i, $1 \leq i \leq n$ that sums to M.

2. (i) Show that the knapsack optimization problem reduces to the knapsack decision problem when all the p's, w's and M are integer and the complexity is measured as a function of input length. (Hint: if the input length is m then $\Sigma\, p_i \leq n2^m$ where n is the number of objects. Use a binary search to determine the optimal solution value).

   (ii) Let DK be an algorithm for the knapsack decision problem. Let R be the value of an optimal solution to the knapsack optimization problem. Show how to obtain a 0/1 assignment for the x_i, $1 \leq i \leq n$ such that $\Sigma\, p_i x_i = R$ and $\Sigma\, w_i x_i \leq M$ by making n applications of DK.

3. In conjunction with formula G in the proof of Cook's theorem (Section 11.2), obtain M for the following cases for instruction i. Note that M can contain at most $O(p(n))$ literals (as a function of n). Obtain M under the assumption that negative numbers are represented in ones complement. Show how the corresponding $G_{i,t}$'s may be transformed into CNF. The length of $G_{i,t}$ must increase by no more than a constant factor (say w^2) during this transformation.

   i) $Y \leftarrow Z$
   ii) $Y \leftarrow V - Z$
   iii) $Y \leftarrow V + Z$
   iv) $Y \leftarrow V * Z$
   v) $Y \leftarrow$ **choice** $(0, 1)$
   vi) $Y \leftarrow$ **choice** $(r{:}u)$ where r and u are variables.

4. Show that the clique optimization problem reduces to the clique decision problem.

5. Let SAT(E) be an algorithm to determine whether or not a propositional formula E in CNF is satisfiable. Show that if E is satisfiable and has n variables $x_1, x_2, \ldots, x_n$ then using SAT(E) n times one can determine a truth value assignment for the x_i's for which E is true.

6. Let SATY be the problem of determining whether a propositional formula in CNF having at most three literals per clause is satisfiable. Show that CNF satisfiability $\propto$ SATY (Hint: Show how to write a clause with more than three literals as the **and** of several clauses each containing at most three literals. For this you will have to introduce some new variables. Any assignment that satisfies the original clause must satisfy all the new clauses created).

7. Let SAT3 be similar to SATY (Exercise 6) except that each clause has exactly three literals. Show that SATY ∝ SAT3.

8. Let F be a propositional formula in CNF. Two literals x and y in F are *compatible* iff they are not in the same clause and $x \neq \bar{y}$. x and y are *incompatible* iff x and y are not compatible. Let SATINC be the problem of determining if a formula F in which each literal is incompatible with at most three other literals is satisfiable. Show that SAT3 ∝ SATINC.

9. Let 3-NODE COVER be the node cover decision problem of Section 11.3 restricted to graphs of degree 3. Show that SATINC ∝ 3-NODE COVER (see Exercise 8).

10. [Feedback Node Set]
    (a) Let $G = (V, E)$ be a directed graph. Let $S \subseteq V$ be a subset of vertices such that deletion of S and all edges incident to vertices in S results in a graph G' with no directed cycles. Such an S is a feedback node set. The size of S is the number of vertices in S. The feedback node set decision problem (FNS) is to determine for a given input k if G has a feedback node set of size at most k. Show that node cover decision problem ∝ FNS.
    (b) Write a polynomial time nondeterministic algorithm for FNS.

11. [Feedback Arc Set] Let $G = (V, E)$ be a directed graph. $S \subseteq E$ is a feedback arc set of G iff every directed cycle in G contains an edge in S. The feedback arc set decision problem (FAS) is to determine if G has a feedback arc set of size at most k. Show that node cover decision problem ∝ FAS.
    (b) Write a polynomial time nondeterministic algorithm for FAS.

12. The feedback node set optimization problem is to find a minimum feedback node set (see Exercise 10). Show that this problem reduces to FNS.

13. Show that the feedback arc set minimization problem reduces to FAS (Exercise 11).

14. [Hamiltonian Cycle] Let UHC be the problem of determining if in any given undirected graph G there exists an undirected cycle going through each vertex exactly once and returning to the start vertex. Show that DHC ∝ UHC (DHC is defined in Section 11.3).

15. Show UHC ∝ CNF satisfiability.

16. Show DHC ∝ CNF satisfiability.

17. [Hamiltonian Path] An i to j Hamiltonian path in a graph G is a path from

vertex i to vertex j that includes each vertex exactly once. Show that UHC is reducible to the problem of determining if G has an i to j hamiltonian path.

18. [Minimum Equivalent Graph]   A directed graph $G = (V, E)$ is an equivalent graph of the directed graph $G' = (V, E')$ iff $E \subseteq E'$ and the transitive closures of G and G' are the same. G is a minimum equivalent graph iff $|E|$ is minimum amongst all equivalent graphs of G'. The minimum equivalent graph decision problem (MEG) is to determine if G' has a minimum equivalent graph with $|E| \leq k$ where k is some given input.
    (a)   Show that DHC $\propto$ MEG.
    (b)   Write a nondeterministic polynomial time algorithm for MEG.

19. [Clique Cover]   The clique cover decision problem (CC) is to determine if G is the union of l or fewer cliques. Show that chromatic number decision problem $\propto$ CC.

20. [Set Cover]   Let $F = \{S_j\}$ be a finite family of sets. Let $T \subseteq F$ be a subset of F. T is a cover of F iff

$$\bigcup_{S_i \in T} S_i = \bigcup_{S_i \in F} S_i.$$

The set cover decision problem is to determine if F has a cover T containing no more than k sets. Show that the node cover decision problem is reducible to this problem.

21. [Exact Cover]   Let $F = \{S_j\}$ be as above. $T \subseteq F$ is an exact cover of F iff T is a cover of F and the sets in F are pairwise disjoint. Show that the chromatic number decision problem reduces to the problem of determining if F has an exact cover.

22. Show that SAT3 $\propto$ EXACT COVER (see Exercise 21).

23. [Hitting Set]   Let F be as in Exercise 21. The hitting set problem is to determine if there exists a set H such that $|H \cap S_j| = 1$ for all $S_j \in F$. Show that exact cover $\propto$ hitting set.

24. [Tautology]   A propositional formula is a tautology iff it is true for all possible truth assignments to its variables. The tautology problem is to determine whether or not a DNF formula is a tautology.
    (a)   Show that CNF satisfiability $\propto$ DNF tautology.
    (b)   Write a polynomial time nondeterministic algorithm TAUT(F) that terminates successfully iff F is not a tautology.

25. [Minimum Boolean Form]   Let the length of a propositional formula be equal

to the sum of the number of literals in each clause. Two formulas F and G on variables $x_1, \ldots, x_n$ are equivalent if for all assignments to $x_1, \ldots, x_n$ F is true iff G is true. Show that deciding if F has an equivalent formula of length no more than k is NP-Hard. (Hint: Show DNF tautology reduces to this problem).

26. [Circuit Realization] Let C be a circuit made up of **and, or** and **not** gates. Let $x_1, \ldots, x_n$ be the inputs and f the output. Show that deciding if $f(x_1, \ldots, x_n) = F(x_1, \ldots, x_n)$ where F is a propositional formula is NP-hard.

27. Show that determining if C is a minimum circuit (i.e. has a minimum number of gates, see Exercise 26) realizing a formula F is NP-hard.

28. [0/1-knapsack] Show that Partition $\propto$ 0/1-knapsack decision problem.

29. [Job Sequencing] Show that the job sequencing with deadlines problem (Chapter 10) is NP-hard.

30. Show that partition $\propto$ minimum finish time non-preemptive 3 processor flow shop schedule. Use only one job that has three nonzero tasks. All other jobs have only one nonzero task.

31. Show that partition $\propto$ minimum finish time non-preemptive 2 processor job shop schedule. Use only one job that has three nonzero tasks. All other jobs have only one nonzero task.

32. Let $J_1, \ldots, J_n$ be n jobs. Job i has a processing time t_i and a deadline d_i. Job i is not available for processing until time r_i. Show that deciding whether all n jobs can be processed on one machine without violating any deadline is NP-Hard. (Hint: Use partition).

33. Let $J_i, 1 \le i \le n$ be n jobs as in the above problem. Assume $r_i = 0, 1 \le i \le n$. Let f_i be the finish time of J_i in a one processor schedule S. The *tardiness* T_i of J_i is $\max\{0, f_i - d_i\}$. Let $w_i, 1 \le i \le n$ be nonnegative weights associated with the J_i's. The total weighted tardiness is $\Sigma w_i T_i$. Show that finding a schedule minimizing $\Sigma w_i T_i$ is NP-hard. (Hint: Use partition).

34. Let $J_i, 1 \le i \le n$ be n jobs. Job J_i has a processing time of t_i. Its processing cannot begin until time r_i. Let w_i be a weight associated with J_i. Let f_i be the finish time of J_i in a one processor schedule S. Show that finding a one processor schedule that minimizes $\Sigma w_i f_i$ is NP-hard.

35. [Quadratic Programming] Show that finding the maximum of a function $f(x_1, \ldots, x_n)$ subject to the linear constraints $\Sigma_{1 \le j \le n} a_{ij} x_j \le b_i, 1 \le i \le n$

and $x_i \geq 0$, $1 \leq i \leq n$ is NP-hard. The function f is restricted to be of the form $\Sigma c_i x_i^2 + \Sigma d_i x_i$.

36. Show that the problem of obtaining optimal finish time preemptive schedules for a two processer flow shop is NP-hard when jobs are released at two different times R_1 and R_2. Jobs released at R_i cannot be scheduled before R_i.

37. Let $G = (V, E)$ be a graph. Let $w(i, j)$ be a weighting function for the edges of G. A *cut* of G is a subset $S \subseteq V$. The *weight* of a cut is

$$\sum_{\substack{i < j \\ i \in S, j \notin S}} w(i, j).$$

A *max-cut* is a cut of maximum weight. Show that the problem of determining the weight of a max-cut is NP-hard.

38. [Plant Location]   Let S_i, $1 \leq i \leq n$ be n possible sites at which plants may be located. At each site at most one plant can be located. If a plant is located at site S_i then a fixed cost F_i is incurred. This is the cost of setting up the plant. A plant located at S_i will have a maximum production capacity of C_i. There are n destinations, D_i, $1 \leq i \leq m$, to which products have to be shipped. The demand at D_i is d_i, $1 \leq i \leq m$. The per unit cost of shipping a product from site i to destination j is c_{ij}. A destination may be supplied from many plants. Define $y_i = 0$ if no plant is located site i and $y_i = 1$ otherwise. Let x_{ij} be the number of units of the product shipped from S_i to D_j. Then, the total cost is

$$\sum_i F_i y_i + \sum_i \sum_j c_{ij} x_{ij}, \quad \sum_i x_{ij} = d_j \quad \text{and} \quad \sum_j x_{ij} \leq C_i y_i.$$

All x_{ij} are non-negative integers. We may assume that $\Sigma C_{ij} \geq \Sigma d_i$. Show that finding y_i and x_{ij} so that the total cost is minimized is NP-hard.

39. [Concentrator Location]   This problem is very similar to the plant location problem (Exercise 38). The only difference is that each destination may be supplied by only 1 plant. When this restriction is imposed, the plant location problem becomes the concentrator location problem arising in computer network design. The destinations represent computer terminals. The plants represent the concentration of information from the terminals which it supplies. Show that the concentrator location problem is NP-hard under each of the following conditions:

  i) $n = 2$, $C_1 = C_2$, $F_1 = F_2$ (Hint: use Partition)
  ii) $F_i/C_i = F_{i+1}/C_{i+1}$, $1 \leq i < n$, $d_i = 1$ (Hint: use Exact Cover)

40. [Steiner Trees] Let T be a tree and R a subset of the vertices in T. Let $w(i, j)$ be the weight of edge (i, j) in T. If (i, j) is not an edge in T then $w(i, j) = \infty$. A Steiner tree is a subtree of T that includes the vertex set R. It may include other vertices too. Its cost is the sum of the weights of the edges in it. Show that finding a minimum cost Steiner tree is NP-hard.

41. a) How should the proof of Theorem 11.14 be modified to permit recomputation of shared nodes.

   b) [Ravi Sethi] Modify the proof of Theorem 11.14 so that it holds for level 1 dags representing expressions in which all operators are noncommutative. Hint: designate the sucessor vertex on a chain to be the left child of its predecessor vertex and use the following $n + 1$ node binary tree to connect together the tail nodes of the n chains:

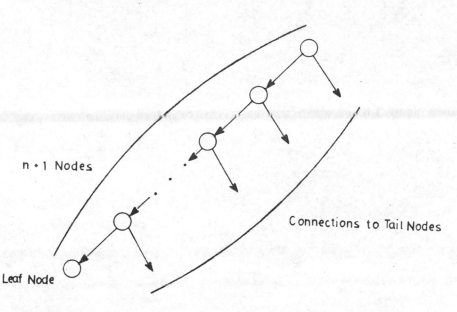

n + 1 Nodes

Connections to Tail Nodes

Leaf Node

   c) Show that optimal code generation is NP-hard for leaf dags on an infinite register machine. (Hint: Use FNS).

42. Assume that P is a parallel assignment statement $(v_1, \ldots, v_n) \leftarrow (e_1, \ldots, e_n)$ where each e_i is a simple variable and the v_i's are distinct. For convenience, assume that the distinct variables in P are $v_1, \ldots, v_m$ with $m \geq n$ and that $E = (i_1, i_2, \ldots, i_n)$ is a set of indices such that $e_{ij} = v_{ij}$. Write an $O(n)$ algorithm to find an optimal realization for P.

43. Let $F = \{S_j\}$ be a finite family of sets. Let $T \leq F$ be a subfamily of F. The

size of T, $|T|$, is the number of sets in T. Let S_i, S_j be two sets in T. S_i and S_j are disjoint iff $S_i \cap S_j = \phi$. T is a disjoint subset of F iff every pair of sets in T are disjoint. The set packing problem is to determine a disjoint subfamily T of maximum size. Show that clique α set packing.

44. Show that the following decision problem is NP-complete.
   Input: Positive integers n; w_i, $1 \leq i \leq n$ and M.
   Decision: Do there exist nonnegative integers $x_i \geq 0$, $1 \leq i \leq n$ such that

$$\sum_{1 \leq i \leq n} w_i x_i = M$$

Chapter 12

APPROXIMATION ALGORITHMS FOR·NP-HARD PROBLEMS

12.1 INTRODUCTION

In the preceding chapter we saw strong evidence to support the claim that no NP-hard problem can be solved in polynomial time. Yet, many NP-hard optimization problems have great practical importance and it is desirable to solve large instances of these problems in a "reasonable" amount of time. The best known algorithms for NP-hard problems have a worst case complexity that is exponential in the number of inputs. While the results of the last chapter may favor abandoning the quest for polynomial time algorithms, there is still plenty of room for improvement in an exponential algorithm. We may look for algorithms with subexponential complexity, say $2^{n/c}$ (for $c > 1$), $2^{\sqrt{n}}$ or $n^{\log n}$. In the exercises of Chapter 5 an $O(2^{n/2})$ algorithm for the knapsack problem was developed. This algorithm can also be used for the partition, sum of subsets and exact cover problem. Tarjan and Trojanowski ("Finding a maximum independent set," *SIAM Computing,* 6(3), pp. 537–546, 1977.) have obtained an $O(2^{n/3})$ algorithm for the max-clique, max-independent set and minimum node cover problems. The discovery of a subexponential algorithm for an NP-hard problem increases the maximum problem size that can actually be solved. However, for large problem instances, even an $O(n^4)$ algorithm requires too much computational effort. Clearly, what is needed is an algorithm of low polynomial complexity (say $O(n)$ or $O(n^2)$).

The use of heuristics in an existing algorithm may enable it to quickly solve a large instance of a problem provided the heuristic "works" on that instance. This was clearly demonstrated in the chapters on bactracking and branch-and-bound. A heuristic, however, does not "work" equally effectively on all problem instances. Exponential time algorithms, even coupled with heuristics will still show exponential behavior on some set of inputs.

If we are to produce an algorithm of low polynomial complexity to solve an NP-hard optimization problem, then it will be necessary to relax the meaning of solve. In this chapter we shall discuss two relaxations of the meaning of solve. In the first we shall remove the requirement that the algorithm that solves the optimization problem P must always generate an optimal solution. This requirement will be replaced by the requirement that the algorithm for P must always generate a feasible solution with value "close" to the value of an optimal solution. A feasible solution with value close to the value of an optimal solution is called an *approximate solution*. An *approximation algorithm* for P is an algorithm that generates approximate solutions for P.

While at first one may discount the virtue of an approximate solution, one should bear in mind that often, the data for the problem instance being solved is only known approximately. Hence, an approximate solution (provided its value is "sufficiently" close to that of an exact solution) may be no less meaningful than an exact solution. In the case of NP-hard problems approximate solutions have added importance as it may be true that exact solutions (i.e. optimal solutions) cannot be obtained in a feasible amount of computing time. An approximate solution may be all one can get using a reasonable amount of computing time.

In the second relaxation we shall look for an algorithm for P that *almost always* generates optimal solutions. Algorithms with this property are called *probabilistically good* algorithms. These are considered in Section 12.6. In the remainder of this section we develop the terminology to be used in discussing approximation algorithms.

Let P be a problem such as the knapsack or the traveling salesperson problem. Let I be an instance of problem P and let $F^*(I)$ be the value of an optimal solution to I. An approximation algorithm will in general produce a feasible solution to I whose value $\hat{F}(I)$ is less than (greater than) $F^*(I)$ in case P is a maximization (minimization) problem. Several categories of approximation algorithms may be defined.

Let α be an algorithm which generates a feasible solution to every instance I of a problem P. Let $F^*(I)$ be the value of an optimal solution to I and let $\hat{F}(I)$ be the value of the feasible solution generated by α.

Definition α is an *absolute approximation* algorithm for problem P if and only if for every instance I of P, $|F^*(I) - \hat{F}(I)| \leq k$ for some constant k.

Definition α is an *f(n)-approximate* algorithm if and only if for every instance I of size n, $|F^*(I) - \hat{F}(I)|/F^*(I) \le f(n)$. It is assumed that $F^*(I) > 0$.

Definition An ϵ-*approximate* algorithm is an $f(n)$-approximate algorithm for which $f(n) \le \epsilon$ for some constant ϵ.

Note that for a maximization problem, $|F^*(I) - \hat{F}(I)|/F^*(I) \le 1$ for every feasible solution to I. Hence, for maximization problems we will normally require $\epsilon < 1$ for an algorithm to be judged ϵ-approximate. In the next few definitions we consider algorithms $\mathcal{C}(\epsilon)$ with ϵ an input to $\mathcal{C}$.

Definition $\mathcal{C}(\epsilon)$ is an *approximation scheme* iff for every given $\epsilon > 0$ and problem instance I, $\mathcal{C}(\epsilon)$ generates a feasible solution such that $|F^*(I) - \hat{F}(I)|/F^*(I) \le \epsilon$. Again, we assume $F^*(I) > 0$.

Definition An approximation scheme is a *polynomial time approximation scheme* iff for every fixed $\epsilon > 0$ it has a computing time that is polynomial in the problem size.

Definition An approximation scheme whose computing time is a polynomial both in the problem size and in $1/\epsilon$ is a *fully polynomial time approximation scheme*.

Clearly, the most desirable kind of approximation algorithm is an absolute approximation algorithm. Unfortunately, for most NP-hard problems it can be shown that fast algorithms of this type exist only if $P = \text{NP}$. Surprisingly, this statement is true even for the existence of $f(n)$-approximate algorithms for certain NP-hard problems.

Example 12.1 Consider the knapsack instance $n = 3$, $M = 100$, $\{p_1, p_2, p_3\} = \{20, 10, 19\}$ and $\{w_1, w_2, w_3\} = \{65, 20, 35\}$. $(x_1, x_2, x_3) = (1, 1, 1)$ is not a feasible solution as $\Sigma \; w_i x_i > M$. The solution $(x_1, x_2, x_3) = (1, 0, 1)$ is an optimal solution. Its value $\Sigma \; p_i x_i$ is 39. Hence, $F^*(I) = 39$ for this instance. The solution $(x_1, x_2, x_3) = (1, 1, 0)$ is suboptimal. Its value is $\Sigma \; p_i x_i = 30$. This is a candidate for a possible output from an approximation algorithm. In fact, every feasible solution (in this case all three element 0/1 vectors other than $(1, 1, 1)$ are feasible) is a candidate for output by an approximation algorithm. If the solution $(1, 1, 0)$ is generated by an approximation algorithm on this instance then $\hat{F}(I) = 30$. $|F^*(I) - \hat{F}(I)| = 9$ and $|F^*(I) - \hat{F}(I)|/F^*(I) = 0.3$. □

Example 12.2 Consider the following approximation algorithm for the 0/1 knapsack problem: consider the objects in nonincreasing order of p_i/w_i. If object i fits then set $x_i = 1$ otherwise set $x_i = 0$. When this algorithm is used on the instance of Example 12.1, the objects are considered in the order 1, 3, 2. The result is $(x_1, x_2, x_3) = (1, 0, 1)$. The optimal solution is obtained. Now, consider the following instance: $n = 2$, $(p_1, p_2) = (2, r)$, $(w_1, w_2) = (1, r)$ and $M = r$. When $r > 1$, the optimal solution is $(x_1, x_2) = (0, 1)$. Its value, $F^*(I)$, is r. The solution generated by the approximation algorithm is $(x_1, x_2) = (1, 0)$. Its value, $\hat{F}(I)$, is 2. Hence, $|F^*(I) - \hat{F}(I)| = r - 2$. Our approximation algorithm is not an absolute approximation algorithm as there exists no constant k such that $|F^*(I) - \hat{F}(I)| \leq k$ for all instances I. Furthermore, note that $|F^*(I) - \hat{F}(I)|/F^*(I) = 1 - 2/r$. This approaches 1 as r becomes large. $|F^*(I) - \hat{F}(I)|/F^*(I) \leq 1$ for every feasible solution to every knapsack instance. Since the above algorithm always generates a feasible solution it is a 1-approximate algorithm. It is, however, not an ϵ-approximate algorithm for any ϵ, $\epsilon < 1$.   □

Corresponding to the notions of absolute approximation algorithm and $f(n)$-approximate algorithm, we may define approximation problems in the obvious way. So, we can speak of k-absolute approximate problems and $f(n)$-approximate problems. The .5-approximate knapsack problem is to find any 0/1 feasible solution with $|F^*(I) - \hat{F}(I)|/F^*(I) \leq .5$.

As we shall see, approximation algorithms are usually just heuristics or rules that on the surface look like they might solve the optimization problem exactly. However, they do not. Instead, they only guarantee to generate feasible solutions with value within some constant or some factor of the optimal value. Being heuristic in nature, these algorithms are very much dependent on the individual problem being solved.

12.2 ABSOLUTE APPROXIMATIONS

Planar Graph Coloring

There are very few NP-hard optimization problems for which polynomial time absolute approximation algorithms are known. One problem is that of determining the minimum number of colors needed to color a planar graph $G = (V, E)$. It is known that every planar graph is four colorable. One may easily determine if a graph is 0, 1 or 2 colorable. It is zero colorable iff $V = \phi$. It is 1 colorable iff $E = \phi$. G is two colorable iff it is bi partite (see Exercise 6.41). Determining if a planar graph is three colorable is NP-hard. However, all planar graphs are four colorable. An absolute approximation algorithm with $|F^*(I) - \hat{F}(I)| \leq 1$ is easy to obtain. Algorithm 12.1 is such an algorithm. It finds an exact answer when the graph can be colored using at most two colors. Since we can determine whether or not a graph is bipartite in time $O(|V| + |E|)$, the complexity of the algorithm is $O(|V| + |E|)$.

procedure *ACOLOR*(*V, E*)
  //determine an approximation to the minimum number of colors//
  //needed to color the planar graph $G = (V, E)$//

    case
     : $V = \phi$: **return** (0)
     : $E = \phi$: **return** (1)
     : *G is bipartite*: **return** (2)
     : **else**: **return** (4)
    endcase
end *ACOLOR*

Algorithm 12.1 Approximate coloring

Maximum Programs Stored Problem

Assume that we have n programs and two storage devices (say disks or tapes). We shall assume the devices are disks. Our discussion applies to any kind of storage device. Let l_i be the amount of storage needed to store the ith program. Let L be the storage capacity of each disk. Determining the maximum number of these n programs that can be stored on the two disks (without splitting a program over the disks) is NP-hard.

Theorem 12.1 Partition α Maximum Programs Stored.

Proof: Let $\{a_1, a_2, \ldots, a_n\}$ define an instance of the partition problem. We may assume $\Sigma\, a_i = 2T$. Define an instance of the maximum programs stored problem as follows: $L = T$ and $l_i = a_i$, $1 \leq i \leq n$. Clearly, $\{a_i, \ldots, a_n\}$ has a partition iff all n programs can be stored on the two disks. $\square$

By considering programs in order of nondecreasing storage requirement l_i, we can obtain a polynomial time absolute approximation algorithm. Procedure PSTORE assumes $l_1 \leq l_2 \leq \cdots \leq l_n$ and assigns programs to disk 1 so long as enough space remains on this tape. Then it begins assigning programs to disk 2. In addition to the time needed to initially sort the programs into nondecreasing order of l_i, $O(n)$ time is needed to obtain the storage assignment.

```
procedure PSTORE (l, n, L)
  //assume l_i ≤ l_{i+1}, 1 ≤ i < n//
  i ← 1
  for j ← 1 to 2 do
    sum ← 0  //amount of disk j already assigned.//
    while sum + l_i ≤ L do
      print ('store program', i, 'on disk', j)
      sum ← sum + l_i
      i ← i + 1
      if i > n then return endif
    repeat
  repeat
end PSTORE
```

Algorithm 12.2   Approximation algorithm to store programs

Example 12.3   Let $L = 10$, $n = 4$ and $(l_1, l_2, l_3, l_4) = (2, 4, 5, 6)$. Procedure PSTORE will store programs 1 and 2 on disk 1 and only program 3 on disk 2. An optimal storage scheme stores all four programs. One way to do this is to store programs 1 and 4 on disk 1 and the other two on disk 2.   □

Theorem 12.2   Let I be any instance of the maximum programs stored problem. Let $F^*(I)$ be the maximum number of programs that can be stored on two disks of length L each. Let $\hat{F}(I)$ be the number of programs stored using procedure PSTORE. Then, $|F^*(I) - \hat{F}(I)| \le 1$.

Proof: Assume that k programs are stored when Algorithm 12.2 is used. Then, $\hat{F}(I) = k$. Consider the program storage problem when only one disk of capacity $2L$ is available. In this case, considering programs in order of nondecreasing storage requirement maximizes the number of programs stored. Assume that p programs get stored when this strategy is used on a single disk of length $2L$. Clearly, $p \ge F^*(I)$ and $\sum_1^p l_i \le 2L$. Let j be the largest index such that $\sum_1^j l_i \le L$. It is easy to verify that $j \le p$ and that PSTORE assigns the first j programs to disk 1. Also,

$$\sum_{i=j+1}^{p-1} l_i \le \sum_{i=j+2}^{p} l_i \le L.$$

Hence, PSTORE assigns at least programs $j + 1$, $j + 2$, $\ldots$, $p - 1$ to disk 2. So, $\hat{F}(I) \ge p - 1$ and $|F^*(I) - \hat{F}(I)| \le 1$.   □

Algorithm PSTORE may be extended in the obvious way to obtain a $k - 1$ absolute approximation algorithm for the case of k disks.

NP-hard Absolute Approximations

The absolute approximation algorithms for the planar graph coloring and the maximum program storage problems are very simple and straightforward. Thus, one may expect that polynomial time absolute approximation algorithms exist for most other NP-hard problems. Unfortunately, for the majority of NP-hard problems one can provide very simple proofs to show that a polynomial time absolute approximation algorithm exists iff a polynomial time exact algorithm does. Let us look at some sample proofs.

Theorem 12.3   The absolute approximate knapsack problem is NP hard.

Proof: We shall show that the 0/1 knapsack problem with integer profits reduces to the absolute approximate knapsack problem. The theorem then follows from the observation that the knapsack problem with integer profits is NP-hard. Assume there is a polynomial time algorithm $\mathcal{Q}$ that guarantees feasible solutions such that $|F^*(I) - \hat{F}(I)| \le k$ for every instance I and a fixed k. Let (p_i, w_i), $1 \le i \le n$ and M define an instance of the knapsack problem. Assume the p_i are integer. Let I' be the instance defined by $((k + 1)p_i, w_i)$, $1 \le i \le n$ and M. Clearly, I and I' have the same set of feasible solutions. Further, $F^*(I') = (k + 1)F^*(I)$ and I and I' have the same optimal solutions. Also, since all the p_i are integer, it follows that all feasible solutions to I' either have value $F^*(I')$ or have value at most $F^*(I') - (k + 1)$. If $\hat{F}(I')$ is the value of the solution generated by $\mathcal{Q}$ for instance I' then $F^*(I') - \hat{F}(I')$ is either 0 or at least $k + 1$. Hence if $F^*(I') - \hat{F}(I') \le k$ then $F^*(I') = \hat{F}(I')$. So, $\mathcal{Q}$ can be used to obtain an optimal solution for I' and hence I. Since the length of I' is at most $(\log k)*(\text{length of } I)$, it follows that using the above construction we can obtain a polynomial time algorithm for the knapsack problem with integer profits.   □

Example 12.4   Consider the knapsack instance $n = 3$, $M = 100$, $(p_1, p_2,$

p_3) = (1, 2, 3) and (w_1, w_2, w_3) = (50, 60, 30). The feasible solutions are (1, 0, 0), (0, 1, 0), (0, 0, 1), (1, 0, 1) and (0, 1, 1). The values of these solutions are 1, 2, 3, 4 and 5 respectively. If we multiply the p's by 5 then ($\hat{p}_1$, $\hat{p}_2$, $\hat{p}_3$) = (5, 10, 15). The feasible solutions are unchanged. Their values are now 5, 10, 15, 20 and 25 respectively. If we had an absolute approximation algorithm for $k = 4$ then, this algorithm will have to output the solution (0, 1, 1) as no other solution is within 4 of the optimal solution value.   □

Now, consider the problem of obtaining a maximum clique of an undirected graph. The following theorem shows that obtaining a polynomial time absolute approximation algorithm for this problem is as hard as obtaining a polynomial time algorithm for the exact problem.

Theorem 12.4 Max clique $\propto$ absolute approximation max clique.

Proof: Assume that the algorithm for the absolute approximation problem finds solutions such that $|F^*(I) - \hat{F}(I)| \leq k$. From any given graph $G = (V, E)$, we construct another graph $G' = (V', E')$ such that G' consists of $k + 1$ copies of G connected together such that there is an edge between every two vertices in distinct copies of G. I.e., if $V = \{v_1, v_2, \ldots, v_n\}$ then

$$V' = \bigcup_{i=1}^{k+1} \{v_1{}^i, v_2{}^i, \ldots, v_n{}^i\}$$

and

$$E' = \left(\bigcup_{i=1}^{k+1} \{(v_p{}^i, v_r{}^i) | (v_p, v_r) \in E\} \right) \cup \{(v_p^i, v_r^j) | i \neq j\}.$$

Clearly, the maximum clique size in G is q iff the maximum clique size in G' is $(k + 1)q$. Further, any clique in G' which is within k of the optimal clique size in G' must contain a sub-clique of size q which is a clique of size q in G. Hence, we can obtain a maximum clique for G from a k-absolute approximate maximum clique for G'.   □

Example 12.5 Figure 12.1(b) shows the graph G' that results when the construction of Theorem 12.4 is applied to the graph of Figure 12.1(a). We have assumed $k = 1$. The graph of Figure 12.1(a) has two cliques.

One consists of the vertex set $\{1, 2\}$ and the other $\{2, 3, 4\}$. Thus, an absolute approximation algorithm for $k = 1$ could output either of the two as solution cliques. In the graph of Figure 12.1(b), however, the two cliques are $\{1, 2, 1', 2'\}$ and $\{2, 3, 4, 2', 3', 4'\}$. Only the latter may be output. Hence, an absolute approximation algorithm with $k = 1$ will output the maximum clique.   □

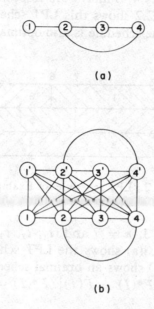

(a)

(b)

Figure 12.1   Graphs for Example 12.5

12.3   ε-APPROXIMATIONS

Scheduling Independent Tasks

Obtaining minimum finish time schedules on m, $m > 2$ identical processors is NP-hard. There exists a very simple scheduling rule that generates schedules with a finish time very close to that of an optimal schedule. An instance I of the scheduling problem is defined by a set of n task times, t_i, $1 \le i \le n$, and m, the number of processors. The scheduling rule we are about to describe is known as the LPT (longest processing time) rule. An LPT schedule is a schedule that results from this rule.

Definition An *LPT schedule* is one that is the result of an algorithm which, whenever a processor becomes free, assigns to that processor a task whose time is the largest of those tasks not yet assigned. Ties are broken in an arbitrary manner.

Example 12.6 Let $m = 3$, $n = 6$ and $(t_1, t_2, t_3, t_4, t_5, t_6) = (8, 7, 6, 5, 4, 3)$. In an LPT schedule tasks 1, 2 and 3 are assigned to processors 1, 2 and 3 respectively. Tasks 4, 5 and 6 are respectively assigned to processors 3, 2 and 1. Figure 12.2 shows this LPT schedule. The finish time is 11. Since, $\Sigma \, t_i/3 = 11$, the schedule is also optimal.

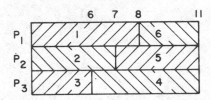

Figure 12.2   LPT schedule for Example 12.6

Example 12.7 Let $m = 3$, $n = 7$ and $(t_1, t_2, t_3, t_4, t_5, t_6, t_7) = (5, 5, 4, 4, 3, 3, 3)$. Figure 12.3(a) shows the LPT schedule. This has a finish time of 11. Figure 12.3(b) shows an optimal schedule. Its finish time is 9. Hence, for this instance $|F^*(I) - \hat{F}(I)|/F^*(I) = (11 - 9)/9 = 2/9$. $\square$

It is possible to implement the LPT rule so that at most $0(n \log n)$ time is needed to generate an LPT schedule for n tasks on m processors. An exercise examines this. The preceding examples show that while the LPT rule may generate optimal schedules for some problem instances, it does not do so for all instances. How bad can LPT schedules be relative to optimal schedules? This question is answered by the following theorem.

Theorem 12.5 [Graham] Let $F^*(I)$ be the finish time of an optimal m processor schedule for instance I of the task scheduling problem. Let $\hat{F}(I)$ be the finish time of an LPT schedule for the same instance. Then,

$$\frac{|F^*(I) - \hat{F}(I)|}{F^*(I)} \le \frac{1}{3} - \frac{1}{3m}$$

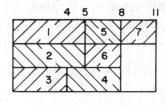

(a) LPT Schedule

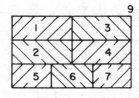

(b) Optimal Schedule

Figure 12.3 LPT and optimal schedules for Example 12.7

Proof: The theorem is clearly true for $m = 1$. So, assume $m \geq 2$. Assume that for some m, $m > 1$, there exists a set of tasks for which the theorem is not true. Then, let $(t_1, t_2, \ldots, t_n)$ define an instance I with the fewest number of tasks for which the theorem is violated. We may assume $t_1 \geq t_2 \geq \cdots \geq t_n$ and that an LPT schedule is obtained by assigning tasks in the order $1, 2, 3, \ldots, n$.

Let S be the LPT schedule obtained by assigning these n tasks in this order. Let $\hat{F}(I)$ be its finish time. Let k be the index of a task with latest completion time. Then, $k = n$. To see this, suppose $k < n$. Then, the finish time $\hat{f}$ of the LPT schedule for tasks $1, 2, \ldots, k$ is also $\hat{F}(I)$. The finish time, f^*, of an optimal schedule for these k tasks is no more than $F^*(I)$. Hence, $|f^* - \hat{f}|/f^* \geq |F^*(I) - \hat{F}(I)|/F^*(I) > 1/3 - 1/(3m)$. (The latter inequality follows from the assumption on I.) $|f^* - \hat{f}|/f^* > 1/3 - 1/(3m)$ contradicts the assumption that I is the smallest m processor instance for which the theorem does not hold. Hence, $k = n$.

Now, we show that in no optimal schedule for I can more than two tasks be assigned to any processor. Hence, $n \leq 2m$. Since task n has the latest completion time in the LPT schedule for I, it follows that this task is started at time $\hat{F}(I) - t_n$ in this schedule. Further, no processor can have any idle time until this time. Hence, we obtain:

$$\hat{F}(I) - t_n \le \frac{1}{m} \sum_{1}^{n-1} t_i$$

So,

$$\hat{F}(I) \le \frac{1}{m} \sum_{1}^{n} t_i + \frac{m-1}{m} t_n.$$

Since,

$$F^*(I) \ge \frac{1}{m} \sum_{1}^{n} t_i,$$

we can conclude that

$$\hat{F}(I) - F^*(I) \le \frac{m-1}{m} t_n$$

or

$$\frac{|F^*(I) - \hat{F}(I)|}{F^*(I)} \le \frac{m-1}{m} \frac{t_n}{F^*(I)}$$

But, from the assumption on I, the left hand side of the above inequality is greater than $1/3 - 1/(3m)$. So,

$$\frac{1}{3} - \frac{1}{3m} < \frac{m-1}{m} \frac{t_n}{F^*(I)}$$

or

$$m - 1 < 3(m-1) t_n / F^*(I)$$

or

$$F^*(I) < 3t_n.$$

Hence, in an optimal schedule for I, no more than two tasks can be assigned to any processor. When the optimal schedule contains at most two tasks on any processor then it may be shown that the LPT schedule· is also optimal. We leave this part of the proof as an exercise. Hence, $|F^*(I) - \hat{F}(I)|/F^*(I) = 0$ for this case. This contradicts the assumption on I. So, there can be no I that violates the theorem.   □

Theorem 12.5 establishes the LPT rule as a $(1/3 - 1/(3m))$-approximate rule for task scheduling. As remarked earlier, this rule can be implemented to have complexity $O(n \log n)$. The following example shows that $1/3 - 1/(3m)$ is a tight bound on the worst case performance of the LPT rule.

Example 12.8 Let $n = 2m + 1$, $t_i = 2m - \lfloor (i + 1)/2 \rfloor$, $i = 1, 2, \ldots,$ $2m$ and $t_{2m+1} = m$. Figure 12.4(a) shows the LPT schedule. This has a finish time of $4m - 1$. Figure 12.4(b) shows an optimal schedule. Its finish time is $3m$. Hence, $|F^*(I) - \hat{F}(I)|/F^*(I) = 1/3 - 1/(3m)$.   □

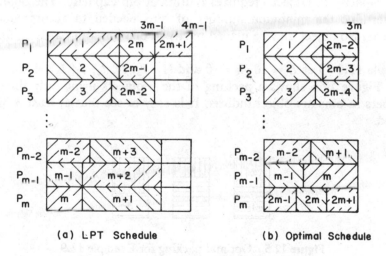

(a) LPT Schedule   (b) Optimal Schedule

Figure 12.4 Schedules for Example 12.8

For LPT schedules, the worst case error bound of $1/3 - 1/(3m)$ is not very indicative of the expected closeness of LPT finish times to optimal finish times. When $m = 10$, the worst case error bound is .3. Two experiments were conducted ("An application of bin-packing to multiprocessor scheduleing," by E. Coffman, M. Garey and D. Johnson, *SIAM Computing,*

7(1), pp. 1–17, 1978.) to see what kind of error one might expect on a random problem for $m = 10$. In the first experiment, 30 tasks with task times chosen according to a uniform distribution between 0 and 1 were generated. $F^*(I)$ was estimated to be $\sum_1^{30} t_i/10$ and $\hat{F}(I)$ was the length of the LPT schedule generated. The experiment was repeated ten times and the average value of $|F^*(I) - \hat{F}(I)|/F^*(I)$ computed. This value was 0.074. In the second experiment task times were chosen according to a normal distribution. The average $|F^*(I) - \hat{F}(I)|/F^*(I)$ was 0.023 this time. These figures are probably a little inflated as $\sum_1^{30} t_i/10$ is probably an underestimation of the true $F^*(I)$.

Efficient ϵ-approximate algorithms exist for many scheduling problems. The references at the end of this chapter point to some of the better known ϵ-approximate scheduling algorithms. Some of these algorithms are also discussed in the exercises.

Bin Packing

In this problem we are given n objects which have to be placed in bins of equal capacity L. Object i requires l_i units of bin capacity. The objective is to determine the minimum number of bins needed to accommodate all n objects. No object may be placed partly in one bin and partly in another.

Example 12.9 Let $L = 10$, $n = 6$ and $(l_1, l_2, l_3, l_4, l_5, l_6) = (5, 6, 3, 7, 5, 4)$. Figure 12.5 shows a packing of the 6 objects using only three bins. Numbers in bins are object indices. It is easy to see that at least 3 bins are needed.

Figure 12.5 Optimal packing for Example 12.9

The bin packing problem may be regarded as a variation of the scheduling problem considered earlier. The bins represent processors and L is the time by which all tasks must be completed. l_1 is the processing requirement of task i. The problem is to determine the minimum number of processors needed to accomplish this. An alternative interpretation is to regard the bins as tapes. L is the length of a tape and l_i the tape length needed to store program i. The problem is to determine the minimum number of tapes needed to store all n programs. Clearly, many interpretations exist for this problem.

Theorem 12.6 The bin packing problem is NP-hard.

Proof: To see this consider the partition problem. Let $\{a_1, a_2, \ldots, a_n\}$ be an instance of the partition problem. Define an instance of the bin packing problem as follows: $l_i = a_i$, $1 \le i \le n$ and $L = \Sigma\ a_i/2$. Clearly, the minimum number of bins needed is 2 iff there is a partition for $\{a_1, a_2, \ldots, a_n\}$. $\square$

One can devise many simple heuristics for the bin packing problem. These will not, in general, obtain optimal packings. They will, however, obtain packings that use only a "small" fraction of bins more than an optimal packing. Four simple heuristics are:

I. *First Fit* (FF)

Index the bins 1, 2, 3, ... All bins are initially filled to level zero. Objects are considered for packing in the order 1, 2, ..., n. To pack object i, find the least index j such that bin j is filled to a level r, $r \le L - l_i$. Pack i into bin j. Bin j is now filled to level $r + l_i$.

II. *Best Fit* (BF)

The initial conditions on the bins and objects are the same as for FF. When object i is being considered, find the least j such that bin j is filled to a level r, $r \le L - l_i$ and r is as large as possible. Pack i into bin j. Bin j is now filled to level $r + l_i$.

III. *First Fit Decreasing* (FFD)

Reorder the objects so that $l_i \ge l_{i+1}$, $1 \le i < n$. Now use First Fit to pack the objects.

IV. *Best Fit Decreasing* (BFD)

Reorder the objects so that $l_i \ge l_{i+1}$, $1 \le i < n$. Now use Best Fit to pack the objects.

Example 12.10 Consider the problem instance of Example 12.9. Figure 12.6 shows the packings resulting when each of the above four packing rules is used. For FFD and BFD the six objects are considered in the order

(4, 2, 1, 5, 6, 3). As is evident from the figure, FFD and BFD do better than either FF or BF on this instance. While FFD and BFD obtain optimal packings on this instance, they do not in general obtain such a packing. □

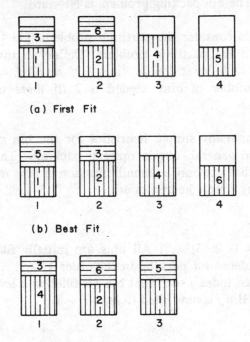

(a) First Fit

(b) Best Fit

(c) First Fit Decreasing and Best Fit Decreasing

Figure 12.6 Packings resulting from the four heuristics

Theorem 12.7 Let I be an instance of the bin packing problem and let $F^*(I)$ be the minimum number of bins needed for this instance. The packing generated by either FF or BF uses no more than $(17/10) F^*(I) + 2$ bins. The packing generated by either FFD or BFD uses no more than $(11/9) F^*(I) + 4$ bins. These bounds are the best possible bounds for the respective algorithms.

Proof: The proof of this theorem is rather long and complex. It may be found in the paper: "Worst-Case Performance Bounds For Simple One-Dimensional Packing Algorithms," by Johnson, Demers, Ullman, Garey and Graham, *SIAM Jr. On Computing*, 3(4), pp. 299–325 (1974). □

NP-hard ε-Approximation Problems

As in the case of absolute approximations, there exist many NP-hard optimization problems for which the corresponding ε-approximation problems are also NP-hard. Let us look at some of these. To begin, consider the traveling salesperson problem.

Theorem 12.8 Hamiltonian cycle $\propto$ ε-approximate traveling salesperson.

Proof: Let $G(N,A)$ be any graph. Construct the complete graph $G_1(V, E)$ such that $V = N$ and $E = \{(u, v) \mid u, v \in V \text{ and } u \neq v\}$. Define the edge weighting function w to be

$$
w(u, v) = \begin{cases} 1 & \text{if } (u, v) \in A \\ \\ k & \text{otherwise} \end{cases}
$$

Let $n = |N|$. For $k > 1$, the traveling salesperson problem on G_1 has a solution of length n if and only if G has a Hamiltonian cycle. Otherwise, all solutions to G_1 have length $\geq k + n - 1$. If we choose $k \geq (1 + \epsilon)n$, then the only solutions approximating a solution with value n (if there was a Hamiltonian cycle in G_1) also have length n. Consequently, if the ε-approximate solution has length $\leq (1 + \epsilon)n$ then it must be of length n. If it has length $>(1 + \epsilon)n$ then G has no Hamiltonian cycle. $\square$

Another NP-hard ε-approximation problem is the 0/1 integer programming problem. In the optimization version of this problem we are provided with a linear optimization function $f(x) = \Sigma\, p_i x_i + p_0$. We are required to find a 0/1 vector $(x_1, x_2, \ldots, x_n)$ such that $f(x)$ is optimized (either maximized or minimized) subject to the constraints that $\Sigma\, a_{ij} x_j \leq b_i$, $1 \leq i \leq k$. k is the number of constraints. Note that the 0/1-knapsack problem is a special case of the 0/1 integer programming problem just described. Hence, the integer programming problem is also NP-hard. We shall now show that the corresponding ε-approximation problem is NP-hard for all ϵ, $\epsilon > 0$. This is true even when there is only one constraint (i.e., $k = 1$).

Theorem 12.9 Partition α ε-approximate integer programming.

Proof: Let $(a_1, a_2, \ldots, a_n)$ be an instance of the partition problem. Construct the following 0/1 integer program:

$$\text{minimize } 1 + k(m - \Sigma \, a_i x_i)$$

$$\text{subject to } \Sigma \, a_i x_i \leq m$$

$$x_i = 0 \quad \text{or} \quad 1, \quad 1 \leq i \leq n$$

$$m = \Sigma \, a_i / 2$$

The value of an optimal solution is 1 iff the a_i s have a partition. If they don't then every optimal solution has a value at least $1 + k$. Suppose there is a polynomial time ϵ-approximate algorithm for the 0/1 integer programming problem for some ϵ, $\epsilon > 0$. Then, by choosing $k > \epsilon$ and using the above construction, this approximation algorithm can be used to solve, in polynomial time, the partition problem. The given partition instance has a partition iff the ϵ-approximate algorithm generates a solution with value 1. All other solutions have value $\hat{F}(I)$ such that $|F^*(I) - \hat{F}(I)|/F^*(I) \geq k > \epsilon$. $\square$

As a final example of an ϵ-approximation problem that is NP-Hard for all ϵ, $\epsilon > 0$, consider the quadratic assignment problem. In one interpretation this problem is concerned with optimally locating m plants. There are n possible sites for these plants, $n \geq m$. At most one plant may be located in any of these n sites. We shall use $x_{i,k}$, $1 \leq i \leq n$, $1 \leq k \leq m$ as mn 0/1 variables. $x_{i,k} = 1$ iff plant k is to be located at site i. The location of the plants is to be chosen so as to minimize the total cost of transporting goods between plants. Let $d_{k,l}$ be the amount of goods to be transported from plant k to plant l. $d_{k,k} = 0$, $1 \leq k \leq m$. Let $c_{i,j}$ be the cost of transporting one unit of the goods from site i to site j. $c_{i,i} = 0$, $1 \leq i \leq n$. The *quadratic assignment problem* has the following mathematical formulation:

$$\text{maximize } f(x) = \sum_{i,j=1}^{n} \sum_{k,l=1}^{m} c_{i,j} d_{k,l} x_{i,k} x_{j,l}$$

$$\text{subject to (a) } \sum_{k=1}^{m} x_{i,k} \leq 1, \; 1 \leq i \leq n$$

$$\text{(b) } \sum_{i=1}^{n} x_{i,k} = 1, \; 1 \leq k \leq m$$

$$\text{(c) } \quad x_{i,k} = 0, 1 \text{ for all } i, k$$

$$c_{i,j}, \, d_{k,l} \geq 0, \, 1 \leq i, j \leq n, \, 1 \leq k, l \leq m$$

Condition (a) ensures that at most one plant is located at any site. Condition (b) ensures that every plant is located at exactly one site. $f(x)$ is the total transportation cost.

Example 12.11   Assume two plants are to be located ($m = 2$) and there are three possible sites ($n = 3$). Assume

$$\begin{pmatrix} d_{11} & d_{12} \\ d_{21} & d_{22} \end{pmatrix} = \begin{pmatrix} 0 & 4 \\ 10 & 0 \end{pmatrix}$$

and

$$\begin{pmatrix} c_{11} & c_{12} & c_{13} \\ c_{21} & c_{22} & c_{23} \\ c_{31} & c_{32} & c_{33} \end{pmatrix} = \begin{pmatrix} 0 & 9 & 3 \\ 5 & 0 & 10 \\ 2 & 6 & 0 \end{pmatrix}$$

If plant 1 is located at site 1 and plant 2 at site 2 then the transportation cost $f(x)$ is 9*4 + 5*10 = 86. If plant 1 is located at site 3 and plant 2 at site 1 then the cost $f(x)$ is 2*4 + 3*10 = 38. The optimal locations are plant 1 at site 1 and plant 2 at site 3. The cost $f(x)$ is 3*4 + 2*10 = 32.   □

Theorem 12.10   Hamiltonian cycle ∝ ε-approximate quadratic assignment.

Proof: Let $G(N,A)$ be an undirected graph with $m = |N|$. The following quadratic assignment instance is constructed from G:

$$n = m$$

$$c_{i,j} = \begin{cases} 1 & i = (j \bmod m) + 1, 1 \le k, j \le m. \\ 0 & \text{otherwise} \end{cases}$$

$$d_{k,l} = \begin{cases} 1 & \text{if } (k, l) \in A, 1 \le k, l \le m. \\ \omega & \text{otherwise} \end{cases}$$

The total cost, $f(\gamma)$, of an assignment, γ, of plants to locations is

$\sum_{i=1}^{n} c_{i,j} d_{\gamma(i)\gamma(j)}$ where $j = (i \bmod m) + 1$ and $\gamma(i)$ is the index of the plant assigned to location i. If G has a Hamiltonian cycle $i_1, i_2, \ldots, i_n, i_1$ then the assignment $\gamma(j) = i_j$ has a cost $f(\gamma) = m$. In case G has no Hamiltonian cycle then at least one of the values $d_{\gamma(i),\ \gamma(i \bmod m+1)}$ must be ω and so the cost becomes $\geq m + \omega - 1$. Choosing $\omega > (1 + \epsilon)m$ results in optimal solutions with a value of m if G has a Hamiltonian cycle and value $>(1 + \epsilon)m$ if G has no Hamiltonian cycle. Thus, from an ϵ-approximate solution, it can be determined whether or not G has a Hamiltonian cycle. $\square$

Many other ϵ-approximation problems are known to be NP-hard. Some of these are examined in the exercises. While the three problems just discussed were NP-hard for ϵ, $\epsilon > 0$, it is quite possible for an ϵ-approximation problem to be NP-hard only for ϵ in some range, say, $0 < \epsilon \leq r$. For $\epsilon > r$ there may exist simple polynomial time approximation algorithms.

12.4 POLYNOMIAL TIME APPROXIMATION SCHEMES

Scheduling Independent Tasks

We have seen that the LPT rule leads to a $(1/3 - 1/(3m))$-approximate algorithm for the problem of obtaining an m processor schedule for n tasks. A polynomial time approximation scheme is also known for this problem. This scheme relies on the following scheduling rule: (i) Let k be some specified and fixed integer. (ii) Obtain an optimal schedule for the k longest tasks. (iii) Schedule the remaining $n - k$ tasks using the LPT rule.

Example 12.12 Let $m = 2$; $n = 6$; $(t_1, t_2, t_3, t_4, t_5, t_6) = (8, 6, 5, 4, 4, 1)$ and $k = 4$. The four longest tasks have task times 8, 6, 5 and 4 respectively. An optimal schedule for these has finish time 12 (Figure 12.7(a)). When the remaining two tasks are scheduled using the LPT rule, the schedule of Figure 12.7(b) results. This has finish time 15. Figure 12.7(c) shows an optimal schedule. This has finish time 14. $\square$

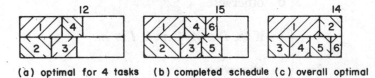

(a) optimal for 4 tasks   (b) completed schedule (c) overall optimal

Figure 12.7   Using the approximation scheme with $k = 4$

Theorem 12.11 [Graham] Let I be an m processor instance of the scheduling problem. Let $F^*(I)$ be the finish time of an optimal schedule for I and let $\hat{F}(I)$ be the length of the schedule generated by the above scheduling rule. Then,

$$\frac{|F^*(I) - \hat{F}(I)|}{F^*(I)} \leq \frac{1 - 1/m}{1 + \lfloor k/m \rfloor}$$

Proof: Let r be the finish time of an optimal schedule for the k longest tasks. If $\hat{F}(I) = r$ then, $F^*(I) = \hat{F}(I)$ and the theorem is proved. So, assume $\hat{F}(I) > r$. Let t_i, $1 \leq i \leq n$ be the task times of the n tasks of I. Without loss of generality, we may assume $t_i \geq t_{i+1}$, $1 \leq i < n$ and $n > k$. Also, we may assume $n > m$. Let j, $j > k$ be such that task j has finish time $\hat{F}(I)$. Then, no processor may be idle in the interval $[0, \hat{F}(I) - t_j]$. Since $t_{k+1} \geq t_j$, it follows that no processor is idle in the interval $[0, \hat{F}(I) - t_{k+1}]$. Hence,

$$\sum_{i=1}^{n} t_i \geq m(\hat{F}(I) - t_{k+1}) + t_{k+1}$$

and so,

$$F^*(I) \geq \frac{1}{m} \sum_{1}^{n} t_i \geq \hat{F}(I) - \frac{m-1}{m} t_{k+1}$$

or

$$|F^*(I) - \hat{F}(I)| \leq \frac{m-1}{m} t_{k+1}.$$

Since $t_i \geq t_{k+1}$, $1 \leq i \leq k + 1$ and at least one processor must execute at least $1 + \lfloor k/m \rfloor$ of these $k + 1$ tasks, it follows that:

$$F^*(I) \geq (1 + \lfloor k/m \rfloor) t_{k+1}.$$

Combining these two inequalities, we obtain

$$\frac{|F^*(I) - \hat{F}(I)|}{F^*(I)} \leq ((m - 1)/m)/(1 + \lfloor k/m \rfloor) = \frac{1 - 1/m}{1 + \lfloor k/m \rfloor}. \quad \square$$

Using the result of Theorem 12.11, we can construct a polynomial time ϵ-approximation scheme for the scheduling problem. This scheme has ϵ as an input variable. For any input ϵ it computes an integer k such that $\epsilon \le (1 - 1/m)/(1 + \lfloor k/m \rfloor)$. This defines the k to be used in the scheduling rule described above. Solving for k, we obtain that any integer k, $k > (m - 1)/\epsilon - m$ will guarantee ϵ-approximate schedules. The time required to obtain such schedules, however, depends mainly on the time needed to obtain an optimal schedule for k tasks on m machines. Using a branch-and-bound algorithm, this time is $O(m^k)$. The time needed to arrange the tasks such that $t_i \ge t_{i+1}$ and also to obtain the LPT schedule for the remaining $n - k$ tasks is $O(n \log n)$. Hence the total time needed by the ϵ-approximate scheme is $O(n \log n + m^k) = O(n \log n + m^{((m-1/\epsilon \cdot m))})$. Since this time is not polynomial in $1/\epsilon$ (it is exponential in $1/\epsilon$), this approximation scheme is not a fully polynomial time approximation scheme. It is a polynomial time approximation scheme (for any fixed m) as the computing time is polynomial in the number of tasks n.

0/1 Knapsack

The 0/1 knapsack heuristic proposed in Example 12.2 does not result in an ϵ-approximate algorithm for any ϵ, $0 < \epsilon < 1$. Suppose we try out the heuristic described by procedure ϵ-APPROX (Algorithm 12.3). In this procedure P and W are the sets of profits and weights respectively. It is assumed that $p_i/w_i \ge p_{i+1}/w_{i+1}$, $1 \le i < n$. M is the knapsack capacity and k a nonnegative integer. In the loop of lines 2-5, all $\sum_{i=0}^{k} \binom{n}{i}$ different subsets, I, consisting of at most k of the n objects are generated. If the currently generated subset I is such that $\sum_{i \in I} w_i > M$ it is discarded (as it is infeasible). Otherwise, the space remaining in the knapsack (i.e., $M - \sum_{i \in I} w_i$) is filled using the heuristic described in Example 12.2. This heuristic is stated more formally as procedure L (Algorithm 12.4).

line **procedure** ϵ-*APPROX*(*P, W, M, n, k*)
      // (i)   the size of a combination is the number of objects in it;//
      // (ii) the weight of a combination is the sum of the weights of//
         //the objects in that combination;//
      //(iii) k is a nonnegative integer which defines the order of the//
         //algorithm//
1     $PMAX \leftarrow 0$;
2   **for** all combinations I of size $\le k$ **and** weight $\le M$ **do**
3        $P_I \leftarrow \sum_{i \in I} p_i$
4        $PMAX \leftarrow \mathbf{max}(PMAX, P_I + L(I, P, W, M, n))$
5   **repeat**
6   **end** ϵ-APPROX
      Algorithm 12.3 Heuristic algorithm for knapsack problem

procedure $L(I, P, W, M, n)$
  $S \leftarrow 0; i \leftarrow 1; T \leftarrow M - \Sigma_{i \in I} w_i$ //initialize//
  for $i \leftarrow 1$ **to** n **do**
    if $i \notin I$ **and** $w_i \le T$ **then** $S \leftarrow S + p_i$
                        $T \leftarrow T - w_i$

    endif
  repeat
  return (S)
end L

Algorithm 12.4 Subalgorithm for procedure ϵ-APPROX

Example 12.13 Consider the knapsack problem instance with $n = 8$ objects, size of knapsack $= M = 110$, $P = \{11, 21, 31, 33, 43, 53, 55, 65\}$ and $W = \{1, 11, 21, 23, 33, 43, 45, 55\}$.

The optimal solution is obtained by putting objects 1, 2, 3, 5 and 6 into the knapsack. This results in an optimal profit, P^*, of 159 and a weight of 109.

We obtain the following approximations for different k:
a) $k = 0$, PMAX is just the lower bound solution $L(\phi, P, W, M, n)$;
    PMAX $= 139; x = (1, 1, 1, 1, 1, 0, 0, 0); W = \Sigma_i x_i w_i = 89$;
    $(P^* - \text{PMAX})/P^* = 20/159 = .126$.
b) $k = 1$, PMAX $= 151; x = (1, 1, 1, 1, 0, 0, 1, 0); W = 101; (P^* -$
    PMAX$)/P^* = 8/159 = .05$.
c) $k = 2$, PMAX $= P^* = 159; x = (1, 1, 1, 0, 1, 1, 0, 0); W = 109$.

The table of Figure 12.8 gives the details for $k = 1$. It is interesting to note that the combinations $I = \{1\}, \{2\}, \{3\}, \{4\}, \{5\}$ need not be tried since for $I = \{\phi\}$ x_6 is the first x_i which is 0 and so these combinations will yield the same PMAX as $I = \{\phi\}$. This will be true for all combinations I that include only objects for which x_i was 1 in the solution for $I = \{\phi\}$. $\square$

Theorem 12.12 Let J be an instance of the knapsack problem. Let n, M, P and W be as defined for procedure ϵ-APPROX. Let P^* be the value of an optimal solution for J. Let PMAX be as defined by procedure ϵ-APPROX on termination. Then,

$$|P^* - \text{PMAX}|/P^* < 1/(k + 1).$$

Proof: Let R be the set of objects included in the knapsack in some optimal solution. So, $\Sigma_{k \in R} p_i = P^*$ and $\Sigma_{k \in R} w_i \le M$. If the number of objects in R, $|R|$, is such that $|R| \le k$ then at some time in the execution of pro-

I	PMAX	P_I	R_I	L	PMAX = max {PMAX, $P_I + L$}	x optimal
ϕ	0	11	1	128	139	(1,1,1,1,1,0,0,0)
6	139	53	43	96	149	(1,1,1,1,0,1,0,0)
7	149	55	45	9	151	(1,1,1,1,0,0,1,0)
8	151	65	55	63	151	(1,1,1,1,0,0,1,0)

*Note that rather than update x optimal it is easier to update the optimal I and recompute x optimal at the end

Figure 12.8   Expansion of Example 12.13 for $k = 1$

cedure ϵ-APPROX, $I = R$ and so PMAX $= P^*$. So, assume $|R| > k$. Let $(\hat{p}_i, \hat{w}_i)$, $1 \le i \le |R|$ be the profits and weights of the objects in R. Assume these have been indexed such that $\hat{p}_1, \ldots, \hat{p}_k$ are the k largest profits in R and that $\hat{p}_i / \hat{w}_i \ge \hat{p}_{i+1} / \hat{w}_{i+1}$, $k < i < |R|$. From the first of these assumptions, it follows that $\hat{p}_{k+t} \le P^*/(k + 1)$, $1 \le t \le |R| - k$. Since the loop of lines 2–5 tries out all combinations of size at most k, it follows that in some iteration, I corresponds to the set of k largest profits in R. Hence, $P_I = \sum_{i \in I} p_i = \sum_{i=1}^{k} \hat{p}_i$. Consider the computation of line 4 in this iteration. In the computation of $L(I, P, W, M, n)$ let j be the least index such that $j \notin I$, $w_j > T$ and $j \in R$. Thus, object j corresponds to one of the objects $(\hat{p}_r, \hat{w}_r)$, $k < r \le |R|$ and j is not included in the knapsack by algorithm L. Let object j correspond to $(\hat{p}_m, \hat{w}_m)$.

At the time object j is considered, $T < \hat{w}_j = \hat{w}_m$. The amount of space filled by procedure L is $M - \sum_{i \in I} w_i - T$ and this is larger than $\sum_{i=k+1}^{m-1} \hat{w}_i$ (as $\sum_{1}^{m} \hat{w}_i \le M$). Since this amount of space is filled by considering objects in nondecreasing order of p_i/w_i, it follows that the profit S added by L is no less than

$$\sum_{i=k+1}^{m-1} \hat{p}_i + \frac{\hat{p}_m}{\hat{w}_m} \Delta$$

where

$$\Delta = M - T - \sum_{1}^{m-1} \hat{w}_i.$$

Also,

$$\sum_{i=m}^{|R|} \hat{p}_i \le \frac{\hat{p}_m}{\hat{w}_m} \left(M - \sum_{1}^{m-1} \hat{w}_i \right).$$

From these two inequalities, we obtain:

$$P^* = P_I + \sum_{k+1}^{|R|} \hat{p}_i$$

$$\le P_I + S - \frac{\hat{p}_m}{\hat{w}_m} \Delta + \frac{\hat{p}_m}{\hat{w}_m} \left(M - \sum_{1}^{m-1} \hat{w}_i \right)$$

$$= P_I + S + \hat{p}_m (T/\hat{w}_m)$$

$$< P_I + S + \hat{p}_m$$

Since, PMAX $\ge P_I + S$ and $\hat{p}_m \le P^*/(k + 1)$, it follows that:

$$\frac{|P^* - \text{PMAX}|}{P^*} < \frac{\hat{p}_m}{P^*} \le \frac{1}{k + 1}$$

This completes the proof.   □

The time required by Algorithm 12.3 is $O(n^{k+1})$. To see this, note that the total number of subsets tried is

$$\sum_{i=0}^{k} \binom{n}{i} \quad \text{and} \quad \sum_{i=0}^{k} \binom{n}{i} \le \sum_{i=0}^{k} n^i = \frac{n^{k+1} - 1}{n - 1} = O(n^k).$$

Subalgorithm L has complexity $O(n)$. So, the total time is $O(n^{k+1})$.

Algorithm ϵ-APPROX may be used as a polynomial time approximation scheme. For any given ϵ, $0 < \epsilon < 1$ we may choose k to be the least integer greater than or equal to $(1/\epsilon) - 1$. This will guarantee a fractional error in the solution vaue of at most ϵ. The computing time is $O(n^{1/\epsilon})$.

While Theorem 12.12 provides an upper bound on $|P^* - \text{PMAX}|/P^*$, it does not say anything about how good this bound is. Nor does it say anything about the kind of performance we may expect in practice. Let us now address these two problems.

Theorem 12.13 For every k there exist knapsack instances for which $|(P^* - \text{PMAX})/P^*|$ gets as close to $1/(k + 1)$ as desired.

Proof: For any k, the simplest examples approaching the lower bound are obtained by setting: $n = k + 2$; $w_1 = 1$; $p_1 = 2$; p_i, $w_1 = q$, $2 \leq i \leq k + 2$, $q > 2$, $M = (k + 1) q$. Then, $P^* = (k + 1) q$. The PMAX given by ϵ-APROX for this k is $kq + 2$ and so $|(P^* - \text{PMAX})/P^*| = (1 - 2/q)/(k + 1)$. By choosing q increasingly large one can get as close to $1/(k + 1)$ as desired. $\square$

Another upper bound on the value of $|P^* - \text{PMAX})/P^*|$ can be obtained from the proof of Theorem 12.12. We know that $P^* - \text{PMAX} < \hat{p}_m$ and that $P^* \geq \text{PMAX}$. Also since $\hat{p}_m$ is one of $p_{k+1}, \ldots, p_{|R|}$, it follows that $\hat{p}_m < \bar{p}$ where $\bar{p}$ is the $(k + 1)$-st largest p. Hence $|(P^* - \text{PMAX})/P^*| < \min\{1/(k + 1), \bar{p}/\text{PMAX}\}$. In most cases $\bar{p}/\text{PMAX}$ will be smaller than $1/(k + 1)$ and so will give a better estimate of closeness in cases where the optimal is not known. We note that $\bar{p}$ is easy to compute.

The preceding discussion leads to the following theorem:

Theorem 12.14 The deviation of the solution PMAX obtained from the ϵ-approximate algorithm, from the true optimal P^* is bounded by $|(P^* - \text{PMAX})/P^*| < \min\{1/(k + 1), \bar{p}/\text{PMAX}\}$.

In order to get a feel for how the approximation scheme might perform in practice, a simulation was conducted. A sample of 600 knapsack instances was used. This sample included problems with $n = 15, 20, 25, 30, \ldots, 60$. For each problem size, 60 instances were generated. These 60 instances included five from each of the following six distributions:

    I.   random weights w_i and random profits p_i, $1 \leq w_i$, $p_i \leq 100$.
    II.   random weights w_i and random profits p_i, $1 \leq w_i$, $p_i \leq 1000$.
    III.   random weights w_i, $1 \leq w_i \leq 100$, $p_i = w_i + 10$.
    IV.   random weights w_i, $1 \leq w_i \leq 1000$, $p_i = w_i + 100$.
    V.   random profits p_i, $1 \leq p_i \leq 100$, $w_i = p_i + 10$.
    VI.   random profits p_i, $1 \leq p_i \leq 1000$, $w_i = p_i + 100$.

Random profits and weights were chosen from a uniform distribution over the given range. For each set of p's and w's, two M's were used; $M = 2 * \max\{w_i\}$ and $M = \Sigma w_i/2$. This makes for a total of 600 problem instances. Figure 12.9 summarizes the results. The figure gives the number of problems for which $(P^* - \text{PMAX})/P^*$ was in a particular range. .5-APPROX is ϵ-APPROX with. $k = 1$ and .33-APPROX is ϵ-APPROX with $k = 2$. As is evident, the observed $|P^* - \text{PMAX}|/P^*$ values are much less than indicated by the worst case bound of Theorem 12.12. Figure

12.10, gives the result of a simulation for large n. Computing times are for a FORTRAN program run on an IBM 360/65 computer.

Method	0 (Optimal value)	$(P* - PMAX)/P*$ *100								
		.1%	.5%	1%	2%	3%	4%	5%	10%	25%
L(ϕ,P,S,M,n)	239	267	341	390	443	484	511	528	583	600
.5-APPROX	360	404	477	527	567	585	593	598	600	
.33-APPROX	483	527	564	581	596	600				

Figures give number of solutions that were within r percent of the true optimal solution value; r is the figure in the column head.

Figure 12.9 Results of simulation for set of 600 problems

Problem size n	100	200	500	1000	2000	3000	4000	5000
Computing Time	.25	.9	3.5	14.6	60.4	98.3	180.	350.
Estimated % difference min{ p/PMAX, .5}*100	2.5%	1.3%	.5%	.25%	.12%	.08%	.06%	.04%

$M = \Sigma w_i/2; \; w_i, p_i \in [1,1000]$; times in seconds

Figure 12.10 Computing times using the .5-approximate algorithm

12.5 FULLY POLYNOMIAL TIME APPROXIMATION SCHEMES

The approximation algorithms and schemes we have seen so far are particular to the problem considered. There is no set of well defined techniques that one may use to obtain such algorithms. The heuristics used depended very much on the particular problem being solved. For the case of fully polynomial time approximation schemes, we can identify three underlying techniques. These techniques apply to a variety of optimization problems. We shall discuss these three techniques in terms of maximization problems.

We shall assume the maximization problem to be of the form:

$$\max \sum_{i=1}^{n} p_i x_i$$

$$\text{subject to } \sum_{i=1}^{n} a_{ij} x_i \le b_j, \qquad 1 \le j \le m$$

$$x_i = 0 \text{ or } 1 \qquad 1 \le i \le n \tag{12.1}$$

$$p_i, a_{ij} \ge 0$$

Without loss of generality, we will assume that $a_{ij} \le b_j$, $1 \le i \le n$ and $1 \le j \le m$.

If $1 \le k \le n$, then the assignment $x_i = y_i$, will be said to be a *feasible assignment* iff there exists at least one feasible solution to (12.1) with $x_i = y_i$, $1 \le i \le k$. A *completion* of a feasible assignment $x_i = y_i$ is any feasible solution to (12.1) with $x_i = y_i$, $1 \le i \le k$. Let $x_i = y_i$ and $x_i = z_i$, $1 \le i \le k$ be two feasible assignments such that for at least one j, $1 \le j \le k$, $y_j \ne z_j$. Let $\Sigma p_i y_i = \Sigma p_i z_i$. We shall say that $y_1, \ldots, y_k$ *dominates* $z_1, \ldots, z_k$ iff there exists a completion $y_1, \ldots, y_k, y_{k+1}, \ldots, y_n$ such that $\sum_{i=1}^{n} p_i y_i$ is greater than or equal to $\Sigma_{1 \le i \le n} p_i z_i$ for all completions $z_1, \ldots, z_n$ of $z_1, \ldots, z_k$. The approximation techniques to be discussed will apply to those problems that can be formulated as (12.1) and for which simple rules can be found to determine when one feasible assignment dominates another. Such rules exist for example for problems solvable by the dynamic programming technique. Some such problems are 0/1-knapsack; job sequencing with deadlines; job sequencing to minimize finish time and job sequencing to minimize weighted mean finish time.

One way to solve problems stated as above is to systematically generate all feasible assignments starting from the null assignment. Let $S^{(i)}$ represent the set of all feasible assignments for $x_1, x_2, \ldots, x_i$. Then $S^{(0)}$ represents the null assignment and $S^{(n)}$ the set of all completions. The answer to our problem is an assignment in $S^{(n)}$ that maximizes the objective function. The solution approach is then to generate $S^{(i+1)}$ from $S^{(i)}$, $1 \le i < n$. If an $S^{(i)}$ contains two feasible assignments $y_1, \ldots, y_i$ and $z_1, \ldots, z_i$ such that $\Sigma p_i y_i = \Sigma p_i z_i$ then use of the dominance rules enables us to discard or kill that assignment which is dominated. (In some cases the dominance rules may permit the discarding or killing of a feasible assignment even when $\Sigma \, p_j y_j$ $\neq \Sigma \, p_j z_j$. This happens, for instance, in the knapsack problem (see Section 5.5). Following the use of the dominance rules, it is the case that for each feasible assignment in $S^{(i)}$ $\sum_{j=1}^{i} p_j x_j$ is distinct. However, despite this, it is possible for each $S^{(i)}$ to contain twice as many feasible assignments as in $S^{(i-1)}$. This results in a worst case computing time that is exponential in n. Note that this solution approach is identical to the dynamic programming solution methodology for the knapsack problem (Section 5.5) and also to the branch-and-bound algorithm later developed for this problem (Section 8.2).

The approximation methods we are about to discuss are called rounding, interval partitioning and separation. These methods will restrict the number of distinct $\sum_{j=1}^{i} p_j x_j$ to be only a polynomial function of n. The error introduced will be within some prespecified bound.

Rounding

The aim of rounding is to start from a problem instance, I, formulated as in (12.1) and to transform it to another problem instance I' that is easier to solve. This transformation is carried out in such a way that the optimal solution value of I' is "close" to the optimal solution value of I. In particular, if we are provided with a bound, ϵ, on the fractional difference between the exact and approximate solution values then we require that $|F^*(I) - F^*(I')/F^*(I)| \leq \epsilon$, where $F^*(I)$ and $F^*(I')$ represent the optimal solution values of I and I' respectively.

I' is obtained from I by changing the objective function to max $\Sigma \, q_i x_i$. Since I and I' have the same constraints, they have the same feasible solutions. Hence, if the p_i's and q_i's differ by only a "small" amount, the value of an optimal solution to I' will be close to the value of an optimal solution to I.

For example, if the p_i in I have the values: $(p_1, p_2, p_3, p_4) = (1.1, 2.1, 1001.6, 1002.3)$ then if we construct I' with $(q_1, q_2, q_3, q_4) = (0, 0, 1000, 1000)$ it is easy to see that the value of any solution in I is at most 7.1 more than the value of the same solution in I'. This worst case difference is achieved only when $x_i = 1, 1 \leq i \leq 4$ is a feasible solution for I (and hence also for I'). Since, $a_{ij} \leq b_j, 1 \leq i \leq n$ and $1 \leq j \leq m$, it follows that $F^*(I) \geq 1002.3$ (as one feasible solution is $x_1 = x_2 = x_3 = 0$ and $x_4 = 1$). But $F^*(I) - F^*(I') \leq 7.1$ and so $(F^*(I) - F^*(I'))/F^*(I)$

≤ 0.007. Solving I using the procedure outlined above, the feasible assignments in $S^{(i)}$ could have the following distinct profit values:

$S^{(0)}$ $\{0\}$
$S^{(1)}$ $\{0, 1.1\}$
$S^{(2)}$ $\{0, 1.1, 2.1, 3.2\}$
$S^{(3)}$ $\{0, 1.1, 2.1, 3.2, 1001.6, 1002.7, 1003.7, 1004.8\}$
$S^{(4)}$ $\{0, 1.1, 2.1, 3.2, 1001.6, 1002.3, 1002.7, 1003.4, 1003.7,$
  $1004.4, 1004.8, 1005.5, 2003.9, 2005, 2006, 2007.1\}$

Thus, barring any elimination of feasible assignments resulting from the dominance rules or from any heuristic, the solution of I using the procedure outlined above would require the computation of $\sum_{0 \leq i \leq n} |S^{(i)}| = 31$ feasible assignments.

The feasible assignments for I' have the following values:

$S^{(0)}$ $\{0\}$
$S^{(1)}$ $\{0\}$
$S^{(2)}$ $\{0\}$
$S^{(3)}$ $\{0, 1000\}$
$S^{(4)}$ $\{0, 1000, 2000\}$

Note that $\sum_{i=0}^{n} |S^{(i)}|$ is only 8. Hence I' can be solved in about one fourth the time needed for I. An inaccuracy of at most .7% is introduced.

Given the p_i's and an ϵ, what should the q_i's be so that

$$(F^*(I) - F^*(I'))/F^*(I) \leq \epsilon \quad \text{and} \quad \sum_{i=0}^{n} |S^{(i)}| \leq u(n, 1/\epsilon)$$

where u is a polynomial in n and $1/\epsilon$? Once we can figure this out we will have a fully polynomial approximation scheme for our problem since it is possible to go from $S^{(i-1)}$ to $S^{(i)}$ in time proportional to $O(S^{(i-1)})$. (See the knapsack algorithm of Section 5.5.)

Let LB be an estimate for $F^*(I)$ such that $F^*(I) \geq$ LB. Clearly, we may assume LB $\geq \max_i\{p_i\}$. If

$$\sum_{i=1}^{n} |p_i - q_i| \leq \epsilon F^*(I)$$

then, it is clear that, $(F^*(I) - F^*(I'))/F^*(I) \leq \epsilon$. Define $q_i = p_i - \text{rem}(p_i, (\text{LB} \cdot \epsilon)/n)$ where $\text{rem}(a, b)$ is the remainder of a/b, i.e., $a -$

$\lfloor a/b \rfloor\ b$ (e.g., rem(7, 6) = 1/6 and rem(2.2, 1.3) = .9). Since rem(p_i, LB$\cdot\epsilon/n$) < LB$\cdot\epsilon/n$, it follows that $\Sigma\ |p_i - q_i| <$ LB$\cdot\epsilon \le F^*\cdot\epsilon$. Hence, if an optimal solution to I' is used as an optimal solution for I then the fractional error is less than ϵ.

In order to determine the time required to solve I' exactly, it is useful to introduce another problem I'' with s_i, $1 \le i \le n$ as its objective function coefficients. Define $s_i = \lfloor (p_i \cdot n)/(\text{LB}\cdot\epsilon) \rfloor$, $1 \le i \le n$. It is easy to see that $s_i = (q_i \cdot n)/(\text{LB}\cdot\epsilon)$. Clearly, the $S^{(i)}$'s corresponding to the solutions of I' and I'' will have the same number of tuples. (r, t) is a tuple in an $S^{(i)}$ for I' iff $((r \cdot n)/(\text{LB}\cdot\epsilon), t)$, is a tuple in the $S^{(i)}$ for I''. Hence, the time needed to solve I' is the same as that needed to solve I''. Since $p_i \le$ LB, it follows that $s_i \le \lfloor n/\epsilon \rfloor$. Hence

$$|S^{(i)}| \le 1 + \sum_{j=1}^{i} s_j \le 1 + i\lfloor n/\epsilon \rfloor$$

and so

$$\sum_{i=0}^{n-1} |S^{(i)}| \le n + \sum_{i=0}^{n-1} i\lfloor n/\epsilon \rfloor = U(n^3/\epsilon).$$

Thus, if we can go from $S^{(i-1)}$ to $S^{(i)}$ in $O(|S^{(i-1)}|)$ time then I'' and hence I' can be solved in $O(n^3/\epsilon)$ time. Moreover, the solution for I' will be an ϵ-approximate solution for I and we would thus have a fully polynomial time approximation scheme. When using rounding, we will actually solve I'' and use the resulting optimal solution as the solution to I.

Example 12.14 Consider the 0/1 knapsack problem of Section 5.5. While solving this problem by successively generating $S^{(0)}$, $S^{(1)}$, ..., $S^{(n)}$ the feasible assignments for $S^{(i)}$ may be represented by tuples of the form (r, t) where

$$r = \sum_{j=1}^{i} p_j x_j \quad \text{and} \quad t = \sum_{j=1}^{i} w_j x_j.$$

The dominance rule developed in Section 5.5 for this problem is: (r_1, t_1) dominates (r_2, t_2) iff $t_1 \le t_2$ and $r_1 \ge r_2$.

Let us solve the following instance of the 0/1 knapsack problem: $n = 5$, $M = 1112$ and $(p_1, p_2, p_3, p_4, p_5) = (w_1, w_2, w_3, w_4, w_5) = \{1, 2, 10, 100, 1000\}$. Since $p_i = w_i$, $1 \le i \le 5$, the tuples (r, t) in $S^{(i)}$, $0 \le i \le 5$

will have $r = t$. Consequently, it is necessary to retain only one of the two coordinates r, t. The $S^{(i)}$ obtained for this instance are: $S^{(0)} = \{0\}$; $S^{(1)} = \{0, 1\}$; $S^{(2)} = \{0, 1, 2, 3\}$; $S^{(3)} = \{0, 1, 2, 3, 10, 11, 12, 13\}$; $S^{(4)} = \{0, 1, 2, 3, 10, 11, 12, 13, 100, 101, 102, 103, 110, 111, 112, 113\}$; $S^{(5)} = \{0, 1, 2, 3, 10, 11, 12, 13, 100, 101, 102, 103, 110, 111, 112, 113, 1000, 1001, 1002, 1003, 1010, 1011, 1012, 1013, 1100, 1101, 1102, 1103, 1110, 1111, 1112\}$.

The optimal solution has value $\Sigma\ p_i x_i = 1112$.

Now, let us use rounding on the above problem instance to find an approximate solution with value at most 10% less than the optimal value. We thus have $\epsilon = 1/10$. Also, we know that $F^*(I) \geq \text{LB} \geq \max\{p_i\} = 1000$. The problem I'' to be solved is: $n = 5$, $M = 1112$, $(s_1, s_2, s_3, s_4, s_5) = (0, 0, 0, 5, 50)$ and $(w_1, w_2, w_3, w_4, w_5) = (1, 2, 10, 100, 1000)$. Hence, $S^{(0)} = S^{(1)} = S^{(2)} = S^{(3)} = \{(0, 0)\}$; $S^{(4)} = \{(0, 0), (5, 100)\}$; $S^{(5)} = \{(0, 0), (5, 100), (50, 1000), (55, 1100)\}$.

The optimal solution is $(x_1, x_2, x_3, x_4, x_5) = (0, 0, 0, 1, 1)$. Its value in I'' is 55 and in the original problem 1100. The error $(F^*(I) - \hat{F}(I))/F^*(I)$ is therefore $12/1112 < 0.011 < \epsilon$. At this time we see that the solution may be improved by setting either $x_1 = 1$ or $x_2 = 1$ or $x_3 = 1$. $\square$

Rounding as described in its full generality results in $O(n^3/\epsilon)$ time approximation schemes. It is possible to specialize this technique to the specific problem being solved. In particular, we can obtain specialized and asymptotically faster polynomial time approximation schemes for the knapsack problem as well as for the problem of scheduling tasks on two processors to minimize finish time. The complexity of the resulting algorithms is $O(n(\log n + 1/\epsilon^2))$.

Let us investigate the specialized rounding scheme for the 0/1 knapsack problem. Let I be an instance of this problem and let ϵ be the desired accuracy. Let $P^*(I)$ be the value of an optimal solution. First, a good estimate UB for $P^*(I)$ is obtained. This is done by ordering the n objects in I such that $p_i/w_i \geq p_{i+1}/w_{i+1}$, $1 \leq i < n$. Next, we find the largest j such that $\Sigma_1^j w_i \leq M$. If $j = n$, then the optimal solution is $x_i = 1$, $1 \leq i \leq n$ and $P^*(I) = \Sigma\ p_i$. So, assume $j < n$. Define UB $= \Sigma_1^{j+1} p_i$. We can show ½ UB $\leq P^*(I) <$ UB. The inequality $P^*(I) <$ UB follows from the ordering on p_i/w_i. The inequality ½UB $\leq P^*(I)$ follows from the observation that

$$P^*(I) \geq \sum_{i=1}^{j} p_i \quad \text{and} \quad P^*(I) \geq \max\left\{\sum_1^j p_i, p_{j+1}\right\}.$$

Hence, $2P^*(I) \geq \Sigma_1^{j+1} p_i =$ UB.

Now, let δ = UB*ϵ^2/9. Divide the n objects into 2 classes BIG and SMALL. BIG includes all objects with p_i > ϵ UB/3. SMALL includes all other objects. Let the number of objects in BIG be r. Replace each p_i in BIG by q_i such that $q_i = \lfloor p_i/\delta \rfloor$. (This is the rounding step.) The knapsack problem is solved exactly using these r objects and the q_i's.

Let $S^{(r)}$ be the set up tuples resulting from the dynamic programming algorithm. For each tuple $(x, y) \in S^{(r)}$ fill the remaining space $M - y$ by considering the objects in SMALL in nondecreasing order of p_i/w_i. Use the filling that has maximum value as the answer.

Example 12.15 Consider the problem instance of Example 12.14. n = 5, $(p_1, p_2, p_3, p_4, p_5)$ = $(w_1, w_2, w_3, w_4, w_5,)$ = (1, 2, 10, 100, 1000), M = 1112 and ϵ = $^1/_{10}$. The objects are already in nonincreasing order of p_i/w_i. For this instance, UB = $\Sigma_1^5 p_i$ = 1113. Hence, δ = 3.71/3 and ϵUB/3 = 37.1. SMALL, therefore, includes objects 1, 2 and 3. BIG = {4, 5}. $q_4 = \lfloor p_4/\delta \rfloor$ = 94 and $q_5 = \lfloor p_5/\delta \rfloor$ = 946. Solving the knapsack instance n = 2, M = 1112, (q_4, w_4) = (94, 100) and (q_5, w_5) = (946, 1000), we obtain: $S^{(0)}$ = {(0, 0)}; $S^{(1)}$ = {(0, 0), (94, 100)} and $S^{(2)}$ = {(0, 0), (94, 100), (946, 1000), (1040, 1100)}. Filling (0,0) from SMALL, we get the tuple (13, 13). Filling (94, 100), (946, 1000) and (1040, 1100) yields the tuples (107, 113), (959, 1013) and (1043, 1100) respectively. The answer is given by the tuple (1043, 1100). This corresponds to $(x_1, x_2, x_3, x_4, x_5)$ = (1, 1, 0, 1, 1) and $\Sigma p_i x_i$ = 1103. $\square$

An exercise explores a modification to the basic rounding scheme illustrated in the above example. This modification results in "better" solutions.

Theorem 12.15 [Iharra and Kim] The algorithm just described is an ϵ-approximate algorithm for the 0/1-knapsack problem.

Proof: The proof may be found in the paper by Ibarra and Kim which is cited at end of this chapter. $\square$

The time needed to initially sort according to p_i/w_i is $O(n \log n)$. UB can be computed in $O(n)$ time. Since $P^*(I) \leq$ UB, there are at most UB/δ = $9/\epsilon^2$ tuples in any $S^{(i)}$ in the solution of BIG. The time to obtain $S^{(r)}$ is therefore $O(r/\epsilon^2) \leq O(n/\epsilon^2)$. Filling each tuple in $S^{(r)}$ with objects from SMALL takes $O(|\text{SMALL}|)$ time. $|S^{(r)}| \leq 9/\epsilon^2$ and so the total time for this step is at most $O(n/\epsilon^2)$. The total time for the algorithm is therefore $O(n(\log n + 1/\epsilon^2))$. A faster approximation scheme for the knapsack problem has been obtained by Lawler (see the references). His scheme also uses rounding.

Interval Partitioning

Unlike rounding, interval partitioning does not transform the original problem instance into one that is easier to solve. Instead, an attempt is made to solve the problem instance I by generating a restricted class of the feasible assignments for $S^{(0)}$, $S^{(1)}$, ..., $S^{(n)}$. Let P_i be the maximum $\sum_{j=1}^{i} p_j x_j$ amongst all feasible assignments generated for $S^{(i)}$. Then the profit interval $[0, P_i]$ is divided into subintervals each of size $P_i \epsilon / (n - 1)$ (except possibly the last interval which may be a little smaller). All feasible assignments in $S^{(i)}$ with $\sum_{j=1}^{i} p_j x_j$ in the same subinterval are regarded as having the same $\sum_{j=1}^{i} p_j x_j$ and the dominance rules are used to discard all but one of them. The $S^{(i)}$ resulting from this elimination is used in the generation of $S^{(i+1)}$. Since the number of subintervals for each $S^{(i)}$ is at most $\lceil n/\epsilon \rceil + 1$, $|S^{(i)}| \le \lceil n/\epsilon \rceil + 1$. Hence, $\sum_{i}^{n} |S^{(i)}| = O(n^2/\epsilon)$.

The error introduced in each feasible assignment due to this elimination in $S^{(i)}$ is less than the subinterval length. This error may however propagate from $S^{(1)}$ up through $S^{(n)}$. However, the error is additive. Let $F(I)$ be the value of the optimal generated using interval partitioning, and $F^*(I)$ the value of a true optimal. It follows that

$$F^*(I) - \hat{F}(I) \le \left(\epsilon \sum_{i=1}^{n-1} P_i \right) / (n - 1).$$

Since $P_i \le F^*(I)$, it follows that $(F^*(I) - \hat{F}(I))/F^*(I) \le \epsilon$, as desired.

In many cases the algorithm may be speeded by starting with a good estimate, LB for $F^*(I)$ such that $F^*(I) \ge$ LB. The subinterval size is then LB$\cdot\epsilon/(n - 1)$ rather than $P_i \epsilon/(n - 1)$. When a feasible assignment with value greater than LB is discovered, the subinterval size can be chosen as described above.

Example 12.16   Consider the same instance of the 0/1 knapsack problem as in Example 12.14. $\epsilon = 1/10$ and $F^*(I) \ge$ LB ≥ 1000. We can start with a subinterval size of LB$\cdot\epsilon/(n - 1) = 1000/40 = 25$. Since all tuples (p, t) in $S^{(i)}$ have $p = t$, only p will be explicitly retained. The intervals are $[0, 25), [25, 50), \ldots$ etc. Using interval partitioning we obtain: $S^{(0)} = S^{(1)} = S^{(2)} = S^{(3)} = \{0\}$; $S^{(4)} = \{0, 100\}$; $S^{(5)} = \{0, 100, 1000, 1100\}$.

The best solution generated using interval partitioning is $(x_1, x_2, x_3, x_4, x_5) = (0, 0, 0, 1, 1)$ and its value $\hat{F}(I)$ is 1100. $(F^*(I) - \hat{F}(I))/F^*(I) = 12/1112 < 0.011 < \epsilon$. Again, the solution value may be improved by using a heuristic to change some of the x_i's from 0 to 1.   □

Separation

Assume that in solving a problem instance I, we have obtained an $S^{(i)}$ with feasible solutions having the following $\sum_{1 \leq j \leq i} p_j x_j$: 0, 3.9, 4.1, 7.8, 8.2, 11.9, 12.1. Further assume that the interval size $P_i\epsilon/(n-1)$ is 2. Then the subintervals are [0, 2), [2, 4), [4, 6), [6, 8), [8, 10), [10, 12) and [12, 14). Each value above falls in a different subinterval and so no feasible assignments are eliminated. However, there are three pairs of assignments with values within $P_i\epsilon/(n-1)$. If the dominance rules are used for each pair, only 4 assignments will remain. The error introduced is at most $P_i\epsilon/(n-1)$. More formally, let $a_0, a_1, a_2, \ldots, a_r$ be the distinct values of $\sum_{j=1}^{i} p_j x_j$ in $S^{(i)}$. Let us assume $a_0 < a_1 < a_2 \cdots < a_r$. We will construct a new set J from $S^{(i)}$ by making a left to right scan and retaining a tuple only if its value exceeds the value of the last tuple in J by more than $P_i\epsilon/(n-1)$. This is described by the following algorithm:

$J \leftarrow$ assignment corresponding to a_0; $XP \leftarrow a_0$
for $j \leftarrow 1$ **to** r **do**
  if $a_j > XP + P_i\epsilon/(n-1)$
      then put assignment corresponding to a_j into J
        $XP \leftarrow a_j$
  endif
repeat

The preceding algorithm assumes that the assignment with less profit will dominate the one with more profit in case we regard both assignments as yielding the same profit $\sum p_j x_j$. In case the reverse is true the algorithm can start with a_r and work downwards. The analysis for this strategy is the same as that for interval partitioning. The same comments regarding the use of a good estimate for $F^*(I)$ hold here too.

Intuitively one may expect separation to always work better than interval partitioning. The following example illustrates that this need not be the case. However, empirical studies with one problem indicate interval partitioning to be inferior in practice.

Example 12.17 Using separation on the data of Example 12.14 yields the same $S^{(i)}$ as obtained using interval partitioning. We have already seen an instance where separation performs better than interval partitioning. Now, we shall see an example where interval partitioning does better than separation. Assume that the subinterval size $LB \cdot \epsilon/(n-1)$ is 2. Then the intervals are $[0, 2)$, $[2, 4)$, $[4, 6) \cdots$ etc. Assume further that $(p_1, p_2, p_3, p_4, p_5) = (3, 1, 5.1, 5.1, 5.1)$. Then, following the use of interval partitioning we have: $S^{(0)} = \{0\}$; $S^{(1)} = \{0, 3\}$; $S^{(2)} = \{0, 3, 4\}$; $S^{(3)} = \{0, 3, 4, 8.1\}$; $S^{(4)} = \{0, 3, 4, 8.1, 13.2\}$; $S^{(5)} = \{0, 3, 4, 8.1, 13.2, 18.3\}$.

Using separation with $LB \cdot \epsilon/(n - 1) = 2$ we have: $S^{(0)} = \{0\}$; $S^{(1)} = \{0, 3\}$; $S^2 = \{0, 3\}$; $S^{(3)} = \{0, 3, 5.1, 8.1\}$; $S^{(4)} = \{0, 3, 5.1, 8.1, 10.2, 13.2\}$; $S^{(5)} = \{0, 3, 5.1, 8.1, 10.2, 13.2, 15.3, 18.3\}$. $\square$

In order to compare the relative performance of interval partitioning (I) and separation (S), a simulation was carried out. We used the job sequencing with deadlines problem as the test problem. Algorithms for I and S were programmed in FORTRAN and run on a CDC CYBER 74 computer. Both algorithms were tested with $\epsilon = 0.1$. Three data sets were used: (p_i = profit; t_i = processing time needed; d_i = deadline).

Data Set A: random profits $p_i \in [1, 100]$, $t_i = p_i$ and $d_i = \Sigma_1^n t_i/2$.

Data Set B: random $p_i \in [1, 100]$; $t_i = p_i$ and random $d_i \in [t_i, t_i + 25n]$

Data Set C: random $p_i \in [1, 100]$; random $t_i \in [1, 100]$ and random $d_i \in [t_i, t_i + 25n]$.

The program had a capacity to solve all problems generating no more than 9000 tuples (i.e., $\Sigma_0^n |S^{(i)}| \leq 9000$). For each data set an attempt was made to run 10 problems of size 5, 15, 25, 35, 45, ... Figure 12.11 summarizes the results.

The exercises examine some of the other problems to which these techniques apply. It is interesting to note that one may couple existing heuristics to the approximation schemes that result from the above three techniques. This is because of the similarity in solution procedures for the exact and approximate problems. In the approximation algorithms of Sections 12.2–12.4 it is usually not possible to use existing heuristics.

At this point, one might well ask the question: What kind of NP-hard problems can have fully polynomial time approximation schemes? Clearly, no NP-hard ϵ-approximation problem can have such a scheme unless $P = NP$. A stronger result may be proven. This stronger result is that the only NP-hard problems that can have fully polynomial time approximation schemes (unless $P = NP$) are those which are polynomially solvable if restricted to problem instances in which all numbers are bounded by a fixed polynomial in n. Examples of such problems are the knapsack and job sequencing with deadlines problems.

Data Set	A	B	C
Total number of problems solved	80	30	30
Number of optimal solutions generated by I	54	20	16
Number of optimal solutions generated by S	53	18	14
Average fracitonal error in nonoptimal solutions by I	.0025	.0047	.0040
Average fractional error in nonoptimal solutions by S	.0024	.0047	.0040
Number of I solutions better than S	3	7	9
Number of S solutions better than I	1	7	6

Figure 12.11 Relative performance of I and S

Definition [Garey and Johnson] Let L be some problem. Let I be an instance of L and let LENGTH(I) be the number of bits in the representation of I. Let MAX(I) be the magnitude of the largest number in I. Without loss of generality, we may assume that all numbers in I are integer. For some fixed polynomial p let L_p be problem L restricted to those instances I for which MAX(I) $\leq$ p(LENGTH(I)). Problem L is *strongly NP-hard* iff there exists a polynomial p such that L_p is NP-hard.

Examples of problems that are strongly NP-hard are: Hamiltonian cycle; node cover; feedback arc set; traveling salesperson, max-clique, etc. The 0/1 knapsack problem is probably not strongly NP-hard (note that there is no known way to show that a problem is not strongly NP-hard) as when MAX(I) $\leq$ p(LENGTH(I)) then I can be solved in time O(LENGTH(I)^{2*} p(LENGTH(I))) using the dynamic programming algorithm of Section 5.5.

Theorem 12.16 [Garey and Johnson] Let L be an optimization problem such that all feasible solutions to all possible instances have a value that is a positive integer. Further, assume that for all instances I of L, the optimal value $F^*(I)$ is bounded by a polynomial function p in the variables LENGTH(I) and MAX(I), i.e., $0 < F^*(I) < p$(LENGTH(I), MAX(I)) and $F^*(I)$ is an integer. If L has a fully polynomial time approximation scheme, then L has an exact algorithm of complexity a polynomial in LENGTH(I) and MAX(I).

Proof: Suppose L has a fully polynomial time approximation scheme. We shall show how to obtain optimal solutions to L in polynomial time. Let I be any instance of L. Define $\epsilon = 1/(p(\text{LENGTH}(I), \text{MAX}(I))$. With this ϵ, the approximation scheme is forced to generate an optimal solution. To see this, let $\hat{F}(I)$ be the value of the solution generated. Then,

$$|F^*(I) - \hat{F}(I)| \leq \epsilon F^*(I) \leq F^*(I)/p(\text{LENGTH}(I), \text{MAX}(I)) < 1$$

Since, by assumption all feasible solutions are integer valued, $F^*(I) = \hat{F}(I)$. Hence, with this ϵ, the approximation scheme becomes an exact algorithm.

The complexity of the resulting exact algorithm is easy to obtain. Let $q(\text{LENGTH}(I), 1/\epsilon)$ be a polynomial such that the complexity of the approximation scheme is $O(q(\text{LENGTH}(I), 1/\epsilon))$. The complexity of this scheme when ϵ is chosen as above is $O(q(\text{LENGTH}(I), p(\text{LENGTH}(I), \text{MAX}(I)))$ which is $O(q'(\text{LENGTH}(I), \text{MAX}(I)))$ for some polynomial q'. $\square$

When Theorem 12.16 is applied to integer valued problems that are NP-hard in the strong sense, we see that no such problem can have a fully polynomial time approximation scheme unless $P = \text{NP}$. The above theorem also tells us something about the kind of exact algorithms obtainable for strongly NP-hard problems. A *pseudo-polynomial* time algorithm is one whose complexity is a polynomial in $\text{LENGTH}(I)$ and $\text{MAX}(I)$. The dynamic programming algorithm for the knapsack problem (Section 5.5) is a pseudo-polynomial time algorithm. No strongly NP-hard problem can have a pseudo polynomial time algorithm unless $P = \text{NP}$.

12.6 PROBABILISTICALLY GOOD ALGORITHMS

The approximation algorithms of the preceding sections had the nice property that their worst case performance could be bounded by some constants (k in the case of an absolute approximation and ϵ in the case of an ϵ-approximation). The requirement of bounded performance tends to categorize other algorithms that "usually work well" as being bad. Some algorithms with unbounded performance may in fact "almost always" either solve the problem exactly or generate a solution that is "exceedingly close" in value to the value of an optimal solution. Such algorithms are "good" in a probabilistic sense. If we pick a problem instance I at random then there is a very high probability that the algorithm will generate a very good approximate solution. In this section we shall consider two algorithms with this property. Both algorithms are for NP-hard problems.

First, since we shall be carrying out a probabilistic analysis of the algorithms we need to define a sample space of inputs. The sample space is set up by first defining a sample space S_n for each problem size n. Problem instances of size n are drawn from S_n. Then, the overall sample space is the infinite cartesian product $S_1 \times S_2 \times S_3 \times \ldots \times S_n \ldots$. An element of the sample space is a sequence $X = x_1, x_2, \ldots, x_n, \ldots$ such that x_i is drawn from S_i.

Definition [Karp]   An algorithm $\mathcal{Q}$ solves a problem L *almost everywhere* (abbreviated a. e.) if, when $X = x_1, x_2, \ldots, x_n, \ldots$ is drawn from the sample space $S_1 \times S_2 \times S_3 \times \ldots \times S_n, \ldots$, the number of x_i on which the algorithm fails to solve L is finite with probability 1.

Since both the algorithms we shall be discussing are for NP-hard graph problems, we shall first describe the sample space for which the probabilistic analysis will be carried out. Let $p(n)$ be a function such that $0 \leq p(n) \leq 1$ for all $n \geq 0$. A random n vertex graph is constructed by including edge (i, j), $i \neq j$, with probability $p(n)$.

The first algorithm we shall consider is due to Posa. This is an algorithm to find a Hamiltonian cycle in an undirected graph. Informally, Posa's algorithm proceeds as follows. First, an arbitrary vertex (say vertex 1) is chosen as the start vertex. The algorithm maintains a simple path P starting from vertex 1 and ending at vertex k. Initially P is a trivial path with $k = 1$, i.e., there are no edges in P. At each iteration of the algorithm an attempt is made to increase the length of P. This is done by considering an edge (k, j) incident to the end point k of P. When edge (k, j) is being considered, one of three possibilities exist:

(i)   [$j = 1$ and path P includes all the vertices of the graph]
    In this case a Hamiltonian cycle has been found and the algorithm terminates.

(ii)   [j is not on the path P]
    In this case the length of path P is increased by adding (k, j) to it. j becomes the new end point of P.

(iii)   [j is already on path P]
    Now there is a unique edge $e = (j, m)$ in P such that deletion of e and the inclusion of (k, j) to P results in a simple path. e is deleted and (k, j) added to P. P is now a simple path with endpoint m.

The algorithm is constrained so that case (iii) does not generate two paths of the same length having the same end point. With a proper choice of data representations, this algorithm can be implemented to run in time $O(n^2)$ where n is the number of vertices in the graph G. It is easy to see that this algorithm does not always find a Hamiltonian cycle in a graph that contains such a cycle. However, Posa has shown the following:

Theorem 12.17 [Posa] If $p(n) \approx (\alpha \ln n/n)$, $\alpha > 1$ then the preceding algorithm finds a Hamiltonian cycle (a. e.).

Proof: See the paper by Posa.   □

Example 12.18 Let us try out the above algorithm on the five vertex graph of Figure 12.12. The path P initially consists of vertex 1 only. Assume edge (1, 4) is chosen. This represents case (ii) and P is expanded to $\{1, 4\}$. Assume edge (4, 5) is chosen next. Path P now becomes $\{1, 4, 5\}$. Edge (1, 5) is the only possibility for the next edge. This results in case (iii) and P becomes $\{1, 5, 4\}$. Now assume edges (4, 3) and (3, 2) are considered. P becomes $\{1, 5, 4, 3, 2\}$. If edge (1, 2) is next considered, a Hamiltonian cycle is found and the algorithm terminates.   □

The next probabilistically good algorithm we shall look at is for the maximum independent set problem. A subset of vertices N of graph $G(V, E)$ is said to be independent iff no two vertices in N are adjacent in G. Algorithm 12.5 is a greedy algorithm to construct a maximum independent set.

procedure INDEP(V, E)
$\quad N \leftarrow \phi$
$\quad$**while** there is a v $\in (V-N)$ **and** v not adjacent to any vertex in N **do**
$\quad\quad N \leftarrow N \cup \{v\}$
$\quad$**repeat**
$\quad$**return** (N)
end INDEP

Algorithm 12.5 Finding an independent set

One can easily construct examples of n vertex graphs for which INDEP generates independent sets of size 1 when in fact a maximum independent set contains $n - 1$ vertices. However, for certain probability distributions it can be shown that INDEP generates good approximations almost everywhere. If $F^*(I)$ and $\hat{F}(I)$ represent the size of a maximum independent set and one generated by algorithm INDEP, respectively, then the following theorem is obtained:

Theorem 12.18 [Karp] If $p(n) = c$, for some constanct c, then for every $\epsilon > 0$ we have:

$$(F^*(I) - \hat{F}(I))/F^*(I) \le .5 + \epsilon \quad (a.e.).$$

Proof: See the paper by Karp. $\square$

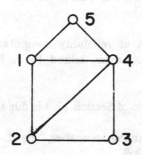

Figure 12.12 Graph for Example 12.18

Algorithm **INDEP** can easily be implemented to have polynomial complexity. Some other NP-hard problems for which probabilistically good algorithms are known are: Euclidean traveling salesperson, minimal colorings of graphs, set covering, maximum weighted clique and partition.

REFERENCES AND SELECTED READINGS

Note: Exercise numbers at the end of a reference indicate that these exercises are based on work reported in this reference. The reference, however, contains more results than covered by the cited exercises.

Our terminology for absolute, $f(n)$ and ϵ-approximation algorithms is taken from the paper:

"Combinatorial problems: reducibility and approximation," by S. Sahni and E. Horowitz, *Op. Res.*, 26(4), 1978.

The terms approximation scheme, polynomial time approximation scheme and fully polynomial time approximation scheme were coined by Garey and Johnson and used in their lecture on approximation algorithms which was presented at the Symposium on Algorithms and Complexity, Carnegie Mellon Institute, Pittsburgh, 1976. Sahni pointed out that for the 0/1 knapsack problem the corresponding absolute approximation problem is also NP-hard. The following paper, contains the remark on the knapsack problem:

"Approximate algorithms for the 0/1-knapsack problem," by S. Sahni, *JACM,* 22, pp. 115–124, 1975. [exercise 18].

This paper also contains the polynomial time approximation scheme for the 0/1-knapsack problem discussed in §12.4. Several other absolute approximation problems are shown NP-hard in:

"A computer scientist looks at reliability computations," by A. Rosenthal, in *Reliability and Fault Tree Analysis,* edited by J. Fussel and N. Singpurwalla, *SIAM,* 1975.

The analysis of the LPT rule of Section 12.3 is due to R. Graham and appears in:

"Bounds on multiprocessor timing anomalies," by R. Graham, *SIAM Jr. on Appl. Math.,* 17(2), pp. 416–429, 1969.

This paper also contains the polynomial time approximation scheme for scheduling independent tasks that was discussed in §12.4. ε-approximate bin packing algorithms may be found in:

"Performance bounds for simple one dimensional bin packing algorithms," by D. Johnson, A. Demers, J. Ullman, M. Garey and R. Graham, *SIAM Jr. on Comput.,* 3(4), pp. 299–325, 1974.

An excellent bibliography on approximation algorithms is:

"Approximation algorithms for combinatorial problems: an annotated bibliography," by M. Garey and D. Johnson, in *Algorithms and Complexity: Recent Results and New Directions,* J. Traub, ed., Academic Press, 1976.

Polynomial time ε-approximate algorithms for many scheduling problems may be found in the following papers:

"Scheduling independent tasks to reduce mean finishing time," by J. Bruno, E. Coffman and R. Sethi, *CACM,* 17(7), 382–387, 1974.

"Algorithms for minimizing mean flow time," by J. Bruno, E. Coffman and R. Sethi, *Proc. IFIP Congr. 74,* North Holland Pub. Co., Amsterdam, 1974, pp. 504–510.

"A level algorithm for preemptive scheduling," by E. Horvath, S. Lam and R. Sethi, *JACM,* 24(1), pp. 32–43, 1977.

"Bounds on LPT schedules on uniform processors," by T. Gonzalez, O. Ibarra and S. Sahni, *SIAM Jr. on Computing,* 6(1), pp. 155–166, 1977 [exercises 4–6].

"Job shop and flow shop schedules: complexity and approximation," by T. Gonzalez and S. Sahni, *Oper. Res.,* 26(1), pp. 36–52, 1978.

"Heuristic algorithms for scheduling independent tasks on nonidentical processors," by O. Ibarra and C. Kim, *JACM,* 24(2), pp. 280–289, 1977 [exercises 8–10].

A 0.5-approximate algorithm for the Euclidean traveling salesperson problem appears in:

"Worst-case analysis of a new heuristic for the traveling salesman problem," by N. Christofedes, *Manag. Sci. Res. Report #388,* Carnegie Mellon University, 1976.

ϵ-approximate algorithms for other NP-hard problems appear in:

"Approximation algorithms for some routing problems," by G. Fredrickson, M. Hecht and C. Kim, *Proc. 17th An. Symp. on Found. of Comp. Sci.,* Houston, Texas, pp. 216–227, 1976.

"Location of bank accounts to optimize float: an analytic study of exact and approximate algorithms," by G. Cornuejols, M. Fisher and G. Nemhauser, *Manag. Sci.* 23(8), pp. 789–810, 1977.

"An analysis of approximations for maximizing submodular set functions—II," by M. Fisher, G. Nemhauser and L. Wolsey, CORE discussion paper #7629, Universite Catholique De Louvain, Belgium, 1976.

"An analysis of approximations for finding a maximum weight hamiltonian circuit," by M. Fisher, G. Nemhauser and L. Wolsey, CORE, University of Louvain, Belgium, 1977.

"Code generation for expressions with common subexpressions," by A. Aho, S. Johnson and J. Ullman, *JACM,* 24(1), pp. 146–160, 1977.

Some $f(n)$-approximate algorithms appear in:

"Approximation algorithms for combinatorial problems," by D. Johnson, *JCSS,* 9, pp. 256–278, 1974. [exercises 11–16].

The approximation algorithm MSAT2 (exercise 12) for the maximum satisfiability problem has also been studied by K. Lieberherr. The *weight* of a CNF formula F is defined to be $w(F) = \sum_i 2^{-|C_i|}$ where $|C_i|$ is the number of literals in the ith clause of F. He shows that MSAT2 leaves at most $\lfloor w(F) \rfloor$ clauses unsatisfied. This result together with a generalization of MSAT2 appears in the paper:

"Interpretations of 2-satisfiable conjunctive normal forms," by K. Lieberherr, Florida State Univ., Tallahassee, to appear in *JACM*.

Lieberherr has also considered the notion of an optimal polynomial time approximation algorithm. A polynomial time approximation algorithm is optimal iff the problem of guaranteeing better solutions is NP-hard. MSAT2 (exercise 12) as well as some heuristics for other NP-hard problems are shown optimal in the following paper:

"Optimal heuristics for combinatorial optimization problems," by K. Lieberherr, Florida State University, Tallahassee, 1978.

Sahni and Gonzalez were the first to show the existence of NP-hard ϵ-approximate problems. Their results appear in the paper:

"*P*-complete approximation problems," by S. Sahni and T. Gonzalez, *JACM*, 23, pp. 555–565, 1976. [exercises 20–26, 29]

Garey and Johnson have shown that the ϵ-approximate graph coloring problem is NP-Hard for $\epsilon < 1$. Their result appears in the paper:

"The complexity of near optimal graph coloring," by M. Garey and D. Johnson, *JACM*, 23, pp. 43–49, 1976.

Some other NP-hard ϵ-approximate problems appear in:

"Traversal marker placement problems are NP-complete," by S. Maheshwari, University of Colorado, Technical report #CU-CS-092-76, 1976.

"Code generation for short/long address machines," by E. Robertson, Univ. of Wisconsin, MRC Report #1779, 1977.

A polynomial time approximation scheme for submodular set functions appears in:

"Best algorithms for approximating the maximum of a submodular set function," by G. Nemhauser and L. Wolsey, CORE discussion paper #7636, Universite Catholique De Louvain, Belgium, 1976.

An approximation scheme for scheduling tasks with precedence constraints appears in:

"Scheduling for maximum profits/minimum time," by O. Ibarra and C. Kim, *Math. of Oper. Res.*, to appear.

Ibarra and Kim were the first to discover the existence of fully polynomial time approximation schemes for NP-hard problems. Their work appears in the paper:

"Fast approximation algorithms for the knapsack and sum of subsets problems," by O. Ibarra and C. Kim, *JACM*, 22, pp. 463–468, 1975. [exercises 27–28]

This paper develops the $O(n(\log n + 1/\epsilon^2))$ algorithm for the 0/1 knapsack problem. An approximation scheme for the integer knapsack problem is also developed. E. Lawler has improved upon these schemes. He has obtained $O(n \log(1/\epsilon) + 1/\epsilon^4)$ and $O(n + 1/\epsilon^3)$ schemes for the knapsack and sum of subset problems. Lawler's work appears in the paper:

"Fast approximation algorithms for knapsack problems," by E. Lawler, *Proc. 18th Ann. Symp. on Foundations of Computer Science*, Rhode Island, pp. 206–213, 1977.

Fully polynomial time approximation schemes for many scheduling problems appear in the papers:

"Algorithms for scheduling independent tasks," by S. Sahni, *JACM*, 23, pp. 114–127, 1976. [exercises 30, 31, 33–37, 39–41].

"Exact and approximate algorithms for scheduling nonidentical processors," by E. Horowitz and S. Sahni, *JACM*, 23, pp. 317–327, 1976. [exercises 31 and 38]

Our discussion of the general techniques: rounding, interval partitioning and separation is from the paper:

"General techniques for combinatorial approximation," by S. Sahni, *Oper. Res.*, 25(6), pp. 920–936, 1977.

The notion of strongly NP-hard is due to Garey and Johnson. Theorem 12.16 is also due to them and appears in:

""Strong" NP-Completeness results: motivation, examples and implications," by M. Garey and D. Johnson, Bell Laboratories Report, Murray Hill, 1976.

The discussion on probabilistically good algorithms is based on the following papers:

"The probabilistic analysis of some combinatorial search algorithms," by R. Karp, University of California, Berkeley, Memo No. ERL-M581, April 1976.

"The fast approximate solution of hard combinatorial problems," by R. Karp,

Proc. Sixth Southeastern Conf. on Combinatorics, Graph Theory, and Computing, Winnipeg, 1975.

"Hamiltonian circuits in random graphs," by L. Posa, *Discrete Mathematics*, 14, pp. 359–364, 1976.

"Probabilistic analysis of partitioning algorithms for the traveling salesman problem in the plane," by R. Karp, *Math. of Oper. Res.*, 2(3), pp. 209–224, 1977.

The following paper contains a "good" algorithm for the general traveling salesperson problem. The algorithms have worked well on all problem instances tested. However, no statistical or probabilistic analysis has been made.

"An effective heuristic algorithm for the traveling salesman problem," by S. Lin and P. Kernighan, *Operations Research,* 21(2), 1973, 498–516.

Analysis of other probabilistically good algorithms appear in:

"Fast Probabilistic algorithms for hamiltonian circuits and matchings," by D. Angluin and L. Valiant, *Proc. 9th Annual Symp. on Theo. of Computing,* pp. 30–41, 1977.

"Analysis of the expected performance of algorithms for the partition problem," by C. Kim, Technical Report, University of Maryland, 1976.

"Maximization problems on graphs with edge weights chosen from a normal distribution," by G. Lueker *Proc. 10th Annual Symp. on Theo. of Computing*, pp. 13–18, 1978.

EXERCISES

1. The following NP-hard problems were defined in either Chapter 11 or 12. For each of these defined in the exercises, the exercise number appears in parenthesis. For each of these problems, clearly state the corresponding absolute approximation problem. (Some of the problems listed below were defined as decision problems. For these, there correspond obvious optimization problems that are also NP-hard. The absolute approximation problem is to be defined relative to the corresponding optimization problem.) Also, show that the corresponding absolute approximation problem is NP-hard.

    i)   Node Cover
    ii) Set Cover (ex. 11.20)
    iii) Set Packing (ex. 11.43)
    iv) Feedback Node Set
    v)   Feedback Arc Set (ex. 11.11)

vi)   Chromatic Number

vii)   Clique Cover (ex. 11.19)

viii)   Max-Independent Set (see Section 12.6)

ix)   Nonpreemptive scheduling of independent tasks to minimize finish time on $m > 1$ processors (Section 12.3)

x)   Flow shop scheduling to minimize finish time ($m > 2$)

xi)   Job shop scheduling to minimize finish time ($m > 1$)

2. Obtain an $O(n \log n)$ algorithm that implements the LPT scheduling rule.

3. Show that LPT schedules are optimal for all task sets that have an optimal schedule in which no more than two tasks are assigned to any processor.

4. A uniform processor system is a set of $m \geq 1$ processors. Processor i operates at a speed s_i, $s_i > 0$. If task i requires t_i units of processing then, it may be completed in t_i / s_i units of real time on processor p_i. When $s_i = 1, 1 \leq i \leq m$ we have a system of identical processors (section 12.3). An MLPT schedule is defined to be any schedule obtained by assigning tasks to processors in order of nonincreasing processing times. When a task is being considered for assignment to a processor, it is assigned to that processor on which its finishing time will be earliest. Ties are broken by assigning the task to the processor with least index.

a)   Let $m = 3$, $s_1 = 1$, $s_2 = 2$ and $s_3 = 3$. Let the number of tasks n be 6. $(t_1, t_2, t_3, t_4, t_5, t_6) = (9, 6, 3, 3, 2, 2)$. Obtain the MLPT schedule for this set of tasks. Is this an optimal schedule? If not obtain an optimal schedule.

b)   Show that there exists a two processor system and a set I for which $| F^*(I) - \hat{F}(I)| / F^*(I) > 1/3 - 1/(3m)$. $\hat{F}(I)$ is the finish time of the MLPT schedule. Note that $1/3 - 1/(3m)$ is the bound for LPT schedules on identical processors.

c)   Write an algorithm to obtain MLPT schedules. What is the time complexity of your algorithm?

5. Let I be any instance of the uniform processor scheduling problem. Let $\hat{F}(I)$ and $F^*(I)$ respectively be the finish times of MLPT and optimal schedules. Show that $\hat{F}(I)/F^*(I) \leq 2m/(m + 1)$ (see exercise 4).

6. For a uniform processor system (see exercises 4 and 5) show that when $m = 2$, $\hat{F}(I)/F^*(I) \leq (1 + \sqrt{17})/4$. Show that this is the best possible bound for $m = 2$.

7. Let $P_1, \ldots, P_m$ be a set of processors. Let $t_{i,j}$, $t_{i,j} > 0$ be the time needed to process task i if its processing is carried out on processor P_j, $1 \leq i \leq n$, $1 \leq j \leq m$. For a uniform processor system, $t_{i,j}/t_{i,k} = s_k/s_j$ where s_k and s_j are

the speeds of P_k and P_j respectively. In a system of *nonidentical processors*, such a relation need not exist. As an example, consider $n = 2$, $m = 2$ and

$$\begin{pmatrix} t_{11} & t_{12} \\ t_{21} & t_{22} \end{pmatrix} = \begin{pmatrix} 1 & 2 \\ 3 & 2 \end{pmatrix}.$$

If task 1 is processed on P_2 and task 2 on P_1, then the finish time is 3. If task 1 is processed on P_1 and task 2 on P_2, the finish time is 2. Show that if a schedule is constructed by assigning task i to processor j such that $t_{i,j} \leq t_{i,k}$, $1 \leq k \leq m$ then $\hat{F}(I)/F^*(I) \leq m$. $\hat{F}(I)$ and $F^*(I)$ are respectively the finish times of the schedule constructed and of an optimal schedule. Show that this bound is best possible for this algorithm.

8. For the scheduling problem of Exercise 7, define procedure A as:

    procedure A
    $f_j \leftarrow 0$, $1 \leq j \leq m$
    for $i \leftarrow 1$ **to** n **do**
        $k \leftarrow$ least j such that $f_j + t_{i,j} \leq f_l + t_{i,l}$, $1 \leq l \leq m$
        $f_k \leftarrow f_k + t_{i,k}$
        print ('schedule task', i, 'on processor', k)
    repeat
    end A

Algorithm 12.6 Scheduling

f_j is the current finish time on processor j. So, $\hat{F}(I) = \max_j \{f_j\}$. Show that $\hat{F}(I)/F^*(I) \leq m$ and this bound is best possible.

9. In the above exercise, first order the tasks so that $\min_j \{t_{i,j}\} \geq \min_j \{t_{i+1,j}\}$, $1 \leq i < n$. Then use algorithm A. Show that $\hat{F}(I)/F^*(I) \leq m$ and this bound is best possible.

10. Show that the results of exercise 8 hold even if the initial ordering is such that $\max_j \{t_{i,j}\} \geq \max_j \{t_{i+1,j}\}$, $1 \leq i < n$.

11. The satisfiability problem was introduced in chapter 11. Define maximum satisfiability to be the problem of determining a maximum subset of clauses that can be satisfed simultaneously. If a formula has p clauses, then all p clauses can be simultaneously satisfied iff the formula is satisfiable. For procedure MSAT, show that for every instance I, $|F^*(I) - \hat{F}(I)|/F^*(I) \leq 1/(k + 1)$. k is the minimum number of literals in any clause of I. Show that this bound is best possible for this algorithm.

procedure *MSAT* (*I*)
   //approximation algorithm for maximum satisfiability. *I* is a formula.//
   //Let x_i, $1 \leq i \leq n$ be the variables in *I* and let C_i, $1 \leq i \leq p$ be the//
   //clauses.//
   $CL \leftarrow \phi$ //set of clauses simultaneously satisfiable//
   $LEFT \leftarrow \{C_i | 1 \leq i \leq p\}$ //remaining clauses//
   $LIT \leftarrow \{x_i, \bar{x}_i | 1 \leq i \leq n\}$ //set of all literals//
   while LIT contains a literal occurring in a clause in LEFT **do**
      let y be a literal in LIT that is in the most clauses of LEFT.
      let R be the subset of clauses in LEFT that contain y
      $CL \leftarrow CL \cup R; LEFT \leftarrow LEFT - R$
      $LIT \leftarrow LIT - \{y, \bar{y}\}$
   repeat
   return (*CL*)
end *MSAT*

Algorithm 12.7   Procedure for Exercise 11

12.   Show that if procedure MSAT2 is used for the maximum satisfiability problem
      of Exercise 11 then, $|F^*(I) - \hat{F}(I)|/F^*(I) \leq 1/2^k$ where k, $\hat{F}$ and F^* are
      as in Exercise 11.

procedure *MSAT2* (*I*)
   //same function as MSAT//
   $w(i) \leftarrow 2^{-|C_i|}$, $1 \leq i \leq p$ //weighting function $|C_k|$ = number of//
                                    //literals in C_i//
   $CL \leftarrow \phi; LEFT \leftarrow \{C_i | 1 \leq i \leq p\}$
   $LIT \leftarrow \{x_i, \bar{x}_i | 1 \leq i \leq n\}$
   while *LIT contains a literal occurring in a clause in LEFT* **do**
      let y $\in$ LIT be such that y occurs in a clause in LEFT
      let R be the subset of clauses in LEFT containing y
      let S be the subset of clauses in LEFT containing $\bar{y}$
      if $\Sigma_{C_i \in R} w(i) \geq \Sigma_{C_i \in S} w(i)$ **then** $CL \leftarrow CL \cup R$
                                           $LEFT \leftarrow LEFT - R$
                                           $w(i) \leftarrow 2 * w(i)$ *for each* $C_i \in S$
                                  else $CL \leftarrow CL \cup S$
                                           $LEFT \leftarrow LEFT - S$
                                           $w(i) \leftarrow 2 * w(i)$ *for each* $C_i \in R$
      endif
      $LIT \leftarrow LIT - \{y, \bar{y}\}$
   repeat
   return (*CL*)
end *MSAT2*

Algorithm 12.8   Procedure for Exercise 12

13. Consider the set cover problem of Exercise 11.20. Show that if procedure SET_COVER is used for the optimization version of this problem then

$$\hat{F}(I)/F^*(I) \leq \sum_1^k (1/j)$$

where k is the maximum number of elements in any set. Show that this bound is best possible.

procedure SET_COVER(F)
    //S_i, $1 \leq i \leq m$ are the sets in F. $|S_i|$ is the number of elements in S_i.//
    //$|\cup S_i| = n$//
    $G \leftarrow \cup S_i$; $R_i \leftarrow S_i$, $1 \leq i \leq m$
    $COV \leftarrow \phi$ //elements covered//
    $T \leftarrow \phi$ //cover being constructed//
    while $COV \neq G$ **do**
        let R_j be such that $|R_j| \geq |R_q|$, $1 \leq q \leq m$
        $COV \leftarrow COV \cup R_j$; $T \leftarrow T \cup S_j$
        $R_i \leftarrow R_i - R_j$, $1 \leq i \leq m$
    repeat
    return (T)
end SET_COVER

Algorithm 12.9 Procedure for Exercise 13

14. Consider a modified set cover problem (MSC) in which we are required to find a cover T such that $\sum_{S \in T} |S|$ is minimum.

(a) Show that exact cover αMSC (see Exercise 11.21)
(b) Show that procedure MSC is not an ϵ-approximate algorithm for this problem for any ϵ, $\epsilon > 0$.

procedure MSC (F)
    //same variables as in SET_COVER//
    $T \leftarrow \phi$; $LEFT \leftarrow \{S_i | 1 \leq i \leq m\}$; $G \leftarrow \cup S_i$
    while $G \neq \phi$ **do**
        let S_j be a set in $LEFT$ such that
        $|S_j - G|/|S_j \cap G| \leq |S_q - G|/|S_q \cap G|$ for all $S_q \in LEFT$
        $T \leftarrow T \cup S_j$; $G \leftarrow G - S_j$; $LEFT \leftarrow LEFT - S_j$
    repeat
    return (T)
end MSC

Algorithm 12.10 Procedure for Exercise 14

15. Consider the following heuristic for the max clique problem: i) delete from G a vertex that is not connected to every other vertex ii) repeat (i) until the remaining graph is a clique. Show that this heuristic does not result in an ϵ-approximate algorithm for the max clique problem for any ϵ $0 < \epsilon < 1$.

16. For the max-clique problem, consider the following heuristic: (i) $S \leftarrow \phi$, (ii) add to S a vertex not in S that is connected to all vertices in S. If there is no such vertex then stop with S the approximate max clique, otherwise repeat (ii). Show that the algorithm resulting from this heuristic is not an ϵ-approximate algorithm for the max-clique problem for any ϵ, $\epsilon < 1$.

17. Show that procedure COLOR is not an ϵ-approximate coloring algorithm for the minimum colorability problem for any ϵ, $\epsilon > 0$.

```
procedure COLOR (G)
    //G = (V, E) is a graph with |V| = n vertices. COL(i) is the color to use//
    //for vertex i, 1 ≤ i ≤ n//
    i ← 1   //next color to use//
    j ← 0   //number of vertices colored//
    while j ≠ n do
        S ← φ   //vertices colored with color i//
        while there is an uncolored vertex, v, not adjacent to a vertex in S do
            COL(v) ← i; S ← S ∪ {v}; j ← j + 1
        repeat
        i ← i + 1
    repeat
    return (COL)
end COLOR
```

Algorithm 12.11 Procedure for Exercise 17

18. Show that if line 4 of Algorithm 12.3 is changed to PMAX $\leftarrow$ max {PMAX, $L(I, P, W, M, n)$} and line 1 of procedure L replaced by the line

$$S \leftarrow 0; \qquad i \leftarrow 1; \qquad T \leftarrow M$$

then the resulting algorithm is not ϵ-approximate for any ϵ, $0 < \epsilon < 1$. Note that the new heuristic constrains I to be outside the knapsack. The original heuristic constrains I to be inside the knapsack.

19. Show that procedure INDEP of Section 12.6 is not an ϵ-approximate algorithm for the maximum independent set problem for any ϵ, $0 < \epsilon < 1$.

20. Consider any tour for the traveling salesperson problem. Let city i_1 be the starting point. Assume the n cities appear in the tour in the order i_1, i_2, i_3, ..., i_n, $i_{n+1} = i_1$. Let $l(i_j, i_{j+1})$ be the length of edge $\langle i_j, i_{j+1} \rangle$. The arrival time Y_k at city i_k is

$$Y_k = \sum_{j=1}^{k-1} l(i_j, i_{j+1}), \quad 1 < k \leq n + 1$$

The mean arrival time $\overline{Y}$ is

$$\overline{Y} = \frac{1}{n} \sum_{k=2}^{n+1} Y_k$$

Show that the ϵ-approximate minimum mean arrival time problem is NP-hard for all ϵ, $\epsilon > 0$.

21. Let Y_k and $\overline{Y}$ be as in Exercise 20. The variance, σ, in arrival times is

$$\frac{1}{n} \sum_{2}^{n+1} (Y_k - \overline{Y})^2.$$

Show that the ϵ-approximate minimum variance time problem is NP-Hard for all ϵ, $\epsilon > 0$.

22. An edge disjoint cycle cover of an undirected graph G is a set of edge disjoint cycles such that every vertex is included in at least one cycle. The size of such a cycle cover is the number of cycles in it.
   (a) Show that finding a minimum cycle cover of this type is NP-hard.
   (b) Show that the ϵ-approximation version of this problem is NP-hard for all ϵ, $\epsilon > 0$.

23. Show that if the cycles in Exercise 22 are constrained to be vertex disjoint then the problem remains NP-Hard. Show that the ϵ-approximate version is NP-hard for all ϵ, $\epsilon > 0$.

24. Consider the partitioning problem:
   Let $G = (V, E)$ be an undirected graph. Let $f: E \to Z$ be an edge weighting function and let $w: V \to Z$ be a vertex weighting function. Let k be a fixed integer, $k \geq 2$. The problem is to obtain k disjoint sets $S_1, \ldots, S_k$ such that:

   (a) $\bigcup S_i = V$
   (b) $S_i \cap S_j = \phi$ for $i \neq j$
   (c) $\sum_{j \in S_i} w(j) \leq W$; $\quad 1 \leq i \leq k$

(d) $\displaystyle\sum_{i=1}^{k} \sum_{\substack{(u,v) \in E \\ u,v \in S_i}} f(u, v)$ is maximized

W is a number which may vary from instance to instance. This partitioning problem finds application in the minimization of the cost of interpage references between subroutines of a program. Show that the ϵ-approximate version of this problem is NP-hard for all ϵ, $0 < \epsilon < 1$.

25. Let $G = (V, E)$ be an undirected graph. Assume that the vertices represent documents. The edges are weighted such that $w(i, j)$ is the dissimilarity between documents i and j. It is desired to partition the vertices into $k \geq 3$ disjoint clusters such that

$$\sum_{i=1}^{k} \sum_{\substack{(u,v) \in E \\ u,v \in C_i}} w(u, v)$$

is minimized. C_i is the set of documents in cluster i. Show that the ϵ-approximate version of this problem is NP-hard for all ϵ, $\epsilon > 0$. Note that λ is a fixed integer provided with each problem instance and may be different for different instances.

26. In one interpretation of the generalized assignment problem, we have m agents who have to perform n tasks. If agent i is assigned to perform task j then a cost c_{ij} is incurred. When agent i performs task j, r_{ij} units of his resources are used. Agent i has a total of b_i units of resource. The objective is to find an assignment of agents to tasks such that the total cost of the assignment is minimized and such that no agent requires more than his total available resource to complete the tasks he is assigned to. Only one agent may be assigned to a task.

Using x_{ij} to be a 0/1 variable such that $x_{ij} = 1$ if agent i is assigned to task j and $x_{ij} = 0$ otherwise, the generalized assignment problem may be formulated mathematically as:

$$\text{minimize} \quad \sum_{i=1}^{m} \sum_{j=1}^{n} c_{ij} x_{ij}$$

$$\text{subject to} \quad \sum_{j=1}^{n} r_{ij} x_{ij} \leq b_i, \quad 1 \leq i \leq m$$

$$\sum_{i=1}^{m} x_{ij} = 1, \quad 1 \leq j \leq n$$

$$x_{ij} = 0 \text{ or } 1, \text{ for all } i \text{ and } j$$

The constraints $\Sigma\ x_{ij} = 1$ ensure that exactly one agent is assigned to each task. Many other interpretations are possible for this problem.

Show that the corresponding ϵ-approximation problem is NP-hard for all ϵ, $\epsilon > 0$.

27. Consider the $O(n(\log n + 1/\epsilon^2))$ rounding algorithm for the 0/1 knapsack problem. Let $S^{(r)}$ be the final set of tuples in the solution of BIG. Show that no more than $(9/\epsilon^2)/q_i$ objects with rounded profit value q_i can contribute to any tuple in $S^{(r)}$. From this, conclude that BIG can have at most $(9/\epsilon^2)/q_i$ objects with rounded profit value q_i. Hence, $r \le \Sigma\ (9/\epsilon^2)/q_i$ where q_i is in the range $[3/\epsilon, 9/\epsilon^2]$. Now, show that the time needed to obtain $S^{(r)}$ is $O(81/\epsilon^4$ ln $(3/\epsilon))$. Use the relation

$$\sum_{3/\epsilon}^{9/\epsilon^2} (9/\epsilon^2)/q_i \simeq \int_{3/\epsilon}^{9/\epsilon^2} (9/\epsilon^2)\ dq_i/q_i = \frac{9}{\epsilon^2} \ln (3/\epsilon).$$

28. Write a SPARKS algorithm for the $O(n(\log n + 1/\epsilon^2))$ rounding scheme discussed in § 12.5. When solving BIG use three tuples (P, Q, W) such that $P = \Sigma\ p_i x_i$, $Q = \Sigma\ q_i x_i$ and $W = \Sigma\ w_i x_i$. Tuple (P_1, Q_1, W_1) dominates (P_2, Q_2, W_2) iff $Q_1 \ge Q_2$ and $W_1 \le W_2$. In case $Q_1 = Q_2$ and $W_1 = W_2$ then an additional dominance criteria may be used. In this case the tuple (P_1, Q_1, W_1) dominates (P_2, Q_2, W_2) iff $P_1 > P_2$. Otherwise, (P_2, Q_2, W_2) dominates (P_1, Q_1, W_1). Show that your algorithm is of time complexity $O(n(\log n + 1/\epsilon^2))$.

29. Show that if we change the optimization function of Exercise 25 to maximize

$$\sum_{\substack{u \in C_i \\ v \notin C_i \\ (u, v) \in E}} w(u, v)$$

then there is a polynomial time ϵ-approximation algorithm for some ϵ, $0 < \epsilon < 1$.

30. Use separation to obtain a fully polynomial time approximation scheme for the independent task scheduling problem when $m = 2$ (see Section 12.4).

31. Do Exercise 30 for the case when the two processors operate at speeds s_1 and s_2, $s_1 \ne s_2$. See Exercise 4.

32. Do Exercise 30 for the case when the two processors are nonidentical (see Exercise 5).

33. Use separation to obtain a fully polynomial time approximation algorithm for the job sequencing with deadlines problem.

34. Use separation to obtain a fully polynomial time approximation scheme for the problem of obtaining two processor schedules with minimum mean weighted finish time (see Section 11.4). Assume that the two processors are identical.

35. Do Exercise 34 for the case when a minimum mean finish time schedule that has minimum finish time amongst all minimum mean finish time schedules is desired. Again, assume two identical processors.

36. Do Exercise 30 using rounding.

37. Do Exercise 31 using rounding.

38. Do Exercise 32 using rounding.

39. Do Exercise 33 using rounding.

40. Do Exercise 34 using rounding.

41. Do Exercise 35 using rounding.

42. Show that the following problems are strongly NP-hard
  i) Max Clique
  ii) Set Cover
  iii) Node Cover
  iv) Set Packing
  v) Feedback Node Set
  vi) Feedback Arc Set
  vii) Chromatic Number
  viii) Clique Cover

APPENDIX A: SPARKS

This section is meant for people who do most of their programming in FORTRAN. FORTRAN has the distinction of being essentially the earliest higher level programming language, developed about 1957 by a group at IBM. Since then it and its derivatives have become established as the primary language for scientific and engineering computation. But, with our greater understanding of the process of creating programs has come a realization of the deficiencies of FORTRAN. Creating a program is properly thought of as taking a real world problem and translating it into a computer solution. Concepts in the real world such as a geneology tree or a queue of airplanes must be translated into computer concepts. A language is good if it enables one to describe these abstractions of the real world in a natural way. Perhaps because of its very early development, FORTRAN lacks many such features. In this appendix we explore the idea of writing a preprocessor for FORTRAN which inexpensively adds some of these missing features.

A preprocessor is a program which translates statements written in a language X into FORTRAN. In our case X is called SPARKS. Such a program is normally called a compiler so why give it the special name preprocessor? A preprocessor is distinguished from a compiler in the following way: the source and target language have many statements in common.

Such a translator has many advantages. Most importantly it preserves a close connection with FORTRAN. Despite FORTRAN's many negative attributes, it has several practical pluses: 1) it is almost always available and compilers are often good, 2) there is a language standard which allows a degree of portability not obtainable with other languages, 3) there are extensive subroutine libraries, and 4) there is a large labor force familiar with it. These reasons give FORTRAN a strong hold in the industrial marketplace. A structured FORTRAN translator preserves these virtues while it augments the language with improved syntactical constructs and other useful features.

Another consideration is that at many installations a nicely structured language is unavailable. In this event a translator provides a simple

614

means for supplementing an existing FORTRAN capability. The translator to be described here can be obtained by writing to the address given at the end of this appendix.

In order to see the difference between FORTRAN and SPARKS consider writing a program which searches for X in the sorted array of integers $A(N)$, $N \le 100$. The output is the integer J which is either zero if X is not found or $A(J) = X$, $1 \le J \le N$. The method used here is the well known binary search algorithm. The FORTRAN version looks something like this:

```
      SUBROUTINE BINS (A,N,X,J)
      IMPLICIT INTEGER (A − Z)
      DIMENSION A(100)
      BOT = 1
      TOP = N
      J = 0
100   IF (BOT. GT. TOP) RETURN
      MID = (BOT + TOP)/2
      IF (X. GE. A (MID)) GO TO 101
        TOP = MID − 1
        GO TO 100
101.  IF (X. EQ. A (MID)) GO TO 102
        BOT = MID + 1
        GO TO 100
102   J = MID
      RETURN
      END
```

This may not be the "best" way to write this program, but it is a reasonable attempt. Now we write this algorithm in SPARKS.

```
SUBROUTINE BINS (A,N,X,J)
IMPLICIT INTEGER (A − Z)
DIMENSION A(100)
BOT = 1; TOP = N; J = 0
WHILE BOT. LE. TOP DO
  MID = (BOT + TOP)/2
  CASE
    : X. LT. A(MID): TOP = MID − 1
    : X. GT. A(MID): BOT = MID + 1
    :ELSE: J = MID; RETURN
  ENDCASE
REPEAT
RETURN
END
```

The difference between these two algorithms may not be dramatic, but it is significant. The WHILE and CASE statements allow the algorithm to be described in a more natural way. The program can be read from top to bottom without your eyes constantly jumping up and down the page. When such improvements are consistently adopted in a large software project, the resulting code is bound to be easier to comprehend.

We begin by defining precisely the SPARKS language. A distinction is made between FORTRAN statements and SPARKS statements. The latter are recognized by certain keywords and/or delimiters. All other statements are regarded as FORTRAN and are passed directly to the FORTRAN compiler without alteration. Thus, SPARKS is compatible with FORTRAN and a FORTRAN program is a SPARKS program. SPARKS statements cause the translator to produce ANSI FORTRAN statements which accomplish the equivalent computation. Hence, the local compiler ultimately defines the semantics of all SPARKS statements.

The reserved words and special symbols are:

BY	CASE	CYCLE	DO	ELSE	ENDCASE
ENDIF	EOJ	EXIT	FOR	IF	LOOP
REPEAT	UNTIL	WHILE	TO	THEN	:
;	//				

Reserved words must always be surrounded by blanks. Reserved means they cannot be used by the programmer as variables.

We now define the SPARKS statements by giving their FORTRAN equivalents. In the following any reference to the term "statements" is meant to include both SPARKS and FORTRAN statements. There are six basic SPARKS statements, two which improve the testing of cases and four which improve the description of looping.

```
IF cond THEN                IF(.NOT. (cond)) GO TO 100
   S₁                          S₁
ELSE                           GO TO 101
   S₂                   100     S₂
ENDIF                   101     CONTINUE
```

S_1 and S_2 are arbitrary size groups of statements. Cond must be a legal FORTRAN conditional. The ELSE clause is optional but the ENDIF is required and it always terminates the innermost IF.

CASE		IF(.NOT. (cond1)) GO TO 101
: cond1 : S_1		S_1
: cond2 : S_2		GO TO 100
$\vdots$	101	IF(.NOT. (cond2)) GO TO 102
		S_2
: condn : S_n		GO TO 100
: ELSE : S_{n+1}	102	$\vdots$
ENDCASE	$100 + n - 1$	IF(.NOT. (condn)) GO TO $100 + n$
		S_n
		GO TO 100
	$100 + n$	CONTINUE
		S_{n+1}
	100	CONTINUE

$S_1, S_2, ..., S_{n+1}$ are arbitrary size groups of statements. Cond1, cond2, ..., condn are legal FORTRAN conditionals. The symbol ELSE surrounded by colons designates that S_{n+1} will be automatically executed if all previous conditions are false. This part of the case statement is optional.

The four looping statements are:

WHILE cond DO	100	IF(.NOT. (cond)) GO TO 101
S		S
REPEAT		GO TO 100
	101	CONTINUE

S is an arbitrary group of statements and cond a legal FORTRAN conditional.

LOOP	100	CONTINUE
S		S
UNTIL cond REPEAT		IF(.NOT. (cond)) GO TO 100

S and cond are the same as for the while statement immediately preceding.

LOOP	100	CONTINUE
S		S
REPEAT		GO TO 100
	101	CONTINUE

S is an arbitrary size group of statements.

preprocessor and then to define each SPARKS statement as a new macro. Such a processor is usually small and allows the user to easily define new constructs. However, these processors tend to be slower than the approach of direct translation. Moreover, it is hard to build in the appropriate error detection and recovery facilities which are sorely needed if SPARKS is to be used seriously. Therefore, we have chosen the first approach. Figure A.1 contains a flow description of the translator.

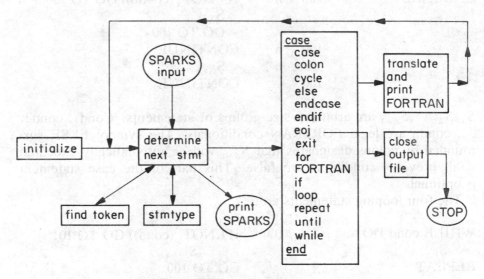

Figure A.1: Overview of SPARKS Translator

The main processing loop consists of determining the next statement and branching within a large CASE. This does whatever translation into FORTRAN is necessary. When EOJ is found the loop is broken and the program is concluded.

The SPARKS translator was first written in SPARKS. The original version was hand translated into FORTRAN to produce our first running system. Since that time it has been used by a variety of people and classes. Thus it is running far better than the original version. Nevertheless, the translator has not been proved correct and so it must be used with caution.

Extensions

Below is a list of possible extensions for SPARKS. Some are relatively easy to implement, while others require a great deal of effort.

E.1 Special cases of the CASE statement

CASE SGN : exp :   CASE: integer variable:

    : .EQ.0 : S_1 : 1 : S_1

    : .LT.0 : S_2 and   : 2 : S_2

    : .GT.0 : S_3 :

ENDCASE   : n : S_n

                      ENDCASE

The first gets translated into the FORTRAN arithmetic IF statement. The second form is translated into a FORTRAN computed go to.

E.2 A simple form of the FOR statement would look like

LOOP exp TIMES
    S
REPEAT

where exp is an expression which evaluates to a non-negative integer. The statements meaning can be described by the SPARKS for statement:

FOR ITEMP = 1 TO exp DO
    S
REPEAT

An internal integer variable ITEMP must be created.

E.3 If F appears in column one then all subsequent cards are assumed to be pure FORTRAN. They are passed directly to the output until an F is encountered in column one.

E.4 Add the capability of profiling a program by determining the number of executions of each loop during a single execution and the value of conditional expressions.

HINT: For each subroutine declare a set of variables which can be inserted after encountering a WHILE, LOOP, REPEAT, FOR, THEN or ELSE statement. At the end of each subroutine a write statement prints the values of these counters.

E.5 Add the multiple replacement statement so that

$$A = B = C = D + E$$

is translated into

$$C = D + E; B = C; A = B$$

E.6   Add the vector replacement statement so that

$$(A,B,C) = (X + Y, 10,2*E)$$

produces $A = X + Y; B = 10; C = 2*E$

E.7   Add an array "fill" statement so that

$$NAME(*) \leftarrow exp1,exp2,exp3$$

gets translated into

$$NAME(1) = expl; NAME(2) = exp2; NAME(3) = exp3$$

E.8   Introduce appropriate syntax and reasonable conventions so that SPARKs programs can be recursive.
      HINT: Mutually recursive programs are gathered together in a module, MODULE (X(A,B,C)(100)) whose name is X, whose parameters are A,B,C and whose stack size should be 100.

E.9   Add a character string capability to SPARKS.

E.10 Add an internal procedure capability to aid the programmer in doing top-down program refinement.

E.11 Attach sequence numbers to the resulting FORTRAN output which relates each statement back to the original SPARKS statement which generated it. This is particularly helpful for debugging.

E.12 Along with the indented SPARKS source print a number which represents the level of nesting of each statement.

E.13 Generalize the EXIT statement so that upon its execution it can be assigned a value, e.g.,
      LOOP
          S_1
          IF cond1 THEN EXIT : expl : ENDIF
          S_2
          IF cond2 THEN EXIT : exp2 : ENDIF
          S_3
      REPEAT
      will assign either exp1 or exp2 as the value of the variable EXIT.

E.14 Supply a simplified read and write statement. For example, allow for hollerith strings to be included within quotes and translated to the nH $x_1 \ldots x_n$ format.

All further questions about the definition of SPARKS should be addressed to:

Chairman, SPARKS Users Group
Computer Science, Powell Hall
University of Southern California
Los Angeles, California 90007

To receive a complete ANSI FORTRAN version of SPARKS send $20.00 (for postage and handling) to Dr. Ellis Horowitz at the above address.

INDEX

350